Look For These Other Products From The Coriolis Group:

RHCE Linux Exam Cram
by Kara Pritchard

Linux IP Stacks Commentary
by Stephen Satchel and HBJ Clifford

Linux Core Kernel Commentary
by Scott Maxwell

General Linux I

Dee-Ann LeBlanc

The Coriolis Group, LLC
14455 N. Hayden Road, Suite 220
Scottsdale, Arizona 85260

480/483-0192
FAX 480/483-0193
http://www.coriolis.com

Library of Congress Card Number: 00-130581

President, CEO
Keith Weiskamp

Publisher
Steve Sayre

Acquisitions Editor
Shari Jo Hehr

Marketing Specialist
Cynthia Caldwell

Project Editor
Stephanie Palenque

Technical Reviewer
Ray Rowden

Production Coordinator
Wendy Littley

Cover Design
Jesse Dunn

Layout Design
April Nielsen

CD-ROM Developer
Robert Clarfield

Printed in the United States of America
10 9 8 7 6 5 4 3 2 1

CORIOLIS

14455 North Hayden Road • Suite 220 • Scottsdale, Arizona 85260

Coriolis: The Smartest Way To Get Certified™

To help you reach your goals, we've listened to readers like you, and we've designed our entire product line around you and the way you like to study, learn, and master challenging subjects.

In addition to our highly popular *Exam Cram* and *Exam Prep* books, we offer several other products to help you pass certification exams. Our *Practice Tests* and *Flash Cards* are designed to make your studying fun and productive. Our *Audio Reviews* have received rave reviews from our customers—and they're the perfect way to make the most of your drive time!

The newest way to get certified is the *Exam Cram Personal Trainer* —a highly interactive, personalized self-study course based on the best-selling *Exam Cram* series. It's the first certification-specific product to completely link a customizable learning tool, exclusive *Exam Cram* content, and multiple testing techniques so you can study what, how, and when you want.

Exam Cram Insider —a biweekly newsletter containing the latest in certification news, study tips, and announcements from Certification Insider Press—gives you an ongoing look at the hottest certification programs. (To subscribe, send an email to **eci@coriolis.com** and type "subscribe insider" in the body of the email.) We also sponsor the Certified Crammer Society and the Coriolis Help Center—two other resources that will help you get certified even faster!

Help us continue to provide the very best certification study materials possible. Write us or email us at **cipq@coriolis.com** and let us know how our books have helped you study. Tell us about new features that you'd like us to add. Send us a story about how we've helped you; if we use it in one of our books, we'll send you an official Coriolis shirt!

Good luck with your certification exam and your career. Thank you for allowing us to help you achieve your goals.

Keith Weiskamp
President and CEO

To my parents, for helping me get where I am today.

᛫

ABOUT THE AUTHOR

Dee-Ann LeBlanc is a technical writer with Renaissoft, Inc. She is the author of a number of books on Linux and other topics, including *Linux Install And Configuration Little Black Book* and the upcoming *Linux System Administration Black Book*, both from The Coriolis Group. She has been using Linux since 1994 as an end user and eventually as a system administrator. Dee-Ann is also one of the instructors for Smart Planet's "Unix: An Introduction" and "Unix: System Administration," and is an RHCE (Red Hat Certified Engineer) as well as on her way to the level one LPIC.

ACKNOWLEDGMENTS

I would like to extend my thanks to LANWrights for their assistance and support, and my husband for putting up with my odd hours during this project.

In addition, this book has many contributors behind the scenes. First of all, thanks to Ray Rowden for a great tech editing job. Next, to the others who contributed chapters to this book, Ed Tittel, Janet Valade, Kyle Findlay, John Kloian, and Nick Estes, thanks for all your hard work and filling in at the last minute!

CONTENTS AT A GLANCE

TABLE OF CONTENTS

CHAPTER 4
BOOT INITIALIZATION, SHUTDOWN, AND RUNLEVELS 93

CHAPTER 6
LINUX ADMINISTRATIVE TASKS 167

CHAPTER 8
LINUX NETWORKING FUNDAMENTALS 265

Chapter 11
Compiling A Custom Kernel 373

CHAPTER 12
MANAGING LINUX SECURITY 407

EXAM INSIGHTS

Welcome to *General Linux I Exam Prep!* This book aims to help you get ready to take—and pass—Exam 101, "General Linux I," which covers the common elements in various Linux distributions. This Exam Insights section discusses exam preparation resources, the testing situation, the three different certification programs in general, and how this book can help you prepare for the Linux certification exams.

Exam Prep books help you understand and appreciate the subjects and materials you need to pass certification exams. I've worked from the exam curriculum objectives to ensure that all key topics are clearly explained. My aim is to bring together as much information as possible about the Linux certification exams.

Nevertheless, to completely prepare for any Linux test, I recommend that you begin by taking the Self-Assessment included in this book immediately following this Exam Insights section. This tool will help you evaluate your knowledge base against the requirements for one of the Linux Level I certifications under both ideal and real circumstances.

Based on what you learn from that exercise, you might decide to begin your studies with some classroom training or some background reading. You might decide to read The Coriolis Group's *Exam Prep* book that you have in hand first, or you might decide to start with another study approach. You may also want to refer to the study guides available from the organizations offering the exams.

I also strongly recommend that you install, configure, and fool around with the software that you'll be tested on, because nothing beats hands-on experience and familiarity when it comes to understanding the questions you're likely to encounter on a certification test. Book learning is essential, but hands-on experience is the best teacher of all!

HOW TO PREPARE FOR AN EXAM

Preparing for any Linux-related test requires that you obtain and study materials designed to provide comprehensive information about the product and its capabilities that will appear on the specific exam for which you are preparing. The following list of materials will help you study and prepare:

➤ The manuals that come with the distribution.

➤ The exam preparation materials, practice tests, and self-assessment exams on the certification Web sites (**www.redhat.com**, **www.linuxcertification. org**, and **www.lpi.org**). Find the materials, download them, and use them! Study the materials for all of the exams. It may just be that a description on another site helps you to understand something better than it did on the site whose exams you are aiming for.

In addition, you'll probably find any or all of the following materials useful in your quest for Linux expertise:

➤ **Study Guides** Several publishers—including The Coriolis Group—offer Linux titles. The Coriolis Group series includes:

  ➤ **The *Exam Cram* series** These books give you information about the material you need to know to pass the tests. *RHCE Linux Exam Cram* is the perfect learning companion to prepare you for the Red Hat Certified Engineer Level I exam. It is also worth considering if you are going to take the LPI Red Hat specialization exam, or even just feel that you need as many preparation materials as you can find.

  ➤ **The *Exam Prep* series** These books provide a greater level of detail than the *Exam Cram* books and are designed to teach you everything you need to know from an exam perspective.

  Together, the two series make a perfect pair.

➤ **Multimedia** These Coriolis Group materials are designed to support learners of all types—whether you learn best by listening, reading, or doing:

  ➤ **The *Practice Tests Exam Cram* series** Provides the most valuable test preparation material: practice exams. Each exam is followed by a complete set of answers, as well as explanations of why the right answers are right and the wrong answers are wrong. Each book comes with a CD that contains one or more interactive practice exams.

  ➤ **The *Exam Cram Flash Card* series** Offers practice questions on handy cards you can use anywhere. The question and its possible answers appear on the front of the card, and the answer, explanation, and a valuable reference appear on the back of the card. The set also includes a CD with an electronic practice exam to give you the feel of the actual test—and more practice!

  ➤ **The *Exam Cram Audio Review* series** Offers a concise review of key topics covered on the exam, as well as practice questions.

➤ **Classroom Training** There are many opportunities to get training in the classroom if that is your favorite venue for learning. Red Hat offers their own courses, and the other certification organizations either offer courses or point to them on their Web site.

➤ **Other Publications** You'll find direct references to other publications and resources in this book, but there's no shortage of materials available about Linux. I've included a complete resource section in Appendices A through F. This should give you an idea of where I think you should look for further discussion.

By far, this set of required and recommended materials represents an unparalleled collection of sources and resources for Linux and related topics. I anticipate that you'll find that this book belongs in this company.

TAKING A CERTIFICATION EXAM

Once you've prepared for your exam, you need to register with a testing center. Each Linux certification track is different, so they are discussed separately here.

Taking A Red Hat Exam

Red Hat offers a combination of courses and exams in multiple testing centers. You have the choice of taking the exam by itself for approximately $750, or as the fifth day of the RHCE week-long course for a combined cost of approximately $2,500. If you don't pass the exam the first time through, you may retest by taking the exam portion only.

The Red Hat exams and courses are available in a number of locations. To get the latest listing of testing centers, prices, and courses, go to **www.redhat. com/training**. You can sign up at the last minute if there is room—because the course and exams are hands on, attendance is limited by number of machines—but the registration will not finish going through until Red Hat receives your purchase order and credit card information.

Taking An LPI Exam

The Linux Professional Institute (LPI) exams are offered through VUE (Virtual University Enterprises) for $100 apiece. You can sign up for a test through the company's Web site at **www.vue.com**. Or, you can register by phone at 877-619-2096 (within the United States or Canada) or at a range of numbers available through VUE's Web site.

Taking A Sair Linux & GNU Exam

The Sair Linux & GNU exams are offered through Sylvan Prometric for $100 apiece. You can sign up for a test through the company's Web site at **www.slspro. com**. Or, you can register by phone at 800-895-6717 (within the United States or Canada) or at a range of numbers available through Sair's Web site at **www.linuxcertification.org**.

Signing Up With VUE Or Sylvan Prometric

To sign up for a test, you must possess a valid credit card, or contact either company for mailing instructions to send them a check (in the U.S.). Only when payment is verified, or a check has cleared, can you actually register for a test.

To schedule an exam, call the number or visit either of the Web pages at least one day in advance. To cancel or reschedule an exam, you must call before 7 P.M. pacific standard time the day before the scheduled test time (or you may be charged, even if you don't appear to take the test). When you want to schedule a test, have the following information ready:

➤ Your name, organization, and mailing address.

➤ Your Test ID. (Inside the United States, this means your Social Security number; citizens of other nations should call ahead to find out what type of identification number is required to register for a test.)

➤ The name and number of the exam you wish to take.

➤ A method of payment. (As I've already mentioned, a credit card is the most convenient method, but alternate means can be arranged in advance, if necessary.)

Once you sign up for a test, you'll be informed as to when and where the test is scheduled. Try to arrive at least 15 minutes early.

THE EXAM SITUATION

When you arrive at the testing center where you scheduled your exam, you'll need to sign in with an exam coordinator. He or she will ask you to show two forms of identification, one of which must be a photo ID. After you've signed in and your time slot arrives, you'll be asked to deposit any books, bags, or other items you brought with you. Then, you'll be escorted into a closed room.

 If you are taking the RHCE exam and this is the last day of a series of courses, you'll find that sign-ins are not so stringent because you are already a known entity.

All exams are completely closed book. In fact, you will not be permitted to take anything with you into the testing area, but you will be furnished with a blank sheet of paper and a pen or, in some cases, an erasable plastic sheet and an erasable pen. Before the exam, you should memorize as much of the important material as you can, so you can write that information on the blank sheet as soon as you are seated in front of the computer. You can refer to this piece of paper anytime you like during the test, but you'll have to surrender the sheet when you leave the room.

If you are taking the RHCE exam, you are also furnished with the materials necessary to complete the hands-on components of the exam, such as distribution CD-ROMs for the installation component.

You will have some time to compose yourself, to record this information, and to take a sample orientation exam before you begin the real thing if you are taking the LPI or Sair exams. I suggest you take the orientation test before taking your first exam, but because they're all more or less identical in layout, behavior, and controls, you probably won't need to do this more than once. If you are taking the RHCE track exam, then your proctor will explain the procedures and guidelines once everyone has settled in.

Typically, the room will be furnished with anywhere from one to half a dozen computers, and each workstation may be separated from the others by dividers designed to keep you from seeing what's happening on someone else's computer. Most test rooms feature a wall with a large picture window. This permits the exam coordinator to monitor the room, to prevent exam-takers from talking to one another, and to observe anything out of the ordinary that might go on. The exam coordinator will have preloaded the appropriate Linux certification exam—for this book, that's Exam 101—and you'll be permitted to start as soon as you're seated in front of the computer for the Sair and LPI exams, or as soon as the proctor announces that it is time to do so.

All Linux certification exams allow a certain maximum amount of time in which to complete your work (this time is indicated on the exam by an on-screen counter/ clock, or by warnings from the proctor, so you can check the time remaining whenever you like). All LPI and most Sair certification exams are computer generated and most use a multiple-choice format, and one of the RHCE exams is also multiple choice. Although this may sound quite simple, the questions are constructed not only to check your mastery of basic facts and figures about Linux system administration, but they also require you to evaluate one or more sets of circumstances or requirements. Often, you'll be asked to give more than one answer to a question. Likewise, you might be asked to select the best or most effective solution to a problem from a range of choices, all of which technically are correct.

For the RHCE exam, you must actually complete some specific tasks as explained by your proctor. One of these tasks involves installing and configuring the distribution on a system to the proctor's specifications, and the other involves diagnostics and troubleshooting on a system set up by the proctor. Taking any of these exams is quite an adventure; they involve real thinking. This book shows you what to expect and how to deal with the potential problems, puzzles, and predicaments.

When you complete a Linux certification exam, the software or the certification contact will tell you whether you've passed or failed, though in the case of the RHCE exam these results are not immediate. Results are broken into several topic areas. Even if you fail, I suggest you ask for—and keep—the detailed report that the test administrator should print for you if you took the LPI or Sair exams. You can use this report to help you prepare for another go-round, if needed.

If you need to retake an exam, you'll have to schedule a new test and pay the fee once again.

 The first time you fail a test, you can retake the test the next day. However, if you fail a second time, you must wait 14 days before retaking that test. The 14-day waiting period remains in effect for all retakes after the first failure.

In the next section, you'll learn more about how Linux test questions look and how they must be answered.

EXAM LAYOUT AND DESIGN

Whichever type of written test you take, questions belong to one of four basic types:

➤ Multiple-choice with a single answer

➤ Multiple-choice with one or more answers

➤ Multipart with a single answer

➤ Multipart with one or more answers

Always take the time to read a question at least twice before selecting an answer. Not every question has only one answer; many questions require multiple answers. Therefore, it's important to read each question carefully, to determine how many answers are necessary or possible, and to look for additional hints or instructions when selecting answers. Such instructions often occur in brackets immediately following the question itself (as they do for all multiple-choice questions in which one or more answers are possible).

The following multiple-choice question requires you to select a single correct answer. Following the question is a brief summary of each potential answer and why it is either right or wrong.

Question 1

Which of the following IP addresses is part of a group that is only assigned to networks that are isolated from the Internet?

○ a. 196.17.13.76

○ b. 192.168.101.6

○ c. 210.170.15.1

○ d. 70.15.141.5

The correct answer is b because any address beginning with 192.168. is slated for isolated networks to the point that TCP/IP will not try to deliver data out to the Internet when given that address. Answers a, c, and d are all viable IP addresses that can only ever belong to one machine on the Internet at a time.

This sample question format corresponds closely to the written Linux certification exam format—the only difference on the exam is that answer keys do not follow questions. To select an answer, you would position the cursor over the radio button next to the answer. Then, click the mouse button to select the answer.

Let's examine a question where one or more answers are possible. This type of question provides checkboxes rather than radio buttons for marking all appropriate selections.

Question 2

Which of the following are commonly used email clients available to Linux users? [Choose all correct answers]

❑ a. pine

❑ b. sendmail

❑ c. elm

❑ d. eudora

Answers a and c are correct. The pine and elm email clients are two popular command line tools Linux users utilize on a daily basis. Sendmail is a mail server that is typically used under Linux, not a client. Therefore, answer b is incorrect. And, Eudora is a Windows and Macintosh based email client. Therefore, answer d is incorrect.

For this particular question, two answers are required. As far as the authors can tell (and the Linux certification committees won't comment), such questions are scored as wrong unless all the required selections are chosen. In other words, a partially correct answer does not result in partial credit when the test is scored. For Question 2, you have to check the boxes next to items a and c to obtain credit for a correct answer. Notice that picking the right answers also means knowing why the other answers are wrong!

LINUX TESTING FORMATS

Currently, the Linux certification groups use the fixed-length testing format for the written exams. All of the LPI and Sair Level I exams are done in this multiple-choice format. One of the RHCE exams is done this way as well, but the other two are performance based, meaning that you must accomplish a particular set of end results.

The tests for Sair and the written exam for Red Hat all have approximately 50 questions apiece. LPI's exams, on the other hand, are the new kids on the block as far as when they came out of the starting gate. Initially their exams will vary from 60 to 100 questions as the bugs get shaken out of the questions—you can still get certified taking the beta exam, you are partially judged against the performance of the other testers—and then will likely also settle down to approximately 50 questions.

STRATEGIES FOR DIFFERENT TESTING FORMATS

Before you choose a test-taking strategy, you must know if your test is fixed-length or performance based. In the case of Linux certification this is simple. For Level I candidates, only RHCE testers have to face performance based exams. How you approach these different types of exams in some ways varies radically, and in some ways is quite similar.

The Fixed-Length Exam Strategy

A well-known principle when taking fixed-length exams is to first read over the entire exam from start to finish while answering only those questions you feel absolutely sure of. On subsequent passes, you can dive into more complex questions more deeply, knowing how many such questions you have left.

Fortunately, the exam software for fixed-length tests makes the multiple-visit approach easy to implement. Each certification track has slightly different software, but they all allow you to move backward and forward through the questions until you are satisfied with the results.

As you read each question, if you answer only those you're sure of and mark for review those that you're not sure of, you can keep working through a decreasing list of questions as you answer the trickier ones in order.

There's at least one potential benefit to reading the exam over completely before answering the trickier questions: Sometimes, information supplied in later questions sheds more light on earlier questions. At other times, information you read in later questions might jog your memory about Linux facts, figures, or behavior that helps you answer earlier questions. Either way, you'll come out ahead if you defer those questions about which you're not absolutely sure.

Here are some question-handling strategies that apply to fixed-length tests. Use them if you have the chance:

➤ When returning to a question after your initial read-through, read every word again—otherwise, your mind can fall quickly into a rut. Sometimes, revisiting a question after turning your attention elsewhere lets you see something you missed, but the strong tendency is to see what you've seen before. Try to avoid that tendency at all costs.

➤ If you return to a question more than twice, try to articulate to yourself what you don't understand about the question, why answers don't appear to make sense, or what appears to be missing. If you chew on the subject awhile, your subconscious might provide the details you lack, or you might notice a "trick" that points to the right answer.

For fixed-length tests, it's wise to budget your time by making sure that you've completed one-quarter of the questions one-quarter of the way through the exam period. For 50 question tests this means you must complete one-quarter of the questions one-quarter of the way through (the first 12 or 13 questions) and three-quarters of the questions three-quarters of the way through (37 or 38 questions).

If you're not finished when only five minutes remain, use that time to guess your way through any remaining questions. Remember, guessing is potentially more valuable than not answering, because blank answers are always wrong, but a guess may turn out to be right. If you don't have a clue about any of the remaining questions, pick answers at random, or choose all a's, b's, and so on. The important thing is to submit an exam for scoring that has an answer for every question.

At the very end of your exam period, you're better off guessing than leaving questions unanswered.

The Performance-Based Exam Strategy

Taking a performance-based exam is slightly different, but similar. Though there may not be a set number of questions to answer, you will have a list of objectives. If it helps you to budget your time properly, take a moment to number them. It also may happen that you do not have a set number of tasks per se, but you do have a final objective to meet. In this case, take the time to get a grasp on what obstacles stand in the way of you meeting this objective.

Once you have a good feeling for how much you have to do, you can budget your time accordingly. Do not get so focused on one task that you neglect all of the others to complete it. In fact, you may find that putting aside a task that is giving you trouble and returning to it later means that you either now realize how to deal with the issue, or completing a different objective makes this other one easier to accomplish.

Also keep in mind that if things seem far too difficult, you may be over-analyzing the problem. Take a step back and start over. Unfortunately, when you get down to the last five minutes of the exam you cannot just guess your way through the rest of the answers. However, make sure to remember what the proctor told you at the beginning about the rules for the examination. You may have access to anything on the system, including man pages!

QUESTION-HANDLING STRATEGIES

Based on exams I have taken, some interesting trends have become apparent. For those questions that take only a single answer, usually two or three of the answers will be obviously incorrect, and two of the answers will be plausible— of course, only one can be correct. Unless the answer leaps out at you (if it does, reread the question to look for a trick; sometimes those are the ones you're most likely to get wrong), begin the process of answering by eliminating those answers that are most obviously wrong.

Almost always, at least one answer out of the possible choices for a question can be eliminated immediately because it matches one of these conditions:

➤ The answer does not apply to the situation.

➤ The answer describes a nonexistent issue, an invalid option, or an imaginary state.

After you eliminate all answers that are obviously wrong, you can apply your retained knowledge to eliminate further answers. Look for items that sound correct but refer to actions, commands, or features that are not present or not available in the situation that the question describes.

If you're still faced with a blind guess among two or more potentially correct answers, reread the question. Try to picture how each of the possible remaining answers would alter the situation. Be especially sensitive to terminology; sometimes the choice of words ("remove" instead of "disable") can make the difference between a right answer and a wrong one.

Only when you've exhausted your ability to eliminate answers, but remain unclear about which of the remaining possibilities is correct, should you guess at an answer. An unanswered question offers you no points, but guessing gives you at least some chance of getting a question right; just don't be too hasty when making a blind guess.

If you're taking a fixed-length test, you can wait until the last round of reviewing marked questions (just as you're about to run out of time, or out of unanswered questions) before you start making guesses. Guessing should be your technique of last resort!

Numerous questions assume that the default behavior of a particular utility is in effect. If you know the defaults and understand what they mean, this knowledge will help you cut through many Gordian knots.

MASTERING THE INNER GAME

In the final analysis, knowledge breeds confidence, and confidence breeds success. If you study the materials in this book carefully and review all the practice questions at the end of each chapter, you should become aware of those areas where additional learning and study are required.

After you've worked your way through the book, take the practice exam in the back of the book and the practice exams on the CD-ROM. This will provide a reality check and help you identify areas to study further. Make sure you follow up and review materials related to the questions you miss on the practice exams before scheduling a real exam. Only when you've covered that ground and feel comfortable with the whole scope of the practice exams should you set an exam appointment. Only if you score 85 percent or better should you proceed to the real thing (otherwise, obtain some additional practice tests so you can keep trying until you hit this magic number).

If you take a practice exam and don't score at least 85 percent correct, you'll want to practice further. Sair provides a free practice exam for each of their four Level I exams on their Web site that you can start with. You also should spend extra time troubleshooting problems where before you might give up and take the easy way out.

Armed with the information in this book and with the determination to augment your knowledge, you should be able to pass the certification exam. However, you need to work at it, or you'll spend the exam fee more than once before you finally pass. If you prepare seriously, you should do well. Good luck!

The next section covers the exam requirements for the various Linux certifications.

THE LINUX CERTIFIED SYSTEM ADMINISTRATOR PROGRAMS

Each of the Linux certification programs currently has its own certification track, which boasts a special acronym (as a would-be certificant, you need to have a high tolerance for alphabet soup of all kinds).

The Red Hat Certification Track

The Red Hat certification track currently takes the following path:

➤ **RHCE (Red Hat Certified Engineer)** Anyone who has a current RHCE is warranted to possess a high level of expertise with Red Hat Linux 6.0. This credential is designed to prepare individuals to plan, implement, maintain, and support machines and basic networking services built around Red Hat Linux 6.0 or later and other Linux products.

This first level certification is attained by completing a single day session of three different exams. One of these exams is the written component, which tests your Linux knowledge in general. The other two are both hands on components taken in a lab. One of these lab exams involves completing a network-based install and configuration for network services on a machine. The other involves fixing a broken installation.

You must pass all three examinations and obtain a certain minimum average score between all three in order to receive an RHCE certification.

➤ **RHCE II (Red Hat Certified Engineer Level II)** Anyone who has a current RHCE II is warranted to possess a high level of expertise with Red Hat Linux 6.0 or later and various Linux programs and products. This credential is designed to prepare individuals to plan, implement, maintain, and support machines and networks built around Red Hat Linux 6.0 or later of products.

The details on obtaining an RHCE II certificate are not yet available. However, the topics will cover advanced system administration, security, and network and server administration. If you are already an RHCE and are interested in proceeding to the RHCE II stage, go to **www.redhat.com/ training** for more details.

➤ **RHCX (Red Hat Certified Examiner)** Red Hat Certified Examiners are individuals who are deemed able to administer, oversee, and grade the

RHCE exam, based on technical knowledge and instructional experience and ability. Thus, it is necessary for an individual seeking RHCX certification to pass the RHCE exam first, to have at least a year of training experience, and a strong background in Linux networking and installation issues.

Once a certificate is awarded, RHCE's typically have a year until they need to recertify on Red Hat's current product version. (If individuals do not recertify within the specified time period, their certifications become invalid.) Because technology keeps changing and new products continually supplant old ones, this should come as no surprise.

The best place to keep tabs on the Red Hat training and certification programs and its various certifications is on the Red Hat Web site. The current root URL for the RHCE program is **www.redhat.com/training**. If this URL doesn't work, try examining the current site index. This will help you find the latest and most accurate information about Red Hat's certification programs.

The Linux Professional Institute Certification Track

The Linux Professional Institute certification track currently takes the following path:

➤ **LPIC I (Linux Professional Institute Certified Level I)** Anyone who has a current LPIC is warranted to possess a level of expertise with Linux in general, as well as a specialty in one distribution. This credential is designed to prepare individuals to plan, implement, maintain, and support Linux machines and basic networking services.

  This first level certification is attained by completing a series of two exams: T1 and T2. Both of these exams are written. The T1 exam tests your Linux knowledge in the areas of networking, text file editing, shell scripting, and other basic abilities that are necessary for a professional Linux system administrator. The T2 exam is broken into two different parts. The first part of the T2 tests your knowledge of installation planning and execution, package handling, devices, and more. Finally, the second part of the T2 is distribution-specific, your choice of one of the following: Caldera, Debian, TurboLinux, RedHat, Slackware, or SuSE.

  You must pass both the T1 and the T2 examinations to receive an LPIC Level I certification.

➤ **LPIC II (Linux Professional Institute Certified Level II)** Anyone who has a current RHCE II is warranted to be capable of administering a LAN of Linux machines connected to the Internet, with or without assistants. This credential is designed to prepare individuals to plan, implement, maintain, and support Linux machines and networks.

The details on obtaining an LPIC II certificate are not yet solidified. However, there will be two exams covering topics such as troubleshooting problems, writing shell scripts with sh and sed, and Internet, LAN, and server administration. There is no distribution specialty planned for this level. If you are already an LPIC I and are interested in proceeding to the LPIC II stage, go to **www.lpic.org** for more details.

➤ **LPIC III (Linux Professional Institute Certified Level III)** Anyone who has a current RHCE III is warranted to be capable of administering a large LAN or Internet site made up of Linux machines, with assistants under their direction. This credential is designed to prepare individuals to plan, implement, maintain, and support large networks of Linux machines or mixed operating systems.

The details on obtaining an LPIC III certificate are not yet solidified. However, there will be a set of five exams from which you choose two specialties: Windows Integration; Internet Servers; Database Servers; Security, Firewalls, and Encryption; Kernel Internals, Device Drivers, C Programming, and Creating Distribution Packages. If you are already an LPIC I and LPIC II, and you are interested in proceeding to the LPIC III stage, go to **www.lpic.org** for more details.

Sair Linux & GNU Certification Track

The Sair Linux & GNUs certification track currently takes the following path:

➤ **LCP (Sair Linux & GNU Certified Professional)** Anyone who has a current LCP certificate is warranted to possess a level of expertise in the installation and administration of individual Linux machines. This credential is designed to prepare junior system administrators with the foundations they need to build their experience and move on to the other levels.

The LCP is actually a sub-level certification given when you pass one of the first two LCA exams. Both of these exams are written. The first exam, Installation and Configuration, covers issues involved in installing Linux, configuring it, and finding your way around. The second exam, System Administration, covers issues such as system tuning, user management, process management, and more. Which of these two you choose to take first to get the LCP is up to you.

➤ **LCA (Sair Linux & GNU Certified Administrator)** Anyone who has a current LCA is warranted to possess a solid level of expertise with Linux in general, as well as an understanding of the plusses and minuses of the more popular distributions. This credential is designed to prepare power users and system administrators for management of individual machines and small networks.

This first level certification is attained by completing a series of four different exams: Installation and Configuration, System Administration, Network Connectivity, and Security. All four of these exams are written. Topics covered are items such as installation steps, user management, kernel compilation, setting up basic networking services and firewalls, working at the command line, and process control.

You must pass all four examinations in order to receive an LCA certification.

➤ **LCE (Sair Linux & GNU Certified Engineer)** Anyone who has a current LCE is warranted to be capable of administering a LAN of Linux machines connected to the Internet. This credential is designed to prepare individuals to plan, implement, maintain, and support Linux machines and networks.

This second level certification is attained by completing another series of four exams, in the same categories as the LCA. As with the other certification tracks, the specifics of these exams are not solidified yet. The issues covered will be more in depth, such as configuring name service. If you have an LCA and want more information, go to **www.linuxcertification.org** for more details.

➤ **MCLE (Master Sair Linux & GNU Certified Engineer)** Anyone who has a current MCLE is warranted to be capable of administering a large LAN or Internet site made up of Linux machines, with assistants under their direction. This credential is designed to prepare individuals to plan, implement, maintain, and support large networks of Linux machines or mixed operating systems.

The details on obtaining an MCLE certificate are not yet solidified. However, there will be a set of four exams structured similarly to the previous two levels. If you are already an LCA and LCE, and are interested in proceeding to the MCLE stage, go **to www.linuxcertification.org** for more details.

TRACKING LINUX CERTIFICATION STATUS

Each of the different Linux certification organizations will handle post-certification issues differently. In general, these solutions will include hardcopy affirmation that you did indeed pass the exam, as well as a way for potential employers and clients to verify this information. For example, once you pass Red Hat's RHCE you receive the following a certificate, suitable for framing, along with a serial number which you or others can use to verify your information on Red Hat's Web site. This information includes whether the certification is up to date as of that time.

ABOUT THE BOOK

Career opportunities abound for well-prepared Linux administrators. This book is designed as your doorway into Linux system administration through a variety of Linux distributions. If you are new to Linux or system administration, this is your ticket to an exciting future. Others who have prior experience with Linux and system administration will find that the book adds depth and breadth to that experience. Also, the book provides the knowledge you need to prepare for the various Linux certification tracks. These exams will take you the entire way toward becoming a certified system administrator.

Because Linux is a network operating system with may network tools available for it, it is marvelously scalable and fits into both large and small organizations. It provides the cornerstone on which to build an Internet Web site, or an intranet, while protecting the rest of your network from the outside world. The success of Linux is reflected in the huge number of software vendors and developers who are flocking develop in this environment, especially those who have switched from other environments to Linux.

When you complete this book, you will be at the threshold of a system administration career that can be very fulfilling and challenging. This is a rapidly advancing field that offers ample opportunity for personal growth and for making a contribution to your business or organization. The book is intended to provide you with knowledge that you can apply right away and a sound basis for understanding the changes that you will encounter in the future. It also is intended to give you the hands-on skills you need to be a valued professional in your organization.

The book is filled with real-world projects that cover various aspects of working with and managing Linux. The projects are designed to make what you learn come alive through actually performing the tasks. Also, every chapter includes a range of practice questions to help prepare you for the Linux certification exams. All of these features are offered to reinforce your learning, so you'll feel confident in the knowledge you have gained from each chapter.

Features

To aid you in fully understanding Linux administration concepts, there are many features in this book designed to improve its value:

➤ **Chapter objectives** Each chapter in this book begins with a detailed list of the concepts to be mastered within that chapter. This list provides you with a quick reference to the contents of that chapter, as well as a useful study aid.

➤ **Illustrations and tables** Numerous illustrations of screenshots and components aid you in the visualization of common setup steps, theories, and concepts. In addition, many tables provide details and comparisons of both practical and theoretical information.

➤ **Notes, tips, and warnings** Notes present additional helpful material related to the subject being described. Tips from the author's experience provide extra information about how to attack a problem, how to set up Linux for a particular need, or what to do in certain real-world situations. Warnings are included to help you anticipate potential mistakes or problems so you can prevent them from happening.

➤ **Hands-on projects** Although it is important to understand the theory behind Linux and system administration, nothing can improve upon real-world experience. To this end, along with theoretical explanations, each chapter provides numerous hands-on projects aimed at providing you with real-world implementation experience.

➤ **Chapter summaries** Each chapter's text is followed by a summary of the concepts it has introduced. These summaries provide a helpful way to recap and revisit the ideas covered in each chapter.

➤ **Review questions** End-of-chapter assessment begins with a set of review questions that reinforce the ideas introduced in each chapter. These questions not only ensure that you have mastered the concepts, but are written to help prepare you for the Linux certification examinations. Answers to these questions are found in Appendix G.

➤ **Sample tests** Use the sample test and answer key in Chapters 14 and 15 to test yourself. Then, move on to the two interactive practice exams found on the CD-ROM.

WHERE SHOULD YOU START?

This book is intended to be read in sequence, from beginning to end. Each chapter builds upon those that precede it, to provide a solid understanding of both Linux and system administration concepts. After completing the chapters, you may find it useful to go back through the book and use the review questions and projects to prepare for the Linux certification tests for your chosen track. Readers are also encouraged to investigate the many pointers to online and printed sources of additional information that are cited throughout this book.

Please share your feedback on the book with us, especially if you have ideas about how I can improve it for future readers. I'll consider everything you say carefully, and I'll respond to all suggestions. Send your questions or comments to us at **cipq@coriolis.com**. Please remember to include the title of the book in your message; otherwise, I'll be forced to guess which book you're writing about. And I don't like to guess—I want to *know*! Also, be sure to check out the Web page at **www.certificationinsider.com**, where you'll find information updates, commentary, and certification information. Thanks, and enjoy the book!

SELF-ASSESSMENT

Linux certification became available quite recently. Professional system administrators all over the world are exploring the certification movement and considering which of the three major exam programs is right for them. On the other end of the spectrum, employers are chomping at the bit to have a way to tell experienced and capable potential employees from those who are not when the applicant does not have a string of work experience to vouch for them.

The reason this Self-Assessment in included in this *Exam Prep* book is to help you evaluate your readiness to tackle Linux Level I certification. It should also help you understand what you need to master the topic of this book—namely the Red Hat, Sair, and Linux Professional Institute's (LPI) Level I certification programs. But before you tackle this Self-Assessment, let's talk about concerns you may face when pursuing an RHCE, LPIC, or LCA, and what an ideal Linux Level I system administration candidate's experience might look like.

RHCEs, LPICs, AND LCAs IN THE REAL WORLD

In the next section, I describe an ideal Linux Level I candidate, knowing full well that only a few real candidates will meet this ideal. In fact, my description of that ideal candidate might seem downright scary. But take heart: Although the requirements to obtain an RHCE, LPC, or LPIC may seem pretty formidable, they are by no means impossible to meet. However, you should be keenly aware that it does take time, requires some expense, and consumes substantial effort to get through the process.

The certification programs are already under way and newly certified administrators are regularly appearing on the scene, so it's obviously an attainable goal. You can get all the real-world motivation you need from knowing that many others have gone before, so you will be able to follow in their footsteps. If you're willing to tackle the process seriously and do what it takes to obtain the necessary experience and knowledge, you can take—and pass—all the certification tests involved in obtaining an LPIC, RHCE, or LCA. In fact, these *Exam Preps*, and the companion *Exam Crams*, are designed to make it as easy on you as possible to prepare for these exams. But prepare you must!

THE IDEAL LINUX LEVEL I CANDIDATE

Just to give you some idea of what an ideal certified Linux system administrator candidate is like, here are some relevant statistics about the background and experience such an individual might have. Don't worry if you don't meet these qualifications, or don't come that close—this is a far from ideal world, and where you fall short is simply where you'll have more work to do.

➤ Academic or professional training in Linux or Unix system administration theory, concepts, and operations. This includes everything from user management, file system management, and working at the command line level.

➤ Three-plus years of professional Linux system administration experience. This must include installation, configuration, upgrade, and troubleshooting experience.

➤ Two-plus years in a networked environment that includes hands-on experience with networking services and Internet or intranet servers. A solid understanding of architecture issues, installation, configuration, maintenance, and troubleshooting is also essential.

➤ A thorough understanding of TCP/IP, addressing, and name resolution.

➤ A thorough understanding of file and print services, both locally and over a network.

➤ Familiarity with key TCP/IP-based services, including HTTP (Web servers), NFS, DNS, SMB, FTP, and NIS (these topics are especially important for the exams, because a system administrator needs to be able to set them up at least at a basic level.)

Fundamentally, this boils down to a bachelor's degree in computer science, plus three years of work experience in a technical position involving system administration: installation, configuration, and maintenance. I believe that well under half of all certification candidates meet these requirements, and that, in fact, most meet less than half of these requirements—at least, when they begin the certification process. But because all of those people who already have been certified have survived this ordeal, you can survive it too—especially if you heed what this Self-Assessment can tell you about what you already know and what you need to learn.

PUT YOURSELF TO THE TEST

The following series of questions and observations is designed to help you figure out how much work you must do to pursue Linux certification and what kinds of resources you may consult on your quest. Be absolutely honest in your answers, or you'll end up wasting money on exams you're not yet ready to take. There are no right or wrong answers, only steps along the path to certification. Only you can decide where you really belong in the broad spectrum of aspiring candidates.

Two things should be clear from the outset, however:

➤ Even a modest background in computer science will be helpful.

➤ Hands-on experience with Linux in a networked, administrative environment is an essential ingredient to certification success.

Educational Background

1. Have you ever taken any computer-related classes? [Yes or No]

   If Yes, proceed to question 2; if No, proceed to question 4.

2. Have you taken any classes on computer operating systems? [Yes or No]

   If Yes, you will probably be able to handle Linux architecture and system component discussions. If you're rusty, brush up on basic operating system concepts, particularly Linux and Unix, especially virtual memory, multitasking regimes, user mode versus kernel mode operation, and general computer security topics.

   If No, consider some basic reading in this area. I strongly recommend a good general operating systems book, such as *Operating System Concepts*, by Abraham Silberschatz and Peter Baer Galvin (Addison-Wesley, 1997, ISBN 0-201-59113-8). If this title doesn't appeal to you, check out reviews for other, similar titles at your favorite online bookstore.

3. Have you taken any networking concepts or technologies classes? [Yes or No]

   If Yes, you will probably be able to handle Linux networking terminology, concepts, and technologies. If you're rusty, brush up on basic networking concepts and terminology, especially TCP/IP and Linux networking configuration and troubleshooting.

   If No, you might want to read one or two books in this topic area. The two best books that I know of are *Computer Networks, 3rd Edition*, by Andrew S. Tanenbaum (Prentice-Hall, 1996, ISBN 0-13-349945-6) and *Computer Networks and Internets*, by Douglas E. Comer (Prentice-Hall, 1997, ISBN 0-13-239070-1).

   Skip to the next section, "Hands-On Experience."

4. Have you done any reading on operating systems or networks? [Yes or No]

   If Yes, review the requirements stated in the first paragraphs after questions 2 and 3. If you meet those requirements, move on to the next section, "Hands-On Experience." If No, consult the recommended reading for both topics. A strong background will help you prepare for the Linux exams better than just about anything else.

Hands-On Experience

The most important key to success on all of the Linux tests is hands-on experience, especially with troubleshooting and long term administration issues. If I leave you with only one realization after taking this Self-Assessment, it should be that there's no substitute for time spent installing, configuring, and using the various Linux packages upon which you'll be tested repeatedly and in depth.

5. Have you installed, configured, and worked with:

   ➤ Linux as a network server? [Yes or No]

   If Yes, make sure you understand basic networking concepts as discussed earlier. You should also study Linux TCP/IP interfaces, utilities, and services.

 You can download objectives, practice exams, and other information about the exams covered in this book from the Web sites for each of the three groups: **www.redhat.com**, **www.lpi.org**, and **www.linuxcertification.org**.

   If you haven't worked with Linux as a networking server, TCP/IP, and the popular Linux server packages, you must obtain one or two machines and a copy of your favorite Linux distribution. Then, learn the operating system, and do the same for TCP/IP and whatever other software components on which you'll also be tested.

   In fact, I recommend that you obtain two computers, each with a network interface, and set up a two-node network on which to practice. With decent Linux-capable computers selling for about $500 to $600 apiece these days, this shouldn't be too much of a financial hardship. You can order a CD-ROM with a Linux distribution from your favorite distributor or download it from the Internet.

   ➤ Linux as a client machine? [Yes or No]

   If Yes, make sure you understand how to use Linux as a user, and the issues a user might need the system administrator to help them with.

   If No, you will want to use the same distribution you obtained to study for system administration issues and utilize it as a user without superuser privileges.

6. For any specific Linux package that is not itself the kernel (for example, the X Windowing System, various desktop environments, and so on), have you installed, configured, used, and upgraded this software? [Yes or No]

   If the answer is Yes, skip to the next section, "Testing Your Exam-Readiness." If it's No, you must get some experience. Read on for suggestions on how to do this.

Experience is a must with any Linux exam, be it something as simple as adding users or as challenging as setting up an anonymous FTP server securely. Take that two node network and treat one machine as a server and one as a user machine and install any service and package you think a user might want, or might be useful for the network. Test your own security measures and services. There are any number of Web sites and books out there with useful information to help you along the way, including this book.

 If you have the funds, or your employer will pay your way, consider taking a class through those authorized by the specific organization offering the exam you have chosen to take. Classroom exposure can be useful for filling in knowledge gaps and clarifying issues that before you only understood at a surface level.

Before you even think about taking any Linux exam, make sure you've spent enough time with the related software to understand how it may be installed and configured, how to maintain such an installation, and how to troubleshoot that software when things go wrong. This will help you in the exam, and in real life!

Testing Your Exam-Readiness

Whether you attend a formal class on a specific topic to get ready for an exam or use written materials to study on your own, some preparation for the Linux system administration certification exams is essential. At $100 or more per try, pass or fail, you want to do everything you can to pass on your first try. That's where studying comes in.

I have included a practice exam in this book, so if you don't score that well on it, study and try it again, as well as any practice tests available on the organization's Web site. I also have built two exams to include on the CD-ROM at the back of this book. If you still don't hit a score of at least 85 percent after these tests, you'll want to investigate the practice test resources listed on the organization's Web site.

For any given subject, consider taking a class if you've tackled self-study materials, taken the test, and failed anyway. The opportunity to interact with an instructor and fellow students can make all the difference in the world, if you can afford that privilege. For information about Linux classes, visit the Training and Certification pages at **www.redhat.com**, **www.lpi.org**, or **www.linuxcertification.org**.

If you can't afford to take a class, visit the sites anyway, because they often include pointers to free practice exams and to recommended study guides and other self-study tools.

7. Have you taken a practice exam on your chosen test subject? [Yes or No]

If Yes, and you scored 85 percent or better, you're probably ready to tackle the real thing. If your score isn't above that crucial threshold, keep at it until you break that barrier.

If No, obtain all the free and low-budget practice tests you can find (see the list above) and get to work. Keep at it until you can break the passing threshold comfortably.

When it comes to assessing your test readiness, there is no better way than to take a good-quality practice exam and pass with a score of 85 percent or better. When I'm preparing myself, I shoot for 90-plus percent, just to leave room for the "weirdness factor" that sometimes shows up on exams.

ASSESSING READINESS FOR LINUX LEVEL I CERTIFICATION

In addition to the general exam-readiness information in the previous section, there are several things you can do to prepare for the Linux system administration exams. As you're getting ready for your chosen path, check out the resources listed in Appendix C. These are great places to ask questions and get good answers, or simply to watch the questions that others ask (along with the answers, of course).

You should also cruise the Web looking for Linux documentation, system administration guides and tips, and more. Of course, not every resource will be accurate. Determining which is and which is not is an excellent way to study.

Linux exam mavens also recommend checking the various Linux distributions' tech support databases for "meaningful technical support issues" that relate to your exam's topics. Although I'm not sure exactly what the quoted phrase means, I have also noticed some overlap between technical support questions on particular products and troubleshooting questions on the exams for those products.

For Linux system administration Level I preparation in particular, I'd also like to recommend that you check out one or more of these resources as you prepare to take your chosen exam:

➤ Douglas Comer: *Internetworking with TCP/IP, Volume 1: Principles, Protocols, and Architecture*, Prentice Hall, Englewood Cliffs, NJ, 1995. ISBN: 0-13-216987-8.

➤ Jochen Hein: *Linux Companion for System Administrators*, Addison-Wesley, Reading, MA, 1999. ISBN: 0-201-36044-6.

➤ Ellen Siever, O'Reilly Staff, Andy Oram (Editor): *Linux In A Nutshell*, O'Reilly & Associates, Cambridge, MA, 1999. ISBN: 1-56592-585-8.

➤ Matt Welsh, Matthias Kalle Dalheimer, Lar Kaufman: *Running Linux 3rd Edition*, O'Reilly & Associates, Cambridge, MA, 1999. ISBN: 1-56592-469-X.

Visit your favorite bookstore or online bookseller to check out one or more of these resources. I believe the first one is the best general all-around reference on TCP/IP available, the second compliments basic system administration knowledge wonderfully, and the last two complement the contents of this *Exam Prep* for test preparation very nicely.

One last note: Hopefully, it makes sense to stress the importance of hands-on experience in the context of the Linux exams. As you review the material for the exams, you'll realize that hands-on experience with Linux commands, tools, and utilities is invaluable.

ONWARD, THROUGH THE FOG!

Once you've assessed your readiness, undertaken the right background studies, obtained the hands-on experience that will help you understand the products and technologies at work, and reviewed the many sources of information to help you prepare for a test, you'll be ready to take a round of practice tests. When your scores come back positive enough to get you through the exam, you're ready to go after the real thing. If you follow this assessment regime, you'll not only know what you need to study, but when you're ready to make a test date at Sylvan, VUE, or another appropriate venue for your chosen exam track. Good luck!

## CHAPTER ONE

HARDWARE AND INSTALLATION

AFTER READING THIS CHAPTER AND COMPLETING THE EXERCISES, YOU WILL BE ABLE TO:

➤ Understand the difference between kernel space and user space

➤ Know what the Linux kernel is and understand its function

➤ Know what a module is and understand its function

➤ Manage processes

➤ Know what libraries are and understand their function

➤ Know what a driver is and understand its function

➤ Determine if a particular piece of hardware is supported in Linux

➤ Initialize devices at boot time using passed parameters to the kernel

To gain an understanding of the Linux operating system, it is important to know the underlying architecture of the system as well as how it interacts with hardware. This introductory chapter covers the various levels of the system and how they interoperate, as well as the basics of the Linux kernel itself.

LINUX AND FREE SOFTWARE

Linux—in its current incarnation—would not exist today if it were not for the free software movement. However, this is a movement that is generally misunderstood. Newscasters crow about how Linux will overthrow Microsoft. They say this will happen because Linux is "free," and without truly understanding what this means, they further confuse the public because they themselves do not appear to understand the issue.

How GNU/Linux Was Born

In 1984, Richard Stallman began to develop what he called "GNU software," because of the need as he saw it to return to the scientific method of software code peer review, rather than the overwhelming standard of nondisclosure agreements and closed code. GNU stands for "GNU's Not Unix." It is tightly interwoven with the Free Software Foundation (FSF), which raises funds for GNU's work.

The combined efforts of Stallman, GNU, and the FSF led first to the tools such as GNU Emacs and GCC (the Gnu C Compiler). As Linus Torvalds' Linux kernel continued to grow and prosper, the GNU team decided in 1992 to build its set of tools around Linux because its own kernel was not yet ready for production use. The Linux kernel combined with the GNU tools is referred to as GNU/Linux, though often folks just use "Linux" to refer to the entire operating system and components.

Other items the Linux community uses regularly thanks to GNU are gzip, the bash shell, the Ghostscript interpreter and its cousin Ghostview, glibc—the GNU C libraries—smail, GNU tar, and more. For a complete listing, go to **www.gnu.org/software/software.html**.

The GNU General Public License

GNU introduced the term "copyleft" to the world. This term is used to prevent code written for the express purpose of being open to the community from being closed off. There are actually multiple legal forms of copyleft, one of which is the GNU General Public License (GPL).

The GPL is the license you most commonly encounter when dealing with open source software. It is important to read it carefully if you have a mind at all toward software development using any GNU or GPL-covered tools. Otherwise, what the GPL primarily means to an end user is that you should have free access to the source code of any GPL-covered package you download or purchase. This clause does not mean that the source will necessarily be included with the purchase. When it is not, in practice, often the source can be found on a Web or FTP site.

An open source license such as GPL starkly contrasts with copyright licenses used by proprietary software developers, which state the owner of the code in question. More importantly, proprietary code—more often than not—is never shown to the public if it can be helped. The software is only made available in binary format.

"Free" Software

The word *free* in the FSF, and when used in reference to Linux and the suite of tools available to it, does not actually refer to cost. To quote Richard Stallman, "*free* refers to freedom, not to price." The FSF defines *free* as:

➤ The freedom to run the program for any purpose.

➤ The freedom to alter the program's source to suit your needs.

➤ The freedom to offer copies of the software, either for free or a fee.

➤ The freedom to distribute your own modified versions of the program.

What is considered radical about this notion is that one can charge for something even though the source is freely available. A quick look at the number of Linux distributions available for sale, noting how many of them are also available for download from the Internet, proves that free software is a viable solution for for-profit ventures.

The concern in the business community is to find a way to make a profit from code written under GPL or other FSF or GNU copyleft statements. Those who cannot see the opportunities in these areas have failed to properly analyze the situation surrounding them. Remember that having the source code available does not mean that a company or group has the knowledge or means to modify it so that it serves their needs. It also does not mean that programmers on staff will understand the code or its implications, or have the time or ability to offer technical support. Therefore, there are a number of revenue-generating oppor-tunities available to those who write free software, such as the following:

➤ Custom programming

➤ Technical support

➤ Custom documentation

➤ Seminars and training

➤ Porting to other platforms

➤ Software packaging and distribution via CD-ROM or the Internet

The terms "free software" and "open source" essentially refer to the same thing.

Choosing The Right Operating System

All operating systems are, at the base level, tools. Each one of those available has its own strengths and weaknesses. When users choose to use one operating system over another, they generally should have a reason for doing so, even if that reason is just to learn how to use it. Therefore, it is important to know why you might want to use Linux rather than another operating system. At some point, you may need to justify the decision to management, or simply to answer questions from users or people who are considering using the operating system for themselves.

Multi-User

Some operating systems are built to assume only one user will ever utilize the machine they are installed on. Examples of such systems are MS-DOS and AmigaDOS, among others. Other operating systems are capable of understanding that there are different users who might use them. These operating systems have a login screen that requests a username and password before allowing a user to do anything. Some examples of these systems are Microsoft Windows, Microsoft Windows NT, Unix, Linux, and FreeBSD.

This issue is important because a machine with no form of user identification and security scheme is highly vulnerable because just anyone can walk up to it and utilize it. Such a setup also does not offer any way of preventing access to administrative functions, private data, or anything else that you might want to prevent people from changing or copying. There is also no way to track who was logged in when, or who created which files.

There is still one more level of distinction to consider. Some operating systems can handle multiple users, but only if there is only one user logged in at a time. For example, because it is intended for use as a workstation, Microsoft Windows is designed this way. One user logs in, does what he or she needs to do, then logs off. Then another user can log in and do his or her thing. Other operating systems are able to handle having more than one user logged in simultaneously, generally using a network connection. These are the systems that you are most likely to see used as network servers, such as Linux, FreeBSD, Unix, and Windows NT.

Multi-Tasking

Another distinction that separates operating systems is how many tasks they can handle simultaneously. An operating system such as MS-DOS can only do one thing at a time. In general, this is not a problem because only one user can use the machine at a time anyway. However, it can be a hassle if you are using it to run a program that takes a long time, and the machine is tied up with that process so that you cannot do anything else until the program completes its task.

Operating systems such as Linux, Unix in general, FreeBSD, and Windows NT can handle more than one task at a time, and so are referred to as multi-tasking. How well each of these systems handles running multiple tasks is an exercise for the reader to determine.

LINUX ARCHITECTURE OVERVIEW

The Linux architecture is made up of two main sections; these sections are known as *kernel space* and *user space*. As one might expect, the kernel space handles all of the low-level functions, and the user space handles all of the high-level functions. Of course, as with many parts of the Linux system, there can be exceptions to this rule, which will be covered in more detail shortly. In the kernel space, lots of interesting things happen. There are various subsystems that live there, and in those subsystems is where all of the various low-level *drivers* can be found. On the other hand, user space is a lot more straightforward and simply exists as a series of *processes*. Once again, there can be exceptions, which make Linux far more interesting and more powerful than meets the eye.

Before continuing, however, you need to understand just what user space and kernel space are. User space and kernel space are not divided physically, they are more of a virtual division in the system processes, much like how a city is divided into zones. These zones serve to both divide the process levels, and to organize the system processes.

User Space

User space is the easiest facet of the Linux architecture to understand; going back to our zoning example, the user space is like a residential zone in a city. When a program is loaded, be it a Web browser, word processor, or even just **ls**, it loads into user space. Once loaded into user space, it uses the services provided by the kernel space to do such things as printing text to the screen, opening a file, and almost every other bit of system interaction that needs to be done. So for every-day interaction with Linux, or any other operating system for that matter, it's the user space that is the easiest to see and understand. The rest of the operating system usually seems a bit mysterious.

Kernel Space

Kernel space is where all the magic happens. When an application wants to print "Hello World" to the screen, it's the code residing in the kernel space that makes it happen. Referring to the zoning example, the kernel space is equivalent to an industrial zone of a city. The processes in kernel space are responsible for taking the raw system resources of a computer and turning them into something usable by your applications. The kernel does the brunt of this work itself. What's missing is a communication link between user space and kernel space. This gap is filled with the low-level system *libraries*. These libraries are equivalent to the commercial zone of a city: They take the demands from user space, buffer them and pass the demands in bulk to the Linux kernel. Although it's generally thought of as being part of kernel space, this is not always the case. These libraries are the bridges that link user space with kernel space and as such they live a little in each part.

Linux Kernel

It is a common misconception that Linux is the entire operating system, when, in reality, Linux refers only to the kernel. Some say calling the operating system Linux when a majority of the user space applications come from the GNU project is wrong; others feel that the operating system should be named for its kernel. However, any way you choose to look at it, the kernel is the heart of Linux.

The kernel is responsible for all low-level tasks; these tasks include communicating with peripherals, writing to the hard drive, even loading applications into user space. This is accomplished with drivers. Every chip, board, and socket in a computer has a driver, which acts as an interface to go between generic system calls and specific hardware instructions. For example, when an application sends a request to initialize the acme whizbang card in the computer, the driver would take the whizbang_init() system call and know to send the word 0x42 to port 0x0489. The benefit of doing this is if someone else uses bob's super whizbang deluxe, the application would still send a whizbang_init() system call, but there would be a different driver there to interpret that into the proper hardware language. The problem that arises with this is that it is not feasible to have the drivers for every single hardware device loaded and ready all the time. This is largely taken care of by *modules*.

The other role that the kernel plays is with low-level functionality that is not hardware-dependent. For example, the ability to manipulate a filesystem is a function of the kernel. Other kernel responsibilities include handling the TCP/IP stack, controlling serial data flow, etc. At any point where a low-level function is needed, the kernel handles the requests. At this point, one might wonder just what counts as low-level. As a rule, any function that is required to make a computer work at a basic level is a low-level function. You will find that everyone interprets what is classified as "low level" differently. The distinction, however, is typically not all that important.

MAJOR SUBSYSTEMS

With user space and kernel space set up and communicating with each other, there are a few subsystems that become apparent. These are the kernel modules, processes, and system libraries. These subsystems are not exclusive to either space in the overall Linux architecture, but rather assist in the linking and management of them.

Modules

When dealing with a large number of devices, the kernel can get quite large. There are two downsides to this increased size; one is that overall system performance degrades slightly. In normal circumstances, this is not a large concern as this performance drop is not noticeable, but in high-load situations, such as a popular Web server or an active file server, the performance drop can become noticeable. The other thing that kernel size impacts is the ability to boot from a floppy disk—after all, if the kernel is larger than a floppy disk, you won't be able to boot from a floppy.

In the first case, modules would be used for drivers that are not in constant use. For example, when running a Web server, the drivers for the CD-ROM drive, tape drive, and serial ports probably would not be used very often, but these drivers would need to be present for when those devices are required. The solution is to make the drivers as modules; this way, the drivers can be loaded into the kernel dynamically on an as-needed basis. This same effect helps us in the second example. The base kernel can have the basic drivers to make the system operational, and then the drivers for the rest of the devices can be loaded from another disk.

The obvious question here is: If most parts of the kernel can be built as modules that can be dynamically loaded and unloaded, why not make everything a module and let the modules load and unload as needed? The reason is that it takes time and resources to load and subsequently unload a module. Therefore, it's generally a good idea to either compile the required drivers directly into the kernel, or load them as modules and leave them in memory once they are there. With these considerations in mind, it becomes apparent that a balance needs to be found somewhere between the benefits and the overhead of using modules. The best bet is if a driver is going to be used frequently, compile it into the kernel if at all possible. The one notable exception to this is when dealing with *Plug and Play* devices, which will be discussed more later in the chapter.

Process Management

In user space, every application is referred to as a process. More specifically, *every thread* is a process. When checking for email, for example, the application may have one thread to interface with the user, a thread to handle the network connection, and a thread to interface the two to the mailbox on the hard drive. In this instance, the application has three processes, each of which has a specific task to complete. When working with a Linux system, the **ps(1)** command can be used to obtain a list of processes and the various information attached to them. Here are some commonly used parameters for **ps**:

```
u list the user that owns each process
a show processes for all users
x show processes without a controlling terminal
c command name from task_struct
w wide output: don't truncate command lines to fit on
one line. Every w that is specified will add another
possible line to the output.
r show currently active (running) processes
txx show processes that are attached to controlling terminal
/dev/ttyxx. For example, if the who command shows that
a user is logged into ttyp0, the command "ps tp0" will
show what processes he or she is running.
```

The most commonly used invocation of **ps** is **ps ax**. This command gets a list of all system processes and the basic information about them. The most important information to know when dealing with a process is the process identification (PID) number. Using this number, signals can be sent to the process. These signals can tell it to restart, pause, terminate, etc. To send a signal to a process, the **kill(1)** command is used:

```
Commonly used kill options:
 pid This option is required. It specifies which process
 is to be signaled.
 -SIGNAL specifies the signal that should be sent, for example,
 use -HUP to send a SIGHUP to a process.
 -l Print a list of signal names.
```

Process management is a very powerful feature of Linux. With other operating systems, if an application goes haywire in the system, the solution is often to restart the system. This is not the case with Linux; when an application runs away, it can be told to terminate itself, and if that doesn't work, the kernel can be instructed to kill the process altogether.

 All of this process information may seem abstract at first, but it becomes quite intuitive once you get the hang of it.

Libraries

Libraries are collections of commonly used functions that applications can share. The libraries can be divided into two categories. These are the system libraries and the user libraries. As mentioned earlier, the system libraries link user space applications with the kernel. The user libraries are just common functions that make programming more convenient for programmers and more consistent for users. An example of this type of library is GTK+; this particular library contains a standard set of functions for drawing and manipulating objects in the X window environment. Programmers like to use it because then they do not have to write the code to manipulate X graphics; they can concentrate on the meaningful part of their program. Users also like it when programmers use the library because they know that when a program uses it, that program will have a consistent look and feel with other programs that also use the library.

HARDWARE AND DRIVERS

A working computer is made up of many different devices that all communicate and cooperate to process, store, and display information. But how do the devices know how to do this in an orderly manner? The answer is: drivers. A driver is piece of software that tells a particular device how to interact with other devices or software (mainly operating systems). This book concentrates on drivers designed specifically to tell an operating system, namely Linux, how to communicate with devices that may be installed on the computer they are running on. However, be aware that drivers are not necessarily pieces of software that you install. There are other types of drivers such as *firmware* that are burned into microchips on a device. For instance, a modem and a motherboard both have firmware. A computer's BIOS is also another example of firmware.

HOW DRIVERS WORK

Drivers work by sitting between the operating system and a given piece of hardware. The driver tells the operating system how to communicate with the device while also interpreting what the device is telling the operating system. For instance, when information is sent out on a network, the kernel bundles the data into packets of a determined configuration based on the protocol being used; the kernel then sends the information to the network interface card (NIC) for transmission over the network. Because there are so many different types of NICs—with more showing up everyday—an operating system can't know how to communicate with every one that exists or will exist. If an operating system could do that, its size would be exponentially increased, making it slow and inefficient. This is where the driver comes in.

A device driver is nothing more than an instruction set telling the kernel how to send information to the device, a NIC in this instance, as well as how to receive information from the device. When you install a device driver, it is kind of like teaching the operating system a new language, the device's language. Just as people have different languages, so does each piece of hardware that is used in a computer.

DETERMINING IF YOUR HARDWARE IS SUPPORTED

There are many great pieces of hardware available these days, with something new coming out almost every day. Unfortunately, the device is all but useless without a driver. Before putting any system together or making an upgrade to an existing system, always check to see if a particular device is supported under the operating system you plan to use.

The first place to look when trying to determine if a piece of hardware is supported under Linux is the Linux Hardware Compatibility *How-To*. It can be located on any site that mirrors How-Tos such as **www.linuxdoc.org/HOWTO.html**. This document is updated fairly often, and is very thorough, but do not expect to see the latest 3D graphics accelerator or hard drive controller listed here. Also, the "Linux Hardware Database" located at **http://lhd.datapower.com** will let you search for a device to see if it is supported under Linux. Another excellent location is the kernel itself and its accompanying documentation. For real-time information on operating system support, try the device's manufacturer. Most manufacturers these days support Linux with their drivers; however, not everyone does at this point in time. And of the ones that do, the Linux drivers usually roll out after the device is released. Typically, if a device has been around for awhile and is popular, it is generally supported under Linux. If a device is brand new, obscure, or implementing some experimental or unstandardized technology, do your research. There is nothing worse than spending hundreds of dollars on the latest device, only to find out that you can't use it because there are no drivers available.

OBTAINING LINUX DRIVERS

If the kernel you are using supports a particular device, you don't have to worry about obtaining a driver. For instance, the 3Com 3c905 is supported in the kernel, and if you tell the kernel that you are using that card while configuring the kernel, it will compile a driver into itself or in a module that it loads at boot time. If a piece of hardware isn't supported in the kernel, then you will have to obtain a driver for that device.

There is no one place to obtain drivers for Linux. The first place to go for a device driver is the manufacturer of the given device. If the manufacturer does not offer a driver, do not give up hope; there are many devices that have drivers for Linux that are not supplied by the manufacturer. For instance, the Intel Ether Express Pro 100 NICs aren't supported by Intel under Linux. Donald Becker at NASA is responsible for writing most of the networking code that is now within the Linux kernel supporting the Ether Express NIC. The Internet, being what it is, is the best place for tracking down drivers for Linux. The first place to look for a Linux driver is at **www.linuxhardware.net**. The site is designed for Linux users to place and retrieve information about various pieces of hardware and their experiences with them. The site also has a driver database that is fully searchable. Next, check **www.kernelnotes.org**. This site has a wealth of links to sites on all facets of Linux including hardware and drivers as well as kernel information, news, and kernel downloads.

WHY NEW HARDWARE IS OFTEN NOT SUPPORTED

When a new piece of computer hardware comes out on the market, as a general rule, it has very few drivers available. These drivers are typically for Microsoft products and, of course, are not compatible with Linux. If a company does not supply Linux drivers for its products, an outside programmer must create a driver before there is one available for distribution. This task of creating device drivers is not necessarily a simple one. If the manufacturer provides a list of specifications for the programmer to work with, the job is much easier than if a driver has to be reverse-engineered.

Often, what all of this means to the end user is that drivers are not immediately available for brand-new hardware. Due to the lag between the arrival of the hardware on the shelves and the driver's completion, it is often recommended that you avoid choosing the latest and greatest components when putting together a Linux box. At the very least, do your homework—you may be pleasantly surprised to find that there is a driver for the new product you want to use.

PLUG AND PLAY CONCERNS

Although someday it will be, at this writing, Linux is not ISA Plug and Play-aware. However, because Plug and Play is a standard for PCI, Linux will detect and attempt to configure most PCI devices rather than the BIOS. Be sure to shut off BIOS PnP autodetection before you install.

Having this feature available does not mean that you should expect to install a new device and have Linux detect and configure the device for you. As stated previously, most devices require a driver to function properly.

The closest Linux comes to supporting Plug and Play on the ISA bus is the isapnp tools. These tools poll the ISA bus and return information from devices present in an effort to help the kernel communicate with them. However, there still must be user intervention to load and configure the isapnp tools to properly set up the device and any drivers needed. Keep in mind that the isapnp tools are a separate package from the kernel, and run in user space, so any drivers for ISA Plug and Play devices must be loaded as modules.

To utilize isapnp after installation, you often need to start with the **pnpdump** command by typing **pnpdump > /etc/isapnp.conf**. This command probes every ISA card that has Plug and Play capabilities and outputs the factory settings. If there are no such cards on board, then you will get a listing that ends in the statement "No boards found," so just running **pnpdump** without the redirection is a good way to see if the system is detecting any ISA Plug and Play devices.

Next, you would use the command **vi /etc/isapnp.conf** to open the file (detailed information on using **vi** is given in Chapter 5). Any line that begins with a hash mark (#) is commented out and ignored. Statements generated for card settings may span multiple lines, and consist of terms in parentheses. Understand that this file is broken down into three sections with the first and last being the simplest.

The first /etc/isapnp.conf section is for device initialization. If the PnP items in your BIOS are shut off, then this segment generally looks like the following:

```
(ISOLATE CLEAR)
(IDENTIFY *)
```

When combined, these two lines ensure that unique numbers are assigned to each card, and that each card is identified properly. The last is the cleanup section that consists of the single line:

```
(WAITFORKEY)
```

This statement resets the cards so that they will wait for further instructions from the operating system.

Use the more-complex middle section for configuration purposes. Each ISA Plug and Play device found by **pnpdump** has an entry here. What you need to do is uncomment those lines you want to use by removing the hash marks. For this, it is important to understand what you are seeing. What follows is a run-through of the **pnpdump** results for a sound card.

The file begins with information from **pnpdump**, and then lines similar to the following:

```
# Trying port address 0203
# Trying port address 020b
# Board 1 has serial identifier fe 10 09 f4 74 28 00 8c 0e
```

In the first two lines of this sample, you see where **pnpdump** tested the available ISA ports. It then found an ISA PnP card and outputted what it found. After this the initialization section continues with the following code:

1

```
# (DEBUG)
(READPORT 0x020b)
(ISOLATE PRESERVE)
(IDENTIFY *)
(VERBOSITY 2)
(CONFLICT (IO FATAL)(IRQ FATAL)(DMA FATAL)
    (MEM FATAL)) # or WARNING
```

 Note that some lines of code are broken here for print purposes only, line continuations are indented following the line to which they belong.

Notice that the DEBUG statement is commented out. If you want diagnostic messages produced for this device—perhaps if you cannot get it working and think that the problem may be the card itself—then remove the comment. Otherwise, leave it be. After this, **pnpdump** locates which address is available to store registry information and assigns it to READPORT. You can set this value by hand if you want to, but be sure that you choose an unused address.

Next is often the ISOLATE option. When used with the PRESERVE argument, all current Plug and Play settings are kept. Earlier the ISOLATE setting was shown with the CLEAR argument. The result of that combination would be to set all ISA PnP devices to the settings they had when the machine was turned on. After this, the IDENTIFY statement with the wildcard tells the machine to determine the Card Select Number (CSN) for each of the installed ISA PnP cards. The CSN is a unique handle assigned to the card for configuration only.

The VERBOSITY option takes arguments from zero to three, with zero providing the least detailed output and three providing the most. Finally, the CONFLICT statement given in this example says that if there are I/O, DMA, IRQ, or MEM resource conflicts with other cards, the program you are trying to use with this card will fail with an error. The last portion of the statement, "# or WARNING", is a comment informing you that you can substitute getting a warning about conflicts instead of forcing the program to exit for any of the four resources.

Now, the actual configuration section begins. The first portion of it is simple identifier information, telling you which card this portion of the code refers to and what registers it is capable of utilizing. This section might look like the following:

```
# Card 1: (serial identifier fe 10 09 f4 74 28 00 8c 0e)
# Vendor Id CTL0028, Serial Number 269087860, checksum 0xFE.
# Version 1.0, Vendor version 1.0
# ANSI string -->Creative SB16 PnP<--
```

```
#
# Logical device id CTL0031
#      Device supports vendor reserved register @ 0x38
#      Device supports vendor reserved register @ 0x3a
#      Device supports vendor reserved register @ 0x3b
#      Device supports vendor reserved register @ 0x3e
#
# Edit the entries below to uncomment out the configuration required.
# Note that only the first value of any range is given,
      this may be changed if required
# Don't forget to uncomment the activate (ACT Y) when happy
```

Notice the next line has two opening parentheses and no closing. This is because your task in editing this file is to uncomment the portions that will make up the rest of the statement. For this specific card, the opening for the code segment is:

```
(CONFIGURE CTL0028/269087860 (LD 0
#      ANSI string -->Audio<--
```

Now you must continue the statement. However, do not be misled. Notice the warning that comes after the opener:

```
# Multiple choice time, choose one only !
```

There is probably more than one opening CONFIGURE statement in the file. Each statement has a different LD (Logical Device) value. You need to configure each of these sections. The first CONFIGURE statement very likely offers a series of statements. Each starts with a line similar to the following:

```
#      Start dependent functions: priority preferred
```

Use these lines to make your choices. Go with the preferred option first, and if the card does not function, you can comment that section again and try the acceptable options, and then the functional options. You might end up with the following code if you go with the preferred section:

```
#      Start dependent functions: priority preferred
#         IRQ 5.
#              High true, edge sensitive interrupt (by default)
(INT 0 (IRQ 5 (MODE +E)))
#         First DMA channel 1.
#              8 bit DMA only
#              Logical device is not a bus master
#              DMA may execute in count by byte mode
#              DMA may not execute in count by word mode
#              DMA channel speed in compatible mode
```

1

```
(DMA 0 (CHANNEL 1))
#        Next DMA channel 5.
#              16 bit DMA only
#              Logical device is not a bus master
#              DMA may not execute in count by byte mode
#              DMA may execute in count by word mode
#              DMA channel speed in compatible mode
(DMA 1 (CHANNEL 5))
#        Logical device decodes 16 bit IO address lines
#              Minimum IO base address 0x0220
#              Maximum IO base address 0x0220
#              IO base alignment 1 bytes
#              Number of IO addresses required: 16
(IO 0 (SIZE 16) (BASE 0x0220))
#        Logical device decodes 16 bit IO address lines
#              Minimum IO base address 0x0330
#              Maximum IO base address 0x0330
#              IO base alignment 1 bytes
#              Number of IO addresses required: 2
(IO 1 (SIZE 2) (BASE 0x0330))
#        Logical device decodes 16 bit IO address lines
#              Minimum IO base address 0x0388
#              Maximum IO base address 0x0388
#              IO base alignment 1 bytes
#              Number of IO addresses required: 4
(IO 2 (SIZE 4) (BASE 0x0388))
```

Notice that if you string all of the uncommented lines together for the
CONFIGURE statement, you have:

```
(CONFIGURE CTL0028/269087860 (LD 0 (INT 0 (IRQ 5 (MODE +E)))
      (DMA 0 (CHANNEL 1)) (DMA 1 (CHANNEL 5)) (IO 0 (SIZE 16)
      (BASE 0x0220)) (IO 1 (SIZE 2) (BASE 0x0330))
      (IO 2 (SIZE 4) (BASE 0x0388))
```

By counting the opening and closing parentheses, you can tell that this statement
is not complete. There are 18 opening and 16 closing parentheses. Skipping over
all of the priority acceptable and priority functional sections, you will eventually
come to the following line:

```
#      End dependent functions
 (NAME "CTL0028/269087860[0]{Audio                }")
# (ACT Y)
))
```

Uncomment the ACT Y line and you have fully set up your first configuration statement. You must uncomment this line to activate the settings! Notice that you also just gained the extra two parentheses you needed to close out the statement. Now, you have the text:

```
#
# Logical device id CTL2011
#       Device supports vendor reserved register @ 0x38
#       Device supports vendor reserved register @ 0x3a
#       Device supports vendor reserved register @ 0x3b
#       Device supports vendor reserved register @ 0x3e
#
# Edit the entries below to uncomment out the configuration
      required.
# Note that only the first value of any range is given, this
      may be changed if required.
# Don't forget to uncomment the activate (ACT Y) when happy.

(CONFIGURE CTL0028/269087860 (LD 1
#       Compatible device id PNP0600
#       ANSI string -->IDE<--

# Multiple choice time, choose one only!
```

The configuration is not over. This is the beginning of configuration settings for Logical Device 1. Treat this section the same way, going with the preferred options unless they cause a problem later. You might end up with the following:

```
#       Start dependent functions: priority preferred
#         IRQ 10.
#             High true, edge sensitive interrupt (by default)
(INT 0 (IRQ 10 (MODE +E)))
#       Logical device decodes 16 bit IO address lines
#             Minimum IO base address 0x0168
#             Maximum IO base address 0x0168
#             IO base alignment 1 bytes
#             Number of IO addresses required: 8
(IO 0 (SIZE 8) (BASE 0x0168))
#       Logical device decodes 16 bit IO address lines
#             Minimum IO base address 0x036e
#             Maximum IO base address 0x036e
#             IO base alignment 1 bytes
#             Number of IO addresses required: 2
(IO 1 (SIZE 2) (BASE 0x036e))
```

Notice that this section was shorter than previous code. Once again, you have the statement close where you need to uncomment the activation line. Below, it is shown uncommented:

```
#      End dependent functions
 (NAME "CTL0028/269087860[1]{IDE                }")
(ACT Y)
))
```

The file continues. In this case, there are still LD 2 and LD 3 to configure. This configuration might look like the following:

```
#
# Logical device id PNPffff
#      Device supports vendor reserved register @ 0x38
#      Device supports vendor reserved register @ 0x3a
#      Device supports vendor reserved register @ 0x3b
#      Device supports vendor reserved register @ 0x3e
#
# Edit the entries below to uncomment out the configuration
      required.
# Note that only the first value of any range is given, this
      may be changed if required.
# Don't forget to uncomment the activate (ACT Y) when happy.

(CONFIGURE CTL0028/269087860 (LD 2
#      ANSI string -->Reserved<--
#      Logical device decodes 16 bit IO address lines
#          Minimum IO base address 0x0100
#          Maximum IO base address 0x03f8
#          IO base alignment 8 bytes
#          Number of IO addresses required: 1
(IO 0 (SIZE 1) (BASE 0x0100))
 (NAME "CTL0028/269087860[2]{Reserved           }")
(ACT Y)
))
#
# Logical device id CTL7001
#      Device supports vendor reserved register @ 0x38
#      Device supports vendor reserved register @ 0x3a
#      Device supports vendor reserved register @ 0x3b
#      Device supports vendor reserved register @ 0x3e
#
# Edit the entries below to uncomment out the configuration
      required.
```

```
# Note that only the first value of any range is given, this
      may be changed if required.
# Don't forget to uncomment the activate (ACT Y) when happy.

(CONFIGURE CTL0028/269087860 (LD 3
#      Compatible device id PNPb02f
#      ANSI string -->Game<--
#      Logical device decodes 16 bit IO address lines
#          Minimum IO base address 0x0200
#          Maximum IO base address 0x0200
#          IO base alignment 1 bytes
#          Number of IO addresses required: 8
(IO 0 (SIZE 8) (BASE 0x0200))
  (NAME "CTL0028/269087860[3]{Game                }")
(ACT Y)
))
# End tag... Checksum 0x00 (OK)
```

Nothing was deleted from this section except the comments for the IO definition lines and the activation lines. Each stage of this file gets shorter and shorter because there are fewer options to set. Finally, we reach the Tidy Up section and the card is told that the configuration is finished, and it should now wait for interaction with the operating system.

```
# Returns all cards to the "Wait for Key" state
(WAITFORKEY)
```

 Use the command **man isapnp.conf** for a complete set of tag and operator definitions.

HARDWARE ISSUES

One reason Linux can be difficult for some people is that it does not work with all hardware. However, it is easy to forget that all operating systems are fussy about the hardware they accept. The key is learning how to quickly make decisions that do not result in costly lost time and returning devices.

SCSI And NIC

As you learned earlier, the kernel configures devices at boot time in kernel space (with the exception of user space programs such as the isapnp tools). If a kernel is configured and compiled correctly, then most devices should not pose any problems at boot time. However, some devices or multiple instances of devices require user intervention to help the kernel set up and configure these devices on a hardware level. Most commonly, SCSI devices and multiple instances of NICs will require some user intervention in the manner of passing the kernel extra parameters at boot time. The way in which a device's driver is set up (i.e., as a module or compiled directly into the kernel) will determine how these extra parameters will be passed to the kernel as it loads and initializes hardware devices. There is no general rule for devices of a particular nature (i.e., SCSI cards) always refer to the device's documentation before attempting to pass parameters to the kernel.

SCSI devices have their own addressing scheme. If there are any such devices on the system you are preparing to put Linux on, you need to ensure that these devices are properly detected by the machine and assigned SCSI IDs. Where you go to do this depends on whether the motherboard has onboard support for SCSI or not. If there is onboard support on the motherboard, chances are that SCSI information is set directly in the BIOS. However, there also may be a separate "SCSI BIOS" that comes up after the computer determines that you do not want to use the main BIOS. Press the key necessary to open the SCSI BIOS and you can configure it from there.

When purchasing NIC devices, be sure to get a PCI networking card. If you utilize an ISA card, then you will have to set up many features by hand. However, Linux can auto detect the PCI version and handle much of the setup for you. This aspect can save some serious headaches.

Winmodems

Winmodems are basically modems without any firmware. This means that the entire modem is operated by software. Compared to a regular modem that has firmware, winmodems require software to tell them how to communicate with other modems, whereas a regular modem already knows how to communicate with other modems because of its firmware.

As stated earlier, kernel drivers act as an interpretation layer between generic system calls and the hardware's native language. With winmodems, because there is no direct translation, complete modem emulation would have to be implemented, causing excessive and unacceptable kernel bloat. Therefore, any support for a winmodem has to come as a user space emulation package. There are projects underway to accomplish this, but at the time of this writing, there are no plans to merge these packages with the kernel.

Sound Cards

Many users run into trouble trying to get their sound cards configured in Linux. The first thing that you may need to do if the sound card is ISA is use the isapnp tools to configure its Plug and Play aspects. Even more daunting to the beginning Linux user is that not all Linux distributions ship sound-enabled kernels as the default option. To check and see if this is the case, use the command **cat /dev/sndstat**. If you get a result that is not an error, and in this result you see a line similar to the following:

```
Load type: Driver loaded as a module
```

Using this saves you from kernel compilation. Otherwise, see Chapter 11 for how to compile a new version of the kernel.

 If you are using the Red Hat distribution or one of its derivatives, a special sound configuration tool is included.

Laptops

There are a number of extra issues that come into play when planning to install Linux on a laptop. Many of these issues revolve around having little control over the hardware inside. It is important to take some additional time before even purchasing the machine to ensure that there is a reasonable chance that it will work with Linux. Not only should you check the standard hardware lists, you should also look at the Linux Laptop HOW-TO at **www.linuxdoc .org/HOWTO/Laptop-HOWTO.html**, and the Linux on Laptops site at **www.cs.utexas.edu/users/kharker/linux-laptop/**. These two Web sites will help you to narrow down which laptops are likely to support the features you require in Linux.

The biggest issue with laptop hardware is typically getting the X server to run. An incompatible video card or display can make this task anywhere from difficult to impossible. Another item to remember when you are preparing to install is that if you are using a PCMCIA-connected CD-ROM or floppy drive during the installation process, you may need to make a special installation disk with the proper PCMCIA drivers. Consult the distribution's manuals for detailed information on what it requires.

RAID

Although the average user is not much concerned with the topic of RAID (Redundant Array of Inexpensive/Independent Disks, the meaning of the "I" is slowly changing from "Inexpensive" to "Independent") storage, a system administrator needs to understand what it is and what it can do. Without this understanding, you cannot make fully educated choices about how to install the file system and what type of error correction, prevention, and recovery methods might best suit your budget and needs.

1

RAID refers to a series of storage options that each has its own capabilities and costs. This series was originally five different standards, each with more features than the previous. More RAID levels are sometimes added, but understanding the base levels gives you what you need to follow the rest.

One of the most important aspects of RAID technology to understand is the concept of media striping. This technique allows data to be spread across multiple drives in a manner similar to that shown in Figure 1.1.

How wide or narrow to make the stripes is a factor of what kind of application the RAID array—as RAID drive groups are called—is meant for. If the array's purpose is to store information in a lot of small records, such as database entries or word processing files, then make the stripes large so that the entries can be stored in their entirety on one physical drive. A large stripe can be megabytes wide. Doing this allows for simultaneous data access because different records will be spread across different drives.

On the other hand, if you are dealing with large items such as video, high-resolution images, or other things that make for huge files, then you want small stripes, which can be as small as 512 bytes. Doing this allows the files to be spread over a number of physical drives, and so speeds up how quickly they are opened and saved.

Along with choosing how many and how large the RAID stripes should be, you also must choose which RAID level to utilize. RAID-0 is the simplest form. It has no manner of error recovery or data redundancy, but uses striped drives as shown in Figure 1.1. Due to the striping, data can be read or written on each of the drives at the same time, which if laid out properly can speed up input/output (I/O) performance.

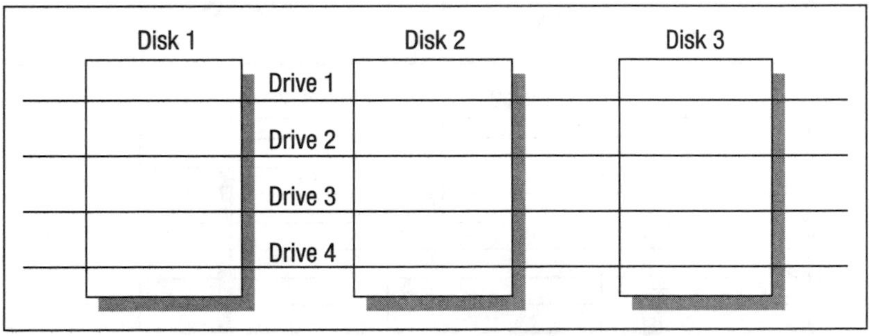

Figure 1.1   RAID striping with three physical disks and four large data stripes to create four logical RAID drives.

RAID-1 is slightly different. It involves using pairs of drives, where each pair appears to the machine as only one hard drive. Rather than spreading sequential data across the pair, the exact same data is written to each drive in the exact same location. Doing this provides data redundancy, so that if one drive fails physically, the other one can pick up the work without a pause. It also allows for fast data access because you can read from both drives at the same time. The problem is, however, that if a data problem creeps into the system, it is mirrored onto both drives as well.

RAID-2 is similar to RAID-0 but has error correction built in. However, this correction type is redundant because modern drives already save it in each sector, so it is currently considered obsolete. RAID-3, on the other hand, is still in use. Its error correction routine is far more thorough than that used in RAID-2, but can only do one I/O task at a time, so is really only useful for small systems with one user. A representation of how it works is given in Figure 1.2. Notice the large number of small data stripes. Data in this RAID level must be stored across all of the drives to maximize I/O speed.

The RAID-4 setup is similar to RAID-3 except for one critical way: The stripes are larger, allowing for files to be stored entirely on one drive. This one change opens this RAID level for use on multi-user systems. The one place where it is still slow is that it can only write to one drive at a time because the parity information must be written as well.

The most complex solution offered among the original RAID levels is RAID-5. Instead of having a single parity drive, as in RAID-4, the parity information is stored among all of the system drives. This immensely speeds up write access along with read access. The size of the stripes you choose for this level determine whether it is better for one (small stripes) or many (large stripes) users.

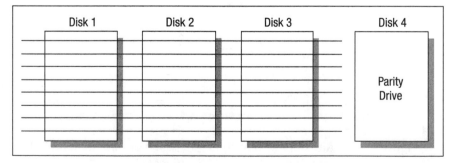

Figure 1.2 RAID-3 with three data drives and one parity drive to store error correction information.

THE MYTH OF THE BENCHMARK

As competition in the operating system world increases, the benchmark is becoming more popular. A *benchmark* is a standard against which programs, operating systems, or machines are compared. If you do research on Linux and benchmarks, you will find many of them out there, and even more frustrating, you will find conflicting results! There are some reasons for this, and for why benchmarks are something to treat with suspicion until you have read their methods and how they came to their results.

First, a benchmark has to clearly state what it is testing for. Testing to see which operating system is faster, for example, is a pretty broad claim. A number of questions come to mind:

➤ What exactly were they testing to produce this benchmark?

➤ Do the items they were testing represent the sum total of what should effect the conclusion they give? For example, if they were testing for operating system speed, did they cover all aspects of the operating systems, or just selected portions?

➤ Was identical hardware used for the tests?

➤ Is the hardware chosen known to be explicitly beneficial to one operating system or the other?

➤ Were the operating systems both fine-tuned by experts with those systems?

➤ Were the operating systems both used as they come out of the box?

➤ What software was used for these tests? Was that software originally written for one operating system then ported to the other by someone who was not an expert?

These are just a few of the questions that come to mind when looking at benchmark reports. The primary issue is that many benchmark tests are biased, either purposely or by carelessness. This problem is especially true in the broader benchmark tests that are meant to prove which operating system is "better" than another. All operating systems are tools. Each has its strengths and weaknesses. Testing those strengths and weaknesses is possible, but "better" is a subjective issue pertaining to what it is being used for.

The most trustworthy benchmark tests are those that are highly specialized. For example, having experts each set up and optimize different Web servers on identical hardware and connections and then fetch identical Web pages from them. A number of response time issues could be tested here, though networking experts may still argue that the setups were not set up specifically enough for testing.

WHAT IS A SYSTEM ADMINISTRATOR?

When preparing for a Linux certification exam, remember that it is imperative that you have real-life experience in system administration. There may be some things you do on a regular basis that you never really considered part of a system administrator's job. You may bear the title of system administrator and never have dealt with some of the things that the job entails. However, it is important that you understand the breadth of what potentially falls under this title, not just the depth of the technology behind it.

Keeping Things Running Smoothly

A system administrator's job can often be boiled down to the phrase: "Keep things running smoothly." In an environment in which you are supporting a LAN in a work environment, or servers that feed information to and from the Internet, you are somewhat like a roadie for a rock band. Your job is to keep things running behind the scenes. It is you who are responsible for keeping the machines up and functional, software installation, network additions and upgrades, and fixing problems when they occur.

Technical Support

One job that you will either love or hate is technical support. A system administrator in an office LAN environment tends to be responsible for all of the hardware, including keeping printers running properly and helping users recover from disk crashes. You may even have to provide email and phone support to users who are having problems, or simply do not know how to accomplish what they need to do. More on the general topic of dealing with users is covered in Chapter 6, but for now it is important to keep in mind that you do not work in a vacuum. The better your setup, configuration, documentation, and troubleshooting skills are, the better off you will be.

Documentation

In the early days of computers and Unix, many programmers and administrators liked to keep what they did somewhat hidden and cryptic. There are many reasons given for this habit, from ensuring job security to elitism. The desire to keep things hidden resulted in there being no documentation for those who came after them, no way to tell what had been done, or what kind of logic was used to set up the system. There is another problem with this though.

If you do not keep detailed documentation, then it will be you who suffers along with everyone else. There is a lot to keep track of in the world of computers today. Good things to document are procedures, for example. Especially complex ones that take you some time to figure out. If you only have to deal with something once every year or so, then it is easy to forget how to do it in the meantime. Well-documented procedures prove their worth in such situations.

Other items to document carefully are machine configurations, including any changes made. This allows you to bring the machine back up quickly if you need to replace it, or to fix things if a user accidentally fouls them up. Keeping track of file system locations as well helps immensely if you lose track of what is where, or are out of the office when something goes down and someone else attempts to fix it.

 A three-ring binder of notes, reminders, and printouts of gathered tips and tricks is often a system administrator's best friend!

Assisting Management

Another important job often given to system administrators is that of assisting management with equipment purchase decisions. There are a number of reasons for this. For one thing, it is not the average manager's job to understand the ins and outs of technology as it evolves at its typically rapid pace. There is also the issue of obtaining the proper hardware for the Linux distribution, let alone choosing the distribution that fits your needs the best.

Simply understanding the underlying premises behind choosing hardware for Linux—for example, checking hardware compatibility lists, and not getting the latest and greatest items—adds immense value to your position. Being available to do some research and at the very least double-check purchasing decisions before hardware turns up on your desk that has to be sent back, makes life easier for everyone, including yourself.

When management does not involve you in purchasing decisions, consider asking if you can at least look over the purchase orders before they are submitted. This request is especially well received when in conjunction with having to report that you are behind schedule because Linux incompatible hardware was purchased.

CHAPTER SUMMARY

This chapter explored the Linux architecture and discussed the differences between user space and kernel space, as well as what the kernel actually does. You saw the major Linux subsystems, including kernel modules, user processes, and system libraries. Also covered was hardware and what function drivers play in making it work correctly with an operating system. You then took a look at ways to determine if a particular device is supported under Linux. Plug and Play devices as well as winmodems were covered, and lastly, you saw how to configure devices at boot time by passing the kernel parameters to help it configure a device correctly and load its appropriate driver.

For Linux certification, nothing in this chapter is more important than understanding what the kernel is and how it operates. Once this concept is mastered, it sets the stage for everything else to fall into place. It is also important to understand the difference between user space and kernel space, especially when dealing with processes. Remember that user space is nothing more than a place where running programs or applications reside, whereas kernel space is where all the actual processing and device interaction take place. Another important thing to know for the purposes of examination, is how to perform successful process management using the **ps** and **kill** commands.

If you are interested in the Sair certification track, be sure to learn the history of Linux, GNU, and the Free Software Foundation. Even if you are not going to follow that track, it is good to have an idea of where things came from. This knowledge will help you better understand discussions on where they're going.

REVIEW QUESTIONS

1. The driver for a device is located in _____ space.
   a. driver
   b. kernel
   c. user
   d. root

2. A driver acts as a (an) _____ between the kernel and a piece of hardware.
   a. linguist
   b. interpreter
   c. go-between
   d. gateway

3. What part of the Linux operating system is actually Linux?
   a. module
   b. library
   c. kernel
   d. driver

4. The kernel is responsible for what kind of tasks?
   a. high-level
   b. mid-level
   c. low-level
   d. menial

5. Which command would be used to kill stop process number 889?
   a. **job –s 889**
   b. **stop 889**
   c. **job –k 889**
   d. **kill 889**

6. Which command would be used to stop all instances of /usr/bin/smbd?
   a. **kill –a /usr/bin/smbd**
   b. **killall /usr/bin/smbd**
   c. **job –k /usr/bin/smbd**
   d. **stop –a /usr/bin/smbd**

7. Which command would be used to restart the daemon with process ID 945?
   a. **kill 945**
   b. **kill –HUP 945**
   c. **killall 945**
   d. **kill –9 945**

8. What part of the Linux architecture holds generic system calls?
   a. user space
   b. libraries
   c. kernel space
   d. threads

9. If a device driver were needed often, what might you make to speed access time?
   a. kernel
   b. library
   c. thread
   d. module

10. Which file would you edit to give the kernel device information for a driver loaded as a module?
   a. /etc/modules.conf
   b. /etc/modules
   c. /etc/lilo.conf
   d. /dev/modules

11. Which file would you edit to pass the kernel device configuration parameters for a driver compiled directly into the kernel?

    a. /etc/modules

    b. /etc/modules.conf

    c. /dev/modules

    d. /etc/lilo.conf

12. What divides user space and kernel space?

    a. virtual zones

    b. different file system formatting

    c. partitions

    d. physical etchings on the hard drive

13. Kernel size makes an impact on which of the following when booting from a hard drive?

    a. remaining hard drive space

    b. number of modules loadable

    c. video capability

    d. system performance

14. What organization produced most of the tools that are used in Linux?

    a. NSF

    b. NAFTA

    c. GPL

    d. GNU

15. Which of the following most accurately describes Linux and how it handles users?

    a. single user

    b. single sequential users

    c. multi-user

    d. multiple simultaneous users

16. Which of the following most accurately describes Linux and how it handles processes?

    a. single process

    b. single sequential process

    c. multi-process

1

17. The person who first wrote the Linux kernel was _____.
    a. Linus Torvalds
    b. Richard Stallman
    c. Matt Welsh
    d. Scott MacNeally

18. When choosing hardware for a new Linux machine, you should always purchase the newest equipment. True or False?

19. _____ refers to the philosophy that programming code should be openly available for all to modify, package, and compile to run?
    a. Free software
    b. Shareware
    c. Public domain

20. What is the financial arm of GNU?
    a. Free Software Fund
    b. Free Software Foundation
    c. GNU itself
    d. GNU Project Financial

HANDS-ON PROJECTS

Project 1.1

For this project, a functional Linux system with the standard GNU tools is needed. This is an example of basic process management. In Chapter 7, the idea of process management will be expanded on.

To start a process, find what PID it is, and then stop the process:

1. Start a process. For this example, the **yes** command will be used. The **yes** command outputs a bunch of y's until it is **kill**ed. Although sometimes useful in certain scripts, simply running it on the console is highly annoying and you will want to get to the part where you **kill** it quickly. Before continuing, note that it is not a good idea to do this project while telnetted in, or over a serial terminal; the **yes** command will quickly flood your buffers and make your life miserable; so do this at an actual console. To start the **yes** command, run:

```
> yes
```

2. The **yes** command is now doing its thing, but it's hard to get anything done while your screen is flashing by with y's. So stop **yes** by pressing Ctrl+C.

3. Let's start **yes** again in a slightly friendlier manner. This time you will tell **yes** to output to /dev/null* instead of the screen, and also put it in the background so you can get a command prompt back.

```
> yes > /dev/null &
```

The > character tells the system to redirect the output, in this case to /dev /null, and the & character tells the system to place the process into the background.

4. Now, you need the PID for the new process so you can send it a signal.

```
> ps ax
```

This command will output a list of processes similar to the one shown here; use the output from your computer to find a similar entry and get its PID for use in the next steps.

```
PID   TTY   STAT   TIME    COMMAND
1     ?     S      0:03    init [3]
2     ?     SW     0:00    (kflushd)
3     ?     SW     0:00    (kupdate)
4     ?     SW     0:00    (kpiod)
5     ?     SW     0:00    (kswapd)
12    ?     S      0:00    /sbin/kerneld
28    ?     S      0:00    /usr/sbin/cron -110
44    ?     SW     0:01    (klogd)
47    ?     S      0:08    /usr/sbin/syslogd
59    ?     S      0:00    /usr/sbin/inetd
61    ?     SW     0:00    (lpd)
66    ?     S      0:00    (sendmail)
95    ?     S      0:00    /usr/local/apache/bin/httpd
102   ?     S      0:00    /usr/sbin/dhcpd eth0
104   ?     S      0:00    /usr/sbin/named
944   4     R      9:53    yes
972   1     R      0:00    ps ax
```

5. Now send a signal to **kill** the process, but first, you need to know what signal to send. To find out what signals are available, run:

```
> kill -l
```

1

It will produce an output similar to this:

```
1) SIGHUP      2) SIGINT     3) SIGQUIT    4) SIGILL
5) SIGTRAP     6) SIGABRT    7) SIGBUS     8) SIGFPE
9) SIGKILL    10) SIGUSR1   11) SIGSEGV   12) SIGUSR2
13) SIGPIPE   14) SIGALRM   15) SIGTERM   17) SIGCHLD
18) SIGCONT   19) SIGSTOP   20) SIGTSTP   21) SIGTTIN
22) SIGTTOU   23) SIGURG    24) SIGXCPU   25) SIGXFSZ
26) SIGVTALRM 27) SIGPROF   28) SIGWINCH  29) SIGIO
30) SIGPWR
```

6. The signal you want to send is #9, or **KILL**.

```
> kill -KILL 944
```

or

```
> kill -9 944
```

Remember, substitute the PID for your process when running that command.

7. Did it work? Use **ps** to find out if it's gone now.

```
> ps ax
PID  TTY  STAT  TIME   COMMAND
1    ?    S     0:03   init [3]
2    ?    SW    0:00   (kflushd)
3    ?    SW    0:00   (kupdate)
4    ?    SW    0:00   (kpiod)
5    ?    SW    0:00   (kswapd)
12   ?    S     0:00   /sbin/kerneld
28   ?    S     0:00   /usr/sbin/cron -110
44   ?    SW    0:01   (klogd)
47   ?    S     0:08   /usr/sbin/syslogd
59   ?    S     0:00   /usr/sbin/inetd
61   ?    SW    0:00   (lpd)
66   ?    S     0:00   (sendmail)
95   ?    S     0:00   /usr/local/apache/bin/httpd
102  ?    S     0:00   /usr/sbin/dhcpd eth0
104  ?    S     0:00   /usr/sbin/named
976  1    R     0:00   ps ax
```

Project 1.2

This project is in two parts. For the first portion of this project, you will need a functioning Linux system and two network interface cards supported under Linux, with the drivers compiled into the kernel. You must also be logged into the system as root. For the second portion, you need access to the World Wide Web, though which operating system you use to get to it does not matter.

The goal of this project is to use the Linux kernel loader, LILO, to pass the kernel parameters that will help it configure these two NICs during boot up.

1. Using a text editor, such as **joe** or **vi**, you first need to add an entry into /etc/lilo.conf:

   ```
   > append="ether=0,0,eth0 ether=0,0,eth1"
   ```

   As you may recall from earlier in the chapter, the zeros in the ether statement tell the kernel to autoconfig the IRQ and BASE_ADDRESS of both NICs.

2. Exit the text editor and issue the **lilo** command:

   ```
   > lilo
   ```

   The resulting dump should look something like this:

   ```
   >Added linux *
   >
   ```

3. Reboot the machine.

Now, you need to learn more about the world of Linux and what it offers. To accomplish this, do the following:

1. Read the GPL document in Appendix B. You may need to read it slowly to be able to make sense of its legalese.

2. Go to the Web site **www.gnu.org** and read the various documents that outline its philosophies and practices.

3. Go to the Web site **www.linuxdoc.org** and look at the wealth of manuals and information there that other Linux users have helped to make available to the general Linux public.

4. Go to the Web site **www.linuxgazette.com** to see the kinds of articles and information that are available to you.

5. Go to the Google search engine's Linux segment, at **www.google.com/ linux** and bookmark it. Try searching on "Certification" and see what comes up.

## CHAPTER TWO

LINUX INSTALLATION AND PACKAGE MANAGEMENT

AFTER READING THIS CHAPTER AND COMPLETING THE EXERCISES, YOU WILL BE ABLE TO:

➤ Determine what hardware will function with Linux

➤ Partition a hard drive with **fdisk**

➤ Install Linux

➤ Perform basic troubleshooting on a Linux installation

➤ Update an existing Linux installation

➤ Compile programs from source code

➤ Take care of the most common modem and sound card issues

As you would assume, installing Linux is an important step in getting a Linux system up and running. When doing so, the first thing to know is which distribution to use. Although many Linux fans disagree on which distribution is best and why, keep in mind that once the system is installed, Linux is Linux is Linux. The main differences lie within the actual installation process.

LINUX PRE-INSTALLATION OVERVIEW

Linux *distributions* such as Red Hat and Caldera have a fairly simple installation process, whereas distributions such as Stampede and Debian give the user more power over the installation and are thus more complex. The best way to choose one if you do not already have a favorite is to close your eyes and pull one out of a hat. Each distribution has installation documentation, so getting one to work is fairly easy. The difficult part of the installation is checking your hardware and ensuring you have everything needed to install before you begin.

Reviewing Your Hardware Specifications

Before installing Linux, it is important to check that your hardware is supported. As a rule, any device that is popular or has been around for awhile is likely to be supported. To be sure of a device's support status, check the hardware compatibility How-To; which is available at your favorite documentation site (try **www.linux.org** if you do not have a favorite yet). One thing to note is that even if your device is not explicitly supported, if it is a fairly common device, the drivers are often incorporated as generic. One example of this is the NE2000 network card driver. In general, unless you have a brand new bleeding-edge proprietary device, odds are it will work under Linux.

Gather Information

As you would expect, it is necessary to gather some information before installing Linux. First, make a list of all the hardware on your system. With many modern distributions, most, if not all, of your hardware will be properly detected. However, when the installer asks what kind of video card you have, you'll appreciate having the list on hand so you do not have to shut down the system and start the installation process all over again.

Next, check with the installation instructions of your specific distribution to see what you need to begin the installation. Many distributions require boot disks to start the installation; some use one, and some use two or more, and others can boot from the CD-ROM. Once everything is gathered, you are ready to boot the system from your boot media and forge ahead in the installation process.

Preparing The BIOS

Sometimes a machine's BIOS does not need adjustment before you can begin installation, but often it does. It is best to take a look at it before getting started just to save yourself the need to go back and change things later. To begin this process, reboot or turn on the machine, and press the key that enters the BIOS—or "setup," as it is frequently called during the boot process. The issues to examine while looking through your BIOS include date and time, SCSI device settings, IRQs, and hard drive issues.

If you want the system to have time to refresh itself properly each time the system reboots, then you need to set the date and time within the BIOS itself. Doing so ensures that Linux is getting its proper date and time from the BIOS chip, and not from you each time you boot. Also, if you are installing from a CD-ROM that can handle the installation, be sure to set the boot sequence so that the CD-ROM is first.

A major consideration is ensuring that Linux can boot properly. The operating system cannot boot properly if you have the boot information—typically kept either in the /boot directory or partition, or in the top of the root partition—above the hard drive's 1023rd cylinder. This is an unfortunate BIOS limitation left over from the days of smaller drives, and only recently has it become a wide-spread inconvenience. Hopefully, this limit will be removed soon. However, for now we are stuck with it. There are a few reliable ways to get around it. One method involves turning on Logical Block Addressing (LBA) in the BIOS. Unfortunately, this method is not guaranteed to help. If you have a machine that you cannot rearrange to make sure that the boot information is below the 1024th cylinder, try using LBA mode and see if the machine is suddenly able to boot.

There are some simple BIOS items that typically need to be disabled. One of these is boot virus detection, which likely would complain if you tried to make a change to the master boot record (MBR) when it came time to install the LInux LOader (LILO). Another involves shutting off or disabling the power management BIOS feature, and if there is an option involving a Plug and Play (PNP) OS, set it to No. Linux is not a PNP operating system, although it can handle some versions.

Getting Hardware Information From The BIOS

You also need to get some information from the BIOS before you continue. You may not need to use it, but it will be invaluable if you do need it. Even more importantly, you need to know how to get this information for the exams.

Where exactly you need to look varies from BIOS to BIOS. Try sections such as Chipset Features or PCI Configuration. Sometimes the information is spread out between multiple sections, so just keep looking until you find everything you need. The details you are looking for are the IRQs and I/O addresses for all of the machine's ports. These addresses are not always clearly labeled, so you also need to know how to recognize them.

This information comes in two different formats. Usually the IRQ addresses are clearly labeled. These items tend to be integers between one and twenty. However, the serial and parallel devices that work through COM and LPT ports might be labeled as "port addresses." These values are usually given with a three-digit number and an "H" on the end.

Once you have located the IRQs and port addresses, write all of this information down. You may need it.

Preparing SCSI And NIC Devices

There are two things you may need to do before installing Linux to ensure that your SCSI drives and devices will work properly. First, you need to enter the SCSI BIOS—or the main BIOS if it supports SCSI—as mentioned in Chapter 1. This BIOS has the ability to detect which SCSI IDs are available and which are already in use. Make sure that unique IDs are assigned to all SCSI devices and drives, and that if the boot information is on a SCSI drive, that it is correctly marked as a boot device.

Once the BIOS information is taken care of, you may need to do a low-level format of the SCSI drive. The manufacturer provides the tools necessary to accomplish this formatting.

A similar issue is involved with NIC devices. You may need to use the disks provided by the manufacturer to set up the card's I/O, IRQ, and DMA information. However, you may not need to use these tools. Keep these items in the back of your mind during the installation in case you run into trouble, and look at both the installation materials and the manufacturer's Web site for information on how well the devices work with Linux. You may be pleasantly surprised and find they have useful data there.

Choosing A Partition Scheme

Although choosing partitions is a simple issue for the average user, this task is more complex for a system administrator. It is important to understand what portions of the filesystem can and cannot be placed off on their own, and why you would want to segregate them.

As a general rule, most user machines only need two partitions, root—mounted at /—and swap. The entire file system can happily sit within the root partition on end-user machines unless there is specific reason to create other partitions. Use the knowledge gained in the rest of this section to decide if there is reason enough to do so.

When installing a server or administration machine, the choices are not always so cut and dried. There are debates in some circles over whether, for example, there is a performance gain or loss when the filesystem is split over many partitions. The answer tends to lie somewhere in the middle ground: Scatter the filesystem over too many partitions and you can actually slow it down.

As stated earlier, there are specific reasons to consider putting some portions on the filesystem on their own partitions. Those portions of a hard drive that contain information that changes rapidly—multiple times a day—are more likely to suffer media wear and tear damage than sections that change only occasionally. These sections are /var/mail, /var/spool, /var/lock, almost everything else in the /var hierarchy, and /tmp.

The concern, then, is the potential for media damage. If wear and tear strikes in the middle of your root filesystem, you might have a serious problem. However, moving the potential culprits off to their own partitions—perhaps /var and /tmp—puts them off where they can only affect themselves. A trade-off, though, is that doing so concentrates the wear and tear in a more focused manner on that one section of the filesystem. Thorough backup procedures can take care of this concern, however.

Another reason to break portions of the filesystem off onto other partitions is the potential for storage problems. For example, sometimes log files run wild and can fill a filesystem entirely. The /tmp directory can either be overrun by buggy programs spewing temporary files, or by users abusing their ability to put files there. Also, there is the issue of enforcing user quotas. A quota, as you will learn in Chapter 3, can be used only on a per-partition basis. So, if you want to create user quotas, you need to separate the home directories onto another partition. In fact, the best way to prevent each of these issues from overrunning the filesystem is by using separate partitions. If /var or /var/log has its own partition, then log files cannot expand past the boundaries of the partition. Your filesystem is safe from them. The same is true with the /tmp directory.

There is yet another reason to place the /home hierarchy off by itself. There may be times when you want to completely reinstall a system, but do not want to lose user information. You can accomplish this by making a /home partition and not making a new filesystem on that partition during the installation.

One more item that you may want to put off on its own—depending on the distribution you are using—is the /boot directory. If your distribution places its kernel in the /boot directory, then it is generally recommended to give this directory a separate small partition, perhaps 16MB. Doing so allows for that portion of the filesystem to remain safe even if the rest crashes, which means that you will still be able to boot the system to fix it.

An interesting issue is directories and hierarchies that can actually be kept remotely. The /usr directory contains programs run by the user population, and is often kept centrally to allow for easier software management. The same is true of /opt, if you choose to use it.

However, you cannot move all directories and hierarchies off by themselves. Some must stay with the root filesystem. The /bin directory, for example, must be kept in the root partition; so must /dev, /etc, /sbin, and /lib.

LINUX INSTALLATION OVERVIEW

This step is where each Linux distribution goes its own direction. Some will automatically start the installation process after booting from the installation media, and others will make you run a setup program. In any case, the distribution's installer will prompt you with questions and give step-by-step instructions to guide you through the installation process with minimal hassle.

Preparing Boot Disks

If the machine you are installing on cannot boot from the CD-ROM drive, or there is some other reason that you need to use a boot disk during the installation, you either need to use the ones provided or create your own. You cannot just copy the boot images onto the floppy; this operation is not precise enough. Instead, you need to write the image sector-by-sector so the disk is exactly what is expected.

You can make an installation boot disk either in Linux—or Unix in general—or in any operating system that can run an MS-DOS program. If you already have Linux machines up and running, then you might choose to do this under Linux. Mount the installation CD-ROM, place a floppy in the floppy drive, and then use the **dd** command in the following format to write the image to the disk:

```
dd if=image of=/mnt/floppy
```

For example, if you were making a Red Hat installation disk, the command would look like the following:

```
dd if=/mnt/cdrom/images/boot.img of=/mnt/floppy
```

Under MS-DOS, you would use the rawrite utility. This program writes the raw image sector-by-sector just like dd. It comes with almost all Linux distributions right on the CD-ROM. Note where the boot image is stored before running the utility; you will need to enter its full path.

 Both of these utilities work slower than a normal copy command. Be prepared to wait longer than usual.

Preparing Drives With **fdisk**

One thing you will have to do during the installation process regardless of distribution is partition and format the filesystem. This chapter discusses **fdisk** because it is the tool that is available across the board, regardless of which flavor of Linux you choose. For a basic setup, two partitions are needed, one for

Linux itself, and one for the virtual memory swap space. To do this, the **fdisk** command is used. The **fdisk** command is run by issuing the **fdisk /dev/*drive*** command. For most users, the drive will be hda, which is the primary master IDE drive. Once **fdisk** is running, several options will be available, as shown in Table 2.1.

With large servers, there are many tricks and techniques for using partitions to increase the security and performance on your Linux system; however, for the purposes of getting a basic system up and running, this chapter will cover only a basic scheme. For a more advanced discussion on filesystems and hierarchy, refer to Chapter 3.

Another partition that many system administrators like to create is the /home partition. There are many reasons behind this preference. For one thing, there is a good chance that somewhere along the way the operating system will be reinstalled, especially if the machine in question is a workstation that will not have a lot of important configuration information on it. Having a separate home partition means that you can format the rest of the filesystem and yet leave /home in place and intact, without losing anyone's information. Also, keeping the home hierarchy on its own partition ensures that nothing any user does in his or her home directory can overrun the rest of the filesystem. The worst that it can do is fill up the /home partition, which then will have to be dealt with for the sake of all the other users.

Table 2.1   fdisk options.

Command	Action
A	Toggle a bootable flag.
b	Edit bsd disklabel.
c	Toggle the DOS compatibility flag.
d	Delete a partition.
l	List known partition types.
m	Print this menu.
n	Add a new partition.
o	Create a new empty DOS partition table.
p	Print the partition table.
q	Quit without saving changes.
t	Change a partition's system ID.
u	Change display/entry units.
v	Verify the partition table.
w	Write table to disk and exit.
x	Extra functionality (experts only).

The following is a transcript of a hard drive being partitioned with a basic setup of just the swap and root partitions. Commands and comments are italicized.

```
# fdisk /dev/hda
Device contains neither a valid DOS partition table, nor Sun or SGI
disklabel
Building a new DOS disklabel. Changes will remain in memory only,
until you decide to write them. After that, of course, the previous
content won't be recoverable.
The number of cylinders for this disk is set to 16383.
There is nothing wrong with that, but this is larger than 1024,
and could in certain setups cause problems with:
1) software that runs at boot time (e.g., LILO)
2) booting and partitioning software from other OSs
 (e.g., DOS FDISK, OS/2 FDISK)
Command (m for help): p
Disk /dev/hda: 16 heads, 63 sectors, 16383 cylinders
Units = cylinders of 1008 * 512 bytes
 Device Boot Start End Blocks Id System
Here we verified that the table is currently empty.
Command (m for help): n
Command action
 e extended
 p primary partition (1-4)
p
Partition number (1-4): 1
First cylinder (1-16383, default 1): 1
Last cylinder or +size or +sizeM or +sizeK (1-16383, default 16383):
+64M
Change the 64 to however large you would like the swap size to be.
Command (m for help): n
Command action
 e extended
 p primary partition (1-4)
p
Partition number (1-4): 2
First cylinder (132-16383, default 132): 132 The default
Last cylinder or +size or +sizeM or +sizeK (132-16383, default 16383):
16383 Also the default
Command (m for help): t
Partition number (1-4): 1
Hex code (type L to list codes): 82
Changed system type of partition 1 to 82 (Linux swap)
Command (m for help): a
Partition number (1-4): 2
We must activate the partition to boot from it!
Command (m for help): w
```

```
The partition table has been altered!
Calling ioctl() to re-read partition table.
 hda: hda1 hda2
 hda: hda1 hda2
Syncing disks.
WARNING: If you have created or modified any DOS 6.x
partitions, please see the fdisk manual page for additional
information.
```

Non-Destructive Drive Preparation

If you are setting up a dual-boot machine for a user, and that machine already has its entire drive given over to an MS Windows operating system, then you cannot simply partition it. Partitioning an active drive destroys the already existing partition. A utility called FIPS—found at **http://bmrc.berkeley.edu /people/chaffee/fips/fips.html**—deals with this problem with great results. It works on FAT16 (Windows 3.x) and FAT32 (Windows9x) drives, essentially changing values in the partition table and boot sector to shrink the existing partition.

 The standard warnings apply to make backups of anything that you cannot afford to lose.

To prepare to break up the drive, first run your favorite MS-DOS or Windows disk-checking program—such as **chkdisk** under DOS or ScanDisk under the Windows 9x Accessories menu, System Tools submenu—to locate any bad clusters on the drive. After this, format a bootable MS-DOS floppy. If you are doing this from an MS-DOS window, type **format a:/s** to create a system disk. There are three files that come with FIPS that together allow you to return the drive to its previous state if anything goes wrong during the reallocation. Copy these files to the formatted system floppy: ERRORS.TXT, FIPS.EXE, and RESTORRB.EXE. Now put this disk aside; you will need it in a moment.

Now you need to consolidate the data on your drive. Items may be scattered all over the hard drive, especially if you have been using it for some time. This data needs to be placed all within the area you are going to leave for your Windows drive. If any of it is still on the section of the drive you want to break off using FIPS it will be lost, if FIPS will even let you do this. In Windows 9x, use the Disk Defragmenter under the Accessories menu, System Tools submenu, or any other defragmentation program to which you are partial.

Boot from the bootable floppy you made earlier. Run the FIPS utility from the floppy drive; you should be able to just type **fips** at the prompt. The program will gather information about which operating system you are currently running and your hard drives. It then displays your partition table and asks which partition you want to split (if you have more than one already).

After displaying your boot sector information and doing a number of checks to ensure that the hard drive is healthy, FIPS allows you to choose which cylinder within the empty portion of the drive the new partition should start on. It does so with an interface that lets you use the cursor keys to increase or decrease the size, and tells you how large or small the resulting partition would be. Once you are happy with what it says, press Enter.

Because FIPS is built to ensure that you cannot easily make mistakes, it now double-checks that this part of the drive is empty and lets you look over the partition table one more time. Pressing **y** puts the changes into effect. At some point, FIPS offers to write some information to disk that allows you to backtrack to your original configuration. Put this information on that bootable floppy. You may need it, though most likely you will not.

If you are the cautious type, reboot with the same boot floppy and run **chkdsk** on your Windows partition to ensure it is okay. After that, you can reboot normally and ensure that everything is working, then proceed to the rest of the Linux installation.

Choosing A Boot Manager

Although some operating systems make the issue of a boot manager transparent, Linux requires that you give it some thought. Many users choose LILO, the LInux LOader. This is especially true of single-boot systems that only run Linux, such as servers.

The choice is not always so straightforward for a dual-boot end-user system. If Linux is sharing with Windows 9x, then LILO often works well as long as you install Linux second—the Windows installer wipes LILO off of the master boot record (MBR). Another alternative is **Loadlin**, which utilizes the Windows 9x boot options menu to allow you to choose Linux instead of Win-dows at boot time. There are also commercial products available for Windows users. System Commander (**www.v-com.com**) can manage multi-boot systems, as can Boot Magic (**www.powerquest.com**).

Other operating systems come with their own boot managers. Microsoft Windows NT and IBM OS/2 both have boot managers that you can use instead of LILO. Just be sure to install them after Linux, or be sure to tell the distribution's installer not to overwrite the MBR.

Choosing Tools And Packages

Regardless of which Linux distribution you choose, there will be a list of pack-ages available for you to install. The first important thing to remember is that if you forget something you can add it later. Also, keep in mind what this machine is going to be used for. Break down your decisions into two categories: Definitely Need, and Definitely Do Not Need.

In the Definitely Need category fall items that are required for the machine to function. If it is going to be on a LAN, then it needs basic networking tools. If the machine is intended to be a Web server, then it needs the Apache server package. Read over the options carefully and choose what makes sense.

On the other hand, you have the Definitely Do Not Need category. A machine that exists only to be a mail server does not need a GUI, so do not install the X Windowing System or any desktop environments. Machines without any GUI do not need any tools that require a GUI, so X games are not necessary. In fact, on any server machine that will see serious use, you should have no games. They waste CPU cycles as badly as a GUI does, if not worse.

Then there are the items in the middle. Those that might be useful, or may not ever be needed. Once again, remember that you can add packages later by hand, or remove them if they prove to be unnecessary.

Troubleshooting The Installation

Sometimes there are problems after installing a Linux distribution. Typically, these are booting problems, or problems with missing files. For booting issues, /etc/lilo.conf is generally the culprit. For our example system setup in the **fdisk** section, the lilo.conf file should look like this:

```
# Global Section
boot = /dev/hda
vga = normal
# End of Global Section
# Begin Linux Parition Section
image = /vmlinuz
      root = /dev/hda2
      label = linux
      read-only
# End of Linux Partition Section
```

If, however, the problem is with missing files, follow the guidelines in the next section on updating an existing Linux installation. Should the problem be too severe to do so, the best way to fix it is to reinstall using the proper options to install the complete system.

Setting Up SCSI And NIC Devices

There are three ways to configure a device with kernel parameters at bootup. The first is to pass the kernel arguments directly at boot time; this method is used if the driver is compiled into the kernel. The second method is to have the kernel load the driver as a module at boot time. The third option is to stop the kernel loader just before the kernel is loaded and pass the parameters directly from the prompt; for **lilo**, this would be accomplished by pressing the

Tab key at the moment the LILO: prompt shows up on the screen. The first two methods are used once a desired configuration has been reached; the third is generally used for testing a given set of parameters or configuring a device that is rarely used.

To pass the kernel arguments through the kernel loader, the configuration file must be edited. For LILO, this file is /etc/lilo.conf. To pass the kernel parameters for devices, the **append** keyword is used. The generic use of the **append** keyword is as follows:

```
append "parameters to pass to the kernel"
```

For instance, if you had two NICs that you wanted to tell the kernel how to configure at bootup, you would use the **ether** command. The generic form of the **ether** command is as follows:

```
ether=IRQ, BASE_ADDRESS(io port), PARAM_1, PARAM_2, DEVICE
```

In the /etc/lilo.conf file, our entry would look like this:

```
append "ether=0,0,eth0 ether=0,0,eth1"
```

By using the zeros for the IRQ and BASE_ADDR (base address) parameters, you are instructing the kernel to automatically configure them. If this doesn't work, you will need to add the specific IRQ and BASE,_ADDR, as in the following example for two NICs that have IRQs 10 and 11 and base addresses of 220 and 330, respectively:

```
append "ether=10,0x220,eth0 ether=11,0x330,eth1"
```

Keep in mind that when referring to I/O ports, they must be referred to in hex (i.e., 0x220), that is, prepend any I/O port address(es) with "0x". You may have noticed that you never stated the PARAM_1 or PARAM_2 in the **ether** statements. This is because those two parameters in the **ether** command are completely optional. Refer to the documentation for your specific card to deter-mine if you need to pass optional parameters to the kernel.

In most cases, the IRQ and BASE_ADDR are all you need to help the kernel configure your cards. The last step in this process is the most important one; you must run **lilo** to add your updates to the configuration file. Failure to run **lilo** results in the additions you have just made not existing as far as the system is concerned. Run **lilo** as follows:

```
> lilo
```

The resulting dump will show you all the additions to /etc/lilo.conf file and your boot partitions. The one with the asterisk (*) is your default boot partition. Assuming you have one boot partition named linux, you should see output similar to the following:

```
> Added linux *
>
```

If you are loading the device driver as a module, the process is similar; just change the location of the arguments that are passed to the kernel. This is usually done by editing the /etc/modules.conf file. Most entries in the /etc/modules.conf file have a structure similar to the following:

```
alias [device] [driver name]
```

In the following example, you are going to configure two NICs, eth0 and eth1, which are going to use the smc-ultra driver loaded as a module.

```
alias eth0 smc-ultra
alias eth1 smc-ultra
```

This tells the kernel that the modular driver smc-ultra is to be used to configure and communicate with devices eth0 and eth1. If you need to pass the kernel additional options for each device (i.e., irq, base address, and so on), you would add the following to the /etc/modules.conf file:

```
alias eth0 smc-ultra
options smc-ultra irq=10 io=0x220
alias eth1 smc-ultra
options smc-ultra irq=11 io-0x330
```

To describe all the possible boot-time parameters for all the possible devices is beyond the scope of this book. However, there is documentation on how to pass the kernel parameters for specific devices at boot time available at **www.linuxdoc.org/HOWTO/BootPrompt-HOWTO/BootPrompt-HOWTO.html**. This How-To contains a wealth of information for some commonly used devices and some not so common. This document should in no way be considered to supercede any documentation from a device's manufacturer.

UPDATING AN EXISTING LINUX INSTALLATION

Like everything else, computer software changes. Over time there will be updates, patches, and new versions to almost every software component that makes up a Linux system. This includes the kernel, libraries, drivers, and applications. Every operating system has some way of being updated. As the operating systems are different so are the methods of updating. The same is true for the different distributions of Linux; most have tools for updating (sometimes called a *package management* tool) and some do not. No matter the method, every distribution has the same goal, to update the existing software to the new software or install a brand-new piece of software.

Which Files To Download

Before updating your system, the first question to ask is: What needs updating? The answer to this question will determine what packages or files you need to download. A simple example of this would be a system that needs an enhancement only found in a kernel of a higher version than the one currently being used. Therefore, the file needed to perform the update would be a new kernel, usually found at **ftp.us.kernel.org**. Although this sounds as easy as downloading a file, it may not always be that simple. Sometimes when you want to upgrade one piece of software, it requires upgrading several others that you may not have considered. Always read the documentation on a piece of software to determine if additional upgrades or installations are needed to install the software in question.

Another thing that must be considered when downloading an updated piece of software is what type of Linux system is being upgraded. As mentioned earlier, every distribution differs in its update method. For instance, Red Hat uses rpms, Debian uses debs, and Stampede uses slps; these are all instances of distribution-specific packages intended to make upgrading or installation easier. With a Linux system that has some sort of package management scheme, there is always a package management tool. For example, with Stampede, the tool is called slpi, and Red Hat uses a tool called rpm. These distribution-specific files are nothing more than the regular *GNU* software put together by the distribution maintainer in such a way as to facilitate the installation; they require no editing of a makefile or running of a configuration script. Simply using the package tool on the new or updated software will configure and install the software where it needs to go for the particular distribution. But where do you get these distribution packages? These packages are usually retrieved from the distribution maintainer. For instance, rpms for Red Hat would be found at **ftp.redhat.com**. Stampede packages would be retrieved from **ftp.stampede.org**.

A Linux box does not need to have a package management tool in order to be updated. You always have the tried-and-true method of compiling and installing software directly from the source available to you. The method may differ, but the outcome is still the same. It may not be as easy, but it will produce the desired result if done properly.

So where do you get these updates and software revisions?

The first place to look for new Linux software and software updates is **http://freshmeat.net**. Next, **www.linuxapps.com** and **www.linuxberg.com** are the places to go. If the software is not found at either of these sites, it probably does not exist. These two sites are renowned worldwide as being the definitive places to go for Linux software. In the event that either of these sites do not have a piece of software that you know exists, then there is only one other place that it could be on the Internet. That is **www.metalab.unc.edu**, the old sunsite site, which is also well known for its extensive Linux software supply. All of these sites have some sort of search engine, which makes finding the desired software extremely easy.

Understanding Packages

There are a number of different package types that you will encounter when looking for software to update your installation. Some are a legacy of Linux's Unix roots, whereas others are relatively new and even being ported for use in other flavors of Unix. It is important for you to understand what each type of package is made of, and how to install files from it.

 A package is a method of bundling programs or files for the ease of getting all components at once.

The primary issue revolves around the type of packaging tool you need. Some of the tools are used to compress files. The **gzip** tool, for example, is a GNU program that compresses files or groups of files. It is used in the format **gzip** *flags files*. For example, to gzip the contents of /var/log into the file /root/archives/logs9.gz, you would type:

```
> gzip /var/log/* /root/archives/logs9.gz
```

To then uncompress the files, use **gunzip**, as in **gunzip logs9.gz**. This tool places the unzipped files wherever the .gz file is.

 Another type of compressed file you will run into in the Unix world is the .Z file, which is created by the **compress** command and opened by the **uncompress** command. However, this type of compression is not as efficient as that of the GNU tools.

Other packaging tools bundle files. The one used in the Linux and Unix world primarily is **tar**. This tool is capable of retaining permissions and locations in a relative manner, so that you can unpack the package in the directory where you want to install it and everything is automatically put into place.

Creating a **tar** package is a little more complex than file compression. Part of the trick to using **tar** properly is understanding how to build the flags. To create an archive, you definitely need to start with **tar −c**. After this, there are some others you might want to use, as outlined in Table 2.2.

A common flag combination for creating a tar archive is **tar cvf file.tar files**. For example, you might type the following to bundle the entire home hierarchy together for easy replacement after an upgrade:

```
> tar cvf homebackup.tar /home
```

The **tar** command assumes that if you give a directory name, you want the whole directory. Extracting files is much the same. The primary difference is that, instead of the **c** flag, you use an **x** for extract. If, for example, you downloaded some source code and want to place it under the /usr/src hierarchy. You would place the file in /usr/src and then type the following:

```
> tar xvf source.tar
```

 A common packaging combination is using **tar** to bundle the files, and then **gzip** to compress them. The result of this is called a Tarball, and either has a **.tar.gz** or **.tgz** extension.

There are other package types as well. Some distributions created their own packaging and management formats. Common ones are .rpm and .deb. For more about these items, see Chapter 15.

Table 2.2 Flags used with the **tar** command.

Flag	Purpose
A	Concatenate the new tar file onto an older one.
f	Put the archive in the specified file.
p	When extracting the files, keep the same permissions as they had when they were archived.
r	Add the listed files to the specified already-existing archive.
u	Update the files in the archive with the given files if the new files are more recent than those in the archive.
v	Give verbose output.
X	Exclude the listed file from the package.
z	Gzip the files as they are placed into the archive, or uncompress while extracting.

Update Issues

As alluded to earlier, a software update or new install may not always be as simple as installing the desired piece of software or update. Every piece of software on a Linux system has some sort of *dependency* on other software. Of these, the most important is the libraries (see Chapter 1); although there are other pieces of software that another may be dependent on.

There are many tools at your disposal for determining whether your system has the required software or software version to perform an update or installation. For instance, if a piece of software's documentation says that you need **make** version 3.77 to *compile* and install, you would verify that you had **make** and that it was the correct version as follows:

To find **make**:

```
> which make
```

The **which** command searches your path and will return the first instance of the executable named **make**. If there are other instances of **make** on your system, **which** will not tell you. The **locate** * or **find** command would be used to find multiple instances of **make**:

```
> locate make
```

 You can update the locate database at any time with the **updatedb** command. Running this program takes a while, but ensures that you have an up-to-date version of the database to use rather than having to resort to the more complex **find** command.

or

```
find / -name make
```

Now, to determine what version of **make** you have, execute **make** with the –v or –version option, in the format "make –v" or "make —version".

If you had **make** version 3.77 on your system, you should see the following:

```
> make -v
GNU Make version 3.77, by Richard Stallman and Roland McGrath.
Copyright (C) 1988, 89, 90, 91, 92, 93, 94, 95, 96, 97, 98
 Free Software Foundation, Inc.
This is free software; see the source for copying conditions.
There is NO warranty; not even for MERCHANTABILITY or FITNESS FOR A
PARTICULAR PURPOSE.
Report bugs to <bug-make@GNU.org>.
```

Almost every executable program on a Linux system will have an option to determine its version, usually –v or –version. If in doubt, refer to the appropriate man page for the command.

There are other dependencies besides executables, usually the libraries. On most Linux systems, the bulk of the libraries are kept in /lib, /usr/lib, /usr/local/lib or any other directory called lib. The file /etc/ld.so.conf contains most of the search paths for libraries. The environment variable **LD_LIBRARY_PATH** may also contain library path information. As a general rule, system libraries are found in /lib; user libraries are found in /usr/lib.

```
> echo $LD_LIBRARY_PATH
```

The previous command will display the contents of the environment variable if any.

Library files are not executables, so we cannot find out what version they are by running them with a –v option. A library's version information is typically contained in its name. For example, if you wanted to determine which version of libc, a system library, was on your system, you would do the following:

1. Change directory to the /lib directory where system libraries are generally kept:

   ```
   > cd /lib
   ```

2. Then search for all instances of libc.so* in that directory:

   ```
   > ls libc.so.*
   ```

3. You should get output similar to the following, assuming that libc 6.0 is installed on your system:

   ```
   libc.so.6
   ```

4. Notice the file named libc.so.6; this is the general format of file version naming (i.e., library name followed by version number). If you had version 5 of libc, you would have received an output like the following:

   ```
   libc.so.5
   ```

If you cannot find a required library on your system, check with the search sites previously listed for a download location.

Enough cannot be said about the importance of thoroughly reading the documentation on a given piece of software. This is never truer than when installing software. Reading the documentation thoroughly will significantly reduce any issues with updates or installations.

2

MAKE AND INSTALL PROGRAMS FROM SOURCE CODE

This is a complicated issue because the method for compiling and installing a program depends entirely on what the programmer decided to do at the time. However, many programs follow a set of standards that make our lives easier. Always remember to read the INSTALL and README files before doing anything to get specific installation notes from the programmer.

With that said, typically, the first thing that must be done is to unarchive the source files. To do this, run:

```
> tar xfvz [filename.tar.gz]
```

Once the source files are unarchived, go into the newly created directory. This is where the README and INSTALL files are usually found. After reading those files, the next step is often to run the following command:

```
> ./configure
```

Not every package includes a configuration script. If this file does not exist, then you will have to go through the entire process by hand. It is useful in this case to keep the INSTALL file that comes with the package open in one virtual terminal and have another open where you follow it step-by-step.

If **configure** has errors, run

```
> ./configure -help
```

to get specific configuration options. The next thing to do is perform the actual compilation, done by running this command:

```
> make
```

The **make** utility automates the compilation process. Large programs can easily have dozens of source files and need hundreds of commands to be executed to compile them; **make** does everything for you! Once **make** finishes, the program is ready to install. Programs that are more complex than just a single executable can often be installed with the following command:

```
> make install
```

whereas simple programs that consist of a single executable sometimes need to be installed manually. To do this, simply copy the executable into a directory somewhere on the path, such as /usr/local/bin.

There is more in-depth coverage of the **make** command in Chapter 5.

CONFIGURING MODEMS AND SOUND CARDS

Of all the devices that can be in a computer, modems and sound cards can be the most difficult to get working in Linux. Due to their popularity and the length of time each has been around, nearly every one is different. Most problems arise because of resource conflicts. Fortunately, PCI versions of these cards are becoming more widely available, so in a few years, nearly all of these problems should be eliminated.

Modem Issues

The most common problem with modems is an IRQ conflict. An IRQ is the mechanism used to tell the computer that data is waiting to be picked up, and if two modems are sharing the same IRQ, the computer may not be able to talk to them individually. This typically occurs when an internal modem is set to the same settings as one of the built-in serial ports on the motherboard. To fix the problem, simply change the settings of one or the other. This is where the other common problem comes in. The problem is that the modem is using a non-standard configuration; to solve this, use the **setserial** programs described below.

```
usage: setserial serial-device [cmd1 [arg]] ...
port 0xXXXX        set the I/O port
irq IRQ#           set the interrupt
uart UART          set UART type (none, 8250, 16450, 16550, 16550A
auto_irq           try to automatically determine irq during configuration
skip_test          skip UART test during configuration
spd_hi             use 56kb instead of 38.4kb
spd_vhi            use 115kb instead of 38.4kb
spd_normal         use 38.4kb when a buad rate of 38.4kb is selected
```

A frequently asked question is: Why doesn't Linux properly recognize serial ports with a non-standard configuration? The answer is, there is no way to *autoprobe* for a serial port in a safe way; the probe is just as likely to crash a system as it is to find a modem. To avoid this, users must use **setserial** to configure non-standard ports.

Sound Card Issues

Sound cards are a bit more difficult to tame than modems. They suffer from the same basic problems as modems, but there is no single way to fix them. When troubleshooting a sound card, the first thing to do is to refer to the documentation that comes packaged with the Linux kernel for the most up-to-date information. Check the pnpdump information as discussed in Chapter 1 if the card is an ISA PNP item. If you know the resource settings, try compiling the driver as a module—compilation is covered in Chapter 5—and configuring the settings using the /etc/modules.conf file as described earlier. Sound card support has only been in the mainstream kernel for a short period of time as of this writing, so until the standards evolve more, your mileage may vary. For best results, use common or popular sound cards, and check the kernel docu-mentation before buying.

The Red Hat distribution and its derivatives include a sound card configuration tool called **sndconfig**. See Chapter 15 for more information on this tool and how to put it to use.

CHAPTER SUMMARY

In this chapter, you learned how to determine what hardware will function with Linux. This is an important step in the Linux installation process. The next thing covered was how to prepare a hard drive with **FIPS** if necessary, and then partition it using **fdisk**. Once the hard drive is partitioned, the next step is to install Linux. Of course, not all installations can go perfectly, so a few basic steps to troubleshoot a Linux installation were discussed.

After having a working Linux system, it is very important to know how to update an existing Linux installation, which includes the ability to compile programs from source code and work with the various packaging software out there. When installing and maintaining a Linux system, the most common problems are with modems and sound cards, so we demonstrated to you how to take care of the most common modem and sound card issues.

For the purposes of a Linux certification examination, the most important things to know are how to partition a drive with **fdisk**; understand the reason behind using **FIPS** and the concerns to watch out for with it; be able to manipulate .tar, .gz, and Tarball files; and understand the basics of how to install and compile programs yourself from the source code.

REVIEW QUESTIONS

1. One can assume that a brand new, just released, super accelerated video card will work with Linux.

   a. True

   b. False

2. What is the minimum number of partitions typically needed to get a Linux system up and running?

   a. 0

   b. 1

   c. 2

   d. 3

3. What class of software is commonly used to update programs in Linux?

   a. package management

   b. library

   c. upgrade

   d. makefile

4. If your distribution does not have a preferred package management tool, you cannot update your system.

   a. True

   b. False

5. A program you are compiling says it cannot find a library; you know where this library is installed on your system. What would you type to find out how to relay this information to the program's configure script?

   a. **configure –help**

   b. **configure —help**

   c. **./configure –h**

   d. **./configure –help**

6. What would you type to locate a file named foo, when you have no idea where it is in the filesystem hierarchy?

   a. **find foo**

   b. **find / –name foo**

   c. **find –name foo**

   d. **find /**

7. Which command could you use instead of **find** if foo was an executable in your path?

    a. **run**

    b. **where**

    c. **which**

    d. **when**

8. When running a program, it has an error stating that there is an invalid path listed in LD_LIBRARY_PATH; what would you type to check to see what path that is?

    a. **lib LD_LIBRARY_PATH**

    b. **LD_LIBRARY_PATH**

    c. **locate LD_LIBRARY_PATH**

    d. **echo LD_LIBRARY_PATH**

9. A program requires libdb version 1.2.17 or higher; which of the following files is acceptable? [Choose all correct answers]

    a. libdb.so.4.2.5

    b. libdb.so.1.2.18

    c. libdb.so.1.2.16

    d. libdb.so.2.1.17

10. What tool simplifies the compilation process?

    a. make

    b. build

    c. run

    d. edit

11. What command would configure a modem with an I/O port of 0x03f8, an unknown IRQ, and a 16450 UART that incorrectly reports itself when probed?

    a. **set serial 0x03f8 uart 16450**

    b. **setserial 0x03f8 16450**

    c. **setserial port 0x03f8 auto_irq uart 16450 skip_test**

    d. **set serial p 0x03f8 auto_irq u 16450**

12. Your sound card's manual says it is 100 percent SoundBlaster-compatible. This means the SoundBlaster driver will work with it.

    a. True

    b. False

13. What options must you look over and adjust before installing Linux on a machine?

    a. RAM

    b. VRAM

    c. BIOS

    d. BEOS

14. Which of the following packages would you be sure to install on a dual-boot end-user machine? [Choose all correct answers]

    a. X Server

    b. NFS client

    c. FTP Server

    d. word processing packages

15. Which of the following information might you get from the BIOS? [Choose all correct answers]

    a. Device SCSI IDs

    b. Device IRQs

    c. Device Ports

    d. Device Flags

16. Which of the following is a device port address from the BIOS?

    a. 13

    b. 153

    c. LUN:0

    d. 261H

17. What tool is available in all Linux distributions for partitioning drives?

    a. fdisk

    b. SCSI

    c. disklabel

    d. Apache

18. Which piece of hardware can you damage by setting your video options too high?

    a. motherboard

    b. video card

    c. video RAM

    d. monitor

19. You have a video card that can display as high as 1024×768, and a monitor that can handle 1600×1200. What is the best resolution you will get on this screen?

    a. 1600×1200

    b. 1024×768

    c. 800×600

    d. 1152×864

20. Which of the following packages would you avoid installing on a machine that will be a high-traffic Web server? [Choose all correct answers]

    a. X Server

    b. X and Console Games

    c. HTML Editor

    d. NFS Server

Hands-On Projects

Project 2.1

Most distributions start the installation process by use of boot disks. Because of this fact, this exercise will go through the process to make them. If you do not have access to any systems running a Unix variant (including Linux), then try the next project to make the disks using Windows.

For this project, you will need access to a working Unix-type system with an Internet connection, a floppy drive, and two high-density 3.5-inch diskettes.

To create installation disks within Linux:

1. Download the boot and root images. For this project, we will use the ones for Stampede's distribution. The two files are at **ftp://ftp.stampede.org/ disks/bare.ide** and **ftp://ftp.stampede.org/disks/stampede.gz**.

2. Put the images onto floppy disks. Insert the first floppy into the disk drive and make the boot disk using the following:

    ```
    > dd if=bare.ide of=/dev/fd0 *
    ```

3. Put the second floppy in the disk drive and make the root disk:

    ```
    > dd if=stampede.gz of=/dev/fd0
    ```

4. Try them out! Insert the boot floppy into the floppy drive and turn on the computer. When asked, insert the root disk.

To create the installation disks using Windows:

1. Download the boot and root images. For this project, we will use the ones for Stampede's distribution. The two files are at: **ftp://ftp.stampede.org/ disks/bare.ide** and **ftp://ftp.stampede.org/disks/stampede.gz**.

2. Download rawrite.exe. This program will write the boot and root disks in the correct format for Linux. The file is located at **ftp://ftp.stampede.org/ disks/rawrite.exe**.

3. Put the images onto floppy disks. Insert the first floppy into the disk drive and make the boot disk:

   ```
   > rawrite bare.ide
   ```

4. Put the second floppy in the disk drive and make the root disk:

   ```
   > rawrite stampede.gz
   ```

5. Try them out! Insert the boot floppy into the floppy drive and turn on the computer. When asked, insert the root disk.

Project 2.2

In this project, you will compile the glib library. When compiled, you will simply delete it without installing it to avoid any potential problems.

For this project, you will need a working Linux system with an Internet connection.

To compile the glib library:

1. Download glib. To do this, use the **ftp** command:

   ```
   > ftp ftp.gtk.org

   Connected to ftp.gtk.org.
   220 ftp.gimp.org NcFTPd Server (free educational license) ready.
   Name (ftp.gtk.org:): anonymous
   331 Guest login ok, send your complete e-mail address as password.
   Password:
   230-You are user #17 of 50 simultaneous users allowed.
   230-
   230 Logged in anonymously.
   Remote system type is UNIX.
   Using binary mode to transfer files.
   ftp> cd /pub/gtk/v1.2
   250 "/pub/gtk/v1.2" is new cwd.
   ```

```
ftp> get glib-1.2.5.tar.gz
local: glib-1.2.5.tar.gz remote: glib-1.2.5.tar.gz
200 PORT command successful.
150 Opening BINARY mode data connection for glib-1.2.5.tar.gz
(409149 bytes).
226 Transfer completed.
409149 bytes received in 26.5 secs (15 Kbytes/sec)
ftp> quit
221 Goodbye.
```

2. Unarchive the file:

```
> tar xfvz glib.whatever.tar.gz
```

3. Change directories to the source directory you just unarchived:

```
> cd glib-whatever
```

4. Configure glib:

```
> ./configure
```

5. Compile glib:

```
> make
```

With this complete you should have a freshly compiled glib.so.whatever in your source directory.

3

DEVICES, LINUX FILESYSTEMS, AND FILESYSTEM HIERARCHY

AFTER READING THIS CHAPTER AND COMPLETING THE EXERCISES, YOU WILL BE ABLE TO:

➤ Add a new unformatted partition to your system

➤ Access temporary data devices such as floppy disks and CD-ROMs

➤ Control filesystem mounting, unmounting, and access

➤ Create and use disk quotas

➤ Work with files and links

If the kernel is the heart of a Linux machine, the filesystem is also a vital organ—perhaps the lungs. Within the filesystem reside the device drivers, data, system files, and all the other pieces that go into a working operating system. Like the lungs, if the filesystem isn't properly cared for or suffers some form of physical crisis, the entire installation is damaged.

Managing Partitions And Filesystems

Partitions and filesystems meld together from the user's point of view. As a system administrator, however, it's important to understand the nuances that differentiate them. A *partition* is a segment of a drive, or a single drive, that's marked into one block. As far as the kernel is concerned, each partition is its own *device*. (Partitions are covered in more detail in Chapter 2.)

The *filesystem* is the entirety of the directory tree that the kernel sees. As you attach partitions and devices to the system to use them, you make them a part of the directory tree, and so a part of the filesystem. Sometimes the current filesystem setup is no longer sufficient and needs to be updated.

Determining Factors

A number of factors influence whether it's time to update your filesystem. Some of these factors include the following:

➤ A physical hard drive failure causes a definite need to update the filesystem. Whether an entire drive fails or only one partition on it, the lost space usually must be replaced by a new unit.

➤ If one or more partitions continually fill their allotted space, you must either use them more efficiently or give them more space. Depending on the partition, you can either move the filesystem to a larger space or split it onto multiple partitions.

➤ Perhaps you want to add a new physical drive or partition that's mountable via NFS or Samba by outsiders, but contains only the data you want accessible by those outsiders.

Adding another hard drive to a machine also requires the creation of partitions if you intend it to be a part of the filesystem.

Adding New Partitions

A number of steps are involved in adding a new partition to the filesystem. It's generally a good idea to follow each step fully to ensure that any problems are found and nullified before putting valuable data on the new filesystem.

Partitioning With **fdisk**

Although some distributions of Linux come with their own partitioning tools, they all come with **fdisk**, which is a command-line partition editor. The partitioning tools are useful when initially installing, but it's often faster to use **fdisk** at this point, when you're making changes to the live filesystem.

To get a list of your current partitions, type the following:

```
fdisk -l
```

3

If you have a simple Linux system installed, your partition list might look something like this:

```
Device      Boot   Start   End    Blocks    Id         System
/dev/hda1    *      1       255    2048256   Linux
/dev/hda2           256     627    2988090   Extended
/dev/hda5           256     272    136521    Swap
```

In this case, the partition labeled Extended contains available space. Look at the start and end sectors of /dev/hda2 and /dev/hda5. Envision them as shown in Figure 3.1.

Now it's time to prepare the new Linux Native partition. Typing **fdisk** brings up the following prompt:

```
Command (m for help):
```

Create a new partition by typing **n** and then pressing Enter. The following prompt appears:

```
Command     Action
l           logical (5 or over)
p           primary partition (1-4)
```

Because the new partition will also be inside the extended partition, type **l** for logical and press Enter. At the First Cylinder and Last Cylinder prompts, the defaults are fine because for this example, the purpose is to fill the rest of the empty space.

This new partition needs to be identified as Linux Native. Linux **fdisk** automatically tags new partitions as this type. It's wise to double-check, however.

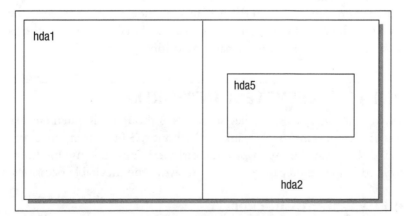

Figure 3.1 Layout of the example hard drive partitions.

If you need to see a list of your partitions while working in **fdisk**, use the **p** command. If you need to see a list of each partition's type, to remember which is Linux Native and which is Linux Swap, type **l**.

When you've finished, type **w** and press Enter to write the new partition table; then type **q** and press Enter to quit. The **fdisk** utility is discussed in detail in Chapter 2.

Formatting

Once the new partition is created and saved in the partition table, you need to format it. To format a Linux Native partition, use the command **mke2fs**. Continuing with the example, to format the new Linux Native partition—which can be seen via **fdisk** or **df** (more about **df** in the section titled "Controlling Filesystem Mounting And Unmounting" later in this chapter)—you would type the following:

```
mke2fs /dev/hda6
```

However, if the new partition is a swap partition, the command is **mkswap**.

You can also format an MS-DOS partition, such as a temporary storage space or floppy disk. The command to do so is **mkfs.msdos**.

Once the formatting is complete, the partition must be mounted for use (see the section "The Mount Process" for further information).

Removing Partitions

Removing a partition is a less complex matter. First, it must be unmounted by hand, and then removed from the mount sequence at boot time (see the section "Understanding /etc/fstab," later in this chapter). Finally, to remove the partition from the drive, use either a third-party partitioning tool or **fdisk**.

MAINTAINING FILESYSTEM INTEGRITY

If filesystem integrity fails, the filesystem fails. Although this statement may seem obvious, it's important to let it sink in. Without the filesystem, the entire Linux box fails. Now that the issue is stated clearly, let's look at some methods that are available to help you prepare for and try to avoid the inevitable occasional failure.

The Filesystem Checker

One of the most important tools in a system administrator's arsenal is **e2fsck**, which examines the filesystem for faults and fixes them as best it can. It's important when shutting down the system not to always suppress the boot time filesystem check. Or, if the system is up for a long period of time (say 100 days), it's wise to run the occasional check manually.

 If you start getting read errors when you try to open files, run this command on the filesystem to see if the media is damaged.

If the filesystem you want to check was marked as clean during the current uptime, you can still force a check by typing the following:

```
e2fsck -f
```

Making Filesystem Backups

Sometimes there's no avoiding it: Drives do and will fail. Sometimes you get a warning in the form of occasional drive problems. Other times, the failure is immediate and catastrophic.

Whether a drive failure is a serious incident or a mere nuisance depends on how much thought and effort you put into planning and implementing your backup scheme. File backups are covered in detail in Chapter 6.

Drive failure isn't the only serious concern for a system administrator. One rampant process or unfortunate typo can wreak havoc if it changes permissions or ownership on vital system files. It's highly recommended that you keep a printout or disk backup of the permission and ownership structure of either selected portions of the filesystem or the entire thing.

The simplest way to back up the file and permission structure of the whole filesystem is by typing the following from the root (/) directory:

```
ls -laR > /filesystem.backup
```

If you prefer to back up only particular portions of the filesystem structure, but you want to store them all in the same file, then you can back up each section individually and append them all to one file. For example, if you wanted to archive the /etc directory and its subdirectories plus the main /bin directory, with the second appended to the first file's listing, you'd type the following:

```
cd /etc
ls -laR > /partial.backup
cd /bin
ls -la >> /partial.backup
```

If you regularly need to back up the same set of directories, then this process would be perfect for you to practice your shell scripting skills (more on shell scripting in Chapter 5).

CONTROLLING FILESYSTEM MOUNTING AND UNMOUNTING

One beauty of the Linux method (which began with Unix) of handling additional media—whether they're floppies, CD-ROMs, Zip drives, or hard drives residing in other machines—is that these various media mesh seamlessly into your own filesystem. In order to add one of these devices to the filesystem you *mount* it.

The Mount Process

To add a media device to your filesystem, you must first create a *mount point* for it. A mount point is the directory within the filesystem where the media's contents will reside. The /mnt directory exists as the base on which you add these items. There are various philosophies on the subject. Some administrators simply mount anything onto /mnt, but this approach works only if you mount one item at a time. Others prefer a more hierarchical approach.

If you prefer to create a mount hierarchy for each type of media (which is the recommended course of action just to help keep things straight when you have more than one item mounted), you need to create a directory for each media. A common set of directory choices would be /mnt/cdrom, /mnt/floppy, and /mnt/zip. Use names that are easy to remember.

Once you've created the mount point, you need to know how Linux sees the device you want to mount. Some distributions create handy aliases and links and some don't. The device files themselves are located in the /dev directory.

The syntax for the **mount** command is as follows:

```
mount -t filesystem_type /dev/device /mnt/mountpoint
```

Commonly used filesystem types are shown in Table 3.1.

If you're mounting a Linux-formatted device, then you can use this command instead:

```
mount /dev/device /mnt/mountpoint
```

For example, to mount a data CD-ROM you might type the following:

```
mount -t iso9660 /dev/cdrom /mnt/cdrom
```

Table 3.1 Frequently used **mount** filesystem types.

Type	System
ext2	The Linux filesystem
iso9660	The CD-ROM filesystem
msdos	The MS-DOS filesystem; otherwise, fat or fat16
nfs	The Network File Server filesystem
ntfs	The Windows NT filesystem
smbfs	The Samba filesystem, based on the SMB protocol
swap	Swap space
sysv	The System V Unix filesystem
vfat	The Windows filesystem; includes the Windows 98 and later format, FAT32

Once you've mounted a filesystem, all you have to do to access it is change directories to the mount point. In the case of the previous example, you would change to the directory /mnt/cdrom. Doing a file listing would show you the top-level directory on the CD-ROM.

The Unmount Process

Before you remove temporary media from your system, you first need to unmount it. Properly unmounting media ensures that the filesystem is aware that the mount point is now empty and writes any data held in RAM before that data is placed on the media.

To unmount a device, use the **umount** command. You can use either of the following two formats:

➤ umount /dev/*device*

➤ umount /mnt/*mountpoint*

Understanding /etc/fstab

The central control for filesystem mounting is the file /etc/fstab. All essential portions of your filesystem are listed here. The format used in /etc/fstab is as follows:

```
Device Mount Point Filesystem Type Mount Options Dump Mount Order
```

When you first install Linux, a default /etc/fstab file is created. This default file contains the mount points and partitions you created during the installation process. Some administrators may need to edit this file by hand. However, as a system administrator, it's important to understand how to best put it to use.

It's possible to create quick shortcuts to allow fast mounting of temporary items. Fill out the information and be sure not to automatically mount. For example, to make a shortcut so you don't have to type out the commands to mount a CD-ROM each time, you might use these values: /dev/cdrom, /mnt/cdrom, iso9660, noauto, 0, 0. Doing so would let you simply type **mount /mnt/cdrom** at the prompt to mount a CD-ROM.

The Device Field

The /etc/fstab Device field contains the name of the device to be mounted. For example, if you created a temp partition (/temp) on the first partition of the first IDE drive, the Device field would contain /dev/hda1.

The Mount Point Field

The /etc/fstab Mount Point field contains the mount point within the filesystem that the kernel assigns to the device. Following the previous example, the mount point listed would be /temp.

Filesystem Type

The /etc/fstab Filesystem Type field contains the type of filesystem to be mounted. Continuing the example, the new partition is Linux formatted, so the filesystem type would be **ext2**.

Mount Options

The /etc/fstab Mount Options field contains the controls and privileges to apply to the mounted partition. Commonly used mount options are shown in Table 3.2. If you're using multiple options, separate them with a comma and no space.

Table 3.2   Frequently used mount options.

Option	Purpose
asynch	Handle filesystem input/output asynchronously.
auto	Mount at boot time.
defaults	Shorthand for the following set of options: rw, suid, dev, exec, auto, nouser, asynch.
dev	Accept both character and block special devices.
exec	Allow binaries on the filesystem to be executed.
noauto	Do not mount at boot time.
nodev	Do not accept either character or block special devices.
noexec	Do not allow binaries on the filesystem to be executed.
nosuid	Do not allow suid on the filesystem.

(continued)

Table 3.2 Frequently used mount options *(continued)*.

Option	Purpose
nouser	Only allow the console or the superuser to mount.
ro	Mount as read only.
rw	Mount as read-write.
suid	Allow suid on the filesystem.
user	Allow users to mount.

If you wanted to mount the filesystem as read-writable, user-mountable, but not automatically mounted, you might use the following string for the options:

```
rw,suid,dev,exec,noauto,user,asynch
```

 Note the "user" entry. A large complaint on single-user or end user machines is that users cannot mount a floppy or CD-ROM on their own. On those machines where you want the person to specifically be able to mount certain items, be sure to add the user item to the options list for that device.

Dump

The /etc/fstab Dump field tells the kernel whether to dump the changes to disk immediately or cache them to memory until there's an idle moment to write the data or until the buffer is filled. You gain speed if dumping is used, but if there's a failure the data may be lost before it's written. A value of 0 in this field means dumping isn't used, whereas a value of 1 means dumping is used.

Mount Order

The /etc/fstab Mount Order field determines when each device is added to the filesystem. A value of 0 means not to mount the item at boot time. Always give the value 1 to the root (/) partition. Use 2 for additional items that need to be added at boot time. The kernel doesn't recognize any number greater than 2 in this field in the fstab file.

Manipulating MS-DOS Files

There is a package called mtools that is good for manipulating MS-DOS floppies. A series of programs comes with it, each of them emulating an MS-DOS command. These programs are listed in Table 3.3. This set of tools expects an MS-DOS floppy to be in the first floppy drive.

For example, you might place a blank floppy in the drive and type the following sequence to format it as an MS-DOS disk, create the MS-DOS subdirectory

Table 3.3   The utilities that come in the mtools package.

Utility	Purpose
mattrib	Change the MS-DOS attribute flag. Available flags are shown in Table 3.4.
mcd	Change active directories on the MS-DOS floppy.
mcopy	Copy files to and from the MS-DOS floppy. These files have to be in MS-DOS naming format.
mdel	Delete a file on the MS-DOS floppy.
mdir	Give a directory listing on the MS-DOS floppy.
mformat	Make an MS-DOS filesystem on a floppy.
mlabel	Assign a volume label to an MS-DOS floppy.
mmd	Create a new subdirectory on an MS-DOS floppy.
mrd	Delete a subdirectory on an MS-DOS floppy.
mread	Copy a file from the MS-DOS floppy to the Linux filesystem.
mren	Rename a file on the MS-DOS floppy.
mtype	Show the contents of a text file on an MS-DOS floppy.
mwrite	Copy a file from the Linux filesystem to the MS-DOS floppy.

"text" on it, and copy the file /usr/src/linux/README into the MS–DOS "text" subdirectory:

```
mformat
mmd \text
mwrite /usr/src/linux/README a:\text
```

Table 3.4   MS-DOS file attributes.

Attribute	Result
+a	Turn on the MS-DOS archive attribute, which marks it to be archived by a backup program.
-a	Turn off the MS-DOS archive attribute, which marks the file as not needing to be archived.
+h	Turn on the MS-DOS hidden file attribute.
-h	Turn off the MS-DOS hidden file attribute.
+r	Set the MS-DOS file as read only.
-r	Set the MS-DOS file as read-write.
+s	Set the MS-DOS system file attribute.
-s	Turn off the MS-DOS system file attribute.

Listing Mounted Filesystems

To quickly see what filesystems you've mounted at any given time, type the following command:

```
df
```

This command also gives the mount point, how much space is in the partition, how much space is left, and the percentage available.

SETTING AND VIEWING DISK QUOTAS

Offering user accounts opens the door to a number of important issues, one of which is disk space. Even a few users can overrun a partition if they don't pay attention to how much data they download over time. One way of counteracting this problem is to put all user space on one partition so that the sum total of data users store doesn't affect the rest of the filesystem. However, this method of space control causes users who are frugal with storage to suffer when less conscientious users fill the rest of the drive.

Another way of dealing with the problem of storage space is to create disk *quotas*. Assigning a quota to whomever you deem necessary prevents them from pushing the limits of disk space.

You must double-check a few preliminaries before you can do any work with quotas. Depending on which kernel version you have and which Linux distribution you have, you may need to do some additional work before proceeding.

The Quota Package

To see if the quota package itself is installed on your system, type the following:

```
which quota
```

If the package is installed, you'll see a listing of where the quota program is located. Proceed to the next section.

If **which** can't find the quota package, you need to install it. The package should be available within the Linux distribution media or through the distribution's Web site (see Chapter 2 for more details on package management).

Kernel Quota Support

The quota package is integral enough that its use must be supported at the kernel level. If you don't have quota support in your kernel, you need to compile a new one (see Chapter 11 for more on the kernel).

Setting Quotas

To utilize the quota package, you must attend to a number of steps. First, set which filesystems to watch. Next, create the quota storage files. Finally, edit the quota data for each filesystem on which a quota will be enforced.

Assigning Quotas To A Filesystem

To alert a Linux box that quotas are assigned to part of the filesystem, edit the /etc/fstab file. Two new mount options are available when you use quotas: **usrquota** and **grpquota**. Which option you use depends on which meets your needs more efficiently.

The **usrquota** option is for situations when you want to limit one, some, or even all users on a filesystem to using a certain amount of space. This option is especially useful in situations such as providing Linux shells or dial-in accounts to the general public when a large number of people are using the system and its available disk space; or, when one or more users insist on using far more than their share of space.

Perhaps a particular partition is used by a number of different project groups to store their work. In this case, a more efficient use of quotas would be to assign the **grpquota** option to the partition. Then, each project group could be assigned a total amount of space available, and each project member would work within that total space. No one group could overrun the partition.

After saving and exiting /etc/fstab, it's then important to create the file(s) that contain each partition's quota information. Each partition using quotas gets its own quota.user file and/or quota.group file (depending on which mount options you assigned, although it doesn't hurt to add both). These files must be placed in the partition's root directory (basically, its mount point). For example, assigning user quotas to the root partition means creating the file /quota.user. Assigning group quotas to a separate partition mounted as /home/project_teams means creating the file /home/project_teams/quota.group.

The owner and group of these empty quota.user and quota.group files must be root, and the files' permissions must be 600. After this process is complete, reboot the system so all of the changes will take effect properly.

Understanding Quota Options

You can assign three different items with a quota: hard limits, soft limits, and a grace period. A *hard limit* is the amount of space a user or group may take up; they may not ever exceed this space. However, a *soft limit* allows a user or group to exceed the limit for a specified amount of time, or *grace period*.

Sometimes all three of these items are used together. Perhaps a particular user abuses the soft limits and exceeds them by unreasonable levels on a regular basis.

A hard limit can be added above the soft limit, and the user can't exceed the limit even for a moment.

Setting Quota Limits

After telling the filesystem to expect quotas and creating the quota storage structure, it's time to assign the quotas themselves. The methodology you use entirely depends on the environment and user base. However, the basics of quota assignment remain the same.

The command used to assign quotas is **edquota**. Its flags are shown in Table 3.5.

The command has a slightly different format depending on the task you want to complete. To set a quota for a single user, type the following:

```
edquota -u username
```

This command opens a temporary file containing settings for the user similar to the following:

```
Quotas for user username:
/dev/hda1: blocks in use: 0, limits (soft = 0, hard = 0)
 inodes in use: 0, limits (soft = 0, hard = 0)
```

Edit the values in the parentheses as you prefer. To limit the quota by size, edit the **blocks** value(s). To limit the number of files, edit the **inodes** value. When you've finished, save and exit the file.

To set a quota for a single group, type the following to get a temporary file very similar to the previous example, but containing group settings:

```
edquota -g groupname
```

One method of building a default quota and then assigning it to other users is to choose a *proto-user*. This proto-user can be an already existing person on your system, or a test account. You can then assign the proto-user's quota settings to anyone else with the following format:

```
edquota -p proto-username -u username
```

Table 3.5   **edquota** command-line flags.

Flag	Function
-p	Assign the quota specified to all users.
-u	The quota assignment that follows is for a user.
-g	The quota assignment that follows is for a group.
-t	Assign the grace period for a soft limit.

To edit the soft limit grace period for users, type the following:

```
edquota -ut
```

This command opens a temporary file that looks similar to the following:

```
Time units may be: days, hours, minutes, or seconds
Grace period before enforcing soft limits for users:
/dev/hda1: block grace period: 0 days, file grace period: 0 days
```

Edit the number and the time unit (if necessary) to set your grace period.

To edit the grace period for groups, type the following to get a group settings file identical to the previous example:

```
edquota -gt
```

Viewing Existing Quotas

The **repquota** command comes with a quota package that allows you to generate reports including relevant information. The simplest use of this command is as follows:

```
repquota -a
```

This usage displays a listing of all users on all filesystems, their limits, and how close or far they are to reaching them. If you specifically want to know only about users or groups on specific filesystems, you also have that option. For example, the following command displays quota information for all users, regardless of usage, on the root filesystem:

```
repquota -u /
```

To see the same information for the groups on that filesystem, you'd use the **-g** flag.

USING FILE PERMISSIONS TO CONTROL FILESYSTEM ACCESS

It's imperative to understand file permissions and their use if you're to have a secure filesystem. Used properly, they're a system administrator's last barrier from attack—but they often also cause accidental mischief.

Understanding Permissions

File permissions in their file listing form consist of a set of nine characters. When you're reading these characters, the set is broken down into three groups of three. The first triad represents the permissions for the owner of the file. The second set of three pertains to the group the owner belongs to. Finally, the third triad refers to every user on the system.

A file permission triad is made up of three permission slots: read, write, and execute. If the slot has a letter in it (**r**, **w**, or **x**), then the permission bit is turned on. If slot is empty—which shows as a dash (-)—the permission is turned off. A fully on triad would look like the following:

```
rwx
```

An example file permission set with full permissions for the user, read and execute for the group, and only read for the world, would be as follows:

```
rwxr-xr--
```

There's also one extra slot directly in front of the triads: the type bit. A variety of characters can appear within this bit, as shown in Table 3.6. These additional characters are used to tighten or slightly alter the meanings behind the permission sets.

Changing Permissions

A common administrative—and even user—task involves changing permissions. The command used to accomplish this is **chmod**. You can use two different approaches when working with permissions. The first (and more cumbersome) involves working with the triad characters and can be used in a relative manner, in steps where you specifically change particular bits.

Changing permissions with this method involves two components within the **chmod** command. One component identifies which triad is referred to: **u** for user, **g** for group, or **o** for other; the other determines which permission bit is turned on or off. The bits are then manipulated by adding or subtracting them from the triad component.

Table 3.6   Some common type permission characters.

Character	Type
-	File
d	Directory
l	Symbolic link
s	Set ID

Say a file with the following permissions exists:

```
-rwxrwx--
```

To remove the group's write bit, but allow others to read the file, type the following:

```
chmod g-x,o+r
```

The second method of manipulating file permissions is much less complex in many ways. It's a matter of understanding that permission sets can be represented by a number, and then explicitly set a new permission based on a new set of numbers. A permission set is by definition an octal value, and each bit within the triad has a specific value. A read permission counts as four, a write permission as two, and execute as one. You total the values within the triad to get the digit for that triad. The three triad digits together make up the permission set's octal value.

Take the example permission set from the previous example (after it was changed). The first triad is **rwx**; its bits have the values four, two, and one, which total seven. The second triad is now **rw-**; its bit values of four and two total six. The third triad is **r--**, which has the value four. So the octal representation of **rwxrw-r--** is 764.

Using The **umask**

The **umask** is the octal file creation mask. It contains the bits that are off by default when a new file is created. The **umask** plus the permission value totals 777.

Here's how to work with **umask**. With this example, you'll create a new file, then change the umask, and then create another file. You'll then change the second file's permissions to match the first file's. To accomplish this task, follow these steps:

1. Change to the root of the new partition. For example:

   ```
   cd /project
   ```

2. Type the following to create the empty file:

   ```
   touch project-file1
   ```

3. Get a file listing (including the permissions) using the following command:

   ```
   ls -l project-file1
   ```

3

4. Change the **umask** to a value it wouldn't normally be by typing the following:

```
umask 011
```

5. Create a second empty file, project-file2.
6. Get a file listing, including the permissions, on both files.
7. Change the permissions on project-file2 to match those on project-file1 using the **chmod** command.

The Art Of Permission Use

It's important to consider the ramifications of the permission combinations chosen for directories and files. Loose permissions on directories jeopardize tightly protected files. Poorly chosen group permissions allow any other user (if all are in a generic "user" group) to see anything any other user owns.

If you find that your users tend to leave their permissions too loose, use the **umask** to turn off bits during file creation to make their new files safer. You can also set the sticky bit on user directories so that every file within them is created by default with their permissions. This type of monitoring can go a long way toward tightening system security on the user end when it comes to sheer lack of understanding.

 Do not set shell scripts to run SUID root. Not only is this dangerous from a security point of view, but it will actually not work. The kernel will not allow it.

MANAGING FILE OWNERSHIP

Along with file permissions, the question of file ownership comes into play. The permission triad refers to what the user, group, and everyone else are allowed to do. The user is the owner of the file, and the group is the group the user is assigned to.

File ownership is a matter of what user the file belongs to, and what group the user belongs to. Only one user and one group can own the file. However, a user can belong to more than one group.

Specialized Groups

If there are many users on the system, it's sometimes worthwhile to create specialized groups for various clusters of users. For example, you might create a special group for project team members who all need access to the same information. Using combinations of tight permissions and special groups can help to keep unwanted users out of sensitive areas of the filesystem (more on the topic of security in Chapter 12).

Changing Ownership

A system administrator often creates files for other users. Leaving a file with the owner and group "root" in a user's home directory without changing ownership means the user won't be able to access the item. To change the ownership on a file, use the **chown** command. The format for **chown** is as follows:

```
chown username.groupname item
```

CREATING AND MANAGING LINKS

One danger with sloppy file management is to have many copies of the same file lying around the filesystem. The problem with this situation is that updating the file in one place doesn't update it everywhere else. There's no guarantee that, unless the administrator is extremely diligent, he won't miss a file somewhere and leave an old version in use. Creating a *link* allows a system administrator to keep duplicate files in check.

Hard Links

A *hard link* creates a file name that points to the exact same **inode** as the original file. Any changes made to the linked file are also made to the original. The link also has the permissions of the original file. Because the link points to the same **inode**, you can't make a hard link from one partition to another. The **inode** on the second partition would point to a totally different item than the **inode** on the first, because each partition's **inodes** start from the beginning and aren't numbered cumulatively.

Even if you delete the original file, the hard link will still exist until it, too, is deleted.

Symbolic Links

A *soft* (or *symbolic link*) creates a file name that points to the original file but doesn't share the same **inode**. A symbolic link, or *symlink*, appears to have a full permission set (**lrwxrwxrwx**) in a file listing, but in fact uses the same permissions as the original. Because the original and the link don't share the same **inode**, you can make a symlink across partition boundaries. Also, if you delete the original and then try to use the link after the original is gone, you'll get a "File Not Found" error. This happens, again, because the files don't share the same **inode**.

Creating Links

The command used to create a link is **ln**. To create a hard link, the format is as follows:

```
ln original link
```

To create a symbolic link, use the following command:

```
ln -s original link
```

To create hard and symbolic links to files within and outside of the test partition:

1. Change to the root of the new partition. For example:

   ```
   cd /project
   ```

2. Create a hard link from project–file1 to linkH by typing the following:

   ```
   ln project-file1 linkH
   ```

3. Create a symbolic link from project–file1 to linkL by typing the following:

   ```
   ln -s project-file1 linkL
   ```

4. Get a full file listing and examine the results. To get the listing, type the following command:

   ```
   ls -la
   ```

5. Try making a symbolic and hard link outside of the new partition.

Listing Links

To see how many links to a file exist, use the following command:

```
ls -l filename
```

The second column of the file listing contains the number of links.

FINDING SYSTEM FILES

When you're doing routine maintenance or trying to fix problems, it's easy to forget where the various scattered system files live within the filesystem. A number of good places to start and useful commands can speed a harried system administrator along on the quest of the moment.

Common Locations

Where to look for an important file depends on the type of file it is. File locations may vary slightly between distributions, but for the most part these items have standard homes (see the section "The Filesystem Standard"). The locations of exact files are covered in more detail where they become relevant.

It's wise to include the directories listed in the following sections in system backups (except, perhaps, for the documentation section, which doesn't change often and is generally easier to replace).

Daemons

Many daemons reside in /etc or in directories within the /etc hierarchy. A popular location is /etc/rc.d/init.d/.

Documentation

Documentation is an important component of the filesystem and a boon when it comes time to learn to use a new package. Most documentation is within /usr/doc and /usr/man.

Kernel

The kernel is a vital part of the system, because the Linux box can't run without it. Its modules are stored in /lib/modules. The kernel itself is stored in /boot.

Logs

Log files tend by default to be in the /var/log hierarchy.

System Configuration Files

System configuration files have several preferred home directories, many residing under /etc. Some of the specific places to look are:

➤ **/etc/sysconfig/** Contains device configuration files

➤ **/etc/sysconfig/network-scripts** Contains network device control scripts

➤ **/var/spool/cron** Contains user crontabs

➤ **/etc/rc.d/** Contains a number of startup scripts

User Configuration Files

Many user configuration files are within the users' home directories, which are in /home/*username*. However, other system-wide files are necessary for user management, as well. These files tend to reside in /etc.

Search Commands

If you know the name of the program or file—or at least part of the name—a number of commands can help you track it down.

3

which

The **which** command looks through the directories listed in the user's PATH environment variable (more on environment variables in Chapter 5) for the program listed, using the following format:

```
which program
```

When using the **which** command, the full name of the program must be used.

This command is especially useful if there's more than one version of the program on the system. The path displayed in the **which** command's output is that of the version run by typing the program name on the command line (because it comes first in the PATH statement).

If you want to run a different version of the program, type its full path to bypass the PATH statement.

locate

The **locate** command looks through its own database to quickly find the items sought. This database, slocate.db, contains the entire filesystem structure from the last time the program **updatedb** was run. Often, the updater runs among the daily **cron** jobs (more on **cron** in Chapter 6) in the wee hours of the morning.

The **updatedb** program is actually just "**slocate –u**", which creates a database of the filesystem starting at the root directory.

The format used with the **locate** command is as follows:

```
locate file
```

The **locate** command accepts patterns with the wildcard characters *, ?, and [ ]. The asterisk (*) stands for an unknown set of characters of unknown length. The question mark (?) stands for a single unknown character, and may be used in groupings to indicate a fixed number of unknown characters. The brackets ([ ]) define a range of letters or numbers separated by a dash and no spaces.

find

The **find** command is a complex and powerful tool that searches the current filesystem structure. Its basic format, when used to search for partial file names from the root directory, is as follows:

```
find / -name 'pattern'
```

 If the entire file name is known, just use it without the single quotes.

Another format for the **find** command searches for files owned by a particular user. This method is an excellent way to root out items belonging to users after their accounts have been deactivated. The format is as follows:

```
find / -user username
```

SITUATING FILES PROPERLY

Although there's no one true way enforced for laying out a filesystem, guidelines exist that can make a system administrator's life easier. Staying within these guidelines allows new programs to find the system files and additional libraries and programs they seek without requiring cumbersome configuration files or source code edits. Following the guidelines also makes it easier to train additional system administrators or assistants on how to maintain the system.

The Filesystem Hierarchy Standard

The Linux Filesystem Standard (FSSTND) is fully outlined at **http://www. pathname.com/**. It specifies the standard layout of a Linux filesystem, and the FSSTND documentation also lays out as best it can where the distributions are more likely to be similar and where they're more likely to be different. This was in some ways a dry run for the next step.

The second and current standard that covers all flavors of Unix is the Filesystem Hierarchy Standard (FHS), which is also outlined at **www.pathname.com/**. The reason to have such a far-reaching set of file location guidelines is to allow developers trying to write software for the growing variety of Unix platforms to have less trouble making versions for all of them. The more scattered the flavors become, the less supported most of them would get until only a few were really feasible. Keep this in mind when you are determining where to place your own packages, especially if you deal with a lot of commercial software.

Of course, there is no one who will force you to follow the FHS. There are even times when it may not make sense to do so. However, it's still wise to be aware of its standard layout. This knowledge helps when it's time to install programs that are looking for files that aren't in the expected locations. Often, a quickly added soft link can rectify the situation.

Permissions Issues

Where files are stored best is partially a factor of who needs to have access to them. If you keep programs or shell scripts that users are supposed to use in a directory that's only usable by the Superuser, you defeat the purpose of having them.

HARD DISK PERFORMANCE

Much of what you do when working in Linux involves the filesystem, so it is important to keep a close eye on your hard disk and what it is doing. There are certain things you can do to optimize its performance, and to ensure that you do not run out of filesystem resources before you should.

Drive Optimization

There is a utility available under Linux called **hdparm**. It comes with most Linux distributions, so you should not need to download it. It is important to understand that you need to be careful with this utility. Each hard drive is different and if you set things wrong you can damage your filesystem. Some basic coverage of fairly safe activities is covered here because it is not possible to know what type of hardware you have in your machine, and this basic knowledge is what the exams require as well.

The **hdparm** command is used in the format **hdparm** *flags device*. The flags you may want to make use of are outlined in Table 3.7. Notice that each flag has its own parameters, so each needs to be used separately. For example, **hdparm −c1 −d1 /dev/hda**.

Table 3.7 Flags commonly used with the **hdparm** command.

Flag	Arguments	Purpose
A	0 or 1	Disable (0) or enable (1) IDE read-lookahead.
c	0, 1, or 3	Disable (0) or enable (1) (E)IDE 32-bit I/O support across a PCI or VLB bus. If necessary, add the sync sequence (3), which is needed by some chipsets but slows down performance.
d	0 or 1	Disable (0) or enable (1) the use of DMA (Direct Memory Access) to send data directly to RAM, if the chipset is capable of this.
i	None	Display drive information, including current multiple sector mode.

(continued)

Table 3.7 Flags commonly used with the **hdparm** command *(continued)*.

Flag	Arguments	Purpose
m	0, 2, 4, 8, 16, 32	Disable (0) or enable multiple sector I/O on IDE drives that support this feature. This option can greatly speed drive performance, but be careful not to push it too hard. To enable, use one of 2, 4, 8, 16, or 32, which are the number of sectors that can be transferred by the I/O interrupt. Try different settings and see which seems to work best for your drive.

Notice that the m flag in Table 3.7 is used per drive, not per partition.

Monitoring Disk Resources

Another issue that can occur on well-used filesystems is getting short on resources. Low disk resources does not always mean that the drive is almost full. An ext2 disk drive is basically made up of a bunch of blocks, and **inodes** are used to map what data is stored in which blocks. The problem is, if you run out of **inodes**, then you cannot store any more files!

The more tiny your files, the faster you use up your **inodes**. Remember, you are using one inode per file.

There are two useful commands that can help you keep an eye on this potential problem: **df** and **du**. The **df** command is fairly quick and dirty. You can type **df** and immediately get a report similar to the following:

```
Filesystem      1024-blocks    Used    Available    Capacity    Mounted on
/dev/hda3         4795616    2409182  2138230        53%           /
/dev/hda1            7496       915     6181          13%         /boot
```

Every item mounted onto the filesystem is included in this quick listing. You can control the type of data you get back. In this case, it is kilobytes. You can also type **df –i** to see data on **inodes**:

```
Filesystem      Inodes    Iused    IFree    %Iused    Mounted on
/dev/hda3      1241088    136950  1104138    11%          /
/dev/hda1         4000        18    3982      0%        /boot
```

Table 3.8   Flags commonly used with the **du** command.

Flag	Purpose
b	Print file size in bytes.
c	Produce a grand total of data listed.
h	Print file sizes in human-readable formats.
k	Print file sizes in kilobytes.
s	Only give the directory totals, not the file sizes.
S	Do not count subdirectories, just stay in the main directory.
x	Stay only on the current filesystem.

or **df –h** to get the answer in the most friendly format:

```
Filesystem     Size   Used   Avail   Capacity   Mounted on
/dev/hda3      4.6G   2.3G   2.0G    53%        /
/dev/hda1      7.3M   915K   6.0M    13%        /boot
```

The **du** command, on the other hand, gives much longer output and is often more useful to redirect into a file. If you just type **du**, the command will output the size of every file recursively down through the current directory, and at the end give a total of how much data is in that directory. Again, there are flags available, and you can only use one at a time. The flags for **du** are outlined in Table 3.8.

CHAPTER SUMMARY

The weight of each item covered in this chapter on the exams partially depends on what exam you'll be taking. Although items such as quotas may be covered only in a vague sense, most of the other items included are likely to appear on any Linux exam you encounter. Be especially sure to become comfortable with the filesystem layout, mounting devices, working with /etc/fstab, and the practices and concepts behind altering file ownership and permissions.

REVIEW QUESTIONS

1. Which of the following are capable of being part of a Linux machine's filesystem? [Choose all correct answers]

   a. partition

   b. floppy drive

   c. Zip drive

   d. monitor

2. Which command allows you to partition a drive?

 a. **e2fsck**

 b. **fdisk**

 c. **chmod**

 d. **stab**

3. Which command allows you to format a partition?

 a. **e2fsck**

 b. **fdisk**

 c. **mke2fs**

 d. **chmod**

4. Which command allows you to scan the filesystem for problems?

 a. **e2fsck**

 b. **fstab**

 c. **mke2fs**

 d. **chmod**

5. What command would you use to mount the first partition of the second IDE drive, which contains Windows 95 data, to /mnt/win?

 a. **mount –t msdos /dev/sda1 /mnt/win**

 b. **mount /dev/hdb1 /mnt/win**

 c. **mount –t vfat /dev/hdb1 /mnt/win**

 d. **mount /mnt/win**

6. After mounting the partition at /mnt/win, what would you type to change to the directory that corresponds to d:\work\faxes\?

 a. cd /mnt/win/work/faxes

 b. cd /mnt/win\work\faxes

 c. cd /work/faxes

 d. cd /dev/hdb1/work/faxes

7. To unmount the /mnt/win partition, what command would you type?

 a. **rm /mnt/win**

 b. **unmount /mnt/win**

 c. **umount /mnt/win**

 d. **del /mnt/win**

8. What file contains important filesystem information, including which partitions have quotas enforced on them?

   a. /etc/mke2fs

   b. /filesystem

   c. /etc/fstab

9. What kind of quota would you assign if you wanted to give someone a warning about exceeding quota limits but let them go over the limit temporarily?

   a. soft

   b. hard

   c. symbolic

   d. block

10. What command would you use to see a listing of quotaed partitions and the status of the users with quotas?

   a. **edquota**

   b. **repquota**

   c. **find**

   d. **df**

11. What is the octal representation of the permission set **rw-r--r--**?

   a. 322

   b. 422

   c. 741

   d. 644

12. Which of the following permission sets belongs to a symbolic link?

   a. drwxrwx--

   b. lrwxrwxrwx

   c. rw-rw-rw-

   d. -r--r--r--

13. Where is the first place you might look when trying to locate a daemon?

   a. /bin

   b. /usr

   c. /etc

   d. /var

14. When trying to determine the home of a particular file, what commands might you use? [Choose all correct answers]
    a. **which**
    b. **find**
    c. **fdisk**
    d. **locate**

15. If you encountered a Linux system you weren't familiar with, what standard would you follow to help you find important system files?
    a. POSIX
    b. DNS
    c. TCP/IP
    d. FSSTND

16. If the permissions on a portion of the filesystem must be restored, which method(s) can you use to retrieve the original settings? [Choose all correct answers]
    a. Full Filesystem Backup
    b. Partial Filesystem Backup
    c. Just leave them as they are
    d. Printout of Filesystem listing

17. What is the mask of permission set rwxr--rw-?
    a. 644
    b. 723
    c. 746
    d. 632

18. What is the umask of permission set rwxr--rw-?
    a. 746
    b. 031
    c. 022
    d. None of the above.

19. What is the umask of permission set rw-r--rw-?
    a. 020
    b. 022
    c. 646
    d. None of the above.

20. To make a link that ensures that the linked file exists even after the original file is deleted, which type of link would you create?

    a. hard

    b. symbolic

    c. soft

    d. virtual

HANDS-ON PROJECTS

These projects require a Linux system running at least kernel 2.0.x. This computer must have a partition available for you to add to the filesystem, quotas must be activated within the kernel, and the quota package must be installed.

Project 3.1

In this project, you'll create a new Linux Native partition using **fdisk**, and then mount that partition using the default options in /etc/fstab.

To add this new partition:

1. Get a listing of the current partition structure by typing the following:

   ```
   fdisk -l
   ```

2. Start **fdisk** with the following command:

   ```
   fdisk
   ```

3. Create the new partition by filling out the prompts similar to the following:

   ```
   Command (m for help): n
   Command action
    l logical (5 or over)
    p primary partition (1-4)
   l
   First cylinder (273-627, default 273): 273
   Last cylinder or +size or +sizeM or +sizeK (273-627, default 627): 627
   Command (m for help): w
   ```

4. Format the new partition by typing the following (fill in the location of your new partition appropriately):

   ```
   mke2fs /dev/hda6
   ```

You may get an error when you try to run this command. If so, reboot the system and try again.

5. Add the new partition to your /etc/fstab file with a line similar to the following:

```
/dev/hda6 /project ext2 defaults 1 4
```

6. Reboot the machine to test the new partition table.

Now, you need to check your root partition for errors and create a backup of some of the more essential parts of the filesystem.

To check and then back up:

1. Change to the root directory by typing the following:

```
cd /
```

2. To force a check of the root partition for errors, type the following:

```
e2fsck -f
```

It's better to run this command on something other than the root partition—one that isn't as important and won't harm your machine if you do run this command. If there is a /usr partition laid out, **umount** it first and then issue the command to **fsck** it. Checking the root partition while the partition is mounted may cause errors.

3. Follow the prompts. It's almost always safe to allow the program to fix errors. If you're concerned for your files, answer No.

4. Back up the /etc hierarchy to the file /backup by typing the following:

```
cd /etc
ls -laR > /backup
```

5. Back up the /var/log hierarchy to the same file by typing the following:

```
cd /var/log
ls -laR >> /backup
```

Project 3.2

In this project, you'll set your new partition to handle quotas. Then, you'll create a proto–user and apply its quota settings to another user's space on that partition.

3

To add and assign the quotas, do the following:

1. To prime the partition to accept quotas, edit /etc/fstab.

2. Change the defaults segment of the listing for the new partition to the following:

```
defaults,usrquota
```

3. Save and exit /etc/fstab.

4. Change to the root of the new partition. For example:

```
cd /project
```

5. Create both of the necessary quota files by typing the following:

```
touch quota.user
touch quota.group
```

6. Change the new files' permission to 600 by typing the following:

```
chmod 600 quota.*
```

7. Reboot to activate quotas.

8. Choose or create a user account to function as the proto–user. Assign a quota to this account by typing the following:

```
edquota -u protouser
```

9. In the temporary file, fill in numbers suitably small for the exercise, such as:

```
Quotas for user protouser:
/dev/hda1: blocks in use: 0, limits (soft = 20, hard = 40)
 inodes in use: 0, limits (soft = 0, hard = 0)
```

10. Save and exit the file.

11. Use this quota setting as a basis for assigning another user his quota by typing the following:

```
edquota -p protouser -u otheruser
```

12. Assign a grace period by typing the following:

    ```
    edquota -ut
    ```

13. In the temporary file, fill in a grace period of 30 minutes by changing the defaults to the following:

    ```
    Time units may be: days, hours, minutes, or seconds
    Grace period before enforcing soft limits for users:
    /dev/hda1: block grace period: 30 minutes, file grace period: 0 days
    ```

14. Save and exit the file.

15. Log in as either the proto-user or the other user and place files into the new partition until you reach the soft and hard limits.

## CHAPTER FOUR

BOOT, INITIALIZATION, SHUTDOWN, AND RUNLEVELS

AFTER READING THIS CHAPTER AND COMPLETING THE EXERCISES, YOU WILL BE ABLE TO:

➤ Customize LILO on your Linux boxes

➤ Set exactly which daemons should start and stop as you enter specific runlevels

➤ Create a custom boot disk and use it to repair a Linux box that won't otherwise boot

➤ Properly shut down a Linux machine

It's important to understand the startup and shutdown behavior of a Linux box. Knowing what tasks happen when, and from which scripts and configuration files, helps when you're trying to diagnose boot problems or configure a system.

LILO, THE BOOT MANAGER

LInux LOader (LILO) is the first program a Linux box encounters after the BIOS (assuming a third-party boot manager isn't in use). As such, LILO has the unique ability to either frustrate the boot process or help it go smoothly. After you get the basic setup functioning properly, several customization options are available.

Using LILO To Boot

To use LILO to boot your Linux system, it must be properly installed. Most PC-based Linux distributions include an option to install it within their installation programs, but it's also important to know how to install it by hand to assist in fixing potential problems.

Installing LILO requires three major steps: installing the LILO package, configuring LILO, and running it. First, the LILO package must be installed. If it isn't available with the distribution CDs or downloaded files, it's easily attainable from a number of Linux download sites.

Once the package is installed, you configure LILO at least at a basic level for test purposes (there's time for additional customization later). To do so, create the file /etc/lilo.conf. At a bare minimum, it must have the basics to boot each kernel and operating system on the machine. The section necessary to boot Linux should look like the following (substituting the partition label appropriate for the system in question):

```
image=/vmlinuz
label=Linux
root=/dev/hda2
```

For another operating system, such as Windows 95, the section might look like this:

```
other=/dev/hdb1
table=/dev/hdb
label=Windows
```

Once the LILO configuration file is saved, the final step involves running LILO to ensure it places the information it needs properly. To run LILO, type the following:

```
/sbin/lilo
```

Be sure to have your emergency boot disk handy in case something goes wrong when rebooting after installing LILO. You'll need the emergency disks to boot without it and fix the problem.

Customizing LILO

Once LILO satisfactorily boots the machine, there are a number of customization options a system administrator can apply to make life easier.

Time Delay

It's possible to add a time delay, allowing a busy system administrator a chance to intercept LILO and make a boot choice without having to hover over a rebooting machine. The parameter used for this goes in /etc/lilo.conf in the global section, which is above the label definitions. The format used is:

```
delay = tenths_of_seconds_to_wait
```

For example, if the delay time should be 30 seconds, then the line would be:

```
delay = 300
```

If this option isn't included, LILO boots immediately.

Default OS

To set which label boots by default, make it the first in the set of label listings.

Comments

It's a good practice to comment everything you do as a system administrator whenever possible. Doing this makes things easier when you're making changes later or relearning how to use a script or program. To comment in LILO, use the hash mark (**#**). If the comment runs multiple lines, a hash mark must appear at the beginning of each line.

Boot Message

A short (65,535 byte) message can be displayed before the LILO boot prompt. If the text file is in the default location of /etc/lilo.msg, then the line to add in the global section of /etc/lilo.conf is:

```
message=/etc/lilo.msg
```

Pass Kernel Options

You can pass kernel options through LILO in two different ways. One way is by hand, typing them in at the LILO prompt. Another method involves adding a statement in /etc/lilo.conf. If you need to pass the same option every time you boot into Linux, go ahead and put it in the configuration file. It saves a lot of typing time and keeps you from forgetting anything.

To pass options at the LILO prompt, type the label for the boot instance you want to use—for example, linux—and then the command for the parameter to pass. For example, it might look like the following:

```
LILO: linux ether=IRQ, BASE_ADDRESS(io port), PARAM_1, PARAM_2, DEVICE
```

When you want to pass options to the kernel in the configuration file, remember that you need to do this in the definition section for the image you need to pass the information for, not in the global section of /etc/lilo.conf. You use an **append** statement to declare what needs to be passed as discussed in Chapter 2. Taking the example above, you would add this statement in the following format:

```
append "ether=0,0,eth0 ether=0,0,eth1"
```

LINUX STARTUP AND RUNTIME BEHAVIOR OVERVIEW

When a computer boots, after it looks at the CMOS and BIOS it turns to its MBR to see what it needs to do. In the case of Linux where you have chosen LILO (or an alternative boot loader) as your boot manager, LILO continues the process according to its configuration. If Linux is the OS you choose from the LILO prompt, then LILO calls the kernel, which in turn calls /etc/rc.d/rc.sysinit in some distributions, others go directly to the next step from the kernel. When its tasks are complete, it calls the program /sbin/init. More than one version of this item is available, depending on the Linux distribution being used. It can be identified by looking at its configuration file, which is /etc/inittab. The inittab file assigns the runlevel, and the proper daemons start, depending on which runlevel is assigned. At the end of all these scripts, /etc/rc.d/rc.local runs; then, the user finally sees the login prompt.

 If the system makes it through LILO but crashes before reaching the prompt, then the problem very likely is in one of these scripts or data files.

System Initialization Scripts

The system initialization scripts execute in a precise order. First, rc.sysinit starts if it exists in the particular distribution in question. It loads basic system and networking information, mounts drives, and turns on quotas. Next, /sbin/init calls the appropriate /etc/rc.d/rc#.d initialization script or the /etc/rc.d/rc runlevel manager—some distributions have this manager and some do not, depending on the runlevel specified. After this, the rc#.d or rc script ensures that only the daemons assigned to the runlevel are active. Finally, /etc/rc.local reads in the information specific to the machine (as opposed to the network).

Init Files

The system init files contain data used during the boot process. Each file is specialized, containing data pertaining to particular tasks and issues. The file /etc/fstab, for example, stores the data and settings necessary for rc.sysinit to mount filesystems at boot time (more on /etc/fstab in Chapter 3). When it comes time to enter a runlevel, the level to use comes from the file /etc/inittab. Finally, the data for the login and Telnet prompts, for console and Telnet users, respectively, is loaded from the files /etc/issue and /etc/issue.net.

LINUX INITIALIZATION BEHAVIOR

Now let's look at boot initialization behavior in more detail. The following sections trace some important system initialization steps.

/etc/rc.d/rc.sysinit

The first thing /etc/rc.d/rc.sysinit does is set the default PATH statement. After this, it looks to see if the file /etc/sysconfig/network exists. If it does exist, then rc.sysinit runs the network script to set the system's networking configuration. If not, rc.sysinit assigns the computer the name "localhost" and tells the system no networking capability is required.

Next, rc.sysinit runs the /etc/rc.d/init.d/functions script, which defines a number of functions called by the shell scripts contained in the same directory. It then runs the program /sbin/loglevel and assigns its output to the environment variable **$LOGLEVEL**. This action determines how much detail the system logs record.

Once this action is complete, rc.sysinit loads the keymap according to the keyboard information selected during system installation. The term *keymap* is fairly self-descriptive—it's a data table that maps what keys on the keyboard output what characters when pressed.

After the keys are mapped, the program /sbin/setsysfont sets the font used to display data to the screen. Next, the system swap space is activated. Now the hostname and domain name gleaned earlier in the process from the /etc/sysconfig/network are assigned to their respective environment variables: **HOSTNAME** and **NISDOMAIN**.

At this point in the rc.sysinit script, it looks to see if the file /fsckoptions exists. If so, it sets the contents of that file to a variable. If the file /forcefsck exists, then the script adds a flag in front of the variable to force a filesystem check with the options set in the variable. The script now looks to see if the /fastboot file exists. If so, it skips the filesystem check. If the /fastboot file doesn't exist, however, the script makes a full check of the root (/) filesystem.

Next is an odd line of code:

```
mount -t proc /proc /proc
```

The /proc portion of the filesystem is stored in RAM, not on disk. This unusual syntax mounts the RAM partition transparently into the filesystem structure.

After this, rc.sysinit checks to see if any Plug and Play (PNP) devices exist. If so, it checks to see if it's expected to automatically configure them. If it's supposed to configure them, it runs isapnp. If not, it continues without configuring PNP.

The script now mounts the root (/) filesystem in full read-write mode, updates quota information if necessary, and then turns on quotas for the root partition. Next, it clears the variable **IN_INITLOG** and, if the file /etc/HOSTNAME doesn't exist, puts the contents of the **HOSTNAME** environment variable into the file.

The rc.sysinit script next clears the mtab, which is a file containing the distilled version of /etc/fstab that the system refers to regularly. Then, it enters the root filesystem and /proc into mtab. After that, it checks to see if the kernel is monolithic or modular (see Chapter 11 for more on the kernel) and runs the appropriate options.

Now the script loads a series of kernel modules, followed by RAID devices. Once finished with these tasks, it runs a filesystem check on all partitions except the root (/), unless the fastboot option was chosen during the last shut-down. Once this check is complete (or skipped), all other partitions are mounted except those requiring NFS; then, nonroot partition quotas are activated.

At this point, a number of files are deleted, both to clean up the system for this boot time and to prepare for the next boot. The fastboot and filesystem-checking option files are deleted. Many lock files are removed from the /var/lock hierarchy. Stale process ID files are deleted from /var/run, and more lock files from /tmp.

The rc.sysinit script now begins setting up the machine for the current session. It sets the system clock, activates swap space, and loads necessary modules such as SCSI handlers. Then, it checks the file /etc/sysconfig/desktop to determine which X display manager to use by default, and sets the system so it sees that manager as the default unless a user's preferences state otherwise.

Finally, /etc/rc.d/rc.sysinit saves a copy of all the messages it displayed during the boot process to /var/log/dmesg.

/etc/rc.d/rc#.d

When /sbin/init declares the default runlevel (0 to 6), the system looks to the /etc/rc.d hierarchy. Within it is a series of numbered directories: rc0.d, rc1.d, through rc6.d. These directories correspond to the runlevels (discussed in more detail in the "Changing And Managing Runlevels" section later in this chapter) themselves, and contain a ranking of the daemons to start and stop when entering that level. To read the ranking, follow the relatively simple format, as described in the following section.

ActionOrderDaemon

The Action component of the ranking file assigns which of two possible things should happen to the daemon upon entering the runlevel: Start the daemon or Kill the daemon. When looking at the Order component, keep in mind that the Order values for the K (Kill) items are separate from the Order values for the S (Start) items. These values are two-digit integers from 00 to 99. The Daemon component is the name of the actual daemon to which the ranking refers.

 These ranking files aren't copies of the daemons themselves. Rather, they're soft links to the daemons.

/etc/rc.d/rc.local

The last initialization script loaded is /etc/rc.d/rc.local. Depending on the distribution in question, the file may be completely empty aside from a few comments, or it may contain code. This is the file in which a system administrator puts custom initialization script code.

LINUX LOGIN BEHAVIOR

When you approach a Linux terminal or machine and face the login screen, you are actually looking at a combination of two things. One of these items is a version of the getty program. Which version depends on the distribution you are using; one popular one for console logins is **mingetty**. For a network login you would need to use another getty program, perhaps **mgetty**. Which getty program you choose is often simply determined by which one the distribution uses. There are also limits on what kind of connections each version can fulfill—some can only handle console connections like **mingetty**, some do not handle modem connections well like **agetty**.

The other item you see on the screen, generally on the top, is the contents of the file /etc/issue or /etc/issue.net. Each of these has a separate function that depends on whether this is a local or network login. Both files are used to display introductory information above the login prompt; it is smart to keep the distribution information out of them, especially from /etc/issue.net, which is what users will see when they try to make a telnet connection. If you give information on the distribution, those who study such things for mischief will already have clues as to what weakness to pursue.

Once you enter a login name, a password, and press Enter, the getty version calls the **login** program. This program verifies the password against /etc/passwd or /etc/shadow. If the password checks out as correct, you are passed to the shell or program assigned in /etc/passwd or /etc/shadow.

CHANGING AND MANAGING RUNLEVELS

Whether you're using them to change to single-user mode to reset a lost root password or to automatically boot into an X window manager on a user machine, runlevels are a useful administrative tool.

Changing At The Command Line

To change runlevels directly at the command line, use the **init** command. This command calls the initial init program, which then calls inittab, which then follows the instructions in the appropriate /etc/rc.d/rc#.d directory to stop and start daemons for the new runlevel.

The format for the **init** command is

```
init x
```

where **x** is the runlevel to change to. Unfortunately, which numbers correspond to what for runlevels is not standard across distributions. Table 4.1 shows the runlevels available for Red Hat, whereas Table 4.2 lists those available in SuSE, according to SuSE's documentation.

Table 4.1   Runlevels and their functions.

Level	Description
0	Halt, or shut down
1	Single-user mode
2	Multiuser mode, no NFS available
3	Full multiuser mode; the default command-line use runlevel
4	No longer used
5	Full multiuser mode with graphical login; the default X-based runlevel
6	Reboot

Table 4.2   Runlevels in SuSE Linux.

Runlevel	Description
0	Halt
S	Single user
1	Multiuser, no networking
2	Multiuser, networking, standard runlevel
3	Multiuser, networking, GUI
4	Unused
5	Unused
6	Reboot

Note that there are some similarities. Across the board, they take advantage of one interesting aspect of using **init**. Typing

```
init 0
```

shuts down the machine, and typing

```
init 6
```

reboots it.

 To boot straight into a runlevel from the LILO boot prompt, type the Linux label and the runlevel number. For example, "linux 5".

Changing Runlevel Defaults

To change the default daemon starts and stops for a runlevel, change the contents of the appropriate /etc/rc.d/rc#.d directory. To remove an item from being affected by a change in runlevel, delete it from the directory listing. To add a daemon to be killed or started when entering the runlevel, create a soft link in the /etc/rc.d/rc#.d directory to the actual daemon file. As discussed earlier, it's important how this file is named.

If **init** needs to kill the daemon as it enters the new runlevel, start the link name with *K*. However, if it needs to start the daemon as it moves to the new runlevel, start the name with *S*. The next part of the daemon's name is an integer from 00 to 99 that places the daemon within the kill or start order. It's important to keep dependencies in mind: If the daemon requires another daemon to be already running before it can start, be sure to place it after the item it depends on.

Automating Application Startup

Often, a system administrator wants to add specific applications and processes that don't ordinarily start at boot time. The approach used to add such items to the boot process depends on what type of program is involved.

Services

Starting a service such as a Web server usually involves running a daemon. To make the daemon run at startup, set it up in the runlevel directory that corresponds to the default runlevel specified in /etc/inittab.

Non-Daemon Applications

To start a program automatically during the boot cycle, take advantage of the /etc/rc.d/rc.local customization script. Using shell scripting commands and techniques (covered in Chapter 5), add the necessary commands, options, and anything else necessary to have the machine boot into its default programs.

You can add other customization aspects within /etc/rc.d/rc.local as well—for example, system-wide environment variables necessary for software and scripts, temporary files that need to be deleted or executed at startup, and anything that needs to run once the system is booted.

System Shutdown

It's highly important to shut down or reboot a system properly. Not all data is written immediately to disk, and that data is lost if someone simply presses the Power or Reset button. Also, there are logs to be halted, temporary files to be created and deleted, network drives to unmount, and many other tasks to attend to in order to shut down cleanly and orderly.

Shutting Down To Power Off

Three commands are available to prepare a Linux machine to be powered off. One of these commands, as mentioned earlier, is

```
init 0
```

This command changes the system to runlevel 0, which corresponds to the **halt** command—the second method of powering down a Linux box. You should avoid both **init 0** and **halt** unless the need to shut down is urgent or no users are logged into the machine in question.

The most graceful method of shutting down a Linux machine is the following command:

```
shutdown -h
```

A number of options are available with this command. They're discussed in more detail in the "Shutdown Command Options" section.

Shutting Down To Reboot

Three corresponding commands are also available to reboot a Linux machine. One of these is the following:

```
init 6
```

This command changes the system to runlevel 6, which corresponds to the **reboot** command—the second method of rebooting a Linux machine. Once again, keep in mind that neither of these commands offers any warning to the users on the machine or its services.

The most graceful method of rebooting a Linux machine is with the same command as before, but using a different flag:

```
shutdown -r
```

Other shutdown options are discussed in the next section.

Shutdown Command Options

The **shutdown** command has quite a number of options, which are shown in Table 4.3. These options allow a system administrator to set wait times, give warning to users, and more.

Table 4.3   shutdown command options.

Flag	Purpose
-c	Cancel the shutdown after it's already started.
-f	Create the /fastboot file so that when the computer comes back up, it won't check the filesystem.
-F	Create the /forcefsck file so that when the computer comes back up, it will check the filesystem.
-h	Halt the system at the end of the shutdown process so it can be powered off.
-k	Print a warning message but do not automatically shut down.
-r	Reboot the system at the end of the shutdown process.
-t	Enter a time in seconds that shutdown should wait before invoking **init**.
hh:mm	The actual time to shut down.
+#m	Shut down in a certain number of minutes, where the hash mark (#) is the number of minutes.

To include a custom message when shutting down, type the message in quotes (" "). For example:

```
shutdown -hf +5m "Shutting down in five minutes."
```

TROUBLESHOOTING BOOT, INITIALIZATION, AND SHUTDOWN PROBLEMS

When a machine won't boot or initialize properly, it's a pretty serious crisis. However, all the information necessary to fix the problems is available in the messages shown during the boot process. It's a matter of knowing how to read the information.

LILO Failures

LILO can fail due to a number of reasons. Fortunately, there's a code behind the way the LILO boot prompt is displayed. As the various stages of LILO progress, parts of the prompt are printed until it's entirely in place. So, the key to diagnosing a LILO failure is understanding what happens before each part of the prompt appears.

Blank Prompt

If no prompt appears, then the computer isn't accessing LILO at all. It could be that the installer forgot to run LILO before rebooting to ensure that all of its pieces were properly in place. In this case, boot with an emergency rescue disk (see the "Creating A Rescue Disk" section later in this chapter for more information) and mount the root (/) partition. Then, run the program /mnt/*mountpoint*/sbin/lilo.

Another issue to check if the boot prompt remains blank is whether LILO (or at least its first stage) is installed on a bootable partition. If not, use your favorite partitioning program to mark the root (/) or boot (/boot) partition as bootable, or boot with an emergency rescue disk, mount the root partition, and use /mnt/*mountpoint*/sbin/fdisk.

L error_code

If the first *L* appears at the prompt followed by an error code, the first stage LILO boot loader (which resides in /boot) loaded properly. It also started. The error refers to the attempt to load the second stage of LILO. The error code itself points to the exact nature of the trouble. Sometimes, solving the problem is as simple as rebooting the machine one or several times. At other times, fixing it involves reinstalling LILO. For one particular error code, 0x04, try removing the word "compact" from your LILO configuration, or adding the word "linear".

LI

If you see *LI* at the prompt and then the process hangs, the second stage boot loader was loaded properly but can't be executed. Try adding the word "linear" to the global portion of /etc/lilo.conf, rerunning LILO, and rebooting.

LIL

If you see *LIL*, *LIL?*, or *LIL-* at the prompt, then the second stage boot loader was loaded properly but some of the files it depends on are out of place. Try adding the word "linear" to the global portion of /etc/lilo.conf, rerunning LILO, and rebooting.

LILO

If the entire *LILO* prompt appears, then LILO has loaded successfully.

Init Failures

Once LILO (or an alternate boot loader) finishes executing, it calls the kernel. The kernel executes and also begins the init cycle. As these kernel and init processes run, a number of messages are printed to the screen and to log files.

Screen Messages

Often, system administrators ignore the messages scrolling across the screen at boot time because there are other things to attend to. However, these messages are invaluable if the machine won't boot properly. Even if the boot failure results in an automatic reboot, the messages are saved to log files (as discussed in the next section).

Generally, the error causing the boot failure is one of the last items shown before the process hangs. There can also be other issues—issues that may not halt the boot process but might cause future problems—that show themselves in the screen messages. It's a good idea to occasionally look through them and check for any tweaks you might need to make.

 Some warnings and errors within the boot sequence actually have little or no effect on the system. Learning which to pay attention to and which to avoid is a matter of experience. A good guide is to deal first with the errors that have an immediate effect on the boot process or on the machine while it's running. You can look into the others when you have some free time to take down the machine and do maintenance.

To move up and down through the information that was sent to the screen, use the key combinations Shift+PgUp and Shift+PgDwn.

You can call up kernel messages at any time with the **dmesg** command.

Boot Logs

As stated before, the boot messages are saved to log files. Even if the boot results in an immediate reboot, these messages are available through booting with a rescue disk (see the "Emergency System Rescue" section for more information) and mounting the appropriate partitions to look at the logs.

Boot-specific messages are saved to the file /var/log/boot.log. The /etc/rc.d/ rc.sysinit script has its own log file called /var/log/dmesg. Another useful log is /var/log/messages, which (although it may contain an overload of information) may show specific messages the others don't.

Abnormal Shutdowns

An abnormal shutdown results whenever proper shutdown procedures aren't followed. This problem may occur due to a user turning off a machine without shutting it down, power outages when there's no uninterruptible power supply (UPS) protection or that last longer than the UPS, a system crash, or some other unforeseen incident.

When a Linux box boots after an abnormal shutdown, it forces a filesystem check. If nothing is wrong, then the boot process proceeds normally. If filesystem errors resulted, you're given the option of allowing **e2fsck** to fix them. It's often good to let the checker do so; but if the explanation of a problem is a cause for concern, then don't fix the particular problem and wait and see how it affects the functionality of the system. Later, if it's still a problem, you can fix it by running **e2fsck** manually.

If the system won't boot after an abnormal shutdown, then a pair of rescue disks is required. See the next section for more information.

EMERGENCY SYSTEM RESCUE

When the Linux box won't boot, it's time for emergency system rescue procedures. These steps involve taking out the custom boot disk and using it to boot the machine. Once booted, you can then mount partitions, check filesystems, and make repairs where necessary.

Creating A Rescue Disk

It's wise to keep a special box of disks at hand for emergencies. These disks aren't the ones that come with the distribution purchased, or the boot disk created to call up the installation program. Once the system is installed, it's important to make a custom boot disk for that machine—and each machine in the LAN, if there's more than one. This disk functions as the emergency rescue disk, or boot disk.

Some distributions have special ways to create this boot disk and special rescue disks to go along with it—some even have rescue disk images right on the distribution CD that you can place on floppy using **rawrite** or **dd**. What is covered here is the most generic method available.

To create a custom boot disk after installation, place an empty floppy disk into the floppy drive. Then use the **mkbootdisk** command to create the boot disk. The command in its most basic format is as follows:

```
mkbootdisk kernelversion
```

The boot disk is then written sector by sector with the kernel version installed on the machine.

Booting Into Rescue Mode

To boot into a mode that allows system repairs, first try booting into runlevel 1. This is accomplished by putting the word "single" after the Linux label in the LILO prompt. For example, if the label was "linux," then you would type **linux single**.

If the system can't boot into runlevel 1, then the rescue disk is necessary. Boot the system with the boot disk in the drive; it will come up in a raw form with only what was installed on the boot disk available to you until you mount partitions.

Rescue Techniques

Once the machine is booted into Linux, the difficult task of tracking down the problem itself begins. You can get a listing of what partitions exist by typing **fdisk –l**, although this will not give you the mount point information. Often, you can tell by size which is which, but if you cannot, it does not hurt to mount the wrong one intentionally. Once you get the root file system mounted, examine the boot messages and logs as discussed in the section "Troubleshooting Boot, Initialization, and Shutdown Problems," earlier in this chapter. These items may or may not give you some hints as to where to start. Trace the runtime behavior and follow whatever clues you find, checking configuration files and scripts for potential problems. Run filesystem checks on the primary partitions and make sure they're flaw-free. Make sure no important files have had their permissions or ownership inadvertently changed.

Common culprits in boot failures are /etc/lilo.conf, /etc/inittab, and /etc/fstab. Another problem may be in the BIOS—sometimes system batteries fail or something gets reset accidentally. Sometimes the problems can be tracked down to a well-meaning user who had just enough knowledge to be dangerous.

Another thing to keep in mind: If you had to boot with boot and rescue disks and then mount even the root file system, you must type **sync**—sometimes more than once—before unmounting the drives to make sure that everything is handled properly. If you have to run LILO off a root partition that is mounted onto the /mnt hierarchy, which would be the case in this scenario, then you need to run /sbin/lilo with the −r flag and tell it the location of the root file system to install itself on. For example, if you mounted it as /mnt/root, then you would type **/mnt/root/sbin/lilo −r /mnt/root**.

Testing System Repairs

It's useful to reboot the system after one or two modifications to see whether it boots successfully, or if signs of trouble are thinning out. Be sure that all of the changes are saved properly before you power down the machine. For example, there's no proper shutdown when you're booted into emergency repair mode. Once again, remember to type **sync** before unmounting all of the partitions mounted during the repair process—many people like to type it more than once just in case. Finally, type **exit** to leave the repair shell, and then power down the machine or reset it to get it to reboot.

Don't make the problem worse by forgetting to close things out properly!

CHAPTER SUMMARY

System boot, initialization, and rescue procedures figure prominently in some exams as a method of distinguishing system administrators from users. It's important to know and be comfortable with issues involving system problem diagnosis and the basic workings of a Linux machine.

Remember that each distribution is going to have its own quirks in the system initialization and runlevel area. Be sure if you are taking an exam that covers specific distributions that you understand the specific twists and turns your chosen specialty takes. This information is especially useful in the system rescue process. Also, examine which rescue process is offered by your chosen distribution. Some offer rescue disk images, some offer rescue tools on the installation CD-ROMs.

REVIEW QUESTIONS

1. Which of the following is not a system initialization script?

   a. /etc/rc.d/rc.sysinit

   b. /etc/fstab

   c. /etc/inittab

   d. /etc/rc.d/rc.local

4

2. Which of the following commands won't prepare your system to be shut off?

   a. **shutdown -r**

   b. **shutdown -h**

   c. **halt**

   d. **init 0**

3. What does the **init** command handle?

   a. Mounting a partition

   b. Starting a program

   c. Formatting a partition

   d. Setting the runlevel

4. What command must you remember to type before unmounting partitions during an emergency rescue situation if you've made any changes in the filesystem?

   a. **sync**

   b. **umount**

   c. **/sbin/lilo**

   d. **init**

5. Which system initialization file contains the default runlevel setting?

   a. /etc/rc.d/rc.local

   b. /etc/lilo.conf

   c. /etc/inittab

   d. /sbin/loglevel

6. Which runlevel corresponds to the multiuser command line interface?

   a. 1

   b. 3

   c. 5

   d. 6

7. Which runlevel corresponds to the multiuser GUI interface?

   a. 1

   b. 3

   c. 5

   d. 6

8. If you forget your root password, which do you type at LILO while reboot-ing to change it, if your LILO label for linux is "Linux"? [Choose all correct answers]

   a. Linux

   b. Single

   c. Linux single

   d. Linux 1

9. What is a good first reaction to LILO hanging during boot time? [Choose all correct answers]

   a. Reinstalling Linux

   b. Booting with a rescue disk and reinstalling LILO

   c. Rebooting and seeing if LILO comes up properly this time

   d. Replacing the hard drive

10. What command do you use to rerun LILO?

    a. **lilo**

    b. **/etc/lilo.conf**

    c. **/bin/lilo**

    d. **/sbin/lilo**

11. If the line "delay = 5000" appears in your /etc/lilo.conf file, how long of a wait is this before the system boots into the default OS choice?

    a. 500 seconds

    b. 50 seconds

    c. 5 minutes

    d. 50 minutes

12. Which of the following lines is not necessary in a basic Linux OS definition in /etc/lilo.conf?

    a. image=/bzImage

    b. label=Linux

    c. root=/dev/hdb1

    d. message=/etc/lilo.msg

13. What is special about the /proc portion of the filesystem?

    a. It contains the settings for which processes should run at what times.

    b. It's totally held in RAM.

    c. It's world–readable.

    d. It must always be on the root (/) partition.

14. Which utility does the OS run at boot time to help configure any Plug and Play devices in the system?

    a. pnp

    b. pnpconfig

    c. setuppnp

    d. isapnp

15. Where can you find the order that the daemons you want to run for runlevel 5 will start in?

    a. /etc/inittab

    b. /etc/rc.d/rc5.d

    c. /sbin/loglevel

    d. /etc/rc.d/rc.local

16. Which flag would you add to the shutdown command to allow your users ten minutes to save their files and log out before the machine goes down?

    a. +10m

    b. +t 10

    c. +t 10m

    d. –t10

17. What command do you use to create a custom boot disk after the installation process?

    a. **bd**

    b. **bootdsk**

    c. **mkboot**

    d. **mkbootdisk**

18. Which item do you not set when creating a boot instance in /etc/lilo.conf for a Windows partition?

    a. label

    b. root

    c. other

    d. table

19. Which environment variable contains a Linux box's domain name?
    a. DOMAIN
    b. DOMAINNAME
    c. NISDOMAIN
    d. DNSDOMAIN

20. Which command do you use to negate a system shutdown?
    a. **kill** *shutdownprocess*
    b. **kill -9** *shutdownprocess*
    c. **shutdown -k**
    d. **shutdown -c**

HANDS-ON PROJECTS

These projects require that a Linux system running at least kernel 2.0.x is already installed, with an X Window manager configured and working properly. The boot manager used must be LILO.

Project 4.1

In this project, you'll customize your /etc/lilo.conf file and reboot the machine to observe its new boot behavior.

To customize your /etc/lilo.conf file and reboot, perform the following:

1. Log in as root.

2. Edit the file /etc/lilo.conf with your editor of choice.

3. In the global segment of the LILO configuration file, add the following line:

```
message=/etc/lilo.msg
```

4. Close and exit the file.

5. Edit the file /etc/lilo.msg.

6. Add the following text:

```
This is where LILO displays my custom comments during boot.
```

7. Save and exit the file.

8. Re-run LILO to make sure all the information is properly put into place:

```
/sbin/lilo
```

9. Reboot the system immediately and skip the filesystem check with the following command:

```
shutdown -rf now
```

10. Watch the messages scroll by as the system shuts down, and then as it reboots. The custom message you added should be displayed directly above the LILO boot prompt. Then, watch the boot messages as your system comes back online.

Project 4.2

In this project, you'll create a boot disk and use it to boot your system and run a filesystem check.

To create a boot disk and use it to boot your system, perform the following:

1. Place a blank boot diskette into your floppy drive.

2. Log in as root.

3. Type **uname –r** to determine your kernel version number.

4. If your floppy drive is at device /dev/fd0 and your kernel version is 2.2.5-15, type the following:

```
mkbootdisk —device /dev/fd0 2.2.5-15
```

You'll see the following text:

```
Insert a disk in /dev/fd0. Any information on the disk will be lost.
    Press <Enter> to continue or ^C to abort.
```

Press Enter.

Some distributions will require you to use a second diskette during the next step. Examine the documentation and see if this is the case for yours. If it is, be sure to create the second diskette as well.

5. Once the process is finished, leave the disk in the drive and reboot the machine.

6. In the sparse emergency shell, type **fdisk –l** to get a listing of the partitions on the machine.

7. Determine which is likely to be your root partition and create a mount point for it; then mount it.

8. Check the filesystem.

9. When finished, type **sync** to ensure that everything is properly saved.

10. Make sure you're outside the mounted partition; then unmount it.

11. Type **exit** to leave the emergency shell.

12. Press the Reset button or shut off the machine.

## CHAPTER FIVE

SHELLS, SCRIPTING, PROGRAMMING, AND COMPILING

AFTER READING THIS CHAPTER AND COMPLETING THE EXERCISES, YOU WILL BE ABLE TO:

➤ Perform basic editing tasks with vi

➤ Form and use search patterns in vi

➤ Analyze and write simple shell scripts

➤ Change and customize the chosen default shell

Although system administrators aren't necessarily programmers, it's useful to have basic skills in scripting and programming. These skills let a system administrator automate tasks and are of great use when installing new packages, some of which must be compiled or slightly altered before they're ready for use.

AN OVERVIEW OF THE UNIX SHELL ENVIRONMENT

All scripting and programming activities are performed within the shell environment, so it's important to understand the basics of this work environment. A *shell* is the interface between the user and the kernel. The shell has a set of tools and features that process what is done at the command line.

There are a number of popular shells within the Linux world. Each different shell has particular areas of specialization that make it appealing to specific groups of people. Three of the most popular shells are as follows:

➤ **Bash shell (bash)**   The default shell in Linux; a derivative of the Unix Bourne shell.

➤ **Public domain Korn shell (pdksh or ksh)**   One of the more popular alternate shells; based on the Unix Korn shell.

➤ **Enhanced C shell (tcsh)**   Another popular Linux shell. This shell's command structure is based on the C programming language, and so it's a favorite among people well versed in C.

TEXT EDITING PRINCIPLES AND PRACTICES

One issue a system administrator must deal with early on is editing text files. Many system configuration and tweaking steps require editing. A number of practices can help this experience go smoothly. The following sections explore some of these practices.

Copy The Original

Before making changes to any system file with which you're unfamiliar, make a backup copy of it in the same location with the same permissions and ownership as the original. Then, if something goes wrong during the configuration process, it's possible to easily return to square one and begin anew.

Save Regularly

Time and time again, users lose work they have done because something happens that doesn't allow them to properly save a file they were working on. Be sure to save files regularly while creating or editing them. It's helpful to develop the habit of saving each time you pause for thought.

This principle goes along well with that of copying the original file before you begin working. Otherwise, what existed in the beginning is quickly lost under a repeatedly saved sea of changes.

PERFORMING EDITING OPERATIONS WITH VI

The *vi (vi*sual editor*)* text editor has as many diehard fans as detractors. Some prefer to use this editor over any other. Others avoid it as much as possible because of its cryptic command structure. However, it has the distinct advantage that it fits on a single floppy disk, isn't memory–intensive, and at times may be the only editor available to use.

Opening Files

To open either an existing file or a new file in vi, type "vi *filename*" (where *filename* is the name of the file you want to open). Be sure you have the proper permissions to both read and write the file if it needs to be edited. It's also possible to open a file with the cursor already positioned on a particular line through one of two methods. First, you can include the **+** flag to declare the specific line number. For example:

```
vi +5 file
```

The second method of using vi to open a file directly to the edit point is to supply a search pattern for vi to look for. If the pattern is found, vi opens with the cursor positioned at its first instance. To open to a search patterned location, use the **+/** flag. For example:

```
vi +/complaint
```

vi Modes

When working in vi, you can use three modes: command, insert, and colon (or last line). Each mode has a specific function when it comes to handling text or files, as follows:

➤ **Command mode** The mode in which vi accepts editing commands. These commands typically begin with a letter or with a number that corresponds to the letter that follows. The editor first opens in command mode. Return to command mode at any time by pressing the Esc key.

➤ **Insert mode** Used to add new text or edit existing text. To enter this mode, type "i" from command mode and press Enter.

➤ **Colon (last line) mode** The mode in which you enter the more complex commands (often file related). To enter last line mode, type a colon. To then execute the command, press the Enter key. This action returns you to command mode.

5

Moving Through Text

The first thing a modern computer user notices about vi is its simplistic interface. Almost all of the commands used are single letters or short combinations of letters that form a complete command. Those accustomed to using a mouse can quickly tire of using a cursor to move through files. Fortunately, vi provides a number of shortcuts to speed up this task. The shortcuts are discussed in the following sections.

Displaying Line Numbers

Most of the vi movement commands involve line numbers. To display the line number for the current line of text, press Ctrl+G. To show all line numbers for the document, you must first enter colon mode. Then, you can type "set nu" and press Enter.

Moving With Line Numbers

Two commands let you move to specific line numbers. One command simply moves to the last line in the file: **G**. The other allows movement to a particular line in the file: Type the line number followed by "G". For example, to move to line 50, type "50G" and press Enter.

More vi Movement Commands

Not all terminal keyboards have arrow keys. Therefore, vi has a set of movement commands that double as arrow keys. Figure 5.1 illustrates the matchup between the arrow keys and the vi movement keys. Knowing these keystrokes is useful in many programs, because this set of characters is used in many other Unix and Linux programs. Not only can you use these commands to move one character or line at a time, you can also use them to jump through things by typing a number before the letter. For example, to move the cursor down twelve lines, you would type "12j".

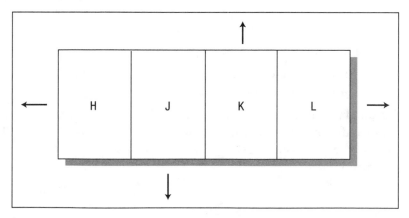

Figure 5.1   The vi arrow key movement commands.

Instead of the up and down arrow keys (or their replacements as shown in Figure 5.1), you can also use the plus (+) key to move up lines and minus (-) to move down. To move multiple lines, type a number before the command as usual.

You can also move in page-sized jumps. Type Ctrl+B to back up a screen's worth of text. Ctrl+F takes you forward a screen's worth. More refined commands allow you to move to the beginning of the current line ("0") or the end ("$"). There are many more movement commands available in the vi editor. Type "man vi" to see a complete command listing.

Inserting Text

As mentioned before, to insert text in general, type "i". However, vi has a rich collection of more specialized commands that can help to speed the file-editing process. To access these items, it's important to be in command mode, not in insert mode.

Appending Text

Two different commands allow a user to append text. Both of these commands first require that the cursor be in place. The first append command is **a**, which directs vi to add new text directly after the cursor. The second is **A**, which tells vi to go to the end of the line the cursor currently sits on and append text.

Beginning A New Line Of Text

Two commands are available to start a new line for text insertion. Once again, these commands require that the cursor already be in place. The first command, **o**, opens a new line below the line where the cursor is located. The second, **O**, creates a new line above the line where the cursor is located.

Changing Text

The change option is a command that requires additional parameters to complete. When invoked, the items marked for change are deleted so they can be replaced.

To begin the change command, type "c" in command mode. After this, type "w" if the change is to apply to a word, or "s" if the change is for an entire sentence. The vi editor determines the end of a word when it sees a space or a punctuation mark; it determines the end of a sentence when it sees a period, exclamation point, or question mark followed by two spaces.

 A shortcut for changing a whole line is typing "C".

It's possible to change multiple words, lines, or sentences by including a number with the change command. For example, to change the next five words, the command would be **5cw**. Typing this command deletes the next five words so they can be replaced.

Overwriting Text

Sometimes you just want to overwrite existing text without having to be specific about how many words, sentences, or lines to replace. Fortunately, vi offers the option to do this, as well. To overwrite text, place the cursor directly before the character you want to begin overwriting and then, in command mode, type "R". However, if you need to replace only a single character without entering insert mode, type "r".

Adding Blank Spaces

The spacebar functions in vi just like it does in almost all other editors, in that it moves to the right and leaves a blank space where the cursor was. However, you can also type a number before pressing the spacebar to create a group of spaces as the cursor shifts that many characters to the right. This is a useful feature for creating columns or simple tables of text.

Substituting Text

Substitution is an editing option available in vi that lies between insertion and deletion. When substituting, the selected characters are deleted; then, vi goes into insert mode until the user chooses to return to command mode. To use the simplest form of this command, you mark the character to replace with the cursor and then type "s". This command deletes that character, after which vi changes to insert mode.

Several options let you substitute multiple characters. If you need to replace a fixed number of characters, type the number followed by "s". For example, to substitute new text for the next nine characters, type "9s". To replace the text for an entire line, type "S" to delete it and then move directly into insert mode.

Deleting Text

The vi editor also offers a suite of deletion options that help to narrow what items to remove. You access these options from command mode.

Deleting Individual Characters

There are two different commands for deleting individual characters. Which to use depends on the direction in which you want to delete. To delete the character the cursor currently rests on, type "x". Otherwise, to delete the character directly behind the cursor (to the left), type "X".

If your goal is to delete multiple characters, type the number and then "X" to delete backward or "x" to delete forward. For example, to delete the previous six characters, type "6X". You can also use the backspace key. You can either back up and erase one character by just pressing the key, or type a number first and press backspace to jump back and erase that many characters.

Deleting Words

If you want to delete the current word, place the cursor on the first letter and type "dw". You can also delete more than one word at a time. To accomplish this, move the cursor to the first letter of the first word, and then type the number and "dw". For example, to delete three words in a row type "3dw".

5

Deleting Lines Of Text

It's possible to delete blocks of text in bulk. To delete a single line, type "dd" in command mode with the cursor positioned on that line. If, instead, your goal is to delete a number of lines, type the number before the **dd** command. For example, to delete the current line and the next three, type "4dd".

Delete To Cursor

There are two different aspects of deleting to the cursor position. The first involves deleting before the cursor, the second after.

The more commonly used feature deletes after the cursor. To delete from the cursor position to the end of the line, type "D". Another useful command deletes to the last line on the screen. To use it, type "dL". To delete to the end of the file, on the other hand, type "dG". To delete from the cursor position to the beginning of the line, type "d^".

Deleting Blocks Of Text

What you need to delete is not always conveniently in a single word, group of sequential words, or all on the same line. You also may not feel like having to count out how many words or characters you want to get rid of. There are a number of options available to help you remove such blocks of text.

To delete from the cursor's current location to the end of a line, type "d". You can also delete from the current cursor location to the beginning of the file ("d1G") or from the current position to the end of the file ("dG"). Perhaps the most practically useful of these, however, allows you to delete from the current cursor position to the end of the listed line. To accomplish this, type "d#$", where the number sign stands for the number of the line to delete to the end of. For example, if you want to delete from the current location to the end of line 20, then you would type "d20$".

Copying And Pasting Text

vi offers many of the features available in modern word processors, including the ability to copy, cut, and paste text. The more of these features you know, the faster your work will go.

Copying And Pasting Lines Of Text

In the course of system administration/shell scripting or makefile editing, you sometimes need to use the same lines again. In that case, you would type the "yy" or "Y" command—these two are identical—to "yank" (copy) lines and then "p" to place them. If you want to copy more than one line, preface the **yy** command with a number. For example, **4yy** copies four lines; then, **p** pastes them in on the line directly under the cursor.

Moving Text

Another useful text editor capability is the ability to move text from one place to another. You can move text in terms of words, rather than full lines. To accomplish this, use the **yw** command to pull the text out of the document—either as a single word, or **#yw** for multiple words, for example **8yw**. The same put command applies to copying. Typing **p** pastes the cut text directly after the cursor's location.

Copying Or Moving Between Documents

Copying or moving text within a file is fairly simple. It uses an unnamed buffer, placing the contents of any copied or deleted text there until another item is copied or deleted. However, the unnamed buffer is specifically bound to the file in question. When you want to copy or move text from one file to another, you need to use named buffers.

You can also use named buffers within a file if you do not want to have to immediately paste what you just cut or copied.

Buffer names consist of a lowercase letter from a to z. You may signify that you want to use such a buffer by typing one double quote (") and then the buffer's name. For example, if you wanted to copy text into buffer e, you would type **e** and then the copy command you wanted to use—perhaps **eyw**. Then you need to open the second document. You cannot do this in a different terminal session, you must open the file in the same session you are currently using. You can open the second file from command mode by typing the command **:e** *filename*. This opens the second file or creates a blank new one with the given name and displays the new file's contents. You can then use the same method to return to the original file.

So, the sequence of items you might type to copy the five lines below the cursor, cursor inclusive, from the file ~/work/data to the new file ~/work/records, and then return to the original document would be:

```
"a5yy
:e ~/work/records
p
:w
:e ~/work/data
```

> Notice that you must save the changes to the file you are currently in before moving to another file.

You must type the buffer name directly after the double quote. Otherwise, the letter given to the buffer name will be interpreted as a **vi** command, not a name.

Creating Patterns In vi

A number of special characters are available for pattern matching within vi. These characters are called *metacharacters*, and they're also used in most other applications in Linux that allow pattern matching.

Any Single Character

To signal one single unknown character within a pattern, add a period. For example, the pattern *mo.se* could match *moose* and *mouse*, but not *mouse's*.

Any Combination Of Characters

To match none or any number of unknown characters within a pattern, add an asterisk. For example, the pattern *n*t* would match *not* and *neat*, but not *notes*.

Match Must Be At The Beginning Of A Line

In order to require that the match be at the beginning of a line, use a caret (^). For example, the pattern *^the* would match the first words in each of the following lines in vi:

```
The quick brown fox jumped over the lazy dog
then ran off with the cat with the fiddle, when
the cow jumped over the moon.
```

Match Must Be At The End Of A Line

If, instead, the goal is to require that the match be at the end of a line, use the dollar sign. For example, the pattern *$read* would match the last word of the highlighted line in vi:

```
I sat down to read the book but fell asleep.
From now on I will stand up when I read
my texts.
```

Ignore This Metacharacter

To ignore any of the metacharacters used in search patterns, *escape* them with the escape character, the backslash (\). For example, to search for this pattern:

```
end. And then,
```

you would need to add an escape character to tell vi that the period is meant as a character, not as a metacharacter. So, the search pattern would look like this:

```
end\. And then.
```

Match One Of A Range

It's possible to provide a specific range of letters or numbers as part of the search term. To do this, surround the range with square brackets. For example, searching for *1[a - d]* would match *1a, 1b, 1c,* and *1d*.

Match Must Be At The Beginning Of A Word

If your goal is to locate items particularly at the beginning of a word, use the metacharacter set **\<**. For example, searching for

```
\<the
```

will match *then* but not *bathe*.

Match Must Be At The End Of A Word

To locate terms at the end of a word, use the metacharacter set **\>**. So, the search term

```
\>the
```

would match *bathe* but not *then*.

Searching Through Text

The vi editor offers a number of search features to help speed the file-editing process. Several of them are covered here, including how to search for text patterns and how to repeat searches.

Searching Forward For Text Or Patterns

There are two different types of searches available in **vi**. One is a simple, quick method of searching forward for patterns or text. You must be in command mode to use this feature. To initiate the search, type a forward slash (/) to search to the right through the text or a question mark (?) to search to the left. Then, type the pattern or text to search for and press Enter.

The second class of search capabilities rests with a group of single-letter search terms. Each of these terms specifies a direction and where the cursor should end up, and is followed by one, and only one, character to look for. To search forward through the file and stop the cursor on the character, use the **f** command, which is essentially the same as using the slash and only typing one character to look for. An example of using this term is **fa** to search for the next instance of "a" to the right of the current cursor position and then stop on the "a". To do the same but to the left, lead with **F** instead.

You may not always want to land immediately on top of the single character search term. To search to the right and move the cursor on top of the character to the left of the search term, begin with **t**. You can also do this to the left, stopping on the character to the right of the search term. Use **T** to accomplish this task.

Once the search is complete, you can repeat it in either direction. To search again for the same character to the right, press the semicolon (;) key. To run the search again to the left, press the comma (,).

Remember that Unix flavors are case sensitive. When searching for characters, be sure to use the proper case that you are looking for.

Repeating Searches

Once a search is complete, there are several quick ways to repeat it. Typing a forward slash (/) and pressing **Enter**—or just typing the letter **n**—repeats a forward search. To repeat the search backward, use **N**.

Searching And Replacing

There are times when the entire reason for searching for text within a file is that you want to replace it with other text. Sometimes these replacements happen in just one or two locations within a file, and at other times you need to do this throughout the whole document. The vi editor includes search and replace functions for your convenience.

A search and replace statement is a colon command, so you invoke it by using **:**. You then have to decide where this operation needs to take place. If you want to search and replace through the entire file, then the statement begins ":%". To run the operation from the current cursor position to the end of the file, start with ":$". You can also tell it which lines to work on. Either use a range, such as ":1–10", a sequence such as ":1,5,10", or a relative value from the cursor position, such as ":+10". If you just use the colon, then the search and replace is only done on the current line.

Now that you have established that you are running a colon command, and designated which portions of the text file the command should affect, you need to tell vi which command to use. The official command for this function is **s**. After this you need to build the rest of the command in the following format:

`/pattern/replace`

We've already discussed the *pattern* part. It needs to match the text that has to be replaced as closely as possible so you do not run into problems where the wrong text is replaced. The *replace* component is what you want the *pattern* portion to be replaced with.

Now for an example to try to pull this all together. Say that you are working on a shell script and realize that you named a variable too generically. You want to change every instance of this item to something more specific so it does not cause confusion with similar variables you now realize you need. The original item is "discount", and you want to change it to "clothing_discount". From command mode you would type:

`:%s/discount/clothing_discount`

If you are unsure of whether there might be conflicts between the search pattern and items that you do not want changed, add "/c" at the end of the term. This addition will cause vi to confirm each replacement before it is made.

UNDOING CHANGES

There is little worse than making a change in your file and, as it goes into effect, realizing that you have just made a major mistake. Fortunately, the vi text editor has functions that allow you to take back the change you just enacted.

Closing Files

As with any editor, you need to understand the various methods of closing files. Some of these methods include saving changes before closing. Others involve closing without saving any changes, which is useful if you have made a mistake that is difficult to fix. Be sure to learn how to use these commands. They are necessary when editing any text file for administrative or other tasks.

Saving Without Closing

First, it is useful to know how to save your changes without closing the file. Doing this allows you to keep a recent copy of the material on the file system, in case there is a crash or some other problem that might cause you to lose your otherwise unsaved work. To save without closing, use the command **:w**.

Saving And Closing

If you are finished editing your file for now and want to save the changes and exit, there are two quick ways to accomplish this task. One of these involves colon mode, using the command **:wq** to save and exit. The other is to use the command **ZZ**.

Closing Without Saving

If for some reason you realize that you need to return to a file's original state, you can close it without saving the changes you have made and then reopen it. To close a file without saving any changes, use the command **:q!**. The exclamation point overrides the save before closing requirement.

 There is much, much more to the vi editor! If you adopt this program as your text editor of choice, then it is worth going thoroughly through the man pages and learning some of the more advanced and involved commands.

CUSTOMIZING THE SHELL ENVIRONMENT

One goal in most work environments is to customize the environment in a way that makes it the most intuitive for the person using it. The same desire applies to system administrators and users with their account shells. Most of the control over the shell environment occurs through *environment variables*.

Introduction To Environment Variables

There are two different sets of variables used in shell programming and day-to-day work within the shell. One of these sets is the *shell variable*. This is a configurable item that is available for use only within that specific instance of the shell. Opening a subshell—a shell inside a shell—or quitting the program that used the variable loses its value.

An environment variable, however, stores values that are accessible to all scripts, programs, and commands run within the shell. Environment variable names are typically typed in all capital letters, mostly to make them distinct from shell variables. How these variables are set and utilized depends in part on the shell being used. Because bash is the default shell, the bash format is discussed here.

Table 5.1   Commonly used environment variables.

Variable	Contents
HOME	The path to the current user's home directory
LOGNAME	The current user's login ID
PATH	The current user's executables search path
PS1	The user prompt
PWD	The current working directory
SHELL	The shell in which the user is currently working

Commonly Used Environment Variables

A number of environment variables are of regular interest and use. A listing is shown in Table 5.1.

Using An Environment Variable

An environment variable is a special kind of variable that, unlike normal shell variables, is global and must be handled differently. Using a variable is a simplified way of referring to the complexities of working with environment variables, and setting and displaying their contents. The methods discussed here for handling environment variables apply to handling variables in general within the shells.

Viewing Contents

To view the contents of an environment variable in almost any shell, use the **echo** command in this format:

```
echo $VARIABLE
```

The dollar sign signals to the shell that the value of **VARIABLE** is the object of the command. For example, **echo $SHELL** displays the shell currently in use.

Setting A Value

To set the value of an environment variable in the bash shell (or korn), use this format:

```
VARIABLE=value
```

Put the value in quotes if it's a string.

For example, this command sets the primary prompt in bash to display the full
working directory:

```
PS1="\w >"
```

In the csh and tcsh shells, environment variables are assigned values with the
following format:

```
setenv VARIABLE value
```

For example:

```
setenv COLOR blue
```

Creating An Environment Variable

It's possible to create new environment variables. First, give the variable a value.
Then—in the bash and korn shells—*export* that variable to the shell environment.
This action ensures that the variable exists outside of this particular shell process.
For example:

```
COLOR="blue"
export COLOR
```

In the csh and tcsh shells, this job is done in one step with the **setenv** command
listed previously.

Storing Shell Settings

User shell settings are stored in a variety of files, because some shells invoke their
own specialty files. The standard shell environment customization data is stored
in two places. The first location is the master file for all logins, configured by
root. The second is the local file over which each individual user has control.

Master Profile

The master shell environment settings are stored as a *profile* in the /etc/profile file.
This file is consulted first by every user's shell during the login process. Within
/etc/profile, you store environment variables that should be set for every user.
For example, it might hold a custom prompt if you don't like the standard prompt
offered by default. If the users are knowledgeable enough to prefer multiple
shells, then a series of **if-then** statements can set different default prompts for
each shell.

The beginning of a sample /etc/profile might look like the following:

```
# /etc/profile
# System wide environment and startup programs
# Functions and aliases go in /etc/bashrc
```

First, the master profile ensures that the directories necessary to run the X client are available to all users with the following statement, which takes the initial PATH value and adds the new item to the end:

```
PATH="$PATH:/usr/X11R6/bin"
```

The next item in the example file sets the default command prompt for login sessions. Because the bash shell is the Linux default, it is generally a good idea to leave this item in bash format. The following sets the prompt to be a string in the format [*user@host currentdirectory*]:

```
PS1="[\u@\h \w]\\ "
```

Notice the extra space before the closing double quote. This space ensures that the cursor at the prompt will not be right up against the end bracket.

Some administrators like to put a limit around the processes a shell session can initiate. Doing this allows them to prevent users from overrunning things, which could wreak havoc on your server. The **ulimit** option allows you to add that type of functionality. In this case, the -c flag is in use, which limits the size of any core dump files that a shell process can create. It is a quick way of ensuring that an unnoticed set of core dumps does not overrun the filesystem.

```
ulimit -c 1000000
```

For more on **ulimit**, type "help ulimit".

Now it is time to set commonly used environment variables. Although the following are all in capital letters to signal to the reader that they are environment variables, just setting them in and of themselves is not enough to make them global.

```
USER='id -un'
LOGNAME=$USER
MAIL="/var/spool/mail/$USER"
```

```
HOSTNAME='/bin/hostname'
HISTSIZE=500
HISTFILESIZE=500
INPUTRC=/etc/inputrc
```

Most of these settings are straightforward. Wherever $USER is included, it breaks down to the specific username of the person logged in—for example, LOGNAME=bob, MAIL=/var/spool/mail/bob. Notice the variety of ways the variables are set. Anything that is just as it appears text-wise is in no form of quotes. Items that include variables that need to be resolved are in double quotes. Finally, items that are actually commands that need to be run are in back quotes.

 The **id** command shown in the USER setting returns information about the login session. When user bob logs in and /etc/profile runs, the command **id -un** runs and prints the user name. If the flag was just -u, then it would print the UID. The **inputrc** file, on the other hand, contains keyboard customization options such as backspace and delete keys.

Now you have to make sure that these variables are environment variables, and therefore global instead of being lost the moment you leave /etc/profile, by implementing the following:

```
export PATH PS1 USER LOGNAME MAIL HOSTNAME HISTSIZE HISTFILESIZE INPUTRC
```

Login Profiles

The individual users' home directories also contain profile statements. There is a collection of files that makes up the complete user profile. All user profiles are consulted after /etc/profile in the login process, allowing users to set their own values for any of the environment variables that may already be set within the master profile. These files are discussed in the order that they are consulted.

First, the /etc/passwd file is consulted to see which shell is assigned to the user. Because bash is the Linux default shell and the primary shell covered in this text, let's assume that bash is the shell assigned to the user in question. When an account is set to the bash shell, the first file Linux looks for is ~/.bash_profile, ~/.bash_login if ~/.bash_profile does not exist, or ~/.profile if neither exists. All three of these files are essentially the same.

Often, the user profile begins with the following statement, which looks to see if the file .bashrc exists in the user's home directory, and if so executes its contents:

```
if test -f ~/.bashrc; then
  . ~/.bashrc
fi
```

Test statements are explained in the section "Testing Values In Scripts."

Continuing with ~/.bash_profile, there may be nothing else present here. It is up to you whether the file stays small or is expanded. Typically, you would add new environment variables—including prompt settings—in this file and then export them in the same manner as done in /etc/profile. One item you may want to call from ~/.bash_profile is ~/.inputrc if you want to customize any key bindings for that particular login session, or for all users in the skeleton ~/.inputrc file.

The ~/.bash_profile file is only executed during login.

Now on to the ~/.bashrc file, which is run each time you open a new instance of the shell. This file may, by default, only call the /etc/bashrc file. Typically, this is where users might set aliases for long commands that they are tired of typing out. A umask value may also be placed in here.

Once ~/.bash_profile finishes executing ~/.bashrc and anything else within the ~/.bash_profile file, then you are completely logged in to the account and looking at a shell prompt.

Logout Profile

You can also have a profile that manages what happens when you log out of the system. This profile for the bash shell is ~/.bash_logout. There is often only one line in this file by default:

```
clear
```

This line ensures that the screen is cleared after the user logs out, leaving the next person to use the machine with only a login prompt and no ability to see what happened last. Setting this item in the logout script also helps people to tell at a glance when a terminal is in use or not.

Remember that you can change all of these default files for all new users—accounts that have not been created yet—in /etc/skel.

INSTALLING AND CHOOSING AN ALTERNATE SHELL

Those who don't want to use the bash shell have the option of changing to a different shell. Some of these shells are installed by default and others aren't, depending on the distribution.

Determine If A Shell Is Present

To see whether a shell is installed on a machine, type the command "chsh –l". This command and flag list the available shells, including their location within the filesystem.

Install Shell

If you desire to use a shell that isn't installed, look first among the files downloaded with the distribution. The shell may be with them, just not part of the packages you installed. If this is the case, install the RPM or .gz.tar file (see Chapter 2 for more on these file formats). Try to make sure the new shells are located in the same place as the old ones.

Change The Default Shell For An Account

To change the shell an account automatically logs in to, use the **chsh** command. First, ensure the shell is there, and install it if necessary. Then, if you're logged in to the user account, use the following command:

```
chsh -s /shellpath
```

For example, if the listing showed the shell was located in /bin/pdksh, then type:

```
chsh -s /bin/pdksh
```

When you're changing the default shell for another account while logged in to root, use the following format:

```
chsh -s /bin/shellpath username
```

For example, changing the shell for user tom to /bin/csh would require this command:

```
chsh -s /bin/csh tom
```

 The default shell for any user can also be changed manually by root by editing the user's entry in /etc/passwd.

Change Shells Temporarily

To change shells only temporarily while logged in to an account, type the full path to the shell (for example, "/bin/csh"). Typically, the only visible change will be that the user prompt is now different. To return to the original shell, type "exit".

SCRIPTING PRINCIPLES AND PRACTICES

Shell scripts are useful tools for a system administrator. They allow administrators to automate processes that otherwise become tedious by hand. Some practices make the process of script writing simpler, and result in scripts that are easier to come back to and edit later.

Be Aware Of Shell Peculiarities

The first thing defined in every script is the shell interpreter in which it should run. It's important that the programmer be aware of the principles of working within that particular scripting language, or at least allocate extra time to test, research, and find the differences in commands and syntax through the errors that result.

One thing that quickly becomes apparent when you're changing shells is that each shell's format for defining a prompt is different.

/bin/bash

Because bash is the default shell, it's a good idea to write scripts for its interpreter first. You'll already be used to working with bash on the command-line level, so writing scripts for the shell requires no transition.

/bin/ksh

The korn shell is a favorite among many shell programmers, because it offers a wide range of features that assist in their work. The function-building and -loading tools are richer than those offered in bash, as are the shell variable tools. A wider range of wildcards for pattern matching are available in ksh. Finally, additional debugging tools are almost always appreciated by programmers.

/bin/tcsh

In the case of the Enhanced C Shell, many of the differences between tcsh and the other shells (except the C shell itself, or csh) involve command syntax, which more closely resembles C programming.

Comments

Comments are a programmer's best weapon against having to reinvent the wheel. Although generally there shouldn't be more lines of comments than code, thoroughly commenting which script segments do what is a good way of ensuring that things learned aren't forgotten. Comments are especially important in situations in which extensive reading or research was required for writing the code.

It's also useful to comment changes as they're made. In these comments, give the reasons for the change and, if it's significant, the date the change was made. This practice can make it simple to return to the previous version of the code—or even to the code as written several versions ago, if you apply comments carefully.

5

Script Storage Practices

It's often a good idea to keep all shell scripts together in a central location (unless they were written for use by all users, in which case they would be better housed somewhere like /bin). When it comes to personal scripts, whether written for system administrators or users, a good storage location is ~/bin. This way, all personal scripts can be well protected with proper use of ownerships and permissions, and there's no need to hunt through the system for them later.

When you add variables to a script, give them meaningful names. This practice prevents guesswork later when you're trying to trace through a script to debug it, edit it, or enhance it. In addition, indent code for loops and other such bundled statements so they're easy to spot as you visually scan the file.

Test The Script

Be sure to test a script before applying it to anything mission-critical. Have it work on dummy items or copies that can be ruined without affecting anything. Depending on how far-reaching the script's commands are, try to avoid running it as root the first time, or make a backup before running it. One typo in an rm statement in root can be devastating to an entire filesystem.

Save the finished script. Move it if necessary to its permanent home. Be sure to set its permissions as executable if it's meant to be run by typing the script's name.

CREATING SIMPLE SHELL SCRIPTS

The basic components used in shell scripting are discussed here; then, in a section later in this chapter "Analysis Of Sample Scripts For Common Tasks," the code is put together into scripts with specific purposes and explained in a walkthrough. An advantage to understanding how to create shell scripts is that this knowledge makes it easier to sidestep toward customizing the scripts already installed on the machine.

Starting A Shell Script

Shell scripts are stored in a text file. The first step in creating one is to determine where to store the file, and then open it in a text editor. The first line in any shell script defines which shell interpreter is used to run the code. This interpreter can be any shell, regardless of what shell the editor is running in. You declare which shell's rules you are using with a line beginning with "#!". These two characters should only appear once in any shell script, on the very first line. They tell the kernel that you are about to declare which program or interpreter to use to run the script. For example, because you are learning the bash (or sh) shell, you might have your script begin with:

```
#!/bin/bash
```

Notice that there is no space between the "#!" and the interpreter declaration.

Basic Script Writing

Let us begin with the basics of writing a shell script. These basics include running commands within the script, accepting input from the command line, and using variables within the bash shell scripting language. Once you understand these initial issues, it is much easier to move on to more complex items, such as loops and testing variable values.

Running a command-line item is as simple as including it within the script code. For example, although you might prefer to do something this short as an alias (more about aliases in Chapter 6) rather than a script of its own, you could write the following:

```
#!/bin/sh
# This script makes sure that my file listings show all long
# form data and files, and do not scroll past when I am trying
# to read them.
ls -la | more
```

Often, /bin/bash and /bin/sh are identical in Linux and are merely links to one another. However, you should be aware that these are not always identical shells. The original shell taken from Unix is sh, whereas bash is the open source version.

All this brief script does is run the **ls** command with the flags "l" and "a", and then pipe it through the **more** command (more on pipes in Chapter 7). If you save it as ~/bin/lsmore and then set it to be executable—for example, by typing **chmod u+x**—then you can just use the command **lsmore** to run the script. The highlighted lines are just comments. Shell script comments begin with a hash mark, after which everything on the line is ignored unless the next item is the exclamation point. In this case, the comments are longer than the actual code!

You can also accept command–line input. Items typed after a shell script name at the command line are read in as shell variables, and assigned an integer of one or greater, each integer being the next in the count. You can then utilize those items by using them as shell script variables. To use a variable, use it in the format "$variable". So, for example, the sample shell script from earlier is now:

```
#!/bin/sh
ls -la $1 | more
```

If you used the command **lsmore /etc/skel**, then you would get a long form file listing of all files, including hidden files, in the directory. The resulting listing would pause if it were longer than a page. It would then wait for you to press the spacebar before advancing through the next page of files.

Scripts can also print information to the screen on their own, they do not need a separate program to print things for them. Take the following script:

```
#!/bin/bash
echo 'The name you entered is $2, $1'
echo "The name you entered is $2, $1"
```

If the script was named names, then you might do the following:

```
> names Joe Smith
> The name you entered is Smith, Joe
> The name you entered is $2, $1
```

Notice the output. In the line where you used single quotes, the values for the variables are shown in the output. However, where you used double quotes, the entire line is treated as straight text with no values. This tactic is one method of making sure that your dollar signs show up properly when you need to use them.

Otherwise, you may end up with items being treated as variables when you did not need them to be. However, this makes getting the following input and output to work properly a bit tricky:

```
> price 12.95
> The price is $12.95
```

You would need the following code to accomplish this:

```
$/bin/bash
echo 'The price is \$$1'
```

The dollar sign is a metacharacter in the bash shell scripting language. You have to escape it if you want it to be taken literally inside of single quotes. The escape character for bash is the backslash, and so in the code above, the first dollar sign is actually printed and the second is assumed to be part of "$1" because it is not escaped.

Not all variables are taken in at the command line. Sometimes it is wise to assign a value to a variable within a script or program instead of hard-coding it in. This practice allows you to quickly change a value used often just once in the program itself, rather than having to change it everywhere it shows up. For example, perhaps you were writing a script that repeatedly had to calculate sales tax for your location. Sales tax does change on occasion, so you decide that this value needs to be assigned to a variable. A short version of the script might look like the following:

```
$/bin/sh
tax=.06
echo 'The tax on this item is ' $tax*$1
```

Notice that the calculation is done outside the quotes. It sometimes makes things simpler to read to put variables outside, especially when something is being done with them. Variables, however, are not always numbers. Sometimes they are strings of characters such as words or sentences. If you are only assigning one word with no spaces to the variable, then you can just do it in the following format:

```
FirstName=Alfred
```

However, if there are spaces in the string, you need to put it in quotes. This rule is appropriate for both strings assigned within the script itself, such as:

```
color="pea green"
```

or strings entered at the command line when invoking the script, such as:

```
> colorsort "pea green" red white "sky blue"
```

You also do not have to assign values to variables directly. A variable can be set to be the output of a command, which allows you to avoid even further having to hard code issues such as dates. To assign such a value within the script code, you need to put the command inside back quotes (' '). Consider this short sample:

```
#!/bin/bash
today='date'
echo 'Today is $today'
```

Even more useful is the concept of command substitution. Command substitution allows you to set the results of one command to be the input for another. To utilize this tool, include the command whose results you want to use as input in back quotes. For example, perhaps you want to copy all files that contain the string "test" in their name to the already-mounted floppy at fd0. You could place the following in the script—or on the command line—to accomplish this task the quickest way:

```
cp 'locate *test*' /dev/fd0
```

Testing Values In Scripts

The bash shell provides a broad range of testing capabilities. These tests range from testing file existence or types, to character and numeric comparison. How you utilize these features is up to you, but it is important to know they are there and what they can do. This is especially true when it comes to adding loops and conditional statements. These are covered in the sections "Adding Loops To A Script" and "Adding Conditional Statements To Scripts" later in this chapter.

The **case** command compares string values to patterns, and then allows you to determine what will happen based on the results. You use this command in the format:

```
case string in
     pattern)
     commands
     ;;
esac
```

In general, the *string* portion of the format is a variable of some sort. The pattern is the wildcard pattern that corresponds to what end value you are looking for. You can have more than one pattern statement, one per line. For an example, perhaps you are writing a script that needs to know whether the person running it has the directory /usr/src/linux in his or her path statement. If he or she does not have it, then it needs to be added. The **case** code segment would be:

```
case $PATH in
    */usr/src/linux*)
        haspath=1
    ;;
esac
```

This statement needs a conditional to complete it. Conditionals are covered in the next section. The **case** statement is especially useful if you want to create a rudimentary menu. Say that you want to create a small menu to offer three file manipulation choices to a user. One way you might write this code is:

```
case $action in
        O|o) echo "You chose option one.";;
        T|t) echo "You chose option two.";;
        R|r) echo "You chose option three.";;
```

Another way of testing items is to use the **test** command. This is a highly versatile command with a large number of flags that allow you to test anything from files to strings to numbers. Due to this level of complexity, each type of testing is covered separately to avoid confusion.

One way to add robustness to a program or script is error correction and detection. A quickly written script might have no double-checking features and so blindly try to write to files when it does not have permission to do so, or write over items that may already exist. When performing **test** operations on a single file, the command is used in the format **test** *-flag file*. The available flags for this type of operation are listed in Table 5.2.

When one of these tests is run, or any of the following ones, a True value returns 0 and a False returns 1. There are also file operators for **test** that allow you to compare files to one another. These options are used in the format "**test** *filea -flag fileb*", and are listed in Table 5.3.

As stated before, **test** does not only run on files. There are a number of flags available to use on strings or to compare them. For individual strings, there are two quick tests available. The first allows you to check to see if a string is empty and is used in the format "**test** **-z** *string*". The second tests to see if the string is not empty, and is used as "**test** **-n** *string*". For string comparison, you also have two tests. The first allows you to test to see if two strings are identical, and is used in the format "**test** *stringa = stringb*". If you want to test to see if the strings are not identical, then use "**test** *stringa != stringb*".

Table 5.2 Flags used with the **test** command on a single file.

Flag	Purpose
b	Tests as true if the item both exists, and is a block special file. Special files are access points between the file system and a device driver. A block special file points to the device driver for a device that requires data in blocks, such as disk drives.
c	True if item exists and is a character special file. A character special file points to the device driver for a device that requires data in characters, such as terminals and tape drives.
d	True if the item exists and is a directory.
e	True if the item exists.
f	True if the item exists and is a file (and not a special file).
g	True if the item exists and is SGID.
G	True if the item exists and is owned by the GID running the process.
k	True if the item exists and has the sticky bit set.
L	True if the item exists and is a symbolic link.
O	True if the item exists and is owned by the UID running the process.
p	True if the item exists and is a named pipe or FIFO (First In First Out). These terms refer to permanent pipes that are named within the file system and are used to pass information between processes.
r	True if the item exists and is readable.
s	True if the item exists and has a size greater than zero.
S	True if the item exists and is a socket, which is a file type used to transfer data between two locations via a network.
u	True if the item exists and is SUID.
w	True if the item exists and is writeable.
x	True if the item exists and is executable.

Table 5.3 Flags used with the **test** command to compare files.

Flag	Purpose
nt	True if the first file is newer than the second.
ot	True if the first file is older than the second.
ef	True if both files have the same device and inode numbers, which means they are hard links or the same file.

Finally, there are the **test** functions that let you compare numbers. These functions are used in the format "**test** *inta -flag intb*". Table 5.4 contains a listing of the flags that are available.

Table 5.4   Flags used with the **test** command to compare integers.

Flag	Purpose
eq	True if both integers are the same.
ge	True if the first integer is greater than or equal to the second.
gt	True if the first integer is greater than the second.
le	True if the first integer is less than or equal to the second.
lt	True if the first integer is less than the second.
ne	True if the integers are not the same.

You can also combine tests by using the last set of flags. The first is used in the format "**test** *test1* -a *test2*", and is True if both tests produce the same result. The second is True if the tests produce opposite results and is used in the format "**test** *test1* -o *test2*". To take this one step further, you can reverse the results of a test by putting an exclamation point in front of the command. For example, "**test !** *test1* -a *test2*" would be True if test1 and test2 were not the same, or the same as using -o.

Examples of running tests are shown in the next section, where they make more sense in the context of conditional statements.

The final basic item you should be able to do is prompt for and accept data from the command line. One command that allows you to accomplish this is the **read** command. You use this command in the following format:

```
read item
```

You can include more than one variable if you want to read more than one item at a time.

Adding Conditional Statements To Scripts

Conditional statements are those that execute specific things depending on what conditions are met. There are two major conditionals available when working on shell scripts. The first is case, which is covered in the testing section because it in itself tests items. The second is the **if** statement.

The most basic **if** statement is usually referred to as **if-then**, and is in the format:

```
if conditions
    then command
fi
```

Essentially, this statement looks at the conditions, and if these conditions are True (zero), then executes the commands after **then**. The **test** command is commonly used in conjunction with **if**. For example, perhaps you are working on a script that requires that a specific file ("scriptdata") exist in the user's home directory so it can write to it. The following line of code would check to see if this file existed, and if not it would create it for you:

```
if test ! -e $USER/scriptdata
    then touch $USER/scriptdata
fi
```

The next level of complication is the **if-then-else** statement, which works in the following format:

```
if conditions
    then command
    else command
fi
```

This statement looks at the conditions, and if they are True, executes the commands after the **then** statement. However, if the conditions are False, it executes the commands after the **else** statement. For example, say that you are trying to calculate royalties on a product, and those royalties are computed on a sliding scale. The first ten thousand copies sold have a royalty of seven percent, and anything above has a royalty of nine percent. Your statement might look like the following:

```
if test $sales -le 10000
    then royalty = $sales * .07
    else royalty = $sales * .09
fi
```

Typing the first line as "if [$sales -le 10000]" accomplishes the same thing. The square brackets are shorthand for the test command.

The most complex form of the **if** statement available in bash is the **if-then-else-elif** statement. You utilize this conditional in the format:

```
if conditions
    then command
    elif conditions
        then command
    fi
    else command
fi
```

This statement looks at the conditions, and if they are True, executes the commands after the **then**. If the conditions are False, it first moves to the **elif** (else if) and checks the conditions there. If those conditions are met, then the script executes the **then** under the **elif**. However, if they are False, the script finally moves to the **else**, and executes that command. For example, consider a situation where you are trying to set purchase discounts for items, and these discounts are calculated on sales volume. If the buyer purchases 1 through 10 items, then he or she gets no discount. However, if he or she purchase 11 through 20 items, he or she get a 5 percent discount. Buying 21 and higher gets a 10 percent discount. The statement would look like the following:

```
if test $volume -le 10
   then discount = 0
   elif test $volume -le 20
        then discount = .05
   fi
   else discount = .1
fi
```

 You can have more than one command after a **then**.

Adding Loops To A Script

There is often a need to add a loop to a script. Perhaps you need to iterate through a sequence of values. Maybe you need to have the script do something until a specific value exceeds a certain amount. The bash shell offers a good variety of loop types that you can use to accomplish your tasks.

A commonly used loop type is the **for** loop, which is an iterative statement that moves through a series of items. A **for** loop is used in two different formats. The first is:

```
for item in list do
    commands
done
```

This statement moves one by one through the list, executing the commands listed until it reaches the end of the list. For example, perhaps you need your script to create a sequence of empty files the first time it runs. The statement you might write to create the files is:

```
for item in file1 file2 file3 file4 do
    touch $item
done
```

The second is:

```
for entry do
     commands
done
```

This statement moves one by one through the arguments given at the command line, executing the commands listed until it reaches the end of the arguments. For a slightly different example from the first, perhaps you have a script where you enter a list of numbers that correspond to file names that have to be created. Your statement might look like the following:

```
for num do
     touch file"$num"
done
```

There are also loop types that operate until certain conditions are met instead of iteratively. The first of these is the **while** loop, which is used in the following format:

```
while condition do
          commands
done
```

Usually some form of test is performed as the condition. This particular loop operates while the condition remains True and then exits. For example, say that you are working on a script that at one point needs to do something only if a certain value remains below the number 20. The statement might look like the following:

```
while [$value -lt 20] do
          newvalue = $value * 9
done
```

The other type of loop that works on conditions instead of iterations is the **until** loop. It is used in the following format:

```
until condition do
          commands
done
```

As opposed to the **while** loop, this one continues until the conditions test as True. To accomplish the same goal as the previous example, the **until** loop would have to be:

```
until [$value -ge 20] do
        newvalue = $value * 9
done
```

Getting And Using A Command's Exit Status

One thing that is useful in a shell script is if a command succeeds or fails, and how it failed if it failed. You can utilize the exit status—also called a return value—of a command with the bash shell variable $?. If the command succeeds, typically **$?** is set equal to zero. If it fails, it is set to a non-zero integer. To merely print the exit status to the screen you would use a line such as:

```
echo $?
```

Conditional statements such as **if** combinations are often used with the exit status. Using these items in conjunction allows you to add error handling to a script. To make the most out of this, you also need to learn how to swap STDERR and STDOUT. This process is done in the format "*number1>&number2*". These numbers are all based on one of three items, as shown in Table 5.5.

Therefore, you can type "1>&2" to have both STDOUT and STDERR stand for the same thing. The purpose of this is to send the error code to the screen instead of losing it somewhere in the background. You might utilize this in the format:

```
echo "Sorry, there was an error: " 1>&2
```

Finishing A Script

Once you finish writing your script, you need to save all of the changes and close the file. As recommended earlier, save the text file in a place that is either already in your path or that you are willing to add to your path. To then make the script executable just by typing its name, change its permissions so that it is executable by the appropriate users.

You may decide that you want to set your script to run as a certain user account by using the SUID bit. However, the system will not allow a script to run as root. There are inherent reasons for this. Some of them are for security, because

Table 5.5   Numbers representing STD items for swapping purposes.

Number	Represents
0	STDIN
1	STDOUT
2	STDERR

any intruder who gained root access could attempt to build shell scripts to run as root and the system administrator may not even notice. Also, you can do much damage by running a script as root that was not thoroughly tested.

ANALYSIS OF SAMPLE SCRIPTS FOR COMMON TASKS

Now, let's take a look at some sample scripts and how they're constructed. These scripts are all written for the bash interpreter.

Adding Users

This script automates adding users to make the process a single-line command with options to fill in, rather than two separate commands. It's incredibly short, written to demonstrate how useful even brief shell scripts can be.

Shell Scripting Language Definition

As stated before, the first line in a shell script defines which interpreter is used. The first line for this script—not counting initial comments—is as follows:

```
#!/bin/bash
```

Request Information From User

The data required to create a user account is the user information and a password. The highlighted statement actually reads in the information:

```
# Getting user ID.
echo "Enter user ID: "
read user
```

Apply The Data

Now that the data is entered, it can be plugged into the commands. It's good practice to provide a way for the user to see that things are working properly, so the script will echo the commands it's entering as it goes. The highlighted statements plug the data into what normally would be typed at the command line:

```
# Echoing back what will happen next.
echo "Creating an account for $user, "
echo "enter password when prompted."
# Creating the user account.
adduser $user
passwd $user
```

Some distributions, such as Slackware, already have a more complex user addition program in place.

Test And Save The File

Testing the script shows that it runs properly. After doing so, log in to the new user account and see if it works. Now, to save the script for future use, give it a meaningful name and location. In the case of this example, good choices would be to save the file as "newuser" in the new directory /root/bin. Finally, change the permissions so the script is an executable.

Backing Up Files

Another common task for system administrators is the regular system backup. This script's purpose is to back up root's home directory to floppy disk.

Shell Scripting Language Definition

Once again, the script's first line is the following:

```
#!/bin/bash
```

Format The Necessary Disks

The first task when making a backup to floppy is ensuring that the floppy disks have been prepared with the ext2 file format. In this case, a loop is used so the administrator can format as many disks as necessary for the task. The code used to make the filesystem is highlighted:

```
# Set the variable to test as true so the if
# statement will begin.
more = "y"
# Begin if statement to continue until there are
# no more disks to format.
while test "$more" = "y"
    do echo "Press Enter to format a disk:"
      # Read an empty variable so the script will
      # pause for the Enter.
      read $foo
      mke2fs /dev/fd0
      # Check to see if any more disks need to be formatted.
      echo "Do you want to format another disk (y/n)?"
      read more
done
```

Back Up The Directory

Now to the meat of the script, which makes the backup. Once again, progress will be indicated by the script so the user can follow what is going on and be sure the script hasn't hung. The code that actually makes the backup is highlighted:

```
echo "Making backup of /root/bin ..."
# Making backup.
tar -cvfM /dev/fd0 /bin/root
```

See Chapter 2 for more on the **tar** command and options.

5

Making Thumbnails Automatically

One popular use for shell scripts is to handle batch operations. This term refers to when you need to do the same thing to a large number of items in bulk. It makes no sense to type the commands one at a time when you can write a quick script that handles it all for you. In this case, you have a special location for your users to upload images, and the shell script's job is to automatically make thumbnail versions of the images, and then move the images themselves into the appropriate locations.

Shell Scripting Language Definition

The script's first line should be the following because we are sticking with the default Linux shell:

```
#!/bin/bash
```

Determine If Any Files Are In The Incoming Directory

You would likely run this script as a cron job, because it would allow you to keep a hands-off approach. Therefore, the first thing this script needs to do is look and see if any files have been added to the incoming images directory, which you have named /Web/incoming.

A quick way to accomplish this task is to place the entire script within a **for** loop. This loop would do one iteration for each file present within the directory. If there were nothing there, then the script would have nothing to work on and would just exit. The outer loop would be:

```
for file in /Web/incoming do
     # The rest of the script goes here!
done
```

Make The Thumbnails

The first thing this script needs to do if there are any files present is to make a thumbnail of that file. A shell script cannot by itself make a thumbnail, but it can call a program that knows how. Assume here that you already have a program downloaded that can do the job called **mkthumb**, and placed it in /usr/sbin. The program's instructions tell you that the proper syntax to use this program is "**mkthumb** *original thumbnail*".

Within the **for** loop, you would add the following code to run the thumbnail creation program:

```
/usr/sbin/mkthumb $file /Web/thumbnails
```

Move The Files

Now that the thumbnail has been created, you need to move the file out of the incoming directory and into the user's designated directory. All users have directories where their images are stored in /Web/users/*user*. First, however, you have to get the name of the user who created the file. To do this, use a segment of code such as:

```
user = 'ls -la $file | cut -d" " -f5'
```

This code does a long file listing of just the file in question. It then feeds that listing to the **cut** command, telling it that the delimiter between fields is a space and that it should cut the fifth field out from the listing. Because the entire command is surrounded by back quotes, this works as a command substitution, so the user variable is set equal to the user who owns the file. Now you can actually move the file. The code to make this move would be:

```
mv $file /Web/users/$user
```

Notice how such a short script takes care of what could be a tedious daily process!

CGI Scripting In The Linux Environment

As Web pages got more complicated, there came a need to make them able to interface with programs which could process information and then feed it back out. CGI (Common Gateway Interface) was created for this purpose. You do not have to use a specific language to write CGI programs or scripts. Languages commonly used to write them are shell scripts in various shells, C, C++, Java, and Perl.

CGI Practices

CGI programs and scripts are typically segmented into a special CGI directory known to the Web server, which is generally called cgi-bin. This directory is the only location from which the server will allow a CGI to be run. After all, programs that run automatically when people access Web pages on your server can be a huge security risk. Although a user making his or her own CGI utility may not have any malicious intent, he or she can still wreak havoc if he or she made a mistake somewhere in his or her code.

Some administrators allow each user to have his or her own cgi-bin directory. The more control you give the users of such things the greater the security risk to the system. Be careful if you decide to offer that service.

Starting A CGI Perl Script

Although the primary programming coverage in this book is on shell scripting, and the Linux certification exams you are preparing for also cover shell scripting, there is also a need to be able to work with CGI scripts and programs. Typically, CGI under Linux is written in Perl. Therefore, this section includes some light coverage of how to use Perl to do forms through CGI.

Perl scripting is actually not much different from shell scripting in many ways. Because a Perl script is also a text file, just like a shell script, you need to let the shell know what it is dealing with. This means the first line of the script will be similar to the following:

```
#!/usr/bin/perl
```

Because Perl is a hybrid between a scripting language and an actual programming language, it is actually capable of loading its own Perl libraries. In this case, you need two specific library modules so that you can process CGI form data and make a timestamp when you save the form data. But first, you have to tell Perl where to look to find these modules. The directories that contain your Perl modules are stored in the @INC Perl array. You place values into arrays in Perl with the **push** command. This command is used in the format:

```
push(@where,what);
```

So, hypothetically speaking, you want to add the directories /usr/local/lib/perl and /usr/local/libdata/perl as the two places Perl should look when you try to load library modules. You would place the directories into the @INC array with the following code:

```
push(@INC,"/usr/local/lib/perl")
push(@INC,"/usr/local/libdata/perl");
```

You then need to explicitly include two different modules. The first of these modules is built to handle forms from the Web. The second you need so you can place a timestamp in the form data file. Now you can actually load the modules, because Perl knows where to look. There are several commands you can use to accomplish this. This example chooses the **use** command, which loads the library module while compiling the Perl script. The **use** command is added in the following format:

```
use "module.pl";
```

This Perl script requires the module **cgi-lib** to process form data, and **ctime** to process the system time for your time stamp. Load these modules with the code:

```
use "cgi-lib.pl";
use "ctime.pl";
```

Building A CGI Script

When you call a CGI from a Web page—instructions are discussed in the next section—the script executes. While performing necessary tasks behind the scenes, any information it needs to send back is done with whatever command in that language sends information to STDOUT—the equivalent of **echo** in bash shell scripting. This process is why CGI is so portable.

Often a CGI is used to process form data, so it is discussed here in that context. First, you need a form to be able to work with. HTML authoring and form creation is outside the scope of this book. If you want to learn more about this subject, consider getting The Coriolis Group's *HTML Publishing on the Internet, Second Edition*, by Brent Heslop and David Holzgang. For the sake of an example, consider the following code:

```
<html>
<head><title>Example Form</title></head>
<body>

<form method="GET" action="/cgi-bin/formprocessor.cgi">
    <p>First Name <input type="text" name="FName"
        size="20"></p>
    <p>Last Name <input type="text" name="LName"
        size="20"></p>
    <p>Gender:</p>
    <p><input type="radio" value="F" checked
        name="Gender"> Female <input type="radio"
            name="Gender" value="M"> Male</p>
    <p><input type="submit" value="Submit"
        name="submit"><input type="reset" value="Reset"
            name="reset"></p>
```

```
</form>
</body>
</html>
```

This code generates the bare-bones form shown in Figure 5.2.

Now you must write the Perl script "/cgi–bin/formprocessor.cgi". This script has to accept the information generated by the form and process it, then return results to the page. Because the METHOD listed in the beginning of the form statement is POST (as opposed to GET, which is the other possibility), the server encrypts the form data within a data block to STDIN and puts the block's size in the CONTENT_LENGTH environment variable. This light form of encryption is not impossible to decode, but is not straightforward either—it would not be worth much if it was. Fortunately, Perl has built-in tools to help, making writing this script a much quicker process than it would be as a bash shell script. One simple line reads the data in for you:

```
&ReadParse;
```

Now, you need to do something with the data. You probably want to write it to a file, so first outside of the script you need to create your data file. For this example, the file is demographics.txt. You might type the following to create the empty file and make it world readable and writeable:

```
> touch demographics.txt
> chmod a+wr demographics.txt
```

Back to the script. First, you have to define your output file. To do this, use the command **$outfile** in the format:

```
$outfile = ">>filename.txt";
```

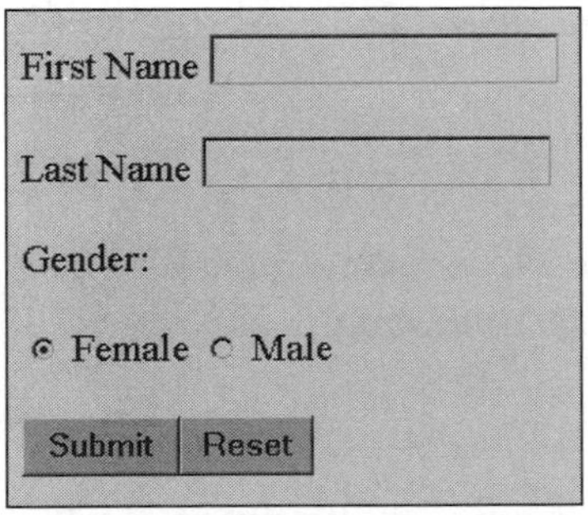

Figure 5.2   A simple form to process with a CGI script.

The double redirection sign signals that if the file exists and has data in it, the new data should be appended onto the end. So the next line in the script is:

```
$outfile = ">>demographics.txt";
```

You now need to open the file. In Perl, you open a file for input with the following code:

```
open(OUTFILE, $outfile);
```

Finally, you can write the data to the file. First, you want to get the current data so you can add your timestamp to the data entry. To grab the date and then remove the newline character from the end of it, a typical problem in Perl, use the following:

```
$date = &ctime(time);
chop($date);
```

The data you brought in with the **&ReadParse** command is stored in the $in variable, each item attached to its name in the format:

```
$in{'name'}
```

To then send the data to the file you might use:

```
print "On $date, $in{'FName'} $in{'LName'} visited and
said they were gender $in{'Gender'}."
```

Now you need to close the file with:

```
close(OUTFILE);
```

Save and exit the script, make it world executable, and you're ready to go!

PROGRAMMING IN THE LINUX ENVIRONMENT

Many programmers like to work in a Unix-like environment. The reasons are many and varied, including familiarity from schooling.

Programming In Linux Vs. Unix

The differences between programming in Linux and Unix aren't so much centered around tool availability, because most tools have at least one version ported to Linux by now. Instead, these issues surround documentation and the fact that Linux is a compilation of different Unix systems.

Documentation Issues

When you're programming in a Unix environment, stacks of documentation usually provide the last word on what is right and wrong within the programming language. However, the documentation isn't nearly as extensive in Linux. Sometimes a programmer must rely on trial and error to determine the proper statements in his or her code.

Unix Mixture Issues

Because Linux is a mix of System V and BSD (Berkeley Software Distribution), all of its tools tend also to be a mix of the two. This fact can be both a plus and a minus to the Linux programmer. If you have access to either System V or BSD documentation, sometimes it will be accurate. If you have access to both, then if one approach doesn't work, you can try the other.

5

Moving Target

Some feel that the hardest aspect of programming for Linux is that they're writing for a moving target. This concern arises because updates are released constantly for various tools and the kernel itself. Whether this fact is something to worry about or a nonissue depends on what the programmer is writing for, and the backward-compatibility of the other tools and programs the software relies on.

Languages Available To Linux Programmers

Almost all programming languages are available for programmers using Linux, and some are available in multiple versions. However, not all of these languages are available freely—some are provided only from commercial vendors.

The most commonly used programming languages under Linux are C and C++—both compiled with the Gnu C Compiler (gcc)—and Perl (a programming/scripting hybrid language).

THE EDIT-COMPILE-TEST CYCLE

When you're writing large, complex programs, it's wise to follow the edit-compile-test cycle. This cycle breaks down the process into small steps to make finding problems along the way much easier.

Cycle Breakdown

The edit-compile-test cycle breaks down into four distinct steps. Follow this cycle until the entire program is written and working properly:

1. Edit the code. In this step, you write one complete segment of the program. "Complete" refers to a section that can be run on its own without needing any more code than is already there.

2. Compile the code. In this step, you run your files through the compiler to see if they compile properly. If not, return to editing.

3. Test the code. The code must give the results required to be able to continue on to its next stage before exiting the testing step. If it doesn't test properly, return to the edit stage and locate the problem.

4. Return to edit. In the final step of the cycle you return to the edit to work on the next section of code.

Debugging Tricks And Tips

You can use a number of tricks and tips of the programming trade when attempting to debug code.

Printing Values

If the problem may be in one of the variables, insert statements to print these variables at each step of the way, or at least at each important juncture. Doing so allows you to watch and see where the variables first begin to appear incorrectly.

Commenting Out

Sometimes it's helpful to comment out pieces of code to see if removing them from the section also removes the error.

Step Through By Hand

If a problem is particularly elusive, consider stepping through the code by hand and seeing if what you do by hand at each point matches what happens on the screen. Sometimes this technique is a good way to find out if a command or function is being used incorrectly.

MANAGING AND MAINTAINING SHARED LIBRARIES

Linux supports *shared libraries*, which consist of a number of functions programs can use that don't need to be compiled directly into the programs. These libraries are a method of keeping program size to a minimum.

Why Update Libraries?

Eventually, a time will come when you're unable to install, run, or compile a program because the libraries on the machine are out of date. This problem is the primary reason to update the system shared libraries. Another might be to utilize library features in software someone is writing on the system, although using this software will require other people to update their libraries, as well.

How To Update Libraries

Although the details of the commands and files for updating libraries may vary slightly from release to release, the process remains the same. First, see if an update is available directly from the distribution installed on the machine. Otherwise, you can get them from Linux sites, where these libraries are often found under a location such as /pub/Linux/GCC; they have names beginning with *lib*. Once you obtain the files, read the instructions included and follow them closely.

Working With Libraries

When you are writing C programs that use library routines and when you write a C program you almost always use library routines. It is either that or reinvent the wheel—you have to load the library that contains the functions you need before you can use them. In C code, this is done with an **include** statement. At the beginning of a file, for example, you will almost always have:

```
#include <stdio.h>
```

This statement gives the program access to the standard C input/output library and its range of functions. Sometimes, however, this one library is not enough. You may not even have the library you need on the system. The **ldd** command allows you to list the shared libraries needed by a program when used in the following format:

```
> ldd program
```

To find which libraries you have on your system, look in the /usr/lib directory. When you do a listing in this location, you will find quite a long list of files. For the most part, all of the files ending in .so are shared C libraries. If you run into an error where you do not have the appropriate library, then place it in this directory once you download it or install it from your distribution media. Once the new shared library is installed, run the **ldconfig** command. This program updates the file /etc/ld.so.conf—which contains a list of directories holding libraries—and /etc/ld.so.cache, which lists the libraries themselves. This last file is another place to go if you are wondering whether you have a library installed or not.

Decided to put your new libraries in some nonstandard directory? Run the **ldconfig** command in the format "**ldconfig** *directory*" and it will include that directory as it builds its files.

WORKING WITH C CODE

It is beyond the scope of this book to teach you all that you need to know about C programming. A system administrator does need to know some basics when it comes time to compile programs downloaded from resource sites. Most of these basics revolve around the **make** package.

Make, The Build Manager

The **make** package is essentially a build manager, meaning that it allows the programmer who originally wrote a program to provide a method for other programmers and users to quickly compile the software without needing to know all the intricate ins and outs concerning how it is compiled. The key to the **make** package is building a *Makefile*, which is something you will encounter in multiple portions of this book. This Makefile contains sets of instructions that automate the compilation process to the point where the user only has to type a few words and everything is then done for him or her.

Customizing A Makefile

Not all Makefiles are created equal, and even a well-made one may not have everything you need. Therefore, you need to be able to read through one and pick out what items might need to be changed, and what would be harmful to touch. If you are familiar with C programming, you will quickly notice that a Makefile is simply a backward version of what you have to do to compile a program. The first section is what pulls everything together, and is in the format:

```
program : one.o two.o three.o
            cc -o program one.o two.o three.o
```

After this portion, you have the smaller components that each assembles the items that are used to build the program. In this case, these are:

```
one.o : one.c
        cc -c one.c
two.o : two.c
        cc -c two.c
three.o : three.c
        cc -c three.c
```

That may be the entire Makefile. With this file, someone could just use the command **./make program** inside the source directory and everything would be compiled for him or her. Of course, this is a very simple version of a Makefile. There really is not even anything for you to edit. To make things more complex, add some macros. A macro is set in the format:

```
macro = string
```

Often macros are used to set various system variables. You may find a macro such as:

```
weblogs = /var/log/web
```

Although this statement is valid in and of itself, maybe your Web server logs are not in /var/log/web. Editing this statement will ensure later in the Makefile that when it is plugged in, using the format $(*macro*) or ${*macro*}, the value is correct.

Typical Make Commands

Over the years a number of programmers have adopted particular Makefile targets to the point where they almost serve as standards. Often, for example, there is an "all" target, which runs everything in the Makefile. Another commonly used target is "clean," which is used to remove the temporary files generated during the previous builds. Most of the time there is a make target which is the same name as the program you are building. This item may or may not be the same as a "make all".

Other common make targets are items like "install", which instead of compiling the program puts it in place and sets all of the proper permissions. Makefiles are quite versatile that way.

CHAPTER SUMMARY

Although scripting and programming may not be featured in the Linux certification exams, some generalities regarding these topics are included. Especially important is the ability not so much to write your own scripts and programs, but to look over other people's offerings and customize them to your own needs (or at least understand what you are seeing and make sure that you are not installing something harmful on your system).

Study the basics of shell scripting and learn how to write your own scripts. The better you are at this, the more sense the exams will make to you. This is especially true when you're trying to diagnose problems in system init scripts. Knowing the basics of CGI Perl programming allows you to evaluate the multitude of Perl scripts out there as well as build your own forms and access the information they pull in.

Knowing where your system libraries are and how to make sure it can find all of them is imperative to a smoothly running system, especially when you are dealing with shared libraries. If the programs that depend on shared library code cannot find those libraries, you have a serious problem on your hands. Remember the **ldconfig** command. You will need it.

Finally, although 9 times out of 10 these days you may never have to touch the inside of a Makefile, it is very important that you can understand it for that tenth time out of 10.

REVIEW QUESTIONS

1. What is a shell?

    a. A compiled program run from the command line

    b. A login work environment

    c. A game available to X users

    d. The outer layer of a program

2. Which of the following isn't a valid shell?

    a. tcsh

    b. bash

    c. ksh

    d. lsh

3. Which of the following is a valid vi mode? [Choose all correct answers]

    a. delete

    b. colon

    c. command

    d. insert

4. Which of the following vi commands result in the user being able to insert text without manually entering insert mode? [Choose all correct answers]

    a. **c**

    b. **R**

    c. **s**

    d. **o**

5. Which of the following isn't a vi pattern metacharacter?

    a. *

    b. .

    c. ^

    d. ,

6. Which of the following environment variables contains the current working directory?

   a. PS1

   b. HOME

   c. PWD

   d. PATH

7. What file are the main user environment settings stored in?

   a. /etc/profile

   b. .profile

   c. .login

   d. /etc/login

8. What command is used to change default shells?

   a. **chgshell**

   b. **chsh**

   c. **shell**

   d. **pwd**

9. What practical features are missing from the example scripts in this chapter? [Choose all correct answers]

   a. Option to skip formatting

   b. Carefully formatted ASCII art

   c. Entry error checking

   d. Menus with all possible entries

10. Why might you write a shell script?

    a. To automate filling in blanks in a GUI program

    b. To automate a process you usually do from the command line

    c. To write a complex binary program

    d. To write a simple binary program

11. The pattern \<.$a\star$ will find which of the following words in vi? [Choose all correct answers]

    a. car

    b. care

    c. bear

    d. bare

12. When writing a binary program, what kind of process is the best to follow?
    a. edit, compile, edit, compile, test
    b. edit, test
    c. edit, test, edit, test, compile
    d. edit, compile, test, edit, compile, test

13. What sequence of characters is used in vi to save a file without closing it?
    a. *:wq*
    b. *:w*[Enter]
    c. *:q*[Enter]
    d. *:!w*[Enter]

14. What format would you use to create the environment variable MYNAME and set its value to Dawn Smith in the bash or korn shells?
    a. MYNAME="Dawn Smith"
    b. MYNAME=Dawn Smith
    c. set MYNAME="Dawn Smith"
    d. export MYNAME=Dawn Smith

15. Which of the following is a valid first line for a shell? [Choose all correct answers]
    a. **ls –la | more**
    b. **#/bin/bash**
    c. **#!/bin/bash**
    d. **#!/bin/ksh**

16. Which of the following commands deletes a line of text but not the line itself, keeping it open and entering insert mode so new text can be entered?
    a. **c**
    b. **C**
    c. **w**
    d. **d**

17. What character do you type to tell vi you want to search for text?
    a. :
    b. \
    c. /
    d. [Esc]

18. What does the **read** command do in a shell script?

    a. Waits for the user to press any key and then continues

    b. Waits for the user to input data and then press Enter

    c. Prints out data on the screen

    d. Prints data to a file

19. What must be done before a shell script can be run by just typing its name?

    a. It must be moved to a special spot in the filesystem.

    b. It has to be compiled.

    c. Its permissions must be changed to executable.

    d. Its ownership has to be root.

20. Which C compiler is most commonly used in Linux?

    a. gcc

    b. gC

    c. cc

    d. c-comp

HANDS-ON PROJECTS

These projects require that you have access to a Linux system with the following shells installed: bash, ksh, and tcsh.

Project 5.1

In this project, you'll create a file in vi, edit it, and then save and exit.

To create a file in vi:

1. Log in to any user account.

2. Edit the file project5-1 in your home directory with vi by typing

```
vi ~/project5-1
```

3. Enter insert mode by typing "i".

4. Enter the following text:

```
How much wood
could a woodchuck chuck
if a woodchuck
could chuck
wood?
```

5. Press Esc to return to command mode.

6. Type a colon (:) to enter colon mode.

7. Type "w" and press Enter to save the file.

8. Move the cursor to the beginning of the third line by typing "3G".

9. Type "o" to insert a blank line beneath line three and enter insert mode.

10. Type "How does a woodchuck chuck anyway?" and press Esc to return to command mode.

11. Type a colon (:) to enter colon mode.

12. Display the line numbers by typing "set nu" and then pressing Enter.

13. Type "1G" to move to the beginning of the file.

14. Open a search by typing the forward slash (/).

15. Type the word "wood" and press Enter. The cursor moves to the first instance of the word.

16. Type a forward slash (/) and press Enter. The cursor moves to the next instance of the word, which is a part of the word *woodchuck*.

17. Go to the line you added (*How does a woodchuck chuck anyway?*) by typing "4G".

18. Delete the line and move the rest of the text up by typing "dd".

19. Type "A" to move to the end of the current line and enter insert mode.

20. Type "a lot of".

21. Type a colon (:) to enter colon mode.

22. Type "wq" and press Enter to save and exit the file.

Project 5.2

In this project, you'll set a custom prompt in the bash shell, korn shell, and enhanced C shell. You'll explore what happens when you return to the original shell, and then make the changes permanent for the bash shell in the user profile.

To set a custom prompt, do the following:

1. Log in to a user account that uses the bash shell.

2. Examine the default prompt.

3. Type

```
PS1="\w> "
```

to change the prompt to something similar to:

```
/home/user>
```

5

4. Type "chsh –l" to see a listing of available shells and their paths.

5. Type "/bin/ksh" or the appropriate path for the korn shell.

6. Enter your password at the prompt.

7. Note the current login prompt.

8. Type the following and then press Enter:

```
PS1="$PWD> "
```

The prompt changes to the same as in Step 3.

9. Type "/bin/tcsh" or the appropriate path for the enhanced C shell.

10. Enter your password at the prompt.

11. Note the current login prompt.

12. Type the following and then press Enter:

```
set prompt = "%/> "
```

13. Type "exit" to leave the subshell.

14. Type "exit" again. Continue doing so until you've returned to the login prompt. Note what a mess of subshells has been left behind by this experimentation.

15. Log back in to the account. Note that the login prompt is back to its original form.

16. Type "ls –la" to see all of the files in the account's home directory.

17. Determine whether the file .profile or .bash_profile already exists.

18. Type "vi .profile" or "vi .bash_profile"—depending on which file is present—to open the user settings file.

19. Type "G" to move to the end of the file if it has content.

20. Type "o" to create a new blank line at the end and enter insert mode.

21. Type the following:

```
PS1="\w> "
```

22. Press the Esc key.

23. Type a colon (:) to enter colon mode.

24. Type "wq" and press Enter to save and exit the file. Note that the prompt hasn't yet changed.

25. Type "logout" to return to the login prompt.

26. Log back into the account. Note that you now have the modified prompt.

## CHAPTER SIX

LINUX ADMINISTRATIVE TASKS

AFTER READING THIS CHAPTER AND COMPLETING THE EXERCISES, YOU WILL BE ABLE TO:

➤ Develop a basic set of user policies

➤ Add new users to your own specifications and remove existing users from the system completely

➤ Configure how much data to keep in system logs and how long the data should be retained

➤ Create timed jobs to automate the work of system administration

➤ Develop a system backup plan

PRINCIPLES AND PRACTICES OF SYSTEM ADMINISTRATION

There are a number of overall principles that many effective system administrators follow. These principles define how to govern user behavior, provide user support, and ensure system security without being too heavy-handed with the users.

Dealing With Users

Although many may look to find a way to avoid dealing with users, this is not possible. Eventually, every system administrator has to deal with the system's end users. How these dealings take place depends on a number of issues, including how much the users understand up front, what their goals are, and the tone of the proceedings.

User Policies

A way to cut down on difficult situations with users is to have a set of policy statements published where all users are able to read them. Even if the person does not read the policies right away, having these documents available gives the system administrator the ability to instruct the user to read the policy statement before continuing discussion.

One of the most important policy statements to have in place is a "Reasonable Use" policy. This document should explicitly spell out what actions can get a user disciplined or his or her account revoked. Items such as spamming, newsgroup or email harassment, hacking or cracking any site, and any general criminal activities are all issues that administrators of large sites must eventually deal with. Thinking out the site's response to such situations beforehand can facilitate smooth going if they happen.

 If the site is an ISP or a corporate site, it is a good idea to have a lawyer examine and approve the policy statement.

New Software Requests

Users often contact administrators when they want services not currently provided, or to install software that requires higher access than a typical user has. Sometimes the request is as simple as asking for access to a newsgroup the site does not carry. At other times, there may be a new commercial, shareware, or freeware product that needs to be installed centrally, or that the user simply does not have the knowledge or access level to install.

There are a number of ways of assessing whether to grant the user's request. Many of these methods are dependent on how many users are on the system, how much room there is for new software, what type of program it is, and how trusted the source is. The most suspect circumstances are programs that were written by the user or when the code does not come from a trustworthy source. If the software the user wants to install offers a value-added service that would be useful to many users, then it might be worth going through the code to ensure that it is safe.

It is often useful for LANs or ISPs with a lot of users to have a policy regarding how to request adding new software to the system.

Customer Service

Customer service is important to any business. If users feel that their problems will be dealt with in a timely manner, they tend to be happier and easier to deal with, and are less likely to leave. Even if the users in question are employees in the same company as the system administrator, an adversarial relationship between system administrators and end users can create counterproductive tension. Offer a specific method of reporting problems or requesting assistance, such as a special email address or phone number. Then, deal with these issues when you are feeling patient and calm.

If customer support and service is not something you care to deal with directly, outsource this task. Assign someone else to the task who has both the technical knowledge to handle many problems on his or her own, plus the people skills to handle frustrated users.

Customer support issues are less likely to be a problem when quality documentation is available.

Scheduled Downtime

If the system must be taken down for upgrades or adjustments, warn the users 48 hours ahead of time, if possible. This time period gives users a chance to back up any data they are concerned about losing, make copies of files they need to work on while the system is down, or adjust their schedules around the lack of projected availability.

Announcing downtime tends to involve giving an estimate of how long the system will be unavailable. When estimating downtime, try to consider the fact that even the smoothest operations can run into unforeseen snags. Double or even triple the time estimates when giving them to users, and include a clause in the announcement stating that the downtime may be longer, if necessary.

Security Issues

System security (discussed in detail in Chapter 12) must be among a system administrator's primary concerns. An insecure system will not function well for long, and will soon suffer from user error or malicious intent, especially if this system (or LAN) is connected to the Internet. High-profile sites are not the only ones in danger of being compromised by hackers or crackers.

Consider no machine completely secure. If your system contains data that must not ever be seen by outside sources, or data that, if altered, would compromise far too much, put it on a machine that is not connected to Internet-accessible computers.

The Superuser

In all flavors of Unix, the term "superuser" is bandied about. This label essentially refers to the root account. The superuser is the person who has access to everything on the system. With this level of power comes certain problems and responsibilities.

Many novice system administrators or hobbyists constantly work on the system while logged in as root. Sending anything but important system administration–related mail, making news posts, or going into chat areas such as IRC as root quickly labels you as one of the following: a clueless new admin who is going to do severe damage to his or her own system at some point, a clueless new admin who is starry-eyed about his or her level of power, or someone who is out to cause trouble in the case of chat areas, because root access allows you to run attack programs you otherwise could not run.

Although these assumptions may seem unfair, there is a basis for them. As stated before, root has the ability to do pretty much anything. There are few system administrators who have not discovered the pain of just how much leeway the system gives this account. Typing "**rm** -rf" in the wrong directory can wipe out large portions of the file system. Typing "**chmod** -R 644" in the wrong directory can widely compromise security, or break a number of programs. Combine these mistakes with sloppy backup procedures or not keeping records of filesystem structure, permissions, and ownership, and you have just lost days of productivity repairing the damage.

There are various beliefs on when you should actually log in as the superuser. Some people feel you should never actually log in as root and instead use the **su** command to briefly access the root account from your own user account. This command is used in the following manner:

```
> su root
Password:
>
```

It may not look like much, but issuing the command from any user account opens up a subshell with you as root. This is not entirely the same as logging in as the superuser. You have the privileges, but none of root's login files are run. One of the biggest problems you may encounter is trying to find the programs you want to run. Using this method does not assign you root's path.

 If you just type "**su**" with no user, it is assumed you are trying to **su** into the root account.

To then leave the subshell, just type "exit". You can, in fact, use **su** to temporarily become any user as long as you have the password. However, root does not need the passwords. Root can use **su** to become any user at will. Use this privilege sparingly.

Another approach to superuser logins is to only log in to root when you genuinely need to use it. Log in as root, get the task done, then log back out and go back to using your own user account.

MANAGING USERS

If there are more than a few users on the system, eventually the issues of user, group, and server management come to the forefront.

The Default User

The system administrator can control the defaults used when creating new users. This is done by changing the settings for the script used, and changing the directory to use when creating a user account's home directory.

Useradd Defaults

The useradd script does what once had to be done by hand when adding new users. It creates an entry in the /etc/passwd (and /etc/shadow if using shadow passwords) file for the new user, creates the home directory for this user, and puts the default files within the home directory. These default files come from the /etc/skel directory, discussed in the next section.

Useradd utilizes the values stored in the file /etc/default/useradd or /etc/adduser.conf, depending on which Linux distribution is involved.

The Skeleton Directory

The /etc/skel directory contains all items that should be automatically put into a new user's account. Although the default contents vary slightly between distributions, the files found there are typically the user's individual .profile, or .bash_profile, which contain the final init settings used during the login process.

The profile files contain the login initialization information over which the user has direct control.

Changing User Defaults

A system administrator can—and often should—change the users' creation defaults to suit their needs. Note that changing these defaults does not change information for already existing users. Instead, it sets the new defaults for adding new users.

Display The Useradd Defaults
To display the current defaults for user creation, type "useradd –D".

Change The Default Home Directory Location
To change where home directories are placed by default, use the format "useradd –Db *newpath*". The new path is the top of the hierarchy where new user directories will be added. By default, the path is /home.

Change How Long An Expired Password Lasts
For security reasons, the system can be set to disable unused accounts. If some-one breaks into an account no longer being used, it can take quite some time before anyone realizes there is a problem.

One way to tell that an account is not in use is if the password expires and is not changed over a period of time. To set the system to automatically enforce the expiration of such accounts, use the format "useradd –Df *days*", where the argument is the number of days the expired password has remained unchanged.

Change The Default Group
In general, new users are often added to the "user" group—except in particular distributions that use a more specialized setup. If there is reason to change the default group, even if to temporarily add a block of special users, first create the group in /etc/group, then use the format "useradd –Dg *groupname*". Remember to change the defaults back to their previous settings if this is a temporary change.

Change The Default Shell
The default shell in Linux is usually /bin/bash. However, sometimes users are more familiar with a different environment, or the system administrator uses a tailor-made shell. To change the default shell assigned to each new user, use the format "useradd –Ds *shellpath*".

Change The Default User Files
Any alterations to the default user files can be made by changing items in or adding files or directories to the directory /etc/skel. Doing this is especially

useful if setting user defaults to a particular shell whose profile variant does not already exist in the skeleton directory.

Understanding /etc/passwd

When created, user accounts are placed in the file /etc/passwd. Although administrators often use tools to avoid editing this file directly, it is important to be familiar with the file as part of system maintenance.

An example of an entry in the /etc/passwd file is:

```
user:password:UID:GID:name:home:shellUser
```

The user entry is the user's login name. A number of different philosophies are employed in naming users, and how closely these are followed depends on the nature of the system and the institution under which it operates. Large institutions such as universities and corporations often use some variant on the user's full name, perhaps a first initial and last name (for example, Bill Smith would be bsmith). ISPs might allow users to use a custom search engine to see if the login name they want is already in use, until they find one they can have. Smaller setups might simply let users choose their names, and if there is a conflict, let them choose another.

Password

The password entry is one of three different things. If it is an "x", it means that shadow passwords are in use, and that the user's password is stored in /etc/shadow. The account may not have a password at all, in which case, its entry will be an asterisk (*). This case tends to be used for daemons and system programs, such as shutdown.

However, if the entry is a series of characters, then the password is encoded directly into /etc/passwd. Do not edit this password manually. Use the **passwd** command instead.

UID

The *UID* (User ID) is a unique number that identifies the user behind the scenes. Just as Internet addresses are strings of numbers associated with their domain names, login names have the UID beneath them. The user creation utilities automatically choose the next available number when adding a new user.

What range of UIDs is available depends on which distribution is in use. Typically, a certain range of lower numbers is reserved for administrative accounts, and numbers beyond that are available for individual users. The user range is easily determined by looking in /etc/passwd to see which numbers were assigned to the user accounts already created.

GID

A *GID* (Group ID) is the unique number that refers to the group to which the user belongs. Each Linux distribution handles this issue in its own manner. As with UIDs, look in the /etc/group file to see how the distribution hands out those already assigned and work within that pattern.

Name

The name entry is the real name or pseudonym assigned to the user. What is put here depends on the policy used for the system. In a work environment, the user's real name is used more often than not. In other environments, users may have the option of choosing what name is assigned to their account, as long as their real identification is provided for billing information.

Home

The home entry is the home directory location. This item is almost always /home/*user*.

Shell

The shell entry is the path to the shell used by default for this account. In Linux, the default is usually /bin/bash unless the administrator uses a custom shell instead for the general user.

Understanding /etc/shadow

If shadow passwords are enabled on the system, then the file /etc/shadow contains the password information that is no longer in the insecure file /etc/passwd. An entry in the /etc/shadow file is laid out as:

```
user:password:lchange:mchange:change:wchange:disable:expire:system
```

Here's the breakdown of the preceding code:

➤ **User**   The user entry is the login name for the account in question.

➤ **Password**   The password entry is the encoded password that would have initially been in the file /etc/passwd. It is now protected within this file, which is not world readable like /etc/passwd.

➤ **Lchange**   The number of days since January 1, 1970, since the password was last changed.

➤ **Mchange**   The number of days before the password can be changed again. This value is set to zero by default.

➤ **Change**   The number of days until the password must be changed.

➤ **Wchange**   The number of days before the password is set to expire that the system will begin warning the user to change the password.

➤ **Disable** Once the password reaches the time when it must be changed, the disable value is the count of days before the account is automatically disabled if the password is not changed.

➤ **Expire** The count of days since January 1, 1970, which equates to the date the account is to expire.

➤ **System** Reserved system value.

Adding Shell Accounts

It is important to consider system security when adding new users. Shell accounts are often considered a security weakness because they provide an opening through which a clever person can worm his or her way into the system itself. So it is important to know not only how to add shell accounts, but how and why to add nonshell accounts.

Shell accounts are necessary for those who need access to a shell itself rather than passthrough for some kind of Internet service. This shell can be one of those that comes with the Linux distribution, an additional one downloaded from a trusted site, or a custom one made by the system administrator to restrict access, or offer a menu-driven shell for those who are not accustomed to using Linux or Unix.

To create a shell account for a new user, use the **useradd** command (sometimes also aliased to **adduser**) in the format "adduser *username*".

Adding Non-Shell Accounts

Not all user accounts need shell access. For those who only want access to *POP* (Post Office Protocol) email, *PPP* (Point-to-Point Protocol), or *SLIP* (Serial Line Interface Protocol), to the Internet, or other such services that do not require an actual shell account, it is possible to assign the user an account without shell access. First, create the account normally. Then, change its shell assignment either directly within /etc/passwd, or with the **chsh** command discussed in Chapter 5, to /bin/false. This tells the Linux system that the user should have no access to any shell.

 A number of the Linux distributions also offer tools within their GUI suites for account creation that include the ability to create nonshell accounts in one step.

Passwords

The useradd tool does not include an option to create passwords, so it is important to not forget this step. To assign—or change—a password to a user as root, use the format "passwd *username password*". For example, to assign the user "marvin" the password "a9b8c5" the **command** would be **passwd marvin a9b8c5**.

It is often wise to assign the users some form of randomly generated password consisting of numbers and letters and direct them to change it immediately during their first login, including instructions on how to do so if they are not familiar with Linux or Unix. Include the new password in a physical mailing to the new users, or give it to them in person or on the phone while the account is being set up. The level of security necessary for the system dictates how much trouble is used to ensure passwords cannot be sniffed by potential intruders.

Removing Users

Users come and go over time: Sometimes they are behind on payments, or are going out of town and want to ensure that no one else can access their account while they are gone. Or perhaps they are moving on to a new location and no longer need the account.

Disabling Users

If the aim is to deny access to a user's account without deleting any of the information associated with it, then open /etc/passwd if not using shadow passwords, or /etc/shadow if using shadow passwords. Change the password entry, which is the second item in the user's listing—after the first colon—to an asterisk (*). This removes the password and makes it impossible to log in to the account from the login screen.

To reactivate the account, create a new password for them as root with the **passwd** command.

Removing Users

If the aim is to remove the users from the system, the process is slightly more complex. It is possible to remove users but keep their files on the system, or to totally remove all traces. It is good etiquette to warn the users of when this removal will take place so they can copy any files they need off of the system first.

Both methods begin with deleting the user's entries from the password and group files. This task is accomplished by using the **userdel** command in the format "userdel *account*". Doing so removes the information from the files, but not the home directory or any of the files. So if some of the files are needed, the directory can be moved or renamed, or the files themselves can be extracted before continuing to the rest of the account removal.

Removing the files involves deleting the users' home directory and tracking the files they left behind throughout the system. The extent of these extras depends on what kind of access the users had, but fortunately there are faster ways to locate these files than manually digging through directories. The **find** command has an option to search for specific file owners. After removing the home directory, issue as root "find / -user *username*". Sometimes this listing is quite long. If this is the case, redirect the output to a file with a format such as "find / -user *username* > ~/*username*_files". Once this is done, a shell script can be written to parse the data from the file and delete the user's files throughout the filesystem.

The key to removing the files belonging to the user is ensuring that they are not being used by others. If the file is a program, one way to do this would be to rename the file. Then, if no one reports any problems within a chosen time span, the file can be deleted with little concern.

MANAGING GROUPS

6

User accounts and new software tend to get most of the focus when considering system management. However, a savvy system administrator will also remember to turn his or her attention occasionally to groups. Although each user account is assigned to a group automatically upon creation, it is possible to utilize the group structure to accomplish what otherwise would require extensive permission assignments.

Group Storage

Group information is stored in the file /etc/group. A user can be assigned to any number of groups. It is often a good practice to put a comment in the file (start a line with # to create a comment) at the end of the default group listing, and then add special purpose groups below it. When it is time to remove old groups, this task ensures that special groups required by the system are not accidentally deleted.

Creating Groups

You can either create your groups manually or with the **groupadd** command. Manual creation is covered in detail so that you understand how to manage the /etc/group file and how to handle what users are in what groups. How you create your groups is a matter of personal preference.

Creating A Group Manually

To create a new group by hand, add it to the end of the listings in /etc/group. The format for this file's entries is similar to that of the /etc/password file. An entry is laid out as follows:

```
name:password:GID:user(s)
```

An example might be:

```
database:*:100:webadmin,root,sally
```

The preceding code can be broken down as follows:

➤ **Name**   When naming groups, try to choose something with a clear purpose, or when it comes time to add users to specialized groups it will take extra time to figure out the group's purpose.

➤ **Password**   At one point in Unix, group passwords were used. The asterisk meant that no password was necessary. This entry is now a legacy feature and no longer functions.

➤ **GID**   The GID (Group ID) here is the same as the GID in the other files, a unique number defining each particular group.

➤ **User(s)**   The user entry contains the list of users who belong to the group in question. Multiple users are separated by a comma with no space; for example, "mary,bob,joe,janice".

Creating A Group With Groupadd

Linux provides a command, **groupadd**, for group creation, though often groups are created manually as described in the previous section. In its simplest format, this command is used in the format **groupadd** *group*, where the GID assigned is the next on the list. You can also specify the exact GID to use with the -g option, using the command in the format **groupadd -g** *GID group*.

Removing Groups

Both the manual and command-based methods of group removal are discussed next. You need to understand the underlying process of what these commands do not only for exam purposes, but to help you do your job as a system administrator, as well. This understanding is especially useful when writing shell scripts.

Removing A Group Manually

There is not much involved in removing groups manually, depending on how they are utilized. Generally, what must be done first is to note the group's GID. Once this is done, the group must be removed from /etc/group, and the users in /etc/passwd that are assigned to that group must be reassigned to other groups. If desired, use the **find** command in the format **find / -group** *group* to locate every file belonging to the group's name or GID.

Removing A Group With **Groupdel**

Removing groups in Linux involves the **groupdel** command. It is used in the simple format **groupdel** *group*. However, it has more considerations involved than just adding a group. The **groupdel** command will not allow you to remove a group that is any user's primary group, as that would cripple the ownership settings for that user. You also need to follow the instructions in the previous section on how to manually find and deal with any files that are left over with that group's old GID.

Group Passwords

There is an extra level of groups that is often ignored. Within this level exists group administrators, passwords, and more. This comes in handy with workgroups and other project-oriented groupings where the system administrator really does not need to be involved beyond the group creation stage; the project manager can be made responsible for the group itself and who belongs to it. Once the group is created, you assign someone group administrator status with the command format **gpasswd -A** *groupadmin group*. The system administrator can also add members to the group, with **gpasswd -M** *user group*.

After this, the group administrator may choose from a set of commands. To add a group member, use **gpasswd -a** *user group*, and to remove someone, **gpasswd -d** *user group*. To add a password to the group to prevent nonmembers from joining it with the **newgrp** command—discussed in the next section—the group administrator uses **gpasswd** *group* and is prompted for the new password.

Changing Groups

In an environment with many users who are organized into work groups, there sometimes comes the problem of the users needing to appear as being in one group for a time, then another, then another. Fortunately, a user can do this for his or her own account. Users who belong to more than one group can change to another group with the **newgrp** command in the format **newgrp** *group*.

MANAGING DAEMONS

Daemons have been mentioned sporadically so far, but have not really been explained in detail. Although users need to understand little or nothing about them, system administrators have to know what they are for, how they work, and how to best utilize them in order to do a good job.

Introduction To The Daemon

A daemon is a program that runs on its own without human interaction. Typically, daemons are servers that wait for clients to send requests and then respond to these requests according to their programming. Quite a large number of network services are daemon servers. You can usually recognize them by the "d" on the end of the program's name. The Web server, for example, is typically Apache on a Linux machine. However, the program itself is httpd, the HTTP daemon.

The daemon, or server, spends a good part of its time listening for connections on a specific address; this process is covered in Chapter 9. The clients, in this case a Web client such as Netscape, are programmed to know how a typical server of their type expects requests to be sent, such as requesting a URL in the case of the Web. When the daemon gets the request, it processes it and then feeds the information asked for back to the client. It is then the client's job to format the data and display it for the user.

Starting And Stopping A Daemon

Daemons are essentially run one of two ways. The first way is manually, which in the case of networking daemons, either means the administrator starts them by hand or gives them to the superdaemon to run—the superdaemon is covered in detail in Chapter 9. The second method of running daemons involves setting them up to run at boot time, and turn off as the system shuts down.

Manually

The manual version of daemon management discussed here is when you actually do things by hand at the command line. An important thing to understand about daemons, especially networking daemons, is that many of them have initialization scripts that are installed with them. These scripts are not stored in the same location, so if you try to locate the daemon by typing for example "which httpd", you are going to find the daemon itself, not its init script.

 You may not find the daemon at all under some distributions with the **which** command. Remember, **which** only finds items that are in your path statement.

Often, the daemon init scripts are stored under the /etc hierarchy, usually under /etc/rc.d. In some cases, they are in a subdirectory of this location: /etc/rc.d/init.d. The scripts are named after the daemons themselves. They may be named exactly the same. The daemon /usr/sbin/httpd may have the init script /etc/rc.d/init.d/httpd under one distribution, whereas the daemon /var/lib/apache/sbin/httpd may use the init script /etc/rc.d/rc.httpd.

Before you start a daemon, it is good practice to see if it is already running—doing so allows you to avoid an error if it is running. To quickly tell if a daemon is running without having to page through processes with **more**, combine the **ps** and **grep** commands as in the following example:

```
ps aux | grep httpd
```

If the daemon is already running, skip ahead to instructions on how to stop it. Then, you can start it properly. These instructions on starting and stopping are necessarily generic due to differences between programs and distributions.

The process of starting and stopping the daemons is pretty straightforward. To start a daemon, often you run the init script in the format "*/path/initscript* start".

For example, if the init script was in /etc/rc.d/init.d, then you would type "/etc/rc.d/init.d/httpd start". Knowing where the daemon actually is located is not required. The script knows.

 If you are already in the /etc/rc.d/init.d directory, then you can just type "./httpd start".

To stop a daemon you do essentially the same thing, except that you would type "/*path*/*initscript* stop". In the case of the example, it would be "/etc/rc.d/init.d/ httpd stop". Some daemons also have a restart option, which allows you to avoid having to both stop and start them by hand.

 An important thing to keep in mind is that every time you change most daemons' configurations you have to restart that daemon before it will load the new settings.

At Boot Time

Starting daemons automatically at boot time involves working with your system's boot process. Somewhere within that process is a place for you to set what daemons need to start. In fact, sometimes there are two methods. The first method places a call to the daemon's init script in the boot files themselves. Typically, the place to put this is /etc/rc.d/rc.local. Type the full path name and command, just as you would to start the daemon from outside the init script's directory. For example:

```
/etc/rc.d/init.d/httpd start
```

The other method is generally the recommended option. This is because you can set the daemons to start and stop depending on what runlevel you are leaving or entering. To accomplish this, you need to look in the /etc/inittab file and see what runlevels correspond to what states in the distribution you are using. Now, look at files or directories that start with /etc/rc.d/rc.# (for example, /etc/rc.d/rc.2 for runlevel 2) or even a letter instead. Some distributions use letters for key runlevels, such as M for multiuser mode with no GUI. If it's a file, then go ahead and use /etc/rc.local or make sure there is a call to the server you want to use in that runlevel's script. If it's a directory, then follow the instructions in Chapter 4 for adding items to the specific runlevel's directory.

CREATING ALIASES

One tool available to you that can make your life easier is the alias. An *alias* is a command that you configure to stand for another command. This tool is not to be confused with a script. An alias is not that complex, just one or several commands on a single line. As the system administrator, you have two options available to you. You can create aliases globally for everyone, and you can create them just for yourself and your accounts.

Creating Global Aliases

To ensure that all people using bash get a particular command alias, set it within the /etc/profile or /etc/bashrc file, depending on which distribution you are using—if there is no /etc/bashrc, use /etc/profile. This action allows more knowledgeable users to replace your alias with their own, but prevents those new to Linux from having to create their own.

An alias is created in the format:

```
alias alias='command'
```

For example, some users like to set an alias that has typing "ls" actually do "ls -a". To create this alias, you would add the following to /etc/bashrc:

```
alias ls='ls -la'
```

Creating User Aliases

As a user, whether while logged in as root or any other account, you can also create your own aliases with the **alias** command. This command is actually used in the same format that you would type it into a login configuration script. So, at the command line you might type:

```
> alias rm='rm -f'
```

Typing just "alias" gives you a list of what aliases you already have set.

SYSTEM RESOURCES

On a hobby machine, system resources are often not much of an issue; things get done when they get done. However, when you are administering servers and services, these resources can mean everything. Bog a machine down badly enough and it becomes useless. There are essentially three types of resources available: memory, processor, and devices such as disks and networking. Each has its own considerations to deal with.

The Memory

The memory resource on a Linux system is both the physical RAM in the machine plus the swap space. When your system is running a group of processes whose memory needs exceed what you have in physical RAM, the kernel begins *paging*. To understand the process of RAM to disk paging you need to understand how the CPU accesses memory.

You are likely familiar with the cards that contain banks of RAM chips. These chips together form your total accessible RAM, as shown in Figure 6.1. This total amount of RAM is divided into equally sized pages, which are somewhat like blocks on storage media. When the system needs to access something in memory, the CPU sends a request down the bus that contains the address for the start of the page it needs. The contents of this page are then loaded into the CPU's internal memory cache, where they can be read or manipulated.

There is of course only a finite amount of physical RAM on the system. Rather than use this capacity as the cap, you create swap space to avoid being limited by your RAM. Paging in the context discussed here is when the kernel first starts accessing that space. When there is no RAM available, individual pages are put in the swap space. Not entire programs, mind you, just individual pages. It is only after the RAM is full but there are many processes still demanding room, causing the system to have to move many pages out to the hard drive, that you start genuinely swapping.

 Swapping is when the kernel starts moving entire processes out to swap space instead of just individual pages.

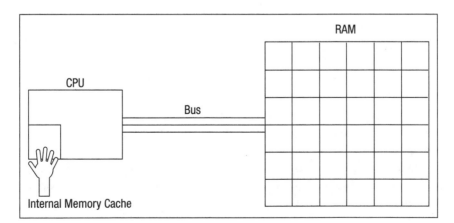

Figure 6.1   The CPU draws pages of memory into its internal cache when it needs to access RAM.

The Processor

A processor, or CPU, is your machine's brain, without it your computer cannot function. These days, your computer may even have more than one CPU. To understand the effect your processor can have on your system, however, you need to understand how it works.

Processors operate within a three-step cycle. In the first step, the CPU gets its instructions from the computer's memory. The second step converts this instruction into a binary value. This value is stored within a register in the processor itself. Now the CPU can access the final step of the cycle. It follows the instruction; going through whatever set of steps is necessary to complete the task. At the end of this cycle, the processor has probably not run the entire program in question. Instead, it has probably completed one aspect of it that returns a value, stores data, or gives instructions to a device. Only when this one cycle is complete can another begin.

It follows, then, that the faster your processor, the faster your machine. However, this is not necessarily always the case. All a processor does is carry out instructions. There are many other items within the machine that can create bottlenecks. It is important to look at the entire machine as a unit, as a sum of its CPU and RAM and drive controllers and more.

The Devices

In the context of system resources, the term *device* returns to any item used for any form of input and output. Although keyboards and mice are I/O devices, these pieces of hardware rarely cause any resource problems unless perhaps they are not configured properly. Other items can, depending on how heavily they are used, both with single data transfers and multiple users at once.

Each device has a combination of features that contributes to its speed. Controllers, drivers, and cables all can limit the bandwidth of device I/O. A device controller is usually a card or a chip on the motherboard. If it is a chip, then you are generally stuck with its capabilities until you upgrade. In fact, the higher end the motherboard, the more controllers are built in. With lower end modern motherboards, you tend to have to purchase SCSI, Ethernet, and video controllers. In many cases, this necessity is actually a good thing because many users like to have control over their desktop hardware. However, for server machines without a need for such things as fancy leading-edge video card technology, it is often considered better to leave card slots open for other things aside from mundane controller use.

The device itself can also be a limitation. Hard drives, for example, each have their own speed specifications for how quickly they can read and write, and indeed how many operations they can perform simultaneously if at all.

TUNING SYSTEM PERFORMANCE

Now that you understand your system resources a bit better, you are in better shape to learn how to tune its performance. Much of this tuning happens in the areas of memory and device I/O. Other aspects you have to watch are processes and daemons, and even the kernel itself. Before you can fix any performance problems, you have to isolate them. Finding and fixing a system's problem areas require knowing the right tools and how to use them. Some of these items will be further addressed in Chapter 7, and so may only be discussed in context here.

Measuring Performance

There are three basic tools available to you when it comes to measuring the kind of load your processes are putting on your system. One of these is the succinct **uptime** program. Type "uptime" and you get a response similar to:

```
12:54am up 6 days, 3 users, load average: 1.00, 2.00, 1.25
```

These items represent:

➤ The current time

➤ How long the system has been up and running

➤ How many users are logged on

➤ Load average one minute ago

➤ Load average five minutes ago

➤ Load average fifteen minutes ago

The important information here is the load average values. A *load average* is the ratio of how many new processes are spawned and how many old processes have been stopped. Although this value may not seem very significant, it is actually quite helpful. The higher the load average, the more processes you have running. The more processes that are running, the harder your system is working, and the slower everything runs. High load averages also make it more likely that items are paging or swapping, which slows system performance as well because disk I/O time is added to how long it takes to do its job.

If you want to see which processes are actually running, use the **ps** command. This item is covered in detail in Chapter 7 so it discussed only briefly here. The results of a full system **ps** command (**ps aux**) are incorporated into the results from the **top** command. This item is also covered in Chapter 7, but there is a special use for it. Many system administrators like to keep **top** continuously running in the background on a particular virtual console. Doing this allows them to take a glance at any time, see which processes are at the high end of the list, as well as data such as load averages, as shown in Figure 6.2.

```
 5:40pm  up 6 days,  4:11,  2 users,  load average: 0.61, 0.18, 0.06
43 processes: 40 sleeping, 3 running, 0 zombie, 0 stopped
CPU states: 13.5% user,  5.0% system,  0.0% nice, 81.4% idle
Mem:   30680K av,  29780K used,   900K free,  20172K shrd,   652K buff
Swap: 128480K av,   7456K used, 121024K free            10132K cached

 PID USER     PRI  NI  SIZE  RSS SHARE STAT  LIB %CPU %MEM   TIME COMMAND
3488 root      16   0  3880 3212   920 R       0  7.2 10.4 371:13 X
5580 dee       18   0  2124 2124  1744 R       0  6.0  6.9   0:00 screenshot
5440 root       5   0  1020 1020   824 R       0  1.7  3.3   0:01 top
3492 dee        3   0  2344 1560  1112 S       0  0.7  5.0   0:22 kwm
3527 dee        1   0  4632 4632  3248 S       0  0.5 15.0   0:27 kpanel
5261 dee        1   0  4104 4104  2956 S       0  0.5 13.3   0:01 konsole
5441 dee        6   0  5604 5604  2596 S       0  0.5 18.2   0:05 gimp
   1 root       0   0   132   68    56 S       0  0.0  0.2   0:03 init
   2 root       0   0     0    0     0 SW      0  0.0  0.0   0:00 kflushd
   3 root       0   0     0    0     0 SW      0  0.0  0.0   0:00 kupdate
   4 root       0   0     0    0     0 SW      0  0.0  0.0   0:00 kpiod
   5 root       0   0     0    0     0 SW      0  0.0  0.0   0:02 kswapd
   6 root     -20 -20     0    0     0 SW<     0  0.0  0.0   0:00 mdrecoveryd
 206 bin        0   0    80    0     0 SW      0  0.0  0.0   0:00 portmap
 222 root       0   0    68    0     0 SW      0  0.0  0.0   0:00 apmd
 275 root       0   0   204  152   124 S       0  0.0  0.4   0:00 syslogd
 286 root       0   0   484  164   132 S       0  0.0  0.5   0:01 klogd
 302 daemon     0   0   144  104    76 S       0  0.0  0.3   0:00 atd
 318 root       3   0   164  108    80 S       0  0.0  0.3   0:00 crond
 338 root       0   0    76    0     0 SW      0  0.0  0.0   0:00 inetd
 354 root       0   0    80    0     0 SW      0  0.0  0.0   0:00 lpd
 392 root       0   0   488  284   236 S       0  0.0  0.9   0:00 sendmail
 409 root       0   0   108   56    36 S       0  0.0  0.1   0:00 gpm
```

Figure 6.2   The output given by the **top** command.

Improving Performance

There are essentially two ways you can deal with the issue of a machine that tends to have a very high load average on a regular basis, say around five or above. One of these methods involves getting programs to share resources better. You can accomplish this with the **nice** command. Using this tool is covered in detail in Chapter 7.

Although people reflexively tend to think that the other method involves upgrading the processor speed, this is an incorrect assumption. You can usually accomplish a lot more by putting more memory in a computer than upgrading the processor. If you have too many processes gumming up the works, they are probably paging and swapping because they are overrunning the system's RAM. Add new memory to an overloaded system if **nice** is not enough to save it. If this still does not fix your problem, then you may want to farm some services off to other machines to ease this one's burden, or indeed try upgrading the processor.

FILE ATTRIBUTES

There is an additional level to the file permissions used by users and even by some system administrators. You need to at least understand this extra level, called attributes rather than permissions, and how to use it; even if you do not find a need for it in your day-to-day functioning. It is included in this chapter because this additional structure tends to be used on some vital system files by administrators but otherwise is ignored. This extra level of control is provided by the Access Control List, or ACL.

Listing And Understanding Attributes

Some distributions may already have attributes set on certain files. Whether they do or not, you can get a list of the attributes set with the **lsattr** command. It works essentially like **ls**, allowing you the same options of listing a file, set of files, or the entire directory. Where typing "ls –l" might give you the output:

```
-rwxrwxr-x   2 root    wheel    4096 Apr 7  1999 filea
-rwxrwxr-x   3 root    wheel    4096 Aug 30 1999 fileb
```

those same two items will show as the following when you type "lsattr".

```
----- filea
----- fileb
```

As you can see, neither of these has any attributes assigned. There are eight components to the attribute set, and each item is either on and is a letter, or off and is a dash. The attributes available are listed in order in Table 6.1.

Setting And Changing Attributes

ACL attributes are added and removed with the **chattr** command. This command is used in the format **chattr** *flags changes files*. There are three different flags available to you with **chattr**, as listed in Table 6.2.

Table 6.1   ACL file attributes listed in the order they are displayed by **lsattr**.

Attribute	Purpose
A	Do not update the atime (last time accessed) value when the file is changed. Not yet in use.
S	Write all file changes to disk rather than caching data to buffers first.
a	The file can only be appended, not written over. This attribute is only available to root.
c	The kernel automatically compresses this file before writing it to disk and uncompresses it before outputting the data upon request. Not yet in use.
d	Do not automatically archive this file when using the **dump** command.
i	The file cannot be deleted, moved, renamed, linked to, or written to. This attribute is only available to root.
s	When this file is deleted its blocks are fully emptied.
u	When this file is deleted its blocks are left intact so it can be undeleted. Not yet in use.

Table 6.2   Flags used with the **chattr** command.

Flag	Purpose
R	The listed changes should be applied recursively throughout the directory tree, ignoring symbolic links.
v	Assign a version value to the file. Used in the format "-v version".
V	Give verbose output, including listing version information.

The changes portion of the format is fairly simple to use. You can either begin this item with a plus (+) or a minus (-). If you start with a plus, then all of the attributes (as shown in Table 6.1) listed are items you want to add. Starting with a minus means you want to remove the attributes listed. Therefore, if you wanted to set the file /webdata/weblog so that it always had its data immediately written to file rather than held in any buffers, you would type the following:

```
chattr +S /webdata/weblog
```

CONFIGURING AND USING LOG FILES

A tool often ignored by beginning system administrators is the *log* file, which contains a record of almost everything that happens. Error messages during system initialization, footprints from attempted or successful intrusions; all of the clues are there for those who know how to use them.

System intrusions and software malfunctions, as much as they are discussed in great detail, are not incredibly common happenings in the day-to-day functioning of a Linux system or network. Familiarizing oneself with the log files under normal circumstances makes tracking system problems and break-ins far easier, as subtle differences in the logs will stand out.

Configuring System Log Files

Log files can be loosely divided into two categories: system logs and software logs. The system logs are those generated during boot and runtime by the kernel and system processes. Software logs, on the other hand, are written by packages such as Web servers, which keep their own log files.

Understanding The System Log **Config** File

The information sent to system logs is defined in the file /etc/syslog.conf. The configuration file is well commented, and although the defaults are sufficient, a system administrator might have the need or desire to change them. An entry in the configuration file is broken into two columns separated by tabs. The first column contains the definition of what type of data should be logged, and the second contains where this data should be logged.

Configuring Which Data To Log

The definition field is divided into two parts, which are separated by a period with no space in between. The first part is the *facility*, which is the type of program that generates the message. Each type of process has a specific logging facility it uses. There is a finite number of terms available to use as the facility, as outlined in Table 6.3. The second is the *priority*, which is the level of logging necessary for the facility. There is a set list of levels, as shown in Table 6.3. When setting the priority, keep in mind that the messages logged are those in the set priority and above. For example, choosing the priority "alert" only logs messages from "alert" and "emerg".

Priority levels available for use are (in order from the most worrisome messages to the least): emerg, alert, crit, err, warning, notice, info, and debug.

Configuring Where To Write The Data

The final portion of /etc/syslong.conf outlines what to do with the logged data. Most often, this entry contains the path of a log file, in the following format:

```
/path/file
```

If a particular program produces verbose logs that are slowing the system down, then put a dash (-) directly before the leading slash (/) for the path. Doing this prevents the system from synching the log file after each instance of writing to it, and so speeds the whole process up. However, if the system crashes, any data not written to the file that was lost from not synching will be irretrievable.

Table 6.3   The facility values available for /etc/syslog.conf.

Facility	Log Messages From
auth	authorization programs
auth-priv	private authorization programs
cron	cron and at
daemon	system daemons not specifically outlined
kern	the kernel
lpr	the print (lpr) daemon
mail	the mail system
news	the news system
syslog	the syslog daemon itself
user	general log output
uucp	the UUCP system
local0 – local7	local software

Putting It Together

Now, to compile all of these pieces into a full statement. The format for a line in /etc/syslog.conf is:

```
facilty.priority              location
```

There are also a couple of tricks and wildcards available to make the process more flexible. To refer to either all facilities or all priorities, put an asterisk in their place (for example, *.priority, or facility.*). Also, to specify that no priority levels should be logged by a specific facility, use the entry "none" (facility.none).

Each portion of the entry has specific operators available to customize the process even further. When dealing with the type of process to log, it is possible to assign more than one process type to the same priority level, and separate them with commas and no spaces, such as "facility1,facility2.priority". With priorities, instead of selecting a level and having every level above it included, the admin can put an equal sign (=) in front of the priority to only log messages of that level, such as "facility.=priority". Another option is to put an exclamation point (!) in the front to say not to include the priority.

Some clever tricks involve using multiple statements to narrow what exactly to log. More than one facility/priority pair can be used together in a statement when separated by a semicolon (;). The reason this ability counts as a clever trick is that when these pairs are combined within the same statement, a following item can cancel out an existing one. For example, the following line in /etc/syslog.conf:

```
kern.*;kern.!info;kern.!notice              /var/log/kernel
```

is the same as using the following combination of statements:

```
kern.=debug                    /var/log/kernel
kern.warning                   /var/log/kernel
```

Principles For Configuring Software Logs

There are a number of programs, often servers, that keep their own log files. When configuring these logs, keep the following in mind.

If the system logs are on a separate partition, then place the software logs on that same partition or create a new one for them. One painful type of system problem administrators run into is the runaway log file. This can happen when a process runs out of control and starts logging at a rapid rate, at which point the file grows until eventually the entire file system partition it rests on is full—an unfortunate circumstance that can literally halt everything when it occurs in the root file system. However, a runaway log file will not jump partitions, so if all of the log files live in a specific partition, their activity cannot adversely affect other partitions.

Also, although it is a good idea to log a large amount of data for new programs, or newly updated ones, after they have proven themselves to be stable, it is better to trim the data saved to include only the necessary items. This factor is especially important if there is a shortage of disk space. Things to trim out are low-level items, such as debugging data. One exception to this rule if the device is connected to the Internet is connection information. Logging accesses and connection attempts to a service that listens to a port is one of the ways to locate intruder footprints at a later date.

Pruning And Archiving Log Files

The very nature of the log file causes it to grow quite large over time. If these files are never cut back, or pruned, then they will eventually overrun the file system. Utilities are provided with Linux to help avoid this problem.

Logrotate

The program /usr/sbin/logrotate *rotates* the log files, removing older logs and creating new empty files to contain the new log information for Red Hat and Caldera installations. It also has a number of other useful log management functions, all of which are controlled from the file /etc/logrotate.conf. Many administrators run this program daily as a *cron job* (discussed in more detail in a later section) to keep the log situation under control.

Introduction To /etc/logrotate.conf

Logrotate's default configuration file is well commented, taking some of the guesswork out of the equation. Default values are often in place while installing the distribution, so some administrators never see the need to edit this file. The beginning of this configuration file contains global settings that apply to each log file referenced. After this, there are specific settings for each of the files in question, which can override the global values.

Where To Send Log Rotation Errors

The first of these settings involves where to email any errors that occur when processing the log files. Generally, these errors are sent to the root account which would just be entered as "errors root", but they could also be sent to a central administration account on the LAN with the format **errors admin@ mainserver** or even out of the domain if this is desirable for some reason with the format **errors admin@domain.org**.

How Often To Rotate Log Files

Another setting of consequence is the one that controls how often to rotate the log files. The possible values to enter for this are: daily, monthly, and weekly. So, to have the log files rotated automatically once a week, the line "weekly" would be included.

Rotate Or Delete Files

How many previous logs should system administrators keep before either deleting or archiving them? With the **rotate** command, enter the number of rotated logs to keep before either deleting or mailing them to the appropriate address. A value of 0 ("rotate 0") keeps the logs from being rotated at all, and instead, no logs will be saved. Use this value only if you're positive that the data in those logs will never be needed.

Compress Old Log Files

Storing old log files can eventually take up an immense amount of space. One way to deal with this issue is to add the **compress** command, which gzips the old logs as they are rotated.

Rotate Files Of A Certain Size

To set a log file to be rotated once it reaches a certain size, use the **size** command in the format **size** *bytes*. To use kilobytes, use **size** *kbytes* or to use MB use **size** *Mbytes*.

Building A Simple /etc/logrotate.conf

Often, a basic /etc/logrotate.conf comes with a Linux distribution. However, walking through the process can help to understand some of the settings. First, to build the global section, all log-related email in this example should go to logadmin; the site in question has low traffic, so rather than rotating on a time basis, the log files are to be rotated automatically when they reach 1MB. So, the global section would look like the following:

```
# Global settings for /etc/logrotate.conf
errors logadmin
size 1M
```

In the local section, in the case of this example, add a section for the hierarchy /var/log/http/. Because these are Web-related logs, they are still interesting to the admin after they have been rotated, so the choice is to keep six copies around before getting rid of them. After this, the old logs are compressed instead of deleted. Once the logs have been rotated, a new log file has to be created. To do this, the http daemon must be stopped and restarted as well.

The segment for this section might look like the following:

```
# Local settings for Web logs
/var/log/http/* {
    rotate 6
```

```
        compress
        postrotate
          /sbin/killall -HUP httpd
    }
```

SCHEDULING JOBS TO AUTOMATE ADMINISTRATIVE TASKS

System administrators have only so many hours in a day. It is unwise to spend these hours doing simple, routine tasks that could easily be automated. Command-line tasks can be automated with shell scripts, but these shell scripts still have to be run by someone or something, which still takes time and a hefty reminder system or memory to not forget.

Even worse, some tasks are best run in the middle of the night when no or few users are around to share the processor time, or be changing files as the program runs. Even the most dedicated system administrator will not want to have to personally attend to these tasks in addition to his or her regular daily activities.

Introduction To cron

The cron daemon is a system administrator's best friend. Any tasks that can be automated—log rotation, backups, building file lookup databases (for example, locatedb), password checks, quota checks, and more—can be set in cron's configuration files to run on a regular basis.

Both the sysadmin and the users have access to cron's features, utilizing different files and tools to set things up.

System cron Jobs

The system's cron jobs for Red Hat distributions are stored in their own directories within the /etc directory and are broken down into the frequency the tasks are run: /etc/cron.hourly/, /etc/cron.daily/, /etc/cron.weekly/, and /etc/cron.monthly/. For other installations, the cron jobs are stored in /var/spool/cron/crontabs/nobody.

When They Run

The file /etc/crontab lists when the scripts in each of the system cron directories are run. To change when this occurs, edit the timing portion of the crontab. Timing is set by the first five items on a line, which are in the order: minutes after the hour, hour, day of the month, month of the year, and day of the week (Sunday is 0, through Saturday, which is 6). These entries are all listed in number format, and are separated with spaces. They can be individual digits, a combination (separated by commas with no spaces), or a series (separated by dashes and no spaces).

For example, to run the programs and scripts in /etc/cron.weekly/ at the zero mark of 12 A.M. and 12 P.M. every Monday, Wednesday, and Friday, the timing format on the file corresponding to /etc/cron.weekly/ would be:

```
0 0,12 * * 1,3,5
```

Determining What Runs

To ensure that a script or program is run as part of the system cron setup, put the file itself or a link to the file in the appropriate directory (hourly, daily, weekly, or monthly). All items inside that directory are run when the timing set in the crontab is reached.

User cron Files

Users do not have access to the master cron configuration files. Instead, they use a program called "crontab" to edit their personal entries, which are stored in /var/spool/cron under their login names.

Display A User cron Entry

Regardless of whether a user's /var/spool/cron entry is empty, the content can be displayed by the system administrator by typing "crontab –u *user* -l". The users themselves can see the contents of their cron settings by typing "crontab -l".

Create A User cron Entry

To add a new entry or edit an existing one in a user's /var/spool/cron entry, the sysadmin can use the format **crontab –u *user* –e** or the user instead can type "crontab -e". A line in an entry consists of the timing and the command to be run. The timing is formatted just as it is in the system cron file. Afterward, add the command that needs to be executed when the time occurs just as it would be typed at the command line. For example, to run the custom script "/root/bin/totaluser" at the beginning of each month, the format might be:

```
0 0 1 * * /root/bin/totaluser | mail -s "User Totals" root
```

Delete A User cron File

To remove a user's /var/spool/cron entry, perhaps while removing his or her account, type "crontab –u *user* –r". The users themselves can also do this if they want to with the format **crontab –r**.

The at Alternative

Another program that runs jobs at specified times is "at". However, where cron handles items that need to run repeatedly, at handles those that only need to be run once.

Add An at Job

To set up a new at job, use the format **at** *time*, then press Enter. This action places the user at the at prompt, at which point the series of commands to run at the time value should be typed. To complete adding the at job, press Ctrl+D. Any output from this job that was not given a specific destination is then mailed to the user.

at Time Formats

There are a variety of ways to express time for at. For numbers, it accepts both twelve-hour time (for example, 1:00 P.M.) and twenty-four–hour time (for example, 1300). There are also a series of time keywords available: midnight, noon, teatime (4:00 P.M.), or now. The now option must include an increment modifier, that tells at when, relative to the current time, to run the job. First, use the plus sign (+) and then the modifier, which is a number with one of the following keywords: minute, hour, day, week, month, or year.

For example, to create an at job that runs a command 20 minutes from when it is entered into the at queue, do the following sequence:

```
at now + 20 minute
at> echo "I am your at job."
at> ^D
```

Then, 20 minutes later, the user who typed in this sequence would get email with the echo text as the email body.

The space between the plus and the number is important for at to parse things correctly.

at Date Formats

To go along with the time options, there are methods of setting the date as well. The keywords for setting a day are: today, tomorrow, the spelled-out day of the week (for example, Wednesday), or the first three letters of the day of the week (for example, Wed). To go even farther, use the following options: the spelled-out month (for example, June), or the first three letters (for example, Jun), or the four-digit year.

For example, to run a command on July 3, 1999 at 4:00 P.M., the format would be:

```
at 4 pm Jul 3, 1999
at> echo "You told me to send you mail right now."
at> ^D
List At Jobs
```

To list what at jobs are in the queue—either all as root, or the user's jobs—type "atq" or "at -l".

Delete An at Job

To delete an at job from the queue, either type "atrm *job*" or "at -d *job*".

CORE DUMP CONTROL

One effective use for the cron command is core dump control. A core dump is a file containing everything that was in RAM at the time of a problem that causes the system to "dump core." Having a machine with 128MB of RAM means that every core dump is 128MB. A lot of core dumps can lead to a large problem with disk space.

These core dump files are only really useful to programmers. If you are not trying to debug programs, then you probably just want to blindly get rid of the things. You can remove or comment out the **cron** job that takes care of them later if they keep showing up and you want to look into the problem. A programmer's tool available on Linux that helps you to examine core dump files is **gdb**, the GNU Debugger.

To hunt and destroy core files, write a shell script that searches through the filesystem for files with the name "core" or some variation on this. Be careful! If you just automatically wipe everything, then you may run into trouble by deleting files you need. Many system administrators just have **cron** notify them of the listing of potential core files, and then either use another script to get rid of the ones they know are safe to delete, or do it by hand.

CREATING EFFECTIVE DATA BACKUPS

To avoid a system crash ending in disaster, it is imperative for any system administrator to create system backups. When adequate backups are kept, even a hard drive failure can be nothing more than a minor annoyance.

Determining Which Data To Back Up

One of the biggest tasks involved in creating data backups is deciding which data is vital enough to back up. The measuring stick is this: How difficult will the data be to replace if it is lost? If the question makes you queasy, then that data should be included in the backup.

Full Backups

In an ideal world, everyone would have up-to-the-minute backups of every byte of hard drive space. However, this level of maintaining backups is not usually possible. So instead, a system administrator often must pick and choose what parts of the file system to back up regularly.

Remember, however, that a full file system backup even occasionally—say, once a month—can work well if the files that tend to change frequently are backed up on a more regular basis.

Home Directories

If the users on the system are active and tend to fill their directories with work or recreational files, then the /home hierarchy is good to include in the backup. This is especially true if the network in question is an ISP where the users expect to be able to recover their data in case of a crash, or in a place such as a university computing lab where the users may put their Linux accounts to serious use.

Configuration Files

Any file that had to be configured to work to the system administrator's specifications should be included in the backup. Otherwise, hours and hours can be lost after a crash and recovery as the administrator finds more and more software that needs to be tweaked and adjusted.

Custom Programs And Scripts

Any custom software—source and binaries—and scripts used in the regular operation of the system or by the customers, employees, or others, should be included in the backup. Although there is a lot of standard software that can be downloaded after a large loss of data, custom items require investment of person-hours to reproduce, if they can be reproduced at all by the people available.

Data Files

Data files kept by the various programs and scripts on the server should be included in the backup. Losing Web access statistics when preparing to justify the price of advertising on a Web page, user traffic and disk usage statistics when it comes time to bill for overuse, or other important blocks of data can be painful to the business. These instances could actually bring forth lawsuits if data that was vital belonged to customers who can show that backup precautions were part of their customer agreement.

Server Files

The files provided by servers—Web pages, FTP server contents, or anything else that servers are configured to offer to users—should be backed up regularly to avoid data loss.

File System Structure

An often-overlooked part of the backup process is the file system structure. As most experienced system administrators know, one ill-thought-out command can change permissions recursively over an entire directory hierarchy. Using the hit and miss method of changing the permissions as errors occur is not the most efficient way of solving the problem and, in the case of vital files, can lead to system downtime. Including the file system structure in the backup scheme allows the system administrator to quickly look up the previous permissions of the altered structure and return them to normal.

Backup Media

As technology advances, a wider and wider variety of backup media becomes available. An important thing to remember is that a system administrator is not limited to items advertised as backup tools, and that sometimes the necessary hardware is already available in-house for other purposes. Before acquiring any new backup drives, be sure to check the hardware compatibility lists and make sure there are drivers available for Linux.

Floppy Disks

For smaller backup circumstances, floppy disks are sufficient. Small text data files, especially, are easily stored to one floppy or a series of them.

Hard Drives

The hard drive is often overlooked as a backup media. In many ways it is deceptively simple. There are no fancy drivers necessary, and a spare may very well just be lying around awaiting use. The primary limitation is whether the machine has room for any more drives.

An especially useful aspect of using hard drives for backing up is that if full backups are created, the backup drive can replace the original if it crashes.

Zip Disks

Zip disks are excellent backup media due to their large storage capacity. They are especially good for situations in which the data is too large to fit on a floppy disk, or would take so many disks that the work involved in tending to the backups and restorations would be too cumbersome.

Writeable CD-ROMs

Writeable CD-ROMs are excellent for storing data that the administrator needs to keep long-term, but a waste of media if the data needs to be backed up on a regular basis (say daily or weekly). Rewriteable CD-ROMs, however, are useful for regular backups because of their reusable nature.

An advantage of using CDs to back up data is that many of them can be stored in a compact space.

Tapes

Tape drives are popular choices of backup media. Part of the reason for this is that today's tape drives come up to the order of holding gigabytes of information, which is just what a usage-intense server machine might need.

Backup Frequency

Once a system administrator knows what needs to be backed up, and to what type of media, one final question remains. When? The first answer to this is that backups should be done during typically quiet system hours, which often means in the middle of the night. Making backups while the system is in use can cause conflicts, or leave the backed up data being inconsistent because changes were being made to files while they were being copied.

Daily

Some system administrators choose to perform daily backups. This tactic is recommended when at all possible unless the Linux system in question is not used very often. When using this method, it is a good idea to alternate media such that the same item is not being continuously overwritten. For one thing, such heavy use will wear out the backup media and reduce its reliability. Also, if a critical error occurs three days before it is caught, and only one or two days of backups are kept around, then there is no clean copy of the system to return to.

Weekly

Those who prefer larger or full-scale backups might choose to do this on a weekly basis. Although individual files in certain areas may change at a rapid rate, overall, a file system remains fairly consistent from week to week. Once again, it is smart to have more than one media and rotate the items to reduce wear and tear, and keep clean copies around.

Custom

What most people choose in the end is a mix of these philosophies. A weekly or even biweekly backup is made of the full system, and daily backups are made of the more active portions of the file system. Some schemes are even fairly complex, involving making a partial backup every day, a larger partial backup once a week, and a full system backup once a month.

Backup Software

You have a number of choices available to you when you prepare to do your backups, though what you decide upon will partially depend on the media you are using. If you are using a tape drive, then you will need to ensure that the **ftape** driver is installed and functioning. For any type of CD-ROM variant, you will need the proper CD-ROM-burning software. The old standby of using **tar** to make backups to a set of floppies or hard drive is always available, and is actually quite effective. You can also use the **dump** tool.

One application that is growing in popularity in administration circles is the Advanced Maryland Automatic Network Disk Archiver (AMANDA). This tool allows you to centralize Linux backups over a LAN, which most would agree is a handy feature—mix it with SAMBA and you can back up Windows machines as well. This package is available via FTP at **ftp.amanda.org** in the directory /pub/amanda. For more information on it, go to **www.cs.umd.edu/ projects/amanda**. There are also commercial backup options available that are worth investigating.

Verifying Backup Success

Many administrators at one time or another make the mistake of trusting their backups in blind faith. Then comes that fateful day when the system fails. Out comes the trusty backup. They put it in the drive, try it out, and to their dismay, it does not work.

There is no way to stress just how important it is to verify that your backups were made successfully, and that you can retrieve the data from them. Work the bugs out in the scripts or wherever else they may be hiding before you rest easy.

CHAPTER SUMMARY

Because almost all of the Linux certification exams involve system administration, it is crucial to have some feeling for what kinds of skills a sysadmin needs to accomplish. Knowledge of both the day-to-day job of administering a Linux machine, and the longterm issues such as making backups and handling old log files will come in handy.

System administration begins with the users themselves. Policies must be in place if the Linux machine or LAN involves large numbers of users. Accounts have to be created for each user, sometimes even more than one if there are different functions involved, and these accounts must be maintained and managed over time. As situations change and patterns reveal themselves, most system administrators begin changing default user creation information to save themselves precious time tweaking items that come up over and over.

In the name of security, different kinds of accounts have to be considered. Users who do not require shell access should only be given access to the services they need. Passwords need to be expired, and accounts disabled if these passwords are not changed within a reasonable amount of time. Every small step toward making a system more secure saves countless hours later repairing damage from intrusion.

As the system operates, it generates an immense amount of information, much of it going into log files on a day-to-day basis. These logs can be routinely pruned and purged without ever having to handle them by hand thanks to a combination of the logrotate program and the cron daemon. Many more tasks can be automated with a combination of custom shell scripts and cron, freeing the system administrator's time to do things other than routine command-line functions.

6

Finally, no system is considered safe without at least some form of backup. What type of backup scheme is used depends on the media involved, how often the system is idle enough to back up, how much money is available for purchasing backup hardware and software, and what portions of the system must be included.

REVIEW QUESTIONS

1. What command is used to create user accounts?
   a. **useradd**
   b. **add user**
   c. **user –add**
   d. **user –a**

2. What command is used to create user passwords?
   a. **password**
   b. **pw**
   c. **passwd**
   d. **pass**

3. What command would you use to see the default new user creation settings?
   a. **newuser –d**
   b. **useradd –D**
   c. **useradd**
   d. **userdefault**

4. Where is the default user directory information stored?

   a. /etc/skel

   b. /etc/skeleton

   c. /home/default

   d. /home/usr

5. What daemon watches configuration files and runs repeated tasks automatically at specified times?

   a. atd

   b. timed

   c. rund

   d. crond

6. What program might a user utilize to set up a process to run at a future date? [Choose all correct answers]

   a. cron

   b. crontab

   c. attab

   d. at

7. Which of the following is an incorrectly formatted /etc/syslog.conf entry?

   a. `mail.notify`   `/var/log/mail`

   b. `news.=debug`   `/var/log/news`

   c. `*.crit`   `/var/log/danger`

   d. `*.*,emerg`   `/var/log/emergency`

8. Which of the following cron entries sets a process to run every Wednesday at midnight?

   a. 0 0 ★ ★ 3

   b. 0 0 0 0 3

   c. midnight Wed

   d. 0 ★ 0 0 Wed

9. What program changes the log files as they reach their specified change state?

   a. **cron**

   b. **logrotate.conf**

   c. **logrotate**

   d. **crontab**

10. What file storage programs might be useful for making file system backups? [Choose all correct answers]

    a. gzip

    b. back

    c. at

    d. tar

11. What program is used to delete user accounts?

    a. deluser

    b. remuser

    c. usrrem

    d. userdel

12. Which of the following directories does not contain files used for the system cron jobs?

    a. /etc/cron.daily

    b. /etc/cron.weekly

    c. /etc/cron.montly

    d. /etc/cron.yearly

13. What format might you use to create an at job that runs the next day at 2 P.M.?

    a. now + 24 hours

    b. 1400 tomorrow

    c. 2:00 tomorrow

    d. 2 pm ★

14. What program is useful for hunting down the last remnants of an old user?

    a. find

    b. which

    c. locate

    d. userdel

15. What happens to errors that occur during system cron jobs or log rotations?

    a. They are lost in the ether.

    b. They are saved to a log file.

    c. They are mailed to root.

    d. They are sent to the screen and often lost in other information.

16. Which of the following media is least useful for making repeated backups?

    a. hard drive

    b. writeable CD-ROMs

    c. zip disks

    d. floppies

17. What shell would you assign to a user who only needed his or her account to check POP email?

    a. /bin/bash

    b. /bin/tcsh

    c. /bin/ksh

    d. /bin/false

18. Which of the following is not a valid cron timing entry?

    a. 40 4 1,15,30 ★ ★

    b. 30 2,4,6,8 12 9 0

    c. 15 14 20–25 15 4

    d. 1–3 2 ★ ★ 9

19. Where is user login information stored?

    a. /usr/login

    b. /etc/group

    c. /etc/passwd

    d. /usr/home

20. Where is user cron information stored?

    a. /var/spool/crontab

    b. /var/spool/cron

    c. /usr/crontab

    d. /etc/crontab

HANDS-ON PROJECTS

These projects require that you have access to a working Linux system in command-line mode. The directory /root/bin should already exist and the mail program (/bin/mail) must be installed.

Project 6.1

In this project, you will create a user, then adjust the default user settings and create another. Then, use one of the user accounts to create a cron job, an at job, and finally, remove one of the new users.

To create a user, then adjust the default user settings and create another, do the following:

1. Log on as root.

2. Create the new user, user1 by typing "useradd user1".

3. Give the new user the password "project61" by typing "passwd user1", then enter "project61" at both password prompts.

4. Change to the directory /home/user1 and examine its contents.

5. Open a new virtual terminal.

6. Log in as the new user. Note the default appearance.

7. Return to the root terminal.

8. Change to the directory /etc/skel.

9. Open the file .profile or .bash_profile, whichever exists.

10. Add the following line of code late in the profile:

    ```
    PS1="\w> "
    ```

11. Save and exit the file.

12. Create the directory /home/classaccts.

13. Look at the user account creation defaults by typing "useradd -D".

14. Change the default home directory location to /home/classaccts/ by typing "useradd -Db /home/classaccts".

15. Create the account user2 by typing "useradd user2".

16. Give user2 the password "project61" by typing "passwd user2" and entering "project61" at both of the prompts.

17. Change to the /home directory and look at its contents.

18. Change to the /home/classaccts directory and look at its contents.

19. Change to another virtual terminal.

20. Log in to the new account.

21. Note the user prompts and new home directory.

22. Change to the root directory.

23. Change the default user directory back to /home by typing "useradd -Db /home".

24. Return to the user1 virtual terminal.

25. Open the user's cron settings by typing "crontab -e". An empty crontab file opens.

26. Create a cron job that prints "This is part of my homework" at 12:30 P.M. each day to a piece of email to the user by adding the code:

```
30 12 * * * echo "This is part of my homework"
```

27. Save and exit the file.

28. Create an at job that will run a file listing of the home directory at 3 P.M. tomorrow by typing:

```
at 3pm tomorrow
at> ls
at> ^D
```

29. Return to the user2 window and log out of that account.

30. Return to the root window.

31. Remove user2's account by typing "userdel user2".

32. Log out of the user1 account.

33. Log out of the root account.

Project 6.2

In this project, you will create a new system log file and configure how it is rotated. After this, you will write a short backup script and insert it into the weekly system cron. Then, locate the large files on the system for file system pruning purposes.

To create a new system log file and configure how it is rotated, do the following:

1. Log in as root.

2. Edit the file /etc/syslog.conf.

3. Go to the end of the file.

4. To log all authorization program usage with the priority debug and higher to the file /var/spool/project61, add the code:

```
auth.debug                                    /var/spool/project61
```

5. Save and exit the file.

6. Edit the file /etc/logrotate.conf.

7. Go to the end of the file.

8. Add a new local rotation definition for /var/spool/project61. This file should be rotated daily; logrotate should keep five old versions on hand, and then compress them for storage. The code you would add looks like the following:

```
/var/spool/project61 {
   daily
   rotate 5
   compress
}
```

9. Save and exit the file.

10. Create the file /root/bin/backup.

11. Add the following text to the file:

```
#!/bin/bash
# This script is a very rudimentary backup script that
# ensures that all files in /home/user1 are backed
# up to the /tmp directory. The script then lets
# root know that its task has been accomplished.

tar -cvf /home/user1/* user1back.tar
gzip user1back.tar /tmp/user1back.tgz
mail -s "Backup complete" root
```

12. Save and exit the file.

13. Make the file executable by typing "chmod +x /root/bin/backup".

14. To add this script to the weekly system cron jobs, create a link to /etc/cron.weekly with the command **ln –s /root/bin/backup /etc/cron.weekly/backup**.

15. Now search for the files on your system that are over 1MB with the format **find / –size +2000**, where the 2000 stands for 2000 blocks, which is approximately 1MB.

16. Are any of the files returned log files? If so, they are candidates for size rotation. Edit the /etc/logrotate.conf file and add the line "size M1" to the section associated with that file. If there is no section for the file, then create one with the format:

```
/logpath {
   size 1M
}
```

Include any other information desired, such as number of rotations before deleting or mailing logs.

## CHAPTER SEVEN

GNU AND UNIX COMMANDS

AFTER READING THIS CHAPTER AND COMPLETING THE EXERCISES, YOU WILL BE ABLE TO:

➤ Use the command-line interface to enter commands

➤ Redirect the input and output of commands

➤ Connect commands to each other for complex operations

➤ Display, compare, subset, and reformat text files

➤ Monitor and manage processes

➤ Organize and manage files and directories

➤ Use regular expressions in programs

Unix has countless commands, developed to perform any imaginable computer task. All the major commands and utilities have been ported to Linux, often resulting in faster and more efficient versions, which offer more features and fewer bugs. Although the GNU project developed many of the improved commands and utilities, other projects and other programmers have also contributed improvements or new commands. The consistent syntax and interface of Unix commands allows them to interface with one another, making the commands powerful, flexible tools that can perform complex operations.

USING THE UNIX COMMAND LINE

Linux allows you to enter commands at a command line, similar to Unix. Most of the commands entered at the command line perform identically or at least similarly to Unix commands. Although some users may accomplish all of their tasks without ever needing a command line, many tasks, especially system administration tasks, are best performed using commands entered from the command line.

The Command Interface

The shell program is the interface between you and the kernel. A prompt is displayed when the shell is ready to receive input. The shell accepts your command-line input and interprets it, decoding syntax as required; for example, expanding file names that include wildcards or replacing variable names with their values. When the command line is processed into a simple, recognizable command, with required arguments, the shell executes the command.

The shell allows you to stop the execution of a command while it is running. Entering Ctrl+C usually exits a command and returns you to the prompt, but not in all cases. If output continues to display after Ctrl+C is entered, it may be that the program has actually stopped and is not generating any new output, but is simply displaying output that has already been generated and buffered, waiting to be displayed. When all of the buffered output has finished displaying, the prompt will be displayed.

 If Ctrl+C does not halt command execution, Ctrl+Z will. Ctrl+Z suspends execution, rather than stopping the command. In a second step, you may either continue its execution or stop it using the kill command.

Several shells are available for Linux, as discussed in Chapter 5. Differences in commands available exist by shell. The default shell for most Linux systems is bash, the shell developed by GNU. The information in this chapter refers to GNU bash commands. You may find differences when using a different shell.

Commands And Arguments

Command-line instructions consist of commands and arguments, entered at the shell command line using the correct syntax.

Format

Commands are entered by typing the command at the command-line prompt. Pressing the Enter key submits the command to the shell. The format for commands is:

```
Commandname arguments
```

where *commandname* is the name of the command being executed and *arguments* are information that the command uses during execution. The number of arguments accepted varies by command. Most commands use a default value for any arguments that are not entered on the command line. For instance, the **ls** command, used to display a listing of a directory, has the following format:

```
ls directoryname
```

If the directoryname argument is not entered, the name of the current directory is used by default. Thus, typing:

```
ls
```

displays a listing for the current directory. Typing:

```
ls /etc
```

displays a listing for the /etc directory, no matter what the current directory is when you issue the command.

In addition to arguments, most Linux commands accept options, requiring the following format:

```
commandname options arguments
```

Options change the way a command executes. Most options (sometimes called flags) consist of a minus sign (-), followed by a keyword consisting of one or more characters. Continuing with the **ls** example, using **ls** without any options displays a listing of file and directory names only. However, if you want your output to include more or different information, to organize and display the listing differently, or to only include specific types of files, you may use options to request that the **ls** command produce a different output. For instance:

```
ls -ld
```

also produces a listing of the directory, but formats the output differently, including much more information, and listing only subdirectories.

 Linux commands that are too long to be typed on one command line can be continued on to a second command line by typing a backslash (\) as the last character in the first line.

Built-in Commands

Shells can execute two types of commands: built-in commands and system commands. The built-in commands are subroutines in the shell program itself that are run when the correct command syntax is entered at the command line. Built-in commands are specific to a shell, but most shells contain similar commands. Some shell commands for the bash shell are **cd**, **alias**, **bg**, **break**, **echo**, **exit**, **for**, **help**, **history**, **if**, **jobs**, **kill**, **pwd**, **trap**, **while**, and many more. To see a complete list of built-in commands for a shell, type "help".

System Commands

Most Linux commands are system commands. System commands are programs, stored as files in the filesystem, that are run by typing the command name. Linux distributions include the Linux command set. If any command is missing or destroyed, you can download and reinstall it. You can replace any specific command with a newer version. You can add commands—those obtained from other sources or those you have written yourself.

As a system administrator, it's your job to be sure that all your user accounts can access the system commands. There are two issues to be addressed: location and permissions. When a command name is typed, the shell will search through the user's path until it finds a file with the specified name. If it searches the entire path without finding the name, it returns a "command not found" error message. If it finds the specified file but the permissions are set so that the user cannot execute the file, it returns a "permission denied" error message.

Normally when Linux is installed, the system commands are installed in a directory on the users' default path with the proper protection set. Usually, the commands are located in /bin, /sbin, and /usr/bin (bin for binary) with read and execute allowed for everyone and the path to the bin directories included in the default user path. In general, user commands are in /bin and /usr/bin and /sbin contains system administration commands requiring system privileges to run. Users can, of course, change their own paths. If a user sud-denly cannot execute commands, /bin or /usr/bin was probably removed from the user's path statement.

If you add commands to the system, you could add them to /bin or /usr/bin; however, local commands are usually stored in a local directory, to distinguish them from the normal system commands. Often, local commands are stored in /usr/local/bin. If you add commands in a local directory, different from the system commands, be sure the user default path includes the local directory.

In the command format, *commandname* can be a path, rather than just the file name. Perhaps there is more than one program with the same name so you need to specify which program file to execute. Perhaps the program file is in a test directory or your home directory, not on your path. Perhaps you intend to improve efficiency by sending the shell directly to the program, saving the search time. Often, the absolute path is specified in shell scripts to save time and to be sure the correct version of the command is called. For instance, to run your own version of the **ls** command, which is located in the current directory, type the following path:

```
./ls
```

The shell will execute the local **ls** command, rather than the system **ls** command.

Help

Linux has a very large number of commands. No one can reasonably be expected to remember the names and syntax of all the commands. Help with the details is available in Linux using the **help**, **man**, and **info** commands.

Typing **help** displays a list of the built-in commands for the shell. You can see additional information on any of the listed commands by typing:

```
help commandname
```

Information on system commands is available using the **man** command. For information on a specific command, type:

```
man commandname
```

If you don't know the name of the command, you can enter:

```
man -k searchterm
```

and **man** displays a list of all the commands that include *searchterm* in their description. For instance, if you enter:

```
man -k copy
```

a listing of all the commands that include the word "copy" in their description is displayed. Some of the lines that might be included are as follows:

```
cp      copy files and directories
dd      convert and copy a file
strcpy    copy a string
uucp    Unix to Unix copy
```

The man pages are divided into nine sections (shown in Table 7.1), depending on the type of command being described.

Table 7.1   Man page sections.

Section	Type
1	Executable program or shell commands
2	System calls (functions provided by the kernel)
3	Library calls (functions within system libraries)
4	Special files (usually found in /dev)
5	File formats and conventions, e.g., /etc/passwd
6	Games
7	Macro packages and conventions
8	System administration commands (usually only for a privileged user)
9	Kernel routines (nonstandard)

If you know the section of the command you are looking up, you can type

```
man 1 rm
```

for faster display.

As system administrator, you will sometimes need to add man pages to the system. Many applications that you may install will include man pages that need to be added. If you write any commands for your users, you'll need to add a man page for the new command. To add a man page, add a file with a specific name to the appropriate subdirectory, checking that the protection codes are set correctly.

The man pages are stored within subdirectories inside the /usr/man hierarchy. This hierarchy is divided into the sections man1, man2, and so on; each man page is kept in a separate file to allow for simple removal and updating. The man page files are named for the command being documented, ending in *.sectionnumber*. For instance, the file containing the man page for the **rm** command is named rm.1, which would be stored in /usr/man/man1. Man pages are written in a special format called nroff. Nroff files are ASCII files with embedded text formatting commands. In some cases, the files are compressed to save space. If so, the file will have a gz extension, for example, rm.1.gz.

When the **man** command is issued, it searches the man directories for a file with a name that matches the argument given in the **man** command. If a section number is included in the command line, **man** searches only the subdirectory for the indicated section. The man program formats the man page using nroff, uncompressing the file if necessary, and displays it using the **less** command.

Configuration information used by the **man** command is stored in /etc/man.conf (or in /usr/lib/man.config in some distributions). The location of the man directories is set in the configuration file. The path to the directories should also be stored in the environmental variable, MANPATH. A likely location for the man pages is /usr/doc.

The **info** command displays online hypertext documentation, consisting of topics arranged hierarchically. If info is entered without arguments, the top-level index of topics will be displayed. Some topics include explanations of bash, utilities, and **gawk**.

Info files are created by writing documents in the Texinfo system format and converting them into info system files using the makeinfo utility. The info files are individual pages stored in files with names that begin with info. They are usually located in /usr/info. The info system includes instructions for creating info pages. Type "info texinfo".

Entering Commands

Linux provides great flexibility when entering commands, allowing you to:

➤ Enter only the first few characters of file and directory names

➤ Enter more than one command on a line

➤ Repeat previous commands

➤ Use variables in commands

➤ Use the output of a command as an argument on the command line

➤ Edit command lines

When you enter a file or directory name, you need to only type enough letters to uniquely identify the file name. Then, press the Tab key and the shell will fill in the rest of the characters.

You may enter multiple commands on a single line by separating the commands with a semicolon (;), as follows:

```
hostname;pwd;ls
```

You may repeat a command in several ways, as shown in Table 7.2.

You may use variables in your commands. A common use is to **echo** the contents of a variable. For instance, the command:

```
echo Hello!
```

produces the following display:

```
Hello!
```

Table 7.2 Repeat commands, their descriptions, and examples.

Repeat Command	Description	Example
!! (two exclamation points)	Repeats the last command entered.	Date
		Thu Aug 12 13:11:48 PDT 1999 !! date Thu Aug 12 13:11:48 PDT 1999
		You typed !! and the shell echoed date and executed it.
Up Arrow	Displays previous commands, one at a time, on the command line.	cp file1 file2
		cd .. date press the up arrow press the up arrow press the up arrow cp file1 file2 is now displayed on the command line. Press enter to submit the **cp** command shown.
!c (one exclamation point and enough of the beginning characters of a previous command to uniquely identify it)	Repeat a previous command beginning with the characters entered.	cp file1 file2
		cd .. date !cp The sequence of commands executed is: 1) cp file1 file2 2) cd .. 3) date 4) cp file1 file2. !cp is required to specify the **copy** command because the **cd** command also begins with c. Typing !c would repeat the **cd** command.

(continued)

Table 7.2 Repeat commands, their descriptions, and examples *(continued)*.

Repeat Command	Description	Example
!*n* (one exclamation point and a number that is the line number of a command in the history file)	Repeats the previous command shown on the specified line of the history file.	Date
		cp file1 file2
		cd ..
		history
		1 date
		2 cp file1 file2
		3 cd
		!2
		cp file1 file2
		The three lines after the history command are the output of the history command. Typing !2 causes command number 2 to echo and execute.

The same display can be produced using a variable. Type the following:

```
var1=Hello!
echo $var1
```

You may use system variables in commands as well. For instance:

```
cd $HOME
```

changes the directory to your home directory.

You can use the output of a command as an argument in a command line. Enclose the command in back quotes (') to identify the argument as a command to be executed. For instance:

```
echo 'date'
```

displays the following output:

```
Thu Aug 12 13:11:48 PDT 1999
```

Some commands are quite long when you include all their options and arguments. Linux allows you to correct an error without retyping the entire command. If you enter a command and receive an error message due to a typing mistake, you can repeat the command with a simple substitution using carats (^). The format is:

```
^oldtext^newtext
```

For example:

```
mv /user/local/bin/file1 /usr/local/bin/file11
file not found
^ser^sr
mv /usr/local/bin/file1 /usr/local/bin/file11
```

The first line is the command, with an error in the pathname—user should be usr. A "file not found" error message is returned. The third line is a substitution command, directing that **ser** in the previous command be replaced with **sr**. The command with the substitution in place is echoed and executed.

In some cases, you'll notice an error in a command before you press Enter. You can correct the mistakes without retyping the entire command. Use the arrow keys to move to the location on the command line that needs correction. Ctrl+A moves the cursor to the beginning of the line; Ctrl+E moves the cursor to the end of the line. Any characters you type will be inserted at the cursor location. Ctrl+D deletes the character under the cursor. Esc+S deletes the word to the right of the cursor.

Running Commands In The Background

Some commands take noticeable time to run. For instance, a **Find** command searching the entire file space for a file name may take up to several minutes to execute. Until the prompt returns, no further commands can be issued. The command executing at the command line is said to be in the foreground. Only one job can be in the foreground at a time. In Linux, you may execute commands in the background as well as in the foreground. Jobs in the background do not tie up the system, leaving the command line available for other uses. You can run many commands in the background simultaneously.

To send a command directly to the background, add an ampersand (&) at the end of the command. A number is assigned and displayed when the job is sent to the background. The first job sent to the background is 1, the next is 2, and so on. The job number is used to monitor the status of the background command. The shell displays a message when the background command completes execution.

You can also send a command to the background while it is running. Two steps are required:

```
Ctrl+z
bg
```

Ctrl+Z suspends the job. The **bg** command moves the job to the background where it resumes execution.

The **jobs** command, with no arguments, displays the job numbers, command executed, and status of your background jobs. You can bring any job to the foreground by typing the following:

```
fg %jobnumber
```

You can stop the execution of jobs in the background using the **kill** command with the following format:

```
kill %jobnumber
```

Creating Command Aliases

Linux allows you to assign an alias (nickname) to a command. When you type the alias, the command is entered. An alias is useful if you enter the same long command frequently.

To create an alias, enter:

```
alias nickname='command'
```

whcre *nickname* is the alias or short name for the command and *command* is the command being aliased. For instance, if you often need to list a directory with a long name, you can create an alias for the command, as shown here:

```
alias lsdir5='ls -l /usr/local/dir1/dir2/dir3/dir4/dir5'
```

Type "alias" without any arguments to display a list of all your current aliases. Any aliases you create during a session are lost when you log out. If you want an alias to be available all the time, add the **alias** command to your .login file.

As system administrator, you may want to create some aliases that are available for all your users to use. Perhaps your Linux system is used for a special purpose. If you know tasks that your users perform repeatedly, you can develop some aliases to assist them.

Loops And Scripting At The Command Line

Now that you understand how to write shell scripts, you do not need to create a script file to be able to utilize all of the functions available there. Remember that a shell script is essentially a string of functions you could perform at the command line if you wanted to go through the entire process.

Say that you want to rename a known series of files. These files are originally named file1, file2, and file3 in the directory ~/images. The problem is that you forgot to include the file type in the name. You can rename each of these by hand, or you can start a quick **for** loop at the command line as follows:

```
$ for file in ~/images/file1 ~/images/file2 ~/images/file3
```

This statement is enough to begin the loop. Notice that you have not included the "do" portion of the for statement here. Once you press Enter, the prompt changes. Here is where you type in the rest of the loop:

```
> do
> mv $file $file".jpg"
> done
```

Now do a directory listing and what was file1, file2, and file3 is now file1.jpg, file2.jpg, and file3.jpg. If you prefer to do things all on one line, you can. This same example can be typed in the following format:

```
$ for file in ~/images/file1 ~/images/file2 ~/images/file3; do mv $file
$file".jpg"; done
```

Making Use Of Environment Variables

Setting and viewing the contents of environment variables was discussed in Chapter 5. These items are useful at a practical, command-line level; they are not reserved for use in login and shell scripts. At any time you can either create or modify an environment variable.

Environment variables are useful whenever you need to enter the same values repeatedly. Shell scripts can set an environment variable for other scripts or commands to use. If you have a network with a number of different types of machines—even if they are all different flavors of Linux or Unix—you can use the environment variables to check and store information necessary for programs to customize their responses.

Remember that environment variables may be considered "global" but they really only last while that environment exists. Even if you log in simultaneously on two different virtual terminals you do not have access to the same environment variables. So, any environment variable you want access to in multiple sessions needs to be set in one of your login files.

COMMON COMMANDS

The most frequently used commands are the text processing and file management commands discussed in the following sections.

Processing Text Streams

Text is stored in files of ASCII character codes. When operations are performed on the files, the text is processed in a stream of single characters, including the character that marks the end of the line. The stream flows into the processing program and out, displaying on the screen. Commands that operate on a text stream are called filters, which are designed to perform specified, distinct operations on text as they pass through the filter.

Displaying Text

The simplest text operation is to display text. The simplest display command is the **echo** command, which displays one line of text, taken either from an argument or from a variable. For example:

```
echo This is a line of text.
This is a line of text.
echo $HOME
/home/user1
```

Commands that display text files are listed in Table 7.3.

To display the text in a file, type the following:

```
command filename
```

Table 7.3   File display commands.

Command	Description
cat	Displays entire file to the screen.
more	Displays file to screen one page at a time.
less	Displays file to screen one page at a time. Has more options than the **more** command.
head	Displays first few lines of a file. Displays 10 lines by default. To specify the number of lines, type: head -30 filename.
tail	Displays last few lines of a file. Displays 10 lines by default. To specify the number of lines, type: tail -30 filename.
zcat	Displays the contents of a gzipped or compressed text file to STDOUT.

If you are not sure that a file contains text, check the file type before displaying it. Only text files should be displayed on the screen. Check the file type by typing "file filename".

The **more** and **less** commands are filters that display one screen of text and pause. Press the spacebar to display the next screen of text. Press **q** to stop the display. Both **more** and **less** have many commands for displaying the text, such as displaying specific numbers of lines, searching for specific text strings, and so on. **Less** starts more quickly and allows backward movement through the file. See the man page for a description of all the commands and options.

Searching Files For Text

Often, you'll need to search through files for a line or so of text. For instance, suppose that operations performed for an application, including errors, are recorded in the log file. You need to know the number of errors that have been logged. The log file, though, is 3MB—you can look at the file and count the errors line by line, or you can use a program to search the file and report the number of times the word "error" was found.

grep is a filter that searches through one or more files to find specified text strings and outputs information resulting from the search. The format is:

```
grep options string filenames
```

where *string* is the text to be matched. *String* can be a string to be matched exactly or a regular expression. Regular expressions are patterns to be matched, such as any uppercase character or any string of three numbers. Regular expressions are described later in this chapter, in the "Editing Text Files Using **sed** And **awk**" section.

The options determine the parameters of the search and the content and format of the output. For instance, **–i** means to ignore the case when searching for the string, **–v** instructs **grep** to output each line that does not match the string, and **–c** instructs **grep** to output a count of the number of lines containing the string. To search for the string, wizard of oz, type the following:

```
grep -in "wizard of oz" *
```

The **i** option instructs **grep** to ignore case. The **n** option instructs **grep** to output the line numbers. The string is enclosed in quotes because it contains spaces. The asterisk instructs **grep** to search all files in the current directory. The output lists the name of the file where the string was found, followed by the line number within the file, followed by the text of the line.

Two variations, **fgrep** and **egrep**, are also available. Both run slightly faster but have less flexibility. **fgrep** searches only for exact text strings, not for regular expressions. **egrep** searches for some regular expressions, but not all.

Sorting Text Files

Linux includes a filter that sorts the lines of text in a file. Used without any options, **sort** orders the file in ascending order by the value of the ASCII code for the character. The special characters are first, numbers second, uppercase letters third, and lowercase letters last. **sort** uses as many characters in the line as necessary to determine the sort order. For instance, the following file, called test1, is shown before and after it is sorted using the command:

```
sort test1
Unsorted File     Sorted File
AAAA              $$$$
aaaa xxxx         ,,,,
aaaa bbbb         ....
....              1111
$$$$              4444
cccc              6666
BBBB              AAAA
bbbb              BBBB
,,,,              XXXX
xxxx              aaaa bbbb
XXXX              aaaa xxxx
rrrr              bbbb
1111              cccc
vvvv              rrrr
6666              vvvv
4444              xxxx
```

sort has many options that affect the sort order and output, as shown in Table 7.4.

Table 7.4   sort command options.

Option	Description
-b	Ignore leading spaces and tabs.
-c	Do not process files if they are already sorted.
-d	Dictionary order.
-f	Ignore case.
-help	Print a help message.
-i	Ignore non-printing characters.
-m	Merge input files and sort the resulting merged file.
-n	Sort in numerical order.

(continued)

Table 7.4 **sort** command options *(continued)*.

Option	Description
-o*filename*	Write the output to a file named *filename*.
-r	Sort in reverse order.
-t*c*	The character, *c*, is used to delimit fields.
-u	Identical input lines are output only once.
-z*recsz*	Provide recsz bytes for any one line in the file. This option prevents abnormal termination of sort in certain cases.
+n [-m]	Sort line using the characters between fields n and m only. If m is not specified, sort using the characters from field n to the end of the line.
-M	Treat the first three characters as a month.

Comparing Files

Often, you need to know whether two files are identical or what the differences are between two text files. The **diff** command provides that information. Type:

```
diff file1 file2
```

to have **diff** compare file1 with file2 and output each line that is different. Lines from file1 are shown with < at the beginning of the line; lines from file2 are shown with >. Using the option **–q** produces output stating that there are differences without printing the lines that differ. Other options include **–i** to ignore case and **–c** to show the lines before and after the lines that differ.

The **diff3** command compares three files. With the **–m** option, it produces out-put that merges the changes in two files into the original file.

Editing Text Files Using **sed** And **awk**

Editing text files interactively, using an editor such as **vi**, was discussed earlier. However, when you need to apply a change or set of changes repeatedly, possibly to more than one file, a filter offers a speedier and more efficient way of editing the file. Linux provides two commands for noninteractive text editing: **sed** and **awk** (usually the GNU implementation of **awk** called **gawk**).

sed is used for simple editing tasks, whereas **awk** can be used for more complicated text editing and formatting tasks. **sed** offers the same basic editing commands that are available for interactive editing, such as inserting text, deleting text, and substituting text. However, when using **sed**, you can create a set of editing instructions and apply them to the entire file in one step. The set of instructions is saved in a script that can be used to edit any number of files. In contrast, **awk** provides a set of programming functions, including use of variables, use of arithmetic and string operators, and use of simple programming constructs, such as loops. **awk** allows complex reformatting of a structured text file. For instance, **awk** can be used to transform data into a report—to add headings and comments, move and reformat columns of data, selectively include or exclude data, and reorganize lines into separate sections.

Both commands have similar formats. Both can apply instructions read from the command line or read from a separate script file. The format to include the instructions in the command line is

```
commandname 'instruction' filename
```

where *commandname* is **sed** or **awk** (or **gawk**), *instruction* is the **sed** or **awk** instruction to be applied to the file, and *filename* is the input text file to be edited. To instruct **sed** or **awk** to apply instructions read from a script file, replace the instruction on the command line with a pointer to the script file, as follows

```
commandname -f scriptfilename filename
```

where *scriptfilename* is the file containing the **sed** or **awk** instructions.

Both **sed** and **awk** process the input text file one line at a time. A line is read; the set of instructions is applied to the line, one instruction at a time; the next line is read; and so on, through the entire file. The difference between **sed** and **awk** lies in the instruction set available for processing each line of text.

sed command syntax is similar to **vi** commands in the following ways:

➤ The command is one character.

➤ Any arguments required by the command follow the command.

➤ Line numbers or regular expressions before the command specify which lines are processed using the command.

The most frequently used **sed** commands are listed in Table 7.5.

You can include line numbers before the command to specify which lines the command should edit. You can specify one line number for the line to be edited (that is, **1d** to delete line 1) or two line numbers to edit all lines between the two line numbers (such as **1,3d** to delete lines 1, 2, and 3). You can use a dollar sign ($) to represent the last line. If nothing is specified before the command, all lines are edited. For instance, the following **sed** instruction would delete all lines in the input file:

```
d
```

Table 7.5 **sed** commands.

Command	Syntax	Description
a	a\ string	Append string following the line.
c	c\ string	Change line. Replace it with string.
d	d	Delete line.
i	i\ string	Insert string before the line.
p	p	Print line. The default is to print each line after processing. If the -n option is used, the lines are not output after processing.
s	s/oldstring /newstring/flag	Substitute newstring for oldstring. Flag can be: g - replace all occurrences of oldstring (the default is to replace the first occurrence) p - print w*file* - write line to *file*

In contrast, the following **sed** instruction would delete all lines from line 5 to the end of the file, keeping lines 1, 2, 3, and 4.

```
5,$d
```

You can also specify lines using regular expressions. Regular expressions are combinations of characters that represent patterns to be matched by text strings. For instance, you might write a regular expression that represented blank lines or all lines that begin with a blank character. The command would then be applied only to lines that match the pattern given in the regular expression. Regular expressions are discussed in detail later in this chapter. Regular expressions are enclosed in forward slashes (/). For instance, the following **sed** instruction uses a regular expression:

```
/^$/d
```

This command deletes all blank lines in the text file.

awk can be used for more complicated processing of the text file. **awk** is a programming language, a simple one that is quite structured with a limited instruction set. The syntax and constructs of **awk** are similar to C or to shell script programming, as described in Chapter 5.

awk provides some built-in variables and allows you to create and manipulate additional variables. When **awk** reads a line, it separates the line into fields. By default, **awk** uses spaces to identify fields, but you can change it to divide the line into fields using any character you specify. You can reference each field as a variable, numbered by its sequence on the line. The first field is $1; the second field is $2, and so on. $0 references the entire line. If you have the following input line

```
The house is red
```

and use the following **awk** instructions:

```
{ print $4 " " $2 }
{ print $0 }
```

your output is:

```
red house
The house is red
```

Other system variables built into **awk** are:

➤ **FS** Field separator (default is space)

➤ **NF** Number of fields in the current line

➤ **NR** Line number of the current line

➤ **FILENAME** Name of the current input file

You can create a variable by assigning a value to it using an expression. For example:

```
a = "Hello"
x = 3
y = x+2
z = y/x
```

awk programs are organized into three sections: the BEGIN section, the main program, and the END section. The main program is the loop that reads each line and processes it. **awk** instructions in the main section are executed each time a new line is read from the input file. The BEGIN section contains instructions to be executed only once, before the program begins processing the input file; the END section contains instructions to be executed once, after the program has completed processing all the records in the input text file. The format of the BEGIN section is:

```
BEGIN { awk instructions }
```

awk instructions are separated by a semicolon. For example:

```
BEGIN { x=1;y=2 }
```

The end section has a similar format:

```
END { awk instructions }
```

The BEGIN and END sections are not required. If **awk** does not see the BEGIN or END keyword, it assumes all the instructions are part of the main text-processing–loop section.

A simple, basic use for **awk** is to selectively output lines from the text file. For instance, perhaps you have a file containing names and ages of people and you want to select only the names of the people who are 21 or older. **awk** can do this easily. Because **awk** does not output the records processed, it would only be necessary to identify the lines containing people over 21 and instruct **awk** to output the selected lines. One if statement would be sufficient for the required task. Suppose the input file contains:

```
John Smith 18
Henry Jones 22
Mary Lewis 15
```

The following **awk** script file is created and run:

```
{ if ( $3 >= 21 ) print $0 }
```

where $3 refers to the third field on each line, >= means greater than or equal to, and $0 refers to the entire line.

The output is:

```
Henry Jones 22
```

The operators that can be used in the if statement are:

➤ > Greater than

➤ < Less than

➤ >= Greater than or equal to

➤ <= Less than or equal to

➤ == Equal to

➤ != Not equal to

Suppose you wanted to reformat the text so that the last name was first on each line. The new **awk** script file is:

```
{ if ( $3 >= 21 ) print $2 ", " $1 " " $3 }
```

Notice that the print statement specifies the exact characters to be placed between each field by enclosing the characters in quotes—a comma and a space between fields 2 and 1 and a space between fields 1 and 3.

The output is:

```
Jones, Henry 22
```

Another way to select lines for output is to look for lines containing text that matches a specific pattern. The pattern can be a specific string or a regular expression. The string to be matched is placed between forward slashes at the beginning of the instruction. For instance, using the same input file above, the following **awk** script is created and run:

```
/Jones/ { print $0 }
```

The output is:

```
Henry Jones 22
```

Remember, this is Linux, so lines containing jones or JONES would not be output. You can use an exclamation point (!) in front of the pattern to mean not. Thus, the script file:

```
!/Jones/ { print $0 }
```

outputs the following:

```
John Smith 18
Mary Lewis 15
```

All lines are output that do not contain the pattern, Jones. Suppose you wanted to select only lines for people whose last names were Jones, but not whose first names were Jones. You can specify which field the pattern must match using the following instruction:

```
$2 ~ /Jones/ { print $0 }
```

You can also use !~. The pattern to be matched can be a regular expression. A regular expression is an expression that provides a general pattern for matching, such as any three numbers in a row or two characters followed by a nine or an eight. For instance, the following **awk** instruction would output all lines that were not blank:

```
!/^&/ { print $0 }
```

Detailed information on creating regular expressions is provided later in this chapter.

You can print variables you create, as well as the system variables. Suppose you have an input file containing students' names and grades and want to print a report of student grade averages. The input file is:

```
Jones 78 70 0
Lewis 99 98 90
Wong 88 94 87
Reyes 80 90 75
```

You could use the following script:

```
{ tot = $2 + $3 + $4
   n = NF-1
   print $0 " The average is " tot/n }
```

The second line uses the system variable NF (number of fields) to determine the divisor (n) to use in the third line. The second line is included to show the use of a system variable. For this example, the second line could have been left out and 3 used as the divisor in line 3, rather than n. The output is:

```
Jones 78 70 0 The average is 49.3333
Lewis 99 98 90 The average is 95.6667
Wong 88 94 87 The average is 89.6667
Reyes 80 90 75 The average is 81.6667
```

You can format the output into a more orderly form using the printf statement, rather than the print statement. The printf statement allows you to specify spacing and tabs. The format is:

```
printf ("format",arguments)
```

To format your output, use the following printf statement instead of the print statement above

```
printf("%s\t\t%d\t%d\t%d\t%s%4.2f\n", $1, $2, $3, $4, "The average = ",
tot/n )
```

where $s indicates a string variable, \t is a tab, %d indicates a decimal integer, $4.2f indicates a floating point decimal number that is four columns wide with two decimal places, and \n is a newline character. The output is:

```
Jones           78     70     0      The average = 49.33
Lewis           99     98     90     The average = 95.67
```

```
Wong              88      94      87      The average = 89.67
Reyes             80      90      75      The average = 81.67
```

This description of **awk** barely scratches the surface of its capabilities. It is a programming language specifically designed to manipulate text and has many tools to fulfill its function. As a programmer, you can use conditional statements, for and while loops, and arrays; pass arguments into the script from the command line; import shell variables into the script; use built-in arithmetic and string functions; and use other programming constructs. If you have many text formatting tasks on your system, you can save yourself considerable time and effort by learning more about **awk**.

Getting Statistics On Text Files

You can get statistics on text files, or even the output of commands, with the **wc** command. When used by itself, it gives the number of lines, words, and characters in the file or STDIN. Flags can also be used to target **wc** to only return a specific count, as shown in Table 7.6.

When used on a file, the syntax for **wc** is straightforward:

```
wc filename
```

You can also use it to analyze the output of commands. For example, if you wanted to know how many processes were currently running, you might type:

```
ps aux | wc -l
```

This command would give you a count of how many lines were output, which would then have to be adjusted for the one header line at the top of the process list.

Basic File Management

As discussed earlier, Linux is organized into a filesystem—a collection of directories organized into a tree, with root (/) at the top of the tree. Directories make it possible to locate files quickly. Files are collections of information (bits) and are physically scattered throughout the storage medium. The file system contains

Table 7.6   Flags available for the **wc** command.

Flag	Purpose
-c	Limit the count to the number of characters.
-l	Limit the count to the number of lines.
-w	Limit the count to the number of words.

information about the files, including pointers to the physical location of the file contents. Access to files is made easier by storing files in directories. A file can be located by following a path down the tree structure, rather than by searching the entire file space.

Directories are special files that contain a listing of the files in the directory. The entry for each file contains the name of the file and a pointer to information about the file. The file name is a sequence of up to 256 characters. The pointer is an index number that points to an individual inode, located in a list (array) of inodes, one inode for each file in the filesystem. The inode contains information about the file and pointers to the physical location of the data in the file (see Figure 7.1).

All directories contain, at minimum, entries for . and .. with pointers to the inode for the entries. The . entry refers to the current directory and points to the inode for that directory; the .. entry refers to the parent directory immediately above the current directory and points to the inode for that directory. Clearly, more than one directory entry can point to the same inode.

File Attributes

The file information stored in the inode includes: file type, file protections, owner and group ids, file size, date and time the file was created, and date and time the file was last modified. To display the file attributes, use the **ls** command, the most used Linux command. The **ls** command has many options that control the output. One of the most useful is –l, for a long listing that lists many of the file attributes. Options allow you to specify which attributes are displayed, the format of the display, which file types are displayed, and the order in which the file listings are displayed. See the man page for a description of all the options.

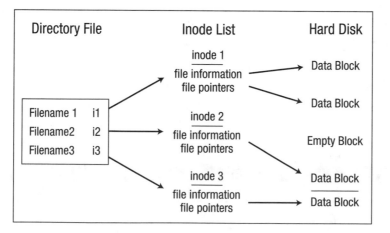

Figure 7.1   Directories in Linux.

The name of a file can be changed using the **mv** command:

```
mv file1 file2
```

file2 is created with the same contents and attributes as file1. file1 no longer exists. The index number in the directory entry for file2 now points to an inode containing the same file information that was stored for file1.

Some commands only work correctly on a specific type of file. To determine the file type before attempting operations on the file, enter:

```
file filename
```

Some of the file types that Linux recognizes are: ASCII text, C program text, shell commands, empty, directory, symbolic link, executable. File protections, owners, and groups are discussed in previous chapters. The file size attribute is displayed in the output from the **ls** –l command, expressed in bytes. The maximum file size on an ext2 filesystem is 2GB.

7

The date attributes of a file can be changed using the **touch** command. Most commonly, the last access and last modified dates are updated to the current date using:

```
touch filename
```

You can specify that only the last access date is updated with the –a option or only the last modified date with the –m option. If the file name given as an argument does not exist, touch creates an empty file with the specified name. The –c option prevents the creation of a new file.

You can specify that touch update the date attributes to a specific date using the –t option. The time specified must be in the format: **MMDDhhmmCCYYss**, where MM is month, DD is day, hh is hour, mm is minute, CC is century, YY is year, and ss is seconds. CC, YY, and ss are optional. For example:

```
touch -t 01031455 file1
```

The date attributes for file1 are updated to January 3, 1999, 1:55 PM. You can also change the dates to equal the dates of another file using the following:

```
touch -r file2 file1
```

The date attributes for file1 are changed to be the same as the date attributes for file2.

Adding, Changing, And Removing Directories

Files are organized into directories. All files are located in a directory, even if it is /, the top directory. A file can be created in a directory or an existing file can be moved from one directory to another. Before a file can be added to a directory, the directory must exist.

Directories are created using the **mkdir** command. The format is:

```
mkdir directorypath
```

where *directorypath* is the path and name of the directory being created. To create a directory, you must have write permission in the parent directory where the directory is being added. The -p option creates any parent directories if they don't already exist. For instance:

```
mkdir -p dir1/dir2
```

specifies a directory called dir1 in the current directory and a directory dir2 in the dir1 directory. dir2 is created in dir1. If the dir1 directory does not already exist, it is created and dir2 is created in dir1. You would need to have write permission in the current directory.

The new directory is created with the permission specified in the system umask. Permissions and the **umask** command are discussed in Chapter 3. The permissions can be set specifically for the directory being created using the -m option.

Files and directories can be moved from one parent directory to another using the **mv** command. To move a file from one directory to another, type:

```
mv dir1/file1 dir2
```

If a directory called dir2 already exists, file1 is moved into dir2 and is no longer in dir1. If there is no directory called dir2, a file called dir2 is created containing the contents of file1, and file1 is removed. To move a directory, type:

```
mv dir1 dir2
```

All the files in dir1 are moved to dir2. If dir2 does not exist, dir2 is created and all the files in dir1 are put into dir2. dir1 no longer exists. If dir2 already exists, dir1 is moved into dir2, along with all its files, for example, the result being dir2/dir1. You can move a directory from one parent directory to another using:

```
mv dir1/dir2 dir3/dir2
```

The command **rmdir** removes directories. The -p option can be used to remove any intervening parent directories. However, **rmdir** only removes empty directories. For example:

```
rmdir dir1/dir2
```

removes both dir1 and dir2, if they are empty. If either directory contains files, the directory is not deleted. You can use the **rm** command to delete directories that contain files. If the –r option is used and the argument is a directory name, **rm** deletes the entire directory and all of its contents, including subdirectories. Use extreme caution with this option… it can be dangerous. Just consider the potential night-mare if superuser were to issue the command: **rm –r /**.

Obtaining User Information

7

There are certain commands available to you that allow you and all of the users to get information on who is logged in to the system, and some information about them. The type of information you can get is limited in some cases to what the user determines.

Who Is Logged In

To get a listing of who is logged in at any given time, use the **w** or **who** commands. Each of these items looks at the utmp file and gives information based on the contents. The shorter command, **w**, gives the most detailed response. An example is shown in Figure 7.2.

In contrast, the **who** command gives much less information, as shown with the same user list in Figure 7.3.

```
[root@deedee /root]# w
 10:20am  up 6 days, 20:51,   4 users,  load average: 2.31, 0.88, 0.33
USER     TTY     FROM            LOGIN@   IDLE   JCPU    PCPU   WHAT
root     tty1    -               4Dec99   1:23   12.63s  0.08s  sh /usr/X11R6/b
dee      tty2    -               Sun 3pm  1:28   0.50s   0.15s  -bash
bob      tty3    -               10:15am  5:20   0.34s   0.13s  bash
mary     tty4    -               10:15am  5:04   0.34s   0.12s  bash
[root@deedee /root]# 
```

Figure 7.2 Output from the **w** command.

```
[root@deedee /root]# who
root     tty1    Dec  4 14:11
dee      tty2    Dec  5 15:25
bob      tty3    Dec 11 10:15
mary     tty4    Dec 11 10:15
[root@deedee /root]# 
```

Figure 7.3 Output from the **who** command.

Getting Information Set By Users

There is also a service that allows users to create a profile for themselves, which other users can then access. This service is **finger**. In some ways this is a legacy service and not used too much today. If you have no use for it, then consider disabling it completely as discussed in Chapter 12. You may also decide to keep it for internal use only, and just not allow anyone outside to send in a **finger** request.

If you send a **finger** request on a machine that has its finger service activated, but the user has no profile in place, then you will receive a response similar to that shown in Figure 7.4. You as the system administrator can configure the finger server for what kind of information it gives out.

A user can add his or her own personalized finger response in ~/.plan. For example, creating a .plan file with the following contents

```
This is my personal plan file.
If I'm not in I'm probably walking my dog.
```

would give a **finger** response such as shown in Figure 7.5.

FIXING SIMPLE INTERFACE PROBLEMS

There are some small troubleshooting issues that seem like a big deal when they occur, especially if you do not know how to fix them. These issues have nothing to do with the GUI or anything particularly fancy. Instead, they deal with everyday problems that might crop up when using your system at a command-line level.

```
[root@deedee /root]# finger dee
Login: dee                          Name: Dee-Ann LeBlanc
Directory: /home/dee                Shell: /bin/bash
On since Sun Dec  5 15:25 (PST) on tty2   18 minutes 33 seconds idle
No mail.
No Plan.
[root@deedee /root]#
```

Figure 7.4   General **finger** command output.

```
[root@deedee /root]# finger dee
Login: dee                          Name: Dee-Ann LeBlanc
Directory: /home/dee                Shell: /bin/bash
On since Sun Dec  5 15:25 (PST) on tty2   38 minutes 13 seconds idle
No mail.
Plan:
This is my personal plan file. If I'm not logged in I'm probably walking my dog.
[root@deedee /root]#
```

Figure 7.5   **finger** command output with plan information.

Fixing The Screen

A couple of things can go wrong with the screen when you are working at the command line. One of these is when you are suddenly stuck with part of the screen inversed: The background is white or gray and the text is black. This problem can occur when you open files or email with particular control characters within them. These control characters can inadvertently activate features you did not want to use. Another issue involves illegible characters. This problem is sometimes caused by the same issue as inversion. That is, control characters that inadvertently activate unwanted features.

How you fix your screen in part depends on what you are currently doing. Some applications have their own keystrokes that tell them to redraw the screen. If you are at the command line and you do not need to retain any information on the screen, begin by typing "clear" to clear away all of the text. If that action does not fix the problem, and often it does not, try typing "reset". Being a touch typist is helpful in these situations if you cannot see your cursor at all.

If you are in a program, try pressing the key combination "Ctrl+L". Many programs use this sequence (the L does not have to be capitalized) to signal that the screen should be redrawn.

Adjusting The Keyboard Repeat Rate

Depending on how fast you type, your keyboard keys may be too sensitive or not sensitive enough. If you find that you are missing a lot of letters as you type, you might want to speed up the keyboard repeat rate. If you are getting a lot of repeated characters from holding down keys too long, you probably want to slow it down.

You can adjust your keyboard's repeat rate with the **kbdrate** command. Just typing it with no arguments gives you the current keyboard rate setting. There are two flags available that allow you to change these settings. Using **kbdrate –d** you can set the delay between accepted keystrokes in milliseconds. These values can, in general, be from 250 to 1000 in steps of 250. So, for example, you could type "kbdrate -d 750". The other flag, used as **kbdrate -r**, controls essentially how many characters per second the keyboard driver will accept. The allowable numbers are listed if you type "man kbdrate". For example, **kbdrate –r 24.0** is an allowable entry.

Fixing The Keyboard LEDs

On most keyboards today there is a small LED (Light Emitting Diode) above the Num Lock key, the Scroll Lock key, and the Caps Lock key. If the light is not above, it is near and labeled as belonging to that key. Sometimes the LED does not properly reflect the key settings. You can fix this option or change it with the **setleds** command.

7

This command allows you to modify the current state of the LEDs, whether by resetting them to match the key states or even changing them so that they do not necessarily match the keys, but instead reflect something else. Type "setleds –L" to return the LEDs to their original state.

USING UNIX STREAMS, PIPES, AND REDIRECTS

Understanding a few concepts allows you to combine commands to accomplish very complicated operations with a single command. Data stream is an important concept in Unix that describes the handling of data. Pipes and redirection are concepts for directing data streams. Using these three important concepts, you can greatly increase the power and efficiency of your system management and programming.

Unix Streams And Their Functions

Data streams are fundamental to the Unix operating system. All data transfers are conducted by means of streams. Text streams, text processed in a single character stream, are discussed earlier in this chapter. In fact, all I/O operations are treated as single byte streams of data.

During I/O operations, data is transferred to or from a device. Communication with devices is handled by the kernel. All devices are included in the filesystem as files in the /dev directory. All devices from the mouse to the video display, keyboard, printer, sound card, or any other device connected to the system are represented by files. The details of transferring data to and from different devices is handled by the device driver, the file in the filesystem that represents the device. To the kernel, all devices look the same. The kernel is only concerned with moving the data to the file that is the transfer point for a specified device. In this way, Unix is not limited to a specific type of computer. All it requires is the correct device driver to communicate with any device.

A stream forms the connection between the application and the device. Data is transferred from the application, through the kernel, to the device file in a single byte stream, as is data moving from the device to the application. The application is at the head of the stream. The direction of the device is considered down-stream; the application is upstream. The stream is a two-directional connection.

As might be expected in Unix, the head of the stream is represented by a file. To output data, the application sends data to a file, which transfers data to the device file using a stream. Whenever a program runs, it is assigned three streams by default: an input stream, an output stream, and an error message stream, referred to as stdin, stdout, and stderr. Normally, stdin is connected to the keyboard and stdout and stderr are connected to the video display. However, you have the ability to redirect any of the standard streams to a different device. Redirection is discussed in the section "Redirecting Streams," later in this chapter.

Stdin is a stream from which programs can read data, but programs can be written to read data from another source, such as a file, rather than from stdin. The program statements determine where the program reads data. For instance, the sort program reads data from a file if one is specified, but looks for data from stdin if no file name is supplied. If you enter sort with no argument, the program maintains control of the shell, not displaying a prompt, just waiting for input from the keyboard. Any characters you type are treated as input for sort until you type Ctrl+D, which signals the end of the data. At that point, the sort program runs, sorting the data you input from the keyboard. For instance:

```
sort
bbbb
aaaa
^d
aaaa
bbbb
```

After the first line, the program waits for you to type the next three lines. After the ^d, sort runs and displays the last two lines—the sorted output.

Redirecting Streams

The stdin, stdout, and stderr streams can be easily redirected to different files. The metacharacters < and > are used for redirection. Input is redirected using <; output is redirected using >.

For output, the metacharacter, followed by the destination, is typed at the end of the command. For instance, to redirect output from the sort filter, type:

```
sort file1 > file2
```

file1 is sorted. The output is saved in file2, not output to the screen. If file2 does not exist, it is created. If file2 already exists, it may or may not be overwritten, depending on the value of a system variable called noclobber. When noclobber is on, an error message is returned saying the file already exists and the command will stop executing. Noclobber is off by default in the bash shell. The command to turn noclobber on or off is:

```
set -o noclobber
set +o noclobber
```

The **-o** option turns noclobber on; the **+o** option turns it off.

To append the output to the end of an existing file, use **>>**.

```
sort file1 >> file2
```

Input is redirected similarly. For instance:

```
mail jane <file2
```

The contents of file2 are used as input by the **mail** command; the contents of file2 are mailed to the email address, jane.

When the shell accepts the command, it recognizes the redirect character. Before it executes the command, the shell creates a new stream for the output, from stdout to the file2, or the input, from file2 to stdin. The redirected stream only applies to the specific command while it is running. It is not a permanent redirection.

Not all output needs to be seen or saved. A useful alternate destination for redirection is /dev/null, a device for discarding output.

Utilizing A Pipe

Pipes, connections directly from one program to another, are a powerful construct of Unix. The stdout of one command can be connected directly to the stdin of another command via a pipe. The metacharacter, |, is used to connect two pro-grams. For instance, suppose you want to select records of Boston residents from a file containing names and addresses and sort the output. You could do that using **awk** and sort, as follows:

```
awk '/Boston/ { print $0 } ' addrfile1 > addrfile2
sort addrfile2 > sortedfile1
```

However, you could obtain the same result in a more efficient manner:

```
awk '/Boston/ {print $0 } ' addrfile1 | sort >sortedfile1
```

You can string as many commands as you want in a row. The commands being piped must accept data from stdin or output data to stdout. Some commands are not able to accept data from stdin or to output data to stdout and, thus, cannot connect in a pipeline. For instance, the **ls** command takes its input from a directory file, not from stdin. Therefore, you cannot pipe data into the **ls** command:

```
sort file1 | ls
```

However, the **ls** command does output to stdout. You can pipe data out of **ls** to another command:

```
ls | lpr
```

Passing Special Characters Among Programs

One use for pipes is when you need to pass special characters—perhaps meta-characters—from one program to another. The difficulty of dealing with special characters in pipes is that different programs see the characters in different ways. The **tr** command, however, can be used to change the special characters from one program's format into what the other program needs to see them as. This command is used in the following format:

```
tr --flags string(s)
```

7

The **tr** command by itself means little. This item is commonly used either in conjunction with a pipe or a redirect. Table 7.7 lists the flags used with **tr** and what they are useful for.

Building the string itself for **tr** is not always straightforward, because it has its own syntax for how it handles special characters. These characters are listed and defined in Table 7.8.

There are also a number of ranges and special character classifications that you can specify with the **tr** command. These items are laid out in Tables 7.9 and 7.10.

As you can see, **tr** is a complex tool. The problem sometimes becomes finding ways to make use of it. One popular way to quickly make use of **tr** is to remove all carriage returns from text files created under other operating systems. These carriage returns can clutter up a Linux text file and in general are a nuisance. To utilize **tr** to accomplish this task, do the following:

```
cat textfileCR | tr --s \r > textfile
```

Table 7.7   Flags used with the **tr** command.

Flag	Purpose
-c	Output the complement of the string, or the individual complements for the series of strings. This complement term refers to everything that does not match the string.
-d	Delete the characters that match the string.
-s	Requires two string entries. Look for instances of the first string where the string is repeated more than once. Reduce these instances to what is listed as the second string.
-t	Truncate groups of characters that match the first listed string down to the size of the second given string.

Table 7.8   Telling the **tr** command to watch for special characters.

Character	Meaning	Character As Used In Other Commands
\a	PC speaker bell	Ctrl-G
\b	Backspace	Ctrl-H
\f	Printer form feed	Ctrl-L
\n	Begin a new line	Ctrl-J
\r	Carriage return	Ctrl-M
\t	Tab	Ctrl-I
\v	Vertical tab	Ctrl-K
\val	The character whose octal assignment is val.	Varies.
\\	Escaped backslash.	Varies.

Table 7.9   Telling the **tr** command about ranges and types to watch for.

Object	Purpose	Example
start-end	The range of characters from start to end.	[L-R]
[item*times]	Display the item character times in a row.	[-*15]
[:charclass]	Display a list of every character in the specified class. A list of classes with examples is shown in Table 7.10.	[:lower]
[=item=]	Display all characters that fall under the same class as item. A list of classes with examples is shown in Table 7.10.	[=a=]

Table 7.10   Character classes available with the **tr** command.

Class	Contains
alnum	Upper- and lowercase letters, and the digits 0–9.
alpha	Upper- and lowercase letters.
blank	Nothing.
cntrl	Control characters.
digit	The digits 0–9.
graph	Any character that can be printed except the space.
lower	Lowercase letters.
print	Any character that can be printed.
punct	All forms of punctuation.

(continued)

Table 7.10   Character classes available with the **tr** command *(continued)*.

Class	Contains
space	Horizontal or vertical empty space.
upper	All uppercase characters.
xdigit	All hexadecimal digits.

As you can see, a solid understanding of pipes and redirections helps when making use of this command.

Redirects In Scripts

You can redirect output in the commands used in a script file. Because each command in a script file runs independently in its turn, the commands are connected to stdin, stdout, and stderr. The < and > commands function similarly in a script.

A common use for redirection in a script file is to write data into a file using the **echo** command. For instance, the following script file is executed:

```
set +o noclobber
total = 1 + 2
/bin/echo -n "The total is " > outputfile1
/bin/echo $total >> outputfile1
```

The file, outputfile1, contains the line:

```
The total is 3
```

The first **echo** command uses the –n parameter which stops the default output of the end-of-line character. The quotations are required so the shell will treat the spaces as characters, rather than as separators. It uses one **>** to create the file. The second **echo** command does not use the –n parameter so an end-of-line character is output after the variable value. A double **>>** is used to append the value of the variable, total, to the previous contents of outputfile1.

Notice that noclobber is turned off in the script so that outputfile1 will be over-written if it already exists. If you do not want to change noclobber for the entire script, but want one statement to overwrite any existing file, use a pipe after the redirect, as follows:

```
echo "start a new file" >| file1
```

If file1 exists, it is overwritten. file1 contains only the new line written by the **echo** command.

In command lines, the standard files are referred to by numbers:

➤ *0*—standard input

➤ *1*—standard output

➤ *2*—standard error

Using the numbers, you can redirect either the stdout, stderr, or both. The redirect commands are:

➤ *> file1*—redirect standard output to file1

➤ n*> file1*—redirect *n* to file1 where *n* is 1 or 2.

➤ *&> file1*—redirect both stdout and stderr to file1

For example:

```
cat infile1 2> file1 | sort
sort infile1 >file1 2> file2
sort infile1 &> file1
```

The first command pipes stdout to the **sort** command but sends any error messages to file1, not to the **sort** command. The second command outputs the sorted file to file1, but sends any error messages to file2, not to file1. The third command sends both stdout and stderr to file1.

Stdin can be redirected so that the input data is read from the script file. A << directive is used, in the following format:

```
mail root <<MESG
Notification:
The script completed normally
MESG
ls
```

The << is followed by a delimiter, in this case MESG. Text is read as input until the delimiter is encountered again. In the above script, an email message is sent to root that says:

```
Notification:
The script completed normally.
```

Then the **ls** command is executed. If the fourth line containing MESG was not present, the **ls** command would be seen as part of the input text and included as a line in the email message rather than executed.

CREATING, MONITORING, AND KILLING PROCESSES

When the shell executes a program, such as a system command, it creates a process. The process includes the running program and its environment. Processes carry out tasks. Running programs need access to resources, such as the CPU, physical memory, and data. The environment in the process provides access to the required resources.

Creating Processes

Each new process is created by an existing process. When you log in to your Linux account, the shell is executed. The shell is a process. Even when you have not issued any commands, the shell process is always running. Any programs you run while logged in to your account run in processes created by the shell process. When a new process is created, it is a child process of the process that created it. The process that created it is its parent process. For instance, if you have a shell script called shellscript1 that contains an **ls** command, when you run shellscript1, two processes are created. The shell creates a process called shellscript1 and the shellscript1 process creates a process called **ls**. The shell process is the parent of shellscript1 and shellscript1 is the parent of **ls**.

One or more processes may be created by a single command-line instruction. A command that runs a single program creates a single process. A command that is a pipe executing more than one program creates a process for each program in the pipe. A set of one or more processes, entered interactively in a single command at the command line, is called a job.

Process Functionality

A child process inherits its environment from its parent process. However, processes run independently of each other. If the environment of a process changes during execution, the changes do not affect the parent or the child processes. The environment includes information about open files, including the standard files, and many shell variables.

When a process is created, it includes stdin, stdout, and stderr, given file descriptors 0, 1, and 2. It also includes any other open files. Thus, if you open a file in a shell script, the following commands in the script include the open file in their environment, because they inherit their environment from their parent, the script. However, the processes run independently, so files opened in either the parent or the child after the creation of the child are not available to the other process.

A program needs information while running, such as the home directory, the current directory, the path or terminal type. A process inherits needed variables from its parent process. Not all shell variables are inherited by default. Variables created in the process are not available for other processes unless explicitly made available using the **export** command. If you create a variable in a script, you must export the variable before it can be used in another program called by the script. To export a variable, type:

```
export varname
```

The programs entered by the user, either from the command line or in a script, are called user processes. The process has a task to perform, with a distinct beginning and ending. When it has completed its task, it exits. Another type of process is called a daemon, which is a system process that runs all the time, listening for certain events. When an expected event occurs, the daemon wakes up and performs its task, returning to its sleep state when its task is completed, waiting for the next event. For instance, lpd is a daemon that handles printing for Linux. It is a process that runs in a sleep state continually, waiting for printer requests. When it senses incoming printer requests, lpd accepts them and copies them to the spooling area. When it has transmitted the request, lpd returns to its wait condition, waiting for the next printer request to arrive.

Monitoring Processes

Each process created has a process id number that is used for monitoring the process. The kernel contains a process table that includes an entry for every process running in the system. The process entry contains information about the process, including owner and group Ids of the user who is executing the program, current status of the process, memory requirements for the process, processing priority, execution time, resource utilization, and other information.

The **ps** command is used to display information about processes. The ps command obtains its information from the /proc filesystem. Typing "**ps**" without options or arguments lists all current processes running under your UID. The output is:

```
PID   TTY    TIME   COMMAND
1916  ttyp1  0:00   bash
1943  ttyp1  0:00   cat
2003  ttyp1  0:00   ps
```

where PID is the process ID number, TIME is the CPU time used, and COMMAND is the command running in the process. Notice that one of the commands listed is the **ps** command that creates the display. If you use the **ps** command when you are logged in as superuser, all the processes for all the users will be included.

The **ps** command has many options controlling the amount and format of information displayed. The –l option gives a long listing with much more information, including the parent process ID number, the size, the User ID, the Status, and the process priority. The possible values for status (STAT) are: R (runnable), T (stopped), D (asleep and not interruptible), S (asleep), Z (zombie), W (no resident pages), and N (positive nice value).

The –A option lists all the processes, showing many system processes. Notice that one process runs the init program and has a PID of 1. This is the first program run after you log in. Notice that there are several processes running *getty*—a command used to set terminal type and options. These are the processes that are waiting for a login on the available ports. Other processes running include system programs and daemons, possibly including **sendmail**, **inetd**, **cron**, **syslogd**, and **httpd.apache**. Other processes may be running that are associated with Xwindows and the KDE desktop.

To see a listing of all the processes, displayed in a tree structure and showing the relationships between parent and child processes, type **pstree**.

Killing Processes

Processes can hang, that is, never exit. Such an occurrence can be the result of programs that are not operating correctly, possibly those that run in endless loops or are instructed to perform impossible tasks. In other cases, processes can sometimes become confused and unresponsive. Such processes need to be killed.

Processes are killed using the **kill** command. To **kill** a process, enter:

```
kill pid
```

where pid is the process ID number. You can only **kill** processes you own, unless you are using the root account which is allowed to **kill** any process. For a particularly stubborn process, you may need to type:

```
kill -9 pid
```

 If you **kill** a parent process, the child processes of that parent will be removed as well.

Sometimes several processes are running the same program. Perhaps you have tried several times unsuccessfully to run a program. The **killall** command allows you to **kill** all processes running a specified command. For example:

```
killall sort
```

All processes running the **sort** command are deleted.

MODIFYING PROCESS EXECUTION PRIORITIES

Numerous processes are running on your system at any given time. However, only one program is actually executing at any given time. A single CPU can only execute one program at a time. One solution would be to execute each program serially, from beginning to end. This solution is inefficient, causing the CPU to wait, doing nothing, when a program is waiting. Programs wait for events such as I/O completion by a peripheral device, the termination of another process, the availability of data or space in a buffer and the freeing of a system resource. Most programs wait frequently—their running time resulting more from the waiting time than from the actual execution of the program code which is much faster than data transfer.

The Unix solution is timesharing—sharing the CPU time among all the active processes, based on a priority number. A program is moved into memory and begins executing. If no waiting time is encountered, the program executes for its designated time slice, a fraction of a second, and is swapped out. Another program is swapped into memory and begins executing. The swapping continues for one process after another. If a program goes into a wait condition during its execution, it is swapped out and another program that is currently in a ready condition is swapped in. By sharing CPU time, Unix ensures that all programs get their required execution time with the most efficient use of the CPU. Because the computer executes instructions at lightening speed and the time slices used by each process are extremely small, programs seem to users to execute continuously and concurrently.

Monitoring Process Execution

As system administrator, system performance is your responsibility. Monitoring and manipulating processes is the major way of managing system performance. Processes can hang, using CPU time while never completing. Processes can contain programs that are poorly written and interfere with system performance. A program can be performing activities that require more system resources than are available on the given system. The system administrator can monitor running processes and intervene when a process is misbehaving. Processes can be killed or their priorities changed. You can expedite certain processes at the expense of others. For instance, a large program can be given a lower priority, leaving more resources for other programs to finish in a more reasonable time.

If your system appears to be having problems a useful option for the **ps** command is –u. The **ps** command with the –u option provides a display that includes the data shown in Table 7.11.

Notice that one process is using 99.4 percent of the CPU. Suspect that a problem with this process might be causing your system problems. A process that is using a large percentage of the available memory might be another source of potential

Table 7.11   Output from the **ps** command with the **-u** option.

USER	PID	%CPU	%MEM	VSZ	RSS	TTY	STAT	START	TIME	COMMAND
user1	964	0.0	0.7	1844	1012	ttyp1	S	10:12	0:00	bash HELP-PATH=/us
user2	1048	99.4	0.2	1068	372	ttyp2	R	10:24	1.57	yes HOST-NAME=nona
user1	1050	0.0	0.2	1076	348	ttyp1	T	10:24	0.00	cat HOST-NAME=nona

problems. Often, changing the priority of a large job so that it allows other processes to run first can free up system problems.

Another useful command is the **top** command. It displays information about the processes currently running that are using the most CPU time. The display frequently refreshes itself to provide up-to-date information. You can interact with the command to change the display of information on the fly.

If you are concerned with particular files or filesystems, the **fuser** command displays the PIDs of all processes that are using specific files or filesystems with the command

```
fuser file1
```

where file1 is the name of the file. The –m specifies that file1 is a filesystem or block device.

Process Execution

The process table contains information for all the current processes. The kernel is responsible for scheduling CPU time for each process. The part of the kernel responsible for timesharing decisions is called the scheduler. The scheduler swaps processes in and out of memory for execution, maximizing CPU usage and ensuring that all processes get some time, no matter how low their priority.

Execution decisions are based on priority numbers. Each process has two priority numbers. One number represents the priority of the process relative to other processes. This number is called the nice number (being nice to allow other processes to use the system) and is set by the user or the system administrator. The other number is the actual execution priority of the process, which is computed dynamically by the scheduler, based on the nice number, the process status, recent resource use of the process, other available processes, and other factors. This number cannot be changed by the user or the system administrator.

Modifying The Execution Order

The actual priority number that determines the execution order of the processes is computed by the system. It is based on several factors, such as the status of the process and how recently it has been given execution time. One of the factors used in determining the priority number is the nice number, a number assigned by the user that assigns relative priority to processes.

The default nice number issued to each process during its creation is 0. Nice numbers can range from 19 to -20. The lowest number, -20, has the highest priority. Processes with higher nice numbers have a lower priority relative to processes with lower nice numbers. The scheduler will give more CPU time to a process with a number of 0 than to a process with a nice number of 6, but will make sure the process with the higher nice number gets some CPU time.

Users may change the nice number of their own jobs to raise the number (lower priority), but not to lower it. The superuser account can change the nice number of any process in either direction, regardless of who owns it.

When a command is entered, it is assigned the default nice number. To enter a command with a nice number different than the default, use the **nice** command. For instance, to enter an **ls** command with a different nice number, type:

```
nice -n 6 ls
```

The **ls** command is executed with a nice number that is higher than the default by six. If the default is 0, the nice number for this **ls** command is 6. If the -n option is not used, the nice number is increased by 10. A privileged user can enter a negative number (for example, -6) to change the nice number to a smaller value.

To display nice numbers, type "nice" with no arguments or options. The nice number for existing processes can be changed using the **renice** command. For instance, to raise the nice number for a process with the PID 800, the owner can type:

```
renice +6 800
```

The nice number for the process is raised by 6 over the current nice number. If +6 was not specified, the nice number is raised by 10. The nice number can be changed for the processes of a specific user by typing the username:

```
renice +8 user1
```

The superuser can increase or decrease the nice number of the processes of any user.

Be careful when changing priorities. Remember that some of the processes are required by the system. Changing priorities drastically can affect system processes.

USING REGULAR EXPRESSIONS

Unix offers many commands that find and/or select specific text for processing in text files. Examples in this chapter are **grep**, **sed**, and **awk**. Other examples are **vi**, Emacs, and Perl. Much of the power and efficiency of the text processing capabilities of Unix comes from its ability to match patterns, rather than only literal strings of text.

Patterns are combinations of literal characters and metacharacters. Literal characters are normal characters, with no special meaning. An a is an a with no meaning other than one of 26 letters in the alphabet. Metacharacters are special characters that are recognized by a program or operating system to have a special meaning when used in an instruction or command. A familiar example of pattern matching is using an asterisk to represent part of a file name. The command:

```
ls *.txt
```

lists all file names that end in .txt, regardless of the letter before .txt. The asterisk here represents a metacharacter and .txt are literal characters.

The * substitution character offered for file-name pattern matching by Unix and by DOS is a convenient, but not very powerful, example of pattern matching. The regular expressions provided for pattern matching by Unix is a powerful tool, almost a programming language. You can do quite complicated text processing given the flexibility of regular expressions.

Expressions And Their Functions

Regular expressions are constructed of patterns that uniquely identify a text string, based on its location or its types of characters.

Beginning And Ending Of Lines

Two very useful metacharacters are ^ and $, that represent the beginning and the end of lines. Using them, you can search for strings that occur only at those locations. For instance, you can search for lines that begin with XX using the regular expression:

```
^XX
```

The search would ignore any lines with XX in the middle or end of the line. A common use of these characters is to search for blank lines using the expression:

```
^$
```

The ^ and $ with no characters between them represent a blank line.

Matching Any Character

The . character is a metacharacter that matches any character. It can be useful in certain situations. For instance, the following string finds any lines that are only one-character long, regardless of what that character is:

```
^.$
```

Matching A Pattern With An Optional Character

Inserting a ? after a character matches patterns with the letter included and with the letter not included. For instance, you could search for June 1 and Jun 1 with the pattern:

```
June? 1
```

You can use parentheses to group characters to be treated as a unit. For instance, the following pattern:

```
Ju(ne)? 1
```

matches June 1 or Ju 1, but not Jun 1.

Matching One Of A Set Of Characters

If you enclose a list of literal characters in square brackets, a pattern is matched if it includes any of the enclosed characters at the specified location. For instance, suppose you are searching for an address in a file and are unsure if it is 111 Green St. or 112 Green St. You can use the following expression:

```
11[12] Green
```

Both addresses are found. The expression means: 1, followed by 1, followed by either a 1 or a 2, followed by a space, followed by G, and so on. You can include as many characters as you want. You can include a range of characters. You can combine characters and ranges. For example, Table 7.12 shows legitimate regular expressions.

Table 7.12   Regular expressions.

Regular Expression	Finds
report[012]	report0 report1 report2
report[0-9]	report0 report1 … report8 report9
report[a-zA-Z]	reporta reportb …reportz reportA reportB … reportZ
report[3-5?!]	report3 report4 report5 report? report!
report[1-9][1-9][A-Z]	report11A report21A … report 99Y report99Z

If you insert ^ at the beginning of the brackets, it negates the character list, finding strings that do not contain the listed characters at the specified locations. For instance:

```
report[^1-7]
```

does not find report1 through report7. It finds only strings that begin with report, followed by any characters except 1 through 7. Notice that while ^ means not while inside the brackets, it means the beginning of the line when placed before a pattern, as follows:

```
^report[^01]
```

The pattern matches an instance of report, followed by a character that is not a 0 or a 1, only if report is the first string of characters at the beginning of the line.

Matching One Of A Set Of Patterns

A pattern that will match one of two or more alternative patterns is signaled by the metacharacter |, meaning "or". The set of alternatives is enclosed in parentheses. For example:

```
(James|Jim|Jimmy)Jones
```

The pattern finds any of the following: James Jones, Jim Jones, or Jimmy Jones. The pipe metacharacter can indicate alternative patterns, as well as literal strings, such as:

```
(Report[12]|File[12])
```

The regular expression finds any of the following: Report1, Report2, File1, File2.

Matching Repeated Patterns

The characters * and + are used to match repeated characters or patterns. The + character means one or more of the immediately preceding items; the * character means zero or more of the immediately preceding item. The difference between the two characters is shown in the following expressions:

```
Report[12]*
Report[12]+
```

Both expressions match any of the following: Report1, Report2, Report11, Report12, Report222222, and so on. However, only the first expression matches Report.

You can use parentheses to enclose characters that are to be treated as a unit. For instance:

```
Report(12)*
```

The expression matches Report12, Report1212, Report121212, but not Report1122 or Report111.

Matching Metacharacters Literally

Sometimes you need to match a $ or a . character, but they are treated as metacharacters in regular expressions. The metacharacter \ is used to remove the special meaning from a metacharacter so it can be matched literally. Using \ to cancel special meanings is called escaping a character. For example, if you wanted to match all dollar amounts at the beginning of a line, you could use the following regular expression.

```
^\$[0-9]+\.[0-9][0-9]
```

The \ before the $ escapes it, removing its special meaning, so that it is treated as a $ character, not as the end of the line. The \ is required in front of the . character also; otherwise, the . would mean any character.

Using Regular Expressions

Regular expressions are used by many commands, utilities, and programs. However, regular expressions do not have exactly the same features in every use. Programs differ in their implementations. Some programs do not recognize some metacharacters or syntax of regular expressions and some programs have additional features, beyond the basic syntax. In addition, the regular expression engines that resolve the expressions can differ in their methods, such as in the order in which they evaluate the expression. Thus, the same expression might produce different results in different programs. The differences do not negate the value of regular expressions as a powerful tool, they simply mean that more study and testing are required when using complex regular expressions in an application to solve a problem.

Regular expressions are placed in programming instructions in different ways. For instance, **grep** requires the regular expression in the command line, delimited by quotes. **awk** expects a regular expression to be located at the beginning of an instruction, delimited by slashes (/). **vi** and **sed** also expect regular expressions to be delimited by slashes.

WORKING WITH COMMAND HISTORY

There is a much-beloved feature in Linux and Unix called the command history. This feature allows you to recall commands you typed previously and reuse them. However, there is also much more to what you can do with the history, depending on the shell you are using and the depth to which you are willing to learn to work with it.

Most people who have been working for a while in Linux have noticed that, while working in the bash shell specifically, if they press the up arrow the last command they used at the command line reappears at the command prompt. This happens because the shell stores a command history. If you want to work more closely with the history, then you need to be sure that you have your command-line editor set appropriately. Because this book and the exams cover the vi editor, you should be sure that the command-line editor is also set to vi. To accomplish this, type "echo $EDITOR". If the response to this command does not give you back the vi editor, then type "export EDITOR=vi". This sets the appropriate environment variable.

Your command history is stored in a file whose name is stored in the HISTFILE environment variable. You can either see its contents by typing **more $HISTFILE**, or by typing **history**. How much information is stored here depends on which distribution you use. If you want to change how many commands are kept, then do so with the HISTSIZE environment variable by typing **HISTSIZE=*newnumber***. This number cannot be more than 500.

Now that you can see what is in the history file, you do not need to use the arrow keys to back up far through the file. Instead, use the command **!*number*** and you can reuse any command in the listing. Another handy history manipulation command is **fc**. You can list the last part of the history file by using the command **fc -l**, and specify how much of the end of the file with **fc -l *howmany***. Even better, if the file is long you can type **fc -l *start end*** to list the commands numbered from start to end.

The **fc** command also lets you search on strings. Use the format **fc -l *string*** to search for commands where you used a certain character string. For example, **fc -l file1** would look for all commands that did any operations on file1 that are still in your history file.

 If you are working with other shells, the process is fairly similar. The pdksh shell does not allow you to use the arrow keys to move through your history, and when dealing with the tcsh shell you have to type "setenv EDITOR vi" to set the environment variable. The tcsh shell also does not have the **fc** command.

READING EMAIL

One thing that many computer users are practically addicted to is reading email. There are two email programs that are popular among Unix and Linux users. These are not the only two email readers available, but are the most widely used. The primary difference essentially is that **pine** reader is menu-driven and **elm** is not. The basics of using these two readers are covered here.

Using Elm To Read Mail

To start the **elm** email client, just type "elm". If this is the first time you have ever run the program, then it will ask whether it should create configuration files and directories for you, and once you have answered, it opens the mail reader as shown in Figure 7.6. This reader lists your mail in the order of newest to oldest, by default, and places letters next to each item to help you determine its status. If you see an "N", then the mail is new and unread. An "O" means it is old but you have not opened and read it yet. If there is no symbol at all next to the email header, then the mail was already read but left in the mailbox.

The commands available in **elm** are shown at the bottom of the screen. To actually read a piece of mail, use the up and down cursors to move to the header and press Enter to open the mail. You can then press **i** or **q** to return to the mail index. If you want to delete this piece of mail, press **d**. A "D" appears next to the mail header. The mail will not actually be deleted until you close the program. This fact is good protection against accidental deletion.

```
 PINE 4.10    MAIN MENU                          Folder: INBOX  2 Messages


         ?     HELP              -   Get help using Pine

         C     COMPOSE MESSAGE   -   Compose and send a message

         I     MESSAGE INDEX     -   View messages in current folder

         L     FOLDER LIST       -   Select a folder to view

         A     ADDRESS BOOK      -   Update address book

         S     SETUP             -   Configure Pine Options

         Q     QUIT              -   Leave the Pine program



      Copyright 1989-1999.  PINE is a trademark of the University of Washington.
                    [Folder "INBOX" opened with 2 messages]
 ? Help                    P PrevCmd              R RelNotes
 O OTHER CMDS > [ListFldrs] N NextCmd             K KBLock
```

Figure 7.6   The **elm** email client.

If you want to move the message from the In mailbox to another one of your mailboxes, press **s**. This gives you the option of saving into a mailbox file of your choice. Be sure to leave the equal sign in the beginning of the mailbox name unless you want the mailbox to be placed somewhere else than inside the **elm** mailbox directory. Once the message is saved it too has a "D" in the listing.

To finally exit **elm**, type **q** to quit the program. You are asked if you want to delete the messages marked for deletion. Choose yes unless you realize you need to keep one or more of them. If the mailbox you wanted to save any of the items to did not exist before, **elm** creates it for you as it saves the file.

 To open a new message to send, press **m**.

Using Pine To Read Mail

To start the **pine** email client, type "pine". If this is the first time you have run the program it will create some directories it needs and then bring you to a welcome screen. Press **e** to exit it and go to the main **pine** menu shown in Figure 7.7.

If you want to read the mail in your "In" mailbox, use the arrow keys to move to the Message Index menu choice and press Enter. This opens the mailbox.

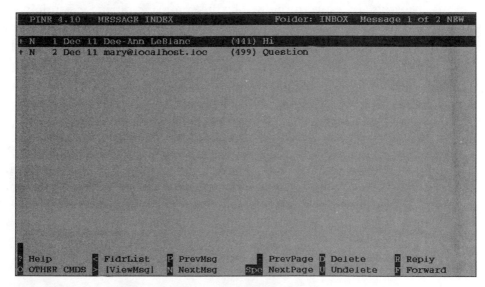

Figure 7.7 The **pine** email client's main menu.

The mail entries have labels almost identical to those in **elm**, except that read messages have plusses next to them. To read a message, press Enter. If you press **d** for delete, then the message is marked deleted but you are not moved out of the message contents display, which confuses some users. Whenever you are in a message, press **<** to return to the index or **n** to move to the next message. Once you are finished, first move to the index out of the message contents, then press **m** to go to **pine**'s main menu. From there, you can leave **pine** by pressing **q** for quit.

To open a new message to send, go to the main menu and choose the Compose Message menu option.

CHAPTER SUMMARY

Linux provides a Unix-like command line for entering commands. The shell provides the user interface that accepts the commands entered at the command-line, processes the commands, and executes them. There are two types of commands: built-in shell commands that are subroutines of the shell, and system commands that are programs stored in the filesystem and executed by entering the file name. The commands are entered in the format: **commandname options arguments**, where *commandname* is the name of the command, *options* determine the way the command is executed, and *arguments* are information used by the command during execution. When a command is executed, it creates a process. All the active processes on a system take turns using CPU time, based on a priority number assigned by the system from available information, a procedure called timesharing.

Data is stored and processed as a stream of single bytes. Files are stored in directories in a tree, with / at the top level. Directories are special files that contain a record for each file, with a pointer to its inode, the data structure that contains the information necessary to access and manage the files.

Many commands are available. The most-used commands are the file management and text processing commands. File management commands include commands to create, locate, move, and remove directories. Text processing commands include filters to display, compare, and reformat text. Commands are also available to monitor and manage processes to enhance system performance.

REVIEW QUESTIONS

1. Which of the following is not a metacharacter used in a regular expression?
   a. $
   b. .
   c. ^
   d. =

2. Which of the following statements is not true about a data stream?
   a. Data streams are one directional.
   b. Data streams transfer one byte of data at a time.
   c. Data streams can be connected to device files.
   d. File descriptors can connect an application to a data stream.

3. How many processes can be created by one job?
   a. 1
   b. 2
   c. 3
   d. unlimited

4. Suppose you need to edit your HTML file and change all <H1> to <H2> through the entire file. Which program would you use?
   a. **diff**
   b. **sed**
   c. **file**
   d. **grep**

5. Which of the following commands is a filter?
   a. **grep**
   b. **cd**
   c. **ps**
   d. **date**

6. Which of the following commands is a valid pipe?
   a. **cat > file1 | lpr**
   b. **sort file1 2> file2 | grep "^A" | lpr**
   c. **ls | ps –aux >file2**
   d. **cat <<XX Hello XX > file1 2>file2**

7

7. Which of the following commands does not accept input from stdin?

    a. **cat**

    b. **ps**

    c. **sort**

    d. **lpr**

8. If you are using **awk**, which of the following instructions will output all lines containing any number anywhere on the line?

    a. /[0-9]*/ { print $0}

    b. /.*/ { print }

    c. /^.[0-9]/ { print $0 }

    d. /.*[0-9]+/ { print $0 }

9. Which of the following information can be found in the inode?

    a. The UID of the owner of a file

    b. The UID of the owner of a process

    c. The protection codes for a process

    d. The name of a file

10. Which of the following commands is a valid command that the owner of process number 800 can enter?

    a. **nice –j +8 800**

    b. **renice +30 800**

    c. **renice 800**

    d. **renice –6 800**

11. Suppose you have a text file called addrfile1 in the format: first name, last name, city, state, age. Suppose you want to create a file with all the entries in California in the format: city: last name, first name, in alphabetical order by city. Which of the following commands is the shortest command that will produce the file you want?

    a. **sort addrfile1 | grep [Cc][Aa](lifornia)? | awk {print $3 $2 $1}**

    b. **awk '/ [Cc][Aa](lifornia)*/ { print $3 $2 $1 } addrfile1 | sort >addrfile2**

    c. **grep "[Cc][Aa](lifornia)" addrfile1 | sed '{ print $3": $2 ", "$1 }' | sort > addrfile2**

    d. **grep "[Cc][Aa](lifornia)?" addrfile1 | awk '{ print $3": $2 ", "$1 }' | sort > addrfile2**

12. Which of the following is true of system commands?

    a. They are subroutines of the shell.

    b. They are functions in the shell.

    c. They are files in the filesystem.

    d. They are subroutines of the kernel.

13. Which of the following commands is most likely to provide you with syntax information about a system command?

    a. **man commandname**

    b. **help commandname**

    c. **info commandname**

    d. **man –k commandname**

14. If each of the following choices was a line in the same text file, which of the lines would be at the top of the file after the file was processed by the **sort** command?

    a. 1111

    b. $$$$

    c. aaaa

    d. AAAA

15. Which of the following statements are true when entering commands at the command line? [Choose all correct answers]

    a. Options are usually placed after the command name, before the arguments.

    b. You can repeat previous commands without typing them in again.

    c. You can type many commands on one line.

    d. You can use variables if you precede their name with a $.

16. What command can you use to convert the special characters used in one command to the format required by another?

    a. **tr**

    b. **grep**

    c. **vi**

    d. **wc**

17. Which command might you use to see the full contents of a .gz text file?

    a. Combination of **gunzip** and **cat**

    b. **gcat**

    c. **zcat**

    d. Combination of **gunzip** and **tail**

7

18. Which command gives you information such as how many lines are in a file?

    a. **w**

    b. **wl**

    c. **w –l**

    d. **wc**

19. Which command allows you to kill a group of processes revolving around the same command the fastest?

    a. **kill**

    b. **kill –9**

    c. **killall**

    d. **kill –all**

20. Which of the following is not a valid sequence of commands?

    a. ps aux | grep http

    b. cp –r /home/bob /home/joe; cd /home/bob; rm –r *; cd ..; rmdir /home/bob

    c. sed s/ab?d/AB?D/g < template.txt

    d. tr –s data.txt

HANDS-ON PROJECTS

Project 7.1

In this project, you will learn about processes and jobs. You will examine and monitor jobs and processes. You will create new jobs and processes, change priorities, and kill them.

To create new jobs and processes, change priorities, and kill them, perform the following steps:

1. Log on to a user account.

2. List all the current processes on your system. Type:

```
ps -el
```

3. Look at all the processes. How many processes are there? Find the PID column. Identify PID 1. Is it running the **init** command? Which UID owns it? Is it root (0)? Identify the process that is running your shell. Does it have a ttyp associated with it? Do the system processes have a ttyp associated with them? Do you see the process that is running the **ps**

command that output the display? Notice the Status column, S. The shell process is sleeping, waiting for the **ps** process to finish running. Look at the column NI. This is the nice number. What do you think the default nice number is?

4. Check to see if any jobs are running in the background by typing "jobs".

5. If you just logged on, no jobs should be running. Create a job to put in the background. If you enter the **cat** command with no arguments, it will continue to run, waiting for input. Type:

```
cat
Ctrl+z
```

6. Type "jobs". Is there a job now? What is its status?

7. Bring the **cat** command back to the foreground by typing "fg". What happened?

8. Stop the **cat** job again with Ctrl+Z. Send it to the background by typing "bg". Now type "jobs". What is the status now? Type "jobs –l". Make note of the PID.

9. Check your processes by typing "ps –l". Is there a process running the **cat** command? Is the PID the same as the PID shown by the **jobs** command? Which process is the parent of the **cat** process (PPID)?

10. Change the nice number of the **cat** process to **renice +6 PID**. Display the processes again. Now what is the number in the NI column for the **cat** process?

11. Kill the **cat** process. Type "kill PID". Display the processes. Is the **cat** process gone? If not, type "kill –9 PID". Is it gone now? Check your jobs? Is the **job** gone as well?

12. Another command useful for testing processes is "yes > /dev/null". The **yes** command output a steady stream of the word yes until you stop it. You need to redirect the output or it will take over your screen. Enter both commands on a single command line and send them to the background by typing:

```
cat ; yes > /dev/null &
```

13. Check your jobs. How many jobs do you have? Check your processes. How many processes do you have for this job?

14. Enter the two commands in a pipe. Type:

```
yes | cat > /dev/null &
```

15. Check your jobs. How many jobs do you have? Check your processes. How many processes do you have for this job?

16. Kill the job by typing "kill %jobnumber". Check your jobs. Is it gone? Check your processes. Are the processes for the job gone?

Project 7.2

In this project, you are going to produce a report from a data file. You have a file containing student names and grades for specific classes. You want to print a report of all the students who have not dropped the class (dropped students show 0 for all tests). You want to sort the report by class. You can do this using **grep** and **sort**.

To produce a report from a data file, perform the following steps:

1. Create an input file called infile1 containing the following data.

```
Mary Smith Math250 90 80 88
Harry Wang Math150 98 96 97
Greg Olson Math250 87 78 80
Tom Valdez Math150 92 95 96
Sally Jones Math250 0 0 0
Bob Hunt Math150 0 70 72
```

2. Use the **grep** command to select the students who completed the class. For instance:

```
grep -v ' 0 0 0' infile1
```

3. Use the **sort** command to sort by class and by last name. For instance:

```
sort +2 infile1
```

4. Combine the operations in one command and redirect the output to a file. For instance:

```
grep -v " 0 0 0" infile1 | sort +2 > report1
```

5. Create an alias for future reports.

```
alias grrep='grep -v " 0 0 0" infile1 | sort +2 report1'
```

## CHAPTER EIGHT

LINUX NETWORKING FUNDAMENTALS

AFTER READING THIS CHAPTER AND COMPLETING THE EXERCISES, YOU WILL BE ABLE TO:

➤ Calculate the proper address information for a TCP/IP network

➤ Know the difference between the three commonly used classes of networks

➤ Be able to configure an interface IP address and netmask

➤ Add routes to the routing table

➤ Calculate subnets

➤ Understand and use common port addresses

➤ Get network status

➤ Trace network routes

➤ Troubleshoot network problems

➤ Setup pppd for both dial-in and dial-out

Networking is one of Linux's strongest points. Because a majority of Linux development occurs over the Internet, the networking code in the Linux kernel is more advanced than that of other operating systems. However, the basic structure of Linux networking is much like other operating systems. TCP/IP (Transmission Control Protocol/Internet Protocol), for example, is TCP/IP regardless of what type of system you are using.

THE TCP/IP PROTOCOL

Networking happens in layers, and nearly every layer is a protocol. The difficulty comes in determining exactly how all of these protocols interact. To get a feel for this interaction, Figure 8.1 shows a diagram of the layers a Web page must go through to be sent to your computer.

It may seem a bit excessive to layer so many protocols for something as simple as loading a Web page, but as you will see, every protocol has a specific role to play in getting your data from one place to another. Protocols used on the Internet are categorized as follows:

➤ **Application:** FTP, HTTP, POP3, SMTP, Telnet, DNS

➤ **Transport:** UDP, TCP

➤ **Network:** IP

➤ **Data Link:** Ethernet protocols, ARP, RARP

The application protocol contains the actual data used by the servers and clients to communicate. Then, the transport and network protocols work together on a logical level to establish the data connection in a platform, hardware, and application-independent way. It is the close interaction between these two layers that spawn phrases like TCP/IP networking, but it is important to remember that these protocols are independent. Finally, once the data packet is ready on the network layer, the data link layer prepares and sends the packet over the physical network interface.

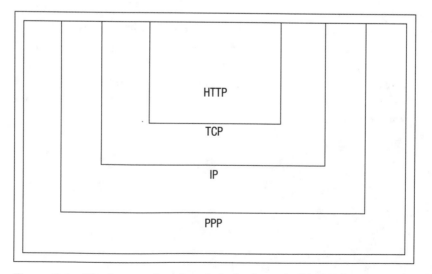

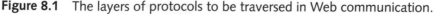

Figure 8.1 The layers of protocols to be traversed in Web communication.

TCP/IP

TCP/IP is the standard protocol of the Internet. Whenever you access a Web page or download a file from the Internet, you are using TCP/IP to do it. Conveniently, TCP/IP is the native protocol in Linux.

When dealing with the IP protocol, two types of packets are common. The most common packet type is TCP. TCP packets are associated with stream-based network connections. These connections are typically used by protocols that need to transfer more than a few bytes at a time such as HTTP (Hypertext Transfer Protocol), FTP (File Transfer Protocol), email, and many others. Not all types of connections require that every single byte of data reaches its destination properly. In situations such as streaming audio or video, networked games, or Internet telephony, it is OK to lose small groups of bytes here and there. The application will still function with sometimes an imperceptible amount of data loss. For these purposes, UDP (User Datagram Protocol) is used instead of TCP, and such traffic is essentially connectionless. There is less bureaucracy involved in a UDP transaction and this protocol uses smaller groups of data, which makes it more desirable for transmitting large amounts of data such as in Internet multimedia applications.

TCP/IP Addressing

Using the IP, each network interface is assigned an IP address. There are two standards for these addresses, IPv4 and IPv6. IPv4 addresses are made up of 4 bytes separated by periods such as 192.168.4.1, and as one might expect, IPv6 addresses are made up of 6 bytes. As of this writing, IPv6 is still in development, but it is expected to replace the current IPv4 standard toward the end of the year 2000.

Just as individual interfaces have addresses, entire networks have addresses as well. A network's addressing scheme is made up of a network address and a *netmask*; this is also known as a *subnet*. To understand a subnet, we must look at these addresses in binary (see Table 8.1). If you have a computer with an IP address of 192.168.4.1 and a netmask of 255.255.255.0, you can use some simple binary math to get the rest of the network information:

```
Network address = IP AND Netmask
Broadcast address = Network address OR (NOT Netmask)
```

Table 8.1 lays out the various addresses used in this example.

Reserved Addresses

More often than not, private LANs are connected to the Internet via IP masquerading or some other *NAT (Network Address Translation)* extension.

Table 8.1   IP, network, and broadcast binary addresses.

Binary Operation	IP	Binary IP	Resulting Address
	192.168.4.1	11000000.10101000. 00000100.00000001	IP
AND	255.255.255.0	11111111.11111111. 11111111.00000000	Netmask
=	192.168.4.0	11000000.10101000. 00000100.00000000	Network
OR	0.0.0.255	00000000.00000000. 00000000.11111111	(NOT Netmask)
=	192.168.4.255	11000000.10101000. 00000100.11111111	Broadcast

In doing so, it is important to assign the LAN addresses in one of the reserved subnets (refer to RFC 1918 for the laws on reserved addresses). The reserved subnets are address ranges that are not used on the Internet; this way you can be sure that there will be no confusion when computers on the LAN talk to computers on the Internet.

Each of the three address classes has its own address space reserved for internal subnets:

➤ 1   Class A   10.x.x.x
➤ 16   Class B   172.16.x.x – 172.31.x.x.
➤ 255   Class C   192.168.x.x

INSTALLING TCP/IP NETWORKING

Installing TCP/IP networking involves configuring each networking device or interface with the appropriate address. It also requires the overall network and subnet address as well as a general understanding of how all this address information interoperates to form a homogeneous TCP/IP network that can successfully communicate with itself as well as the outside world.

Setting Machine Addresses

Every device that is to communicate on a network must have an address. If it is a physical device, there are two addresses, a hardware address and an IP address. The hardware, or MAC (Media Access Control), address is hard-coded into a device, such as a network interface card (NIC). In most cases, the MAC address can be ignored, unless DHCP (Dynamic Host Configuration Protocol) or BOOTP (Boot Protocol) is used. But how do you know what IP address to use? Unless the interface that is to be assigned an IP address is public, and therefore an address has usually been given to you or is preconfigured when online, it is up to you to determine an interface's IP address.

As mentioned earlier, there are blocks of reserved IP addresses. It is typically a good idea to use one of the three classes of reserved network addresses for private network interfaces, to avoid any potential security issues or address conflicts. The question is, which class of network is right for a given situation? At this point, a discussion on the differences of the three common classes of networks should help answer the question.

There are three commonly used classes of IP addresses:

➤ **Class A IP addresses** These use the leftmost 8 bits of the *dotted quad* (IP address) to identify the network. This leaves the three rightmost 24 bits or three bytes to identify hosts on the network. On a bit level, a Class A address has the leftmost bit of the first byte always set to 0 (decimal value of 0 to 127 for the byte). This means that the rightmost seven bits of the first byte can either be a 1 or a 0, which gives us 2^7 possible combinations or 128 different networks, with $(2^{24})-2$ or 16,777,214 possible interfaces. You are probably wondering why we subtracted 2 from the possible interface combinations. The reason is this: There must always be a network and broadcast address on a given network, typically 0 and 255 respectively, thus reducing the number of possible interfaces by two. It is important to note at this point that the networks 0.0.0.0 (the default route) and 127.0.0.0 (the loopback device) have special meanings and are not available for use to identify networks. So, there are only 126 available Class A network addresses.

➤ **Class B IP addresses** These use the left two bytes of the dotted quad to identify the network, leaving the last two bytes to identify interfaces. On a bit level, a Class B address has the leftmost 2 bits of the first byte set to 10. This leaves 14 bits left to specify the network address, giving 16,384 possible networks. Therefore, Class B networks have a decimal range of 128 to 191 for the first byte, and 0 to 255 for the second byte, with each network containing up to 65,534 possible interfaces.

➤ **Class C IP addresses** These use the three leftmost bytes of the dotted quad to identify the network, leaving the last byte to identify interfaces. Class C addresses always start with the leftmost 3 bits of the first byte set to 110 for a decimal range of 192 to 253 for the leftmost dotted quad. Raising 2^8 there are 254 possible interfaces (remember to subtract two from the possible 256 interfaces for the network and broadcast addresses of a network). Note: Class C networks with a first byte greater than 223 are reserved and therefore unavailable for use.

There are also Class D and Class E networks. Class D networks have the leftmost bits set to 1110. Class D addresses are used for IP multicasting, and Class E addresses are reserved for experimentation. Table 8.2 summarizes these points.

8

Table 8.2 The three primary classes of IP network addresses.

Network Class	First Byte Decimal Range	Possible Networks	Possible Interfaces Per Network
Class A	1-126	126	16,777,214
Class B	128-191	16,384	65,534
Class C	192-223	2,097,152	254

The number of possible interfaces is always two less than the total possible interfaces to allow for broadcast and network address.

It should be clear to see from the previous discussion on network classes that it is very important to pick a class of network that is capable of handling the number of interfaces you expect to have on any one network.

The IP address of a network interface is typically configured and assigned by the kernel through the **ifconfig** command. It is important to note here that **ifconfig** will fail unless the interface is already configured and online (i.e., drivers loaded as in the case of a NIC or a link brought up and online as in a PPP connection). To assign an IP address of 192.168.0.1 to device eth0 using a netmask of 255.255.255.0, the following command would be issued:

```
> ifconfig eth0 192.168.0.1
```

Notice in the above command that the netmask was not specifically stated. This is because the desired netmask was 255.255.255.0. **ifconfig** automatically assumes a netmask of 255.255.255.0. If a different netmask were desired such as 255.255.255.242, the following command would have been used instead:

```
> ifconfig eth0 192.168.0.1 netmask 255.255.255.242
```

ifconfig is used as follows:

```
> ifconfig interface [aftype] options | address ...
```

The interface component consists of the network device to which the settings you are adding should point. Usually, these interfaces are Ethernet cards. Your first Ethernet card is typically eth0. The second is eth1, and so on. After this comes—only if you need it—the type of addressing scheme you are using. Because we are discussing TCP/IP here, you do not need to include this option. The **ifconfig** program recognizes the TCP/IP addressing format by default.

A range of options is available for use with the **ifconfig** command. These options are outlined in Table 8.3.

Table 8.3   Commonly used options available with the **ifconfig** command.

Option	Additional Option	Purpose	Argument
add	None.	Add an address to the database.	The IP address to add to the database.
address	None.	Assign a specific IP address to the interface you named.	The IP address to attach to the card.
allmulti	-	Turn on (or off if you use the minus sign) the ability for the machine to receive special packets sent to everyone on the network.	None.
arp	-	Turn on (or off if you use the minus sign) ARP for this interface. ARP is typically used for Ethernet interfaces.	None.
broadcast	-	Set (or clear if the minus sign is used) the broadcast address for the interface.	Broadcast address.
del	None.	Remove an address from the database. The opposite of add.	The IP address to remove.
down	None.	Shut down the interface's driver.	None.
hw	The hardware class: ether, ax25, ARCnet, and netrom.	Set the hardware address for the interface.	Hardware address in a form appropriate for the class.
interface	None.	List which interface you are defining.	Interface driver, such as eth0.
io_addr	None.	Set start I/O address for the interface.	Address.
irq	None.	If the device is capable of being set in this manner, set the IRQ address for the interface.	Address.
netmask	None.	The network mask for this interface.	IP address for netmask.

(continued)

8

Table 8.3   Commonly used options available with the **ifconfig** command *(continued)*.

Option	Additional Option	Purpose	Argument
pointtopoint	-	Set (or unset if the minus sign is used) a direct connection between this interface and the one listed.	IP address for the outside interface.
promisc	-	Set (or unset if the minus sign is used) promiscuous mode, which tells the interface to receive all packets crossing through the network instead of ignoring those not for itself.	None.
tunnel	None.	Create a tunnel between this interface and the one listed. A tunnel is a method of creating a virtual dedicated connection across the Internet, used to create a VPN (virtual private network). This is a popular method for adding outbased machines to the local LAN.	IP address for tunnel end.
up	None.	Activate the driver for the interface. Opposite of the down option.	None.

Stringing these options together to form useful commands is the trick with **ifconfig**. Some examples were given earlier. You do not, however, have to go through this process every time you boot the machine. Physical devices are usually configured at boot time by the init scripts. These scripts are located in the
/etc/rc.d/ tree.

Before Routing

Before data can be routed to a particular machine, the router needs to know what hardware corresponds to the given IP address. When you boot a Linux machine that is on a LAN or directly on the Internet, this machine runs the **ifconfig** command during the network initialization component. This command maps the machine's Ethernet card to its IP address. If there are multiple Ethernet cards within the machine, the command maps each of the MAC addresses to its respective IP address, as defined when you configured this information.

You can see the contents of your ARP cache at any time by using the command **arp -a**. Remember that more specific routing issues give way to more generic ones. If you have specific ARP information set, this information can override things you set later when routing. Make sure your ARP information is accurate.

Setting Up Routing

Now that you have a properly configured network interface, you need to tell the kernel how to route outbound packets. Assume, for the sake of argument, that the eth0 interface is configured with IP address 192.168.4.5. We need to first add a route for the network 192.168.4.0. Issuing the **route** command as follows will accomplish this:

```
> route add -net 192.168.4.0 netmask 255.255.255.0 eth0
```

The following command will add the appropriate route for the interface to the desired network. Following along with the previous example, say that eth0 is plugged directly into a hub that is a gateway to the Internet which IP address 192.168.4.10 is also plugged into. What you need to do now is tell your Linux system how to get out onto the Internet using the gateway. To do this, you need to make an entry in the system's routing table. Use the **route** command to do this.

```
> route add default gw 192.168.4.10
```

If you issue **route** with no arguments, you should see a routing table similar to this one:

```
Kernel IP routing table
Destination Gateway Genmask Flags Metric Ref Use Iface
192.168.4.5 * 255.255.255.0 U 0 0 0 eth0
192.168.4.0 * 255.255.255.0 U 0 0 0 eth0
loopback * 255.0.0.0 U 0 0 0 lo
default 192.168.4.10 0.0.0.0 UG 0 0 0 eth0
```

The routing table is essential for any TCP/IP networking to occur. If the routing is configured incorrectly, networking will not work because data packets have no idea of how to get where they need to go.

Setting Netmasks

A netmask is nothing more than a bit mask ANDed with an IP address to determine which part of the address is the network and which part is the interface. In a standard non-subnetted Class C IP address the netmask would be 255.255.255.0. On a bit level, the netmask would look like this:

```
11111111.11111111.11111111.00000000
```

Basically, this means that all the bits from left to right that are a 1 signify that this part of an interface's address refers to the network. The 0 bits are possible interface addresses. For standard non–subnetted classes of networks, the corresponding netmasks would be:

➤ **Class A**   255.0.0.0

➤ **Class B**   255.255.0.0

➤ **Class C**   255.255.255.0

You will see in the next section where the netmask is more useful.

Setting Up Subnets

The previous section discussed what the netmask was for. It determines which part of an IP address was the network and which part was the interface. To better utilize IP address space, you will apply your knowledge of the netmask to create network subnets. Subnetting is the division of a single Class A, B, or C network into at least two parts.

Basically, subnetting divides the standard interface space into at least two parts: the subnet number and the interface number on that subnet. Subnetting helps solve the problem of expanding routing tables by ensuring that the subnet structure of a network is never visible outside of the private network.

To implement a subnet, you must first determine how many networks and interfaces are needed now and in the future. These numbers will help determine how a network is divided into subnets. For ease of illustration, take the Class C network of 192.168.0.0. On a bit level, the address and standard netmask would look like the following:

```
11000000.10101000.00000000.00000000 - Address
11111111.11111111.11111111.00000000 - Netmask
```

For the purpose of this illustration, say you have determined that you want 4, or 2^2, different subnets on the base network. To accomplish this, take the first two bits of the last byte and use then to designate the four different subnets. This will leave the last six bits of the last byte to identify interfaces. This will give you a netmask of:

```
11111111.11111111.11111111.11000000 or 255.255.255.192
Subnet 1-4 Addresses
Network1: 11000000.10101000.00000000.00000000 or 192.168.0.0
Broadcast1: 11000000.10101000.00000000.00111111 or 192.168.0.63
Network2: 11000000.10101000.00000000.01000000 or 192.168.0.64
Broadcast2: 11000000.10101000.00000000.01111111 or 192.168.0.127
Network3: 11000000.10101000.00000000.10000000 or 192.168.0.128
Broadcast3: 11000000.10101000.00000000.10111111 or 192.168.0.191
```

```
Network4: 11000000.10101000.00000000.11000000 or 192.168.0.192
Broadcast4: 11000000.10101000.00000000.11111111 or 192.168.0.255
```

These four different subnets can each have $(2^6)-2$ or 62 interfaces. The broadcast address for each subnet has the last six bits all set to 1s and the network address of each subnet has the last six bits all set to 0s. When working out how to subnet a network, it is always a good idea to work out the design in bitwise fashion. Although the decimal dotted quads were designed to be an easy way for people to understand IP addressing, configuring subnets in base ten can be extremely confusing.

IP Multicast

To understand the concept of IP multicasting, consider your radio. Each station is broadcast on a reserved frequency. Anyone who tunes a radio to that station can listen to it in an ideal world—if it helps, think of all Internet users as being in the same radio time zone or broadcasting zone.

IP multicasting is an option that is in fact ingrained in the very structure of IP addressing. Class D addresses, which range from 224.0.0.0 to 239.255.255.255—bitwise, all addresses that begin with 1110—are specifically allocated for multicasting. In fact, the 224.0.0.0 to 224.255.255.255 are locally reserved multicasting addresses, where 225.0.0.0 to 239.255.255.255 are valid across the Internet and each can only have one unique sender.

Some of these addresses are reserved for internal use locally or Internet-wide. Others are already owned by broadcasters. For a full list see RFC 1700—one location for this document is **www.landfield.com/rfcs/rfc1700.html**, search down for the text "INTERNET MULTICAST ADDRESSES".

IP multicasting is accomplished with the UDP packet type. You can limit the broadcast range to a number of different groupings, including staying within your own LAN or continent. This is in many ways a service that the average system administrator does not implement, but you do need to know what it is and what the Class D addressing segment is for. If you want more information on IP multicasting, check out **www.cs.washington.edu/homes/esler/ multicast**.

DEFINING AND MANAGING COMMON PORT ADDRESSES

When dealing with networking, you will run into the same port numbers again and again. This is because all common services have standard port numbers. Table 8.4 shows some commonly used port numbers; for a complete list, take a look at the /etc/services file.

Table 8.4   Commonly used port numbers.

Service	Definition	Port
DNS	Name service	53
FTP Data	File transfer	20
FTP Control Information	File transfer	21
HTTP	Web data	80
IMAP	Remote email access	143
POP3	Email pickup	110
NetBIOS	Non-TCP/IP network application communication	139
NNTP	News service	119
SMTP	Email service	25
SNMP	Network device management	
Telnet	Remote shell access	23

Why To Use Standard Ports

When you open up your Web browser to access a Web page, it establishes a connection on port 80 because it knows that 80 is the standard port for HTTP connections. The same is true for nearly every other network service. Having the ports work in this way is a good thing; it means that anyone can visit a Web page without having to know specific details about it. However, as one would assume, there are times when it is good not to use standard port numbers.

Why To Deviate From Standard Ports

Any situation in which a server is not intended for the general public is a good candidate for using a non-standard port. For example, let's say your company wants its employees to be able to log in to the Web server to check their email. At the same time, you do not want to advertise to the world that this functionality is there. A good way to do this is to place the WWW email gate-way server on a port other than 80.

 One thing to keep in mind while doing this is that a non-standard port number is not a replacement for good security. On the other hand, it could, and often is, used to augment a good security scheme.

USING TCP/IP WITH LINUX

Every Linux distribution comes with a plethora or networking tools. Most of these tools are essential for the maintenance and troubleshooting of a network. Among the many tools available, the three most commonly used and vital tools are **PING**, **netstat**, and **traceroute**.

PINGing Hosts

PING is probably the most used TCP/IP tool. This program uses the ICMP protocol, which sends UDP packets. The reason ICMP is UDP-based is that the entire purpose of PING is to see whether or not packets make it to their destination and back. **PING** is most commonly used to determine if an interface is up and communicating. **PING** uses the ICMP protocol's ECHO_REQUEST to elicit an ECHO_RESPONSE from network interfaces. For instance, if you wanted to determine if an interface with IP address 192.168.0.2 is communicating on the network, you would issue the following command:

```
> PING 192.168.0.2
```

If the interface is in fact online, you would receive back responses like the following:

```
> PING 192.168.0.2
PING 192.168.0.2 (192.168.0.2): 56 data bytes
64 bytes from 192.168.0.2: icmp_seq=0 ttl=128 time=1.0 ms
64 bytes from 192.168.0.2: icmp_seq=1 ttl=128 time=0.9 ms
64 bytes from 192.168.0.2: icmp_seq=2 ttl=128 time=0.9 ms
64 bytes from 192.168.0.2: icmp_seq=3 ttl=128 time=0.9 ms
64 bytes from 192.168.0.2: icmp_seq=4 ttl=128 time=0.9 ms
```

With the **PING** command that was issued, this stream would continue until stopped with ^C. If you wanted to only send a specific number of **PING** packets, you would use the -c option with the **PING** command:

```
> PING -c 5 192.168.0.2
```

This would only send out five packets and terminate.

Network Status

As an administrator of a network, it is important to view the status of your network. In Linux, the **netstat** command is used. **netstat** displays network connections, routing tables, interface statistics, masquerade connections and netlink messages. For instance, suppose you wanted to see your local routing table. Using **netstat**, you would issue the following command:

```
> netstat -re
```

You will receive a data output of the kernel IP routing table:

```
Kernel IP routing table
Destination Gateway Genmask Flags Metric Ref Use Iface
default * 255.255.255.0 U 0 0 0 eth0
```

```
25.232.55.0 * 255.255.255.0 U 0 0 0 eth1
loopback * 255.0.0.0 U 0 0 0 lo
default hostname 0.0.0.0 UG 0 0 0 eth1
```

Table 8.5 shows some of the common options used when issuing the **netstat** command.

Route Tracing

Sometimes it is useful to know which path your packets are taking to a given destination. Also, if your packets are being dropped, you can determine where your packets are being dropped. You can also find out where a given route is broken to a given host. In Linux, the command to perform these diagnostics is **traceroute**. Say for instance you wanted to find out what path your packets took to get to amazon.com. You would issue the following command:

```
> traceroute www.amazon.com
```

You would get back a line-by-line list of all the different hosts your packets traveled through on their way to **www.amazon.com** and their associated **PING** times. If for some reason there were no route to **www.amazon.com**, **traceroute** would show you the last host reached while trying to get to **www.amazon.com**.

Table 8.5 **netstat** options and their descriptions.

Option	Optional Option	Function
-r	—route	Display routing table
-i	—interfaces	Display interface table
-s	—statistics	Display networking statistics (like SNMP)
-M	—masquerade	Display masqueraded connections
-v	—verbose	Be verbose
-n	—numeric	Don't resolve names
-N	—symbolic	Resolve hardware names
-e	—extend	Display other/more information
-c	—continuous	Continuous listing
-l	—listening	Display listening server sockets
-a	—all, —listening	Display all sockets (default: connected)
-o	—timers	Display timers
-F	—fib	Display Forwarding Information Base (default)
-C	—cache	Display routing cache instead of FIB

TROUBLESHOOTING TCP/IP PROBLEMS

Problems will inevitably occur in Linux networking, and when this happens, it is important to know how to handle them. To narrow and subsequently fix the problem, one must know how to view the network settings, test the network, and interpret the results of the previous two steps.

Viewing Current Network Settings

For software to communicate over a network, two sets of settings must be in place. The first is the interface settings, and the other is the routing table. To accomplish this, take another look at the commands **ifconfig**, **netstat**, and **route**.

To look at the interface settings, run the **ifconfig** program without any parameters. The resulting screen will have blocks of information about each configured interface, which is explored in more detail in the following section.

To examine the routing table, there are two possibilities: **netstat** and **route**. Simply running **route** without any parameters will output the routing table. By default, **route** will reverse DNS lookup all of the addresses in the table to make it easier to read; however, if there is a network problem, route may hang indefinitely when attempting to do so. To avoid this, the -n switch can be used to force **route** to just output the IP address. **netstat** can also output the routing table when called with the -r switch. The same -n switch can also be used with **netstat** as it is used with **route**.

Test Routing

The first thing to do when there is a network problem is to make sure there actually is a network problem. The best way to do this is with the **PING** command. For example, if the problem is on the 192.168.4.0 network, **PING** another host on that network with a command such as:

```
> PING -c 5 192.168.4.3
```

If the **PING** works as it would normally, there isn't a network problem. In that case, refer to the documentation for the network program that is malfunctioning. If **PING** shows that there is a problem, the next step is to examine the interface settings. To do this, look at the output from **ifconfig**; it should look something like the sample output shown here:

```
eth0 Link encap:Ethernet HWaddr 52:54:00:DF:FC:F5
 inet addr:192.168.4.1 Bcast:192.168.4.255 Mask:255.255.255.0
 UP BROADCAST RUNNING MULTICAST MTU:1500 Metric:1
 RX packets:35315620 errors:0 dropped:0 overruns:0 frame:0
 TX packets:33712487 errors:0 dropped:0 overruns:0 carrier:0
 collisions:12984 txqueuelen:100
 Interrupt:9 Base address:0x6000
```

It may also be a good idea in this situation to run **netstat -r**. If the only routes that exist are the network and loopback, without an eth0 route, then the interface is not up. It's a way of checking routes and interfaces at the same time.

The first settings to check here are the address settings, such as IP address and netmask, that were discussed earlier. If one or more of these are incorrect, or if the device is not even listed, follow the steps in the section "Installing TCP/IP Networking" to set it up correctly. If the device still is not listed after doing so, check the kernel to determine if the device driver is present for the given interface. Also, examine if the numbers listed next to RX and TX packets are very low and the number listed next to collisions is very high; if so, there is most likely a hardware problem with the physical network infrastructure.

If the interface is configured properly, then the problem is with routing the data to where it needs to go. First, view the routing table with the **route –n** command. Tracking a problem with the routing table is quite simple; it should exactly reflect the physical topology of the network. For example, if the eth0 device is physically hooked to the network 192.168.4.0, there should be a routing table entry to reflect that. Figure 8.2 shows a diagram of a sample network. Here is the routing table that would go with it.

```
Kernel IP routing table
Destination Gateway Genmask Flags Metric Ref Use Iface
192.168.4.0 * 255.255.255.0 U 0 0 0 eth0
192.168.7.0 * 255.255.255.0 U 0 0 0 eth1
192.168.6.3 * 255.255.255.255 U 0 0 0 eth2
207.98.129.1 * 255.255.255.255 U 0 0 0 ppp0
127.0.0.1 * 255.0.0.0 U 0 0 0 lo
172.18.0.0 192.168.7.3 255.255.0.0 UG 0 0 0 eth1
0.0.0.0 207.98.129.1 0.0.0.0 UG 0 0 0 ppp0
```

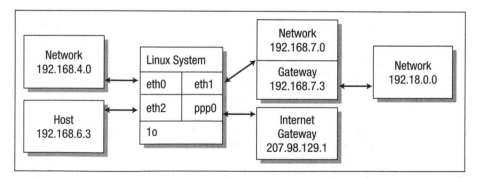

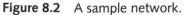
Figure 8.2 A sample network.

To fix a route, delete it with **route del** *destination*, and then re-create it using instructions in the "Installing TCP/IP Networking" section.

Common Problems

There are two problems that typically occur with Linux networking: operator error and hardware malfunctions. In five years of Linux networking, I have seen only a handful of problems that were not one of the two. If address information is consistently incorrect, check your scripts for typos, and if smoke is pouring out of the computer, shut it down, unplug it, and take a look inside.

CONFIGURING AND USING PPP

Commonly in the /etc directory is a directory called PPP. This is where all the scripts associated with bringing up and taking down a PPP connection reside. Typically, pppd uses these files to allow easier management of a PPP connection, but be aware that a PPP connection requires zero files to be established and or taken down; the entire process can be accomplished from the command line. pppd commonly uses six scripts to help bring up, establish, and take down a PPP connection. These scripts are as follows:

➤ A chat script of any name

➤ Options

➤ pap–secrets

➤ chap–secrets

➤ ip–up

➤ ip–down

 ISDN is just another type of modem connection. You can use **pppd** for ISDN as well.

Setting Up The Chat Script

The chat script is the script responsible for setting up the pairs of expectations and responses for successful negotiation of the modem connection. For instance, when you issue the **ATZ** command to a modem, you expect to receive an OK from the modem. In the chat script, this would look like the following:

```
"" "ATZ"
"OK" "ATDT5551234"
```

The first empty set of "" says that you expect nothing and respond to that with an "ATZ". Following that, you expect to receive an "OK". If the "OK" is received, then we send the tone dialing string "ATDT5551234". See if you can determine the set of expectations and responses in the following chat script:

```
""  "ATZ"
"OK" "ATDT5551234"
"login" "username"
"password" "password"
```

You already know what the first two lines accomplish, but have you determined what the second two do? The "login" says that you expect to receive through the modem the string "login" from wherever it is you are dialing in to. Having successfully received the login prompt from your provider, you send your username for authentication. Having sent your username, expect to be prompted for your password. That is what the first string on the fourth line says, expect "password" from your provider. Having received the password prompt, send your password. If this last step is accomplished successfully, you have a link established with your provider. If for some reason your provider prompted you for a username and password differently than the previous example, such as "hello" for username and "authenticate" for password, you would change your expectations in the script accordingly.

At this point, your PPP connection is not complete. You still need to configure your local and remote IP addresses and add an entry into your routing table so information can flow both upstream and downstream along your PPP connection.

Connecting With pppd

As mentioned earlier, pppd uses six different scripts to bring up, establish, and take down a PPP connection. In the previous section, you learned how to set up the chat script. Use that chat script along with the other pppd scripts to successfully dial in to a network such as an ISP.

To properly use pppd, make a minor change to your chat script. Remove all lines associated with authentication from the chat script (i.e., username and password). Use two other files, pap-secrets and chap-secrets, to do the authentication during the dial-up process. Next, set up the /etc/ppp/options file. This file contains lines that tell pppd what serial port to use to make the connection, how to make the connection, and how to configure the connection when it is up. A standard /etc/ppp/options file may look something like this:

```
#use serial device ttyS1 (cua1) for the ppp connection
/dev/ttyS1
#lock the device while in use
lock
#remote end does not need to authenticate itself
noauth
```

```
#Username used when authenticating this ppp session
name "username"
#Tells pppd to automatically bring this link up when needed
demand
#Take link down if idle for 600 seconds (10 minutes)
idle 600
#Use server assigned local IP address
ipcp-accept-local
#Use server assigned gateway IP address
ipcp-accept-remote
#Automatically place an entry in the routing table for the ppp connec-
tion
defaultroute
#Use modem, lock link at 115200 using hardware flow control
modem 115200 crtscts
#Chat line used to dial modem
connect '/usr/sbin/chat -v -f /etc/ppp/[name of chat script]'
#Local and remote IP address, overwritten by the ipcp options
192.168.0.1:192.168.0.3
```

This /etc/ppp/options file is more or less a standard file when using a PPP connection to dial in to an ISP.

Next, tell pppd how to authenticate itself once it has dialed in. This is where the /etc/ppp/pap-secrets and /etc/ppp/chap-secrets files come in. These files contain the username referred to in the /etc/ppp/options file along with the associated password. A pap and chap-secrets file for user name "bob" with password "hello", would look like this:

```
# PAP authentication file: /etc/ppp/pap-secrets
# This file should have a permission of 600.
# ~# chmod 600 /etc/ppp/pap-secrets
# Username Server Password IP addresses
"bob"     *      "hello"    *
# CHAP authentication file: /etc/ppp/chap-secrets
# This file should have a permission of 600.
# ~# chmod 600 /etc/ppp/chap-secrets
# client    server     secret          IP addresses
"bob"     *      "hello"    *
```

Two things are very important to remember: The username must be the same as the name line in the /etc/ppp/options file, and each entry in the secrets files must be separated by a tab character.

There are two more files associated with pppd: the ip-up and ip-down scripts. These scripts are automatically executed by pppd when the connection comes and goes down, respectively. These files do not need to exist to successfully establish ppp links with pppd, such as dialing in to an ISP. However, if you wish to do something special or out of the ordinary every time a PPP connection comes up and goes down, these two files are the place to put these sorts of things.

Providing Dial-in Service

Providing ppp dial-in service is much the same as dialing out to make a ppp connection. In fact, the only major change is in the chat script. This example will set up the server 192.168.4.1 to accept a dial-in from a computer that will then receive the IP address 192.168.4.2. The authentication will be performed using pap, and the IP address for the DNS server will be served to the client using ipcp protocol requests. In addition to the following two files, you will also create a /etc/ppp/pap-secrets file as outlined previously. The following steps outline how to create a script for a basic ppp dial-in service:

1. Make a /etc/ppp/options file:

```
#Lock the modem while is use by pppd
lock
#require authentication from the dialing in peer
auth
#use local IP 192.168.4.1 and assign remote IP of 192.168.4.2
192.168.4.1:192.168.4.2
#Use serial port ttyS1 (cua1)
/dev/ttyS1
#lock ppp connection at this speed
115200
#use hardware flow control
crtscts
#assign a dns server IP address to client
ms-dns 192.168.4.100
#keep listening for connections after link has gone down
persist
#use this chat command line with chat scipt /etc/ppp/pppscript
connect "/usr/sbin/chat -v -f /etc/ppp/pppscript"
```

2. Make a suitable chat script to initialize the modem and then wait for a phone call. For this example, your chat script is called /etc/ppp/pppscript:

```
"" "ATZ"
"RING" ""
"RING" "ATA"
"CONNECT" ""
```

3. After initializing the modem, the script will answer the call after two rings and then pass the call to pppd after a connection has been established. As with most things in Linux, there are several other ways to go about establishing dial-in services. For a basic PPP dial-in, this is the easiest way to go about it.

PPP Alternatives

Not all dial-in services utilize PPP. Another connection method that used to be more popular was SLIP (Serial Line Internet Protocol). SLIP is an older protocol without as many error correction and data transmission type capabilities. The tool used to make a SLIP connection is **dip** (Dialup IP). In fact, the **dip** program can do PPP connections as well.

Another version of SLIP that is available is CSLIP, or Compressed SLIP. This protocol is also something you can handle through **dip**.

Getting The Most Out Of Serial Connections

Sometimes your modem may not work as quickly as it should, even though all your settings may be correct. In these cases, the problem may actually be with where your modem is in the IRQ hierarchy. You can move it up in the priority listing with the **irqtune** tool, which is available at **www.best.com/~cae/ irqtune**. The modem's serial port also may simply not be configured to the right speed. Use **setserial -a** to check the current settings. If you have a 56Kbps modem, then the serial speed should be 115.2Kbps.

DOMAIN NAMES

This entire book is sprinkled with domain names. Everywhere you turn on the Internet there is yet another name to memorize. As a system administrator, you will eventually have to deal with the issue of getting your own domain name. You also need to understand the purpose for these names and how they are used.

Registering A Domain

A domain name consists of two parts: the domain and the extension. Together, these two parts form a unique entity that only one person can register. Where you go to register this name, however, depends on the extension. There was a day when any .com, .net, or .org domain had to be registered through one specific organization: InterNIC, now Network Solutions at **www.network solutions.com**. This limitation is no longer in place. A number of alternative registrars exist. However, all of these other name registration organizations must at some point register the new name with the central listing at Network Solutions.

The general process for registering a new .net, .com, or .org name is first you must see if that name is already taken. Use the **whois** tool discussed in the "Getting Information About Domains" section to look up the information on whatever name and extension combination you want to register. If nothing comes up, then you can register it. However, if it is taken, then you have to find some variation on the name that is not yet taken.

There are also a series of extensions available that specify which country the domain is within. Each of these extensions is registered through its own organization. You can either locate the registry for the country on your own or utilize a registrar who will take care of the process for you.

Domain Name Translation

Once a domain name and its respective IP information is entered into the Internet name databases, it can be quickly translated back and forth by name resolver routines. When you try to access a domain, Linux looks to your list of name resolution rules. It first tends to look locally to see if you already have that domain's IP information entered on the machine or in its cache from a previous lookup. If not, it goes to a domain name server specified in the rules. This server may or may not have the addressing information. If it does, then your query is complete and the IP values are returned.

If the local domain server does not have the information you need, then it looks to the zone server for the address in question. Zone servers come in a number of varieties but in this case the domain server looks to any zone server for that particular domain extension. This server keeps a list of the zone servers for each specific domain's site and passes the request on to them. These local zone servers then have the IP information for the specific machine on that domain and return the IP information.

BASIC NETWORKING TOOLS

There is a certain collection of networking tools that any system administrator should be familiar with. This set of tools has nothing to do with the networking services you will set up later in Chapter 9. Instead, they help in a variety of areas, such as getting information about other domains and addresses, and connecting to your own machines remotely.

Getting Information About Domains

There are two primary tools used to get information about domains and IP addresses. The first of these is **whois**. If you want more information on where a domain is or who owns it, then you can get the information with this command. Typing "**whois** domain.extension" gets you the registered address for the site, the contact information for the administrator, the registered domain servers for the site, and other such administrative information necessary to register the domain in the first place.

If you have an IP address and want to know what domain it belongs to, then you can often get this information with the **nslookup** command. Typing "**nslookup** *IPaddress*" gives you what information it can get—depending on where the address is in its network, sometimes **nslookup** is not incredibly useful. It also has further capabilities, however. You can get information on the domain and its name servers with this command and more.

Remotely Accessing Machines

There are two different commands used to remotely access a Linux machine. One of these is **telnet** and is used across pretty much every operating system. Typing "**telnet** *host.domain.extension*" allows you to get a login prompt for that machine if it has the telnet service enabled. If you have a shell account there, you can then log on to it. However, you cannot log in to a root account in this manner unless the machine is explicitly set up for that. Allowing root telnet access is a major security hole.

Another command available if you want to access other machines that are on the same network—and those machines have the service enabled—is **rlogin**. These machines need to be similar, with the same terminal types and screen sizes. You can either type "**rlogin** *host*" to remotely log in to a specific machine with the same username, or "**rlogin** *host* -l *username*" to remotely log in to a different account.

It is possible to create an .rhosts file in your home directory on the host you want to be able to **rlogin** to, in which you make a list of the machines you trust yourself to log in from to that account. Doing this saves you from having to enter a password on your way in. However, it is also a security hole because if someone breaks into the trusted machine, he or she can immediately get into your account on the other one.

Transferring Files

If you need to transfer files between machines, a tool such as **telnet** will not do. Instead, you need to use **ftp**. Whether you want to move or copy files within your own network or between it and an outside location, you can utilize **ftp** as long as there is an **ftp** server listening on the machine you want to connect to and you have an account there or there is some form of anonymous access. Type "**ftp** *host.domain.extension*" to open the connection. Then, either log in with your username and password or use the anonymous or guest account if available to you. If you are logging in anonymously and this service is activated, then use the username "anonymous" and enter your email address for the password.

8

Once you connect you get a command prompt. Use the **cd** command to change to the directory you want to transfer the files to. Either use the command **ascii** (text file) or **binary** (compiled program) to tell **ftp** which type of file you are about to transfer. The **dir** and **ls** commands allow you to get a directory listing. To actually transfer your data, either use the **get** (single file) or **mget** (multiple files using wildcards) commands to download files, or the **put** (single file) or **mput** (multiple files using wildcards) commands to upload.

 Be sure that if you are transferring files in groups they are all text or binary items and not mixed. Otherwise, there may be files missing in the end.

When you are finished with your session, use the command **quit** or **bye** to close the connection.

TAYLOR UUCP

One service that used to be far more popular but is waning as connection time becomes more affordable—and therefore is still popular in areas where connection time is expensive—is UUCP, or Unix-to-Unix Copy. This service allows you to transfer mail and news in bulk on a regular basis and then close the connection, rather than needing to keep it open while users read and answer messages.

All Linux distributions come with some form of UUCP software, with Taylor UUCP being the most popular. Install this from its Web sites or installation media, and then go to the directory /etc/uucp in most cases to find the configuration files. If the instructions are different for the distribution you are dealing with, then follow those instructions instead. One key consideration is that you need to create a user and group both by the name "uucp" so that you can ensure there are no permission problems.

The Linux UUCP HOWTO at **www.linuxdoc.org/HOWTO/UUCP-HOWTO-4.html** contains detailed information for ensuring that your Taylor UUCP installation works properly if you want to know more.

CONFIGURING AND USING BOOTP

Linux provides a few alternatives that automate giving addresses to network machines. The most basic of these alternatives is **bootp**, or the Bootstrap Protocol. Essentially, the bootp tool dynamically gives IP addresses to machines at boot time, according to which MAC address they have. This protocol is not only used in the Linux environment, but is common across a number of network operating systems.

Although **bootp** can also be used to direct diskless machines to the network information they need to start up, the discussion of **bootp** here will only cover assignment of network addressing information.

Installing bootp

To use the bootp tool, you must first install the bootp daemon. This daemon may have already been installed when you put the distribution on your machine. Use the command **which bootp** to see if the program is installed. If it is not there, you will need to locate it within your distribution CD-ROM or download it from the distribution's Web site.

Generally speaking, if you installed most of the networking tools available to you, the bootp daemon may very well be on the machine already.

Configuring The bootp Server

There are a number of issues to consider when configuring bootp. These issues range from how it is run, to how many clients it needs to manage, to which exact clients it manages and what range of IP addresses the daemon can hand out. Be careful when you configure this daemon, because doing so incorrectly can cause a lot of confusion on the clients.

The first issue to consider when configuring bootp is whether to run it as a standalone daemon, or under the auspices of inetd. Unless the daemon is serving addressing information for large banks of machines—say, 50 or more—it makes sense to run it as part of the superdaemon. Otherwise, be sure to include a statement that starts the daemon at boot time in the bootp server. The actual bootp daemon is bootpd.

Once you have added bootpd to either your startup scripts or inetd's configuration file, open the file /etc/bootptab with your favorite text editor. A line in this file follows the format:

```
name:argument1:argument2:
```

There are essentially two types of name entries: direct naming and templates. Direct names represent the individual machines that the statements define, and can have dashes or periods in them as long as they begin with a letter. Templates, on the other hand, always begin with a period. A template contains information that is relevant to more than one machine.

Arguments can be made up of a number of elements. The options available are listed in Table 8.6.

8

Table 8.6   Arguments available for /etc/bootptab host definitions.

Argument	Purpose	Example
dn	The domain name for the item.	dn=colors.org
ds	The domain name server or list of servers the item should look to.	ds=192.168.15.14
gw	The gateway address, or list of addresses. This gateway is typically a proxy or IP masquerading server.	gw=192.168.12.1
ha	The twelve-digit hardware address that identifies the particular client in question—typically the MAC address for the Ethernet card.	ha=56248F67AD449
hn	Transmit the host name assigned to the client. This name is what you use to name the individual machine's entry.	hn
ht	The type of hardware the host is using, according to RFC 1340.	ht=RS-232
ip	The IP address to assign the host.	ip=192.168.162.9
lg	The address for the server that logs the host's information, or a list of addresses.	lg=192.168.173.5
lp	The address for the print server, or a list of addresses.	lp=192.168.12.5
sm	The subnet mask to pass to the host.	sm=255.255.255.0
tc	Points to a template you want referenced to fill in the blanks.	tc=.all

Consider the following code:

```
.all:sm=255.255.255.0:lp=192.168.12.61:hn:ds=192.168.12.4:dn=colors.org:
blue:tc=.all:ha=153A632E628F:ip=192.168.12.10:
green:tc=.all:ha=1276B25FE276:ip=192.168.12.11:
purple:tc=.all:ha=A5163F62BE16:ip=192.168.12.12:
```

The highlighted portion is the template. All of the data within this template—subnet mask, print server, host name passing to machine, DNS server, and the domain name—is identical for each of the machines defined afterward. Only the machine-specific information, such as the name itself, the hardware address, and the IP address, is explicitly defined each time.

This is a very basic approach to using bootp. It is also possible to utilize this service across subnets.

Once the configuration is complete, save and exit the file. If you are running bootpd on its own, be sure to stop and restart the daemon.

Configuring The bootp Client

The bootp client is a program called bootpc. You have to create a shell script to go along with this client, so that it knows what machine to ask for information and what data to ask for. This script must run among your initialization scripts, and so is often with the other rc items as rc.bootp. A sample rc.bootp comes with the bootpc package.

Edit the sample rc.bootp script so that it matches what you need on your client machine. This script has many comments to explain what is happening at each stage, and a lot of code that is commented out by default. Your job as the administrator is to determine what you need to keep and what you do not need.

Once you have rc.bootp set to the format you need it in, be sure to reference it within your startup scripts.

8

CONFIGURING AND USING DHCP

A more commonly used tool for providing addressing and domain information during install or boot time is DHCP (Dynamic Host Configuration Protocol). This tool is more advanced than its cousin bootp, although it is backward compatible with the older protocol. A major distinction between the two tools is that DHCP can assign lease times. Leases refer to how long a machine is allowed to keep the IP address assigned to it by the DHCP server.

The discussion of DHCP here is limited to handing out network addresses at boot time.

Installing DHCP

To use the DHCP tool, you must first install the bootp daemon. If you have a kernel newer than version 2.2—type "uname -r" to see what kernel version you are using—then you need to make sure that you have a client daemon (dhcpcd) that is at least version 1.3. The 2.2 kernel does not function properly with the older dhcpcd. For the server end, if the distribution came with a server, then use that version. Otherwise, FTP the latest version from ftp://ftp.isc.org/isc/dhcp/.

This daemon may have already been installed when you put the distribution on your machine. Type **which dhcpd** to see if the server is installed, and **which dhcpcd** to see if the client is installed. If it is not there, you will need to locate it within your distribution CD-ROM or download it from the distribution's Web site. If you installed most of the networking tools available to you, the dhcpc daemon is probably on the machine already.

You can determine which version your DHCP server is from the full package name among the distribution materials.

Configuring The DHCP Server

Assuming that you already have the rest of your networking set up, what you need to do from here is edit the file /etc/dhcpd.conf. There are a number of graphical tools available to handle the job, depending on which desktop environment you prefer to use. However, it is important to know how to do this by hand before you move on to the fancier tools. Because the goal for the Linux certification exams is to understand the basics of DHCP, the following walkthrough covers how to set a server up that only hands out IP addresses and other necessary networking information. For further information, type **man dhcpd.conf**.

First, set the lease times. The reason that IP addresses are leased rather than permanently assigned is that this goes against the function of the DHCP server. When a client requests an IP address, the server offers an address out of its available bank of choices. The client can have this address for a certain amount of time, which is the lease period. Once this lease expires, or is about to expire, the client contacts the DHCP server again.

A lease is expressed in seconds, so get out your calculator!

Generally, you would set two different lease times. The default is what the server will assign if the client does not request a specific lease time. Add a line that looks something like the following if you want to set a two-week default (60 seconds in a minute, 60 minutes per hour, 24 hours per day, 14 days in two weeks):

```
default-lease-time 1209600;
```

You can also set the maximum lease time that is the longest lease the server will assign. Add a line of code that looks like the following if you want to set a long maximum, say a month (60 seconds in a minute, 60 minutes in an hour, 24 hours in a day, then average 30 days per month):

```
max-lease-time 2592000;
```

After you set the lease times, you need to set the global options. Global DHCP options are values that are the same for all of the machines the server handles. For example, this section might look like the following:

```
option domain-name-servers 192.168.13.4, 192.168.13.13, 192.168.13.42;
option domain-name "colors.org";
option subnet-mask 255.255.255.0;
option routers 192.168.13.1;
option broadcast-address 192.168.13.255
```

Now you have to create the statement that actually hands out the IP addresses. You can use the following format to hand out this information dynamically, meaning that no machine is promised a specific IP address. This example demonstrates handing out a range of addresses between 192.168.13.50 and 192.168.13.200:

```
subnet 192.168.13.0 netmask 255.255.255.0 {
        range 192.168.13.50 192.168.13.200;
}
```

If you want to have each IP address assigned to a specific host, then use this format instead. This example is for the machine named "pink", to which I want to assign the address 192.168.13.50:

```
host pink {
        hardware ethernet 01:5A:61:68:FE:01;
        fixed-address 192.168.13.50;
}
```

Mix and match these two assignment methods as your needs require. Once the /etc/dhcpd.conf file is finished, save and exit it.

You now need to start the server, or restart it if it is already running. The daemon is dhcpd. Before your next reboot be sure to set the daemon up to start automatically at boot time, either by adding it to the runlevel symlinks or to the system initialization scripts.

Configuring The DHCP Client

The main issue when it comes to configuring your DHCP client is making sure that the client machine contacts the DHCP server for networking information at boot time. This step is most definitely a case where you must understand the distribution's initialization scripts so you know where to insert the client call.

 It is wise to back up system files before you start changing them. Also, make sure you have emergency recovery disks (boot and rescue/root).

Essentially, you need to locate the network initialization script if there is a separate one, or the network init portion of another init script, and replace it with new code—but leave the section that assigns the host name and loopback information. The entire code necessary to tell the client to get its network information over the primary Ethernet card (eth0) is similar to:

```
/sbin/dhcpcd
```

Be sure that you have the correct path to the DHCP client daemon, dhcpcd. However, if you are using a Red Hat distribution, the command used by default for the clients is **pump**. The code in this case might look like:

```
/sbin/pump -I $DEVICE -h $HOSTNAME
```

Now, be sure that the DHCP server is running, and reboot the client machine. Typing **ifconfig** will show you whether the DHCP client got its information.

CONFIGURING AND USING NIS

At a basic level, the NIS (Network Information Service) is used to centrally manage user accounts and passwords on LANs. NIS is invaluable on larger networks whose users may be using any machine at any time, because maintaining the accounts on each machine individually would require much annoyance and perhaps even assistants so you could get real administrative work done.

Before Installing NIS

The NIS server and client typically come along with the distribution. You also need to install the RPC Portmapper, which will translate program information to port numbers. This daemon is not only included with the distributions, but often is already installed by default.

First, check for the Portmapper. Type **ps aux | grep portmap** to see if it is running on its own. Also, look in /etc/inetd.conf. The Portmapper is often run from the superdaemon, so check to see if it is both present and uncommented. If you do uncomment it, remember to restart inetd. If the Portmapper is nowhere on the system, be sure to install it from the distribution CDs and then be sure it is activated.

Setting Up The NIS Server

The NIS server should be available with your distribution materials, or might already be installed depending on what packages you chose. However, the package will not likely have the letters N-I-S in its name. Instead, look for ypserv. This name comes from the fact that the server was once called the Sun

Yellow Pages, but had to be renamed for phone company trademark reasons. You will need both the ypserv and makedbm programs, which are very likely packaged together.

Once these packages are installed, there are two files you need to edit. The first is /var/yp/securenets—if you cannot find it at this location, do a search on "securenets." This file is used to set what range of hosts has access to your NIS server. Use a combination of IP address and hostmask to describe this range. In a simple example, you may want to ensure that the machine itself can access its own NIS server, plus perhaps all machines in the 192.168.150.* range, then you would include the following text in the file:

```
host 127.0.0.1
255.255.255.0 192.168.150.0
```

After saving and exiting this file, edit /etc/ypserv.conf. This file is not as straightforward as the previous one. There are two different types of lines you can create: options, and rules. An option is in the format:

```
option: value
```

There are essentially two different options available. The first is dns and is used in one of two formats: "dns: yes" or "dns: no". If you set this option to yes, then the NIS server will do a DNS lookup to get the host name of machines that are not explicitly defined in its own files. The default for this option is no because, generally, it is more secure for the system administrator to explicitly lay out exactly which machines are welcome to use the server. The second option is xfr_check_port, which is used in the same formats as the dns option. If you set this option to yes, which is the default, the NIS server must run on a port lower than number 1024.

A rule is used to define who can access the server at what level, and is in the format:

```
host:names:security:mangle:which
```

Some of these fields are required, and others are optional. The host field is the IP address or a range of addresses to which the rule applies. You can specify them as an IP and netmask combination, or a wildcarded range. For example, "192.160.250." and "192.160.250.0/255.255.255.0" both refer to the same range of addresses. The names field lists the file that maps the individual IP addresses to domain names. This feature allows you to securely manage who has access to what as mentioned earlier. Use the full path to the file. The format necessary for this file is discussed later in the chapter.

Table 8.7   The /etc/ypserv.conf security options when defining access rules.

Option	Purpose
deny	If the host requesting NIS information matches the address group listed, refuse to send information.
none	Always allow access to the host map file.
port	Allow access if the requests come from a port below 1024 on the originating machine. If they come from a higher port, refuse them.

The security field offers a number of choices, which are outlined in Table 8.7. Choose the feature most appropriate to the considerations surrounding the hosts you are defining with the rule. Remember that you can have more than one rule in the file.

The mangle field should contain either "yes" or "no". If you put a "yes" in this slot, then the item referred to by the final field will be "mangled," or changed to an "x" if the access in question matches the rule. This method is used to prevent unauthorized people from being able to guess people's passwords. By default, mangle is set to "no".

Finally, the "which" field is used to say which item should be changed to an "x" if the mangle field is set to "yes". The items you choose are fields in an /etc/ passwd entry. The second field is the default, which is the password itself.

Once all of this information is configured, restart the NIS server if it is already running.

 As you might guess, the NIS tool does not work well in conjunction with shadow passwords. This is one of the few instances where you are better off deactivating the shadow suite.

Setting Up The NIS Client

The base program that you need in order to make a machine an NIS client is **ypbind**. This program needs to run all the time so the machine can talk to the server, so you need to either add it to the init scripts or the runlevel daemon listing. There is also a collection of client programs that may come packaged together, or separately. The important items for the user are those that take the place of existing commands. From a user's point of view, the important one is **yppasswd**, which is what they need to type to change their password on an NIS client.

You also must ensure that NIS is one of the programs used to look up host information by the machine. To do this, open the file /etc/host.conf and look for the line that probably says:

```
order hosts,bind
```

Change this line so somewhere within it the term "nis" also appears in the order. For example:

```
order nis,hosts,bind
```

Now, make a backup copy of the /etc/passwd file, then erase the contents of the original. It helps to build the new NIS file from scratch. For example, say that you want to centrally manage user accounts and passwords. Add the following line to /etc/passwd:

```
+:*:::::::/etc/NoShell
```

This line of code tells the NIS client machine to consult the NIS server for all logins. However, this is probably not what you want to do. Each machine, for example, should have its own root account. To remove a user definition from being centrally managed, include an explicit line like the following:

```
+root:::::::
```

You can also explicitly block logins to certain accounts by putting a minus sign (-) in front of them.

CHAPTER SUMMARY

This chapter discussed the fundamentals of Linux networking. Among the major points along the way were network protocols and how they interact, and a great deal about TCP/IP networking. The addressing scheme of subnets and netmasks was discussed, as well as how the standard ports are often used. In addition, steps to troubleshoot network problems were discussed. Then, you stepped through the process of how to create a ppp connection, both outgoing and incoming. For the purposes of studying for a certification exam, it is most important to know how to successfully configure and diagnose network interfaces using **ifconfig**, **route**, and **netstat**.

After the networking itself is configured, you can set up networking services. These services allow you to centrally control issues such as IP address assignments and login information. Only the basics of these services were covered in this chapter because during the exam it is more important to know what the service is and what it is capable of than to be able to use it in great detail. Remember that this book covers Level I exams, which involve individual machines and small networking issues. Network centralization services are most useful for larger LAN's where it would be horribly time-consuming to have to deal with machines in a one-on-one basis for routine matters.

REVIEW QUESTIONS

1. A Linux program requests a status report via _____.
   a. SNMP
   b. NNTP
   c. SMTP
   d. TCP

2. Which of the following is a transport protocol?
   a. TCP/IP
   b. SNMP
   c. UDP
   d. IPX

3. A TCP connection is a _____-based network connection.
   a. Linux
   b. datagram
   c. stream
   d. application

4. Why is the phrase "TCP/IP networking" misleading?
   a. Class A
   b. Class B
   c. Class C
   c. Class D

5. IP addresses are assigned to a(n) _____.
   a. module
   b. interface
   c. network
   d. CPU

6. A network interface has an IP address of 172.16.0.24 and a netmask of 255.255.0.0. What are this interface's broadcast and network addresses?
   a. broadcast = 172.16.0.255, network = 127.0.0.1
   b. broadcast = 172.16.255.255, network = 172.16.0.0
   c. broadcast = 172.16.0.0, network = 255.255.255.255
   d. broadcast = 172.16.255.255, network = 255.255.0.24

7. The IP address in the previous question is accessible from the Internet.
   a. True
   b. False

8. What class of network is the address in Question 6?
   a. A
   b. B
   c. C
   d. D

9. To allow the interface in Question 6 to access the Internet it would have to go through:
   a. NAT
   b. PPP
   c. SNMP
   d. TCP/IP

10. What do the first two bits of a Class B network look like?
    a. xxx
    b. xxx.xxx
    c. xxx.xxx.xxx
    d. xxx.xxx.xxx.xxx

11. Which addressing class are you most likely to be able to get, if you can get an entire class?
    a. Class A
    b. Class B
    c. Class C
    d. Class D

12. What commands are used to configure interface eth0 with an IP address of 192.168.0.4 using a netmask of 255.255.255.0? [Choose all correct answers]
    a. **ifconfig eth0 192.168.0.4 netmask 255.255.255.0**
    b. **route eth0 192.160.0.4 255.255.255.0**
    c. **route eth0 192.160.0.4**
    d. **ifconfig eth0 192.168.0.4**

13. Which of the following is the command used to add an entry in the routing table for an Internet gateway with an IP address of 172.4.25.3?

    a. **route add defgw 172.4.25.3**

    b. **route add default 172.4.25.3**

    c. **route add gate 172.4.25.3**

    d. **route add default gw 172.4.25.3**

14. Which command would you use to delete the routing table entry added in Question 13? [Choose all correct answers]

    a. **route del 0.0.0.0**

    b. **route del default**

    c. **delroute default**

    d. **route -d gate**

15. What is the non-subnetted netmask for a Class B network?

    a. 255.0.0.0

    b. 255.255.0.0

    c. 255.255.255.0

    d. 255.255.255.255

16. What command will send six PING packets to interface 172.4.0.23?

    a. **PING 172.4.0.23**

    b. **PING 6 172.4.0.23**

    c. **PING -n6 172.4.0.23**

    d. **PING -c 6 172.4.0.23**

17. What command would you use if you suspected packets were being dropped enroute to their destination?

    a. **netstat (no options)**

    b. **PING**

    c. **traceroute**

    d. **route**

18. What service would you implement if you wanted to centrally control user accounts?

    a. NFS

    b. DNS

    c. NIS

    d. DHCP

19. What tool would you use to get the contact information for a site's technical administrator?

    a. nslookup

    b. netstat

    c. ifconfig

    d. whois

20. What command would fix the problem in the previous question?

    a. **route mask 255.0.0.0**

    b. **ifconfig eth0 netmask 255.255.0.0**

    c. **netmask 255.255.0.0**

    d. **ifconfig netmask 255.255.0.0**

21. What directory contains the files associated with pppd?

    a. /etc/pppd

    b. /etc/ppp

    c. /usr/local/ppp

    d. /var/pppd

22. The PPP login chat script contains which of the following? [Choose all correct answers]

    a. prompts

    b. login password

    c. responses

    d. user shell

23. What line(s) would you add to the /etc/ppp/options file to tell pppd to use serial device ttyS1 with hardware flow control? [Choose all correct answers]

    a. demand

    b. crtscts

    c. /dev/ttyS1

    d. lock

24. What is the major difference between dial-in and dial-out ppp services using pppd?

    a. chat script

    b. password prompt

    c. userid prompt

    d. specialized software

8

HANDS-ON PROJECTS

These projects require a Linux system running at least kernel version 2.0.x. This computer must also have a network interface card with the appropriate drivers activated within the kernel.

Project 8.1

In this project you will configure network interface eth0 with a new IP address and netmask. Also, we will add an entry into the routing table, as well as an entry for a gateway to the Internet.

To change eth0's IP address and netmask:

1. Issue the **ifconfig** command with the new IP address and netmask:

```
> ifconfig eth0 192.168.0.1 netmask 255.255.255.0
```

2. Add a route to the routing table for the new IP address of eth0:

```
> route add -net 192.168.0.0
```

3. Add an entry into the routing table for an Internet gateway at IP address 192.168.0.100:

```
> route add default gw 192.168.0.100
```

Project 8.2

In this project, you will configure and initiate a PPP connection. This connection will be much like one that would be used to dial in to an ISP.

To configure and initiate a PPP connection:

1. Make an /etc/ppp/options file to connect using the modem on /dev/ttyS1. This file should include an entry to log in as "joe":

```
#use serial device ttyS1 (cua1) for the ppp connection
/dev/ttyS1
#lock the device while in use
lock
#remote end does not need to auhenticate itself
noauth
#Username used when authenticating this ppp session
name "joe"
#Automatically place an entry in the routing table for the ppp
  connection
defaultroute
```

```
#Use modem, lock link at 115200 using hardware flow control
modem 115200 crtscts
#Chat line used to dial modem
connect '/usr/sbin/chat -v -f /etc/ppp/[name of chat script]'
```

2. Make a chat script to establish the modem connection:

```
""        "ATZ"
"OK"      "ATDT5551212"
"CONNECT"      ""
```

3. Make a pap-secrets file to hold the password information:

```
joe       *         password       *
```

4. Test the connection to see if it works:

```
> pppd
```

8

LINUX NETWORKING SERVICES

M any computer users choose the Linux operating system as an inexpensive and stable way to implement Internet or intranet services. Setting up these services correctly is not only important in the sense that they provide what is needed by the system administrator, but is also imperative for system security. Take the time to ensure that you learn how to set up these services, and then, if possible, experiment with the user access options to ensure that you fully understand how to best set up these files for your needs.

THE LINUX MODEL FOR NETWORKING SERVICES

There are two methods for invoking network daemons within Linux. In the first method, a central daemon monitors the *ports* used by a service, then awakens its controlling process when necessary. The second method is more processor-intensive but appropriate for particular services. In this case, the daemons run continuously in the background listening for attempted accesses.

The inetd Superdaemon

The central daemon in charge of most networking services is inetd, otherwise referred to as the *superdaemon*. This daemon is controlled by a combination of files that, in total, tell it what services are under its domain, and what ports these services use to talk to the outside world.

Introduction To /etc/inetd.conf

The file /etc/inetd.conf tells the superdaemon what services it is responsible for handling. This file contains the list of services inetd listens to incoming connections for. The file is segmented into sections with services put into groups, and the default is usually well-commented. Most common inetd-run Internet and network services are listed even if they are commented out and not used, meaning that the administrator often only needs to go through and uncomment what is needed, and comment out what is unnecessary.

Introduction To /etc/services

The file /etc/services tells the superdaemon which port each service owns. These port assignments often follow a certain standard so that the clients trying to access them know where to look. See Chapter 12 for a discussion on when not to follow the standards in the name of system security.

Individual Networking Daemons

Sometimes, a network services daemon needs to run on its own so that it is always active. Often, this is the case when a service will have a lot of requests, such as httpd (the Web server daemon). There is a certain amount of overhead when starting a daemon, including RAM and hard drive usage. If a high-demand daemon is run through inetd, it must be restarted each time a new request comes in on its port.

In the case of such services, it makes more sense to run them as standalone daemons. Overall, the system usage cost is far lower than leaving them on constantly.

Stopping And Starting Daemons

When changes are made to daemon configuration files, it is important to restart the daemons so they will take on the new settings. To accomplish this, the daemon's control script needs to be located. Using the **which** command will not work, as this action will point to the daemon itself. Instead, as with most networking daemons, go to /etc/rc.d/init.d, which is where many of those scripts are located. Type *./daemon* and it will give a list of the commands it accepts. For more information about controlling daemons, see the "Creating, Monitoring, and Killing Processes" section in Chapter 7.

The networking daemons have two or three options. The two most common options are **start** and **stop**, and the third is **restart**:

➤ **Stop** After changing a daemon's configuration files, issue the command **/etc/rc.d/init.d/*daemon* stop**. This directive shuts the daemon down properly. If any errors occur while stopping the daemon, issue the same command again.

➤ **Start** After successfully stopping the daemon, issue the command **/etc/rc.d/init.d/*daemon* start**. This directive puts the daemon back into place. If any errors occur, issue the **stop** command and start again.

➤ **Restart** Some daemons include the shorthand command of **restart**. Those that have it use the format **/etc/rc.d/init.d *daemon* restart**. This directive shuts down the daemon, then immediately runs it. If any errors occur, issue the **restart** command again, or use **stop** and **start** instead.

9

CONFIGURING AND MANAGING INETD

Configuring inetd to operate according to the system's needs involves altering its two configuration files, /etc/inetd.conf and /etc/services. Many administrators have no need to change /etc/services, but often /etc/inetd.conf needs to be adjusted to provide desired network services.

Understanding /etc/inetd.conf

The /etc/inetd.conf file is primarily made up of service definitions and comments. A service definition line is formatted as follows:

```
Service  Socket  Protocol  Flags  User-Run-As  Path  Arguments
```

Here is a breakdown of the preceding code:

➤ **Service** The name of the service being defined. This name must match the one listed in /etc/services.

➤ **Socket** A virtual connection between two network applications, consisting of an IP address and a port number. There are only two types of sockets used in Linux, and the type of socket needed depends on which protocol is used. TCP uses a socket type of *stream*, whereas UDP uses a socket type of *dgram*.

➤ **Protocol** The language used to communicate between two services. The two protocol choices available are usually TCP and UDP.

➤ **Flags** A UDP flag that controls what inetd does once it receives a connection request. The choices **wait** or **nowait** are available. If the socket type is not dgram, then be sure this value is **nowait**.

➤ **User-Run-As** The user ID of the account the service runs as. More often than not this value is root. See Chapter 12 for a discussion on when this default is a bad idea.

➤ **Path** The location of the program that runs when the service is accessed. Although it may differ in other flavors of Unix, the path in Linux is almost always /usr/sbin/tcpd.

➤ **Arguments** The command and flags passed to the tcpd server when this service is activated.

Changing any daemon setting means that the inetd must be stopped and restarted before these settings will take effect.

Understanding /etc/services

The /etc/services file is primarily made up of service port assignments and comments. A port definition line is formatted as follows:

```
Service  Port  Aliases
```

The preceding code breaks down as follows:

➤ **Service** The name of the service to which the port is being assigned. This name must match what is in the /etc/inetd.conf file.

➤ **Port** The port number assigned to the service. Often, this port number is the standard used across the Internet. This practice makes it easier for clients to find servers, because they know where to expect them. When using a non-standard port (see Chapter 12 for security reasons for doing so) the user on the client side must specify the port number to connect to the non-standard port server.

➤ **Aliases** Alternative names for the port, if any. Separate these with a single space.

Changing any daemon settings means that the inetd must be stopped and restarted before these settings will take effect.

SETTING UP AND CONFIGURING BASIC DNS SERVICES

Although it is possible to run most network services without Domain Name Service (DNS) configured, they would have to operate completely with IP addresses. So, before configuring the rest of the network services, take the time to configure at least the basic *nameservice* on the machine. At the very least, it makes the rest easier to test along the way. In fact, consider having at least two nameservers on the machine or network, a primary and a backup. Doing this can save many headaches if one of the nameservers goes down.

Why To Run named

The named daemon is part of the BIND (Berkeley Internet Name Domain) name service package. It is used by the vast majority of Internet sites to achieve name resolution, which is a testament to its reliability. Because every access to the Internet requires name lookups, it is a good idea to run named as a stand-alone daemon rather than through the superdaemon.

BIND Version Differences

You need to be aware of some differences between BIND 4 and BIND 8. For one thing, there are no more patches coming out for BIND 4. BIND 8 is the new standard, so if you are setting up a new system, this is the version to use. Also, choosing BIND 8 over BIND 4 gives you at the very least a version that has most of the bugs in BIND 4 fixed from the beginning and the security patches for BIND 4 built in.

The new version of BIND offers dynamic DNS updates, a feature that makes the DNS system able to change more quickly. It used to rely on zone masters to edit its zone files before the days of heavy Internet use. As more sites piled on to the Internet, however, this practice became problematic. When BIND 8 was introduced in 1997, the zone administrator's life got a lot easier. Another feature offered is when the master zone servers have changes in their data, they actually notify the slave servers that a change has been made. This ensures that the slave servers send in a query to determine what the changes are and get them added to their own databases. These notification and query loops immensely improved the propagation of name changes throughout the DNS system.

9

Smaller changes that were just as interesting to BIND users included issues such as a new configuration syntax and better scalability for large nameservers.

Running named At Boot Time

The named daemon may or may not be configured by default to run at boot time, depending on the distribution installed. Examine the contents of the rc directories in /etc/rc.d to see whether this package is already set to automatically run at boot time. If it is not, then create the necessary **start** and **kill** links. Also, examine the contents of /etc/inetd.conf to see if named is configured to be managed by the superdaemon. If this is the case, comment out the line that declares this and restart the superdaemon.

Why To Install A Caching Name Server

A *caching nameserver* keeps a record of recently resolved name and IP address combinations. Having these resolution logs available takes some of the load off of the resolver and the system, speeding up overall lookup accesses. This item comes in a separate package and installs four new configuration files, one of which is a modified /etc/named.conf.

If you do not have a dedicated IP address and your name server is not in the root server cache, it's best to run a caching only server.

The named Configuration Files

The named daemon requires a number of configuration files. Each file contains specific information necessary for name resolution. Because configuring named itself can be such a complex task, it is not covered in the first-level certification exams. Regardless, it is important to understand the basics involved.

/etc/named.conf, The Main BIND Configuration File

The primary file used to configure the named demon is /etc/named.conf. This configuration file is made up of a series of statements in the following format:

```
parameter {
settings;
settings;
};
```

Some important parameters within /etc/named.conf are outlined in Table 9.1.

/etc/named.boot

The configuration file /etc/named.boot contains a list of where the named server can find the information it needs to identify all of the machines it

Table 9.1 Some parameters for the named configuration file /etc/named.conf.

Parameter	Description
acl	Stands for access control list; defines who can access the nameserver.
key	Assigns a particular security key to the server, which is sent when requested.
logging	A feature that lets the admin configure the server's logging facilities to a high degree.
options	Catch-all statement which includes the various settings that can be assigned to the server.
server	Used to assign particular characteristics to specific outside DNS servers.

provides service for. It is broken down into one-line entries in the following format:

```
servicetype    domainserved    lookupfile    backupfile
```

As the named daemon starts, it looks to this file and loads the information from the following lookup files:

➤ **/var/named/named.ca** This file is downloaded from internic.net. Its purpose is to initialize the caching portion of the named server. The cache file from the root name servers includes names from the top level in the hierarchy.

➤ **/var/named/named.local** This file stores the data for all of the machines in the domain. It is referenced in the file /etc/named.boot and loaded by the named server as it starts.

/etc/hosts

The file /etc/hosts is one place where you can set some shortcuts for name resolution. In this file, you explicitly assign IP addresses to specific computers, whether to their fully qualified domain name or just their host name. This is typically where you would enter the names of all the machines in your domain so the machine does not have to look them up. A set of /etc/host entries might look like the following:

```
192.168.150.20    dog.animals.org        dog
192.168.150.21    cat.animals.org        www cat
192.168.150.22    fish.animals.org       ftp fish
192.168.150.23    monkey.animals.org monkey
```

/etc/resolv.conf

The file /etc/resolv.conf is where you tell the machine up to three name servers to look to. You can also tell it the domain name for your network so that the resolver can automatically append that value when you only specify a host name, and list which domains to search for a host under if an explicit local entry cannot be found. An example entry set in /etc/resolv.conf might be as follows:

```
nameserver 192.168.150.4
domain animals.org
search animals.org
```

/etc/host.conf

The file /etc/host.conf is a brief file that quickly tells your system how it should handle name resolution. More often than not it contains the following:

```
order hosts,bind
multi on
```

The reason this file tends to contain these lines is that you are telling it to first look in the /etc/hosts file and then utilize bind to resolve names into IP addresses. It also tells your machine that there may be more than one IP address assigned to a specific machine. Of course, if you are using more than one IP address, you need to have an interface for each—for example, for two IP addresses you need two Ethernet cards, typically eth0 and eth1.

/etc/nsswitch.conf

The Name Service Switch file /etc/nsswitch.conf is used to keep a central listing of various domains and other related databases. The databases you can list in this file are detailed in Table 9.2.

Once you have defined the database you are referring to, you can then specify what service is used to get information from the database. The services available to use in /etc/nsswitch are listed in Table 9.3.

Once you have set what type of service's information should come from where, there is one more refining step available. In this step, you can specify the action that should occur depending on the output of what you said should happen. The output status options are: SUCCESS, NOTFOUND, UNAVAIL, or TRYAGAIN. The available actions are return and continue.

Table 9.2   Databases available in the /etc/nsswitch.conf file.

Database	Contains
aliases	Sendmail mail aliases.
ethers	Ethernet hardware addresses.
group	User groupings.
hosts	Host names and IP addresses.
netgroup	A list of the users at each host.
network	Network names and numbers.
passwd	A list of user passwords.
protocols	The protocols used on the network.
publickey	Keys needed for NIS+ and NFS if you are using encrypted transfers.
rpc	Procedure call names and numbers.
services	A list of network services.
shadow	List of passwords protected with the shadow suite.

Table 9.3   Services available to access databases within the /etc/nsswitch.conf file.

Service	Purpose
compat	Option used only with passwd, group, and shadow if the lookup should be done on the local machine.
dns	Go to the domain name server to get this information.
files	Go to the appropriate file to get this information.
nis	Get this information from the NIS server.
nisplus	Get this information from the NIS+ server.

Putting these items together, you might have an /etc/nsswitch.conf that looks like the following:

```
passwd: compat
group: compat
shadow: compat

hosts: files nfs dns
networks: files
ethers: files
services: files [NOTFOUND=return]
```

Potential Problems With Caching Only Nameservice

The problem with caching only nameservice is that if an address changes, or if incorrect information was gleaned the first time, this data stays in the cache and is not refreshed. The issue of changing information is problematic enough that you should update your cache on a regular basis every few weeks using the **dig** tool. The **cron** tool and a quick shell script can easily take care of this task.

Nameservice cache data is not actually stored in a file. If you run into any problems with your machine's memory, it is wise to rebuild your cache manually. This fact also means that each time your nameservice daemon (named) stops running, you need to rebuild the cache as well.

CONFIGURING AND OPERATING SENDMAIL

Sendmail is a powerful SMTP mail server, and one of the more complex programs to configure. It is generally run as a standalone daemon because mail traffic tends to be constant. There are two methods of configuration for this server. One of these, the new one, is via the m4 macros. This is the recommended method of configuring sendmail unless the administrator is familiar with the cf file.

Sendmail versions 10 and above have a new filesystem storage location: /etc/mail. Also, it is a good idea to move your mail spool to another partition or disk. Mail tends to be I/O intensive and slows down processing of other important OS tasks if you leave it on the root partition; also, there is always the possibility of it damaging the filesystem, so a good recommendation would be to put only the OS on the root partition and keep all of the user applications on a /usr partition. For example, you could create a /dev/hdb1 partition on a second hard drive, and mount it under /etc/mail. That would guarantee that no user could fool your root filesystem with a large mail message.

Introduction To SMTP

SMTP (Simple Mail Transfer Protocol) is not actually the only method of handling email; other methods are discussed in the section "Other Mail Servers And Services," later in this chapter. However, SMTP is the primary method through which mail is moved across the Internet through the use of Mail Transport Agents (MTAs). Sendmail is one highly prevalent MTA.

When a user sends a piece of email, the MTA first looks at the address to which the mail is sent. If it is a local address, sendmail is smart enough to handle these items without much fuss. However, if the mail needs to leave the domain, then the sendmail passes the mail through the SMTP protocol to whatever mail server it is configured to feed to. In this day of Internet email spam (junk email) problems, this upstream mail server tends to be the SMTP server at your Internet Service Provider (ISP). The message proceeds through the SMTP protocol through mail servers across the Internet until it reaches the destination mail server. This server first confirms that the user the mail is meant for exists, and then accepts and delivers that mail.

Mail Exchange (MX)

One item you hear much about when dealing with email is MX (Mail Exchange) records. An MX record allows email going to a domain to be directed to specific hosts that manage mail for that domain. You can create your own MX record for your domain by using your nameserver, named. Edit the file /etc/named.hosts (it may be in /var instead), or create it if it does not yet exist. Create an entry in the following format:

```
hostoriginallyto   IN   MX   importance  mailhost
mailhost   IN   A   mailhostIP
```

You can have more than one line of each type, and, if you have multiple listings governing the same machine, priority is determined by numbering (the lowest number has the highest priority). The thing to remember is all of your mail hosts must have a record pointing to their IP address so they can be quickly found. For example, you might have an MX record set such as:

```
dog.animals.org.   IN   MX   0   mail.animals.org.
cat.animals.org.   IN   MX   0   mail.animals.org.
*.animals.org.   IN   MX   5   mail.animals.org.
mail.animals.org.   IN   A   192.168.0.15
```

Notice the periods at the end of all the domain names. You must include these when working with this file. Also, notice that in one spot a wildcard was used to point all traffic to the animals.org site to the specific mail server listed. This line was given less importance—a five instead of a zero—than the others because specific entries should be used before more general ones. At the end of the statement, the mail server's IP information is listed.

Mail Servers Vs. Forwarders

One important thing to understand is that sendmail must be configured on every machine that gets mail service. However, not every machine needs a full mail server. In most cases, a network or Internet-connected box will have a single full server. Other machines connected to the server box only need to be set up as *mail forwarders*. A forwarder does not even need to run in daemon mode because its only job is to relay mail between the machine and the mail server. The mail server, however, must run as a daemon or the performance hits will be quite draining to the machine.

Configuration With m4 Macros

For years, system administrators have been plagued with the sendmail.cf file, which, although flexible, is incredibly difficult to configure. Today, however, the option of m4 macros has greatly simplified the mail server configuration process, negating the necessity of writing complex sets of rules that can take years to fully understand. Some Linux distributions install the m4 files by default and some do not. However, m4 is almost always included somewhere within the package list. Sometimes finding it just takes a moment or two of investigation.

The advantage of the m4 configuration method instead of sendmail.cf is that with m4 configuration, data is broken down into tables instead of rule sets. In fact, the more simple the needs of the mail setup on the machine or LAN, the less chance there is of even needing to edit any of this material.

Fortunately, the m4 sendmail tool comes with a series of sample configuration files to make things easier for the harried system administrator.

Locating The Files

The location of the m4 configuration files depends on what Linux distribution is installed. Either use the Red Hat Package Manager (RPM) utility to list where its contents were installed, or use the **find** command and search for the text **m4**. Ultimately, there is a directory usually called cf filled with files ending in .m4, .mc, and .cf. The instructions for working with this configuration format are generally found in the README file.

Choosing The Generic .mc

Look through the listing of available .mc files and choose the one that lists the necessary operating system. If a "linux" or distribution-specific file is not listed, then choose one of the generic options such as tcpproto.mc. If a generic file is chosen that is not of the exactly right operating system, copy the file to ensure a safe version is still available and then change the OSTYPE value to "linux". Ensure that the other values look correct.

The list of the available operating system types is found in the ostype subdirectory of the current parent directory.

Personalize The .mc File

The sendmail.cf can be built any time from now on. However, there are many more customization features to utilize to ensure the sendmail server functions as required. First, the admin sets the macros that define the system itself, as well as features and definitions. The more complex the network situation, the more digging necessary to find the configuration pieces that work best for the setup.

Sendmail Standalone Macros

One of the important features in the m4 version of sendmail configuration is the macro. These macros allow the administrator to set values quickly and easily. A macro consists of a term, in all capital letters, with its value in parentheses and sometimes further information on the end. No spaces separate these terms. The macro GENERIC with the value "value" would be written as:

```
GENERIC(value)
```

Table 9.4 lists commonly used macros in .mc files. These macros appear in the order they should be used in the .mc file.

Sometimes these macro definitions have the characters "dnl" directly after them. For example, adding it to the GENERIC definition would be done in the format:

```
GENERIC(value)dnl
```

Table 9.4 Macros used in the personalized .mc file used to generate sendmail.cf.

Macro	Purpose
MASQUERADE_AS	Show all mail as coming from one particular name. This item tends to be used to label all mail as coming from the domain itself, not a particular machine. The **MX record** for your domain or the domain name itself.
OSTYPE	The operating system installed on the computer sendmail is being configured to run on. Already included in the generic .mc files provided with the distribution. Use "linux" or the specific distribution if the generic file contains that setting.
DOMAIN	The domain name the server resides on. The full domain name (for example, animals.org) or the word "generic" if the server lives on an independent machine.
MAILER	The type of program sending mail through the server. One or more than one of local, smtp, uucp, usenet, fax, pop, procmail, mail1 1, phquery, and cyrus with a separate statement for each one. Almost all Internet-based sites should use at least local and smtp.

These characters stand for "delete new line" and cause the program that creates the sendmail.cf to erase everything from that point to the end of the line. This feature is primarily used to prevent growing the sendmail.cf to an unnecessary size with a lot of blank lines.

Sendmail Definition Macros

Another way to assign values to macros in sendmail is to use the **define** feature in the format **define(macro, value)**.

Features

The "feature" statement tells the m4 processor which blocks of rulesets to include or not include in the sendmail.cf file, and what files to examine to find further information. A feature is used in the format FEATURE(featurename). Table 9.5 lists features commonly used in the macro file.

Putting It All Together

The first line of the .mc file must be:

```
include('../m4/cf.m4')
```

This line ensures that any macro invoked has a definition when it comes time to convert the .mc file to the .cf file. The next portion of the file might be:

```
OSTYPE(linux)dnl
FEATURE(nouucp)
MASQUERADE_AS(ANIMALS.ORG)
DOMAIN(animals.org)dnl
MAILER(local)dnl
MAILER(smtp)dnl
```

Creating The .cf File

Within this same directory is a Makefile. Type:

```
m4 personalized.mc > sendmail.cf
```

Table 9.5   Features used in the personalized .mc file used to generate sendmail.cf.

Feature	Purpose
nouucp	Don't include uucp-related rulesets in the sendmail.cf.
nullclient	Forward all mail to the mail server. Use this feature on non-server machines.
use_cw_file	Look in the file /etc/sendmail.cw for a list of all the hosts or domains the mail server is handling mail for. Create this file and at least put the site domain name within it.

The resulting file is necessary to provide the configuration values that the sendmail daemon needs to handle mail properly.

Testing The .cf File

Test the new sendmail.cf by typing

```
/usr/sbin/sendmail -Csendmail.cf
```

inside the directory where the file was created.

Installing The New sendmail.cf

Locate the old sendmail.cf—use the **find** command if necessary—and make a backup of it just in case. Then, copy the new sendmail.cf into its place. After this, restart the sendmail daemon unless it is running from inetd on that machine.

/etc/sendmail.cf

Although it is no longer recommended to work directly with the sendmail.cf file, it is good to understand the file's structure in case it becomes necessary. This file is separated into well-marked segments, such as local information and how to parse mail headers. Each sendmail configuration option is only one-letter long. After this comes any other data it needs, such as flags, values, or cryptic sets of characters relating to rules for how to rewrite mail addresses. If a time comes when a few values must be changed in the sendmail.cf file, back it up before making the changes or make the changes to a new version of the default .mc file.

There are certain items in sendmail.cf that you may find yourself interested in quickly changing. For example, if you change which machine is your domain's primary mail server, then you need to change the DR option in each client machine's sendmail.cf file. Change DR to DR*fullname*. For example, change it from DRcat.animals.org to DRmail.animals.org. Another item that you might need to change if you move a machine from one network to another is which domain it uses. If you move the machine from animals.org to fruit.org, then you need to change the DD value from DDanimals.org to DDfruit.org.

If you begin splitting off who administrates what tasks, and there end up being various people running different machines, then you may want to remove masquerading from certain addresses. This would ensure that mail from root@dog.animals.org does not appear to be mail from root@animals.org when root@cat.animals.org is a different person. Each account that should not be masqueraded should appear with a CE line. You might, for example, have the following set of code:

```
CEroot
CEadmin
Cewebmaster
```

Some people are quite comfortable manipulating the sendmail.cf file. If you find that you prefer to work with sendmail's configurations this way rather than through the macro builder, be sure to learn more about the command structure in this file.

MAIL MANAGEMENT

A separate issue from configuring and running the mail server is mail management. Day-to-day mail server operations can include moving massive amounts of data through mail spools. There is also the problem of junk email, complaints about users, and other nuisances that are the domain of the postmaster, which may or may not be the same person as the system administrator.

The Mail Queue

One way to tell how your mail server is doing is to take a look at the mail queue. If there are many items in the queue that have been sitting there for quite some time, then there could be a problem with upstream mail service, or the mail server itself may be malfunctioning. To list the contents of the mail queue, type either **mailq** or **sendmail –bp**. These are essentially the same command.

If there is nothing in the queue, then either mail service is working fine and everything has been sent, or mail is not being queued properly in the first place. Look in the /var/spool/mqueue directory to see what is queued. Each piece of mail in this directory has two different parts with the same number. Generally speaking, one of these files is the header information and the other is the mail's body. If there are 20 files in the directory and 10 pieces of mail in the mailq listing, everything is working fine. If there are 20 files and there is nothing in the mailq listing, the queue is not working properly. Try restarting the mail daemon.

Mail Aliases

One useful item in the mail administrator's arsenal is the mail alias. You create these items in the file /etc/aliases. A mail alias allows you to reroute mail that comes in to a particular address to end up going somewhere else. These aliases are added in the following format:

```
alias:      username
```

A common item to alias is that of the "postmaster" address. Every site should have at least one postmaster, which is the address to which outside users write to reach some form of administrative mail contact. If you wanted to point postmaster to root, you might include the following:

```
postmaster:    root
```

In fact, that alias is likely already in the file. It is in many cases, considered a requirement. Another excellent use for aliases is mail for people whose addresses are typically misspelled. If one of your staff members is named "Jon" and has the username "jond", people might be likely to spell it "johnd" by accident. The following simple line can take care of this problem rather than dealing with a lot of bounced email:

```
johnd:    jond
```

You can also uses aliases to send email coming to one address instead of to a number of addresses, a kind of de facto mailing list. To create a multiple address alias, use the following format:

```
alias:    user1, user2, user3, user4
```

9

OTHER MAIL SERVERS AND SERVICES

Sendmail is not the only mail server available to Linux system administrators. Also, SMTP mail service is not the only form of mail service available on Linux or the Internet. Although SMTP is how mail moves across the Internet from one place to another, there are some other protocols used for mail fetching that are of interest to admins such as yourself.

The Smail SMTP Mail Transport Agent

A popular alternative to Sendmail is a server called Smail. This program is also an SMTP MTA and many people find it much easier to work with than sendmail. Although most of the Linux certification exams focus on sendmail rather than smail, it is important to at least know the alternative exists and something about how to use it. This option is not quite as scalable as sendmail, meaning that for large-scale mail service, smail may not be able to handle the load. For personal sites or small business sites, however, it should be fine.

 The smail server is included in most Linux distributions because it is such a popular alternative to sendmail, so you likely will not have to download it. However, if you need to get the sources you can find them at the FTP site **ftp.planix.com** in the directory /pub/Smail.

Once you have smail installed, edit the file /usr/lib/smail/config. The variables you may want to change are outlined in Table 9.6.

Table 9.6 Commonly changed variables in /usr/lib/smail/config.

Variable	Purpose	Example
delivery_mode	Sets whether the primary mail server delivers mail immediately (foreground), lets a subprocess handle it (background), or queues the mail until it reaches its next queue processing time (queued).	delivery_mode=queued
postmaster	Set who mail coming to the mail server meant for the mail administrator should go.	postmaster=root
smart_host	Define the machine on your LAN that is the primary mail handler. Do not set this value if you are configuring the primary mail server.	smart_host=cat
smart_path	Used to tell the primary mail server what machine name it uses as the mail host. This name must be properly configured to point to this machine on your network.	smart_path=mail
smart_transport	Used to tell the primary mail server and its slave servers what protocol to use to talk to one another.	smart_transport=smtp
max_message_size	If messages are above a certain K in size, truncate them to save on disk space.	max_message_size=500k
visible_domain	Your domain name and extension so smail can determine if mail is local or not.	visible_domain=animals.org
visible_name	Often, you do not want the mail going out from your domain to show as coming from any particular host. Set this variable to your domain name so the host portion is removed.	visible_name=animals.org

Because smail is not one of the primary methods of mail delivery, many programs do not look for it properly. You need to make soft links from /usr/bin/smail or /usr/local/bin/smail—depending on your installation—to the following locations to ensure proper mail functionality: /usr/bin/rmail, /usr/bin/sendmail, /usr/bin/mailq, and /usr/bin/smtpd.

The Qmail SMTP Mail Transport Agent

Another SMTP MTA available for the Linux community is qmail. There are a number of reasons some people choose qmail over sendmail or smail. These reasons range from perceived security benefits to ease of administration, to built-in mailing list features. For more information on this package and its full range of capabilities, see the qmail home page at **www.qmail.org**.

You generally have no choice but to install qmail by hand. Fortunately, this package comes with useful documentation. The FAQ and a series of INSTALL files walk you through creating the necessary home directory, users, and groups, then run the setup make target. After this you use the auto-configuration script to set up your system information, and do the other pre-use configuration steps listed in the files. Finally, once you are ready, you can disable sendmail and test qmail out.

Do not completely remove sendmail from your system until you are sure qmail is working properly. Just disabling it for now will allow you to test everything with a minimum amount of fuss.

Your qmail configuration files are in /var/mail/control. For an excellent break-down of the specific steps involved in a solid qmail installation, check out the Qmail HOWTO at **www.flounder.net/qmail/qmail-howto.html**.

The POP3 Mail Transport Agent

Another method of getting email that is popular among those who do not have permanent connections to the network containing the mail server, or may work from multiple locations, is POP (Post Office Protocol) service. This form of mail delivery does not use SMTP. Instead, it uses the POP3 protocol, which functions more like a post office box than a mail delivery unit. Instead of automatically delivering your email to your email client, it holds the email until you connect to it and request the latest items with a client such as elm or pine.

Fortunately, you probably do not even need to go out of your way to install a POP3 server. Most Linux distributions include one by default, and you can activate or deactivate it at will in /etc/inetd.conf. Keep in mind that if you do not want to offer POP3 service, it is probably best to remove the service. Unnecessary software is a potential security hole.

You cannot send mail with POP3, only receive. You still need access to an SMTP server to send.

IMAP Mail Transport Agent

Although POP transfers email to the client machine so that the user can read and respond offline before uploading later via SMTP, Internet Message Access Protocol (IMAP) leaves the messages initially on the server and downloads only the headers. The primary difference between POP and IMAP is that POP is an excellent solution for those who do not have permanent connections, whereas IMAP requires a connection while mail is being dealt with.

When you connect to an IMAP server with an IMAP client, you download a set of message headers. You can then choose which messages to download. Everything you do is reflected on the server itself, not just handled on the client end. If you save mail, it is saved in your account mailbox on the server. For those who need roving access to email but do not need or even desire copies of items on their machines, this option is also available.

 Once again, you cannot send mail with IMAP, you can only receive. You still need access to an SMTP server to send mail.

An IMAP server is also installed by default, and can be activated or deactivated in /etc/inted.conf.

Mailing Lists

Sometimes mail aliases are not enough. For a discussion email list where users can join and leave as they please, and the list can be managed by the specific individual running it rather than by the mail administrator, you need full-fledged mailing list software. There are three major players in this field: Majordomo, LISTSERV, and ezmlm.

Mailing List Features

There are a variety of features that people look for in mailing list software. Which features you need really depends on what you want out of the software. One of the more commonly desired features are items such as archiving, which keeps copies of the posts and allows list members to retrieve these old posts when needed. Another is list digesting, which lets list members choose to receive posts grouped in a single email message rather than as individual messages. This is one way system administrators manage to keep cluttered email boxes under control.

A feature that has gotten more popular and now is almost a necessity these days is subscription confirmation. When someone sends in a subscription request, the mailing list software sends email to the newly subscribed address asking for a reply that confirms that this person actually wants to join the list. Unfortunately, there are people who think it is funny or cute or have darker reasons to subscribe people to lists they never asked to be on, and this can cause administration headaches. A misplaced subscription will never get to this stage if you have software that performs confirmations.

Majordomo

The majordomo mailing list manager allows its mailing lists to almost entirely be administered through email. This feature ensures that the system or mail administrator does not have to be involved with the day-to-day operations of any of the lists. Majordomo supports list message archiving, digesting, and subscription confirmation.

Majordomo's latest version, as well as documentation for it, is available at **www.greatcircle.com/majordomo**.

LISTSERV

The LISTSERV mailing list has variable capabilities depending on which version you get. This is a commercial product, but a free version is available for those who do not need more than 10 mailing lists nor the ability to have more than 500 subscribers. The key to the license for the free version is that you cannot use it to run a list that you make money from. LISTSERV's free version is meant for people who just want to have their own discussion lists, not pay services.

The features are slightly different between the free and commercial versions, but both versions are feature-rich. Scalability is a major factor, as well as the com-mercial component of the license. To find out more, go to **www.lsoft.com**.

Ezmlm

The Ezmlm (EZ Mailing List Manager) software and its Ezmlm-idx add-on are meant for use specifically with the Qmail mail server. The features that are today considered essential in mailing list servers are all offered with this program as well. This program works slightly differently than Majordomo and LISTSERV, and the documentation that comes with it clearly spells out how. One of the features is the useful ability to address commands directly to the list instead of through a request address. The main Web site containing documentation and source for this package is at **www.ezmlm.org**.

CONFIGURING AND OPERATING WU-FTP

A commonly used FTP server within the Linux community is in.wuftpd. It provides access for remote users on both an account basis and, with some minor additions for some distributions, anonymous access. This is a service that runs within inetd, so be sure that it is uncommented in /etc/inetd.conf and that inetd is restarted before attempting to test it. Not all distributions come with this server by default.

wu-ftp Configuration Files

There are a number of configuration files available for use with the wu-ftp package. These files control a number of issues, such as who has access to the server and from what locations. How carefully these settings must be attended to depends on the level of security necessary for the FTP server and its file area.

/etc/ftpaccess

The file /etc/ftpaccess is the main configuration file for the FTP server. It is highly flexible, and offers a wide range of configuration options to take advantage of if the FTP implementation needs to serve a number of functions. Within this file, a system administrator can create classes of users and rules for these classes to operate within while FTP-connected to the server, set limits on bandwidth and data usage of the server or user classes, set locations for informational files, and more.

/etc/ftphosts

The /etc/ftphosts configuration file is used to prevent particular accounts from logging in from certain hosts. By default, this file is empty of anything but comments.

/etc/ftpusers

The file /etc/ftpusers contains a list of what users are not allowed to FTP in. These users in this case do not refer to specific people's accounts. Instead, they refer to users such as root which might otherwise gain too-privileged access entering as anyone but anonymous. A default set of users is already entered in this file.

Setting Up An Access-Controlled FTP Site

The wu-ftp server is an access-controlled FTP server by default, meaning that it requires logins from valid users. If, for some reason, implementation of access-controlled logins is not desired but an anonymous server is, be sure to block all but anonymous logins during the configuration process. The anonymous setup is covered in the section "Setting Up Anonymous FTP Access" found later in this chapter. Perform the following steps to set up an access-controlled FTP site:

1. Install the server. Before it can be configured, the server must first be installed. If it is not already present (look for the daemon /usr/sbin/in.wuftpd) the files should be available with the Linux distribution data.

   If not, the definitive download location is through FTP at ftp.wu-ftpd.org/pub/wu-ftpd/. Source, binary, and RPM versions (for some distributions) are all found here.

If the distribution already has the ftpd daemon installed, either use it instead or remove it and replace it with the wu-ftpd package.

2. Prepare to configure the server. There are a large number of settings controlled through server configuration. The basics are covered here, as well as some of the more interesting options.

3. Create a class. To create a class of users, edit the file /etc/ftpaccess. Determine a short but descriptive name to assign the class. Then, choose the types of users who are included in this class (a listing of valid types is given in Table 9.7).

4. Decide on an addressing scheme. After giving the class its name and assigning the types of users in it, determine the addressing scheme assigned to this class. The simplest form of address is the wildcard asterisk (*), which means "everyone from everywhere". Other wildcarded formats such as partial domain names (for example, *.animals.org), IP ranges (for example, 192.168.15.*), and more, are allowed. On the other hand, to block an address range from having access, precede it with an exclamation point (!). For example, !*.animals.org.

   Once all of the parameters are in place, add a statement in the following format:

   ```
   class classname usertype addressrange
   ```

5. Add a virtual host. In general, to add virtual FTP servers, the wu-ftpd software must be recompiled with the VIRTUAL flag. Then, the directory structure must be created such that the virtual FTP host has its own directories, and ftpaccess must be modified to handle the server and its log files.

6. Activate the server. To be sure that in.ftpd starts and stops automatically when entering specific runlevels, add the appropriate links to the /etc/rc.d /rc#.d hierarchy.

Table 9.7   Valid user types in /etc/ftpaccess.

Type	Purpose
anonymous	Allows anonymous access. Do not use this type if anonymous FTP entry is not desired.
guest	Assigns all users that are valid users on the system to "guest". This type is useful if—for security reasons perhaps—allowing full access to the file system to incoming users is not desired.
real	Maps incoming FTP users to their existing accounts on the system.

Setting Up Anonymous FTP Access

Some distributions come with an anonymous FTP package ready to install. With others, administrators must install it from scratch. Support for anonymous FTP access should not be installed unless there is a specific reason to use it. Otherwise, the service is a security risk. To set up an anonymous FTP site, perform the following steps:

1. Create a user and group. First, those accessing anonymously need a user account. Create a user "ftp" with a home directory of /home/ftp, a shell of /bin/true, and an asterisk (*) for a password. Assign the FTP user to its own FTP group, or to the wheel group if in use.

2. Create the base directory. Create a home directory for FTP at the location just mentioned (/home/ftp). Change its ownership to root and the group "ftp" or "wheel", then change the permissions to r-xr-xr-x.

3. Create and fill the directory /home/ftp/bin. Create the directory /home/ftp/bin. Change its ownerships and groups to match those of the home directory, and its permissions to --x--x--x. Then, copy the "ls" program into this directory—do not use links, they will not work properly—and give it the same permissions.

4. Create and fill the directory /home/ftp/etc. Create the directory /home/ftp/etc. Give it identical permissions and ownerships to the /home/ftp/bin directory. Now, create a small version of the file "passwd" in this directory with contents such as:

```
root:*:0:0:System Administrator::
daemon:*:UID:GID:System Daemons::
ftp:*:UID:GID:FTP Site::
```

where UID and GID are the actual values for those statements in the /etc/passwd file. If specific users own files within the FTP hierarchy, then add special accounts for them as well. When finished, give the file the permissions r--r--r--.

5. Create /home/ftp/etc/group. Create /home/ftp/etc/group and inside it make a copy of the FTP statement from the /etc/group file. Then save and give the file the same permissions as the new passwd file.

6. Create the downloads public directory. Create the directory /home/ftp/pub. Assign it owner root and the same group as FTP, with permissions sr-x-rx-rx (2555) so that all files created within the public directory have the same permissions as the directory itself.

7. Create the uploads public directory. Create the directory /home/ftp/pub/ incoming. Assign it owner root and the same group as FTP. The permissions should be trwx-wx-wx (1733) so that no one can overwrite the files that are already there.

8. Restart the superdaemon because it controls the FTP daemon.

CONFIGURING INCOMING TELNET ACCESS

There is little to configure if you want to offer incoming telnet access. This is a fairly simple service that has few options. However, you first need to decide whether you want to offer it at all. It may be wise to shut off telnet on all or some specific machines that you cannot afford to offer such a potential security hole to—after all, if people can telnet into your incoming telnet port, they can start trying to guess username and password combinations. Shutting off this service, however, makes remote maintenance on that machine difficult.

The superdaemon controls whether telnet is running or not, so look in the file /etc/inted.conf for a line similar to:

```
telnet  stream  tcp  nowait  root  /usr/sbin/tcpd  in.telnetd
```

If there is no hash mark in front of the line—as in the example—then the telnet service is active. A hash mark in place means it is commented out and inactive. Change this line to either activate or deactivate the service if you need to.

 If you make any changes in /etc/inetd.conf, don't forget to restart the superdaemon.

When you keep telnet, you could technically continue on without needing to configure anything. One option if you find that telnet requires specific options to work properly on your system is to create a .telnetrc file in /etc/skel to contain the startup conditions as outlined in the telnet man page.

CONFIGURING AND OPERATING APACHE

The most widely used Web server in the Linux world is Apache. Most of the Linux distributions come with this server which is based on the original httpd, but eventually grew into its own package.

Apache Configuration Files

Older versions of Apache (versions 1.3.3 and earlier) have three different configuration files, each with its own focus. The file access.conf controls what services can be run in what directories (such as CGI scripts) and who can access them. The httpd.conf file is the actual daemon configuration file and contains items like virtual hosting information, the port to listen on, and logging assignments. The third configuration file is srm.conf, which holds information such as where the server should look for Web documents.

In Apache 1.3.4, the contents of the three server configuration files (httpd.conf, srm.conf, and access.conf) have been merged into a single httpd.conf file. The srm.conf and access.conf files are now empty except for comments directing the Webmaster to look in httpd.conf. In addition, the merged httpd.conf file has been restructured to allow directives to appear in a hopefully more intuitive and meaningful order.

srm.conf

The primary item set within the srm.conf configuration file is the document root location. The Web server looks in this directory for the documents it needs to access. It also contains settings indicating where the server should look to find icons, and CGI scripts. Those who are happy with the defaults need not change any items within this file.

The document root assigned within srm.conf is /home/httpd/html. This is where all top-level Web files should be stored, and any subdirectories for the Web site should be added. Check to see if this directory was created by the package installer. If not, create it by hand.

access.conf

Often, the access.conf file does not need to be changed. This section is primarily an issue if one section of the Web documents is intended to only be used internally, or by a specific group of people.

httpd.conf

This is the main server configuration file, which often references the other two files. The behavior of the server itself is defined clearly within this file. Also, virtual hosting information is added here so that the server knows where to look when requests come in for Web data that is not hosted under the main network domain name.

Setting Up A Web Site

Many aspects of Apache are preconfigured. It is only necessary to change configuration values if there is a desire to customize, or if virtual hosting setup is necessary. Some distributions may slightly modify where files are placed, so make use of the **find** or **locate** command if necessary to locate the configuration files. To set up a Web site, perform the following steps:

1. Install the server. To prepare the Web site, first, install the Apache server if it is not already installed. The files should be available with the Linux distribution data. If not, the definitive download location is **http://www.apache.org/**.

2. Prepare to customize the configuration files. Customizing the Apache server configuration files first requires the administrator to take stock of what needs to be done. Typically, a default configuration is already in place, so the question is whether or not to change from the default. The most common changes are discussed here.

3. Change the document root location. To change where the Web server looks for its root level files, edit the srm.conf file and change the value for DocumentRoot. This value must be the full path to the base location for the server to find Web files.

4. Change the contact information. By default, the Web administrator contact information displayed by the server is root@localhost. However, many people like to have this address point to an assigned Webmaster who may or may not be root. To change this setting, edit the file httpd.conf and change the value of ServerAdmin to the address of the Web administrator.

5. Set the server to look up host names. By default, the Web server only records IP addresses and not the actual host and domain names of the machines. This setting is the default because it speeds up the entire process of Web accesses. However, many are quite willing to take a small performance hit in trade for logging the actual names of sites instead of their IP addresses.

   To change this default setting, edit the file httpd.conf and change the value of HostnameLookups to "on".

6. Change the default port. In general, it is best to leave the Web server at the default port. Otherwise, people have to use the port number as part of the URL. However, if a proxy server is currently listening on that port instead, or the Web server is for internal use and not meant for the general public, or perhaps is a secondary Web server with a more limited purpose, then changing the port is a good idea.

   To change the default port setting, edit the file httpd.conf and change the value for Port to a new number. Examine the file /etc/services to determine what ports are available for Web server use.

7. Deny access to outside clients. If the Web server is only meant to serve the intranet and not the Internet in general, but the intranet is connected to the Internet, then it is important to set the server not to allow outside users to access the site. This is done by setting the access to only allow clients on the hosting domain.

9

To set the server to only allow internal network accesses, edit the file access.conf and examine the beginning of the file. The value for "order" should be "deny,allow" and the "allow" statement beneath should list .domain.suffix (for example, .animals.org).

It is also possible to refuse access to only certain directories to outside users. To build the proper directory statement, follow the format:

```
<Directory path>
    order: deny,allow
    deny from all
    allow from .domain.suffix
</Directory>
```

The key is partially in the order statement. For permissive access, list allow first. To limit access to the site, list deny first.

8. Add a virtual host. If the Web server has to handle files for more than one domain name, then virtual hosting has to be configured. The important thing to consider when creating this virtual host is that its documents and logs must be different from the main hosts. Or, at least should be different. An example of the code that might be added at the end of httpd.conf to create a virtual host's settings is:

```
<VirtualHost domain.suffix>
    ServerAdmin webmaster@domain.suffix
    DocumentRoot /home/http/www.domain.suffix
    ServerName www.domain.suffix
    ErrorLog /var/log/httpd.domain.suffix
    TransferLog /var/log/htmlaccess.domain.suffix
</VirtualHost>
```

Note that the items referring specifically to the virtual host are labeled for that particular host. This practice can significantly reduce hassles later, such as access reporting and having a large number of virtual hosting users.

Virtual hosts must be added to the DNS tables as well.

9. Restart the server. Now that all the settings have been changed, the Web daemon must be restarted. This daemon is httpd.

If you want Apache to start by default at boot time be sure to either add it to your runlevel directories, or rc.local. Many distributions configure this server to run by default.

MOUNTING AND EXPORTING NFS FILE SYSTEMS

The NFS (Network File System) program allows a system administrator to offer specific partitions on specific machines as mountable across a Linux network. This setup is useful for providing distribution files during an installation for those distributions that support NFS installation, storing files centrally for project teams, and many other purposes.

/etc/exports

To offer partitions for NFS mounting, these items must be configured as accessible by outside users. This task is accomplished through editing the file /etc/exports. Each line in this file contains either a comment or a path to a directory or partition. The entry must completely define access privileges to the share on a single line of text, and so is written in a kind of shorthand in two parts: the exported partition and the rules for exporting.

Export Partition

The first part of an NFS export statement is what partition or portion of the file system is offered to share. All subdirectories inside the shared directory are covered by the definition, so be careful about what is within them.

Export Rules

How the export rules are written is very important. If not enough thought goes into them, the NFS exports become a massive security hole. A single export rule contains no spaces. A space character is treated as a divider to separate export rules from one another. There can be as many export rules assigned to an export item as can all fit on the definition line.

The rules themselves are segmented into two parts. The first part of an export rule defines who is allowed to access the exported area. The second part sets the rules for what those accessing the partition are allowed to do.

Assigning The Who

The options for how to assign who is allowed access to the exported share are fairly flexible. To begin with, both names and IP addresses are valid entries. Also, how narrowly or widely focused these settings can be tweaked ranges all the way from a single machine to the entire Internet (although usually this is not advisable).

Assigning The How

The options for what is allowed or disallowed in many ways are the most important items set in this file. This is because if these options are too permissive, then the NFS export becomes a security risk, but if they are too restrictive, then it may not serve the purpose for which it was created. The options available are shown in Table 9.8.

Putting It All Together

The contents of the /etc/exports file might look like the following:

```
/          cheetah(rw,root_squash)
/incoming  *.animals.org(rw,all_squash)
```

The first line creates an NFS statement that allows users from the machine "cheetah" to NFS mount the root (/) partition, but root is automatically mapped to be an anonymous user. This machine is in the administrator's office which is kept under lock and key when no one is around, and so is fairly trusted, and is given read-write access to the full file system.

The second line creates an NFS statement that allows anyone from the domain to NFS mount the special directory "/incoming" with read-write access. However, everyone who mounts this item is forced into anonymous user permissions.

Managing The NFS Server And Related Daemons

There are three daemons that must be running for an NFS server to function: portmap, nfsd, and rpc.mountd. It is important when upgrading one of these daemons to keep in mind that it may not work with the others, meaning that

Table 9.8 Access options commonly used while setting NFS exports.

Option	Purpose
all_squash	All visitors are set to be anonymous users.
insecure	No limits on which port NFS mounts can originate from.
noaccess	The visitor is not allowed to descend into subdirectories.
ro	The visitor is given read-only access.
root_squash	Accessing the mount with as the user root is forcibly mapped to the user nobody for security reasons (default).
rw	The visitor is given full read-write access (default).
no_root_squash	Visitors are allowed to retain root privileges while on the partition via an NFS mount.
secure	Requires all NFS mounts to originate from a port below 1024 (default).

they will all have to be upgraded, or that the admin keeps backup copies of the originals before trusting they work properly together before new versions of the others come out. Some system library upgrades can also break these daemons.

Daemon Start Order

The portmap daemon needs to be started before the nfs daemon because of inter-service dependencies. An additional daemon called rpc.statd can be used to test that all three programs are loaded properly. With this daemon running, type "rpcinfo -p" to get a listing and see if all of the programs register. On an NFS client machine that is not offering any shares to the other machines on the network, only the portmap daemon is necessary.

Listing Exported NFS File Systems

It is possible to see a list of what clients currently have a system's NFS shares mounted. While logged in as root on the machine in question, type "showmount -e" to see the list of currently exported shares.

Mounting An Exported NFS File System

To mount an NFS share, use the following command structure: **mount -t nfs** ***NFSservername:/sharepath* /mnt/*mountpoint***. For example, to mount the share /users on the machine "gorilla" to the mount point "share", type "mount -t nfs gorilla:/users /mnt/share".

9

OFFERING SAMBA FILESYSTEMS AND PRINTERS ACROSS MULTI-OS NETWORKS

Samba is a boon to every system administrator who needs to connect machines running a number of operating systems all to a single LAN. Once configured, it integrates almost seamlessly into the LAN workings, allowing Linux users to mount non-Linux drives across the network, and non-Linux boxes to see Samba shares in their network drive listings. For the purposes of the first level certification exams, a basic knowledge of Samba is useful.

Samba

Samba is based on the SMB (Server Message Block) protocol which is used for transmitting drive and printer information and data across networks. It is used in Linux because there are tools that understand SMB under Windows NT, OS/2, MS-DOS, Windows, Apple Macintoshes, and other operating systems, allowing file systems and printers to be shared across multi-OS networks. The file /etc/smb.conf is the only configuration file Samba uses. It is where all drive shares and print shares are defined and configured, and where user access is assigned. The Linux Samba client is *smbclient*. This package is similar to FTP, except that it allows access to both drives and printers.

Setting Up Samba Shares

Configuring Samba in almost any form involves editing the file /etc/smb.conf. There are two different forms of shares to set up: those that allow users to connect to portions of the file system, and those that allow people access to network printers. Each of these segments is covered separately.

Comments within the default configuration file start in one of two ways. Any comments that describe the content that follows begin with a hash mark (#). On the other hand, comments that start a line of code to block it from being activated begin with semicolons (;). To activate the deactivated code, delete the semicolon.

Configuring Global Settings

The first segment of /etc/smb.conf contains the Global parameters. These parameters define the default behavior for the shares to follow. Global parameters can be added anywhere from the line following the text "[global]" to the line beginning the Share Definitions section. Definitions added to the Global section generally use the format:

```
setting = value
```

Commonly used Global definitions are listed in Table 9.9.

Setting Up Drive Shares

Each segment of the file system being offered for remote access over Samba needs to be defined as its own share. The format used for a share definition is roughly:

```
[sharename]
  setting1 = value1
  setting2 = value2
  ...
  settingX = valueX
```

Table 9.9 Frequently used Global definitions in /smb/conf.

Definition	Description	Default Value	Possible Values
Default Service	Sets which share is connected to when the remote user does not request a specific share.	None.	The name of the share but not within the brackets.
Load Printers	Make every printer defined in /etc /printcap available for printing over Samba.	Yes.	None.

Table 9.10 Frequently used share definitions in /smb/conf.

Definition	Description	Default Value	Possible Values
Browseable	Sets whether the share is visible when users look at the list of available shares.	Yes.	Yes or No.
Comment	A short string of text used to label the share with something more descriptive than the share name itself.	Empty.	Any string of text.
Deny Hosts	The addresses not allowed to access the share(s).	None.	Full domain or IP addresses, partial addresses with no wildcard necessary (for example, 192.168.15.).
Don't Descend	Lists the subdirectories within the share that remote users are not allowed to enter.	None.	Relative paths, such as ./bin for the /smbshare /bin subdirectory.
Follow Symlinks	Sets whether remote users can follow symbolic links that are within a share.	Yes.	Yes or No.
Guest Ok	Guests are allowed to access the share, instead of just users with accounts.	No.	Yes or No.
Read Only	Remote users may not write to the share.	Yes.	No.
Writeable	Remote users may write to the share.	No.	Yes.

Commonly used share definitions are listed in Table 9.10. The individual share definitions can also be used in the Global definition section, in which case they default the default behavior for all shares unless set differently in a particular share.

Setting Up Print Shares

Each printer needs to have its own share created if it needs special permissions or rules assigned. The format used for a printer definition is roughly the same as that for a drive share, except the following two options need to be included:

```
path = /pathtospool
printable = yes
```

For example, a typical printer entry might be:

```
[mainprinter]
  path = /usr/spool/print
  writeable = no
  guest ok = no
  printable = yes
```

Accessing Shared Items

To access SMB shared items from within Linux, use the tools provided with the Samba package. First, a list of what is available has to be obtained. This task is accomplished by typing "smbclient -L". After this, all that is necessary is to mount the share, or print to it.

Mounting Shared Drives

When mounting an SMB share, use the filesystem type "smb". Mounting a Microsoft Windows share requires using the proper format so that the Windows network understands the location requested. For example, when mounting the shared directory C:\SAMBA on the machine PROJECT, use the format:

```
mount -t smb '\\PROJECT\SAMBA'
```

Or, if not using single quotes, each of the backslashes has to be escaped because the shell will otherwise not understand them properly, meaning that the format must be as follows:

```
mount -t smb \\\\PROJECT\\SAMBA
```

Printing To Shared Printers

To print to an SMB shared printer, use smbclient to first connect to the printer, and then print to it. Connecting to a printer is similar to mounting a service; it is done with the format "smbclient //*server*/*printer*". The printing itself is done with the format "smbclient print *filename*".

Configuring Samba With SWAT

There are several GUI tools available to help you with configuring Samba—see **www.samba.org** for more information. One of these tools, the one that actually comes with Samba, is Samba Web Administration Tool (SWAT). As the name suggests, this tool works within a Web browser rather than having its own custom launcher. This tool is installed along with the rest of the Samba package in most Linux distributions.

If for some reason you must install SWAT manually, be sure to add entries for it in /etc/services and /etc/inetd.conf. SWAT is managed by the superdaemon.

To start SWAT, open your favorite Web browser on the Samba server and go to **http://127.0.0.1:901/**. If going to this URL gives you an error, first try **http://127.0.0.1/** to see if this works. If it does but not with the port number, then SWAT is probably not active in the superdaemon's configuration file. Edit /etc/inetd.conf and remove the comment from in front of the swat entry. Save and close the file, then restart the inetd daemon.

Once SWAT is found correctly, the first thing you get is a login dialog box. Log in as root or to whatever Samba administrator account you created, then click OK. See Figure 9.1 for an illustration of SWAT.

9

Netscape: Samba Web Administration Tool

File   Edit   View   Go   Communicator   Help

samba

HOME   GLOBALS   SHARES   PRINTERS   STATUS

VIEW   PASSWORD

Welcome to SWAT!

Please choose a configuration action using one of the above buttons

Documentation

- **Daemons**
    - smbd – the SMB daemon
    - nmbd – the NetBIOS nameserver
- **Administrative Utilities**
    - smbstatus – monitoring Samba
    - SWAT – web configuration tool
    - smbpasswd – managing SMB passwords
    - make_smbcodepage – codepage creation
    - testparm – validating your config file
    - testprns – testing printer configuration
- **General Utilities**
    - nmblookup – NetBIOS name query tool
    - smbtar – SMB backup tool
    - smbclient – command line SMB client
- **Configuration Files**
    - smb.conf – the main Samba configuration file
    - lmhosts – NetBIOS hosts file
    - smbpasswd – SMB password file
- **Miscellaneous**
    - Samba introduction

http://127.0.0.1:901/shares

Figure 9.1   The home screen of the SWAT Samba configuration tool.

Click the Global button to work on your Global configurations; the Shares button to create, remove, or edit existing file shares; or the Printers button to add, delete, or edit existing print shares. This tool can be a good way of learning a bit more about how to configure Samba. Make some changes, then click the View button to see what your configuration file looks like once they are made.

OTHER NETWORK SERVICES

There are a number of other network services that you may or may not choose to utilize, but you need to at least be familiar with for the Linux certification exams. Some of these services are only needed by particular kinds of network setups, whereas others use a large amount of resources, and so are often only set up by ISPs and others who have the financial incentive to provide them to their users.

The Caching Proxy Server

You may decide after reading Chapter 12 that you need to secure your LAN or part of it behind a proxying firewall. If this is the case, then you are not locked into one choice for a proxy server. Part of the server choice depends on how much traffic you expect to have between the LAN and the Internet, and what type of traffic that is. If your users tend to generate a lot of traffic between certain Web and FTP sites, then a caching proxy might be your answer, either as the entire proxy solution or just part of it.

The Squid proxy server handles specifically HTTP and FTP traffic, and can also cache DNS lookups. This tool is under continuous development. For the latest version and information see **http://squid.nlanr.net**. Some distributions come with Squid already included on their installation media whereas others do not. Take a look at the distribution media or documentation to find out whether yours includes it.

The News Server

A news service works over Network News Transfer Protocol (NNTP). Many sites these days get their Usenet news feeds from other sites rather than invest in the many gigabytes of disk space necessary for a well-rounded news feed. You may find, however, that you have a use for a local server. The server most often used on Linux for news feeds is INN (INternet News). Because this tool is complex and often not needed, it is not covered in the first level Linux certification exams.

The INN server innd comes with most Linux distributions. What makes the setup so complicated is that first you must configure the server itself to work properly on your machine. Then, you have to set up how it interacts with its newsfeeds. There is also the issue of how it handles the news that it already has on the site.

The Time Server

For various reasons, including the strength of system batteries, time does not remain consistent for long across networks. Each machine slowly creeps out of sync with the others, and not even in the same amount or direction. Even if you manage to keep your network completely together with its time values, it may not be accurate with the rest of the world. The network itself may creep.

Enter the Network Time Protocol in the form of xntpd. This service goes to an outside source to periodically check for the accurate time value, and then updates the machine(s) it is configured to handle. Using xntpd or another time service helps avoid the dual problem of BIOS clocks that tend to drift out of sync with real time, and the kernel clock that also may drift. For more information on time service, go to **www.eecis.udel.edu/~ntp**.

Virtual Network Computing

Virtual Network Computing (VNC) is a GUI remote administration tool. This tool allows you to view and manipulate the desktop of another machine within a window on your own desktop. Even better, you can view and work with the desktops of machines that are not running Linux. In a way it is a graphical version of telnet.

VNC is a free open source tool. It was originally written by ORL, the Olivetti Research Laboratory, which is now a part of AT&T in Cambridge, England. The home page is at **www.uk.research.att.com/vnc**.

9

CHAPTER SUMMARY

The Linux certification level-one exams require an understanding of networking services at a basic level. It is important to understand how to set up each of the services discussed for simple tasks, but in-depth treatment of subjects like configuring named and Samba will not be tested until the level-two exams. After saying that, it is useful to understand as much of these topics as possible. The more you understand in depth, the less chance there is that some detail will elude you.

Among the network services, the most important for exam purposes and the most often used are inetd, FTP, and Apache. This is because the services, although they have their complex aspects, are relatively simple to set up and are functioning at a basic level quickly once you understand them. Subsequently, be aware of the differences between the services, such as the formats used for allowing and denying access between the various configuration files.

All in all, the more experience you have working with the various network services the better off you will be. There are a lot of nuances and small steps involved with working them that are easy to forget if you have not practiced using them hands on. This is one area where it definitely pays to take the time and set up a full-fledged test site.

REVIEW QUESTIONS

1. Which file is used to configure the processes the superdaemon controls?

    a. /etc/services

    b. /etc/inetd.conf

    c. /etc/hosts

    d. /etc/hosts.allow

2. Which file is used to configure which ports the network processes on a machine?

    a. /etc/services

    b. /etc/inetd.conf

    c. /etc/hosts

    d. /etc/hosts.allow

3. Which daemon is used to manage a machine's DNS?

    a. inetd

    b. dnsd

    c. named

    d. bind

4. Which extension would you look for when choosing the initial file to begin configuring sendmail using m4?

    a. .m4

    b. .cf

    c. .mc

    d. .sd

5. Which of the following is not a valid FTP server configuration file?

    a. /etc/ftpaccess

    b. /etc/ftphosts

    c. /etc/ftpusers

    d. /etc/ftpdeny

6. Which of the following is not a valid Apache server configuration file?

    a. srm.conf

    b. hosts.conf

    c. access.conf

    d. httpd.conf

7. Which service would you install if you wanted to offer remote mounting of Linux partitions on a Linux-only network?

    a. SMB

    b. FIPS

    c. DNS

    d. NFS

8. Which service would you install if you wanted to offer remote mounting of Linux partitions on a mixed-OS network?

    a. SMB

    b. FIPS

    c. DNS

    d. NFS

9. Which is the cleanest way to close down the daemon /sbin/daemon which has an init script in /etc/rc.d/init.d/daemon and currently is running as process 1022?

    a. **kill -9 1022**

    b. **kill 1022**

    c. **/sbin/daemon stop**

    d. **/etc/rc.d/init.d/daemon stop**

10. If you wanted to prevent inetd from listening for incoming talk requests because you have no intention of using that service, what is the recommended way of doing so?

    a. Delete the line containing the talk service data from /etc/services.

    b. Delete the line containing the talk service data from /etc/inetd.conf.

    c. Comment out the line containing the talk service data from /etc/inetd.conf.

    d. Comment out the line containing the talk service data from /etc/services.

11. What do the letters "dnl" mean in a sendmail.mc file?

    a. Domain name license.

    b. Delete blank characters through the end of the line.

    c. Ignore this line.

    d. Run a macro.

9

12. What must the first line in a sendmail.mc file be?

    a. include('../m4/cf.m4')

    b. #sendmail.cf

    c. #!/bin/sh

    d. OSTYPE(linux)

13. How do you create the sendmail.cf file from the sendmail.mc file?

    a. m4 sendmail.mc sendmail.cf

    b. m4 sendmail.mc

    c. m4 sendmail.mc > sendmail.cf

    d. m4 sendmail.mc < sendmail.cf

14. If you want to add support for virtual hosts to your Web server, which Apache configuration file do you edit?

    a. access.conf

    b. httpd.conf

    c. srm.conf

    d. smb.conf

15. Which variable do you change in the Apache configuration files to move the base directory where the Web server looks for the files it offers to Web clients?

    a. Home

    b. RootDir

    c. BaseDir

    d. DocumentRoot

16. What program do you use to see what Samba shares are available to you?

    a. smbclient

    b. mount

    c. fstab

    d. smb

17. What program do you use to access a Samba share?

    a. smbclient

    b. mount

    c. fstab

    d. smb

18. What file do you edit to create an NFS share?

    a. /etc/smb.conf

    b. /etc/nfs.conf

    c. /etc/exports

    d. /etc/access.conf

19. What file do you edit to create a Samba share?

    a. /etc/smb.conf

    b. /etc/nfs.conf

    c. /etc/exports

    d. /etc/access.conf

20. Which file sharing protocol also handles print sharing?

    a. SMB

    b. NFS

    c. FTP

    d. HTTP

HANDS-ON PROJECTS

These projects require that you have access to a working Linux system in command-line mode. The following packages must already be installed—but not configured—according to the method used with your distribution: wu-ftp, Apache, a working GUI, a working Web browser such as Netscape, NFS, and Samba. If the machine you are working on is a production machine, be sure to work with backup versions of the configuration files, or make backups of the existing ones before doing these exercises.

Project 9.1

To set up a user-only FTP server, and a customized Web server:

1. Log in as root.

2. Edit the file /etc/inetd.conf by typing "vi /etc/inetd.conf".

3. Search for the text "ftp" by typing "/ftp" then press Enter.

4. Be sure that the FTP server is not commented out. If the line begins with a hash mark, delete the mark.

5. Save and exit the file by typing ":wq", then press Enter.

6. If you made changes, then you need to restart the inetd superdaemon. Even if you didn't make changes, it is good practice to go ahead and do so now.

First, confirm the location for the inetd script. It should either be in the directory /etc/rc.d/init.d or one near there if your distribution is slightly different. Use the Locate tool if necessary in the format "locate inetd", and be sure that you do not choose /sbin/inetd which is the actual daemon.

7. Change to the directory containing the script.

8. Stop the daemon by typing "./inetd stop".

9. Start the daemon by typing "./inetd start".

10. To test the server, log in under a user account on the same machine.

11. Type "ftp localhost" to connect to the server.

12. Log in to the FTP server with any user's ID and password.

13. Type "exit" to close the connection.

14. Return to the root login.

15. Now, to configure the Apache server. Use the locate tool to find where your distribution stores the file httpd.conf with the format "locate httpd.conf".

16. Edit the file by typing "vi /*path*/httpd.conf".

17. Search for the text ServerAdmin by typing "/ServerAdmin", then press Enter.

18. Change the text root@localhost to a different address, say root@*servername.domain.extension* (for example, root@aardvark.animals.org).

19. Search for the text "ErrorLog" by typing "/ErrorLog", then press Enter.

20. Change the text "logs/error_log" to "logs/httpd_log".

21. Save and exit the file by typing ":wq", then press Enter.

22. The server comes with a default Web page to test it with. First, see if httpd is already running on your system by typing "ps aux | grep httpd". If it is, continue. If not, skip to Step 26.

23. Locate the script that handles management of httpd. It is likely in the same place as the inetd management script.

24. Change to the management script's directory.

25. Type "./httpd stop" to stop the server.

26. Type "./httpd start" to start the Web server with its new data.

27. Enter the GUI, likely with the command **startx**.

28. Open your Web browser.

29. Access the Web server by typing either "localhost" in the URL line or typing the server's full URL.

Project 9.2

To create and mount both NFS and Samba shares:

1. Log in as root.

2. Create the directory /projects.

3. Create the directory /projects/public.

4. Edit the file /etc/exports by typing "vi /etc/exports".

5. Allow users logging in on your specific machine to NFS mount the /projects directory with read-write access by adding the following line:

```
/projects  localhost(rw)
```

6. Allow members of your domain read-only access to the /projects directory, where any root accounts are treated as nobody accounts, by adding the next line:

```
/projects *.domain.extension(ro,root_squash)
```

7. Allow the world read-only, non-root access to the /projects/public directory by adding:

```
/projects/public (ro,root_squash)
```

8. Save and exit the file by typing ":wq", then press Enter.

9. See if the NFS daemon is already running by typing "ps aux | grep nfsd". If it is running, continue. If not, skip to Step 13.

10. Locate the nfsd controlling script, which should be in the same location as the inetd and httpd controlling scripts.

11. Change to the script's directory.

12. Stop the daemon by typing "./nfsd stop".

13. Restart the daemon by typing "./nfsd start".

14. Create the mount point /mnt/nfs.

15. Test the NFS setup by typing "mount -t nfs localhost:/project /mnt/nfs". The format "mount localhost:/project /mnt/nfs" will likely work as well.

16. Now to create the SMB share. Edit the file /etc/smb.conf by typing "vi /etc/smb.conf".

17. Locate where to create your new share by searching for the text "Share Definitions" with the command **/Share Definitions** and pressing Enter.

18. Type "O" to create a new line below the section banner and then go into insert mode.

19. Create a share for the /projects directory. The share should be writeable by anyone in your domain but not accessible by anyone outside. The code might look like:

```
[projects]
  path = /projects
  writeable = true
  allow hosts = .domain.extension
```

20. Save and exit the file by typing ":wq", then pressing Enter.

21. See if the SMB daemon is already running by typing "ps aux | grep smbd". If it is running, continue. If not, skip to Step 15.

22. Locate the smbd controlling script, which should be in the same location as the inetd and httpd controlling scripts. It also may be called "samba" in some distributions.

23. Change to the script's directory.

24. Stop the daemon by typing "./smbd stop" or "./samba stop".

25. Restart the daemon by typing "./smbd start" or "./samba start".

26. Create the mount point /mnt/smb.

27. Test the SMB setup by typing "smbclient –L".

28. Mount the partition offered by typing "mount –t smb /*path*/project /mnt/smb".

## CHAPTER TEN

PRINTING IN THE LINUX ENVIRONMENT

AFTER READING THIS CHAPTER AND COMPLETING THE EXERCISES, YOU WILL BE ABLE TO:

➤ Add a new printer to a machine or LAN at a basic level.

➤ Make printers and print queues available and unavailable when necessary.

➤ Move print jobs around in the queue, and remove them when necessary.

Unless you are working in a completely paperless environment, you will eventually have to face printers and printing. Everything from installing the printers to making sure they work smoothly on a day-to-day basis comes under the system administrator's job description.

Install Printers

Printers are one of the more difficult components to get working properly under Linux. Although some of the distributions offer tools within the GUI to simplify the process, it is important to understand how this process works at the command-line level. Only then will an administrator be able to deal with the nuances of problems that may develop, or configure printing on a server that has no GUI installed. This fact is a major consideration because not all of the exams allow the use of GUI tools.

Add A Local Printer Entry

Adding a printer entry is a multi-step process that involves creating not only a pointer to the printer in the proper configuration files, but also defining where the home for the print spool and other such items is found. The basics of how to add a new printer to the system are covered here.

/etc/printcap

The file /etc/printcap holds the data necessary for Linux to know what type of printer it is dealing with, where to send print jobs to be added to the printer's queue, and what factors to take into consideration in handling these print jobs. Each entry in this file follows this format:

```
printername|printeralias:\
  :definitions:\
  :lastdefinition:
```

It is within the definitions that the details of how to handle the print jobs themselves reside.

Add A Printer To /etc/printcap

Adding a printer to /etc/printcap involves building the statement and setting the definitions. The first portion of an /etc/printcap statement opens the section for the particular printer, and therefore, does not have a leading colon. If there is only going to be one printer listed, its first given name should be lp. If there is more than one printer, then choose the one that print jobs should be sent to by default and assign the name lp to that one.

Say, for example, that the printer you want to use as the default is a laser printer. One way to write the beginning of the printer configuration is:

```
lp|laser:\
```

The backslash (\) at the end of the line signals that the statement is not yet complete. This function is a carryover from the fact that the backslash is used in many programming and scripting languages to signal that the code continues down to the next line. Next, type the code that specifies the device being printed to. This line equates the first name listed on the previous line with the driver's location, such as:

```
:lp=/dev/lp0:\
```

Note the leading colon (:) at the beginning of the line. All definition statements have this leading colon. Once again, the line ends in the backslash to indicate that the full statement is not yet finished. What comes after the device driver entry is typically the *print spool* location. This directory is usually in either /var /spool/lpd or /usr/spool/lpd, and then within a specific subdirectory named after the printer itself. The naming scheme is especially important if there is more than one printer, because the spool directories have to be kept separate for management purposes.

A spool directory definition for this example might look like:

```
:sd=/var/spool/lpd/laser
```

There are no additional statement-ending characters on this line because these three lines of code are all that's absolutely necessary in a *local printer* listing. Table 10.1 shows a number of other definition types commonly used in printer statements.

10

Table 10.1 Commonly used printer definitions in /etc/printcap.

Variable	Purpose	Arguments	Example
if	Filter the print job before it is sent to the printer itself.	Path to input filter shell script.	:if=/var/spool/lpd/ laser/input:\
lf	Print error log file.	Path to existing log file.	:lf=/var/spool/lpd/ laser/errorlog:\
lo	Lock file created when printer is in use.	Useful for printers that are accessed by many users at once.	:lo=/var/spool/lpd/ laser/laser.lock:\
mx	Maximum size of print job allowed.	Size limit in blocks, or a zero (0) to indicate no limit.	:mx#0:\
rm	Used if printer is attached to another machine on the LAN.	Address of machine printer is attached to.	:rm=dog.animals.org:\
rp	Used if printer is attached to another machine on the LAN.	Pointer to remote printer.	:rp=inkjet:\
sh	Don't print banner pages.	None needed.	:sh:\

Add A Network Printer Entry

If you want to print across a network, there is a bit more configuration to do. You need to configure the local machine to send to the remote printer, and the print server to accept print jobs from other machines. How you approach this issue depends partially on whether you are trying to print over Samba or just to other Linux machines. Samba was discussed in previous chapters. This section specifically covers printing to remote Linux print servers.

Setting Up The Print Server

Open the file /etc/hosts.lpd on the print server. This is where you will list exactly which machines are allowed to use the attached printers, or even limit printing to specific users on certain machines. If you are setting up a print server on fruit.org and only want to allow the machines apple, mango, and peach to print, then your /etc/hosts.lpd file might look like the following:

```
apple.fruit.org
mango.fruit.org
peach.fruit.org
```

To restrict access to this machine's printers to certain users from any of these machines, add the user name after the machine listing. For example, to let user "jen" print from apple, user "joe" print from mango, and user "admin" print from all three, you would edit this file as follows:

```
apple.fruit.org jen admin
mango.fruit.org joe admin
peach.fruit.org admin
```

 Keep in mind that if you put a user restriction in there, no one else can print to the machine without being explicitly listed.

Save and exit the file and restart lpd.

Setting Up The Print Client

When you want to configure a Linux box on your LAN to print to another machine, you need to make some changes to /etc/printcap. In the printer definition you have to include an rm line to define the remote machine to print to, an rp line to define the printer name set for this printer in the remote machine's /etc/printcap file, and reset this print defintion's lp line, all in the format:

```
:rm=printserver.domain.extension:\
:rp=printername:\
:lp=/dev/null:\
```

You do, however, need to keep your local print spool in that printer definition. Any print job sent from a print client machine to a print server machine will end up being spooled twice; once on the client, then once on the server.

Create The Print Spool

The directory containing the printer's queue has to be created manually. In the case of the example, the command to do this is **mkdir /var/spool/lpd/laser**. Then, this directory has to have its group set (it's fine to leave the directory owned by root). In general, the group with permissions for this directory should be daemon, or in some cases, lp if a specific printer group exists. To set the group to daemon, type "chgrp daemon /var/spool/lpd/laser". Finally, the proper permissions have to be set. These permissions should be 775 (rwxrwxr-x). This setting ensures that various queue management programs and daemons can also access the print spools.

Create The Log File

The log file for the specific printer's activities also has to be created manually. Use the **touch** command to make an empty file to contain the logs in both the exact location and name used in the /etc/printcap printer definition. For example, touch /var/spool/lpd/laser/errorlog. Give it the same ownerships as the print spool (owner root, group daemon) and the permissions 466 (r--rw-rw).

Choose A Flexible Print Filter

If the administrator and users only want to print text files, then there is no need to use a print filter. However, this is typically not the case. Those who want to print graphs, charts, or graphics will need access to nontext printer features. This is where print filters come into play.

 If you want to use a filter in a network setting, be sure to install it on the print server machine and not on the local machines.

Choose Whether To Write Or Download

The administrator has two options. First, he or she can write a print filter. Those who are comfortable with writing shell scripts (see Chapter 5 for more on writing shell scripts) and who have experience with the many potential types of files that users print, may often opt to write their own. Others might want to have full control over how print jobs are handled on their LAN or machine, and so, take on the task of developing their print filter as necessary.

The second option is to download a ready-made print filter from the Internet. There are two print filters available on the Internet that are commonly used on Linux systems: APS filter and magicfilter. Both of these filters are available at **metalab.unc.edu/pub/Linux/system/printing/**.

It is important to be familiar with writing simple print filters and utilizing these two ready-made ones.

Install APS Filter

The APS Filter comes with a menu-driven configuration and installation script that not only installs the filter, but sets up your /etc/printcap file for you. As with any useful script, you can learn a lot by examining the installer's code and becoming comfortable with its inner workings. If you are having difficulty understanding how to set up printers in a more complex setting, consider reviewing how the APS Filter configures your /etc/printcap, as shown in the following steps:

1. **Unpack APS filter**   Once you have downloaded the script package from the site listed at the end of the previous section, place it in your preferred source or download directory. Use the gunzip and tar -xvf programs to uncompress and unpack the source, and then change into the resulting directory.

2. **Run the install script**   Because this new directory likely will not be in your path statement, use the command **./SETUP** to run the configuration and installation script. Be sure to read the two initial screens before you press Enter to go past them. It is important to pay attention to what the program will and will not do.

3. **Configure the printer driver**   To begin your printer configuration, press "1" to configure the printer driver you need, and then press Enter. You are presented with a menu of printer brands to choose from. If your printer clearly falls into one of the categories listed, type the number corresponding to the menu option and press Enter. If not, choose a likely candidate and do the same. You can search through the various menu options until you find a printer driver that looks promising, and then select that one.

   Once you choose the driver you want to use, type the number corresponding to its menu item and press Enter. You will be asked to confirm that this is the driver you want to use. Press "y" and then Enter to confirm and return to the main menu. If you decide during the rest of the configuration process that you need to choose a different driver, you can go back and change it.

4. **Configure the printer interface**   Once you have chosen the printer driver, you need to configure the printer interface. From the main menu, press "2", and then Enter to pull up the short interface menu. There are two options available: parallel and serial. Chances are that you have a parallel interface, and as you can read in the Interface Selection section, parallel is also the preferred choice. However, if the printer is connected as a serial device, then choose serial. When you're ready to proceed, type the number for the menu option and then press Enter.

After you tell APS Filter which interface to use, it brings you to the device configuration section. Enter the device that refers to your printer. In general, if you have a parallel printer on the first parallel port, this device will be /dev/lp0. Type in the device path and press Enter, and the script returns you to the main menu.

5. **Test the printer**   Although testing the printer without needing special soft-ware is discussed elsewhere in this chapter, the APS Filter setup script also gives you the option of printing a test page. If you choose to do this, you need to configure the menu options for printer resolution, monochrome or color, and the type of paper used. Be sure to read all of the text given for each of the items before making your selection. Once you are finished and back at the main menu, press the "T" key and press Enter. If the test page does not print correctly, see the section "Troubleshooting Print Problems" for assistance.

6. **Compile APS filter**   After things are configured and the test page is printed—or you have decided to skip that part—it's time to compile the program. Press the "C" key and press Enter. The compilation process is automated, and occasionally pauses either to ask questions, or give information. Be sure to read everything carefully as you proceed through this task. Once the process is complete, the setup script returns you to your prompt.

7. Examine /etc/printcap. Use a tool such as **more** or **vi** to look at /etc/printcap now that APS Filter has altered it.

Once you have the program compiled, the files for APS Filter are installed into various places. Where some of these files are installed depends on where you put the source code. The end results will be in the /bin subdirectory inside the apsfilter source directory as well as the /etc/apsfilterrc file for configuration purposes.

Install Magicfilter

The Magicfilter program does much less of the work for you during the installation stage, which is a positive aspect for some users and a negative aspect for others. The package does come with an auto-configuration script, which saves you the trouble of editing config files, and is compiled using the **make** tool. However, you will have to add it to /etc/printcap by hand. Here's how:

1. **Unpack Magicfilter**   Once you have downloaded the script package from the site listed at the end of the "Choosing A Flexible Print Filter" section earlier in this chapter, place it in your preferred source or download directory. Use the gunzip and tar -xvf programs to uncompress and unpack the source, and then change into the resulting directory.

2. **Configure Magicfilter**   Use the command **./configure** to run the configuration script because its location is not likely to be within your path statement. The shell script displays each step of the configuration process so you can see if there are errors, and their location.

3. **Compile Magicfilter**   Compiling Magicfilter follows a fairly standard process. Use the command **make** to compile the filter. Once again, a stream of text scrolls down the screen to keep you apprised of where the compiler is in the process. Once the program finishes compiling, use the **make install** command to put it and its documentation into place.

For the sake of good programming practice, issue the command **make clean** to clean out the temporary files generated during the compilation process.

4. Add Magicfilter to /etc/printcap. A print filter is not added as an item unto itself. Instead, you would add a line pointing to the printer within an existing or new /etc/printcap statement. If the command **make install** was not clear as to where it placed the new print filter, use the **find** command to search for "magicfilter".

Once you have the program compiled, the files for Magicfilter are installed into /usr/local/bin.

MANAGE PRINT SERVICES

Once a printer and its services are properly installed, tested, and working, what is left in the long run is management. Not only do the printers have to be kept working smoothly, but so do the spools and queues.

Manage Printers

Once the printers are set up, configured, tested and running, they must be managed over time. Access to printers must be disabled temporarily, perhaps while being repaired, or blocked off from receiving new jobs due to a long queue backup. Printer management is accomplished primarily through the lpc program.

List All Available Printers

To list the printers that are configured and available for use, use lpc in one of two different formats. One method is to type "lpc" itself and, then, at the command line it gives you type "status all". The other is to type "lpc status all". If the choice is to use lpc so that it displays its prompt, both the commands **quit** and **exit** close the program.

Enable A Printer

To enable a printer so that it is open to receive print jobs, use the lpc enable option. Typing "lpc enable all" makes all of the printers available, whereas typing "lpc enable printername" makes a specific printer available for use. For example, if the first line of one of the entries in /etc/printcap is

```
ij|inkjet:\
```

the format for the command would be "lpc enable inkjet".

Disable A Printer

One method of disabling a printer is to comment it out of the /etc/printcap file by placing hash marks (#) at the beginning of each line in its definition statement, and then restarting the print daemon. See the section earlier in this chapter "Manage The Print Daemon" for more information on this topic.

The cleaner method, however, is to use the **lpc** command in the format "**lpc** disable printername".

Manage Print Queues

All of the data sent to a printer is listed within the queue. Each print queue is a list maintained by the print queueing daemon lpq which corresponds to the specific printer in question. These queued jobs wait within the printer's spool directory until it is time to be printed, or, in the case of a network printer, they wait on the local machine's spool directory until the network machine hosting the printer can receive the files in its spool directory. The daemon that handles print queue functions is lpq.

List The Contents Of A Print Queue

To see what is in the default print queue—the queue corresponding to the printer with the name lp in /etc/printcap—type "lpq". The output given is in the format:

```
Active/Inactive  User Printing  Job Number  File Name  Size
```

In order to list the contents of a specific print queue among many, use the format lpq -Pprintername. For example, if the first line of one of the entries in /etc/printcap is

```
ij|inkjet:\
```

the format for the command would be lpq -Pij.

10

Rearrange Entries In A Print Queue

Moving an entry in the print queue requires more than one step. Once the print job number of the item that needs to move to the top of the list is obtained, use the lpc program in the format "lpc topq printername job1 job2." For example, "lpc inkjet 25 41 63" would move print job 25 to the top of inkjet's queue, 41 below 25, and then 63 below 41.

Obtain A Queue Status Report

To get the status of a printer and its queue status, type "lpc status printername" or "lpc status all". Using the continuing example, the command might look like "lpc status inkjet".

Disable A Print Queue

To disable a print queue so that nothing will be spooled to a specific printer, type "lpc disable printername" or "lpc disable all". For the example, the usage might look like "lpc disable inkjet".

No jobs will be sent to the printer until the print queue is re-enabled.

Enable A Print Queue

To enable a print queue so that print jobs are accepted into the printer's spool—or any printer's spool—type "lpc enable printername" or "lpc enable all". For the example, this usage might look like "lpc enable inkjet".

MANAGE THE PRINT DAEMON

There is only one daemon involved in the printing process, though other programs that are used to manage print tasks also handle some daemon management tasks. Because printing is not a network services task per se—even when it involves printing over a network—the print daemon is not controlled by the superdaemon. This daemon has to be handled separately.

lpd

The print spooling daemon in Linux is lpd. When a user sends a print job to a printer, lpd takes the job, processes it according to any filtering specified in /etc /printcap, places the job in the printer's spool directory, and adds it to the printing queue. At times, there may be more than one session of lpd running as lpd spawns a child daemon while a printer is printing a job.

Run The Print Daemon

Those who are not using any printing facilities need not run the print daemon. In fact, a single user working at a single machine who never prints more than one document at a time does not need to run a print daemon, technically speaking.

However, it is lpd that feeds documents into the spool directory and into the printer's queue. This daemon is essential for network printing, and multi-user or single-user setups where more than one job may be printing.

Here's how to start the print daemon under the following conditions:

➤ **Manually** The **lpd** initialization script typically resides alongside the other daemon init scripts, for example, in /etc/rc.d/init.d. To start the print daemon manually, run the init script with the start option. For example, type "/etc/rc.d/init.d/lpd start".

➤ **After a daemon crash** If the print daemon crashes for some reason, first check to see if there are any jobs still left in the queue by typing "lpq" or "lpq -Pprintername". If there are no jobs in the queue, then stop the daemon by typing "/etc/rc.d/init.d/lpd stop" if possible; otherwise, get the process number and kill it, and then start it manually as usual. However, if there are jobs in the queue, stop the daemon as stated before, and start it with the **lpc restart all** or **lpc restart printername** command.

➤ **At boot time** Because the lpd daemon is not managed by the super-daemon, it must be specifically started at boot time. This task is accomplished either by adding lpd to the start and kill statements in the runlevel daemon directories (/etc/rc.d/rc#.d) or adding a statement to the final system init script rc.local in the same format the daemon is invoked manually.

10

PRINT FILES

The Linux printing setup is based on the Unix method of handling print jobs, and so treats every printer like it is a line printer. Print filters are used frequently because they preprocess data to avoid its being printed in its encoded format.

Test A Newly Installed Printer

Before trying anything fancy with a printer, test it and make sure that it is working. There are two different aspects of printing to test initially. The first is just a raw data dump to the printer to see if anything comes out onto paper. The second involves the printer's /etc/printcap definitions.

To test to see if data gets to the printer properly at the most basic level, print a simple file. Create a short text file and redirect it to the printer device with the **cat** command. For example, use the following:

```
cat printtest > /dev/lp0
```

Print A Text File

Printing raw ASCII (text) files is relatively simple. Although it is possible to **cat** the contents of the file to the printer, it is better to utilize the print spooling daemon to avoid any conflicts with other users. To send text to the lpd print spooler, use the **lpr** command, the basic format is as follows:

```
lpr Pprintername file
```

If you want to print to a printer that is on another machine on the LAN and you have already configured this printer in /etc/printcap, then send the print job exactly like you would locally. Use the printer's local name, that is the one assigned to it in the /etc/printcap file on the machine you are on.

Print A PostScript File

The Ghostscript package (available on the distribution CD and at **www.cs.wisc .edu/~ghost/**) is an incredibly useful tool for printing PostScript files under Linux. PostScript is a page description language that ensures that text formatting and graphics appear as expected, regardless of what printer or monitor they are sent to. Although this format is not used commonly in the Windows world and is replaced by document formats such as RTF and PDF, it is still in common use within the Unix world.

Create A Ghostscript /etc/printcap Entry

Linux users generally print more text files than PostScript files, unless they are heavily into word processing and formatting. Because of this preference, it is often useful to have to separate entries for the same printer. The first entry might be a simple one that passes text into the print queue, whereas the second routes the print job through a PostScript processor. Doing this saves print overhead, because the text files will not be preprocessed when it is not necessary. Instead of naming the printer after its type—for example, "laser"—you would name it for the jobs the /etc/printcap entry is set up to process. One print definition might be named "text" and the other might be "postscript".

To create a PostScript-processing entry, create a new statement in /etc/printcap with the Ghostscript program as the input filter. This statement might look like the following:

```
ps|postscript:\
  :lp=/dev/lp0:\
  :sd=/var/spool/lpd/laser:\
  :mx#0:\
  :if=/var/spool/lpd/laser/ghost_filter
```

Create A Simple Ghostscript Input Filter

There are many tweaks and settings available to use with Ghostscript when it comes to fine-tuning the output that goes to the printer. What is discussed here are the very basics of how to set up an initial filter just to get things running.

There are also a number of input filters available on the Internet that handle a wide range of file types.

Create the filter at the location specified in the printer definition's input filter line. Within this file, create a shell script similar to the following:

```
#!/bin/bash
# Invoking ghostscript to process the file.
# The word path refers to the full path to the gs program.
cat $1 | /path/gs -dSAFER
```

Save the file and change its permissions to rw-rw-rw- (666), then make sure it is set at an owner of root and group daemon.

The **gs** (Ghostscript) tool can either be used on the command line, or with its companion **ghostview**, which is a GUI interface that helps to navigate the complex program. It is important to know how to use Ghostscript at the command line.

If for some reason Ghostscript is not included with your distribution, go to **www.cs.wisc.edu/~ghost** to download it. This location is also useful for the latest in Ghostscript documentation and information. Ghostview is included at this site as well.

The **gs** tool is complex, with many options that allow refinement of the final product. It is worth further investigation at a later date.

Convert A Text File To PostScript

It is necessary to know how to convert a file into PostScript format by hand. Often, Linux and Unix documentation items are available directly in PostScript on the Internet, but this is not always the case. In fact, if you have a PostScript printer, you cannot just send it raw ASCII text. So, even text must be converted before you can use it.

A tool that is commonly used for this purpose is **a2ps**. This package is available in many distributions, and if it is not within your file system, then you should be able to find it on the Internet. Use the command **a2ps –h** to get a full listing of the many options available, which are useful in fine-tuning the look and functionality of the PostScript document created.

At a basic level, utilize the program to send a text file to a PostScript printer as follows:

```
a2ps -o - textfile | lpr
```

To send the text file to a PostScript file without printing, use:

```
a2ps -o psfile textfile | lpr
```

MANAGE PRINT JOBS

There is a subtle difference between managing print queues and the print jobs themselves. Handling the queues involves controlling whether or not they feed jobs to specific printers, reordering jobs within queues, and other such larger-scale tasks. Managing print jobs, however, involves removing individual jobs from the queue, or groups of jobs.

Canceling print jobs that are already spooled is done with the **lprm** command. The effects of the command and its flags vary with who is using it, whether the person invoking it is the superuser or just a regular user.

Cancel Individual Print Jobs

To cancel an individual print job on the default printer, first look at the printer's queue and get the job number for the document. Then, type "lprm job". Users can look at the queue at their own jobs and cancel their own jobs, whereas superusers can list and delete anyone's jobs.

If there is more than one printer or print queue, cancel the job with the following format:

```
lprm -Pprintername job
```

 A user can cancel all of his or her print jobs at the same time by typing "lprm -" for the default printer, or "lprm -*Pprintername* -" to cancel jobs for a specific printer. Beware, however, of using this format as the superuser, because using the dash (-) will cancel all jobs in the queue for root.

TROUBLESHOOTING PRINTING PROBLEMS

Sometimes printer installations go flawlessly, and at other times they are rife with problems. Fortunately, most printer problems fall into specific categories. Do not fall into the trap of assuming a problem must be something complex when it in fact may be something as simple as someone having tripped over and disconnected a power cord.

lpd

If the printer will not work or inexplicably stops working, check and make sure that the printer daemon (**lpd**) is running. The daemon may have crashed for some reason and may just need to be restarted. On the other hand, the issue may be more subtle than simply a stopped daemon.

If lpd appears to be unstable, set it to log its transactions to help in tracing the problem. The –l flag tells the daemon to log. In the lpd init script, find the section that handles the "start" option and the line within that section that contains the text "daemon lpd". Change this line to daemon lpd –l. The lpd daemon logs through the **syslog** command, so configure the information levels and locations desired through /etc/syslog.conf.

Be sure to remove the –l flag later once the problem is solved.

The Queue

Another potentially simple problem is that the queue might have somehow been disabled. Use the tools at hand to examine the print queues. Begin by typing "lpc status all" to get the status on all of the printers, or "lpc status *printername*" for a specific printer. If the printer queue is disabled, which would prevent any new jobs from being sent, re-enable it. If the printer is listed as "down", which completely removes the printer from action, then type "lpc up *printername*" or "lpc up all".

The Printer

Check the printer itself. Be sure that it is plugged into an active power supply, that its cable is properly plugged into the server machine, and that the printer is on. Although this may seem a rather unlikely event, it is not uncommon for some passerby to trip over a cable and jiggle it loose.

If you suspect that there is something wrong with the printer itself, hook it up to another computer if possible and **cat** a file to the printer device in order to test the hardware itself. Even if the new computer prints only gibberish due to an incorrect printer driver or other system mismatch, at least you'll be able to discern if the printer is capable of receiving commands from the machine.

Also try the printer with a different cable if possible.

This advice works well for any form of hardware troubleshooting. Sometimes, problems may seem to be at the kernel or software level and in fact turn out to be the motherboard, an internal card, a cable, or some other hardware item.

/etc/printcap

Open the /etc/printcap file—especially if this is the first time you have tried to use this printer or you recently made some /etc/printcap changes—and double-check all of the entries. Be sure that every line except the first begins with a colon and every line except the last ends in a colon and then a backslash (:\). If there are multiple printers configured within the file, be sure that the definitions do not accidentally overlap. For example, be sure that two printers are not sharing the same spool directory or name.

Be sure that the /etc/printcap entries are actually correct. If the device definition does not point to the right printer device, or the maximum print job size has accidentally been set to some small value, these aspects will interfere with the proper operation of the printer.

One part of double-checking /etc/printcap is making sure that all files and directories referred to within the printer configuration file actually exist, and exist with the proper user, group, and permission settings. If one of the following conditions exists, then lpd may not be able to spool the print jobs into the queue:

➤ The spool directory was never created

➤ The spool directory was not assigned to the root user or daemon group

➤ The spool directory's permissions are not 775

The Filters

Those who are unfamiliar with using print filters may find that their basic assumptions of how filters work are incorrect. There are a number of issues where a print filter can cause problems. One of these is the simple issue of whether the permissions and ownerships on the filter are correct.

A print filter can either be a binary or a shell script. The purpose of a filter is to process the data being sent to the printer. Be sure that the filter is set to call the commands it runs with the necessary flags and correct paths.

 If you are trying to utilize a filter while network printing, be sure that the filter is on the server machine and not on the local machine you are trying to print from.

Space Availability

One way that printer problems can sneak up on a system administrator is lack of disk drive space. Verify that the partition containing the print spool is not low on storage space. If a lot of print jobs pass through the system, it may be worth giving the print spool directories their own partition to avoid overrunning the main system partition.

The LAN

If you are trying to print across a network connection, there may be a problem with the network itself. Try testing the machine you are printing from by PINGing other machines, accessing services on other machines, or performing other actions that will determine whether the Linux box and the LAN are communicating properly.

CHAPTER SUMMARY

How much printing you need to know, if any, depends on which Linux certification exam you attempt. In general, it is important to understand the basics of printing. These basics include installing a printer to work under Linux, printing to it, and managing the printers, queues, drivers, and jobs on the individual machine or network.

To send a print job to a printer, the printer needs to be installed and configured. Editing the file /etc/printcap and creating a printer definition entry including the necessary options for making sure the files come through properly takes care of this issue once the printer daemon is started up. Then, to print a job and get it into the printer queue, use the lpr command.

The lpd daemon, and the programs lpc, lpq, and lprm are all important when it comes to dealing with printers. The daemon itself handles moving print jobs into the appropriate print spools. The lpq program allows close inspection of the queues for each printer, seeing which jobs are present and what their job IDs are. Then, the lpc program handles printer and queue management tasks such as making them available or unavailable for use, and rearranging jobs within the queues. If the goal is to remove a print job from the queue, **lprm** is the tool of choice.

Be sure to experiment with print filters. Install the two discussed in this chapter—APS Filter and Magicfilter—and investigate others. Practice writing your own. You do not need to be able to write anything as all-inclusive as one of the two you are directed to download, but you should be able to write something simple for a single task.

REVIEW QUESTIONS

1. Which of the following is the print daemon?
   a. lpc
   b. lpd
   c. lpr
   d. lpq

2. Which file contains printer configuration information?

   a. /etc/services

   b. /etc/printcap

   c. /etc/lp

   d. /etc/lp.conf

3. Which of the following is not a valid **lpc** command?

   a. up

   b. enable

   c. stop

   d. remove

4. Which of the following is used to add a document to the print queue?

   a. lpc

   b. lpd

   c. lpr

   d. lpq

5. With what command(s) do you use the format *printername* to specify the printer?

   a. **lpr**

   b. **lprm**

   c. **lpq**

   d. All of the above.

6. Which group should own the print spool directory?

   a. root

   b. daemon

   c. wheel

   d. print

7. Which of the following is a valid entry in a printer definition in /etc/printcap, one that is not the first or last line in the definition?

   a. sh:

   b. :sh:

   c. :sh:\

   d. :sh\

8. Which of the following is used to list what is within the print queue?

   a. lpc

   b. lpd

   c. lpr

   d. lpq

9. Which of the following is not a valid variable to define in an /etc/printcap statement?

   a. if

   b. of

   c. lo

   d. lq

10. What command is often used to test a printer without testing the print daemon at the same time?

   a. **cat**

   b. **lp**

   c. **lpr**

   d. **print**

10

11. Which of the following files do you edit to configure the general logging for lpd?

   a. /var/spool/*printer*/log

   b. /etc/lpd.conf

   c. /etc/syslog.conf

   d. /usr/spool/*printer*/log.conf

12. Which of the following is used to manage printers and queues, and move print jobs within a queue?

   a. lpc

   b. lpd

   c. lpr

   d. lpq

13. Which of the following can be used to start lpd automatically at boot time? [Choose all correct answers]

   a. /etc/inetd.conf

   b. /etc/rc.d/rc.local

   c. /etc/rc.d/rc3.d/

   d. /etc/services

14. What command is used to print a PostScript file? Consider all potential circumstances. [Choose all correct answers]

    a. **gs**

    b. **lpd**

    c. **ps**

    d. **lpr**

15. What unit is the maximum job size set in?

    a. bytes

    b. kilobytes

    c. blocks

    d. bits

16. What printcap definition variable would you use to make sure a page of user identification information is not printed before each print job?

    a. of

    b. mx

    c. rm

    d. sh

17. Which of the following are quick checks to see why your print job isn't going through? [Choose all correct answers]

    a. Is the printer on?

    b. Are the cables firmly in place?

    c. Is the print daemon running?

    d. Is there a bug in the print filter?

18. Which of the following is a valid print filter file type? [Choose all correct answers]

    a. Compiled C++ program

    b. Shell script

    c. Plain text file

    d. Compiled C program

19. Which command sequence—ignoring issues of flags and values—would you use to get the job number for a specific job on the default printer and then cancel that job?

    a. lpq, lpr

    b. lpq, lprm

    c. lpc, lprm

    d. lpc, lpr

20. What do you type when invoking the print daemon if you want it to log information?

 a. pd lf /*loglocation*

 b. lpd –log

 c. lpd –L

 d. lpd –l

Hands-On Projects

These projects require that you have access to a working Linux system in command-line mode. The printer packages must be installed, and you have to have at least a short text file on hand to use to test the setup. Because a specific make and model of printer cannot be expected, you will set up for a fictional printer.

Project 10.1
To install and configure a fictional test printer, do the following:

1. Log in as root.

2. Open the printing configuration file by typing "vi /etc/printcap".

3. Go to the bottom of the file by typing "G".

4. Open a new line by typing "O".

5. Begin the printer entry by adding a short and long name for the printer. Because this is a test setup and should not interfere with any other printers already configured on the site, you will not use the default printer "lp". Instead, add the text:

```
tst|test_printer:\
```

6. Because you don't want this entry to point to a real printer, do not enter a device.

7. Point to the spool directory with:

```
:sd=/var/spool/lpd/tst:\
```

8. Add a maximum cap on output of approximately 1MB. One MB is 1024Kb, and one block is 512b, and 512b is one half of one KB. So, this means that 1MB is 2,048 blocks. The definition line is then:

```
:mx#2048:\
```

10

9. For the last line, because this is a single user test printer, suppress banner pages to save on disk space:

```
:sh:
```

10. Save and exit /etc/printcap by typing ":wq" and pressing Enter.
11. Create the spool directory by typing "mkdir /var/spool/lpd/tst".
12. The directory's owner should already be root. Change its group by typing "chgrp daemon /var/spool/lpd/tst".
13. Change the directory's permissions to rwxr-xr-x by typing "chmod 755".
14. Type "ps aux | grep lpd" to see if the print daemon is currently running.
15. If the daemon is running, then you need to stop it so you can get it to re-read /etc/printcap. To stop the daemon cleanly without causing any problems with current printers that may be running on the machine or LAN, type "lpc down all Restarting the print daemon". Anyone who attempts to print while the daemon and queues are down will get the "Restarting the print daemon" message.
16. Type "lpc up all" to start a new printer daemon and enable all of the print queues.
17. Now, to test the setup with the text file you already have prepared, type "lpr -Ptst *filename*".
18. Type "lpq" to see if the print jobs made it into the queue.
19. Use the **lprm** command to remove the jobs from the queue.

Hands-On Project

Project 10.2
To set up an entry to handle printing to a network printer:

1. Log in as root.
2. Edit the printcap file by typing "vi /etc/printcap".
3. Go to the bottom of the file by typing "G".
4. Open a new line by typing "O".
5. Begin the print statement by assigning the printer's name:

```
tstnet|network_test_printer:\
```

6. Point to the local spool directory:

```
:sd=/var/spool/lpd/tstnet:\
```

7. Tell the printer daemon which machine hosts the remote printer with:

```
:rm=printhost.networkprinttest.org:\
```

8. The machine that hosts the remote printer (printhost.networkprinttest.org) has to have this printer already defined in its own /etc/printcap. This printer is the default printer on the machine, so it can just be referred to as "lp". Tell the local printer daemon which printer on the remote machine the file should go to:

```
:rp=lp:\
```

9. The device to open for this print job does not exist on the local machine, so set it to /dev/null:

```
:lp=/dev/null:\
```

10. For the last line, because this is a single user test printer, suppress banner pages to save on disk space:

```
:sh:
```

11. Save and exit /etc/printcap by typing ":wq" and pressing Enter. After restarting the print daemon you could now print to the remote printer if it existed.

To allow outside machines to print to your local test printer:

1. Edit the file "hosts.lpd" with the command **vi /etc/hosts.lpd** to allow outside hosts to print to your machine.

2. Press "I" to enter vi's Insert mode.

3. Add the following entry:

```
.networkprinttest.org
```

4. Save and exit the file by typing ":wq" and pressing Enter. Now, remote printers can print to the fictional printer.

Although remote printers can print to your printer, they cannnot access the input filters.

## CHAPTER ELEVEN

COMPILING A CUSTOM KERNEL

AFTER READING THIS CHAPTER AND COMPLETING THE EXERCISES, YOU WILL BE ABLE TO:

➤ Distinguish between various kernel sources available to you

➤ Apply patches to kernel sources

➤ Configure a custom kernel

➤ Compile and install a custom kernel

E very system administrator is eventually faced with the need to compile a new kernel. Installing a custom kernel is a complex process involving selecting just the right source code version, refining the kernel configuration, and more. The better you understand the method and methodology behind why you would create a custom kernel, how one is created, and how to optimize the kernel for a Linux system, the more effective you will be.

REASONS TO COMPILE A CUSTOM KERNEL

Although it is certainly not necessary to compile a custom kernel in order to run a Linux system right out of the box, doing so is in some ways unavoidable. Even if the goal is not to add features that are not included by default or optimize the default kernel, the only way to upgrade the operating system is to eventually compile the new kernel desired. Installing kernel binaries is not often a good idea because that action puts too much reliance on whether those binaries take into account all of the system's hardware and software needs.

Access To Features Not Included

What drives many administrators to compile their first custom kernel is a message on their screen that declares the kernel does not support a particular feature, or README files that state nonstandard kernel features are required. Although sometimes these issues can be handled by manually inserting kernel *modules*, there comes a time when it is more efficient to build a whole new kernel.

Kernel Modules

The modern Linux kernel is not designed to be one massive piece of code. Instead, the core portion of the kernel is compiled into a single unit, and the rest is stored as modules. Each module handles one piece of kernel functionality and is loaded when needed, then unloaded when no longer in use. For example, the parport module handles parallel port functionality. Because printers are typically not used on a continuous basis—except on busy print servers—this module is often loaded and unloaded on the fly.

Inserting A Module By Hand

The **insmod** command loads a kernel module. These modules are stored in the directory /lib/modules/*version* and broken down into subdirectories. Table 11.1 lists examples of common subdirectories and the usual contents of each. Many of these modules are device drivers.

For example, perhaps you have an IDE tape drive that you rarely use. The script that handles your backups might have a line such as:

```
insmod /lib/modules/version/block/ide-tape.o
```

This line would load the module before running the backup routine.

One command that particularly comes in handy is **modinfo**. With this command, you can get information about loaded modules in the format "**modinfo** *module*", or those you have not loaded yet in the format "**modinfo** /lib/modules/*version*/*moddir*/*module*.o". However, this command does not always provide the information requested, and in some distributions in fact, appears to be broken. The flags used with **modinfo** are listed in Table 11.2.

Table 11.1   Kernel module directories.

Directory	Contains
block	Modules for handling *block* devices, such as floppy and tape drives.
cdrom	Modules for handling CD-ROM devices.
fs	Modules for handling file system types, such as vfat and smbfs.
ipv4	Modules for handling IP addressing issues.
misc	All modules that do not specifically belong in any of the other module directories, such as sound handlers.
net	Networking modules, such as PPP handlers, LAN handlers, Ethernet handlers, and more.
pcmcia	Modules deal with PCMCIA devices.
scsi	Modules deal with SCSI devices.
video	Modules deal with video output.

Table 11.2   Flags available for the **modinfo** command.

Flag	Purpose
-a	Display information about the person who wrote the module.
-d	Display a description of the module.
-p	Display a list of the parameters you can use with this module.
-h	Display help for the **modinfo** command.
-V	Give version information for **modinfo**.

11

A reliable way to get information on a module is to look in the file /usr /src/linux/Documentation/Configure.help if you have the kernel source installed. Many distributions install it automatically.

Removing A Module By Hand

The **rmmod** command removes a kernel module that is not currently in use, or does not have other modules that need it in order to run. In order to see which modules are currently loaded, use the command **lsmod**. For example, in the script previously discussed, you need to unload the module after the backup routine completes unless you intend to leave it until the next time you reboot the machine. The line to do this might be as follows:

```
rmmod ide-tape
```

Setting Modules To Load Automatically

You can set modules to load automatically without recompiling your kernel. To do this, first locate the file /etc/conf.modules or /etc/modules.conf. The file name varies between these two from distribution to distribution. This file is where you can list the modules to load and what options to use with them.

Optimizing The Default Kernel

Each distribution produces a default kernel that runs the machine adequately. However, this kernel can and should be refined for each system it is installed on. The default kernel has to cover a wide range of hardware and configuration issues in order to please the majority of people who are going to install the distribution. Each of these additional features increases the size of the kernel.

Upgrading To A New Kernel Version

Kernel development in the Linux world proceeds at a rapid pace. As a general rule, it is not a good idea to try to keep up with the latest and greatest in kernel versions. Doing so means that the OS is constantly in flux and very likely will lead to stability problems. Keep in mind the fact that with each kernel upgrade it is possible that things that were working fine only minutes before can suddenly break.

CHOOSING A NEW KERNEL VERSION

To make an educated choice among the kernel versions available, it is important to understand how the kernel development process works. Without this knowledge, it is easy to think one is choosing the best kernel available and end up with something that is, in reality, completely unreliable.

Kernel Development

Linus Torvalds, the initial author of Linux, retains control over what goes into the kernel itself. However, the development of the kernel is done by people all over the world. When someone has something he or she would like to contribute he or she sends it to Linus in the form of a kernel *patch*, which he then takes under consideration and may or may not approve.

Kernel development is split into two streams. One of them is *bleeding edge*, which means that the patch contains brand-new items that need to be tested for stability. The other is *tried and true*—code deemed good enough for use on production machines.

Kernel Numbering

The kernel numbering system is relatively simple to follow. In today's kernels both streams begin with the same initial number. After this major version number comes a dot (.) and then the minor kernel version number. If this minor version is an even number, then the kernel is a production-level type and is considered stable. The odd numbered ones are, instead, the experimental.

After the minor version number comes the build number, which is the number of patches added onto the *major.minor* kernel version thus far. This number is separated from the major and minor with another dot (.), for example, *major.minor.patch*. Sometimes if there are minor changes or distribution-specific alterations to the kernel, there will be a dash on the end with another number listing how many changes were made there as well. Figure 11.1 further illustrates the kernel numbering system.

The Experimental Stream

Choosing to use an experimental kernel (for example, 2.3.14) on a production machine is not recommended. Although the development kernels are mostly stable, there is no guarantee of stability. Remember that this stream is used for testing bleeding-edge code and so there is no pretence that it is ready to be used on machines that are necessary for providing essential services.

However, those who have the need to use features or device drivers that are only available in the experimental stream do take the chance, and are often happy with the results. Just kccp in mind that the kernel may fail. Do not remove the old kernel from the system until the machine has been put through its paces for a few weeks and has demonstrated it is trustworthy.

11

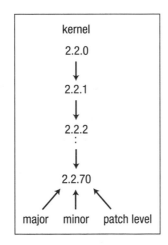

Figure 11.1   The kernel numbering system.

The Production Stream

The production branch of the kernel tree is the stable, proven code that has survived the rest of the kernel development process. If the goal is to carefully choose the exact kernel version that meets the needs of the system, instead of just getting the latest production version (for example, 2.2.52), then it is important to read the change documents that go along with each version increment. Just because the kernel is from the production stream does not mean that everything will work.

A problem for any software developer is the fact that adding one thing sometimes breaks another. This problem explodes exponentially when it comes to an entire operating system. Research what each kernel change fixes, and what it breaks. Eventually the right combination of what pieces need to work will appear. If not, get the latest version or the one closest to the system's needs and keep a close eye on further kernel advances.

Figure 11.2 illustrates the kernel development process in more detail, showing how the two streams interact.

PRE-COMPILATION PREPARATIONS

The same general procedure is used regardless of the reason for replacing the kernel. The source code has to be installed on the machine, and updated if there is a need to apply patches. If the machine is not commonly used for programming

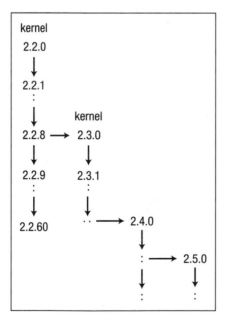

Figure 11.2   The kernel development process.

tasks, then there are likely a number of related packages that need to be installed or updated as well. Often, a newer kernel requires newer versions of the C *compiler* or *shared libraries*.

Obtaining The Kernel Source

The kernel source is available in a number of places. The source used to build the kernel installed by the distribution is available on the distribution CDs. Otherwise, there are archive sites that store kernel source down to the level of each official patch, and also there are other sites that store unofficial patches. All of these items are available on the Internet.

Getting The Distribution's Source

If the aim in compiling a custom kernel is to optimize the current system's operation without actually updating to a new version of the operating system, then obtain the source directly from the CDs that came with the Linux distribution being used.

Most distributions today come with at least two CDs. The first of these CDs is generally the distribution itself. The second is typically the source code for every *Open Source* item on the distribution CD. Whether the source for the kernel is on the distribution CD itself or on the source CD is a question of which distribution is installed.

Getting The Non-Distribution-Specific Source

If the goal is to install source that is newer than what is already installed, there are a number of sites that provide the kernel source on the Internet. One definitive source of kernel information—and pointer to the sources themselves—is on the Open Source Web site at **www.kt.opensrc.org**. This page is a newsletter that outlines the previous week's discussions on the linux-kernel mailing list, which is where Linus and those who assist with kernel development discuss additions and issues such as how the latest source is shaping up. Pointers to kernel-related documents and source sites are also available on this page.

There are two different ways to get a newer version of source. One of these methods is to download the source package for the particular version. If this is not available, download the closest version of the source and the patches necessary to bring it up to the version desired. For example, if the goal is to install kernel 2.4.5, the first step would be to download the source for version 2.4 (which is, essentially, 2.4.0), and then the patches 2.4.1, 2.4.2, 2.4.3, 2.4.4, and 2.5.5.

Adding The Source Patches

If a main source package and a collection of patches is the end result of obtaining the kernel source, then the patches must be applied sequentially. Each patch alters the code of the main package such that, once the patch is applied, the source

11

matches the kernel version the patch is written for. A patch must first be un-compressed and unzipped before being applied, and then placed in the source directory, generally /usr/src/linux. Once this task is accomplished, use the patch program to add it to the kernel source. Use the command **patch –p0 <** *patchfile*.

It is critical that this is done sequentially. To patch kernel 2.4.0 up to 2.4.5 after the patch files are decompressed and unpacked, the sequence of commands would be:

```
$ patch -p0 < patch2.4.1
$ patch -p0 < patch2.4.2
$ patch -p0 < patch2.4.3
$ patch -p0 < patch2.4.4
$ patch -p0 < patch2.4.5
```

Updating Or Installing Related Packages

When you update the kernel, there are sometimes many programs that have to be updated as well. How many there are really depends on how large of a jump is made between the current kernel and the new one. Another issue is that packages that otherwise might not need to be installed to perform every-day operations—say, compiling C code if the machine is not used to do that—are suddenly necessary when it is time to compile things, especially the kernel.

Rather than waiting for error messages to list which packages need to be replaced or installed, read the documentation that comes with the kernel itself. These documents are usually in the documentation subdirectory of the source directory.

The Compiler

In order to replace the current kernel with a new kernel from source, the source must be compiled. If no compiler is installed, then it needs to be added to the system. The compiler used in Linux to build the kernel is GCC, or the *GNU C Compiler*, which currently comes under the package name EGCS (usually egcs). The home page for the organization that provides this package is located at **egcs.cygnus.com**, if a newer version of the package is required and not available from the Linux distribution's Web site.

The Preprocessor

One tool used when preparing to compile C source code is the cpp, or C Preprocessor. This program works with the C compiler to add functionality and automation to the compilation process. Although cpp may not need to be upgraded, it definitely needs to be installed if it is not already.

The Libraries

Compiling the kernel also requires access to the proper libraries. GNU's version of the C libraries is referred to as glibc, and these also need to be installed or upgraded, depending on the version of the kernel involved and what is said in its documentation.

The Build Manager

The *make* build manager assists the user when it comes time to compile software like the kernel sources. All the administrator needs to know are the *make targets*, and most of the compile process is automated by the build manager. This package needs to be installed in order to run the compile, but often does not need to be upgraded.

Other Packages

Other packages you may need, depending on how you go about compiling the kernel and which distribution you are using, are the ncurses packages and the kernel headers. If you download the kernel source, then the headers are included. However, pay attention to the files included with the distribution. If there is a kernel source and kernel header package on the CD, install them both.

The ncurses packages contain cursor control libraries, which allow the use of the cursor while not within a GUI. This set of packages may be necessary if one specific method of kernel configuration is chosen.

11

COMPILING THE KERNEL

One process that makes most people who are not programmers nervous is the compile process. Fortunately, most of the kernel compilation process is automated with the make package. What follows is the step-by-step process necessary to compile a kernel from source.

Understanding The Makefile

The Makefile used for the kernel compilation is located in /usr/src/linux/Makefile. Although most of this document is not necessary for you to understand, there are specific portions that are of interest. This section's purpose is to give you a feeling for what the file contains and what it does in case you need to modify it to suit your purposes. It also serves the greater function of showing you the more advanced capabilities of what you can do in a Makefile.

The very beginning of the Makefile—the first four lines to be precise—is the section you will most likely need to modify. These lines define the version number assigned to the kernel. The following lines refer to kernel 2.2.80:

```
VERSION = 2
PATCHLEVEL = 2
```

```
SUBLEVEL = 80
EXTRAVERSION =
```

If there were an item under the extraversion, this would correspond to the last number after a dash. An extraversion of 12 would change this kernel version to 2.2.80-12. You would change the extraversion if you did some minor adjustments on the Makefile or to any part of the kernel source. Doing this makes it clear later when you are looking through code, which is the one you changed and which is the original.

The next line may be something like:

```
ARCH := $(shell uname -m | sed -e s/i.86/i386/ -e s/sun4u/spark64/ -e s/
arm.*/arm/ -e s/sa110/arm/)
```

Any line with the := grouping is a macro definition. In this case, the variable ARCH is set to the value of the statements within the parentheses. These statements are essentially in three parts, and are not actually evaluated right now. They will be evaluated each time $ARCH is referenced. However, for the sake of example, you will get a walkthrough of the evaluation process.

The first of the three parts is the shell term. This term stands off on its own, because it is not a command by itself. It will be interpreted as $shell, which is a variable that must be defined later within the Makefile. The second part is **uname –m**, which returns the type of processor the current kernel is compiled for. On modern machines, this often returns "i586". Finally, the output of the **uname –m** command is piped as input to a **sed** statement.

The **sed** statement looks prohibitively complex at first glance, but actually it is pretty straightforward. When you want to include more than one editing statement all in the same **sed** command, you lead each statement with -e. So, first the sed statement breaks down into four different editing commands: **s/i.86/i386/, s/sun4u/spark64/, s/arm.*/arm/, and s/sa110/arm/**. All of these editing commands are of the same type, the "s" stands for search and replace. Because we are dealing with the PC architecture and not another such as Sparc or Alpha, the first editing statement is what will be used: s/**i.86/i386**. Therefore, if **uname –m** returns i586, this value will be changed to i386.

The next statement is as follows:

```
.EXPORT_ALL_VARIABLES:
```

There are certain variables you can set within Makefiles by declaring them as targets that do not actually have to have options. A full list of these setting targets is available in the GNU make manual, a menu which is at **www.gnu.org/manual/make-3.77/make.html**. This option exports all of the values of the variables set in the Makefile to the child processes created by this Makefile, such as each of the compilation processes.

After this comes more macros and variable settings. Finally next comes the first make target:

```
all:    do-it-all
```

If you remember from previous coverage of make, you can reference other make targets in this manner. In this case, only one make target is referred to because of the following set of code:

```
ifeq (.config,$(wildcard .config))
      include .config
      ifeq (.depend,$(wildcard .depend))
              include .depend
              do-it-all:    Version vmlinux
      else
              CONFIGURATION = depend
              do-it-all:    depend
      endif
else
      CONFIGURATION = config
      do-it-all:    config
endif
```

This code is not typically indented in the kernel Makefile, but it is indented here to make it more apparent where the loops are. First, there is the issue of the make conditional **ifeq**. This command tests whether the two items within the parentheses are identical. In this case, the first test looks to see whether the .config file—which contains your default kernel configuration—exists or not, first as literally ".config", and then the value of .config with the wildcard function, which expands any wildcards it finds. If there is a default configuration file, the make program reads the contents of that file and then returns to where it left off.

There is no "then" statement with **ifeq**. Instead, including another **ifeq** is treated as a then. Therefore, If the first condition fails, it goes to the second condition, where it tests for a .depend file in the same manner. If it exists, then make reads the contents of the .depend file and assigns the value of the do-it-all target to "Version vmlinux".

If neither if statement is true, then both the CONFIGURATION variable and do-it-all target are set to .depend. Now we break out of the inner loop. If the initial if statement was true—there was a default configuration file—then the CONFIGURATION variable and do-it-all target are set to .config.

Now more variables are set, and then you come across the following:

```
ifdef CONFIG_SMP
CFLAGS += -D__SMP__
AFLAGS += -D__SMP__
endif
```

There are two new items here. First is the **ifdef** statement. This conditional tests to see if the variable—in this case CONFIG_SMP—has any value assigned. If so, it continues to what is inside the **ifdef** statement. If not, it jumps ahead. The second item to discuss is the += definitions. The plus then equal sign together allow you to append items onto text variables. So, for example, no matter what CFLAGS was already, it now has –D__SMP__ on the end of it.

More and more of the types of statements in here are familiar at this point. Scroll past variable and macro definitions, comments, and **ifdef** and **ifeq** statements. At one point you encounter an **ifneq** statement, which is simply the opposite of **ifeq**. It is true if the items in the parentheses do not match.

Now, finally, you reach another new item. The following lines

```
.S.s:
        $(CC) -D__ASSEMBLY__ $(AFLAGS) -traditional -E -o $*.s $<
.S.o:
        $(CC) -D__ASSEMBLY__ $(AFLAGS) -traditional -c -o $*.s $<
```

might look like targets but actually are called suffixes. Anything in the format ".c" or ".o" or ".c.o" is a suffix. People who are familiar with C programming are already familiar with .c which is a source file, or .o which is a nonexecutable compiled object before it is linked to become an executable. However, the two-part suffix is new. A two-part suffix comes in when the person building the Makefile cannot be sure that intermediate files have not changed somewhere along the way. To break down .c.o make, look for a .SUFFIXES line and see if there are any .c files whose source has changed by the time make was ready to make the object files.

Now we get into the actual setting of make targets. The version, boot, vmlinux, symlinks, oldconfig, xconfig, menuconfig, config, and other targets are all assigned here. Notice that some of the targets have information directly after the colon and some do not. If a target has nothing after the colon, then it simply continues with the instructions after it. If there is something after the colon, no matter how many items, all of these items have to be made before it can continue. Consider, for example, the following:

```
boot: vmlinux
        @$(MAKE) -C arch/$(ARCH)/boot
```

Before "make boot" can happen, "make vmlinux" has to already have happened. If it has not, make runs "make vmlinux" and then proceeds to the instructions for "make boot".

 If you see slashes (/) in make targets, these refer to relative paths to where the Makefile is.

The Makefile continues. You should be at the very least able to recognize the components you see in the rest of it, whether or not you fully understand what each does.

Building The Default Configuration File

Within the main kernel source directory, which is likely /usr/src/linux or something similar, begin the compile process by building the default configuration file. This default file contains all of the options used the last time the kernel was configured, making the process of configuring it this time much quicker because every single item does not have to be set from scratch.

To build this initial configuration file, use the **make oldconfig** command. Even if the kernel was compiled by the distribution installer or installed directly as a binary file, there is a default configuration set in place to start with. As mentioned earlier, this configuration file is /usr/src/linux/.config.

Preparing To Configure The Kernel

There are three different programs that handle kernel configuration. Which of these programs are used depends on a combination of issues. The primary considerations are the hardware installed and the system's function within the LAN if connected to one. If there is no GUI installed on the machine—for example, because it is meant to be a function-specific server, such as a mail server—then the X-based configuration tool is not an option. Also, the decision among the three depends on how much of the kernel the administrator needs to configure.

Choosing The Text Kernel Config

The fully text-based kernel configuration option is config, shown in Figure 11.3. This option is by far the most time-consuming and confusing for those who are not used to configuring the kernel. The config tool walks the user through a long question-and-answer session about what features should be compiled in, left out of, or available as modules. Understanding some of these options can require a certain amount of research if the goal is to highly fine-tune the resulting kernel.

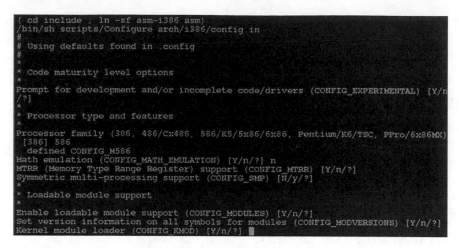

```
( cd include ; ln -sf asm-i386 asm)
/bin/sh scripts/Configure arch/i386/config.in
#
# Using defaults found in .config
#
*
* Code maturity level options
*
Prompt for development and/or incomplete code/drivers (CONFIG_EXPERIMENTAL) [Y/n
/?]
*
* Processor type and features
*
Processor family (386, 486/Cx486, 586/K5/5x86/6x86, Pentium/K6/TSC, PPro/6x86MX)
  [386] 586
  defined CONFIG_M586
Math emulation (CONFIG_MATH_EMULATION) [Y/n/?] n
MTRR (Memory Type Range Register) support (CONFIG_MTRR) [Y/n/?]
Symmetric multi-processing support (CONFIG_SMP) [N/y/?]
*
* Loadable module support
*
Enable loadable module support (CONFIG_MODULES) [Y/n/?]
Set version information on all symbols for modules (CONFIG_MODVERSIONS) [Y/n/?]
Kernel module loader (CONFIG_KMOD) [Y/n/?] ▮
```

Figure 11.3   The "config" kernel configuration option.

Choosing The Menu Kernel Config

A hybrid configuration option, which provides a menu-driven interface that does not require X to be running, is menuconfig, shown in Figure 11.4. This is the option that needs the ncurses set of packages to run properly. Its interface is far friendlier for those who are unfamiliar with the cryptic names and terms used to refer to various kernel features. The menuconfig tool is an especially good choice for those who want to change a few features, or want a more top-down approach to facing kernel configuration, but do not have access to a GUI on the machine.

```
Linux Kernel v2.2.5 Configuration
                            Main Menu
    Arrow keys navigate the menu.  <Enter> selects submenus --->.
    Highlighted letters are hotkeys.  Pressing <Y> includes, <N> excludes,
    <M> modularizes features.  Press <Esc><Esc> to exit, <?> for Help.
    Legend: [*] built-in  [ ] excluded  <M> module  < > module capable

              Code maturity level options  --->
              Processor type and features  --->
              Loadable module support  --->
              General setup  --->
              Plug and Play support  --->
              Block devices  --->
              Networking options  --->
              SCSI support  --->
              Network device support  --->
              Amateur Radio support  --->
              IrDA subsystem support  --->
              v(+)

                  < elect>    < Exit >    < Help >
```

Figure 11.4   The menuconfig kernel configuration option.

Linux Kernel Configuration		
Code maturity level options	IrDA subsystem support	Partition Types
Processor type and features	Infrared-port device drivers	Native Language Support
Loadable module support	ISDN subsystem	Console drivers
General setup	Old CD-ROM drivers (not SCSI, not IDE)	Sound
Plug and Play support	Character devices	Additional low level sound drivers
Block devices	Mice	Universal Serial Bus (USB)
Networking options	Watchdog Cards	Kernel hacking
QoS and/or fair queueing	Video For Linux	
SCSI support	Joystick support	Save and Exit
SCSI low-level drivers	Ftape, the floppy tape device driver	Quit Without Saving
Network device support	Filesystems	Load Configuration from File
Amateur Radio support	Network File Systems	Store Configuration to File

Figure 11.5 The xconfig kernel configuration option.

Choosing The Graphical Kernel Config

The X version of the kernel configuration option is xconfig, shown in Figure 11.5. For many, this tool is the preferred method of configuring the kernel. Whereas menuconfig reduces the confusion when it comes to sorting out what kernel options refer to what pieces of hardware or services, the xconfig option offers a wider range of menus to further refine and speed up the configuration process. Of course, this option is only available on machines which have X up and running.

Modular Or Monolithic

It's important to understand when dealing with the kernel that it has modular capabilities. Kernels can be huge today with all of the information they need to contain. However, not all of this information is needed all of the time, or even one half or one quarter of the time. So, having a massive kernel that contains all the information the operating system might ever possibly need is a waste of RAM, because the kernel has to be held in memory.

It is highly recommended that you create a modular kernel. When doing this, there is an option of whether to compile a feature into the kernel itself, not have it at all, or include it as a module that can be loaded and then released all on the fly. Keep these subtleties in mind when configuring the kernel. If a driver or capability is going to be used less than half the time, add it modularly. If it will be used almost always, or at least on a very regular basis, then include it.

Configuring The Kernel

Now that the choice is made of which tool to use while configuring the kernel, use the command **make *configoption*** to open the configuration tool. For

11

example, to configure using the X tool, make sure you are in the GUI, then use the command **make xconfig**. The specific process involved for configuring the kernel differs depending on the tool chosen.

Using config

Start the config tool by entering the command **make config**. This tool is a step-by-step adaptive walkthrough of kernel configuration. It is adaptive in the sense that the top-level questions pertain to whether a broad feature type is desired, and if the answer is yes, more specific questions are asked to determine which aspects of this feature to use and what settings are appropriate for the system.

Each question offers a collection of answers. If there is only one, or one of the answers is uppercased, then this is the option that will be used as the default if Enter is pressed without typing anything. The most important thing to keep at hand is a collection of resources that help to understand what some of the options refer to. Some of these resources are:

➤ **www.kernelnotes.org**

➤ **www.kernel.org**

➤ **metalab.unc.edu/linux-source**

Although it is useful to work with this tool and get to understand the kernel at a more basic level, it is not necessary for the first-level Linux certification exams. These exams focus more on actually accomplishing the kernel configuration task, and so menuconfig or xconfig are both faster tools to use.

Using menuconfig

Start the menuconfig tool by using the command **make menuconfig**. This tool allows you to navigate through the kernel options in a hierarchical format. Use the up and down arrow keys to move from menu to menu and then press Enter when ready to choose a menu option. Then, use the up and down arrow keys once again to choose which item within that menu to edit. When you reach a screen that gives you configuration choices (an example of this is shown in Figure 11.6), instead of just a menu of types of kernel configuration options (as shown in Figure 11.4), use the up and down arrow keys to move to the item and then press the spacebar to select the configuration choice.

To move backward through the menus, either use the right or left arrow keys to choose the Exit item and then press Enter, or press the Esc key twice. Finally, when the process is completed, use the right and left arrow keys to choose the Exit menu item from the main menu, and save the new configuration information on the way out.

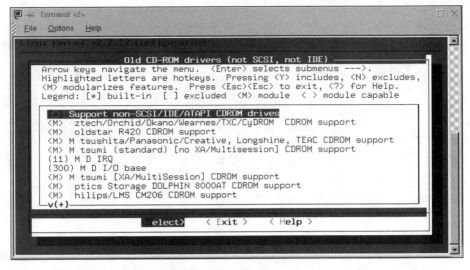

Figure 11.6 Configuring kernel capabilities using menuconfig.

Using xconfig

Start the xconfig tool by typing the command **make xconfig** from within the GUI. This tool is fully graphical. Click the button for the segment of the kernel desired. A new dialog box opens containing the options for this part of the kernel's configuration. On the right of each option is a Help button which, if clicked on, displays a dialog box with information on the item. The Help button will also note the best choice if the user is otherwise unsure.

To close a kernel segment's dialog box, click the Main Menu button. This action will return the administrator to the central kernel configuration menu. When configuration is complete, click the Save and Exit button.

There are a number of options that often can stand to be changed when kernel reconfiguration occurs. These items are listed in Table 11.3.

Compiling The Kernel

The actual act of compiling the kernel is fairly simple. It is a matter of following a series of steps automated by the make package. Once completed, you will have a brand-new kernel ready for use. Each step may take some time because this is the meat of the operation.

➤ **Building The Dependency List** To build the list of which sections of the source depend on other sections of the source, use the **make dep** command.

➤ **Cleaning Out Temporary Files** To clean out the temporary files created during the configuration and dependency building process, use the **make clean** command.

Table 11.3 Frequently changed kernel configuration options.

xconfig Section	Option	Reason To Change	New Value
Processor type and features	Processor family	The default is a 386. Change if the machine in question is not a 386.	The current processor type in your machine. Choose one of the options listed.
Processor type and features	Math emulation	Any machine that is a 486DX and up has a math coprocessor built in. Change if the machine in question is this speed or higher.	"n"
Amateur Radio support	Amateur Radio support	Unless you actually are an amateur radio enthusiast, this option is not necessary.	"n"
Infrared-port device drivers	All items	Not needed unless there are infrared-port devices used with the machine.	"n"
ISDN subsystem	ISDN support	No need for this if ISDN is not the networking connection used.	"n"
Old CD-ROM drivers	Support non-SCSI/ IDE/ATAPI CDROM drives	This option is not necessary unless a CD-ROM drive that is so old that it does not fall under one of these umbrellas is included.	"n"
Joystick support	Joystick support	Not necessary on a server that will not have games on it, or if there is no joystick.	"n"
Ftape, the floppy tape device driver	Ftape, the floppy tape device driver	Not needed if there is no tape drive.	"n"
Native Language Support	Any	Remove the language support modules you do not need, which should be most of them.	"n"
Sound	Sound card support	Not necessary if the machine is not meant to use for multimedia purposes and has no sound card.	"no"

➤ **Building The Kernel** To compile the main portion of the kernel, use the command **make bzImage**. Sometimes this file is **zImage** instead. The **bzImage** file is a more compressed kernel and is used more and more often because the **zImage** kernels rarely fit on a single floppy disk anymore. A kernel that cannot fit on one floppy can then not be put on an emergency boot disk.

➤ **Building The Modules** To compile the modules that the kernel will load and unload as they are needed, use the command **make modules**.

INSTALLING THE KERNEL

Your task is not complete once the kernel is compiled. It now has to be installed, and a smart system administrator installs a new kernel in such a way that it is easy to back up and return to the previous one. After all, there is no guarantee that the kernel will function properly, or at the very least as expected. So, follow this process carefully and do not burn any bridges until you are quite sure everything works.

Moving The Kernel Into Place

The compiler does not automatically overwrite the old kernel with the new one. Although this fact may be an annoyance for some, it is best that the compiler does not try to read the administrator's mind. Overwriting the old kernel accidentally could be, if not catastrophic, a serious headache if the new kernel proves unreliable. Follow these steps to install the new kernel once you have it compiled:

1. The new kernel should be located in an area such as /usr/src/linux/arch/i386/boot/bzImage. If it is not there, then try the command **find / –name 'bzImage'**. The **locate** command will not suffice, because its database has likely not been updated since the compile completed. Neither will the **which** command, because the kernel image will not be within your path statement.

2. Determine whether your current kernel rests in the /boot or root partition. You can do this either with the **ls** command, or the **find** command.

3. Copy the kernel file to the appropriate directory or partition. This is the directory that contains the items that LILO—or an alternate boot manager—calls during boot time.

4. At this point, it is common to rename the kernel. Use the format **vmlinuz-version**, where *version* is the full version of kernel installed, no matter how many extra components are tagged onto the name.

5. The system map file is not buried quite as deeply as the kernel after compilation. The map should be located in /usr/src/linux/System.map. Once again, use the **find** command if necessary, and search on the term "System.map".

6. Copy the system map file into place in the /boot directory or partition. Keep its name the same.

Moving The Modules Into Place

Now that the compiled kernel and system map are in place, it is necessary to move the modules where they need to reside so the kernel can load and unload them when they are needed. The make package fortunately handles this job for the administrator. To accomplish this task, first return to the source directory /usr/src/linux, and then use the command **make modules_install**.

11

The ramdisk

A *ramdisk* is a version of the kernel that is loaded into RAM at boot time. Whether this step is necessary depends on the makeup of the kernel and the system itself, and what components are necessary for the actual boot process.

If every kernel module, including drivers, necessary to boot the system is compiled into the main kernel, then skip making a ramdisk. For example, if there is a SCSI external drive on the system that holds the root (/) partition, and the SCSI handler modules are compiled into the kernel, then move on to the next section. However, if the SCSI handler modules were left as modules, this step must be followed in order to boot the system. The kernel will not be able to load modules before mounting the root (/) partition.

However, if you do find it necessary to make an initial ramdisk, this special version of the kernel will contain the modules necessary to boot even if they are not compiled directly into the main kernel. This ramdisk version will then be unloaded when the boot process is complete and the main kernel will be loaded. To make this ramdisk type "mkinitrd /boot/initrd-*version version*", where *version* is the full version of kernel installed, no matter how many extra components are tagged onto the name.

Building New Module Dependency List

If you ever want to use the commands that allow module manipulation by hand such as **insmod** or **rmmod**, you need to have a proper module dependency list in place. This list, located in /lib/modules/*version*/modules.dep, contains the entire dependency tree for the kernel modules you have installed and built.

To build your new dependency list, type "/sbin/depmod –a". You only need to do this once for each time you build new modules on the machine.

Reconfigure LILO

Building and installing a new kernel does not mean that the machine will actually boot with this kernel automatically. LILO must be configured so that it sees the new kernel and offers a boot option for it. The smart approach is to not get rid of the old boot option, and instead offer boot choices for both the old kernel that is known to work, and the new kernel that is as yet untested.

Open The LILO Configuration File

The LILO configuration file is /etc/lilo.conf. Open this file and examine its contents. This configuration file is covered in depth in Chapter 4. Let's say the current entry for the kernel is:

```
image=/boot/vmlinuz-2.2.5-25
    label=Linux
```

```
root=/dev/hda2
read-only
```

Adding The New Option By Hand

What you do here depends on which distribution you are using. Type "ls /sbin /liloconfig". If the file exists, then skip down to the section "Adding The New Option With /etc/liloconfig". However, it is important to know how to do this by hand regardless.

Insert a new section that is identical to the section pointing to the previous kernel. Do not erase the old section. Then, make sure that the two image lines point to the new and old kernels (vmlinuz file), respectively.

To ensure that it is easy to tell the difference between the two kernel instances during a reboot, change one or both of the label lines. Labels such as "Linux-*version*" or "Linux-new" are useful in keeping things separate. The final version might look like:

```
image=/boot/vmlinuz-2.2.5-25
    label=Linuxtwo2
    root=/dev/hda2
    read-only
image=/boot/vmlinuz-2.4.12
    label=Linuxtwo4
    root=/dev/hda2
    read-only
```

11

Adding The New Option With /etc/liloconfig

If you are using a distribution—such as Slackware—that offers the /etc/liloconfig tool, you can allow this tool to do the work for you. Be sure that the vmlinuz file is in the root directory instead of in /boot, then type "/etc/liloconfig" to change the LILO configuration file.

Be sure to have an emergency disk pair available in case the new kernel does not boot properly.

Rerun LILO And Test The New Kernel

Changes in LILO's configuration file do not take effect until the lilo program is run. Typing "/sbin/lilo -v" runs LILO, which then puts the files it needs exactly where it needs them.

If after shutting down the machine and choosing the new kernel boot option, the machine runs steadily and seems to have no problems, edit /etc/lilo.conf once again and remove the option for the old kernel. Also delete the kernel's vmlinuz file from the /boot directory or partition. After doing this, rerun LILO once again and give the new kernel the default name so that during the next boot the new menu will show.

However, if the new kernel does not function properly, then examine the error messages carefully, then reboot the machine once again, this time choosing the older kernel as the LILO boot option. Depending on the error messages, the kernel may need to be recompiled or the installation may not have been completed properly. In any case, if this new kernel is eventually abandoned, be sure to remove its files from /boot and change LILO so it is no longer an option, then rerun LILO.

CHAPTER SUMMARY

Almost all of the Linux certification exams cover configuring, compiling, and installing the kernel at some level. It is important to run through this process a number of times, trying the different methods at your disposal, so that you really understand how it all works. The process is rather long and complex so it does generally not need to be memorized, but the better you understand it, the faster you will be able to recall what has to be done next. Also spend some time examining the kernel configuration options and giving thought to what options can be cut out to save on how much RAM your kernel takes up, and how much hard drive space the modules take up.

The first and sometimes most difficult part of installing a new kernel is choosing which source package to use. There are subtle nuances between each patch level, features that were added, removed, or disabled that affect which is the best version for your setup and needs. Even the experimental source has to be considered for those who need access to bleeding edge features or drivers.

Once the source is downloaded and patched—if necessary—you have to ensure that the packages you need are installed on the machine. These packages mostly involve items required for compiling the kernel, so if you do a lot of C programming, then they may already be on your system. If you run into strange errors during any of the steps during the compile process, consider the fact that you may be missing a required program.

Configuring the kernel is the least set in stone part of the steps. There are three options of tools to use for configuration, and the most popular is the GUI tool xconfig. Explore the menu options in xconfig and learn which items you can do without in your kernel and which you need. For example, if you don't have an ISDN connection or an old CD-ROM drive, then you won't need either of these services supported.

Then, there is the series of **make** commands used to build the kernel and its modules. These commands each have their own special purpose and must be done in the proper order. Once the kernel and modules are built, they have to be moved into place, and then LILO has to be informed of where to find the new files. Remember that it is rarely a good idea to fully get rid of the previous kernel until you are sure that the new kernel works correctly.

REVIEW QUESTIONS

1. What word is used to refer to the operating system itself?
   a. LILO
   b. kernel
   c. ramdisk
   d. ncurses

2. Which of the following is an experimental kernel number? [Choose all correct answers]
   a. 2.12.52
   b. 3.12.49
   c. 4.11.25
   d. 5.15.12

3. Which command is used to load a kernel module?
   a. **addmod**
   b. **insmod**
   c. **lsmod**
   d. **mod add**

4. Which command is used to list all loaded kernel modules?
   a **lsmod**
   b. **ls –mod**
   c. **mod –list**
   d. **make list**

5. Which command is used to unload an unnecessary kernel module?
   a. **delmod**
   b. **mod –del**
   c. **moddel**
   d. **rmmod**

11

6. Which of the following is a production kernel number? [Choose all correct answers]

   a. 2.14.52

   b. 3.15.49

   c. 4.13.25

   d. 5.10.12

7. Which package is used to manage the kernel build process?

   a. make

   b. mk

   c. compile

   d. run

8. Which package is used to incrementally upgrade the kernel source to a new version?

   a. addsource

   b. make

   c. patch

   d. insmod

9. Which package contains the actual compiler used to build the kernel?

   a. patch

   b. egcs

   c. make

   d. vmlinuz

10. If you wanted to configure the kernel within the Linux GUI, which make option would you run?

    a. oldconfig

    b. xconfig

    c. menuconfig

    d. config

11. Which make option do you use to build the default configuration file, which is then used to set the base for the new configuration?

    a. config

    b. menuconfig

    c. xconfig

    d. oldconfig

12. Which make option do you use to build the kernel itself?
    a. bzImage
    b. kernel
    c. vmlinuz
    d. version

13. To what directory do you need to move the compiled kernel and System.map files? [Choose all correct answers]
    a. /
    b. /boot
    c. /root
    d. /kernel

14. What do you change the name of the kernel to once it is properly placed (not including the version numbers)?
    a. bzImage
    b. kernel
    c. vmlinuz
    d. initrd

15. If you wanted to configure the kernel with a somewhat graphical interface but not within the GUI, which make option would you run?
    a. config
    b. menuconfig
    c. xconfig
    d. initrd

16. What command moves the kernel's modules into place after they're compiled?
    a. **insmod**
    b. **cp modules**
    c. **make modules**
    d. **make modules_install**

17. Which command do you need to run (not including its arguments) if not all of the hardware required for the boot process has drivers compiled into the kernel?
    a. **mkinitrd**
    b. **make initrd**
    c. **make ramdisk**
    d. **mkdisk**

11

18. If you wanted to configure the kernel using a raw text interface, which make option would you run?

    a. config

    b. menuconfig

    c. xconfig

    d. initrd

19. Which file do you need to edit in order to ensure that the machine can boot with the new kernel?

    a. /boot

    b. /etc/lilo

    c. /etc/lilo.conf

    d. /sbin/lilo

20. Which program do you need to run in order to make sure the machine can boot with the new kernel?

    a. make install

    b. make kernel

    c. /sbin/lilo

    d. /etc/lilo

HANDS-ON PROJECTS

These projects require that you have administrative (root) access to a working Linux box and the CD-ROM for the distribution that came with the box. Ability to use the X GUI is preferable but can be worked around if necessary.

Project 11.1

In this project, you will prepare your machine for a change in kernels.

To get ready to change your kernel, do the following:

1. Log in as root.

2. Type "ls –la /usr/src/linux". If the directory exists, look to see if it is a symlink or on its own, and then do one of the following:

   ➤ If /usr/src/linux is a symlink, then delete it.

   ➤ If it is a standalone directory, then use the **mv** command to rename it. A sample new name is /usr/src/linux-old.

3. Download the new kernel source you want to install, or get a copy of the current kernel's source off the distribution CD.

If you find while going through this process that there are a lot of programs that need to be updated, it is a good idea to consider making a backup of some sort. This issue is especially true if you are updating to a newer version of the distribution. For the sake of this exercise, feel free to use the kernel source that comes with the distribution you have installed in order to avoid complications on your current machine.

4. Unzip and unpack the new source inside the /usr/src directory, or install the source RPM, depending on which distribution you are using.

5. Type "ls -a" in the /usr/src directory and see if the source code created a /usr/src/linux directory, or a /usr/src/linux-*version* directory. If there is no /usr/src/linux directory, then type "ln -s /usr/src/linux-*version* /usr/src/ linux" to create a soft link to /usr/src/linux.

6. If necessary, unzip and unpack any patch files you need to apply into the directory the source package created. Be sure that you have every patch file necessary.

7. Change into the new /usr/src/linux directory.

Depending on where this package came from, it may go into /usr/ src/linux or /usr/src/linux-*version*.

11

8. One by one–apply the patches if you are updating source. To apply a patch, type " patch -p0 < *patchfile*" where patchfile is the file name for the specific patch.

More often than not, you should not need to patch a kernel; instead, you should be able to download a full version from a trusted source such as **www.kernel.org**.

9. Use the command **more README** or **less README** to read through the installation instructions that come with the kernel itself.

Leave this file open in another virtual terminal if you are unfamiliar with the kernel build process.

10. Use the command **cd Documentation** to change to the /usr/src/linux/ Docmentation directory.

Take some time at some point to at least skim through the files in this directory.

11. Use the **more Changes** command to read through the document that lists what versions of programs are necessary to compile the kernel properly. An example of what you might find in Changes is shown in Figure 11.7.

 If you look further through this file, you will find more detailed pointers to the issue of what needs to be upgraded and where to find it!

12. In the software versions portion of the Changes file, there is a list of what packages are needed, what versions are necessary, and how to determine which version you have on your machine. Go through this listing and check on each package. For example, the listing in Figure 11.7 first says you need the Kernel modutils version 2.1.121. To check what version you have of this program you would use the command, according to the right-hand column, **insmod –V**.

Keep a list of each package you need to update.

 Caution! It is highly important that you update the packages outlined in the Changes file! Otherwise, you will have no end of trouble trying to get everything to work properly. Often, people install a new version of the distribution along with updating the kernel rather than having to update everything by hand.

```
Current Minimal Requirements
****************************

   Upgrade to at *least* these software revisions before thinking you've
encountered a bug!  If you're unsure what version you're currently
running, the suggested command should tell you.

- Kernel modutils        2.1.121         ; insmod -V
- Gnu C                  2.7.2.3         ; gcc --version
- Binutils               2.8.1.0.23      ; ld -v
- Linux libc5 C Library  5.4.46          ; ls -l /lib/libc*
- Linux libc6 C Library  2.0.7pre6       ; ls -l /lib/libc*
- Dynamic Linker (ld.so) 1.9.9           ; ldd --version or ldd -v
- Linux C++ Library      2.7.2.8         ; ls -l /usr/lib/libg++.so.*
- Procps                 1.2.9           ; ps --version
- Procinfo               16              ; procinfo -v
- Psmisc                 17              ; pstree -V
- Net-tools              1.50            ; hostname -V
- Loadlin                1.6a
- Sh-utils               1.16            ; basename --v
- Autofs                 3.1.1           ; automount --version
- NFS                    2.2beta40       ; showmount --version
- Bash                   1.14.7          ; bash -version
- Ncpfs                  2.2.0           ; ncpmount -v
- Pcmcia-cs              3.0.7           ; cardmgr -V
```

Figure 11.7 The Changes software version listing, software versions section.

13. Often, the fastest way to upgrade packages is to get new versions from the Web site for the distribution you installed, or even to purchase the latest version of the distribution if one is available. Otherwise, get the packages from their home sites or from trusted download locations like the **sunsite.unc.edu** anonymous FTP site, beginning in the /pub/Linux directory tree.

14. Install the downloaded packages. Each should come with its own documentation to refer to if you run into trouble. Remember that you open a gzipped file with the **gunzip** command, you unpack a tar file with the **tar –xvf** command, and you install an RPM with the **rpm –ivh** command.

Project 11.2

In this project, you will compile and install the new kernel.

To build and install your new kernel, set the machine so it can boot into the new kernel, and then test this kernel, do the following:

1. Log in as root.

2. Change to the /usr/src/linux directory, or the directory where you unpacked the kernel source.

3. Use the command **make oldconfig** to put together the default configuration file.

4. Use the **make xconfig** command to run the configuration tool shown in Figure 11.5. If you cannot run a GUI on the system you're using, use the **make menuconfig** command instead.

Now you can begin configuring the kernel. The steps discussed here are just a few examples. Feel free to configure it further on your own before saving and exiting.

5. Click the Amateur Radio support button to open the Amateur Radio support configuration dialog box shown in Figure 11.8.

6. Click the "n" next to the first listing to not include this option in the kernel, unless you want to support it.

7. Click Main Menu to close the dialog box.

8. Click the Mice button to open the Mice configuration dialog box shown in Figure 11.9.

9. Click the "n" next to the listing for each mouse type you don't need support for.

10. Click Main Menu to close the dialog box.

11

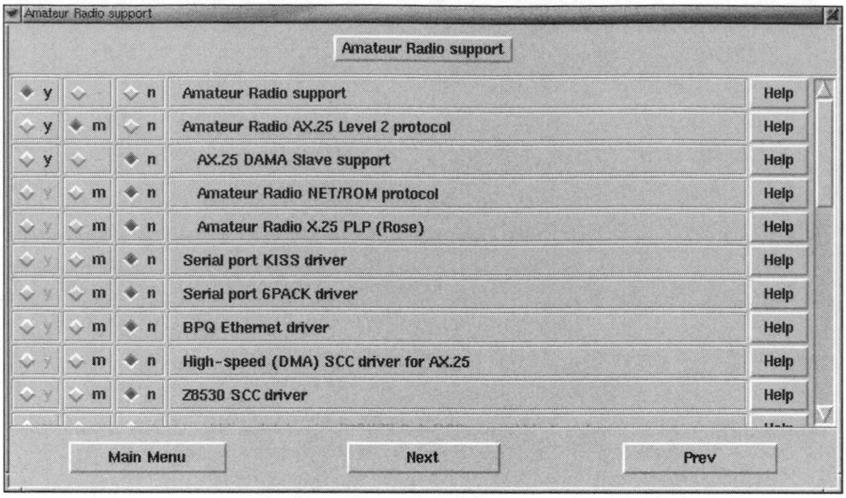

Figure 11.8 The xconfig Amateur Radio support kernel configuration dialog box.

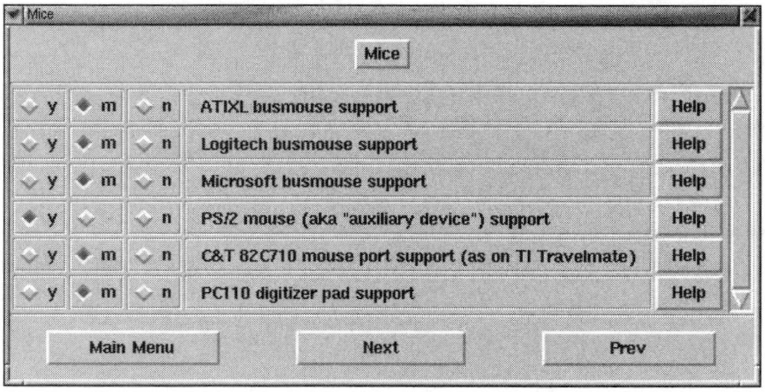

Figure 11.9 The xconfig Mice kernel configuration dialog box.

11. Click the Processor type and features button to open the Processor type and features dialog box shown in Figure 11.10.

12. Click the 386 button to pull up the Processor family dropdown list box shown in Figure 11.11.

13. Click the choice that corresponds to your particular machine's CPU.

14. If the machine is a 486DX or later, click "n" for the Math Emulation option.

15. Click Main Menu to close the dialog box.

16. Continue this process if you want to, disabling the kernel options you don't need.

17. Click the Save and Exit button to close the xconfig tool and save the new kernel configuration file.

18. Read the dialog box shown in Figure 11.12 and click OK to close it.

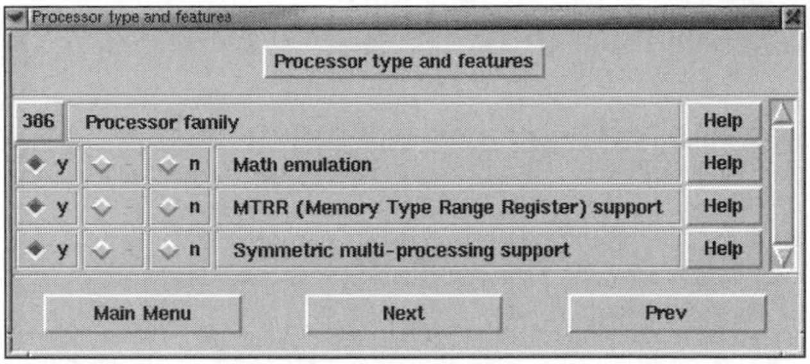

Figure 11.10   The xconfig Processor type and features kernel configuration dialog box.

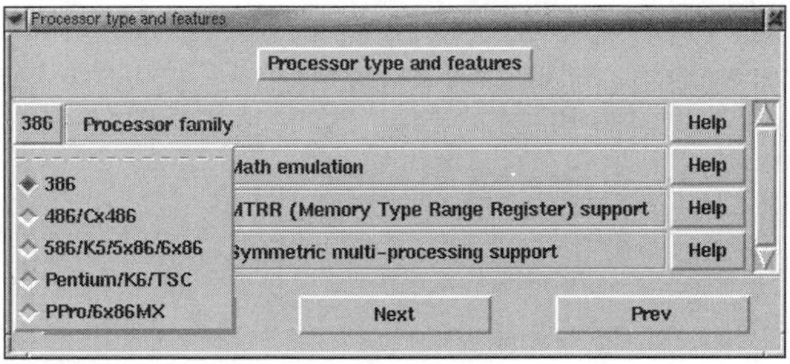

Figure 11.11   The xconfig Processor family dropdown list box

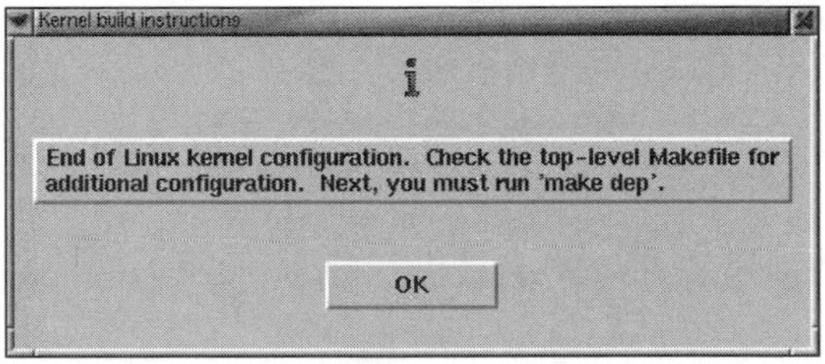

Figure 11.12   The xconfig closing dialog box.

19. Use the **make dep** command to build the code dependency list.

Each of these make steps can take some time to run through.
Prepare to watch a lot of code and messages scroll by.

20. Use the command **make clean** to remove all of the temporary files created so far.

21. Use the **make bzImage** command to compile the kernel itself.

22. Use the command **make modules** to compile the modules that go with the kernel.

23. Change to the directory /usr/src/linux/arch/i386/boot/, or its equivalent if you put the files elsewhere.

24. Use the command **cp bzImage /boot/vmlinuz-*version*** to copy and rename the kernel, where *version* is the full version number of the kernel you just compiled. For example, if the kernel version is 2.2.12 then you would type "cp bzImage /boot/vmlinuz-2.2.12".

25. Change to the /usr/src/linux directory.

26. Use the command **cp System.map /boot** to copy the new map to the /boot directory.

27. The command **make modules_install** will instruct the Makefile to place the modules where they need to be.

28. If you need a ramdisk, use the command **mkinitrd /boot/initrd-*version* version** to make this ramdisk. For example, if the kernel you just made is 2.2.12 you would type "mkinitrd /boot/initrd-2.2.12 2.2.12".

29. Log off the machine.

30. Log in as root.

31. Use the command **vi /etc/lilo.conf** to edit the LILO configuration file.

32. Choose whether you want the new kernel to boot by default or not. If you want to boot into it by default, then add it in front of any other images listed. If not, then make sure it's not the first image listed.

33. Move the cursor onto the line where you want the new definition to begin.

34. Type "O" to create a new line where the cursor is, and change to Insert mode.

35. Type in the new listing for the new kernel. It should look something like:

```
image=/boot/vmlinuz-version
    label=Linux-new
    root=/dev/location
    read-only
```

36. Press the esc key to return to Command mode.

37. Key the command **:wq** or **ZZ** to save and exit LILO.

38. Use the command **/sbin/lilo -v** to run LILO in verbose mode. This action writes all of the data where it must be in order to boot with the settings you just added.

39. Issue the command **shutdown -r now** to reboot the machine immediately.

40. At the LILO prompt, press the Tab key to list the menu options.

41. Type the entry for the new kernel—"Linux-new" according to the example in step 6—and press Enter.

42. Watch the boot process. Hopefully the machine will boot properly and all will be well. If this is so, continue. If not, examine the errors and reboot into the old kernel. You may need to recompile.

 Do not proceed past this point unless you trust the new kernel.

43. Use the command **cd /boot** to change to the /boot directory.

44. Use the command **ls –la** to list the contents.

45. Use the command **del vmlinuz-*oldversion*** to delete the old kernel image.

46. Use the command **vi /etc/lilo.conf** to edit the LILO configuration file.

47. Move the cursor to the first line of the old kernel image entry.

48. Use the command **dd** to delete the lines, one at a time, until the old entry is gone.

49. Rename the new kernel entry to your preferred Linux boot menu option.

50. Use the command **:wq** to save and exit the file.

51. Use the command **/sbin/lilo –v** to run LILO and rewrite its files once again.

52. Use the command **shutdown –r now** to reboot the machine.

53. Press the Tab key to see the menu when you reach the LILO prompt.

54. Type in the menu option for the new kernel. The machine will now boot into the new, working kernel.

11

## CHAPTER TWELVE

MANAGING LINUX SECURITY

AFTER READING THIS CHAPTER AND COMPLETING THE EXERCISES, YOU WILL BE ABLE TO:

➤ Understand the many aspects that fall under the label "system security"

➤ Devise an appropriate security plan for your setup

➤ Determine whether a firewall is appropriate for your system, and implement one

➤ Apply security fine-tuning principles to the machines on your network

Network administrators cannot afford to be lax with system security. If the administrator is careless during setup, or does not keep up with the latest security advisories, the system can be breached through one of many well-known security holes. If a system administrator gets so busy that there is only one aspect of the system they can keep up to date, keeping abreast of the latest security information should be it.

THE LINUX SECURITY MODEL

Security in Linux involves a combination of physical concerns, such as controlling who has hands-on access to machines; network security, where service access is tightened and watched over; and software security, such as continuously updating packages when bug fixes are released. Dealing with security issues is an especially time-intensive process during the initial system setup. Eventually, however, the efforts pay off in terms of the time the admin saves by not having to repair intruder damage and explaining how important data got into outside hands.

The Big Picture

System security is an important topic for any network connected to the Internet, or even those which are not but contain valuable data that must be protected. This security has a multifold purpose. Not only is it trying to keep out those intruders who want to do damage to the system or steal information. Its function is also to protect the network from mistakes that could otherwise prove harmful.

Physical Security

If a machine is in an easily accessible area where there is a lot of traffic, physical security becomes a concern. Security must also be closely monitored if a machine holds any critical data. Even if the users are completely trustworthy and are not going to steal any data, there is a chance that they may unwittingly cause problems by doing things they should not be doing at that machine.

Network Security

Possibly the greatest fear in computer security these days are crackers or other malicious types breaking in through network connections. Each port left open to listen for outside connection attempts is a weak spot. Once Linux is up and running, the administrator should take the time to go through and strengthen each machine's settings to minimize the options available to potential intruders.

For those highly vulnerable networks that need additional protection, there are options such as *firewalls*, but only if the restrictions are not worse than the risk of a break-in.

Security Updates

As soon as any program is released, especially network-oriented ones, someone in the world begins pounding on it to find a weakness. Soon after the weakness is found, whether this is by intruders or people testing a package for security robustness, alerts are sent throughout the Internet among a number of channels. It is imperative to keep a close eye on at least one of these notification services, whether through a security agency or the distributor who made the specific Linux version used locally.

SETTING UP AND MANAGING PHYSICAL SECURITY

Physical security is an issue from the day the machines enter the building to the day those machines are replaced by new ones. The need for tight physical security depends on how available a machine is to the general public, to the users who work for the company that owns the machine, and what kind of information that machine contains and has access to. Those machines that are fairly isolated from harmful or curious hands do not need as much consideration on this security front.

Console Access

The first line of defense when it comes to physical system security is where the machine is physically placed, and who has physical access to it. A haphazardly placed machine can be stolen, but may also be vulnerable if meddling users can touch a keyboard, power cord, power button, or the system's *UPS*; anyone doing so has its fate in his or her hands.

Secured Equipment Rooms

One method of assuring that no one but authorized staff has access to a particular machine is to set up a special access room to contain the apparatus. Whether this room is a person's office that is kept locked when the resident is absent—and this policy must be strictly adhered to if it is to be considered a security measure—or a room with racks for the machines that handle network services in the background, is up to the administrator and their needs.

Secured Cabinets

If a whole room is not available, a rack of computer storage cabinets with locks is another good choice. These racks can be used to store all of a computer's components, or only partial computers if there is a large collection of machines. After all, why have twenty monitors when there instead can be a large switchbox allowing network machines to share one? Even keeping a few monitors on wheeled carts to roll from cabinet to cabinet will save space and money.

Anti-Theft Devices

Machines cannot always be just locked away from the world. In an environment where there are many users moving in and out and no one can supervise the situation on a continuous basis, the issue of equipment theft becomes just as much of a problem as data theft. This situation is especially common in a university environment, and educational institutions in general.

One solution for this issue is the *cable lock*. In this case, the cable is not literally locked onto the hardware, but is actually super-glued to the hardware, and then attached to a secure surface such as the floor or a wall.

12

Secured Cases

Another problem that occurs when machines are available to the general public is that users can open hardware cases with a screwdriver and steal internal components, such as RAM. It is possible to purchase special screws that require a unique screwdriver to replace the default case screws with. Although such an action can prevent the theft of internal components, it may inadvertently encourage thiefs to take the whole machine in lieu of the parts—so be sure to use other security precautions as well.

Local Login Access

There are two types of local login protection. The first type involves the initial login process, and the second is related to what happens when a user leaves a machine after logging in. Remote login issues are a host security issue.

Securing The Login Process

The first line of software defense for a machine is the login prompt, where the users enter both his or her user ID and password. Although the screen does not actually display the password as it is typed in, this form of protection is not enough to keep out intruders…especially if the password is poorly chosen. It is important to make sure that both the administrators and the users understand how to choose a secure password. Strategies for choosing passwords and for ensuring that the users are not risking system security with his or her own poor choices, are discussed later in this chapter in the section "Testing For Bad Passwords."

Securing Idle Machines With Open Sessions

Sometimes users forget to log off a machine or walk away from it to attend to something away from their desk. That short errand can turn into a long one, and if the circumstances are just right could lead to another user working on the idle machine. That user may not even be an intruder, it may be an employee not intending anything malicious.

Maybe someone in the office has something very fast they need to do and is invited to use someone's machine who happens to be at lunch. However, this account owner's permissions might be higher than this person's, opening his or her access privileges and ability to do accidental harm. Remember the phrase: "A little knowledge is a dangerous thing."

A method of avoiding this problem is implementing a password-protection scheme that activates after a certain amount of idle time. Some distributions have one enabled by default within their GUI. Implementing such protection is discussed later in this chapter in the section "Securing Accounts When Idle."

Data Access

Ultimately, what is important to many companies and organizations is that their data is secure. Machines and components are replaceable. Data that is vital to the day-to-day running of the business, financial information, employee records, inventory and stock information, and other important records could bring a company to its knees if it were lost. Take the time to identify and protect the important data.

Permissions

Be sure that vital data is protected by a solid set of permissions and ownerships. Do not leave any holes that can be exploited. If necessary, log in as a regular user and test to see what can be broken into.

 Managing permissions and ownerships is covered in Chapter 3.

Backups

The first thing most users ask the administrator after hearing that there was a machine crash is: "Did you make a backup?" If there is any data that would cause hardship to lose, whether this is specific data or configuration files, source code, or programs, be sure to create a backup as often as is deemed necessary. Determining how often is usually a factor of how much work would not cause intense hardship if it had to be duplicated.

 Creating data backups is covered in Chapter 6.

12

Storage

Theft happens. Fire happens. Even floods have been known to work their way into computer rooms and wreak havoc. Keeping backups is one way to prevent data loss, but if these backups are kept on the same premises as the data, acts of nature can do away with them along with everything else. Although this issue is not a concern to many—after all, if the building is suddenly swept away, the data is the least of the problems—in some industries the data is the core of the business. Or, loss of an important customer's data can bring lawsuits.

On a less catastrophic front, anything that is openly sitting around or in an unlocked cabinet can be stolen, mistakenly taken, or misplaced. Keep important backups in a secure place, either in a fire- and flood-proof safe, or a safe-deposit box somewhere else if they do not need to be kept on site. Or use an Internet connection to store them at a remote location.

Removable hard drives are the most interesting application of the issue of locking up data. These drives are installed in cartridges, and then plugged in and out of the computer as necessary. One of the largest advantages of such setups is that the drives themselves can be locked up for their own protection.

TIGHTENING HOST SECURITY

The care taken to make each machine on the LAN secure contributes to overall network security. Once a particular host is breached, then the entire network may fall soon after. Consider tending to a variety of tasks with each machine before thinking the LAN setup is "complete."

Disabling Unnecessary Network Services

One of the first things to do is look through the list of services that are listening on various ports and determine which are not going to be used. Once the unneeded services are identified, the services should be disabled. These services need to be removed because potential intruders will hammer on any ports that are open to listen to the world, and may even know weaknesses inherent to the particular daemon in use. Minimizing which ports are open and listening is the first step toward host security. Perform the following steps to accomplish this task:

1. Open the /etc/inetd.conf file with the vi editor by typing "vi /etc/inetd.conf".

2. Locate all active services by looking at all lines that do not begin with a hash mark (#). Each of these lines constitutes a service that the superdaemon listens for connections on, hence a weak spot.

3. Give serious consideration to each service and decide which ones are not useful for the particular machine or LAN. Commonly unnecessary services are listed in Table 12.1.

4. Disable the services you decide you do not need by commenting them out. To do this, add a hash mark (#) at the beginning of the declaration line.

 It is simple enough to change which services are available at a later date if they prove to be necessary. Just come back and remove the hash marks, then restart the superdaemon.

5. When finished editing the superdaemon's configuration file, type "ZZ" and press Enter to exit the vi editor.

6. Restart inetd by typing "/etc/rc.d/init.d/inet restart". Modify the path if necessary to account for the structure of the distribution being used.

Table 12.1   Often unused network services managed by the superdaemon.

Service	Function	Recommend Disabling?
finger	A tool that allows people to see whether a particular user is logged on, and get other information about them such as name, office location, phone numbers, and any information the user chooses to make available.	This tool is often abused by potential intruders and it is highly recommended to disable it unless there is a specific need for it.
ftp	A service that allows for file transfer between machines.	If there is only a central FTP server on the LAN, or there is no reason to allow people to FTP into the specific machine, then this service is unnecessary. Be sure, though, that there are other ways to move files between this machine and others if there is a need to do this.
gopher	A text-based information retrieval service that was far more popular before the days of the Web.	Unless there is a specific need or desire to run a gopher server, disable this item.
imap, pop2, pop3	The Internet Message Access Protocol server, and the Post Office Protocol version 2 and 3 daemons. These are the tools that handle email requests from POP and other remote email fetching clients.	Although this service is often necessary, it is not needed on every single machine if there is a central mail server. This is a case of if you need them you need all three, or if you do not need them you do not want any.
talk	The talk program allows users within the LAN or outside of it—who are using Linux or Unix—to chat with one another within a text interface.	If this program is not required, disable it. In general, talk is not often used because tools like email, IRC (Internet Relay Chat), and the telephone all can do the same job of getting information across.
ntalk	The ntalk program is a newer version of the talk program.	If this program is not required, disable it. In general, talk is not often used because tools like email, IRC (Internet Relay Chat), and the telephone all can do the same job of getting information across.
telnet	A service that allows people to log into shell accounts on other machines.	If this is a vital machine where no remote logins are desirable, then this service is not needed. Remember, however, that disabling this service means that even the administrator cannot telnet into the machine remotely.

12

(continued)

Table 12.1 Often unused network services managed by the superdaemon
(continued).

Service	Function	Recommend Disabling?
uucp	The Unix to Unix CoPy service. A specialized tool allowing data to be moved in bulk, once frequently used to provide intermittent news and email service.	As connection time costs have gone down, this service has gone out of fashion in many places. If there is no specific reason to use it, be sure uucp is disabled.

Special User Groups

Careful utilization of account groups can help to limit access to specific portions of the file system, as mentioned in Chapter 3. This method is especially useful for isolating critical data onto its own segments of the file system, because an administrator can specifically build the groups to hold the exact people who should have access. On systems that have all users as a member of the "user" group, for example, specialized groups are especially useful.

Groups For Individual Users

One way of tightening up file security is to create a special group for each user. For convenience, this group can be named the same as the user's login ID. Some distributions (such as Red Hat) do this by default.

The reason for using such specialized groups is that, by default, no one has access to anyone else's files or directories. Additionally, all of the users can be assigned to the group "user".

Special Project Groups

A good way to isolate data files with access for only particular people is to create special groups for those who need to access the file system area. For example, perhaps the administrator is using NIS to centralize the user data files so that everyone has accounts on all of the machines. On the machine 192.168.12.2 there is a partition at /dev/sdb1 mounted as /ProjectX. Creating the group "projectx" in /etc/group and adding the project members to it, and then making the permissions on the mount point owner root, group projectx, then giving group read and write permissions would restrict entry to the data directory to only those who were assigned to the group, and the administrator.

The project team can then NFS mount the partition across the Linux LAN, or work at the machine itself, and both open and save its data to the specialized partition.

 If there is no simple way to accomplish this group creation method with the tools that come with the distribution, write a shell script to handle adding new users instead.

The Nobody User

Rather than always making special accounts for various daemon services, a common practice is to have a user called "nobody" that has a non-shell account. Often, these packages assume this identity by default. If so, leave this setting in place unless you have a different type of secure user account you would rather use. Services that benefit from being changed to the nobody account if they are not already are those that no one should be able to log in to, but that will not be hindered by the limited privileges of the nobody user.

Screening Incoming Packets

It is possible to restrict access to the network services that a particular machine offers. This additional security measure is accomplished by telling the machine to analyze incoming *packets* according to where they came from out on the LAN or Internet. To accomplish this task, use the tcp_wrappers tool.

Determining If tcp_wrappers Is Installed

To see if tcp_wrappers is installed on the machine, type "which tcpd". If tcpd is already installed, then skip the next two sections.

Acquiring The tcp_wrappers Tool

The tcp_wrappers tool may already be included on the distribution CD-ROM. If it is not, then download the source from the FTP site **ftp.cert.org**, in the directory /pub/tools/tcp_wrappers.

Installing The tcp_wrappers Tool

The method used to install the tcp_wrappers tool depends on whether the package is in RPM form, or is a tarred and gzipped source code file. Installing the RPM version is done with the standard RPM install format "rpm –ivh *fullpackagename*". However, the source code version—after untarring with "tar –xvf" and unzipping with "gunzip"—must be compiled into a temporary or source storage directory.

 You need to install the programming tools—at the very least, the make and gcc (egcs) tools (discussed in Chapter 11)—before continuing.

Change into the new tcp_wrappers directory and then open the Makefile with the vi editor. Search for the text "REAL_DAEMON_DIR" and change the value after the equal sign (=) to "/usr/sbin". After saving and exiting the Makefile, type **make linux** to build the program, and then "make install" to install the files where they are needed.

Determining Security Levels

At this point an administrator must decide how restrictively to set access to the machine. If the Linux box in question needs to be tightly secured, follow the security mantra of "Deny all access, and then allow specific groups into specific areas." However, if there is a single service or there are just a few services that need to be restricted, then deny all access to those services only, and then allow the specific groups in that need to use it.

Configuring Packet Screening

The configuration files used for tcp_wrappers are the files /etc/hosts.allow and /etc/hosts.deny. Any rules set in the deny file are used to block entry, and any set in the allow file are used to let packets in. The hosts.allow file is sought first, and if the incoming packet is not covered by an allow rule, then the hosts.deny file is consulted. If no explicit deny rule is found, then the packet is allowed in.

Building a definition is the same for both configuration files. The format used is:

```
daemon: who_allowed
```

The asterisk (*) wildcard is not used in either of these files. For either the daemon or the who_allowed portion of the rule, a selection of specialized wildcards exists as shown in Table 12.2.

To begin with, those who want to use strict security levels should begin by opening the file /etc/hosts.deny and adding the text "ALL: ALL". Save and exit the file and then open the /etc/hosts.allow file and start explicitly adding rules that allow people to access services. One additional term is allowed in the who_allowed segment, and that is the EXCEPT function. For example,

Table 12.2   The /etc/hosts.allow and /etc/hosts.deny wildcard variables.

Variable	Purpose
ALL	Everything applies. Useable for daemons or who_allowed.
KNOWN	The rule applies to any user whose name can be resolved, as well as the machine's name or IP address.
LOCAL	The rule applies to all machines that are on the local network. This distinction is determined by whether there are any dots (.) in the machine's name.
PARANOID	The rule applies to any machine whose resolved name does not match up to its resolved IP address.
UNKNOWN	The rule applies to any user or machine whose name or address cannot be resolved. This resolution refers to host name resolution, user name resolution, and even IP address resolution.

to allow everyone from the local network and from the IP range 192.168.61.*
but not the machine 192.168.61.4 because it is in an insecure location, the
rule might look like:

```
ALL: LOCAL 192.168.61. EXCEPT 192.168.61.4
```

Configuring Welcome Messages

It is possible to include a custom welcome banner for each service that will be
wrapped. To do this, first create the directory /usr/local/etc/banners with the
mkdir command. Each service gets its own specific banner. The banner file is
a text file named the same as the daemon itself. For example, the FTP welcome
banner if the FTP service is restricted with tcp_wrappers would be in /usr/
local/etc/banners/in.ftpd or /usr/local/etc/banners/wu-ftpd.

 These daemons are in the /usr/sbin directory. Type "ls /usr/sbin/
in*" to see the majority of them.

Updating The Log Files

Because tcp_wrappers is monitoring all of the incoming connections, it is possible
to have the tcpd daemon log access information. These logs can be immensely
helpful in detecting attempted break-ins, or to sift through when considering
tightening access restrictions. Because log files were covered in detail in
Chapter 6, the instructions in this section are brief. Edit the file /etc/
syslog.conf and add an entry for the item auth.info wherever seems appropriate
for the system. An example entry might be:

```
auth.info     /var/log/authlog
```

Using The New Configuration

In order to utilize the new configuration settings, the daemons whose files have
changed have to be restarted. In this case, the daemons that need to be restarted
are inetd and syslogd.

Secure Telnet Logins

It is possible that potential hackers could be watching the network packets, looking for anything they can use to get in. One problem is that the *telnet* program
transmits the password in plain text across the network—perhaps even over the
Internet if the connection is coming from outside the LAN. An alternative to
telnet, then, is the ssh (secure shell) program.

12

Obtaining And Unpacking The Secure Shell Source

Encryption laws prohibit the ssh program from being shipped with U.S.-based Linux distributions. A full (not patched) version of the program can be downloaded from **ftp.replay.com** by visiting the site and changing to the directory /pub/crypto/crypto/SSH.

There are two different development streams for this program. Versions beginning with "1." are freely available for any non-commercial use. However, versions beginning with "2." are only freely available for personal or educational use, and must be purchased for commercial use. Unpack the source and enter its directory.

Compiling The Secure Shell

Begin by reviewing the README file in the main ssh directory to see if its instructions conflict with those printed here. Then, type "./configure" to run the auto-configuration program. This program can take a while to do its job, but in the end it produces the customized information necessary to properly compile ssh on the particular machine in question. After that process is complete, type "make" to actually compile the program.

Installing The Secure Shell

Once the compilation is finished, use the **make install** command to install all of the components. This is also when the ssh installer generates the public and private encryption keys used while encrypting the password for transmission.

Configuring The Secure Shell Server

To configure the secure shell server's behavior, the administrator must be logged in as root. Use the command **ssh-keygen** to run the public and private *key* generation program. When it has done most of its work it will ask for a passphrase. Be sure this phrase is not just a dictionary word. Often it is good to use a sentence with no punctuation. After confirming the passphrase, the keys are saved into root's ~/.ssh directory with file names beginning with the text "id_dsa_1024". The public key is the one that ends in ".pub".

Next, have each user who needs to have access to the machine through the secure shell log in to it and run the keygen program within his or her own accounts. Once his or her keys are generated, the contents of their public key file must be copied into the file /root/.ssh/authorized_keys, one public key per line.

 Install the server on every machine that needs to be able to accept secure shell connections.

Configuring The Secure Shell Clients

To connect to a secure shell server, you must have a secure shell client installed. Even without root access the ssh package can be installed in the Linux account that needs to have secure access. Follow the preceeding instructions to set up the ssh files if the machine does not already have its own ssh server. Then, send a copy of the public key file generated with the **ssh-keygen** command to the administrator of the machine that has to be connected to.

Connecting With The Secure Shell

To telnet securely once everything is set up properly, type "ssh *host.domain. extension*". Just using the standard telnet program does not access this same tool unless you create an alias to change typing "telnet" to call ssh instead. However, doing this creates its own set of problems. Remember that you can only use ssh to connect when you have it set up on both ends. If you wanted to telnet to another account that was not set up for security from that machine, creating such an alias would stand in the way initially.

Security And Set IDs

Turning on the set bit for any file or directory is a useful way to get a process to run as a particular user (SUID, or Set User ID) or group (SGID, or Set Group ID). However, it is also a security hazard. As mentioned in Chapter 5 you cannot actually set a shell script to run as either SGID or SUID—or, more accurately, you can assign set bits but they will not be used.

Whenever you feel the desire to SUID or SGID, take a moment to consider the other options available. Ask yourself why this file or directory needs to be set ID. Is it equivalent to creating a new group that contains both the owner of the file or directory and the user it needs to run as? If so, definitely use this option instead.

It is sometimes worthwhile to do a search on set ID files and directories and see what is out there. The important thing is to do one early on if not right after installing your system so you know which items should be set ID. If you have a backup file of the originals, then it is easier to spot those that may not belong. After all, if an intruder gains root or other access he or she can put programs on the system that run set ID that you may never notice, especially if they run in the wee hours of the morning while you are asleep.

To search the entire file system for files that SGID, type "find / -perm g+s" and to search for items that are SUID, type "find / -perm u+s".

Removing Hints For Crackers

The less information outsiders can get about your system, the better. There is a file called /etc/issue.net that by default contains text about what version of

Linux runs on the machine and what release it is. The problem is that this text is then displayed to anyone who tries to telnet into the system as part of the login prompt, whether or not they manage to get in. Once they know the distribution and release, the cracker can look up the various weaknesses in what you are running and start seeing which you fixed and which you did not.

Therefore, it is highly recommended to remove references to the Linux distribution, the release, and the kernel version from /etc/issue.net.

Downloading From Trusted Sites

Many Linux users feel safe from viruses and other hostile programs because the impression today is such issues are the worry of the Microsoft Windows and Apple Macintosh world. Therefore, not as much care is taken when downloading files from the Internet. A lax security practice in this regard is dangerous for a number of reasons.

There is more than one way to compromise system security with downloads. Aside from viruses, you also have to worry about Trojan horses and worms. Each of these concerns has specific features that make them troublesome. A virus, for example, is a hostile program that attaches itself to other software and then replicates within your computer system. What this virus program then does once it is run depends on what the programmer initially intended. Its purpose may be simply to do some minor nuisance task and then pass itself on to others, or it may actually go as far as to make a new file system on your hard drive or alter your partition table. Hopefully viruses will not become a problem to the Linux community, but if they do—and it is likely that people will try at the very least—then having a trusted virus checker will become imperative, as will keeping it up to date.

On the other hand, a Trojan horse is an intrusion tool that masquerades as programs that you usually find on your system. Someone breaking into your system and gaining root access may change some of your standard programs—such as ls, find, login, and passwd—so that you cannot see any of the changes he or she has made. A Trojan horse also may find its way into your system when someone alters a package on a download site to contain his or her own custom back doors. Although viruses are not much of a problem as yet for Linux users, Trojan horses are alive and well. These are one of the prime reasons for being sure to download from trusted software sites such as:

➤ Linux distribution Web sites.

➤ The Sunsite FTP site at **unc.sunsite.edu**, in the directory /pub/Linux.

➤ **www.linuxhq.com**

➤ **www.slashdot.org**

➤ **www.freshmeat.net**

➤ **www.lwn.net**

Finally, there are the worms. A worm does not hide behind another executable. Instead, it is a standalone program that wreaks whatever harm it is designed to do once, or if, the user runs it.

Limiting User RAM And Process Usage

One way of ensuring that no individual user or user processes—including rogue user processes such as buggy software, viruses, worms, or Trojan horses—is to put limits on both how much RAM a user may utilize at one time and how many processes a user can have running at once. Doing these two things ensures that your system cannot be overrun by rogue processes to the point where it is too bogged down for you to fix anything.

The PAM (Pluggable Authentication Modules) tool—also discussed later in the section "Other Password Security Enhancements"—serves this function. An excellent page for getting a full listing of what PAM is capable of is available at **www.kernel.org/pub/linux/libs/pam/index.html**. The module used to set up these limits is called pam_limits. In order to configure this module, you need to create the file /etc/security/limits.conf. Each line in the limits.conf file is in the format:

```
WhoToLimit    TypeOfLimit    WhatToLimit    WhatLimit
```

The WhoToLimit field can be one of three options:

➤ A login name, such as "bart".

➤ A group name with an at symbol on the front, such as "@users".

➤ A wildcard asterisk meaning "all".

Although you may sometimes want to limit only one particular user or everyone, often it is most useful to limit the user base and not also the daemons and programs.

 These limits do not apply to root even if you explicitly attempt to set them to root.

The TypeOfLimit field can be one of three options that will immediately remind you of setting file system quotas:

➤ The term "soft", which sets the soft limit, or the point at which the user or group being defined first has to become concerned with running out of room to move.

➤ The term "hard", which sets the hard limit, or the point at which the user or group can no longer request any more of the specified resource.

➤ The character "-", which turns off limits for the item being defined.

You can set both hard and soft for the same WhoToLimit, though they have to be created in separate statements. This option and the previous are the only two that are absolutely required. If you also include the next option, then you have to add the last as well.

The choices for WhatToLimit related to processes and RAM are:

➤ The term "memlock" to set the maximum amount of RAM available to the defined user or group. The value associated with this option must be in KB.

➤ The term "nproc" to set the maximum number of processes the user or group can run.

➤ The term "priority" to set the **nice** level at which the defined user or group's processes run at by default.

Finally, the WhatLimit item's value is related to what is required by the WhatToLimit item.

For example, to limit everyone in the group "users" to a **nice** level of 13 and a maximum of a nice of 9 then you would enter the following lines:

```
@users    soft    priority    13
@users    hard    priority    9
```

Once you have this information set as you need it, save and exit the file. Then, you need to tell PAM that these limits exist, and what services to apply these limits to. Open the file /etc/pam.conf and add lines in the format:

```
Service    session    required    pam_limits.so
```

So, you might include a line such as:

```
OTHER    session    required    pam_limits.so
```

Save and exit this file and you are ready to go.

THE FIREWALL

"Firewall" is one of the biggest buzzwords in the area of network security, a word tossed around as though it is a cure-all for concerns about intruders. However, a firewall is just a tool like any other service. There are purposes for which a firewall is very effective, and then there are those where such a measure hampers regular network use more than it helps. Implementation is also a huge factor when it comes to whether a firewall really does cure security woes.

A firewall is a tool that centrally regulates what goes in and out of the network. No data goes directly to any machine behind it. Instead, incoming packets must be examined by the firewall first. If they are deemed appropriate, they are sent to where the administrator configured the tool to send them. Sometimes, as far as the outside world is concerned, they can see nothing past the firewall.

This tool comes in a number of forms. Some companies sell ready-made boxes that can be plugged into a network and regulate traffic. There are also commercial products that can be installed in a regular computer, and freely available open source software can be used as well. The software firewalls can usually be installed either on a dedicated firewalling machine, or on a computer that has more than one purpose.

Firewall Drawbacks

Installing a firewall is not the answer to every network security problem. Sometimes network requirements render the firewall negligible, and at other times it is far more of a hassle than it is a help.

Think of a firewall as a large sheet of cardboard hanging in front of a light. Each time the administrator must configure the firewall to allow data to pass in or out, this action requires opening a bit more of the network to the outside world. Doing this is equivalent to punching a hole in the cardboard, allowing a small beam of light to shine through. The more information that has to pass through the firewall, the more holes have to be punched, and the more light shines through. If a lot of data has to be allowed in and out, the firewall starts to look like swiss cheese. At some point along this process its use is severely diluted and other security options should be considered instead.

Some of the software necessary for routine tasks may not be able to utilize the firewall correctly. If the program is open source, then it can be modified to adapt to the firewall's needs if someone is available who is able to alter the code. Sometimes patches are available as well to modify the source. However, if the source code is not available and the initial programmers cannot or will not provide a firewall-capable version, then there is a quandary. Either a firewall is not an option, or another program will have to be used that can work within its restrictions.

Types Of Firewalls

There are essentially two types of firewalls: a proxy firewall, which handles all Internet services for the users protected behind it, and the IP Filtering firewall, which examines all incoming and outgoing TCP/IP packets and handles them according to the rules set within it.

Proxy Firewalls

A proxy firewall handles all Internet traffic for the network. When a user behind the firewall tries to access a Web page on the Internet, for example,

12

the request goes to the proxy server. The firewall in turn uses its own HTTP client to open the URL requested, and then passes this information to the user's client. So, basically, the destination servers on the Internet see all requests as coming directly from the firewall itself.

An advantage of using a proxy firewall is that every connection and attempted connection can be easily logged. A disadvantage is that no one can get into the network from outside even for legitimate purposes.

Filtering Firewalls

An IP filtering firewall works similarly to the tcp_wrappers tool but at a larger level. It is capable of allowing the administrator to have every incoming and outgoing packet examined and then handled according to his or her specifications. The advantage to this tool is that someone who spends the time to build the rules properly can very carefully configure who can do what. A disadvantage is that there is a lot of room to be sloppy with this tool.

IMPLEMENTING A PROXY FIREWALL

The proxy firewall covered here is the SOCKS V5 protocol. This server is freely available for download and with care and attention protects any network well. Although the installation is a fairly simple process, it is important to pay attention to detail during the configuration in order to maximize the security benefits of using the proxy.

Administrators can get the SOCKS V5 proxy server at **www.socks.nec.com**. Click the Download socks5 button and then read the information on the various packages available. There is no Linux-specific source version. Download the Unix source to a download or temporary directory.

 The Web server requires users to enter information before down-loading the software.

After the package is downloaded, follow the patches link to see if there are any patches available. If so, clicking on the patch opens it within the Web browser because it is a text file. Use the browser's Save As function to save the patch out to a file.

Installing The SOCKS V5 Server

In order to install the server, the firewall code has to be compiled. Fortunately, the SOCKS V5 tool comes with an auto-configuration script and a well-done Makefile. If there are no problems during the compilation stage, then getting this tool installed is fairly simple. Follow these steps:

1. **Unpack the source**—Use the gunzip and tar programs to unpack the source into part of the /usr/src or the temporary or download directory preferred for source code.

2. **Examine the text files**—Look at the README and INSTALL files to see if the instructions differ from those here.

3. **Run the auto-configuration script**—Change into the directory created when unpacking the source code, then type "./configure" to begin the auto-configuration script. This script collects information about the hardware and software on the system to feed to the Makefile. It also helps to ensure that everything necessary is installed. The GNU C compiler egcs needs to be installed in order to complete the server installation, and so does the make package, and likely the C libraries as well.

4. **Compile the code**—Once the auto-configuration script completes, type "make" to begin the compile. Hopefully this process will go smoothly. If not, look back at Chapter 11 where the packages that need to be installed are discussed. A package containing necessary libraries—kernel source and headers, for example—might be needed.

5. **Install the SOCKS V5 server**—Once the compile completes, type "make install" to move the binaries and libraries into place.

Building An /etc/socks5.conf Statement

It is important to understand how a SOCKS V5 configuration statement is laid out in order to make the most of the configuration possibilities. It is sometimes helpful to practice on a specific machine, denying all access by default and then letting in specific types of data.

A statement in the /etc/socks5.conf file begins with one of the six options shown in Table 12.3. Each of these options is complex to implement properly.

12

Table 12.3 Configuration statement types for /etc/socks5.conf.

Type	Use
ban	Forbid entry to the entity defined by the rule.
auth	Explicitly defines the type of authentication necessary for a connection to be accepted from the entity defined by the rule.
interface	On a machine that has more than one IP address, explicitly defines where that interface will accept connections from or to.
set	Defines a SOCKS V5 environment variable.
proxytype	Explicitly defines what a proxy needs to be used for, with a type of either socks5 or noproxy.
accesstype	Explicitly defines if a connection will be accepted or not, with a type of either permit or deny.

Building Host And Port Patterns

When an incoming connection arrives at your proxy firewall, it can be analyzed to determine whether the originating machine and process is acceptable. When referring to a host or set of hosts in a SOCKS V5 configuration file, there are a number of ways to narrow exactly which machines to include. The terms available are outlined in Table 12.4.

Because the proxy firewall looks at the incoming and outgoing connections down to the ports themselves, it is important to carefully define which ports are referred to by the rules. Table 12.5 outlines the terms available for adding a port entry.

 The bracket types can be mixed to get the desired end result.

Table 12.4 Host pattern types in the SOCKS V5 configuration files.

Format	Meaning	Example
-	Everything matches.	-
.domain.extension	Any host from the specified domain.	.colors.org
IPbeginning	Any host from the specified IP segment.	192.168.
host.domain. extension	The connection must originate from this particular host.	green.colors.org
IP/Mask	Any host within the range defined by the IP and Mask.	192.168.10.0/ 255.255.255.12

Table 12.5 Port pattern types in the SOCKS V5 configuration files.

Format	Meaning	Example
-	Everything matches.	-
service	The service that uses the port in question	httpd
port	The port number the rule applies to.	90
[start,end]	The range of port numbers listed between the brackets.	[70,90]
(start,end)	The range of port numbers listed between the parentheses, not including the numbers themselves.	(69,91)

Building An Authentication Pattern

Depending on how secure you need the network behind the firewall to be, you may or may not choose to require authentication for incoming connections. There are a couple of different types of authentication available with a proxying firewall. An authentication pattern allows the administrator to define what types of user authentication to use when making a connection. The options available for this pattern are shown in Table 12.6.

When listing more than one item to create the pattern, separate them with commas and no spaces. For example, "k,n".

Setting An Environment Variable

The set statement allows the administrator to initialize environment variables. Some of these variables are outlined in Table 12.7. A full listing is available by typing "man socks5". To set an environment variable, use the format:

```
set variable value
```

Table 12.6   Authentication pattern types in the SOCKS V5 configuration files.

Type	Meaning
-	Any authentication method.
k	Accept Kerberos 5 authentication.
n	No authentication necessary. Only use this setting for services intended for the general public, and use with caution.
u	Accept username and password authentication.

12

Table 12.7   Commonly used environment variables for the SOCKS V5 server.

Variable	Purpose	Values
SOCKS5_MAXCHILD	Sets the maximum number of child processes the SOCKS V5 server can spawn. The default is 64.	The number of child processes that should be allowed.
SOCKS5_NOIDENT	Tells the SOCKS V5 server not to request an ident from incoming connections. This option reduces wasted time if most of the incoming connections are going to come from Unix machines.	No values.

(continued)

Table 12.7   Commonly used environment variables for the SOCKS V5 server (continued).

Variable	Purpose	Values
SOCKS5_REVERSEMAP	Always resolve host names. Using this option slows down performance but creates richer log files.	No values.
SOCKS5_SERVICENAME	Always resolve port service names. Using this option slows down performance but creates richer log files.	No values.
SOCKS5_PASSWD	Sets the password value the SOCKS V5 server gives to another SOCKS V5 server when trying to make a connection.	The password itself.
SOCKS5_USER	Sets the login name the SOCKS V5 server gives to another SOCKS V5 server when trying to make a connection.	The login name itself.

Building The Rule Statements

Now that you know how to build the various patterns that are used in the rules, you can move on to building the statements that configure the proxy firewall's behavior. There are a variety of statements available: ban, auth, interface, proxy, and access. The ban statement refers to what hosts the SOCKS V5 server should not accept connections from. This statement is in the format:

```
ban hostfrom portfrom
```

The *hostfrom* and *portfrom* portions of the statement—and the statements in the rest of this section—refer to where the connection originated. The most restrictive version of this statement would be "ban - -", which would mean to ban outside connections from anyone at any port. However, usually a ban statement is not so restrictive.

The auth statement refers to what types of authentication the SOCKS V5 server accepts from particular hosts. This statement is in the format:

```
auth hostfrom portfrom authpattern
```

The most permissive form of this statement would be "auth - - -", and this format is not uncommon to see.

The interface statement, as mentioned earlier, is only necessary on machines that have two IP addresses—and, hence, two Ethernet cards. This statement is used to tell the SOCKS V5 server which Ethernet card to send the data through. An interface statement is built in the format:

```
interface host port address
```

The *host* and *port* portions of the statement refer to where the connection originated or where it is going. Both must refer to the same item. The *address* portion is the IP or MAC address for the interface the server is to send the data through. The statement "interface - - -" makes no sense.

A proxy statement does not actually begin with the word "proxy". Instead, the term refers to a type of statement that sets whether requests for a particular service on a particular host go directly to it, or are handled by a proxy. These statements are in the format:

```
proxy hostto portto proxyhost:proxyport
```

The first term is either "noproxy" if the request should go directly to the machine in question, or "socks5" if it needs to go through a proxy. The *hostto* and *portto* terms refer to the destination machine specified by the incoming connection—both here and elsewhere in the section. Finally, the *proxyhost: proxyport* entry defines the proxy server itself. This proxy can be a single server or a comma-delineated list in order of preference.

Access statements are used to explicitly define who can access what services. The format used is the same for either:

```
access authpattern command hostfrom hostto portfrom portto users
```

The first term is either "permit" or "deny". The *authpattern* is the authentication pattern defining which types of authentication are accepted for the rule. With the *command* term, set the commands that those who match the rule can run, if it is a permit rule—or not run, if it is a deny rule. The available commands are shown in Table 12.8; to use more than one, list them separated by commas and no spaces.

The *hostfrom, hostto, portfrom,* and *portto* items are all the same as they are elsewhere. Finally, the *users* portion is optional. It is in the format of a comma-separated list of user names with no spaces in between, where the only wildcard available is to just use a dash (-) to signify all users.

12

Table 12.8 Commands recognized by the SOCKS V5 access statements.

Command	Description
-	All commands match.
b	Attach special uses to key combinations.
c	Connect to the service.
p	PING the service.
t	Perform a traceroute.
u	Use the UDP protocol.

Configuring The SOCKS V5 Server

When configuring the SOCKS V5 server, keep in mind that the best security involves denying all connections and then slowly poking holes to allow the necessary items through. Although it might be easier to take a more laid back approach, such an attitude risks making the firewall ultimately useless. However, the restrictions on machines that are all behind the firewall together can be much lighter than those on the machines outside the protective zone.

Create The Configuration File

Log in and use the vi editor to open the file "/etc/socks5.conf". This is where the firewall configuration for the proxy system takes place.

Configure The SOCKS V5 Server

Often, the machines that are behind the firewall are all considered "trusted" by the administrator, or at least to a good degree. For this reason, often they will not be required to use a proxy server for most services. They likely even have access to servers and services that are not at all accessible to the outside world.

The section of /etc/socks5.conf representing the inside network might look something like the following—which, for the sake of example, spans the B class address range from 172.16.10.0 to 172.16.10.15, with the SOCKS V5 server on the machine 172.16.10.20:

```
# The proxy server accepts any form of authentication.
auth - - -
# The proxy server does not regulate internal LAN connections.
permit - - 172.16.10.0/255.255.0.15 - - -
# The proxy server will not accept connections from
# educational institutions because of previous problems
# with attempted intrusion.
ban .edu -
```

Note that because of the ban statement, users inside the protected portion of the network will not be able to access services at educational institutions.

Building An /etc/libsocks5.conf Statement

The SOCKS V5 client configuration file, /etc/libsocks5.conf, has one type of statement in it. However, this statement is complex and must be configured properly to ensure that the machines can access the information they need, and that security is not compromised. The statements in this file are all proxy definitions built in the following manner:

➤ **Proxy Statement Format** A proxy statement in /etc/libsocks5.conf is formatted differently than in /etc/socks5.conf. The format for the client configuration file is:

```
proxy command hostto portto users proxies
```

➤ **Proxy Types** The values for *proxy* are either "socks5" or "noproxy". Use "noproxy" for any services that the client is trusted to access within the safe zone, and socks5 for services that even this machine must use a proxy server to access.

➤ **Available Commands** The *command* options are the same as those listed in the earlier Table 12.8. As usual, these commands can be mixed and matched by using them in a series with commas and no spaces.

➤ **Host And Port** The *hostto* and *portto* items are, once again, the destination host and port patterns for the rule.

➤ **Optional User List** If desired, narrow the focus by including the specific user names covered by the rule. No wildcards are allowed except the dash (-), which stands for all users.

➤ **Optional Proxy Server** The *proxyhost:proxyport* that the rule points to, if not the default.

12

Configuring The SOCKS V5 Clients

The machines behind the firewall will not know how to behave if they are not configured as SOCKS V5 clients. Take a moment to consider whether the machines behind the firewall are all trusted to talk to one another without interference. Then, consider what outside services the clients are allowed to access and configure them to go through the proxy. Otherwise, the network structure will not be properly protected. Follow these steps to configure your SOCKS V5 clients:

1. Create the configuration file. Log in and use the vi editor to open the file "/etc/libsocks5.conf". This is where the machine's clients are told how to utilize the proxy system.

2. Configure the SOCKS V5 client. Often the client machines behind the firewall server are all considered "trusted" by the administrator, or at least

to a good degree. For this reason, often they will not be required to use a proxy server for most services. They likely even have access to servers and services that are not at all accessible to the outside world.

The section of /etc/libsocks5.conf representing the inside network—which, for the sake of example, spans the B class address range from 172.16.10.0 to 172.16.10.15, with the SOCKS V5 server on the machine 172.16.10.20—might look something like:

```
# Here are the settings for how the protected network
# talks within itself.
noproxy - 172.16.10.0/255.255.0.15 - -
socks5 - - - - 172.16.10.20
```

The reason there is no :*proxyport* on the end of the proxy address is that all proxied services are being sent to the firewall, and each service runs through its standard /etc/services port.

IMPLEMENTING A FILTERING FIREWALL

The IP filtering firewall covered here is ipchains. This package often comes with the Linux distributions themselves, and if not it is freely available over the Internet. At one time it was necessary to recompile the kernel before implementing IP filtering with a tool called ipfwadm, but the IP filtering tool—ipchains—is enabled by default in kernels 2.1.102 and up.

If the ipchains package is not installed already, then it first must be installed on the machine. Type "man ipchains" to see if the package is on the system. If no man page exists for this program, then look on the distribution CD-ROM. If for some reason it is not included there, then try the distributor's Web site. A fresh copy of the package is available from the IP Firewalling Chains home page at **www.rustcorp.com/linux/ipchains/**.

IP Chains

An IP *chain* is a set of related TCP/IP packet handling rules. The ipchains package always has at least three chains: input, forward, and output. All rules can be placed under one of these three chains, or new chains can be created if that is what the administrator prefers. There are no stipulations for how to divide the rules into the various chains. The main requirement is to keep related rules together so they can be checked against one another.

Chain ordering is important as well. For incoming data, the first chain applied is the input chain, and then the forwarding chain examines it and passes it on to the appropriate local machine. On the other hand, for outgoing data the first chain applied is the forwarding chain, and then the output chain.

Setting Chain Policy

Each initial chain (input, forward, and output) needs to have an overriding policy. This policy is what handles items that are not specifically covered by the rules set into place by the chains. The choice of policies available is shown in Table 12.9.

To set the policy for a chain, use the format:

```
ipchains -P chain policy
```

Once a chain's policy is set, it is time to start creating rules. For example, it is smart to start with the line:

```
ipchains -P input REJECT
```

From there, the administrator can start adding rules for what must be allowed to pass through.

Rule Parts

Creating a rule can be a complex process, depending on how specific it needs to be in order to regulate traffic. The basic format to add a rule to the end of a chain is:

```
ipchains -A chain rule
```

Address Specification

One class of rule flags refers to the addresses in the packet headers. Some of these flags are shown in Table 12.10.

Table 12.9 Overriding policies available for the default IP chains.

Policy	Result
ACCEPT	If the packet is not covered by any specific rule, then allow it through.
DENY	If the packet is not covered by any specific rule, do not allow it through but do not send an error message.
MASQ	Only available for the "forward" chain. If the packet is not covered by any specific rule, allow it through using IP Masquerading.
REJECT	If the packet is not covered by any specific rule, do not allow it through and send an error message to the originating machine.

12

Table 12.10   Flags used with ipchains to specify address requirements.

Flag	Purpose
d	Test the address the packet is going to.
i	Test the interface, which is the MAC address or IP address through which the data travels.
j	When used along with the REDIRECT target, specifies which port to redirect the packet to.
s	Test the address the packet is coming from.

Address Formats

Addresses in a rule can be in one of the formats used throughout this book. The first is the full domain name, such as martin.names.org. The second is an IP address, such as 10.153.16.25. Third is the IP address and netmask combination, such as 172.19.12.0/255.255.0.19, and fourth is a short form of the IP address and netmask where the entire class range is used. To prepare the fourth type, consider each of the portions of the netmask as a separate entity. A 255 is eight bits, and a 0 is none. So 255.0.0.0 is 8, 255.255.0.0 is 16, 255.255.255.0 is 24, and 255.255.255.255 is 32. The format used for this case is the IP address class base and then the bit size. For example, 192.168.15.0/32 means 192.168.15.0 through 192.168.15.255.

Packet Type Specification

Another class of rule flags refers to the type of packets passing through. Two of the flags are shown here:

➤ **p** This flag tests the protocol used to handle the packet. This protocol is generally either TCP or UDP.

➤ **y** This flag tests to determine if the data is specifically a SYN TCP packet.

Special TCP And UDP Protocol Treatment

If TCP or UDP ports are referenced in the rule, a specific port or range of ports can be specified as well. To list a single port, just use the number. For a range, separate the numbers with a colon (:).

Another TCP-specific item is the SYN packet, which is used to request a connection. If the aim is to block incoming connections from certain places and yet allow internal users to connect to those same machines from inside, then blocking SYN packets does the job nicely. To block these packets, add the -y flag to the TCP protocol rule.

Special ICMP Treatment

If ICMP (Internet Control Message Protocol) is specified in the rule, then there is the opportunity to specify which ICMP service the rule applies to.

Table 12.11 Terms used with ipchains to specify which type of ICMP packets to test.

Name	Provides
destination-unreachable	An umbrella term referring to TCP or UDP traffic which cannot get where it needs to go.
echo-reply	The "pong" response to a ping.
echo-request	A ping.
host-unreachable	TCP or UDP traffic cannot reach the actual host machine which is its destination.
network-unreachable	TCP or UDP traffic cannot reach the network containing its destination.
port-unreachable	TCP or UDP traffic cannot reach the port which is supposed to be listening at its destination.

These names must be used in conjunction with the –s option. Table 12.11 lists an example of the ICMP services available. To get a full listing, type "ipchains –h icmp".

 If the goal is to reverse a rule—that is, use its opposite—then add an exclamation point (!) between the flag and its value, with a space in between the two. For example, "-p ! UDP".

Rule Targets

12

Once the rule itself is set, the last portion of it defines the target, or what should happen if the rule has a match. The six targets available when building an ipchains rule are:

➤ ACCEPT: Allow the packet through.

➤ DENY: Do not accept the packet, and do not send an error message.

➤ MASQ: Change the packet's headers so that it looks like it came from the firewall itself. Only useful if IP Masquerading is running.

➤ REDIRECT: Send a TCP or UDP packet arriving along the input chain to a local port instead of to its declared destination.

➤ REJECT: Do not accept the packet, and send an ICMP packet in return declaring the destination unreachable.

➤ RETURN: Treat the packet like it has just hit the end of the rules in the chain, even if it has not, and apply the test results to the chain policy.

Building Rules

With so many parts, it can be hard to even know where to start when building a rule for ipchains. A good general process involves going from the general to the specific until the rule defines exactly what it needs to regulate. Overly broad ipchains rules can either restrict accesses they are not meant to restrict, or lead to lax security. Follow these steps to build your chain rules:

1. **Choose the chain**—Choose which chain the rule should go in. For many the default chains are enough, and so it is a matter of determining whether the rule regulates incoming data, outgoing data, or data that needs to be passed onto somewhere else. If there is reason to create a new specialized chain, use the command **ipchains -N** *newchain*.

2. **Consider the chain policy**—The default chain policy determines how the rule must be eventually phrased. Any packet that does not match a rule is handled by the default policy. The rule must, then, give a result that is different than the default policy.

3. **Choose the target**—Rather than working through the rule from left to right, take a moment to determine the end result. The target decides what happens if the packet happens to match the rule, so what needs to happen to the packet is paramount and determines issues like whether any of the items need to be reversed.

4. **Build the criteria**—The most complex part of adding a rule is determining the series of criteria necessary to identify the packets it needs to effect. When first starting out using ipchains, it may be worth setting very narrow rules for specific situations as far as what traffic is allowed in, rather than making quite general rules that might let too much in.

5. **Put it together**—Putting it all together, the sequence should be "*chain criteria target*". For example, consider a situation where the administrator wants to prevent any incoming TCP/IP connections. As discussed earlier, this issue creates a problem because when people connect to services outside of the protected area, those services must be able to send packets back to hold up their part of the connection. The solution to this problem is to prevent only the packets that are used to initiate a TCP/IP connection. These packets are referred to as SYN packets.

In order to build the statements, the following steps must be taken:

1. The initial step requires a choice of chains. Because incoming connections need to be regulated, the chain is "input".

2. Next, the chain is new and so has no policy set yet. By default, all chains are set to ALLOW which is not the most secure method of using a firewall. So, chain policy needs to be set to REJECT for incoming connections.

3. Now that the input chain is chosen and its policy is defined to REJECT, the criteria can be built. The rule applies to TCP SYN packets outside the firewall's protected zone. Any TCP packets that are not SYN packets should be sent through.

Now, the statement itself can be built. To build a statement, the steps below must be followed:

1. The default policy needs to be double-checked. The administrator would type "ipchains -L" to get a listing of the chains that exist and what their policies are. Then, to set the input chain's default policy to REJECT he or she would type "ipchains -P input REJECT".

2. With the policy set to REJECT, then the target would be ACCEPT. So the rule's criteria must match what the packets need to contain in order to pass through. The packets must not be TCP SYN packets from outside the network. If the network was on, say, the C class IP address range con-tained in 192.168.162.*, then the rule criteria might look like "-p TCP -s 192.168.162.0/32 -y".

3. In the end, the final statement typed at the command line would look like:

```
ipchains -A input -p TCP -s 192.168.162.0/32 -y ACCEPT
```

Keeping Rules Between Boots

Those who make serious use of ipchains need to keep in mind that the rules are not saved for posterity. When the machine is shut down or rebooted, these rules are lost and have to be rebuilt the next time the machine comes up. The ipchains package comes with the following two scripts to help with this otherwise frustrating issue:

➤ **ipchains-save** After making any rules changes, be sure to run this script, which saves the rules. For example, to save the rules to the file /root/ ipchains-rules, type "ipchains-save > /root/ipchains-rules".

➤ **ipchains-restore** This script reads the rules saved from the last shutdown and re-implements them so they are put back in place. Rather than running this script by hand—a policy that risks the administrator forgetting to run it after a reboot—add it to the init files. For example, at the end of /etc/rc.d/ rc.local add the line "/sbin/ipchains-restore < /root/ipchains-rules".

TIGHTENING USER SECURITY

Once the issues of physical and host security have been addressed, it is time to consider user security. This form of security management is finer, more detailed than the others. The key here is to try to prevent simple user errors that can compromise their accounts, which weakens the security of the host, and so on.

Setting The umask

The set of permissions for a file or directory is its *mask*. There is also the *umask*, which is the reverse of the permissions. The umask contains the permission bits

12

that are turned off by default. It may be a good idea to return to Chapter 3 for a review of file permissions if how to determine the numeric value is unclear.

To get the umask that is currently set on a machine, type "umask". Often the default is 022, which means that no bits are turned off for the first triad, two are turned off for the second, and two for the third. This number translates into a mask of rwxr-xr-x. Now, you need to decide what umask you want to use on your system.

Allowing members of the group and other (all users) to read files by default is not secure. The user's data can be accessed by anyone else on the system. Even worse, if this is the default setting and a lot of the users do not understand issues such as file permissions, then almost every user is going to have a wide-open set of files. Anyone who breaks in to the machine would be able to access anything he or she pleased.

Therefore, one of the first things to do is remove read permissions for the other triad, making the umask 026. If there is reason to do so, then remove them for members of the same group as well, which gives a umask of 066.

To implement the new default permission set, use the **umask 066** command. From that point on, files created by users and root will be created with the permissions rwx--x--x.

Shadow Passwords

One serious problem with most machines by default is that if a user account is breached, the intruder now has access to some vital files. One of these files is /etc/passwd. It is easy to think that the file should simply be kept more secure if it is so vulnerable. The permissions could be changed so it is only accessible to root. However, any program that needs to authenticate users has to have access to /etc/passwd. Making the permissions more restrictive could cripple the system.

The Shadow Password Suite

Converting a system to use shadow passwords means moving the actual password information from /etc/passwd to the new file /etc/shadow. The other account information remains in /etc/passwd. Only the passwords themselves are removed. The security benefit of this action is that the passwords themselves no longer need to be inside an insecure file. Permissions on the /etc/shadow file make it available only to root.

Programs that handle user authentication have to be able to deal with shadow passwords. Fortunately, this suite has been around for some time and most Linux software is shadow-capable. If the source is available, then any software that cannot use /etc/shadow can be modified to do so. The primary problem occurs when software is not able to understand the shadow password setup, and the source code is not available.

Checking To See If Shadow Is Installed

Most distributions install shadow passwords by default, so there may not be any need to install it by hand. A quick way to tell if the suite is already installed is to type "ls /etc/shadow". If the file already exists, then the suite is installed. Then, to see if it is in use type "more /etc/passwd". If the second field in the account entries is always or almost always an "x" instead of an encrypted password, then the shadow suite is already activated.

Installing And Converting

The shadow passwords suite is most likely included amongst the packages that come on the Linux distribution CD. Locate the packages on the CD and then install them as is appropriate for the particular distribution. Once the packages are installed, type "pwconv" to convert the machine to using shadow passwords.

Whether shadow was installed by hand or by default, it can be deactivated with the command **pwunconv**.

Keep in mind that converting to shadow passwords does nothing about the /etc/ groups file. You may have no need to hide your master group file. If for some reason you do, use the **grpconv** command to convert to shadow groups and the **grpunconv** command to return to normal groups. The new group listing is contained in /etc/gshadow.

12

Other Password Security Enhancements

There are actually a number of enhancements that are often used by default in Linux distributions to add to the difficulty of cracking passwords. It is important to understand these additions so you know what the basic password package is capable of, and when you may need to disable the enhancements or alter the code so a specific program can work with them.

PAM, Pluggable Authentication Modules

One password program enhancement is PAM (Pluggable Authentication Modules). This package is not directly applied to the password verification scheme. Instead, PAM allows for the modular handling of system functions. The way this feature applies to password verification is that it prevents the programs themselves from having to know exactly how you have your passwords verified.

If you are using PAM, then programs that require user authentication talk directly to it rather than any specific authentication routines. The file /etc/pam.conf contains the information that sets the redirections.

MD5, Message-Digest Algorithm 5

MD5 refers to a type of 128-bit encryption, which in this context is applied to your user passwords. An additional advantage of using this authentication enhancement is that it allows you to use long passwords. The longer your password is, the longer it will take a random character-generating program to guess it. There is also a checksum involved, meaning that it includes a value at the end of the password field that is derived from the sum of all of the individual bytes within the password.

All of these items together add up to a much more secure system.

Testing For Bad Passwords

No matter how often an administrator explains the need for secure passwords, some users will use passwords that are easy-to-decode. The reasons for doing so vary from a fear of forgetting complex passwords to sheer laziness. If system security is a serious concern, it is important to occasionally check to be sure that the passwords for all accounts on the machine are secure.

Crack

The crack program has been used for years by administrators to hammer at the passwords on their systems and test for poorly chosen ones. This program checks passwords against dictionary words, which is exactly what most people trying to break into a system will do as well. It then reports any accounts whose passwords it was able to obtain.

If crack can figure out someone's password, so can a potential intruder.

The crack program is available at the FTP site **sunsite.unc.edu**, in the /pub/ Linux/system/security folder. Unpack the program into where it needs to be stored—preferably a secure portion of the file system—then change into the resulting directory.

Customizing The Output

Crack is a shell script, and it needs to be edited. Use the **vi Crack** command to open this file. Inspect the value of the variable CRACK_HOME. If it is not the same as the current directory, then change it to the appropriate location.

 To get the current location from the command line, use the command **pwd**.

Another variable that likely needs to be changed is CRACK_OUT. If the end result should not be stored in the CRACK_HOME location, then change this value to the directory where the resulting files should go. If this directory does not currently exist, be sure to create it before running the shell script. Now, save and exit the script.

Editing The Automated Mail File

One of the useful aspects of the crack program is that it can automatically mail those whose passwords it is able to discover with a notice that they have a weak password that potentially compromises system security. The text for this mail file is contained within a file in the Scripts subdirectory of the crack program directory, and the file is named "nastygram". A template version of the letter already exists. Simply edit it with the "vi" editor and change the text to suit the system's needs.

 The crack program also creates a long file each time it runs. A shell script or program can be written to track which users consistently show up as having bad passwords.

Running Crack

Once the crack files are fully configured, choose the format for the command that needs to be run. The basic format is "./Crack *flags* /etc/passwd /etc/shadow" if shadow passwords are in use—for example, "./Crack -m /etc/passwd /etc/shadow". Otherwise, leave the /etc/shadow term out. The flags available are shown in Table 12.12.

Securing Accounts When Idle

One problem that occurs when people are using machines that are readily accessible by others is that they walk away without logging out because they are in the middle of some form of work. When the machine is a terminal in a computer lab, in an open cubicle-style office, or in some other situation where it is easily used by others, there is the chance that either someone else in the office or someone who otherwise does not have access might try to utilize that login session.

Table 12.12 Crack program flags.

Flag	Purpose
f	Run crack in the foreground instead of automatically back-grounding the process. All output is sent to the screen instead of a log file.
m	Send mail to the users who have passwords that the program can guess.
n*value*	**Nice** the program so that it does not bog down the system.

Which program you use to lock down a terminal depends in part whether you are in the GUI or at the command line. If you are running a GUI, look in its main menu for an option such as "Lock Screen"—the menu option available in GNOME. Typing **xlock** at the command line in GUI terminal often has the same effect without needing to use the mouse. The program **vlock** is what you would use if you were not within the GUI and wanted to lock down your virtual consoles. Remember that if you only lock one down, people can log in to the others. However, that may not matter to you if the others are all showing the login prompt.

UTILIZING LOG FILES

Depending on how the log files on the system are configured, they may hold a wealth of information. A very good intruder knows how to cover tracks left in the log files. If someone has already broken in and removed all traces of his or her intrusion, then it may be too late to catch his or her using any of the system logs. However, a review of the logs will tell you if a potential intruder has been sniffing around available ports or whether a new problem with the machine is caused by program bugs or something more sinister.

Failed User Logins

The first thing someone may do if they want access to a machine is either try to break into a root account, or try to divine some account names on the system. Once a hacker has the names of at least one account, he or she can begin trying to figure out that account's password. Although some may try this by hand, often potential intruders use a program or script that goes through dictionary words—perhaps the crack program itself.

Although most users at some point or another forget a password or mistype it while trying to log in, a forgetful user will rarely continue attempting a password 30, 40, or more times in a row without contacting the administrator for assistance with the forgotten or lost password. There is a specific log file that records failed user logins. You can easily utilize this file to help you see if there are large listings of failed logins to the same account all only minutes apart.

There are actually two log files that contain data related to user logins. The first is /var/log/wtmp, which tracks who logs in to the system and keeps a record of it. The more useful log file, however, is /var/log/btmp. This is the file that contains information on failed logins.

Use the commands **ls /var/log/wtmp** and **ls /var/log/btmp** to create the log files that track login information. Although the wtmp file is not necessary unless there is a reason to track login times and durations—and in fact if there is heavy login traffic this file could get large quickly—the btmp file is crucial for helping to watch for attempted break-ins. If this file does not exist, use the **touch /var/log/btmp** command to create it. The system will then utilize it automatically.

To see what is in the wtmp file, type "last". The btmp file requires a different command, **lastb**. With either of these commands, the format "*command* -n *number*" will give a longer listing. For example, **lastb -n 10**.

A useful strategy for tracking attempted break-ins without needing to manually peruse the btmp file on a regular basis is to write a shell script that sends the output of **lastb** to a file—for example:

```
lastb -n 100 > btmp.output
```

and then parses the information for excessive repeating of particular accounts.

Tracking Attempted Port Entries

The tcp_wrappers tool allows logging of incoming data to ports. If there is reason to believe that someone has been hammering at a machine's ports, or that he or she may, then it is a good idea to utilize this tool and make the most of its features. Otherwise, port accesses are not logged.

Configuring tcp_wrappers To Log Attempts

Assuming that tcp_wrappers is already installed as discussed earlier in this chapter, all that must be done is to add additional logging features. Edit the file /etc/hosts.allow and at the end of each line add the text ": severity auth.info: allow". Then, edit the file /etc/hosts.deny and at the end of each line add the text ": severity auth.info: deny". Finally, restart syslogd and the new logging structure is in place.

Now, all of the accepted and rejected connections are logged to the log file assigned to tcp_wrappers in syslogd—in the case of the example earlier, this file is /var/log/authlog.

It is useful to write a script to watch over the /var/log/authlog file similar to the one used to watch over btmp. This script should watch for excessive connections, whether attempted or failed. It will take some time to perfect this script, however, because most packets passing through will be completely legitimate.

 Be sure to make good use of the logrotate function when it comes to the /var/log/authlog file. If there is a lot of traffic to the machine, then this file will become huge fairly quickly.

The SWATCH Log Analysis Tool

Looking through log files manually is an onerous task. Fortunately, there is a tool available for system administrators called SWATCH (the Simple WATCHer and filter). This Perl program removes the need for visually digging through logs and trying to spot irregularities. If this program did not come with your Linux distribution, get it from the FTP site **ftp.stanford.edu** in the directory **/general/ security-tools/swatch/**.

Unpack the file in your preferred source storage directory, enter the directory containing the SWATCH files, and then run the installation script by typing "sh install.sh". This script walks you through the SWATCH installation process. Once the actual program is in place, you can go immediately to setting up the configuration file /etc/swatchrc. Unfortunately, actually setting up this file takes some time and serious thought. You have to determine what kind of suspicious activity you want to watch for in which log files, and then what kind of regular expression will let SWATCH catch the problem. When a problem is spotted— and it will be spotted immediately since SWATCH monitors in real time—the administrator receives an email with the message pre-set to go along with the problem.

Consider your SWATCH configuration to be an ongoing process. Over time, you will gain more and more understanding of what to watch for in your log files that can help you to see problems before they become serious. A line in /etc/swatchrc looks similar to the following:

```
instruction=expression action=options
```

The instruction can be one of three different choices:

➤ **watchfor** Signals that any item matching the expression immediately requires the following action.

➤ **ignore** Signals that any item matching the expression is of no consequence.

➤ **waitfor** Signals that nothing should be done until this particular expression is matched.

 It quickly becomes apparent that how you structure your /etc/ swatchrc is imperative to getting it working smoothly. Many people just use watchfor and leave the other two instructions alone until they understand the process more fully.

The expression value, on the other hand, is a regular expression. See Chapter 7 for a review of how to build these items efficiently. Once SWATCH finds the regular expression and knows from the instruction how to react to it, you need to define an action as laid out in Table 12.13.

Table 12.13   Actions available in /etc/swatchrc.

Action	Purpose	Option	Option Value	Value Required?
bell	Display the contents of the line that matches the expression, then ring the bell.	The number of times to ring the bell.	positive integer	No, default is 1.
echo	Display the contents of the line that matches the expression.	Formatting for the text.	bold, blink, inverse, normal, or underscore	No, default is normal.
exec	Execute the following command if the expression matches.	The command to run.	None.	No.
mail	Send email to the address(es) listed if the expression matches.	The addresses to mail.	Address(es) separated if necessary by colons with no space.	No, default is the user running the program.
pipe	Pipe the line containing the matched expression to the following command.	The command to pipe the information to.	None.	No.
throttle	Do not perform the same action multiple times for identical expressions with identical options.	The option to watch.	None.	No.
write	Display the matched expression on the given user's terminal.	The user to notify.	None.	No.

So, now to put this information all together. Notice that nowhere in the file did you tell SWATCH where to look! You need to have a separate version of swatchrc for each log file you want to watch. Say that you want to watch /var/log/btmp, and be notified by email and an echo to your screen whenever someone tries to log in as root and fails. Since /var/log/btmp logs all failed login attempts you only need to watch for the text "root". However, you do not want to email the results to root because if the intruder gets into the root account he or she can just erase the evidence from the mailbox. Instead, you want it to send the mail to your account "joe".

First, you need to create the configuration file. Open it as /etc/swatchrc_btmp and enter a line similar to:

```
watchfor=/root/ echo mail=joe
```

Once you save and exit this file, you then need to run SWATCH to watch it—or restart it if you just changed the configuration file. To accomplish this, type:

```
swatch -config-file=/etc/swatchrc_btmp —tail-file=/var/log/btmp
```

DETECTING AND REMOVING INTRUDERS

There is somewhat of an art to noticing that your systems have been compromised and then removing all of the intruder's access. This section discusses some of the basic tactics to use and problems to watch for. The type of issues you encounter will invariably depend on the invader's reasons for breaking into the system. Some will have a goal of doing damage or snooping on your system whereas others may be using your machines as a jumping point to attack elsewhere.

One of the main things to remember is that you—or the cron daemon, in the case of things that can be easily automated—should be performing daily checks on your system for anything suspicious. Utilize everything you have learned in this chapter and elsewhere to build a security routine and follow it vigorously. Other-wise, you may not know your system has been breached until an administrator from another site angrily points out that he or she is being attacked from your own site!

Intruders often leave some telltale signs if you know what to look for. One of the biggest of these is the stealth file name. These are file names that at a quick glance do not appear alarming. Only when you stop and blink do you realize they are out of place. The most popular is "…". There is no "…" directory reference. Having a single line in a daily cron check running find on that file name is a good start for security purposes. In fact, file names that begin with a period at all are suspicious because they are not shown in a quick file listing. Also look for files that are out of place, such as /usr/bin/.profile.

Another helpful item for sysadmins everywhere is the checksecurity script available through Debian.

Once you have actually found an intruder, it can be very difficult to remove him or her. You have to find all of his or her backdoors, all of the accounts he or she has broken into, and more. This is where backups (see Chapter 6) are imperative. If you have a long legacy of backups available to you, then you can use them to contrast and compare your vital programs such as ls, find, and ps and make sure they are unchanged. It is generally recommended that you un-network the infected machine until you get it all straightened out.

TRACKING SECURITY UPDATES

It is important to stay up to date in the fast-paced world of system security. There is a constant cycle in which hackers test the limits of Internet, networking services, and other applications. The person who can overwhelm the software or service has a good chance of gaining access to the system. Fortunately, there is a network for getting the information out to system administrators when new weaknesses are discovered.

Getting The News

There are a number of places to watch in order to get the latest news on security problems and fixes. One of these is the home of the distribution in use. Many distributions offer a place to download the latest updates, and even a mailing list which notifies users of security fixes and other uploads.

Web sites to go to for security news are:

➤ **www.cert.org**

➤ **www.ciac.org**

➤ **www.sans.org**

➤ **www.rootshell.com**

   Do not forget to check the distribution Web site too!

There are a number of mailing lists available for getting Linux security news. Table 12.14 shows some of these lists and how to join them.

When a security alert arrives, it usually contains a pointer to the fix for the problem. Sometimes, this pointer is to one specific Linux distribution that may or may not be what is in use on the machine in question. If it is not, go to the appropriate distribution Web site and see if it has its own version of the fix or patch.

12

Table 12.14 Security mailing lists containing Linux information.

List Name	Subscription Address	Subject	Body
bugtraq	listserv@securityfocus.com	(Empty)	SUBSCRIBE BUGTRAQ *LastName, FirstName*
cert-advisory	cert-advisory-request@cert.org	SUBSCRIBE email@address	(Empty)
linux-alert	linux-alert-request@redhat.com	subscribe	(Empty)
linux-security	linux-security-request@redhat.com	subscribe	(Empty)
SANS Network Security Digest	digest@sans.org Network Security	subscribe	(Empty) Getting The Updates Digest

Sometimes it is possible to use a fix or patch for another distribution. This fact especially might be true for the distributions that are based upon others, where the parent's fixes and patches may work on the child's.

CHAPTER SUMMARY

System security is a complex topic where the physical and virtual blend together to create the whole picture. How much each facet affects the overall security of your system depends on where it is located, how many users there are, and how visible it is to the outside world.

Most security topics are only touched upon in the first-level exams. Physical security, for example, is not an exam issue and will likely be saved for security specialist exams. Instead, issues surrounding network security are covered, some of the basic items that can be quickly taken care of while setting up a machine. These tasks are things like disabling unnecessary network services in /etc/ services, the basics of configuring tcp_wrappers and ipchains, and the difference between using shadow passwords and not.

Other important issues for some of the exams are less how to do things than why. How to determine whether a firewall is useful for your particular situation or not, for example, what makes a bad password, which organizations to look to for security advisories and why.

The biggest thing to remember as far as certification and performance as a system administration goes is this: The world of system security is always changing. Do not be left behind.

REVIEW QUESTIONS

1. In what file would you create a custom group?
    a. /etc/passwd
    b. /etc/shadow
    c. /etc/groups
    d. /etc/group

2. What tool restricts what packet traffic goes into and out of one specific machine?
    a. ifconfig
    b. ipchains
    c. tcp_wrappers
    d. socks

3. Which file is used to set what traffic is not allowed to enter a machine with tcp_wrappers in use?
    a. /etc/hosts.deny
    b. /etc/deny
    c. /etc/tcp_deny
    d. /etc/inetd.conf

4. Which file is used to set which traffic may enter a machine with tcp_wrappers in use?
    a. /etc/allow
    b. /etc/hosts.allow
    c. /etc/inetd.conf
    d. /etc/tcp_allow

5. Which of the following is not a valid tcp_wrappers rule?
    a. ALL:LOCAL 192.168.
    b. ALL: UNKNOWN
    c. ALL EXCEPT in.smtpd: 172.16.
    d. All are valid.

6. What tool provides secure telnet connections along with other secure remote connections?
    a. tcp_wrappers
    b. ssh
    c. stelnet
    d. inetd

12

7. Where is this secure connection tool located [Choose all that apply]?
   a. Distribution CDs
   b. ftp.replay.com
   c. www.ssh.fi/sshprotocols2/
   d. Distribution Web sites

8. Which tool is used to control all packets that come in and out of a LAN?
   a. tcp_wrappers
   b. ipchains
   c. SOCKS
   d. ssh

9. Which tool is used to mask what machines are within the LAN and prevent any connections directly to them?
   a. tcp_wrappers
   b. ipchains
   c. SOCKS
   d. ssh

10. Which wildcard in SOCKS configuration is used to mean "all"?
    a. ALL
    b. ★
    c. –
    d. .

11. Which of the following is not a valid SOCKS configuration statement?
    a. auth 192.168.14.0/32 – –
    b. socks5 192.168.14.0/32 – –
    c. ban 192.168.14.15 –
    d. deny – – 192.168.194. 192.168.14.21 – – –

12. What would you type to list what chains exist and what their policies are for an IP Filtering firewall?
    a. ipchains –L
    b. ipchains –A
    c. ipchains –P
    d. ipchains --list

13. Which of the following statements is not valid for setting the policy for a chain?

    a. ipchains –P input DENY

    b. ipchain –P output ALLOW

    c. ipchains –P output MASQ

    d. ipchains –P forward REDIRECT

14. Which flag is used to signal that the following rule definition item is either TCP or UDP?

    a. –s

    b. –p

    c. –d

    d. –t

15. Which flag is used to prevent TCP connection initiation packets from passing through an IP Filtering firewall?

    a. –p

    b. –s

    c. –y

    d. –d

16. Which flag is used to specify that the address referenced refers to where the packet came from for an IP Filtering firewall?

    a. –s

    b. –d

    c. –p

    d. –t

17. Which flag is used to specify that the address referenced refers to where the packet is going for an IP Filtering firewall?

    a. –s

    b. –d

    c. –p

    d. –t

18. Which of the following is not a valid statement for adding a rule to an existing chain?

    a. ipchains –A –p UDP –s ! 192.168.62. REJECT

    b. ipchains –A –p TCP –y –d 192.168.62. DENY

    c. ipchains –A –d 192.168.62.1 www ACCEPT

    d. ipchains –A 192.168.62. www ACCEPT

12

19. What is the command that actually converts a machine so that it uses shadow passwords?

   a. **shadow**

   b. **/etc/shadow**

   c. **pwconv**

   d. **spass**

20. Which file must exist for failed user logins to be recorded?

   a. /var/log/utmp

   b. /var/log/btmp

   c. /var/log/login

   d. /var/log/failed_log

21. Which command is used to view the most recent contents of the failed login log?

   a. **last**

   b. **lastb**

   c. **more**

   d. **tail**

HANDS-ON PROJECTS

These projects require that you have administrative (root) access to a working Linux box with a kernel 2.2.x or higher, and a connection to the Internet through which software can be downloaded—which does not necessarily need to be directly onto the Linux box. Be sure that several user accounts exist, at least one of which has a poor password, something directly from the dictionary. Also, a Web server must be installed on the machine, though nothing more than a default Web page needs to exist in its Web page directories. A clean implementation of ipchains is also necessary.

Project 12.1

In this project, you will examine the minor security weaknesses on your system and fix any that need to be dealt with.

To accomplish this task, do the following:

1. Log in as root.

2. Open the superdaemon configuration file by typing "vi /etc/inetd.conf".

3. Examine the file. What services in there that are not commented out do you actually use?

4. Comment out any services that you do not use, such as finger, by putting a hash mark (#) at the beginning of the line.

5. Double-check the location of the superdaemon init script. In many distributions it is in /etc/rc.d/init.d with the file name inetd.

6. Type "/etc/rc.d/init.d/inetd stop" to stop the superdaemon, adjusting the path if necessary.

7. Type "/etc/rc.d/init.d/inetd start" to start it back up with the new settings.

8. Now, type "ls /etc/shadow" to see if you are using shadow passwords.

9. If the file exists, you are using shadow passwords; skip to step 16.

10. If the file does not exist, then mount the distribution CD and look for the shadow package, which may have a name such as "shadow-utils".

11. Install the shadow package according to its package type—RPM, .tgz, or other format.

12. Type "pwconv" to implement shadow passwords.

13. Type "more /etc/passwd" to see how this file has now changed.

14. Type "more /etc/shadow" to see the new file.

15. If you do not want shadow passwords on your system for any particular reason, then type "pwunconv" to remove them.

16. Now, download the crack tool from **sunsite.unc.edu** in the /pub/Linux/ system/security folder.

17. Choose where you want to store this tool. It is not something that you want the average user to necessarily have access to, it is solely a tool for the administrator. Therefore, having it somewhere in the /root hierarchy is probably a good idea. For example, /root/bin.

18. Unpack the tool. It will create the directory Crack-*version* wherever it is unpacked.

19. Change into the Crack-*version* directory with the **cd** command.

20. Use the command **vi Crack** to open the Crack shell script.

21. Use the command **/CRACK_HOME** and then press Enter to search for the CRACK_HOME environment variable.

22. Change the value assigned to CRACK_HOME to match the current directory location. For example, change it to /root/bin/Crack-*version* if that is currently where the shell script is stored.

23. Use the command **:wq**, then press Enter to save and close the file.

24. Use the command **cd Scripts** to change to the crack Scripts subdirectory.

25. Use the command **vi nastygram** to open the automated mail file.

12

26. Edit the contents of the file to match what you need them to say.

27. Use the command **:wq**, then press Enter to save and close the file.

28. Use the command **cd ..** to return to the main crack directory.

29. Use the **./Crack –m /etc/passwd /etc/shadow** command to run the Crack password scanner and have it automatically mail those who have chosen poor passwords.

30. When this script finishes running, examine its output files.

31. Log in to the user account with the bad password and make sure that it received a copy of the mail.

Project 12.2

In this project, you will install and configure a SOCKS V5 Proxy firewall.

To accomplish this task, do the following:

1. Log in as root.

2. Use a browser to go to the Web site **www.socks.nec.com**.

3. Download the latest Unix source for the SOCKS V5 Proxy firewall into your preferred location for source package, such as /usr/src.

4. Uncompress the source with the **gunzip** command.

5. Unpack the source with the **tar –xvf** command.

6. Use the command **cd socks5-*version*** to change to the new directory.

7. Use the command **./configure** to run the auto-configuration script.

If the script fails, then ensure that you have the programming tools such as gcc (egcs) and C libraries installed.

8. Use the **make** command to compile the source.

9. Use the **make install** command to install the proxy firewall.

10. Type "vi /etc/socks5.conf" to open the proxy firewall server configuration file.

11. Now you have to decide on your firewalling strategy. Because this is an exercise, you will just be configuring a service to see how it works, but in reality the issue is much broader. Determine what machines you want to protect, whether it is the entire network or just part of it, or what services need to be protected. Continue from there.

12. Set the server to accept any type of authentication, as long as some form of authentication is used, by adding the line:

```
auth - - -
```

13. Tell the server to prevent any access to the local Web server from the local machine with the line:

```
deny - - 127.0.0.1 127.0.0.1 - www -
```

14. Use the **:wq** command, then press Enter to save and close the file.

15. Use the **vi /etc/libsocks5.conf** command to open the proxy firewall client configuration file.

16. Tell the client to not use proxies for any requests that come directly to this particular machine:

```
noproxy - 127.0.0.1 - - -
```

17. Use the **:wq** command, then press Enter to save and close the file.

18. Start the SOCKS V5 server by typing the command **socks**.

19. Open a Web browser.

20. Type "http://127.0.0.1/" to access the local Web server.

21. The result should be an access error.

22. Use the **ps aux | grep socks** command to get the process ID for the SOCKS V5 daemon.

23. Use the **kill** *process_ID* command to stop the server.

Project 12.3

In this project, you will install and configure an IP Filtering firewall.

To accomplish this task, do the following:

1. Log in as root.

2. Use the command **man ipchains** to ensure that the ipchains package is installed. If not, install it from the distribution CD.

3. Use the command **ipchains -L** to list what chains currently exist and what their policies are.

4. Set the input chain's policy to REJECT by using the command **ipchains - P input REJECT**.

5. Start a Web browser on the machine.

6. Type "http://127.0.0.1/" to access the local Web server. This access attempt should be denied.

7. Add a rule that allows access to the Web server on the local machine when it comes from the local machine by using the command **ipchains -A input -s lo -d lo www ACCEPT**.

 The "lo" address refers to "local loopback" in ipchains. It is a great cheat instead of typing 127.0.0.1.

8. Use the command **http://127.0.0.1/** to access the local Web server. This access attempt should now work.

9. Use the command **ipchains-save > /root/saved_ipchains_rules** to save the new rule structure.

10. Use the command **vi /etc/rc.d/rc.local** to edit the local system initialization file.

11. Use the **G** command to go to the end of the file.

12. Use the command **/sbin/ipchains-restore < /root/ipchains-rules** to add rule restoration to the boot process.

13. Use the command **:wq**, then press Enter to save and close the file.

14. Reboot the machine with a command such as **shutdown -hf now**.

15. When the computer comes back up, log back in as root.

16. Use the command **ipchains -L input** to list the rules in the input chain. You should see the rule you added earlier in there.

17. Use the command **ipchains -F input** to flush the rule(s) out of the input chain.

18. Use the command **ipchains -P input ACCEPT** to reset the input chain's policy and return your system to normal.

## CHAPTER THIRTEEN

THE LINUX X ENVIRONMENT

AFTER READING THIS CHAPTER AND COMPLETING THE EXERCISES, YOU WILL BE ABLE TO:

➤ Install and configure the X window system

➤ Select and install the appropriate window manager

➤ Configure the user interface for individual needs

The X window system was developed to provide an easy-to-use interface for Unix. For the many Linux users who began computing in the Windows and Mac environment, a familiar user interface is essential. The X window system is similar enough to seem familiar and immediately usable, but the design is very different and the interface is much more configurable to individual needs and tastes.

An X Overview

When Unix was developed, computers were accessed using character-based terminals, capable of displaying characters from the ASCII character set, but not graphics. Unix was accessed using a character-based user interface. Over time, high-resolution bitmap display devices, such as Unix workstations and X terminals, capable of displaying graphics, were developed and used to access Unix. X was developed to access the graphics capabilities of display devices to provide a graphical user interface (GUI). The X Window System is a hardware-independent, distributed windowing system. It is portable, network-transparent, and runs on almost all types of computers. X provides a GUI to make computer use easier and more intuitive for users.

GUIs

Without a GUI, Unix treats the display device as a basic character terminal. A GUI that provides a windowing system is easier to use and more familiar to most users. The windowing system called X is widely available and runs on almost all types of hardware. Although the X Window System started to emerge around the same time as the Macintosh and MS-Windows and provides a GUI that appears and behaves in a manner somewhat similar, the design of the X Window System is very different.

Basically, a window is an area of the screen allocated to a given application program. X allows multiple open windows with applications running concurrently. X allows the use of a pointing device, usually a mouse, to move from window to window and to select objects on the screen.

When X was designed, the look of the graphics was not specified. The details of the visual display were left to the programmers. As a result, different styles of GUI are available. In addition, the X Window System was designed to be extremely configurable, allowing users to customize their X displays to suit their own preferences. Consequently, X Window System displays can look very different from one computer to another, with different colors, window styles, window borders, buttons, fonts, and icons.

X11 And XFree86

X was developed at the Massachusetts Institute of Technology (MIT). Project Athena, a 100 million-dollar project established in conjunction with DEC and IBM, was initiated in the early 1980s to design a computing environment for education. The goal was to transform the existing assortment of incompatible workstations from various vendors into a network of graphical workstations that allowed students and faculty to work at any computer on the campus and have access to their own files. This was a pioneering educational and computing development. X was developed to be the user interface for the network of workstations.

During the mid–eighties, while GUIs gained rapid acceptance among computer users (sparked by the release of the first Macintosh in 1984), X was developed and used primarily inside MIT and DEC. First released in 1984, X evolved rapidly through several versions. In 1986, in response to requests for X from outside organizations, X was first released commercially. X11, the widely released eleventh version, 1987, initiated popular acceptance of X and its continuing position as the dominant standard for Unix systems. Successive releases of X11 have added extra functionality while attempting to remain largely backward compatible. The current release is Release 6 (X11R6), specifically, X11R6.4.

X was open source from its beginning. MIT holds the rights to X, but gives it away for free. With the release of X11R2 in 1988, the X consortium, called X.Org, assumed management of the X standards. X.Org is the worldwide consortium empowered with the stewardship and collaborative development of the X Window System technology and standards. Official releases of X are provided through X.Org (**http://www.x.org**).

The version of the X Window System that is provided with all Linux distributions is XFree86. Unless you specifically acquire and install a different version, such as a commercial version like Motif, your Linux system installation will include XFree86. It is free software—designed, implemented, and distributed by The XFree86 Project, Inc., a not-for-profit corporation, initiated in 1992 by four developers who were unhappy with the existing support for Intel-based Unix platforms and funded by contributions. The XFree86 Project is a member of the X consortium and provides enhancements to the X Window System software, with ports to many Intel-based Unix and Unix-like operating systems. XFree86 includes all of the required binaries, support files, libraries, and tools.

13

X Window System Architecture

The X Window System follows the general Unix paradigm of separate components, rather than one huge piece of software, allowing a particular part of the system to be changed by replacing the relevant component without affecting the other parts of the system. The X Window System software consists of multiple cooperating parts that run independently and concurrently.

The X Window System is client/server software. Client/server computing is a model in which the client software requests a service (processing or data) from the server software and the server software responds to the request with the appropriate service. The client and server software can be located on the same computer or on different computers. One common client/server application is the WWW. The browser is the client and the HTTPD server is the server. The browser sends the request for a file to the HTTPD server and the workstation downloads it to the browser, which then displays the information.

The center of the X Window System is the X server, which is one specific component made up of a set of XFree86 packages aimed at various graphics levels such as SVGA. The X server is located on your Linux system and drives the graphics and input hardware. The server is windowing software that can organize the physical display area into sub-areas known as windows and can control and manage many activities simultaneously. The server monitors input and renders drawings on the display. The server is hardware-dependent and knows how to communicate with your video card, keyboard, and pointing device.

A multitude of clients are also available. Any application that requires the use of display graphics is an X client. The client is the software that performs the operations, such as a database application or email application. When the client requires a graphics display, it sends a request to the X server, which paints the requested display. The server sends a confirming or error message in response to the request. The client also accepts messages initiated by the server. The X server listens for input and sends messages containing input, such as keyboard input or mouse clicks and coordinates, to the client. The client accepts and processes the events sent by the server.

The X server communicates with an X client using the X protocol. For the client and the server to communicate, they must "speak" the same language. Just as spoken languages have rules (grammar, word definitions, spelling), computer communication has rules called protocols. Protocols specify the format and meaning of the data transmissions exchanged by client/server software. The X protocol is the language used to communicate between X server and X client. The X protocol is freely available so computer vendors can implement their own X server and/or clients. As long as the software understands the X protocol, the programs will work with any other X servers or clients. Thus, X client programs can be written to run on any system and the display will work with any hardware under any operating system that has an X server running.

The X server does not care where the client is located. It can communicate equally well with a client on the same computer, or via network connection with a client located on the other side of the country. As long as the client understands the X protocol, the X server can communicate with it and respond to its requests for a display. In addition, the X protocol is an open standard allowing communication between different types of computers. An application can run on one computer, using its CPU, and display output on another computer, even when the other computer is a different type of computer. For instance, an X server running on MS-Windows can display graphics on its local display in response to X protocol messages from an X client application located on a remote Unix computer via a network connection.

X client/server applications running over a modem can result in long response times. A faster network connection, for example, cable modem, is a practical requirement.

If you are familiar with client/server computing in other applications, you may find the X Window System model confusing. Most client/server applications consist of client software on the local computer and server software on a remote computer. The user interacts with the client software and the client software communicates with the remote server to obtain data or services. The preceding Web model example is a more typical client/server application. The user interacts with the client, the browser, and the browser communicates with the remote server, the HTTPD server, to request file downloads. In the X Window System, the user interacts with the server, the local software; the remote software is the client software that sends requests to the X server for services—painting a graphical display.

The X server is responsible for display management. This includes opening a window and painting the display requested by the client. Window management, such as positioning and sizing windows, displaying borders, and moving from one window to another, is handled by client software called a window manager.

Window Managers

General X clients are split into more than one category. The first of these categories is the window management X component. A window manager is an X client program to help you manage multiple windows and use them effectively. The window manager controls the appearance of windows and provides the means by which you interact with them. The window manager is responsible for positioning a new window, providing window titles and borders, moving the location of an existing window, changing window size, iconifying windows, switching the focus from one window to another, and removing a window.

13

Unix is user-centered, providing users with the ability to customize their environments. The X Window System, embodying the Unix philosophy, is designed to be maximally customizable. People are different and like different interfaces. The separation of the window management software from the hardware-dependent server software allows window management software to be developed more easily. Consequently, many window managers have been developed, including window managers that emulate other windowing systems, such as Windows 95, NeXTStep, or Amiga. You may choose which window manager you want to run, based on your individual preferences and needs. In addition, many window managers build flexibility into their software, allowing considerable customization within the window management software itself. This is quite different from the Windows or Macintosh systems, where the window manager is built in, leaving you little control over the look of your display.

Your window manager defines the GUI and determines the look and feel of your X Window system. A window manager may provide only a basic set of functions (move, resize, hide, or close windows) or an extremely elaborate and/or configurable interface. More elaborate interfaces use more resources—memory, screen real estate, time to display, and disk space. Different window managers implement the basic functions differently. For instance, there are three different ways the window manager can handle the initial placement of a window on the screen:

➤ Show an outline of the new window which you are allowed to position

➤ Random placement decided by the window manager

➤ Display every new window in the same place, determined by the user

Other functions handled differently include how many and which programs are started when X is started; how you change the window focus; how you move or resize windows; how overlapping windows are handled; how you edit files; if, how, and where icons are placed; how you maximize windows; and many others.

More elaborate features include configurable buttons, backgrounds, menus, borders, button panels, audio features, user-specified key and pointer button bindings, and animation. Additional functions offered by some window managers include virtual screens or workspaces. A user might design a virtual workspace for a specific purpose, such as email, that includes the applications needed, and display the appropriate workspace when needed, such as a dock or a wharf—a location where commonly used applications can be stored for immediate access.

OPEN LOOK is a GUI standard that was developed by Sun to provide a unified look and feel to different workstations. OPEN LOOK was fairly widely used in the Unix world and was the standard used in Sun's Open Windows graphical interface. Motif was developed as an alternative to OPEN LOOK and is now provided on almost all standard distributions of Unix. Some window managers for Linux follow the OPEN LOOK or Motif standards.

Some widely used window managers that can be installed on Linux are:

➤ **AfterStep** AfterStep was based originally on the look and feel of the NeXTStep interface, the operating system developed for NeXT computers, but has been significantly altered in response to user feedback. It has a small footprint, meaning that it does not take up a lot of RAM, and so is not a drain on system performance. (**http://www.afterstep.org**)

➤ **AMIwm** Amiga Window Manager tries to make your display look and feel like an Amiga Workbench screen. (**http://www.lysator.liu.se/~marcus/amiwm.html**)

➤ **BlackBox** BlackBox emphasizes minimalism and speed. It has the basic set of features, but does not include extended features or decorative features which detract from the main goal: speed. It has a small code base, written in C++. (**http://blackbox.alug.org/**)

➤ **ctwm** Claude's Tab Window Manager features up to 32 multiple virtual screens, called workspaces. Each workspace can be customized using different colors, names, backgrounds, and buttons and you switch from one workspace to another. It is based on twm from the MIT X11 distribution, modified to accommodate the use of several virtual screens. (**http://brugd.ctrl-c.liu.se/~dl/ctwm/**)

➤ **Enlightenment** Enlightenment, often called E, emphasizes configurability in both look and feel. It is color-intensive and you can design your own window borders, menus, and other screen elements. Enlightenment is an elaborate window manager with many features. It is large and runs best on high-end machines. (**http://www.enlightenment.org**)

➤ **FLWM** Fast Light Window Manager emphasizes space, aiming to take up as little screen space as possible. It has borders and titles as thin as possible and minimized programs are picked from a pop-up menu, not wasting space with icons. Small, fast code. (**http://www.cinenet.net/users/spitzak/flwm**)

➤ **fvwm** F Virtual Window Manager is the most common window manager for Linux. (F can stand for anything you like—famous, fantastic, fabulous, flashy, fine, feeble, funky, Fred's.) Provides a 3D look to window frames and a simple virtual desktop. It was derived from twm, and redesigned to minimize memory consumption. The current version is called fvwm2. A version called fvwm95 is available, designed to emulate Windows 95. (**http://www.fvwm.org**)

13

➤ **GWM** Generic Window Manager allows users to build a window manager by writing to files that describe objects on the screen, used as decorations around X applications windows, as pop-up menus, or as independent windows. It should be able to emulate efficiently other window managers, and play the same role for window managers as EMACS does for text editors. It comes with already-defined profiles (standard, vtwm-like, twm-like, mwm-like) or users may design exactly what they want. It is not meant for use by novice computer users. (**http://www.inria.fr/koala/gwm**)

➤ **IceWM** The goal of IceWM is to provide a small, fast, and familiar window manager, compatible with the mwm where appropriate. It is designed to emulate the look of Motif, OS/2 Warp 4, OS/2 Warp 3, and Windows 95. It has been coded from scratch for speed and flexibility, rather than derived from another window manager. (**http://icewm.tux.nu**)

➤ **LessTif** LessTif is a free Motif clone that provides a Motif interface and will run Motif applications. (**http://www.lesstif.org**)

➤ **MWM** Motif Window Manager is a commercial product, not available for free. It is the standard window manager on most commercial Unix workstations.

➤ **OLWM** Open Look Window Manager implements parts of the OPEN LOOK graphical user interface. OLVWM is a version that has been modified to support virtual desktop that is larger than the actual screen.

➤ **twm** Tab Window Manager is an older window manager that provides basic capabilities. It was released by the X consortium with the X Window System and predates MS Windows 3. It is the default window manager released with the X source. It is fairly large. Many newer window managers are modifications of twm.

➤ **vtwm** Virtual Tab Window Manager has the look and feel of twm, modified to support virtual windows.

➤ **WindowMaker** WindowMaker is designed to emulate the look and feel of part of the NeXTStep GUI. It's meant to be fast, relatively small, feature-rich and easy to configure. (**http://windowmaker.org**)

➤ **wm2** Window Manager 2 takes the minimalist approach, providing only five functions:

➤ Move windows around the screen

➤ Resize windows, both horizontally and vertically

➤ Hide windows

➤ Restore hidden windows

➤ Delete windows

➤ **wm2** Does not provide any configurability, icons, a virtual desktop, Nor button panels. It simply adds an attractive frame to each window. It is simple, fast, and small.(**http://123.org/wm2**)

Display Managers

The second part of the general X client component is the display manager. There is less flexibility here, as your choice of window manager or choice of desktop environment (discussed in the next section) often determines this item for you. The most common display managers encountered are:

➤ **gdm** The display manager for the GNOME desktop environment.

➤ **kdm** The display manager for KDE.

➤ **xdm** The general X Window System display manager.

Desktop Environments

The most recent development in providing Unix and Unix-like systems with a GUI that is easy for desktop users is the desktop environment. Desktop environments are more than a window manager. They are a suite of applications that include, in addition to a window manager, a file manager, a panel control center, and many other components. There are two major desktop environments for Linux: GNOME and KDE.

GNU Network Object Model Environment (GNOME) is part of the GNU Project, started in 1984 to develop a completely free Unix-like operating system. GNOME is a desktop environment built entirely of free, open source software. It includes a panel (for starting applications and displaying status), a desktop (where data and applications can be placed), and a set of standard desktop tools and applications, such as a calendar and an address book. GNOME is distributed with the Red Hat distribution, as shown in Figure 13.1.

GNOME is not a window manager. In fact, GNOME must be run in conjunction with a window manager. GNOME is not dependent on any one window manager. Instead, GNOME provides standards so that window managers can be GNOME-compliant. Window managers that are not GNOME-compliant will not provide all the functionality of GNOME. GNOME is distributed with Enlightenment. In addition, some small window managers have been written specifically for GNOME. A list is available at the GNOME Web site at **http://www.gnome.org**.

13

Figure 13.1   The GNOME Desktop Environment in Red Hat 6.1.

K Desktop Environment (KDE) is a complete, integrated desktop environment that is both free and open source and runs on most flavors of Unix. It includes a file manager, a help system, a configuration system, a terminal emulator, tools and utilities, and an ever increasing number of applications, including mail and news clients, drawing programs, a PostScript and a DVI viewer, etc. KDE is available in several languages. KDE is shown in Figure 13.2, and is distributed with Su.S.E., Caldera, and Red Hat.

KDE is not a window manager either, but includes its own window manager called kwm. However, if you wish to use another window manager, you can change. KDE provides a development environment so that software can be developed to run with KDE.

Application Clients

Another client component of the X Window System is the wide range of applications available for use with X. These applications run the gamut of Internet interfaces such as Web clients, solitaire games provided with desktop environments, graphics programs and tools, and more. Any program that runs graphically within X is a client.

INSTALLING AND CONFIGURING XFREE86

In order for the GUI to work correctly, it must be able to accept information from the keyboard and the pointing device and to display information correctly for your particular video card and monitor. Consequently, the X server must be

Figure 13.2 The KDE Desktop Environment in Red Hat 6.1 for the superuser.

installed that knows how to communicate with your hardware. The installation procedure for XFree86 includes configuring it for the correct types of hardware.

Obtaining The Current Version Files

XFree86 is part of every major distribution of Linux. The current release is XFree86-3.3.5, based on X Window System X11R6.3. When XFree86-4.0 is released, it will be based on X11R6.4. To see what version you currently have, enter the following:

```
X -showconfig
```

XFree86 is developed and released through The XFree86 Project. Both source and binary files and documentation are available at its Web site (**http://www.xfree86.org**). Release notes for new releases describe the changes. Check the release notes to determine whether you want or need to upgrade to the newer version. At the current time, the Web site recommends that users upgrade to Xfree86-3.3.5 because some problems were fixed.

Installing The X Window System

XFree86 is installed by default in all the major distributions of Linux. In most initial installations of Linux, you do not need to install XFree86 separately. However, you can install XFree86 separately in your existing Linux system, for instance, if you need to upgrade to a newer version of XFree86.

Before installing XFree86, you need to determine if it runs on your hardware and to identify the X server that is appropriate for your hardware. The release notes and README files provided with the XFree86 distribution contain a list of the video cards supported. Unless you have an old or unusual card, your card is probably supported.

13

Because the X server is the driver for your hardware, you need to download and install the appropriate X server. The information that you need to identify the appropriate server should be in the manual for your video card. The following servers are currently available:

➤ **X8514.tgz** Server for 8514-based boards.

➤ **XAGX.tgz** Server for AGX-based boards.

➤ **XI128.tgz** Server for the Number Nine Imagine 128.

➤ **XMach32.tgz** Server for Mach32-based boards.

➤ **XMach64.tgz** Server for Mach64-based boards.

➤ **XMach8.tgz** Server for Mach8-based boards.

➤ **XMono.tgz** Server for monochrome video modes.

➤ **XP9K.tgz** Server for P9000-based boards.

➤ **XS3.tgz** Server for S3-based boards.

➤ **XS3V.tgz** Server for the S3 ViRGE and ViRGE/VX (considered beta).

➤ **XSVGA.tgz** Server for SuperVGA-based boards.

➤ **XVGA16.tgz** Server for VGA 16.

➤ **XW32.tgz** Server for ET4000/W32-based boards.

If you are unable to identify a server for your specific hardware, select the generic XVGA16, or possibly XSVGA, server.

 Installing an X server with the wrong specific video card driver can damage your system! Incorrect settings can cause harm to your monitor. Monitors driven at the wrong clock rates will physically burn up.

XFree86 can be downloaded from **http://www.xfree86.org**. Several files must be downloaded, in addition to the appropriate X server. Download the XVGA16 server because it is used by the configuration utility. Download the other files from the download directory, e.g., preinst.sh (pre-installation script), Xbin.tgz (the rest of the binaries), Xcfg.tgz (config files), Xdoc.tgz (documentation), and so on.

XFree86 should be installed in /usr/X11R6. If this directory does not exist, create it from the root account. Be sure to unpack the downloaded files in this directory, since the filenames are relative to this directory. Unpack the files using a command such as:

```
gzip -dc Xbin.tgz | tar xfB -
```

After the files are unpacked, you will have several subdirectories in the X11R6 directory, for example, bin and lib.

After installation, be sure that /usr/X11R6/bin is on your path. Also, be sure that the /usr/X11R6/lib can be located by the runtime linker. To do this, add the line

```
/usr/X11R6/lib
```

to the file /etc/ld.so.conf and run /sbin/ldconfig as root.

Before proceeding to configure your X Window System, as described in the next section, run the script, preinst.sh. It will check your system and notify you of missing files and other problems.

Installing The X Font Server And Fonts

Another component of the X Window System is the X Font Server. This program's job is to keep track of all the fonts that are installed and display them when they are requested. It can actually operate across a network, keeping a centralized archive of fonts on one machine so that not all machines have to spare hard drive space for them. To install the Font Server, place the file Xfsrv.tgz into the /usr/X11R6 directory and unpack it with the same procedure as with the other programs, using a format such as:

```
gzip -dc Xfsrv.tgz | tar xfB -
```

Once the server is installed, all X Window System font definition files go into subdirectories within /usr/X11R6/lib/fonts. If you like to keep your additions separate from the main package, then type something similar to "mkdir /usr/X11R6/lib/fonts/added" and put the fonts in this folder.

Font files have names such as "helvB08.pcf.gz". Leave them in this format, it saves quite a bit of space on a font server to have all of the font definition files compressed. Once you have all of the ones you want installed, type "mkfontdir /usr/X11R6/lib/fonts/added" to update the font listing file for that directory, and then "xset fp rehash" to tell the X server to revisit the font path and load the new font database files.

Configuring Your X Window System

When the X Window System is started, it reads a configuration file called /etc /XF86Config. The utility, XF86Setup, provides a GUI interface to create and modify the configuration file. If your video card is not VGA-compatible, you need to use the text-based setup utility, xf 86config, instead. The setup procedure is basically the same, but with a different interface.

If you are using a fixed-frequency monitor, you need to do the configuration manually.

In order to configure XFree86, you need to know the following information about your hardware which should be available in the hardware manuals:

➤ **Video card** Model name, chipset, clock chip, amount of memory, and whether it is VGA-compatible

➤ **Monitor** Horizontal sync rate and vertical refresh rate

➤ **Mouse** Protocol

The Red Hat distribution provides its own configuration utility called Xconfigurator that performs similarly to XF86Setup.

Configuring Your System Using XF86Setup

When you start XF86Setup, it will look for an existing configuration file. If it finds one, it will ask if you wish to use the existing settings. If you have a working setup, you probably want to use the current settings, just changing selected settings. You may want to make a backup copy of the existing configuration file before you start making changes.

Run XF86Setup to configure XFree86 for the appropriate hardware. It will start the X server VGA16 and display the graphical main setup screen shown in Figure 13.3. This screen provides buttons for each configuration that is required:

➤ Mouse

➤ Keyboard

➤ Video Card

➤ Mode

➤ Monitor

➤ Other

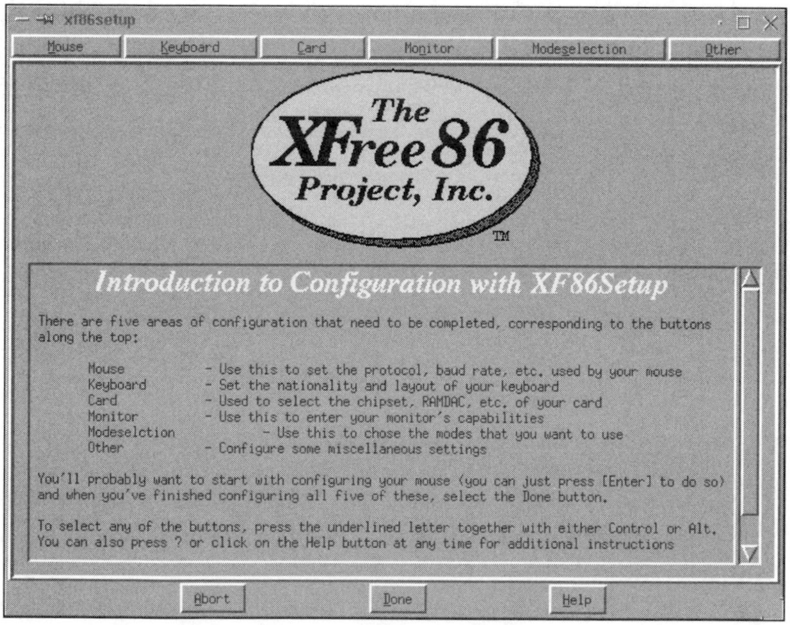

Figure 13.3 The XF86Setup utility, main screen.

At any time, you can press Abort to end the program without saving any settings, with the exception of the mouse settings. Mouse settings become effective as soon as they are set.

You need to configure the mouse first so that it will work correctly while you configure the other devices. In the mouse section of the XF86Setup program (shown in Figure 13.4), a mouse with three buttons is displayed on the screen.

If you move your mouse around, the program should display coordinates. If you press a button, the program should turn the corresponding screen button black. Your mouse configuration is done if this all works correctly. If it does not, you need to change the configuration.

You can select a different mouse device or a different protocol. To select a different mouse device, press the N key, followed by a Tab. Press the P key to try a different protocol. If the mouse pointer does something when you move the mouse, but does not move correctly, try a different protocol. The most common mouse protocol is Microsoft; the second most common is Mouse-Systems. Press the A key to apply the changes.

If your mouse only has two buttons, select Emulate3Buttons. Clicking both buttons at once should emulate clicking the third button. You can also try changing the ChordMiddle setting.

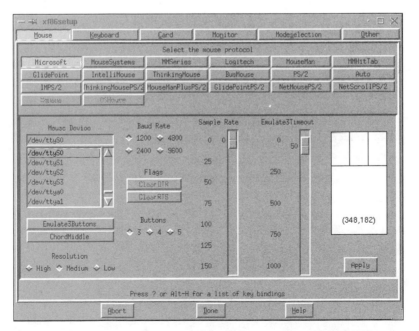

Figure 13.4 The XF86Setup utility, Mouse configuration screen.

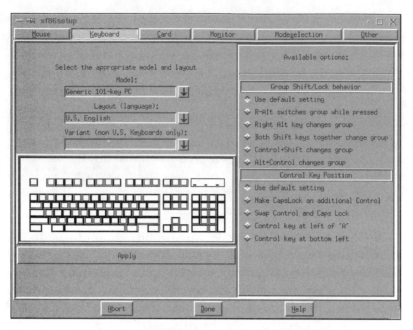

Figure 13.5   The XF86Setup utility, Keyboard configuration screen.

In the keyboard configuration section (shown in Figure 13.5) select the model and layout of your keyboard. A graphical representation of the selected keyboard is displayed and changes when you select a different model.

In the video card configuration section (shown in Figure 13.6) select the model name for your card. If there is a README file button for your model, click the README button. Click Detailed Setup to see the selected settings. If your card is not listed or if the detailed settings are not those given in the README file, you can use detailed setup to set options. Select the appropriate X server. If the server did not probe correctly, select the correct chipset for your card and the Ramdac. Select the clockchip. Set the maximum speed of your Ramdac. Select the amount of RAM on your video card.

In the modeselection section (shown in Figure 13.7), you can select the depth you prefer to use (how many colors can be displayed at once) and select all of the modes you want to use. If your hardware cannot support all of the depth and mode combinations you select, the server will reject the combinations when it tries to start.

In the monitor configuration section (shown in Figure 13.8), enter the horizontal and vertical frequency ranges that your monitor supports. If your monitor supports several different frequencies or ranges, list them all, separated by commas.

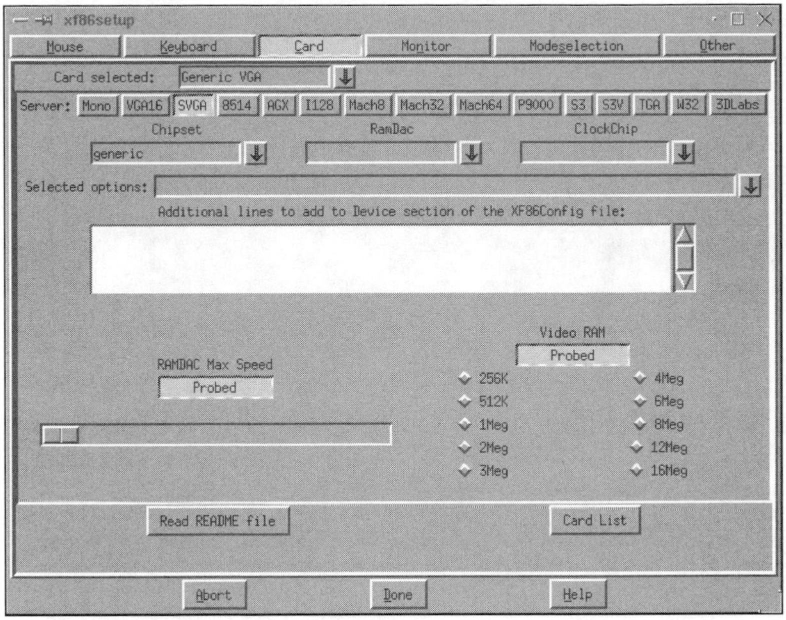

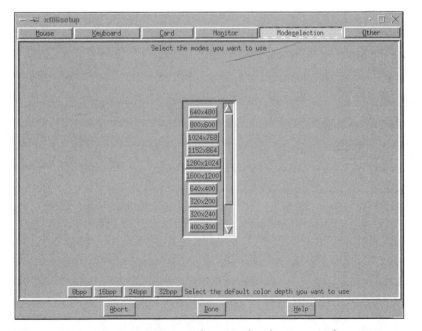

Figure 13.6   The XF86Setup utility, video Card configuration screen.

When you have completed all of the configuration to your satisfaction, press Done, followed by ok. XF86Setup will return to text mode and will attempt to start the X server. If it is unable to start the server, you will be asked if you

Figure 13.7   The XF86Setup utility, Modeselection configuration screen.

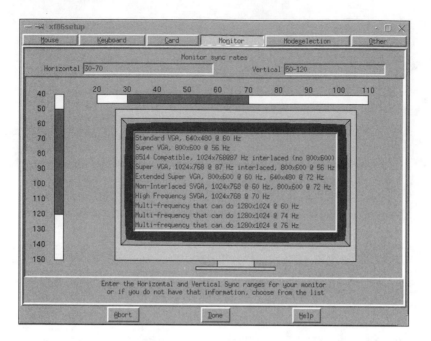

Figure 13.8 The XF86Setup utility, Monitor configuration screen.

would like to return to setup and try again. If the server starts, you can click a button that saves the configuration settings to the configuration file. Finish by clicking OK.

If the server starts but the display doesn't look exactly right, you can use xvidtune (shown in Figure 13.9) to make adjustments. You can access it by clicking a button in XF86Setup or by entering xvidtune at a command line. Read the warning and click OK. Click Auto. Click whatever changes are needed to adjust the

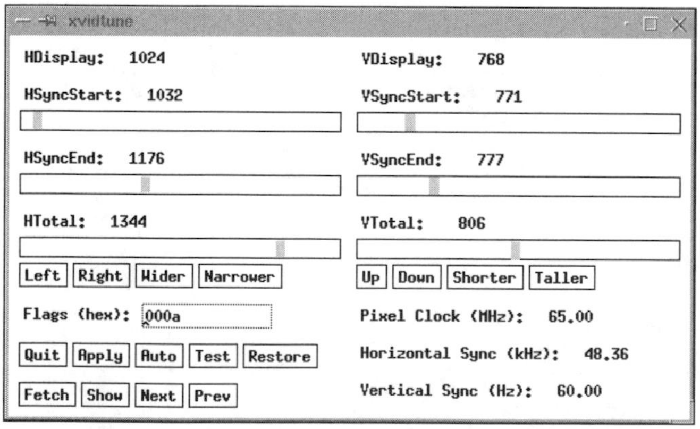

Figure 13.9 The xvidtune configuration tool.

display, for example, Up, Left, Taller, etc. When you are satisfied, press Show to see a **ModeLine** command. Copy the **ModeLine** into the XF86Config file. When you are finished, click Quit to exit the program.

Introduction To XF86Config

Although almost all X server configuration is done with tools today, it is still important to be able to scan your way through /etc/X11/XF86Config and tweak it if necessary. This file is broken down into a series of sections that are often started and ended with the following code:

```
# ****************************************************************************
# SectionName section.
# ****************************************************************************

Section "SectionName"

# This is the actual meat of the section. In this case
# the meat is only a comment.

EndSection
```

The following sections exist in XF86Config, listed in the order they typically appear:

➤ **Files** Path settings for RGB (Red Green Blue) and Font data.

➤ **ServerFlags** This section is often blank, but could contain flags that shut off various server features, such as key combinations for resizing the screen.

➤ **Keyboard** The data corresponding to your particular keyboard.

➤ **Pointer** The definition of which pointing device—mouse, pen, or other supported item—and the parameters necessary for using it.

➤ **Monitor** The necessary statistics for your monitor so that X knows what it is capable of.

➤ **Device** Information on your graphics device or video card. There can be more than one Device section.

➤ **Screen** The video resolution and color depth modes you chose for your X settings. There is one section for each mode you want.

Networking

The X Window System allows you to run an X client program on one host and display the output on another host. You can distribute computing among a group of networked computers. The client program does not generate the graphics and send bitmaps across the network to be displayed. The bandwidth required would be prohibitive. Rather, the X client uses the X protocol to

13

send display requests (for example, display a circle of a specified size at the specified location) to the X server, which then generates the graphics.

Because an X client can send display requests to any X server to which it has a TCP/IP connection, the destination display must be specified. When discussing X, the term display refers to a collection of monitors accessed by a single keyboard and pointing device. A single keyboard can control more than one monitor. Thus, a designator for the output location needs to specify the exact screen. The format of the screen designator is

```
host:displaynumber.screennumber
```

where host is the host name or IP address of the computer where the X server is located. If you have a single server and a single screen on the target display, it is designated as 0.0. If you have more than one, you indicate which one using the displaynumber and the screennumber.

The screen designator is stored in the environment variable, DISPLAY. X clients send display requests to the X server specified by DISPLAY. You can see the DISPLAY value that sends your display to your own screen by typing:

```
echo $DISPLAY
:0.0
```

DISPLAY values that send the display to another computer might look like the following:

```
197.134.15.2:0.0
host2.mynet.com:0.0
```

If you set the DISPLAY on a remote computer to display on your system, you also need to set your computer to accept the display from the remote computer. To give permission to a remote host to display on your system, enter

```
xhost host
```

where host is the name or IP address of the computer you are allowing to display on your system. For instance

```
xhost host2.mynet.com
```

permits the remote host, host2, to display on your system. The command:

```
xhost +
```

allows anyone to display on your Linux screen. You can explicitly prevent a host from displaying on your system using the command:

```
xhost -host2.mynet.com
```

Managing User Window Environments

When the X Window System is started, a configuration script determines the opening environment of your screen. It can start programs that you want to run automatically, such as an xterm terminal emulator session or a clock, and starts your selected window manager. As system administrator, you can determine whether a system configuration script or a configuration script in the individual users home directory is run on X startup.

X is started with the command:

```
startx
```

Startx is a shell script located in /usr/X11R6/bin. As system administrator, you can modify the startx script. The only requirement for the startx script is the command:

```
exec xinit
```

The **xinit** command starts the X Window System, starting the X server and one client program. You can specify which X server and which client to start or you can allow **xinit** to start a default server and client.

If no server is specified on the command line, **xinit** looks in the users home directory for a script named .xserverrc and runs that script to start the server. If it does not find the script, it runs the server X:0. It searches the users path for X. As system administrator, it is your responsibility to ensure that **xinit** can find X. Create a link called X in /usr/X11R6/bin that is a link to the correct X server file (for example, XVGA16).

If no X client is specified on the command line, **xinit** looks in the users home directory for a script named .xinitrc and runs that script to start the client programs. If it does not find the script, it runs the following command to start an xterm session as the first client.

```
xterm -geometry +1+1 -n login -display :0
```

You can specify the X server on the **xinit** command line in the startx script with -- and the path. For example:

```
exec xinit -- /usr/X11R6/bin/Xsvga  :0
```

13

You can specify the first client on the command line also. The client program and its arguments should be the first **xinit** arguments on the command line.

For the client and/or server program names to be recognized as program names, they must begin with a slash (/) or a dot (.). Otherwise, **xinit** treats them as arguments.

As system administrator, you can define one central configuration script. You can create a default .xinitrc to be installed in each user account that references a system startup file. Or, you can specify the configuration script on the **xinit** command line in the startx script. For instance:

```
exec xinit /etc/X11/xinit/xinitrc
```

For the client and/or server program names or script names to be recognized as program names, they must begin with a slash (/) or a dot (.). Otherwise, **xinit** treats them as arguments.

X Application Resource Management

The system administrator or even individual users can configure the resources consumed by the various X applications. For global X resource configurations, go to the directory /usr/X11R6/lib/X11/app–defaults/. Each file in this directory is named for the X application it regulates. The key to these files is that you can change them globally here, or use them to create an .Xresources file in /etc/skel for new user accounts where only specific information is changed.

An example of the contents of one of these files will serve to show you how to quickly pick out items that you may want to change. Take the application GV—GhostView, the Ghostscript file viewer available under X—which has a file in this directory. This file begins with:

```
!
!  gv_user.ad
!  User specific application defaults for gv
!  Copyright (C) 1995, 1996, 1997  Johannes Plass
!


!########## gv_user_res.dat
```

The statements beginning with exclamation points are all comments. Hash marks only serve as placeholders or show emphasis. Next, you have a section prefaced with:

```
!##### Application specific Resources
```

This label tells you that you are about to get into the value assignments that apply only to a specific application. Because you are in the middle of an application–specific file, it is not terribly surprising to discover that the entire contents are devoted to GV. Even nicer, however, is that you can take any one of these lines and simply duplicate it in ~/.Xresources. All of the variables in an X resource file are specifically named in two parts: the program in question (GV in the examples that follow), and then the variable name.

Take this first section of the file:

```
GV.pageMedia:           automatic
GV.orientation:                 automatic
GV.fallbackOrientation:     portrait
GV.swapLandscape:       False
GV.autoCenter:          True
GV.antialias:           True
GV.respectDSC:          True
GV.ignoreEOF:           True
GV.confirmPrint:        True
GV.reverseScrolling:    False
GV.scrollingEyeGuide:   True
GV.autoResize:          True
GV.maximumWidth:        screen-20
GV.maximumHeight:       screen-44
GV.minimumWidth:        400
GV.minimumHeight:       430
GV.confirmQuit:                 1
GV.watchFile:           False
GV.watchFileFrequency:          1000
GV.showTitle:           True
GV.miscMenuEntries:     redisplay       \n\
                        # update        \n\
                        stop            \n\
                        line            \n\
                        toggle_current  \n\
                        toggle_even     \n\
                        toggle_odd      \n\
                        unmark          \n\
                        line            \n\
                        print_all       \n\
                        print_marked    \n\
                        save_all        \n\
                        save_marked
```

Notice that the format for each entry is "program.variable: value". In addition, you can see that the item GV.miscMenuEntries has more than one value. One of these ("update") has a hash mark in front of it, meaning that it is commented out within the value tree. The rest all have the value \n\ after them. This \n\ actually tells X that the definition continues down to the next line.

If you wanted to change just a few items for your own account, you would create a file ~/.Xresources and perhaps add code such as:

```
GV.maximumWidth:     screen-25
GV.maximumHeight:    screen-50
GV.confirmQuit:      0
GV.orientation:      portrait
```

Utilizing The X Environment

The X Window System consists of a hierarchy of windows. The top-level window, called the root window, is opened at startup. The root window fills the entire display. It is different than other windows and cannot be moved or resized. The root window is the backdrop on which all other windows are opened.

Starting Programs

When the X Window System starts, one or more programs may be started from the configuration script, .xinitrc. Some standard command-line arguments are available to set window characteristics for X clients. Table 13.1 lists the arguments available.

Colors are specified using reasonable names, for example, red, blue, green, red3. A list of all the color names available is stored in the file, /usr/X11R6/ lib/X11/rgb.txt. The –display argument can specify a host where the output will be displayed, using the format described in the previous section. A display

Table 13.1 Arguments for X client applications.

Argument	Description
-bw *num*	border width in pixels
-bd *color*	border color
-fg *color*	foreground color (for text or graphics)
-bg *color*	background color
-display *display-name*	specifies location of X server to display the output
-fn *font*	specifies font
-geometry *offsets*	location on screen where window opens.
-iconic	starts with icon, not open window
-rv	switches background and foreground colors
-title *string*	title for window title bar
-name *string*	name for the application
-xrm resource-*string*	specifies resource value

value specified on the command line overrides the display value specified in the DISPLAY environment variable.

The locations for the geometry argument are given in the format

```
-geometry charxlines+leftoffset+rightoffset
```

where *char* is the number of characters in a line of the window, *lines* is the number of lines in the window, *leftoffset* is the number of pixels from the left side of the screen and *topoffset* is the number of pixels from the top. For example, you can start your xterm session with the following command:

```
xterm -geometry 80x25+10+40
```

The xterm window would open with 80 characters per line and 25 lines in the window. 80 × 25 is the default in char and lines are not specified. The window will open 10 pixels from the left side of the screen and 40 pixels from the top of the screen.

Any program can be started from the command line in an xterm terminal emulation window. The arguments just listed can also be entered at the command line.

Using Windows

The functionality of your X environment is determined by your window manager. The functions, buttons, and menus available on the screen and the methods you use to move and resize windows depend on which windows manager you are using. Theoretically, you can run X11 without a window manager, but you will simply have a plain open window that cannot be moved or sized.

All window managers provide a basic set of functions. You can display many windows, usually overlapping if necessary. You can change focus from one window to another, either by just moving the mouse pointer over a different window or by clicking in a different window. Window managers allow you to move a window by dragging it to a new location with the mouse. They allow you to resize a window, usually by dragging an edge of a window to a new size. Some allow you to resize the window, keeping the same dimensions, by dragging the corner of the window. A means, usually a button in a top corner, is provided to close a window. Also, a method is provided, usually a button in a top corner, to shrink a window and store it, often as an icon on a taskbar. The window manager allows you to redisplay a minimized application, usually by clicking on an icon. Most window managers provide a menu of available functions when you click on the right mouse button.

13

For example, fvwm, the most common window manager, paints a border around most windows that consists of a bar on each side and a small L shaped section on each corner. There is an additional top bar called the title bar which displays the name of the window. Some basic mouse functions are shown in Table 3.2.

Press the right mouse button to display a menu of window operations. By default, there are buttons on the title bar. The left one brings up a list of window options. The right one iconifies the window.

All of these are configurable. The mouse clicks can be configured to perform different functions. Buttons can be defined to perform any available function. For instance, there can be up to 10 user-defined buttons on the title bar. The buttons can execute configuration functions as well as window manipulation functions.

Here are some additional functions offered by different window managers:

➤ A control panel that allows you to configure the window manager.

➤ A taskbar with iconized applications.

➤ Button panels with sets of functions.

➤ An application menu. You can configure the menu to include the applications that you might want to use.

➤ Virtual screens. You can create several different virtual screens. You can set up a screen that provides the needed features and applications for word processing and another screen that provides an environment for Web surfing. You can switch between the screens.

➤ An application dock. A place where you can store frequently used applications for easy access.

The more features and functions a window manager has, the more resources it requires, in terms of memory and disk space, and the slower it displays. You need to take the resources available on your Linux machine into account when deciding which window manager to use. Some users require advanced functionality, others do not require it.

Table 3.2   Basic mouse functions.

Function	Description
Press left mouse button when pointer is located in the title bar or the side bars	To move the window
Press the left mouse button when the pointer is located in the corner	To resize the window
Press the right mouse button	To display a menu of window operations

The **xman** Command

X provides a utility for viewing man pages in a GUI. To access this utility, type:

```
xman
```

You first get a small dialog box containing several buttons, shown in Figure 13.10. When you click the Manual Page button, an information screen is displayed as shown in Figure 13.11.

Dragging down from the Options button to the Display Directory choice gives you a menu of man pages, as shown in Figure 13.12. You can browse through a listing of all the available man pages and select a man page to view using the mouse.

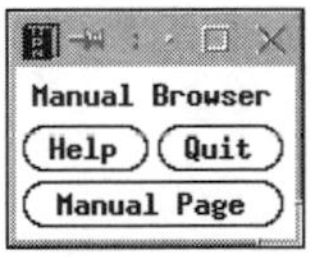

Figure 13.10   The xman tool.

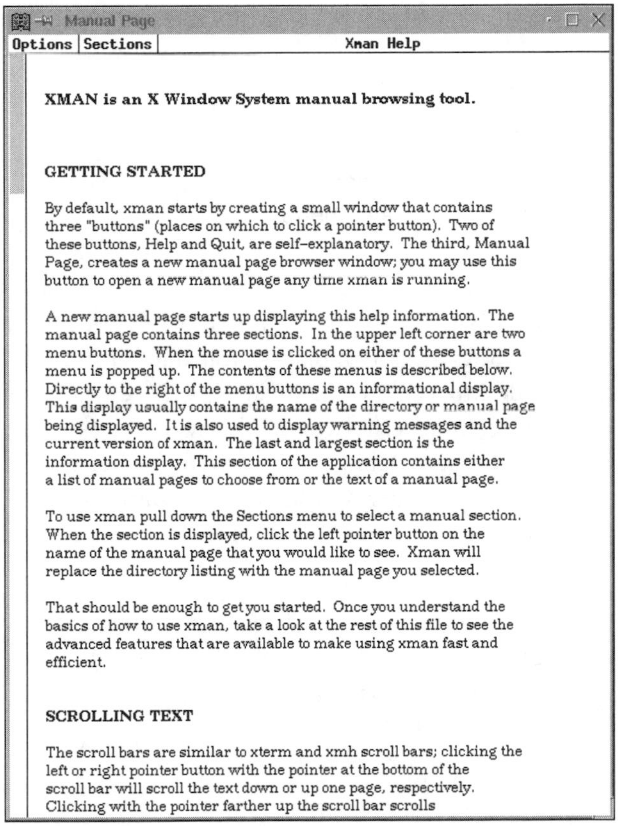

13

Manual Page

| Options | Sections | Xman Help |

XMAN is an X Window System manual browsing tool.

GETTING STARTED

By default, xman starts by creating a small window that contains three "buttons" (places on which to click a pointer button). Two of these buttons, Help and Quit, are self-explanatory. The third, Manual Page, creates a new manual page browser window; you may use this button to open a new manual page any time xman is running.

A new manual page starts up displaying this help information. The manual page contains three sections. In the upper left corner are two menu buttons. When the mouse is clicked on either of these buttons a menu is popped up. The contents of these menus is described below. Directly to the right of the menu buttons is an informational display. This display usually contains the name of the directory or manual page being displayed. It is also used to display warning messages and the current version of xman. The last and largest section is the information display. This section of the application contains either a list of manual pages to choose from or the text of a manual page.

To use xman pull down the Sections menu to select a manual section. When the section is displayed, click the left pointer button on the name of the manual page that you would like to see. Xman will replace the directory listing with the manual page you selected.

That should be enough to get you started. Once you understand the basics of how to use xman, take a look at the rest of this file to see the advanced features that are available to make using xman fast and efficient.

SCROLLING TEXT

The scroll bars are similar to xterm and xmh scroll bars; clicking the left or right pointer button with the pointer at the bottom of the scroll bar will scroll the text down or up one page, respectively. Clicking with the pointer farther up the scroll bar scrolls

Figure 13.11   The xman tool information screen.

Manual Page			▫ ✕
Options	**Sections**	**Directory of: (1) User Commands**	
Mail	a2p	addftinfo	addr2line
afmtodit	ali	anno	anytopnm
apm	apmsleep	apropos	ar
arch	as	as86	asciitopgm
ash	at	atktopbm	atq
atrm	audiocompose	audiosend	autoexpect
awk	basename	bash	batch
bc	bcc	bioradtopgm	bison
bmptoppm	brushtopbm	bsh	bunzip2
burst	byacc	bzcat	bzip2
c++decl	c++filt	c2ph	cal
captoinfo(m)	cat	cccp	cdecl
chage	charset	chattr	chfn
chgrp	chmod	chown	chroot
chsh	chvt	ci	cjpeg
cksum	clear	cmp	cmuwmtopbm
co	col	colcrt	colrm
column	comm	comp	compress
convfont	cp	cpio	cpp
cproto	crontab	cryptdir	csplit
ctags	cut	cvs	date
dc	dd	ddate	deallocvt
decryptdir	depmod	df	diff
diff3	dir	dircolors	dirname
dislocate	dist	djpeg	dlpsh
dnsdomainname	doexec	domainname	du
dumpkeys	dumpreg	echo	ed
egcs	egrep	eject	elks
elksemu	env	eqn	ex
exmh	expand	expect	expectk
expr	extcompose	false	fax2ps
fax2tiff	fgconsole	fgrep	file
find	fitstopnm	fix132x43	flex
flex++	flist	fmt	fold
folder	formail	forw	free
fstopgm	fuser	g++	g3topbm
gawk	gcc	gdb	gedit
gemtopbm	geqn	getfilename	getopt
getty	ghostscript	gif2tiff	giftopnm
gindxbib	glib-config	glookbib	gnp
gnroff	gouldtoppm	gpasswd	gpg
gpic	gpm-root	gprof	grefer

Figure 13.12   The xman tool, man page menu.

The Terminal Emulators

A terminal emulator is what you use to get a command-line prompt in the X Window System. There are a few main emulators available with most Linux distributions. If you use a desktop environment such as GNOME or KDE, then they come with their own terminal emulators. Otherwise, the option tends to boil down to either **xterm** or **rxvt**. The primary difference between these two programs is that **rxvt** is smaller, quicker, and has less graphics options. However, **xterm** is what comes standard with most distributions, perhaps because it has more capabilities.

A general rule is that if you find that your terminal emulator really crawls, try **rxvt**. The problem may extend from a slow graphics card, low RAM, or other such items that might limit GUI performance.

SETTING UP XDM AND CUSTOM X ENVIRONMENTS

The X environment was intentionally designed to be customizable. The Unix philosophy dictates maximum flexibility with the ability for users to create the environment that suits the individual. Every aspect of the X environment from startup to shutdown is customizable.

The X Environment

The X environment consists of its visual presentation and its functionality. Different methods of entering the X environment offer different visual and functional aspects. The look and feel of the environment is determined by the window manager. As discussed in a previous section, the interfaces provided by window managers can look very different. In addition, many window managers are very configurable so that the interface provided on different systems by the same window manager can also look very different. Some window managers offer so much configurability that you almost expect them to make your coffee while you work.

The Startup Environment

So far, only one method of starting X has been described—using the **startx** command. **startx** can be entered at the command line or run automatically when the user first logs in. Using **startx**, the X Window System is started individually for each user account after the user logs in.

Alternatively, your environment can be set up so that X starts when the system is booted and users log in through an X login screen, a useful setup for multi-user machines. The X Display Manager called xdm is used to start X at boot time. Xdm provides services similar to init, getty, and login on character-based terminals. It prompts for login name and password, authenticates the user, and starts a session.

Whether xdm starts at boot time or not is determined by the runlevel. The run-level is set in the inittab file and determines the system state while running. Different runlevels have different meanings for different distributions of Linux. For Red Hat and Caldera, the runlevels are:

➤ halt (do *not* set initdefault to this)

➤ Single user mode

➤ multiuser, without NFS (the same as 3, if you do not have networking)

➤ Full multiuser mode

13

➤ unused

➤ X11

➤ reboot (do *not* set initdefault to this)

The runlevel that starts xdm for SuS.E. is 3, which means full multiuser mode with xdm. Your /etc/inittab file will include a description of the runlevels for your system.

The runlevel for the system is set at boot time by setting initdefault in the inittab file. To use xdm at boot time, you need to set the correct runlevel. Look in your inittab file. You will find a statement similar to the following:

```
id:3:initdefault
```

The 3 is the runlevel. In Caldera or Red Hat, you would change the 3 to 5.

When a user logs in through xdm, a script file, /usr/lib/X11/xdm/Xsession, runs that configures the user session. Xsession is often set up to run a script from the user's home directory called .Xsession. This file is used to configure the X Window System session, similar to the file .xinitrc when X is started using **xinit**. You can include similar commands to start X clients and to start the window manager.

Customizing Your Environment

The first step in customizing your X environment is selecting a window manager. A previous section described some major window managers. Read the information at the Web sites. Decide which window manager will best meet your needs.

All Linux distributions include window managers. The most common window manager is fvwm (currently, fvwm2). Many distributions include the twm window manager. Other window managers may be included with various distributions. If you decide to use a window manager that is not included in your Linux distribution, you can download the software and installation instructions at the window manager Web site. The installation might be an rpm procedure or simply unpacking the downloaded files in the correct directory, usually /usr/X11R6/bin. In some cases, some libraries may be needed, such as libg++ or xpm.

The window manager is started in the configuration script, .xinitrc. If you are using xdm, the script, Xsessions, starts the window manager. The last line of the script should be:

```
exec wmname
```

where *wmname* is the window manager being started, e.g., fvwm2 or twm.

Most window managers allow some configuration. Many window managers allow a great deal of configuration. After the window manager is installed and started, it can be configured to individual preferences. Configuration methods differ. Some require manually editing a configuration file, while some configuration can be done through the window manager interface and control panel. Each window manager has its own configuration files that may be in different locations. Configuration of fvwm, the most common window manager, is discussed in this section.

Fvwm uses a configuration file called fvwm2rc. An example configuration file is provided when fvwm is installed, located in /var/X11R6/lib/fvwm2/ system.fvwm2rc. This can be used as a system-wide configuration file or copied into the user home directory as .fvwm2rc. Fvwm runs this script when it is started. It looks first for .xfvwm2rc in the user's home directory and then in the system configuration directory. If it doesn't find the file, it looks for the file system.fvwm2rc in the system configuration directory. You can specify a different configuration script as a command-line argument when fvwm is started. For example:

```
exec fvwm2 -f /etc/myconfig
```

This command tells fvwm to run myconfig when it starts, instead of .fvwm2rc.

Fvwm provides the ability to add functionality using modules. A module is a separate program which runs as a separate process (child of fvwm) but transmits commands to fvwm to execute. Several modules are available or users can write their own modules. For instance, the FvmwGoodStuff module allows the creation of button panels. Modules allow extra features for users who need them without making the program larger for users who don't need the extra features.

13

The functions of fvwm are defined in the configuration file. Fvwm provides many functions for actions, such as resize, scroll, or beep. Statements in the configuration file bind the functions to buttons or keystrokes. For instance, a menu would be created using the following statements.

```
AddToMenu Utilities "Utilities" Title
 + "Xterm"        Exec  exec xterm -e tcsh
 + "Calculator"   Exec  exec xcalc
 + "Xman"         Exec  exec xman
 + "Mail"         MailFunction \
                  xmh "-font fixed"
 + "Exit Fvwm"    Popup Quit-Verify
Mouse 1 R A Popup Utilities
```

The menu being created is called Utilities with the title "Utilities" displayed. Exec specifies to run the following command. For instance, clicking the X term menu item executes the command:

```
exec xterm -e tcsh
```

The last line binds the created menu as a pop-up menu to mouse button 1. The R and A specify a mouse click anywhere in the root menu. You can also create your own functions. The menu item for Mail is a user-defined function. The description of all the functions available and their format is provided in the fvwm man page.

The configuration file also defines the appearance of your GUI, using functions such as ButtonStyle and BorderStyle. The possible styles can be built-in styles or graphical images, called pixmaps, supplied by you. Pixmaps must be in the XPM format.

Thus, the appearance and functionality of the GUI is customizable. Some window managers are more customizable than others. Enlightenment is one of the more customizable window managers. A well-developed combination of settings that define a specific look and combination of functions is called a theme.

Themes

The customized look and feel of an X Window Screen is defined in the configuration file for the window manager. The configuration file can be distributed to other users who can load it on their system, running the configuration in their own X Window System. Many themes are in the public domain, available for anyone to use. Themes range from a simple combination of colors and simple windows to very elaborate, artistic, fully developed thematic interpretations of a subject.

One type of theme is organized around a color, a combination of shades that are esthetically pleasing, perhaps providing a mood, such as a blue theme or a burnished copper theme. Another type of theme presents a look, such as shiny metal. Another type of theme presents an environment, such as a nature theme or a space theme. A popular type of theme provides an emulation of a different system. For instance, a Mac theme would make a Linux machine look and function exactly like a Mac computer. Another type is organized around an entertainment theme, such as a cartoon character, a computer game, or a movie. For instance, you might expect to find a theme for Star Wars, the movie, Matrix, or Buffy the Vampire Slayer.

Numerous themes are available for download from the WWW. A central site for obtaining themes is **www.themes.org**. You can look at many themes there, perhaps finding one that suits you perfectly. When browsing screenshots of themes, remember that a theme is created with a thematic look, but also with features that the theme author considers useful, organized and functioning in a specific way. The look of the theme is important, but so is its usability.

Themes are specific to a window manager, because each window manager formats its configuration files differently. An Enlightenment theme is not likely to work correctly, or at all, if you are using fvwm. However, a theme is often converted so that similar themes are available for different window managers.

Downloading themes is free and relatively simple. Most downloads consist of the necessary ASCII configuration files, often packed as tar and/or gz files. You need only put or unpack the files in the correct location. If you have a current working window manager setup, make a backup copy of the configuration file before overwriting it with a downloaded theme. In some cases, you might need to provide a command-line argument in your window manager startup command that points to the configuration file that contains the theme. Often, themes contain many configuration files that need to be located in one or more specific directories, with a main configuration file that points to the other configuration files. Some window managers allow you to set up several themes and switch between themes using buttons or menu items.

If you can't find a theme that suits you, you can create your own theme. The exact method depends on the window manager you use. In general, you create a configuration file that defines the features and appearance. If you want an elaborate or artistic look that requires more than background and foreground colors, you need to supply pixmaps—graphic images. The graphics must be in XPM format. Graphics programs, such as the GIMP, can save programs in the XPM format.

13

Fvwm allows some themes, but not as elaborate as some window managers, such as Enlightenment. In fvwm, you can define an integrated appearance for all the elements of the GUI by defining a décor. You define it using functions in the .fvwm2rc configuration file. You create a décor using the AddToDecor function and apply it using the Style function, as follows:

```
AddToDecor try1a
 + ButtonStyle All pixmap image1.xmp
 + TitleStyle -- flat + BorderStyle -- HiddenHandles NoInset
 + HilightColor white navy
Style "try1" UseDecor try1a
Style "xterm" UseStyle try1
Style "*" UseStyle try1
```

The décor is named try1a. The + lines define the appearance of the décor. The first Style function assigns the Décor, try1a, to the style, try1. The next Style function applies the style try1, which uses the Décor, try1a, to all xterm windows. The last Style function applies the style, try1, to all windows.

The functions, ChangeDecor, UpdateDecor, and DestroyDecor are also available.

To create a theme, you need to know the configuration methods for the specific window manager. Documentation is available in the software download or can be read on the window manager Web site. A description of all the built-in functions available for fvwm is provided in the fvwm man page.

MAINTAINING AN X ENVIRONMENT

In most cases, you installed your Linux system from a distribution that included and installed XFree86. You did not install it separately. Also, in most cases, the distribution included and installed many X clients. In many cases, the installation procedure for the Linux distribution installed all the software you required. You have an operational Linux system that provides all the software you need and you did not specifically download and/or install X or any X clients.

Maintaining your X Window System and X clients will not be as simple. You or your users will need a software package that has not been installed. Or, a newer version of a software package will be released with added features you want to use. Or, a problem with a software package will arise and reinstalling the software seems like a possible solution. You will need to download and install software.

As system administrator, it is your responsibility to keep informed of the current status of the software your users require. You need to know when new versions are available and if there are problems with new releases. The WWW is the best source for up-to-date information. In particular, monitor the Web sites of your important X client application software and related user groups.

When a new release of source code is available for distribution, you download it and install it. For most software, the general procedure is:

```
./configure
make
make install
```

As an example, the commands to install the GIMP are listed below. The GIMP is a graphics package that runs under X.

```
tar xvfz gimp-1.0.0.tar.gz
cd gimp-1.0.0
./configure
make
make install
```

The configure script examines your system, and adapts the GIMP to run on it. The **make** command builds whatever is necessary and, assuming the build was successful, the **make install** command installs the software.

The Web site for the software application is the best source for the information you need. Release notes are provided for new releases. Problems with releases are identified. Installation instructions are provided.

WHEN TO AVOID X

It is important to remember that there is always a performance trade-off when you choose a graphical route over command-line tools. Even if you have your X server on a different machine, the client also consumes CPU cycles and memory. In situations where speed is precious, it is sometimes best to avoid using X all together.

The primary example of this type of concern is the single-purpose server. These servers are typically created for heavy use situations such as Web, email, or database services. In these cases, every CPU cycle is precious. Web page viewers may give up and move on to another site if your Web pages load slowly. Mailing lists can bog down the machine if there is not enough RAM and a fast enough machine to get the post processed in a hurry.

Another perhaps obvious issue is monitor type. In some server rooms, only a basic, low-resolution monitor is installed on a switchbox so the administrator can deal with the machines when necessary. If the video card and/or monitor are not up to the task, then do not tempt fate by installing an X server and client.

13

TROUBLESHOOTING

Most problems specific to the X Window System produce symptoms related to the video display. The GUI is not painted at all or is drastically or marginally weird. The first suspect is an error in the configuration. The hardware is not defined quite correctly. Possibly, the X server is not the best choice for your video card.

If you see a minor distortion of the image, try fine-tuning with xvidtune. If the problem is major, check that /usr/X11R6/bin/X is linked to the correct X server. You can reconfigure to see if that corrects the problem, using different settings or installing a different X server. You might try examining the /etc/XF86Config file to see if the settings are what you expect.

Sometimes X applications do not properly shut down. If you are having performance problems, or are being told that you cannot open an application because you already have an instance open, take a look at your process listing. A "kill –9" may be required, although you should always use caution with this command.

Some software writes log files containing possibly useful error messages. For instance, if you are having problems getting xdm to work, the file xdm-errors might contain helpful information for diagnosing the problem.

Also, there are a large number of libraries used by X and the applications that go with it. There is always the chance when you add a new application that was not included with your Linux distribution that you will have to upgrade a library, which in turn may not be backward-compatible with other programs. Be sure to always read the documentation that comes with a package before installing it, and give some serious thought about which packages are worth upgrading the entire X suite of packages and which are not.

The WWW is the best source for troubleshooting information. The Linux XFree86 HOWTO is a good source for information on hardware problems. It lists supported hardware and hardware problems. If you have a newer video card, the information in this document is important (**http://www.linuxdoc .org/HOWTO/XFree86-HOWTO.html**). In addition, the X Window User and the XFree86 HOWTOs contain useful information.

Web sites for specific software are another good source for troubleshooting information. They usually contain FAQs and, sometimes, searchable databases of problem reports and fixes. For instance, the XFree86 Project Web site at **http://www.xfree86.org/FAQ** provides an excellent FAQ discussing such problems as "How do I know which X server to use for my video card," "Why does the server reject my mode lines," and "Why don't menus work properly."

Another resource is Linux discussion lists and newsgroups. Many Linux experts are available to help with problems through the lists and newsgroups. If you have exhausted the online documentation and still are unable to fix your problem, try the newsgroups. Undoubtedly, someone has encountered the problem and knows the solution. There are many, many Linux groups, some general groups and some groups for specific applications or application areas.

X APPLICATIONS

Although you do not need to be an expert in using the various applications available in X for the exams or be a system administrator, it is important to understand some of the options available to you and your users. The types of applications to mostly be concerned with here are office productivity software such as word processors, spreadsheet programs, and more, as well as graphics programs. These are the two groups of applications most frequently wanted by the end user for day-to-day work.

Office Productivity Programs

There are three packages out there that are interesting for those who want to use a Linux box as an office PC. The range of office applications available in each varies, as well as their license agreements and the features offered in each. Take some time to read about each of them, go to their Web sites, and seriously consider trying them out before you tackle the exams.

Applixware

The Applixware Office suite (**www.applix.com/applixware/**) is one option for those who want office productivity tools available to their users that are integrated with one another, allowing for easy sharing of information between applications. This suite consists of a collection of office tools. The WYSIWYG applications included in this suite are: Applix Words for word processing, Applix Spreadsheets for number crunching, Applix Presents for preparing presentations, Applix Graphics for creating graphics, Applix Data for databases, Applix Mail for your email needs, Applix Builder for visual software creation, and a set of filters that allow information from other office tools in Linux and other operating systems to be converted into Applixware format, and vice versa.

Demo versions of the Applixware suite are available at the home site, as well as on CD-ROMs released by various companies. The software itself is not free, but it also is not outrageously expensive with the Deluxe suite being $99. Hardcopy manuals and technical support are also available for those who are interested.

"But this is Linux," you might say. "Where is the Open Source?" Do not despair. The Open Source issue brings us to a new package called SHELF. This package offers an Open Source—under the GPL—version of Applix's object-oriented ELF (Extension Language Facility) programming language. The effect this might have on your business needs is explained at **www.applixware.org** in the SHELF project FAQ. The SHELF package is a full ELF development environment.

StarOffice

Another integrated office suite available to Linux users is StarOffice (**www.sun.com/products/staroffice**), which is currently owned by Sun Microsystems after purchasing the program's creator, Star Division Corporation. The WYSIWYG applications included with this suite are: StarOffice Writer for word processing, StarOffice Calc for spreadsheet needs, StarOffice Impress for preparing presentations, StarOffice Draw for creating graphics, StarOffice Base for databases, StarOffice Schedule for project management and calendar functions, StarOffice Mail for email, and StarOffice discussion for Usenet newsgroup reading. This suite is capable of reading most popular applications' file formats. It is also not only available on Linux. StarOffice is available for most major operating systems.

13

StarOffice is freely downloadable off of Sun's Web site, and also available on a CD-ROM with hardcopy documentation for somewhere around $40. This suite is also available in a number of languages other than English: Dutch, French, German, Italian, Portuguese, Spanish, and Swedish. The source code for this suite falls under the CSL (Community Source License, available for viewing at **www.sun.com/software/communitysource/**).

WordPerfect

Although Corel offers an entire office suite containing the WordPerfect (**http://linux.corel.com/linux8**) word processor, the Linux portion of its offering is currently limited to the WordPerfect program itself. This fact may change sometime in the near future because Corel has placed more of its efforts into Linux development. The WordPerfect product in and of itself is a boon to Linux users as it is a fully functional WYSIWYG word processor that has been around for quite some time.

 Although WordPerfect for Linux is only the word processor component of the overall Corel office suite offering, this product does have spreadsheet table features and other items that make up for this fact for some purposes.

There is a free, downloadable version of WordPerfect for Linux and also packaged versions that include the program on CD-ROM and hardcopy manuals.

Image Manipulation Programs

There are many programs available to the Linux community that allow users to create, convert, and manipulate graphical images. Presented here are three of the most popular options: The GIMP, ImageMagick, and X-Fig.

The GIMP (GNU Image Manipulation Program) package is available under the GPL. This tool, whose home page is located at **www.gimp.org**, is a feature-rich graphics manipulation program. Not only does it come with a good set of brushes, palettes, plug-ins, filters, and more, there are also additional items available for download on the Internet through the program's home page.

ImageMagick (**www.imagemagick.org**) is another functional graphics tool available for Linux users. This program has many similar features to The GIMP as far as the casual user is concerned. It is also chock full of brushes and other such necessities, and has the ability to interface with other programs and scripts. Generally, someone who wanted to choose between these two programs would need to try the two of them out and see which one he or she prefers.

Last but not least, there is X-Fig. This program is not quite as all-encompassing as the previous two. It is more of a basic drawing program for those who need to get the job done without a bunch of layers and effects and shading.

CHAPTER SUMMARY

The X Window System is a hardware-independent windowing system for Unix and Unix-like computers, developed to provide functionality similar to Windows and Mac and distributed for free. The X Consortium provides official releases of X, currently version 11 release 6 (X11R6). The XFree86 Project provides enhancements and ports of X11 to many operating systems. The XFree86 software is included and installed with almost all distributions of Linux.

X is client/server software. The server is located on the local Linux system and communicates with the hardware—paints the display via video card and monitor and accepts input from keyboard and pointer. An X client sends display requests to the X server which responds by painting the display. Any application that requires a graphics display is an X client. X clients can be located on the same computer or on remote computers. Thus, you can use an application on one computer but display the GUI on a different computer across a TCP/IP connection.

A major X client is the window manager, responsible for moving, resizing, hiding, and closing windows and for the look and feel of the GUI. Different window managers offer different features and most are extremely configurable, providing very different appearance and functionality on different computers, determined by their individual configuration script files. Configuration files for the various window managers are available that provide complete coordinated themes, such as Ice or Star Wars, are available for download or you can create your own theme.

Be sure to experiment with different window managers and environments. A number of the exam options require you to know how to install these items, navigate through them, and customize them.

13

REVIEW QUESTIONS

1. Which is the current version of the X Window System?
   a. X10R6
   b. X11R6
   c. X11R5
   d. X11R5.9

2. Which of the following is not a window manager?
   a. Window Maker
   b. twm
   c. xdm
   d. Enlightenment

3. Which of the following is not a command that can be used to start X?

   a. **xdm**

   b. **startx**

   c. **xinit**

   d. **xinit /usr/mycon**

4. Which of the following statements is false?

   a. XFree86 is derived from X11.

   b. XFree86 is an enhancement of X11.

   c. XFree86 is released by the X Consortium.

   d. XFree86 is derived from the X Window System.

5. When you configure XFree86, it is recommended that you configure which device first?

   a. video card

   b. monitor

   c. sound card

   d. mouse

6. When you are dragging a window to a new screen location, which software are you using?

   a. X11

   b. window manager

   c. display manager

   d. server manager

7. Which of the following is a window manager?

   a. OPEN LOOK

   b. X11

   c. KDE

   d. wm2

8. Which of the following is the X server responsible for? [Choose all correct answers]

   a. Displaying the root window

   b. Resizing a window

   c. Closing a window

   d. Starting an application in a window

9. Which of the following statements are true with respect to the following string: 197.134.15.2:0.0? [Choose all correct answers]

    a. This is a valid value for the DISPLAY environment variable.

    b. 0.0 indicates that the computer has no monitor.

    c. 0.0 instructs the X server to display the output on the local display.

    d. The IP address is not valid in this statement; a host name is required.

10. Which of the following is not a utility used to configure XFree86?

    a. XF86Setup

    b. xvidtune

    c. Xconfigurator

    d. XF86Config

11. Which of the following statements is true?

    a. The X protocol is used to send bitmaps from the X client to the X server.

    b. The X protocol is used to send bitmaps from the X server to the X client.

    c. The X protocol can be used to send bitmaps across the network.

    d. The X protocol has nothing to do with bitmaps.

12. Which graphics format must be used for graphic images for most window managers?

    a. GIF

    b. XMP

    c. JPG

    d. EPS

13. What is the xhost command used for?

    a. To send graphical output to a remote computer

    b. To send graphical output to the local computer

    c. To accept X protocol display requests from a remote computer

    d. To send X protocol display requests to another host on your network

14. Which of the following statements is true?

    a. **startx** is a system command, stored in binary format in /bin.

    b. **startx** is used to start X when xdm is not used.

    c. **startx** is run by **xinit** when it starts X.

    d. **startx** is the startup table for X.

13

15. Which of the following is not a configuration file?

    a. xinit

    b. xsession

    c. X86Config

    d. inittab

16. Suppose you are a system administrator who is setting up your system to start the X Window System at boot time. Which file do you edit?

    a. xinitrc

    b. fvwmrc

    c. inittab

    d. X86Config

HANDS-ON PROJECTS

Project 13.1

In this project, you will familiarize yourself with your current configuration and window manager. You will learn to change your X environment.

To customize how you interact with the X environment, do the following:

1. Look at the startup script that is run when X is started. Look for a file, .xinitrc, in your home directory or xinitrc in a system directory, usually /etc /X11/xinit/xinitrc. You can use the **find** command to locate the xinitrc file. If you cannot find one, perhaps a different file was specified as an argument for the **xinit** command. Look at the **xinit** command in the startx script to identify the startup script used by **xinit**. If X is started on your system using xdm, look for a file called Xsessions. Examine the configuration script to see how your current environment is set up.

2. Notice that one or more X clients are started in the configuration script. Add a line that starts another program, just to see what happens, for instance:

```
xterm -geometry 80x10+50+50
```

You should make a backup of the file before changing it.

3. What other commands are there? Is there a command that sets background or foreground colors? Try changing the name of the color to see the effect.

4. What window manager are you using? The command that starts the window manager is usually the last command in the file. Identify the window manager used.

5. Identify the configuration script used by the window manager. It usually has a name related to the name of the window manager. It may be in your home directory or in the system configuration directory, e.g., /etc. If you are unable to locate the file, read the documentation on the Web page for the window manager to determine where to find the configuration file.

6. Examine the window manager configuration file. See if you can identify the commands and their effects. Try changing things to see what happens. (You probably want to make a backup of the file before changing it.) For instance, change color designations. Try more elaborate configurations. Read the documentation for the window manager, such as the man page, to learn the format of the configuration commands. Try making some major changes.

Project 13.2

In this project, you will download and install a window manager. You will install the fvwm95 desktop environment because it was probably not included with your distribution, and for some of the exams it is useful to know how to go through the entire process of downloading and installing the environments. Fvwm95 is a variation of fvwm, which probably was included with your distribution. If you do not have fvwm and wish to download it instead, the procedure is very similar to what is listed below.

13

To download and install fvwm96, do the following:

1. Log in to your system as root.

2. Change directory to /usr/local/src.

3. Download the file.

```
ftp mitac11.uia.ac.be
anonymous
email address
cd pub
cd fvwm95
get fvwm95-2.0.43b.tar.gz
```

4. Unpack the file: tar zxvf fvwm95-fvwm95-2.0.43b.tar.gz.

5. A new directory is created—fvwm95-2.0.43b. cd to the new directory and compile and install the package.

```
cd fvwm95-2.0.43b
./configure
make
make install
```

6. Everything is installed in /usr/local. You can change this. Read the installation instructions. A configuration file, system.fvwm95rc, is created that should work without modification. However, you can copy it to $HOME/ .fvwm95rc. The file contains paths: ModulePath, IconPath, and PixmapPath. Make sure the paths given are correct.

7. Change your .xinitrc or .xsession file to call fvwm95, instead of the window manager it currently calls. There is likely already a line that begins with the term "exec". Usually, the window manager is started on the last line of the file, so if you are using **vi**, type "G" to immediately move to the end, and see if the exec line is there. If there already is an exec line, put a hash mark (#) in front of the line to comment it out and then add a new line beneath it with the text "exec fvwm95".

8. Experiment with your new window manager. Read the documentation. Modify the fvwm95rc configuration file to configure your preferences. The syntax for fvwm, described in this chapter, should also work for fvwm95.

## CHAPTER FOURTEEN

SAMPLE TEST

Questions 1 through 14 utilize the same background information: You need to install a new mail server for the LAN. The old one has gotten too slow for the high volume of mail it has to handle, such as mail for the individual users and mailing lists.

Question 1

Which two documents should you consult before making any final purchasing recommendations?

- ❑ a. The overall Linux hardware compatibility listing.
- ❑ b. The hardware compatibility listing for the distribution you have chosen.
- ❑ c. The installation instructions for the distribution you have chosen.
- ❑ d. System administration documentation.
- ❑ e. Linux user documentation.

Question 2

Which hardware considerations should you keep in mind when putting together this mail server's list of components? [Choose all correct answers]

- ❑ a. Monitor resolution
- ❑ b. RAM size
- ❑ c. VRAM size
- ❑ d. CPU speed
- ❑ e. Large, fast access hard drives

Question 3

Which partitions might you create on the mail server's hard drive(s) other than the root, swap, and boot partitions? [Choose all correct answers]

☐ a. /var/spool

☐ b. /tmp

☐ c. /proc

☐ d. /bin

☐ e. /home

Question 4

What type of server is used to remotely assign IP addresses to machines during the installation process?

○ a. SMB

○ b. NFS

○ c. DHCP

○ d. FT

○ e. HTTP

Question 5

What type of local file server can you use to provide the distribution installation materials to the new machine during a network installation?

○ a. Inetd

○ b. FSSTND

○ c. DNS

○ d. NNTP

○ e. NFS

Question 6

List four popular Linux distributions.

Question 7

Which partitioning tool is available in all distributions?

○ a. Disk Druid

○ b. fdisk

○ c. Partition Magic

○ d. FAT32

○ e. System Commander

Question 8

Which X configuration tool is available in all distributions?

○ a. XF86Setup

○ b. XF86Config

○ c. XConfigurator

○ d. Xconfigurator

○ e. xconfig

Question 9

Install one of the following Linux distributions such that he or she will have as many graphical tools available as they might want and all networking tools are included for use by the administrator: Caldera, Debian, Red Hat, Slackware, SuSE, or TurboLinux. Verify that it was installed properly, and set the machine to boot directly to the GUI.

Question 10

Which of the following are X-based system configuration tools available in some distributions? [Choose all correct answers]

❏ a. COAS

❏ b. KConf

❏ c. Linuxconf

❏ d. Yast

❏ e. GnoConf

Question 11

Which first-level segment of the file system contains a majority of system and server configuration files within its subdirectories?

○ a. /var

○ b. /etc

○ c. /bin

○ d. /sbin

○ e. /lib

Question 12

Which file do you edit to set partitions to mount at boot time?

○ a. /etc/fstab

○ b. /etc/services

○ c. /etc/smb.conf

○ d. /etc/fstab.conf

○ e. /etc/mount.conf

Question 13

Which file do you edit to set up a printer?

○ a. /etc/printtab.conf

○ b. /etc/print.conf

○ c. /etc/lp.conf

○ d. /etc/printtab

○ e. /etc/printers

Question 14

Configure the Apache Web server such that it looks for Web pages within the /data/html hierarchy, which sits on the /data partition. Also have the contact information, **webmaster@chapter14.exam.org**, displayed on all Web pages offered by the server.

Question 15

Which of the following sequences results in the output of the **ls** command being mailed to the recipient?

○ a. **ls** > mail bob

○ b. **ls** | mail bob

○ c. **ls** < mail bob

○ d. **ls** >> mail box

○ e. **ls** || mail bob

Question 16

Which of the following sequences results in the output of the **who** command being saved to the file whonow?

○ a. **who** | whonow

○ b. **who** < whonow

○ c. **who** > whonow

○ d. **who** -> whonow

○ e. **who** whonow

Question 17

Which of the following commands can you use to search within the file system by file names? [Choose all correct answers]

❑ a. **locate**

❑ b. **which**

❑ c. **where**

❑ d. **look**

❑ e. **find**

Question 18

What do you type to join the text contents of the files "start" and "end" into the file "whole"?

○ a. **join** start end > whole

○ b. **cat** start end > whole

○ c. **join** start end whole

○ d. **cat** start end whole

○ e. **merge** start end whole

Question 19

Which command tells you what partitions and devices are mounted onto the file system?

○ a. **mount**

○ b. **fstab**

○ c. **fs**

○ d. **mount -l**

○ e. **df**

Question 20

What would you type to send the last 20 lines of a text file to STDIN?

○ a. **end** -n 20 filename

○ b. **last** -n 20 filename

○ c. **head** -20 filename

○ d. **end** -20 filename

○ e. **tail** -20 filename

Question 21

Which two commands can you use to delete directories?

❏ a. **rm**

❏ b. **rm -rf**

❏ c. **rmdir**

❏ d. **rd**

❏ e. **rd -rf**

Question 22

Which command do you use to change runlevels?

○ a. **initlevel**

○ b. **runlevel**

○ c. **level**

○ d. **run**

○ e. **init**

Question 23

What do you type to stop a hung process that resists the standard attempts to shut it down? [Choose all correct answers]

❑ a. **kill PID**

❑ b. **quit**

❑ c. **kill -9 PID**

❑ d. **exit**

❑ e. **Ctrl+C**

Question 24

Which of the following commands can you use to cleanly restart a Linux machine? [Choose all correct answers]

❑ a. **reboot**

❑ b. **init 6**

❑ c. **init 0**

❑ d. **shutdown -r**

❑ e. **shutdown -h**

Question 25

Create the user account "chap14" with the password "TesTing", and then set the system to ensure that the user cannot use more than 300 blocks of space in the /tmp directory.

Question 26

What command would you use to create an empty file without opening it to edit it?

○ a. **open**

○ b. **vi**

○ c. **pico**

○ d. **touch**

○ e. **edit**

Question 27

Which shell do you assign to a POP3 mail-only account?

○ a. /bin/false

○ b. /bin/sh

○ c. /bin/bash

○ d. /bin/pop

○ e. /bin/pop3

Question 28

Set up a machine so that both Windows and Linux machines on the exam.org domain have read-write access to the /home hierarchy.

Question 29

Set up a machine so that it mounts the NFS share /policy from the machine "fileserver" on the local LAN at boot time with read-only access. This share should be mounted to the location /docs/policy.

Question 30

Which of the following contrasts and comparisons about the services in questions 28 and 29 are true? [Choose all correct answers]

❑ a. 28 does file locking, 29 does not.

❑ b. Both 28 and 29 can be used on a multi-OS LAN to serve files to all machines.

❑ c. 29 does file locking, 28 does not.

❑ d. Both 28 and 29 have special file system types for **mount** purposes.

❑ e. 29 has a special file system type for mounting, but 28 does not.

Question 31

Which mail service controls mail pick-up but is not in itself the server that controls dissemination across the network?

○ a. sendmail

○ b. pop3

○ c. inetd

○ d. smail

○ e. qmail

Question 32

Which daemon controls the network service in question 31?

○ a. inetd

○ b. pop3d

○ c. maild

○ d. nntpd

○ e. pmaild

Question 33

Which **vi** command allows you to delete a single character?

○ a. **d**

○ b. **dd**

○ c. **r**

○ d. **x**

○ e. **D**

Question 34

Which **vi** command deletes an entire line of text?

○ a. **dl**

○ b. **D**

○ c. **dd**

○ d. **d**

○ e. **DL**

Question 35

What do you type to exit a text file in **vi** without saving the changes you've made?

○ a. q

○ b. Q

○ c. :q

○ d. :Q

○ e. :q!

Question 36

What commands allow you to search the contents of a text file without having to open the file? [Choose all correct answers]

❑ a. **vi**

❑ b. **grep**

❑ c. **ex**

❑ d. **sed**

❑ e. **more**

Question 37

What command allows you to see the contents of an environment variable in the bash shell?

○ a. **vi**

○ b. **echo**

○ c. **more**

○ d. **list**

○ e. **print**

Question 38

Which of the following permission sets would allow a shell script to run just by typing its name at the command line, not considering who is typing the command? [Choose all correct answers]

❑ a. 755

❑ b. 644

❑ c. 744

❑ d. 666

❑ e. 664

Question 39

Save a text list of the modules loaded on your workstation to the file /root/my_modules. Once you have done so, locate three modules who have dependencies. Save their dependency lists to the file /root/module_dependencies.

Question 40

Choose the names of the two different kernel development streams.

- ❑ a.   alpha
- ❑ b.   production
- ❑ c.   beta
- ❑ d.   test
- ❑ e.   experimental

Question 41

Which of the following kernel versions would you choose for a Linux server that does not have bleeding edge technology or needs? [Choose all correct answers]

- ❑ a.   4.15.9
- ❑ b.   3.52.101
- ❑ c.   7.12.52
- ❑ d.   6.15.8
- ❑ e.   5.2.55

Question 42

Compile a new version of the kernel that came with the distribution. Optimize this kernel version for the machine it resides on, and remove unnecessary services within it. Verify that the machine boots properly into the new kernel.

Question 43

Set the system such that it specially logs all emergency messages produced by the kernel to the file /var/log/kernel_problems.

Question 44

Which of the following are quick commands you can use to see if a machine is properly networked? [Choose all correct answers]

❑ a. **ifconfig**

❑ b. **ping**

❑ c. **netcheck**

❑ d. **netstat -nr**

❑ e. **eth0**

Question 45

Which command do you use to see which daemons are running, so you can check to see if a troublesome service is up?

○ a. **ps**

○ b. **jobs**

○ c. **daemon**

○ d. **ps aux**

○ e. **dconfig**

Question 46

Which of the following files would you check if names were not properly resolving on your network? [Choose all correct answers]

❑ a. /etc/hosts

❑ b. /etc/nsswitch.conf

❑ c. /etc/resolv.conf

❑ d. /etc/named.conf

❑ e. /etc/hosts.allow

Question 47

Which of the following are issues to examine before turning to a computer to resolve a printing problem? [Choose all correct answers]

❑ a. Is the printer plugged in?

❑ b. Is the printer properly configured?

❑ c. Is the printer on?

❑ d. Are the printer cables properly connected?

❑ e. Is the machine properly talking to the network?

Question 48

Which command can you use to disable a printer while you debug its problem (just the command, no flags)?

○ a. **lpr**

○ b. **lpc**

○ c. **lprm**

○ d. **lpq**

○ e. **lpd**

Question 49

What format of commands can you use to send a text file directly to a printer with no processing?

○ a. **lpr -nofilter file**

○ b. **lpr file**

○ c. **more file > /dev/printer**

○ d. **print file**

○ e. **cat file > /dev/printer**

Question 50

You have a machine that hangs on LI during boot time. Which of the following might you try to fix the problem?
[Choose all correct answers]

❑ a. Reboot the machine.

❑ b. Re-run LILO.

❑ c. Boot into rescue mode and re-run LILO.

❑ d. Boot into rescue mode and examine the file /etc/lilo.conf.

❑ e. Boot into single user mode and examine the file /etc/lilo.conf.

Question 51

Which log file contains the text that scrolls along the screen during the boot process?

○ a. /var/log/bootmsgs

○ b. /var/msgs

○ c. /var/log/messages

○ d. /usr/msgs

○ e. /var/log/syslog

Question 52

What two items do you need to boot an otherwise non-booting Linux box, so you can fix it?

❑ a. boot disk

❑ b. rescue disk

❑ c. installation media

❑ d. spare machine

❑ e. blank, spare hard drive

Question 53

Which command works in almost all distributions to create a boot disk?

- ○ a. **mkboot**
- ○ b. **make bootdsk**
- ○ c. **make boot**
- ○ d. **mkbootdsk**
- ○ e. **mkbootdisk**

Question 54

Which password package should you install to ensure that the central password file couldn't be stolen easily?

- ○ a. PAM
- ○ b. tcp_wrappers
- ○ c. shadow
- ○ d. securepass
- ○ e. ssh

Question 55

Which package can you use to regulate which network traffic is allowed to enter a specific machine, but not on any other machines?

- ○ a. tcp_wrappers
- ○ b. ipchains
- ○ c. SOCKS 5
- ○ d. TCP/IP
- ○ e. ipfirewall

Question 56

Disable all intermittent network services that are typically not used.

Question 57

Which package provides secure remote login sessions, such as secure telnet logins?

○ a. securetelnet

○ b. ssh

○ c. shadow

○ d. ipchains

○ e. SOCKS 5

Question 58

Which tool is commonly used to create an IP filtering firewall in Linux?

○ a. ipchains

○ b. SOCKS 5

○ c. tcp_wrappers

○ d. ipblock

○ e. IPX

Question 59

Which of the following Web sites would you go to in order to keep up with the latest Linux security information? [Choose all correct answers]

❑ a. **www.ilda.org**

❑ b. **www.cert.org**

❑ c. **www.ciac.org**

❑ d. **www.sans.org**

❑ e. **www.lsfa.org**

Question 60

Why is it important to keep up on Linux security information?

○ a. Keep up with the latest trends.

○ b. It is best to always install the latest releases.

○ c. Security holes are sometimes discovered and plugs are made available.

○ d. The latest software has the least holes.

○ e. When you know where the holes are you can create patches yourself.

Question 61

What can users realistically do to help maintain system security?

○ a. Help to install the latest patches.

○ b. Try to break into the system and point out security problems.

○ c. Install their own security measures.

○ d. Choose secure passwords.

○ e. Make sure their passwords revolve around a common theme.

Question 62

Which tool can you run to ensure that users are choosing relatively secure passwords?

○ a. passcheck

○ b. crack

○ c. chkpass

○ d. passtst

○ e. passwdtst

Question 63

Which tool can you use to make sure that users who do not understand permissions are not creating unprotected files by default?

○ a. umask

○ b. chmod

○ c. mask

○ d. perms

○ e. setmask

Question 64

What is a secure philosophy to use when setting up machine or network security?

○ a. Keep everything out.

○ b. Let everything but specific traffic through.

○ c. Deny all and only let specific traffic through.

○ d. Add blockades as you see a need for them, not before.

○ e. Prevent users from ever accessing the outside.

Question 65

What happens to your ipchains settings when you reboot a machine?

○ a. They are automatically saved.

○ b. They are automatically saved if you set them to be.

○ c. They cannot be saved.

○ d. They cannot be automatically saved unless you do something like make an alias for the shutdown routine that ensures this happens.

○ e. You have to specifically type out the command to save them each time.

Question 66

In what top level directory would you find mail spools, print spools, and log files?

○ a. /etc

○ b. /bin

○ c. /usr

○ d. /var

○ e. /opt

Question 67

What file would you edit in your home directory to change which window manager you want to use?

○ a. Xinit

○ b. .xinitrc

○ c. XF86Setup

○ d. xstart

○ e. xf86init

Question 68

What term would you look for in a process listing in order to find the PID for the main GNOME process?

○ a. kdm

○ b. gnome

○ c. xdm

○ d. XGDM

○ e. gdm

Question 69

What would you type to create a file containing all of the items beginning with the letter "a" from the /bin directory?

○ a. ls /bin/a* > file

○ b. ls /bin/a? > file

○ c. ls /bin/a? | file

○ d. ls /bin/a* | file

○ e. ls /bin/a* file

Question 70

What type of value is always different for every Ethernet card?

○ a. IP address

○ b. Host name

○ c. MAC address

○ d. Domain name

○ e. Gateway

Question 71

Which of the following IP addresses is likely a broadcast value?

○ a. 192.168.12.254

○ b. 192.168.176.0

○ c. 192.168.3.1

○ d. 192.168.51.255

○ e. 192.168.255.0

Question 72

What command allows you to set a processor-intensive job to use less CPU time?

○ a. **ps**

○ b. **nice**

○ c. **chps**

○ d. **less**

○ e. **more**

Question 73

Which of the following commands can be used to get information about a package? [Choose all correct answers]

❑ a. **man**

❑ b. **list**

❑ c. **apropos**

❑ d. **info**

❑ e. **more**

Question 74

Where is a good place to store shell scripts that are for use by the author?

○ a. ~/bin

○ b. /bin

○ c. /usr/bin

○ d. /root

Question 75

Under what hierarchy are man pages stored?

○ a. /usr/man

○ b. /man

○ c. /bin/man

○ d. /etc/doc/man

○ e. /usr/doc

## CHAPTER FIFTEEN

ANSWER KEY

1. a, b
2. b, d, e
3. a, b, e
4. c
5. e
6. See discussion of answer in this chapter
7. b
8. a
9. See discussion of answer in this chapter
10. a, c, d
11. b
12. a
13. d
14. See discussion of answer in this chapter
15. b
16. c
17. a, b, e
18. b
19. e
20. e
21. b, c
22. e
23. a, c, e
24. a, b, d
25. See discussion of answer in this chapter

26. d
27. a
28. See discussion of answer in this chapter
29. See discussion of answer in this chapter
30. a, d
31. b
32. a
33. d
34. c
35. e
36. b, d
37. b
38. a, c
39. See discussion of answer in this chapter
40. b, e
41. b, c, e
42. See discussion of answer in this chapter
43. See discussion of answer in this chapter
44. a, b, d
45. d
46. a, b, c, d
47. a, c, d
48. b
49. e

50. a, c, d
51. c
52. a, b
53. e
54. c
55. a
56. See discussion of answer in this chapter
57. b
58. a
59. b, c, d
60. c
61. d
62. b
63. a
64. c
65. d
66. d
67. b
68. e
69. a
70. c
71. d
72. b
73. a, c, d
74. a
75. e

Question 1

Answers a and b are correct. The distribution's hardware compatibility listing and the general Linux hardware compatibility listing. These two documents should be consulted before purchasing any equipment for a Linux box. The simplest way to get things set up is to use hardware covered in the distribution itself. However, if you need something that outside drivers are available for, you will find that kind of information in the general hardware listing.

Answers c, d, and e are all premature. Installation, use, and administration instructions are not necessary until you actually get to the point where the system is already installed, which is far after the equipment is procured.

Question 2

Answers b, d, and e are correct. A mail server benefits from a large amount of RAM, a fast CPU, and large amounts of fast-access hard drive space. The reason it benefits from having a lot of memory is that it can then handle groups of mail messages all at once. A fast CPU helps it move through processes more quickly, especially when it comes to generating postings to large mailing lists. Having a lot of hard drive space ensures that the mail spool will not run out of free room.

Answers a and c are unimportant on a machine that is meant to provide mail service. A Linux box serving such a purpose would only be slowed down with a GUI running, and the GUI is the reason to be concerned with both the monitor resolution and video RAM.

Question 3

Answers a, b, and e are correct. Separating /var/spool onto its own partition helps to ensure that if something goes wrong with the mail server or spool, the output cannot overrun the file system. Putting /tmp on its own partition prevents either software or user items in the /tmp directory from overrunning the file system. Placing /home off on its own is mostly useful for system re-installs or upgrades, allowing you to not have to wipe the /home hierarchy along with other areas.

Answers c and d are not possible, as the /proc portion of the file system is virtual—held in RAM—not placed on the hard drives, and the /bin hierarchy is necessary for basic system functionality and, therefore, not one that you can place on a different partition.

Question 4

Answer c is correct. You can use a DHCP server to assign IP addresses to individual machines during the installation process.

Answers a, b, d, and e list legitimate Linux servers, but these servers do not provide IP addresses. The SMB, or Samba, tool is used for file and print sharing across multi-OS networks. An NFS server is for file sharing across Linux networks. FTP is a file storage server that allows people to browse and retrieve information by logging in to it, and HTTP is for the Web.

Question 5

Answer e is correct. You can use an NFS server to provide the distribution installation materials to the machine on which you are performing the installation.

Answers a, b, c, and d are all valid items but none of them are file servers. Inetd is the superdaemon which controls all intermittently used network services. The FSSTND is the Linux File System Standard. DNS provides domain name resolution, and NNTP is the transfer protocol for usenet news.

Question 6

Some popular Linux distributions are Debian, SuS.E., Red Hat, Caldera, TurboLinux, and Slackware.

Question 7

Answer b is correct. The fdisk partitioning tool is available in all Linux distributions.

Answers a, c, and e all handle partitioning, but do not come with all distributions. Disk Druid is made by Red Hat and used in its distribution along with some derivatives. Partition Magic and System Commander are tools made by third-party companies. Answer d is not a tool, but a file system type. Specifically, FAT32 is the file system type used in Windows 98.

Question 8

Answer a is correct. The XF86Setup program is an X configuration tool that comes with the X server, and therefore, all distributions that use the X server.

Answer b is actually the file that contains the results of running XF86Setup. Answers c and d both refer to Red Hat's Xconfigurator, though c is typed incorrectly. Answer e refers to a nonexistent X configuration tool. However, you might recognize the term as a kernel configuration tool.

Question 9

There are multiple actions necessary to complete this item:

1. During the installation process, take care to make sure that GUI tool and networking tool packages are included amongst those installed.

2. If the machine boots properly into Linux, then the installation is verified.

3. Some distributions offer the ability to configure the machine to boot into the GUI during the installation process and some do not. If necessary, edit the file "/etc/inittab" as root and be sure that the following line near the beginning has a 5 and not a 3:

```
id:5:initdefault
```

Question 10

Answers a, c, and d are correct. GUI-based configuration tools available in some distributions are COAS, Linuxconf, and Yast.

Answers b and e are not valid tools.

Question 11

Answer b is correct. The /etc portion of the file system contains a number of system and daemon configuration files.

Answers a, c, d, and e are valid first-level directories, but are incorrect. The /var directory contains items that change on a regular basis, such as log files and print and mail spool directories. The /bin directory contains system binaries, whereas the /sbin directory contains binaries that run with SUID privileges or as a specific user. The /lib directory contains system libraries, both shared and non-shared.

Question 12

Answer a is correct. The file /etc/fstab manages which partitions are automatically mounted onto the file system.

Answers b and c refer to valid items, but they are not used to manage the file system. The file /etc/services maps networking services to the ports they utilize, and /etc/smb.conf is the configuration file for the Samba service. Answers d and e point to files that do not exist.

Question 13

Answer d is correct. The file /etc/printab contains printer configuration information.

Answers a, b, c, and e point to files that do not exist.

Question 14

There are multiple actions necessary to complete this item:

1. The file containing the data on where the Web server should look for documents is srm.conf, which in some distributions is within the /etc/httpd/conf directory. If you need to, use the **find** command in the format "find / -name srm.conf" to locate the file and then change to that directory.

2. Use the command **vi srm.conf** to open the file.

3. Use the command **/DocumentRoot** and press Enter to begin a search for the variable that tells the Web server where to look for the Web files it offers.

4. Use a command such as **x** to delete the default DocumentRoot value.

5. Enter insert mode—press **i**—and type in the new location of /data/html.

6. Press the Esc key and then type **:wq** to save and exit the file.

7. The file containing the server contact information is httpd.conf. The variable containing the contact information is ServerAdmin. Follow the same process you did to change the DocumentRoot in order to change the ServerAdmin item.

8. Now that you have made the changes, you have to restart the Web server in order for them to go into effect. The exact path for Apache's init script may differ, but in general the command might look like **/etc/rc.d/init.d/httpd stop**.

9. Restart the Web server. In general the command might look like **/etc/rc.d/init.d/httpd start**

Question 15

Answer b is correct. The **ls** command is run, and then the results are piped to the **mail** program, which sends them to bob. Answers a, c, and d generate errors. Answer e displays the output of the **ls** command.

Question 16

Answer c is correct. The **who** command is run, and the results are saved to the file whonow. Answers a and b generate errors. Answers d and e generate nothing.

Question 17

Answers a, b, and e are correct. The three search tools that look at file names are **find**, **locate**, and **which**. Answer c is not a command, except in specifically one shell (tcsh). Answer d is a command, but not a file system search command. The **look** command is used to search the contents of text files.

Question 18

Answer b is correct. To join these two files, you would use the command **cat start end > whole**.

Answers a, c, d, and e all use valid commands, but not necessarily valid syntax. Also, the commands do not do what is required by the question. The **join** command exists in the **ex** editor, and is used to join individual lines of text. This command does not use redirection in its syntax, nor does it use file names. The **cat** command, however, requires a redirection unless you want the output to go to STDOUT, which is the screen. Finally, the **merge** com-mand is used to combine two files that are slightly different, incorporating the sum total of what is there. It does not simply tack the files together like the **cat** command does.

Question 19

Answer e is correct. The **df** command lists the devices and partitions that are mounted onto the file system. Answers a and d refer to a valid command, though there is no -l flag for **mount**. However, the **mount** command adds devices to the file system, it does not give a listing of those devices. The answers b and c refer to nonexistent commands.

Question 20

Answer e is correct. Use the command **tail -20 filename** to see the last 20 lines of a file. The answers for a and d both point to an invalid command. The answer for b points to a valid command. Typing this answer in with a valid file name will even give you some output. However, the last command tells you who is logged in, it does not actually list the contents of any file named in the command. The answer for c, the **head** command, is used to look at the beginning of a file, not the end.

Question 21

Answers b and c are correct. You can use **rmdir** or **rm –rf** to delete a directory. Answer a is incorrect, because the **rm** command without any specific flags will not delete a directory, it will only delete files. Answers d and e point to a nonexistent command.

Question 22

Answer e is correct. The command used to change runlevels is **init**. Answers a, c, and d point to invalid commands. Answer b is a valid command, but does not set the current runlevel. The **runlevel** command displays the current runlevel, and the one that was used directly before entering this one.

Question 23

Answers a, c, and e are correct. The **kill** command by itself tries to allow a process to exit cleanly. You type **kill –9 PID**, on the other hand, to abruptly stop a process that will not quit by any other means. Also, pressing Ctrl+C works for many programs.

Answers b and d are only valid in some contexts, and even in those contexts will not work on a hung process.

Question 24

Answers a, b, and d are correct. The commands used to restart a Linux box are **shutdown –r**, **reboot**, and **init 6**. Answers c and e are incorrect. Both of these are used to shut down a Linux box, not restart it.

Question 25

There are multiple actions necessary to complete this item:

1. To create the user account, use the command **useradd chap14**.

2. To add the password, use the command **passwd chap14** and then type "TesTing" at both of the password prompts.

3. Look at the contents of the file /etc/fstab by typing "more /etc/fstab" to see which portion of the file system /tmp is under. If it is not under a special partition, then it is in the root (/) partition.

4. Use the **cd** command to change to the base of the partition /tmp is under.

5. Use the command **touch quota.user** to create the file that will store the user quotas for that partition.

6. Use the command **chmod 600 quota.user** to properly set the permissions.

7. Use the command **vi /etc/fstab** and go to the fourth column of the entry referring to the partition containing the /tmp directory.

8. Use the command **i** to enter Insert mode, and then add the text ",usrquota" to the section containing the mount options.

9. Press the Esc key, and then use the command **:wq** and press Enter to save and exit the file.

10. Restart the machine by typing "reboot".

11. After logging back in as root, use the command **cd /tmp**.

12. Use the command **edquota –u chap14** to open the quota assignment file for that user.

13. Press **i** to enter Insert mode.

14. In the line containing the text "blocks in use", replace the text "hard = 0" with "hard = 300".

15. Press the Esc key, and then use the command **:wq** and press Enter to save and exit the file.

Question 26

Answer d is correct. You use the **touch** command to create an empty file without needing to open it. Answers a and e point to invalid commands, though either of these might actually be aliased to point to a real command. Answers b and c utilize editors, and so do not satisfy the requirements of the question.

Question 27

Answer a is correct. You assign a POP3 only account to the /bin/false shell. Answers b and c both point to the same shell, the bash shell. However, assigning this shell to a POP3 only user gives him or her login access, which is what you are trying to avoid. Answers d and e are both invalid options in a standard setup.

Question 28

There are multiple actions necessary to complete this item:

➤ The Samba tool allows file and print sharing across multi-OS networks. The configuration file for this tool will either be /etc/smb.conf, or /etc/samba.conf. Type "vi /etc/smb.conf" or the appropriate path to open this file. If the configuration file does not exist, then you need to install the Samba server and then repeat the previous step.

➤ There is a trick to this item. Samba contains a special section called [homes] which you can use to have the server create a share for the user's home directory on the fly. Some default /etc/smb.conf files already have this share in place, and some do not. Be sure the share exists, is not commented out, and contains the line "writeable = yes".

Question 29

There are multiple actions necessary to complete this item:

1. To configure a machine to mount a partition at boot time, you need to open the file /etc/fstab. Use the command **vi /etc/fstab** to accomplish this step.

2. Use the **G** command to go to the end of the file.

3. Use the **o** command to open a new line at the end of the file and enter Insert mode.

4. The format used in an /etc/fstab line is "*device mountpoint fstype options dump order*". In this case, the device is an NFS share, and so uses the format "*machine:/path*". Determine the line of code to be close to:

```
fileserver:/policy /docs/policy nfs user,noauto,ro 0 5
```

5. The last item, the mount order, should be the next number in the list of mount orders you already have. It must have an order number or it will not be mounted automatically.

Question 30

Answers a and d are correct. NFS does not perform file locking but Samba does. Both NFS and SMB have their own file system types (nfs and smb) for **mount** or /etc/fstab.

Answer b is incorrect. NFS only works for other Linux machines. Answer c is incorrect. Its statements about the services are reversed. Answer e is incorrect. Both NFS and SMB have special file system types for mounting.

Question 31

Answer b is correct. The POP3 service functions as a mail pick-up site but not a network mail server. Answers a, d, and e are all valid services, and even valid mail servers. However, they are SMTP mail servers, not POP servers. Answer c is a valid service but not a mail server.

Question 32

Answer a is correct. The inetd superdaemon controls the POP3 mail service. Answer b is incorrect. The POP3 mail service runs through the superdaemon, not on its own. Answers c and e point to nonexistent, or at least nonstandard daemons. Answer d points to the Usenet news daemon.

Question 33

Answer d is correct. The **x** command deletes the current character. Answers a, b, c, and e are all valid **vi** commands, but not the answers to this question. The **d** command begins a deletion statement, but causes no action by itself. On the other hand, the **dd** command deletes the entire selected line of text. The **r** command replaces the selected character with the next one you type, and the **D** command deletes from the cursor location to the end of the line.

Question 34

Answer c is correct. The **dd** command deletes the current line. Answers a and e are invalid **vi** command combinations. Answers b and d are both valid commands, but do not satisfy the requirements for the question. The **d** command begins a deletion statement, but causes no action by itself, and the **D** command deletes from the cursor location to the end of the line.

Question 35

Answer e is correct. You type **:q!** to exit the file without saving changes. Answers a and d are invalid **vi** commands. Answer b closes **vi** and opens the older editor ex in its place. Answer c fails with an error if the file has not been saved.

Question 36

Answers b and d are correct. The **grep** and **sed** commands can be used to search the contents of a text file without needing to open it. Answers a and c both refer to text editors, which would have to open the file. Answer e would have to display the file before it could search the contents.

Question 37

Answer b is correct. The **echo** command allows you to display the contents of an environment variable in the bash shell. Answers a and c are text manipulation commands, not variable manipulation. Answers d and e are not bash shell commands.

Question 38

Answers a and c are correct. The executable bit has to be turned on for the shell script to run at the command line on its own. Answers b, d, and e all have the executable bits turned off.

Question 39

There are multiple actions necessary to complete this item. What follows is one way to accomplish the task:

1. Use the command **lsmod > /root/my_modules** to save the module listing to the required file.

2. Use your preferred browsing command or text editor—**more**, **less**, **vi**, or another tool—to view the contents of /root/my_modules.

3. For each of the modules, type "depmod *modulename*".

4. For the first module that has a dependency, type "depmod *modulename* > module1".

5. For the second module that has a dependency, type "depmod *modulename* > module2".

6. For the third module that has a dependency, type "depmod *modulename* > module3".

7. Type "cat module1 module2 module3 > /root/module_dependencies".

See if you can find a faster way to do this.

Question 40

Answers b and e are correct. The two different kernel development streams are the experimental stream and the production stream. Answers a, c, and d are not valid kernel production streams.

Question 41

Answers b, c, and e are correct. The production stream's second part is an even number, and you would want a production kernel for such a server. Answers a and d are experimental kernels, which you would not want on such a server.

Question 42

There are multiple actions necessary to complete this item. It is important that you are able to complete this task unassisted, as compiling the kernel is heavily covered in all of the Level I certification programs. One method of completing this task is:

1. Use the **mount** command to add the distribution CD-ROM to the file system, or go to the distribution's FTP or Web site.

2. Use the **rmdir** command to delete the /usr/src/linux directory.

3. Install the kernel source to /usr/src/linux. You may also need the kernel headers package, and perhaps even the kernel SRPM.

4. Be sure that the following packages are installed: the gcc compiler (egcs), the C libraries, make, and ncurses.

5. Change to /usr/src/linux with the **cd** command.

6. Choose which of the kernel configuration tools you want to use: config, menuconfig, or xconfig. Type "make *tool*" to open it.

7. Optimize the machine for its CPU type.

8. Remove modular support for items such as amateur radio, old CD-ROMs, and joysticks, which will likely not be needed on a server.

9. Remove support for other hardware that is not on the machine.

10. Save and exit the kernel configuration tool.

11. Use the command **make dep** to build the source dependencies.

12. Use the command **make clean** to make sure no temporary files are in the way.

13. Use the command **make bzImage** to build the kernel.

14. Use the command **make modules** to build the kernel modules.

15. Locate the new kernel. Its file name should be "bzImage" if you need to search for it.

16. Copy the new kernel to /boot.

17. Rename the new kernel to "vmlinuz-*version*".

18. Copy the new system map—System.map—to /boot.

19. Change back to /usr/src/linux if you left it.

20. Use the command **make modules_install** to install the modules.

21. Use **vi** to open /etc/lilo.conf.

22. Add a section to boot with the new kernel.

23. Keep the section with the old kernel. Be sure to make sure they are both labeled such that you can tell which is which.

24. Save and exit the file.

25. Type "/sbin lilo –v" to run LILO and activate the changes.

26. Type "shutdown –r now" to reboot the machine.

27. When LILO comes up, choose the option for the new kernel.

28. If the machine boots properly, the new kernel is verified for the purposes of the question.

Question 43

There are multiple actions necessary to complete this item. One method for completing this task is:

1. Use the **vi** editor to open the file /etc/syslog.conf.

2. Use the **G** command to go to the end of the file.

3. Use the **o** command to create a blank line at the end of the file and enter Insert mode.

4. Build the the logging line. Then kernel's facility is "kern", and the emergency priority is "emerg". Therefore, the line begins with "kern.emerg". The entire line would then be:

```
kern.emerg                 /var/log/kernel_problems
```

5. Save and exit the file by pressing the ESC key and then typing ":wq".

6. Stop the system logging daemon by typing "/etc/rc.d/init.d/syslog stop", adjusting the path if necessary.

7. Start the system logging daemon by typing "/etc/rc.d/init.d/syslog start", adjusting the path if necessary.

Question 44

Answers a, b, and d are correct. The **ifconfig** command displays network interface configurations. The **ping** command lets you see if a machine is reachable by the network. Finally, the **netstat** command with the nr flag displays network address and routing information. Answer c points to an invalid command. Answer e points to the default Ethernet device, not a command.

Question 45

Answer d is correct. The **ps** command displays all running processes, and hence which daemons, when you use it with the aux flag. Answers a and b are incorrect. Just typing **ps** without any flags only displays the processes you are directly running. The **jobs** command, once again, only lists the jobs you specifically have running in the background. Answers c and e point to invalid commands.

Question 46

Answers a, b, c, and d are correct. You might check one or more of the following files if names on a LAN are not resolving properly: /etc/hosts, /etc/resolv.conf, /etc/nsswitch.conf, or /etc/named.conf. Answer e is incorrect. The /etc/hosts.allow file determines which machines are allowed to access services through the tcp_wrappers security package.

Question 47

Answers a, c, and d are correct. Check to see if the printer is plugged in, if it is on, and whether its cables are properly attached before resorting to computer-based print problem solutions. Answers b and e require computer intervention, and so are incorrect.

Question 48

Answer b is correct. The **lpc** command lets you disable a printer or its queue when necessary. Answers a, c, d, and e are all valid items. However, **lpr** sends a file to the print queue, **lprm** removes a job from the print queue, **lpq** lists the print queue items, and **lpd** is the print daemon.

Question 49

Answer e is correct. Type "cat file > /dev/printer" to send a file directly to a printer. Answers a, b, and c all involve valid commands, but none of these produces the result you are looking for. The **lpr** command queues a file, and has no "-nofilter" flag. The **more** command would not properly send the file to the printer, and if it did it would sit and wait for you to press a key to complete the process. Answer d is an invalid command.

Question 50

Answers a, c, and d are correct. A quick method of trying to solve any LILO boot problems is to reboot the machine several times and see if the problem persists. If this method fails, then boot into rescue mode and ensure that there are no errors in the LILO configuration file. If /etc/lilo.conf looks fine, then try re-running LILO to ensure that all of the boot files are placed properly, and reboot.

Answers b and e are not correct based on the phrasing of the question. You have to boot into rescue mode before you can edit the file /etc/lilo.conf, and you cannot boot into single user mode if the machine hangs on LI during boot time.

Question 51

Answer c is correct. The file /var/log/messages contains boot output. Answers a, b, and d, point to invalid log files. Answer e points to a log file that potentially belongs to the system logging daemon.

Question 52

Answers a and b are correct. You need a boot disk and a rescue disk to fix a machine that will not boot properly.

Answer c is a drastic measure, which is not considered actually "fixing" the problem. Answer d is incorrect. A spare machine is not necessary in order to fix a non-booting machine. In fact, it will likely be of no assistance in the absence of networking functions. Answer e is incorrect. While it does not hurt to have spare hard drives, the spare drive cannot be used to fix the machine's boot problems.

Question 53

Answer e is correct. The **mkbootdisk** command creates a boot disk. Answers b and c are incorrect. The make package is used to compile software, not create boot disks. Answers a and d point to invalid commands.

Question 54

Answer c is correct. The shadow password package moves the central password file to a more secure location. Answers a, b, and e all point to valid packages, but none of these places the password file in a more secure location. Answer d points to an invalid package.

Question 55

Answer a is correct. The tcp_wrappers package is used to regulate the TCP/IP network traffic coming in and out of a machine.

Answers b and c both point to valid firewalling packages, but these packages are used for an entire LAN, not just one machine. Answer d points to the commun-ications protocol used to transmit data over the Internet. Answer e points to an invalid package.

Question 56

There are multiple actions necessary to complete this item:

1. Use the command **vi /etc/inetd.conf** to open the superdaemon's configuration file.

2. Place a comment marker (#) at the beginning of the lines for the following services: finger, gopher, talk, ntalk, and uucp, as well as other services such as ftp and telnet that may or may not be necessary under your specific circumstances.

3. Press the Esc key and then type ":wq" and press Enter to save and exit the file.

4. Stop the superdaemon. The exact path for inetd's init script may differ, but in general the command might look like "/etc/rc.d/init.d/inetd stop".

5. Restart the superdaemon. The exact path for inetd's init script may differ, but in general the command might look like "/etc/rc.d/init.d/inetd start".

Question 57

Answer b is correct. The ssh package allows you to configure secure telnet sessions and other remote logins. Answer a points to an invalid package. Answer c points to a valid package, but shadow handles passwords, not data encryption. Answers d and e point to firewalling packages, which regulate what passes in and out of a LAN, but do not handle data encryption.

Question 58

Answer a is correct. The ipchains tool is used to create an IP Filtering firewall.

Answer b refers to a Proxying firewall tool, not IP Filtering. Answer c is an IP filtering tool, but not a firewall. Answer d is an invalid tool. Answer e is a Novell networking protocol, not a TCP/IP firewalling tool.

Question 59

Answers b, c, and d are correct. The Web site most commonly watched for security updates is **www.cert.org**. Two others are **www.ciac.org** and **www.sans.org**.

Answers d and e do point to real Web sites, but neither of them is Linux related, let alone Linux security related.

Question 60

Answer c is correct. New security holes are always being found, and those who want to break in keep track of them too. If you don't plug them, someone will exploit them.

Answers a and b are a poor way to approach Linux. Updates come out at a rapid pace. Continuously updating a Linux machine can make it unstable. Answer d is a dangerous assumption. New software cannot be guaranteed to be foolproof until it has withstood the test of time, and rarely is any package foolproof. Answer e could be correct, but unless you are a security programming expert, is not the best approach, nor is it recommended.

Question 61

Answer d is correct. They can make sure to use secure passwords.

Answers a, b, and c are incorrect. Users should not have the necessary access to install security patches, and should not be encouraged to break into the system unless there is a good reason. Even if they mean well, inadvertent prob-lems could be caused if they succced. As far as users installing their own security measures goes, anything useful would have to be installed on the entire system, and users should not have that kind of access. Answer e is a poor way to choose passwords. Using any form of recognizable pattern for a password is dangerous.

Question 62

Answer b is correct. The Crack tool tests how secure user passwords are. Answers a, c, d, and e are all invalid commands.

Question 63

Answer a is correct. The **umask** command is used to change the default file creation permissions.

Answer b is a valid command, but just changes a specific item's permissions. Answers c, d, and e are invalid commands.

Question 64

Answer c is correct. Deny all, then allow specifics to pass through. Answers a and e are overly restrictive. Answers b and d are overly permissive.

Question 65

Answer d is correct. Settings for ipchains are lost during a reboot or shutdown and there is no "setting" to ensure they are automatically saved. Answers a, b, and c are completely incorrect. Answer e is incorrect, but you can save them by hand if you choose to.

Question 66

Answer d is correct. The /var top level directory contains files that change on a regular basis, such as log and spool files. Answers a, b, c, and e are all valid top-level directories. However, their contents do not include the files listed in the question.

Question 67

Answer b is correct. The ~/.xinitrc file allows you to set which window manager you want to use when logging in to X from that account. Answers a, d, and e are all invalid files. Answer c is the main X server configuration file.

Question 68

Answer e is correct. The GNOME desktop manager's main process is gdm. Answers a and c are valid desktop managers, but not for GNOME. Answers b and d are invalid desktop managers.

Question 69

Answer a is correct. The **ls** command lists the contents of directories, and the asterisk (★) wildcard allows you to specify all files beginning with a in the particular directory. Redirecting the results of the **ls** command into a file completes the requirements for the question. Answer b will only save the file names that are two letters, with the first letter a. Answers c and d will generate errors, because they will expect file to be a program. Answer e will list all files in /bin that start with a to the screen, and the file listing if it exists.

Question 70

Answer c is correct. Every Ethernet card has a unique MAC address assigned by its manufacturer. Answers a, b, d, and e are all valid items, but none of these is necessarily unique to all Ethernet cards.

Question 71

Answer d is correct. Broadcast addresses tend to be at the very end of the available IP range. Answers a, b, c, and e are all valid IP addresses but are likely not broadcast addresses.

Question 72

Answer b is correct. The **nice** command is used to change a job's priority level, so that it runs slower or faster. Answers a, d, and e are valid commands but are not used to change process information. Answer c is an invalid command.

Question 73

Answers a, c, and d are correct. The **man** command pulls up man pages, the **info** command pulls up texinfo pages which have replaced the man pages for some packages, and the **apropos** command helps you to find related commands. Answers b and e are not methods of getting information about a package.

Question 74

Answer a is correct. It is best to keep scripts meant only for your account under ~/bin. Answers b, c, d, and e are all valid locations, but not the best places to keep user-specific scripts.

Question 75

Answer e is correct. The /usr/doc hierarchy contains the man pages for the system. Answers a, b, c, and d are all invalid directories.

OBJECTIVES

Each of the major Linux certification exams has its own set of criteria. This appendix outlines what the study objectives for each exam are, and where to find them within this book. It also points to additional resources to find more information on each exam as well as to sites with useful information that can further help toward study objectives. An excellent way to prepare for any of these exams is to study the combined material for all of them.

THE RED HAT CERTIFIED ENGINEER EXAM

The RHCE (Red Hat Certified Engineer) certificate only requires one day's worth of examinations. However, it comprises three exams within that same day, back-to-back. To prepare for these exams, be sure to know the information outlined in this section.

Installation Issues	Chapter
Pre-installation checklist issues	2
Choosing what partitions to create	2
Partitioning drives with fdisk	2
Recovering from LILO problems	4

Configuration Issues	Chapter
Configuring X after the installation	13, F
Configuring the mouse after the installation	F
Configuring authentication after the installation	F
Configuring time zones after the installation	F
Configuring the keyboard after the installation	F

Using Linux	Chapter
File system layout and standards	3
Searching for files	3
The boot process	4
Red Hat Package Manager use	F
X Window System	13

Administration	Chapter
Understand the Linux boot process	4
Be able to write and analyze shell scripts	5
Manage user accounts	6
Manage groups	6
Create and configure quotas	3
Create **cron** and **at** jobs	6
Be able to generate and understand a Kickstart file	F
Kernel administration and installation	11
Networking basics	8
Networking services	9
Log files	6
Security issues	12
System rescue	4

THE LINUX PROFESSIONAL INSTITUTE (LPI) LEVEL I EXAMS

The LPIC level I program is a series of two exams taken at different times. For this reason, each exam is treated separately. When preparing for each exam, be sure to know the information outlined in its specific section.

T1a: General Linux I

This exam covers half of the distribution-neutral Linux system administration issues. You must pass this exam before you continue to the T1b.

Using Linux	Chapter
Working with Linux at the command line	7
Using the shell	5
Understanding the file system	3

Administration	Chapter
Boot and initialization	4
LILO	4
Configure and administer printing	10
Build and understand documentation	D

T1b: General Linux II

This exam covers half of the distribution-neutral Linux system administration issues.

Installation Issues	Chapter
Hardware and architecture issues	1
Linux installation and package management	2

Using Linux	Chapter
Use the vi editor	5
X Window System	13

Administration	Chapter
Kernel administration and installation	11
Writing and understanding shell scripts	5
Working with source code	11
Working with devices	3
Managing users	5
Managing groups	5
Log files	6
Networking basics	8
Networking services	9
Security issues	12

T2: Distribution-Specific

This exam covers one specific Linux distribution of your choice, out of: Caldera, Debian, Red Hat, Slackware, SuSE, or TurboLinux. Once you pass this exam, you receive your LPI certification for level 1.

Installation Issues	Chapter
Linux installation and package management	E
Locating system files	E
Administrative tools	14

SAIR LINUX & GNU CERTIFIED ADMINISTRATOR EXAMS

The Sair level 1 program is a series of four exams taken at different times, though completing one of the first two earns the LCP certificate. For this reason, each exam is treated separately. When preparing for each exam, be sure to know the information outlined in its specific section.

Although some of the issues for these exams may sound similar or identical, remember the title for the exam in question and use that as your focus. For example, the topics covered in the Installation and Configuration exam focus on the installation and setup of those items.

Installation And Configuration Level 1

This exam focuses on the installation and configuration of Linux in general. Passing it earns the LCP certificate if this is the first exam you take and pass.

Basics	Chapter
FSF history	1
GNU history	1
Linux history	1
Tasking issues	1
User issues	1
GUI trade-offs	13

Using Linux	Chapter
Linux commands	7
X issues	13

Administration Issues	
Understand devices and file systems	3
The Linux boot process	4
Managing users	5
Managing groups	5

System Administration

This exam focuses on Linux system administration. It is the second of the four exams you must pass to get your level one LPIC. Passing it earns the LCP certificate if this is the first exam you take and pass.

Using Linux	Chapter
Advanced Linux commands	7
Creating, monitoring, and killing processes	7
Printing	10

System Administration	Chapter
Quotas	3
Backups	6
Cron and **at** jobs	6
Managing users	5
Managing groups	5
Runlevel management	4
Mounting and unmounting	3
Programming and scripting	11
Shutting down	4
Log files	6
Issues when updating	2
Checking the file system	3
X administration and configuration	13

Network Issues	Chapter
Routing	8
Boot and initialization in depth	4
Network printing	10

Networking

This exam focuses on Linux networking. Because it is more narrowly focused, it is important to study the networking materials in depth, and so this section is not broken down into subsections. To prepare for it, focus on:

Networking Fundamentals	Chapter
TCP/IP basics	8
Linux networking basics	8
Linux networking setup	8
Network service setup	9
Server setup	9

Security

This exam focuses on Linux security. Because it is more narrowly focused, it is important to study the security materials in depth, and so this section is not broken down into subsections. To prepare for it, focus on:

Security Fundamentals	Chapter
Security quick fixes	12
Host security	12
LAN security	12
User security	12

ONLINE SOURCES FOR LINUX SOFTWARE AND UPDATES

Although there are more Linux resources online than you could possibly imagine, this appendix provides pointers to some of the best information resources in a busy, crowded, and informative Web space. Don't be afraid to jump beyond the limits of these resources, and remember that a good search engine can be your best tool when looking for specific documents, tools, source code, or whatever else you might need.

GENERAL LINUX RESOURCES AND CLEARINGHOUSES

The following provide downloads of general Linux information:

➤ **Linux.com: http://www.linux.com** A multidimensional online Linux resource with pointers to all kinds of interesting information. The site is operated and maintained by volunteers, and may occasionally show a broken link or two, but don't let this slow you down.

➤ **LinuxHelp Online: http://www.linuxhelp.org** A stunning collection of information, pointers, tutorials, and a great deal more data about Linux, this site is as easy to appreciate as it is to navigate. A good place to start looking for answers for just about any kind of Linux-related questions.

➤ **#Linuxhelp: http://www.linuxgeek.org** The official Web site of the #linuxgeek help channel on the EFNET IRC network, this site is another great general Linux reference online, with pointers, FAQs, tips and tricks, and more. It also has a great general list of online Linux software download or access sources.

➤ **Gnu is Not Unix: http://www.gnu.org** Although many open source Unix implementations freely acknowledge their inclusion of the Linux kernel, not as many pay equal credit to their most common source for tools, GUIs, and much more. Go straight to the source for all things GNU and interesting at this site!

➤ **Linux Online: http://www.linux.org** An excellent general Linux information site, with pointers to everything from sellers of pre-installed Linux systems, to the latest on Linux in the media.

➤ **Slashdot: http://www.slashdot.org** A popular source for the latest news and software available for the Linux community. Often the first or second site listed at Linux gatherings when people are asked where they go for their information!

ONLINE LINUX SOFTWARE RESOURCES

The following provide downloads of various versions of Linux:

➤ **Linux Kernel Archive Mirror System: http://www.kernel.org/ mirrors** International and national mirror sites (copies of the master Linux kernel distribution) at 89 sites for 45 countries, where 75 other countries or territories are supported remotely.

➤ **Caldera OpenLinux: http://www.calderasystems.com** An open source version of Linux is available from Caldera for download, plus all kinds of information, updates, and code from the company's commercial products division site.

➤ **Debian: http://www.debian.org** An open source operating system based on the Linux kernel is available from Debian for download.

➤ **The Embeddable Linux Kernel Subset (ELKS): http://www.elks.ecs .soton.ac.uk/cgi-bin/ELKS** Downloadable versions of Linux for 8086 and 80286 PCs, plus palmtops, single-board microcomputers, embedded controller systems, and more.

➤ **Linux Mandrake: http://www.linux-mandrake.com** The folks at BeroLinux recently merged with Linux Mandrake. This site offers a free Linux download of their distribution, which won LinuxWorld's product of the year award for 1999.

➤ **Linux for Power PC Systems: http://www.linuxppc.org** This company offers versions of Linux for Power PC platforms from Apple, IBM, Motorola, and other vendors that conform to the CHRP. Downloads available, or you can order the CD-ROM.

➤ **Red Hat Linux: http://www.redhat.com** Red Hat will be happy to sell you its products online, and you can also download additional documentation, updates, fixes, and errata information from its Web site if you already own a copy of its software.

➤ **Slackware: http://www.slackware.com** The "official home" of the Linux slackware distribution; jump to the "GetSlack" button to grab your copy.

➤ **Linuxmafia.org: http://www.linuxmafia.org** Another online source for slackware Linux, the self-professed "industrial strength" Linux distribution online.

➤ **Stampede: http://www.stampede.org** A Linux distribution designed for speed, but also to be "easy for the new user, and awesome for the power user," according to the organization's home page.

➤ **SuSE: http://www.suse.com** The leading distributor of Linux in Europe, SuSE offers both commercial and open source distributions at its Web site, plus a whole lot more.

➤ **TurboLinux: http://www.turbolinux.com** An Asian import that is making great inroads in the U.S. and Europe, TurboLinux is another new Linux distribution that is attempting to capitalize on ease of installation and use in a busy marketplace.

The following provide downloads of Linux GUIs:

➤ **GNOME: http://www.gnome.org** Gnome is an emerging copyleft standard for open source Unix desktops, including many flavors of Linux. Yet another great piece of GNU software.

➤ **WindowMaker: http://www.windowmaker.org** An X11 Window manager for Linux and other open source Unix distributions, this GUI attempts to deliver the look and feel of the NeXTSTEP desktop. Supports both GNOME and KDE windowing environments. WindowMaker now also belongs to the GNU project.

➤ **Xfree86.org: http://www.xfree86.org/3.3.3.1/ftp.html** Source patches are available to upgrade X11R6.3 PL2 from the X Consortium (now The Open Group) to XFree86 3.3.3.1. Binaries for many operating systems are also available.

➤ **Themes: http://www.themes.org** Although themes have more to do with how a desktop looks than how it behaves, they are part and parcel of any well-designed Linux GUI environment. As its name should suggest, this site is the motherlode for desktop themes and designs.

The following provide downloads of Linux software packages:

➤ **Freshmeat.net: http://www.freshmeat.net** One of the premier sources of information about all kinds of Linux-based applications, including a hypertext preprocessor called PHP, often used for serving up Web-based information about all kinds of things—including Linux.

➤ **LinuxApps.Com: http://www.linuxapps.com** One of several general sources for Linux application downloads, this site has the reputation of being among the most complete and up to date of its kind. Its category-based search area can be quite useful.

➤ **GNU Software List: http://www.gnu.org/software/software.html** Be sure to browse the "Descriptions Of GNU Software" available on this page for one of the most complete lists of tools and software available anywhere for Linux.

➤ **FreeCode: http://www.freecode.com** Peruse and download the source code to a wide range of software. An excellent resource for those who learn best by looking at and playing with other people's code.

ONLINE LINUX CERTIFICATION RESOURCES

More than just an open source implementation of the Unix operating system, Linux is well on its way to becoming a marketing phenomenon in its own right. Although its market share still remains relatively low compared to Microsoft's line of Windows products, Linux has gained enough major momentum to attract serious interest from organizations, individuals, and vendors.

Unfortunately, there's still some confusion in the marketplace about which Linux certification really matters. Although there are probably more Linux certifications available than the ones we mention here, there are at least three players who've mounted Linux certification efforts at present, with varying degrees of success:

➤ Red Hat is the largest commercial vendor for Linux (with about 70 percent of that market) and is clearly a major player in the Linux certification game. Right now, Red Hat has launched its own certification program, which creates RHCEs (Red Hat Certified Engineers).

It costs $2,498 (not including travel and lodging) to obtain an RHCE these days, if you take the official fast track preparation class before you take the exam. The exam without the class takes a full day, and costs $749. For more information, visit Red Hat's Training home page at **www.redhat.com/ products/training.html** (or search on "certification" using its search engine).

➤ Sylvan Prometric (a leading purveyor of certification tests of all kinds, as you may already know) and Software Architecture Realization and Implementation (a leading Unix and Linux training company) have teamed up to define and deliver a global, vendor-neutral form of Linux and GNU certification. (Their program has since been endorsed by Caldera, the number two commercial provider of Linux.) This effort has produced a complex certification scheme, with four levels of Linux and GNU certification. These levels span the range from a single test Linux Administrator credential to a Master Linux Engineer who has passed a battery of tests, including a day-long exam that incorporates essay questions, oral testing, and a hands-on component.

Lower-level tests are multiple choice and may be administered at any Sylvan testing center. They cost around $100 each. Costs and locations for the Level IV test remain to be determined, but have been estimated at around $400 For more information, visit the Sylvan/SAIR Linux certification pages at **www.linuxcertification.org**.

➤ The Linux Professional Institute is a vendor-neutral Linux certification group that has nevertheless managed to garner major support from a variety of Linux vendors—including companies like Caldera Systems, SuSE, LinuxCare, and Starnix—while at the same time designing a multi-tiered set of Linux exams. This group's focus is to develop certification criteria and tests to match through the same kind of committee-driven, consensus-building approach that the Internet Architecture Board used so successfully to design and maintain TCP/IP and key related Internet technologies.

In a move that flattened the playing field a bit more for certification issues, Digital Metrics, a small California-based company that launched an entirely Web-based Linux testing and certification effort, merged its efforts with LPI's. The Digital Metrics team brought along its experience with exam development and delivery and served to further enhance LPI development.

LPI's exams are delivered by Virtual University Enterprises (VUE) at **www.vue.com**. This company has testing centers worldwide, which you can locate through its Web site. It costs $100 to take each of the three exams for the first LPI level. The rest of the pricing scheme will be mapped out as the exams are completed, but it is expected that each exam will be priced in the same range.

Under Dan York's able stewardship, and with support from major Linux vendors, not to mention companies like IBM, CompUSA, and ExecuTrain (all of whom are members of LPI's advisory board), we expect great things from this organization, but not until some time well into the year 2000 and beyond.

Although the fate of each of these various Linux certifications is somewhat uncertain, it's pretty clear that some form of Linux certification (perhaps even more than one) is bound to attain market acceptance in the next year or two. When that happens, look out! We strongly believe that Linux certification may very well become the next "big thing" in the certification trade, which explains why so many training providers, publishers, and other interested parties are starting to invest in this niche. Please stay tuned to the various Web sites for more details!

LINUX DOCUMENTATION

By now, you have probably read about many advantages and superior characteristics of the Linux operating system, but documentation for Linux is perhaps its weakest aspect. For early generations of Linux, the only manuals to be found were the built-in documentation, referred to as the "man" pages (man is shorthand for manual). In fact, the first incarnations of the Linux kernel only had screenshots of the directory tree; the user had to manually insert the files according to those reference shots in order to install the system.

In recent years, the documentation process has taken a turn for the better with online reference projects and the Linux HOWTOs. More and more people are becoming involved in Linux, not as programmers but as users, thanks to succinct and comprehensive documentation, manuals, and tutorials.

THE MANUAL PAGES

The man pages are the built-in documentation for the Linux and Unix operating systems. These are usually created by the author of the file or function covered or by the manufacturer of the Linux distribution being used. The man pages can be accessed at either the command line or through most GUIs, as covered in Chapter 13. Although the man pages provide command information, programming notes, and other instructions, they can be difficult for end-users to interpret because they are often quite brief, and originally written for users who have a Unix background.

The man pages can be accessed from any user level, and different versions of the man pages can be found in varying directories. For instance, the manual found in /usr/local may be different than the manual found in /usr/local/docs. The reason for this is that the manual directory index searches specific, predetermined places for man pages and may not look in a /local/man directory installed by a particular application. There is a command to specify directories for the manual, which will be covered in the next section.

Accessing The man Pages

The most common way to access the man pages is via the command line using the **man** command. Like all other commands, this command requires an argument, usually the file or function that is being queried.

Use the command **$ man mkdir**. This brings up the name of the command, a synopsis of the command's syntax, a description of the information found on that manual page, and the options for the command. Other manual pages may go into specifics such as authors, caveats, copyrights, and distribution/permissions policies.

A colon at the bottom of the page signifies that there are multiple pages in the document. Press the spacebar to access the next page. To quit the man page and return to the command line, type the letter *q*.

The man pages are divided into the following different sections:

➤ 1 User Commands
➤ 2 System Calls
➤ 3 Library Functions
➤ 4 Devices
➤ 5 File format
➤ 6 Games
➤ 7 Miscellaneous
➤ 8 System Administration
➤ 9 More kernel documentation
➤ n New documentation
➤ o Old documentation
➤ l Local documentation: machine-specific information

To find a command in a specific section, simply use **man *x***, where *x* is the section number you want to access. This is helpful when commands may be used for different tasks, such as a command that can be used on the user level and the kernel level. For example,

```
$ man 1 ls
```

gives you the manual page for the **ls** command from the first section of the man pages.

These non-command-specific arguments are also available for use with the **man** command:

➤ **man man** Brings up the documentation for the manual itself.
➤ **man info** Contains information on the manual. It can also be used for specific sections of the manual, for example, **$ man 5 info** reports the

information on the games section of the manual pages. This is especially helpful when you can't remember what information a section covers. You should also note that the existence of a section does not ensure any information in that section. A section will only have information if it was installed by program or file packages; that is, if there are no games installed, there will be nothing in the games section.

Using the **apropos** command, you can search the man pages for keywords. This command returns any name lines that contain the keyword you requested:

```
$ apropos edit
```

This syntax searches for the word **edit** in all the name strings found in the man pages. There are other ways of accessing the man pages. X Windows contains a program called **xman**, which provides a graphical interface for the pages. This program is discussed in Chapter 13. The manual pages can also be found on the Internet in HTML format. The online resources are quite reliable and may be more current than the man pages on your system. One such repository can be found at **http://www.linuxpowered.com/html/tutorials/tutoindx.html**. As previously mentioned, the man pages only index specific directories. If an application installs man pages in a directory such as /usr/local/manpage, the manuals may not search that directory. This is especially true if you ever receive the message No Manual Entry when looking for a man page that should be there. For example, the following code updates the man pages to include the documentation from the usr/local/manpage directory:

```
$ export MANPATH=/usr/man:/usr/local/manpage
```

Moving Within Man Pages

Once you have a man page open, you need to be able to move within it. Fortunately, the man page format is fairly easy to move through. After all, if you are trying to find help, the last thing you need to deal with is a complicated interface!

To just read a man page, press the spacebar to advance through the text a screen at a time; or use Page Down to advance ahead a screen and Page Up to back up a full screen. You can also use the up and down arrows to advance or retreat line by line. There is also the ability to search the page by keyword. This feature works identically to many of the other viewers you have learned about in this book. Type / to indicate that you want to do a search, type the search term, and then press Enter. Man advances to the first instance of this term and moves it to the top of the screen, highlighting all visible instances.

Appendix D

Administering Man Pages And Other Documentation

There is actually more than just the man page system on your Linux box as far as help features go. If you have a system with many novice users, or even just people who are inquisitive and like to try to figure things out on their own, then it is wise to have a well-fleshed-out help system. There are a number of components to accomplishing this goal.

First, you have to be sure that you have the man pages installed. All of your man page system is kept in /usr/local/man, or in /usr/man, depending on your setup—in fact, there may be a full directory set in /usr/local/man that is empty. Take a look through your man page listings. Most have fairly self-explanatory names like gunzip.1. If you do not find man pages in the appropriate sections that you think you should have, install them from your distribution media, download them from the distribution's Web or FTP site, or find them elsewhere on the Internet.

There are also the files in /usr/doc to contend with. Here is where the non-man help information goes. Not only may you find a directory named "howto" here with a version of the Linux Documentation Project's HOWTOs, you also will find program documentation for various installed packages in a folder named, hopefully, "packages".

Creating Man Pages

When a programmer or administrator has made changes in a distribution or created something new, he or she might want to add a man page. Created with text editors, source files for the man pages are named by command name, then a point, and the section identifier. For example, a game command of fire would be named **fire.6**. If a man page is to be used with X Windows, the author may add an "x" at the end, that is **fire.6x**, so the system will utilize it properly. The non-numerical sections (n, o, l) are deprecated by the File System Standard, so they should be avoided.

As for formatting source files, the only required field is **NAME**, as the information in that field is used for searching by the **apropos** command. The **NAME** field consists of a list of the function names, separated by commas, then a short, hyphenated description of the file or command's function. The following is an example of a man page:

```
NAME
fire - blast the aliens to save the human race
SYNOPSIS
_fire [-blast]
DESCRIPTION
_fire_creates a burst of energy leveled at the enemy,
harmless to humans, deadly to the aliens.
```

```
FILE
/local/fire.conf
This is the file that informs the game of the strength
of your shots.
COPYRIGHT
        LANWrights, Inc. 1999-07-01 info@lanw.com
```

The following list contains descriptions of some, but not all, fields used in man pages.

➤ **SYNOPSIS** Gives a short list of options, formatted inside brackets; it can also give programmers additional information.

➤ **DESCRIPTION** Should be the most detailed description of the function or program. This section provides all the knowledge necessary to understand your work, and should include items such as algorithms, formats, and explanations of various arguments.

➤ **OPTIONS** Lists all options and their effects.

➤ **FILE** Lets you know about any files used by the program/function.

➤ **AUTHOR** Gives the author's name, usually with his or her email address, as a digital signature.

➤ **SEE-ALSO** A very nice addition for referencing other files and functions that relate to the current man page.

➤ **COPYRIGHT** Included to provide information on copyright and distribution policies of a given man page.

Of course, you may add fields to the man page as you wish. Only the **NAME** field interacts with other parts of the system; any other field is read only by the user.

The man pages contain a wealth of information, but are not aimed at novice users. The man pages are usually written by experienced Unix users for experienced Unix users and are not friendly to others. Their brevity and assumption of a reader's knowledge can sometimes make man pages very frustrating. Fortunately, there are other places to get highly descriptive and user-friendly documentation. The following section provides pointers to and discussion about these resources.

ONLINE DOCUMENTATION

Once again, the Internet is a great resource for the Linux community. Various sites have HOWTOs, frequently asked questions (FAQs), and tutorials for every user level. They are available any hour of the day and are updated often by programmers and others interested in documentation for the Linux community. There are even online searchable repositories of man pages.

The Linux HOWTO

HOWTOs were created as expanded documentation for Linux topics by users who kept copious notes and converted them to user-friendly documentation. The authors' own experience gathered tackling different aspects of the Linux environment inspired them to share the information and helpful insights gathered through their struggle. The HOWTOs also represent the entire knowledge base for Linux, collecting more information than any book could encompass and being much more detailed than any man page. Thus, the HOWTOs are excellent tools for new users to learn the Linux operating system and its environment. The HOWTOs are also unique to Linux, another great accomplishment by the Linux community.

HOWTOs document specific aspects of Linux, including configuration and operation of elements such as the Point-to-Point Protocol (PPP), Ethernet, and upgrading the kernel. Although a HOWTO may resemble a FAQ, it is not in question-answer format. Instead, it is laid out as a complete discussion of one topic. Also available are mini-HOWTOs, which cover short, specialized topics, such as Internet Protocol (IP) masquerading, multiboot, and coffee.

The University of North Carolina's MetaLab site contains all the HOWTOs at **http://metalab.unc.edu/metalab.shtml**. HOWTOs are in both HTML format (**http://metalab.unc.edu/mdw/HOWTO/HOWTO-INDEX.html**) and ASCII format (**http://metalab.unc.edu/mdw/HOWTO/HOWTO-INDEX.html**). The ASCII files are much easier to print and archive. The HTML files are broken up into specific sections and are easier to navigate.

FAQs And Tutorials

FAQs are usually the best resources for specific questions. Easily searched and navigated, these databases contain the most common issues posed as questions and answers on how to resolve them. FAQs are arranged by program or function, topic, then questions linked to the tutorial that discusses that topic.

Tutorials are helpful in covering a broad topic about which an individual wishes to have an in-depth understanding, because they usually provide step-by-step instruction. Tutorials are perhaps the best way to learn, as most create a course-like education.

There are many sites that have Linux FAQs and tutorials available, and instead of listing them all here, the following provides a few online sites that reference many other resources:

➤ *http://www.cse.unsw.edu.au/~conradp/linux/test.html*   Linux Life is a nice, bare-bones site, full of links to documentation, tutorials, and news.

➤ *http://www.linux.com*   Recently opened, Linux.com provides much information in various formats and links to other sites.

➤ *http://metalab.unc.edu/LDP*   The Linux Documentation Project (LDP) is available at this site, UNC's MetaLab.

Online Man Pages

A searchable version of the man pages can be found online as part of LinuxPowered's tutorial pages at **http://www.linuxpowered.com/html/ tutorials/tutoindx.html**.

These man pages are updated frequently and contain man pages for all distributions of Linux. The search engine is also quite user-friendly as there are no additional commands to use—a simple keyword will do the trick. The data from a keyword search is linked to the command or file referenced via HTML, making it much easier to find the specific item you are looking for.

Appendix D

PREPARING FOR DISTRIBUTION-SPECIFIC EXAMS

The third LPI level-one exam is the distribution specialization exam. For this exam, you have to choose one of the following distributions:

➤ Caldera (**www.caldera.com**)

➤ Debian (**www.debian.org**)

➤ Red Hat (**www.redhat.com**)

➤ Slackware (**www.slackware.com**)

➤ SuSE (**www.suse.com**)

➤ TurboLinux (**www.turbolinux.com**)

Each of the specialization exams is patterned the same way, regardless of the distribution, so studying for them is a matter of understanding what LPI is looking for. Really, it is worthwhile to follow this process for the other exams as well, especially for the Red Hat exam because that counts as distribution-specific.

EXAM PARTS

The distribution-specific exams are broken down into four major parts:

➤ Installing the distribution.

➤ Using the package and software management tools included with the distribution.

➤ Identifying where the distribution stores its main configuration files.

➤ Implementing the administrative tools included with the distribution.

None of the parts is particularly difficult to address. If you are genuinely familiar with the distribution, then you likely know much of the required information already.

PREPARING TO STUDY

To prepare for the LPI specialization exam, you need to do the following:

➤ Get the distribution that you want to focus on. Although you could download it, in this case, it might be worth purchasing so you can have all the documentation to study.

> ➤ Obtain access to a machine where you can install the distribution multiple times, even if you have to totally wipe the machine each time.

> ➤ Locate the URL for the distribution's technical support database. Bookmark it and refer to it with any questions you have.

The preceding steps might seem like a lot of fuss to go through, but remember, this is a full exam and entirely focused on a specific distribution.

STUDYING FOR THE EXAM

Now that you have what you need, it is time to study. There are general instructions that work for preparing for all the specialization exams, and there are specific instructions for each distribution, so be sure to read both the general and specific section for your distribution of choice.

General Study Guidelines

In general, when you are preparing for a distribution-specific exam, you need to do the following:

> ➤ Install the distribution. Repeatedly. Explore the various options offered in the installation, including:

>> ➤ Installation classes or categories

>> ➤ Methods of disk partitioning

>> ➤ Automation versus custom setups

>> ➤ Installation methods if possible

>> ➤ Dual boot setups with a form of Windows and Linux on the same machine

> ➤ Read the manual. If you don't want to read the manual cover to cover, then work through its instructions. Read the warnings and cautions and the reasons for any specific recommendations they provide.

> ➤ Choose one or more than one installation to manipulate. Learn what is on the machine by default and what is not. See what GUI you get by default and what other options are available.

> ➤ Locate the files used in the boot process. One place to start looking is in /etc/inittab.

> ➤ Locate the files that contain the basic networking information used at boot time.

> ➤ Determine the package-management scheme used by the distribution and become familiar with it.

> ➤ Locate any system administration tools included with the distribution and become familiar with them.

Preparing For The Specific Exams

As previously stated, each of the specialization exams is laid out similarly. After all, they each have to be just as difficult as the others. Because the specialization exams are not yet completely developed, at this point, there can only be conjecture about some of the material that might be on the exams. The first four items in the following list are solidly laid out across the exams and the rest are chosen from observations of the kinds of questions that are under discussion. Be sure to examine the LPI Web pages for the latest exam focuses before you tackle the distribution-specific exam of your choice.

To pass these exams, you must:

➤ Be familiar with the subtle differences between the handling of kernel modules in each of the distributions. Table E.1 outlines the specific files in question for each distribution, as well as the commands and scripts available for working with the kernel modules.

Table E.1 Kernel module management in each Linux distribution.

Distribution	Files And Directories	Commands	Scripts
Caldera	/lib/modules/*version* /modules.dep, /etc /modules/*version* /default, /etc/modules /options/, /etc /modules.conf, /etc /rc.d/rc.modules	**depmod, modinfo, modprobe, insmod**	None
Debian	/lib/modules/*version* /modules.dep, /etc /modules, /etc /conf.modules, /etc /modutils/	**depmod, modinfo, modprobe, modconf**	/sbin/update-modules, /etc/ init.d/modutils
Red Hat	/etc/rc.d/rc.sysinit, /etc/conf.modules, /lib/modules /modules.dep, /boot/module-info	**lsmod, depmod, ksyms, insmod, rmmod, modprobe**	None
Slackware	/etc/rc.d/rc.modules, /etc/conf.modules	**depmod, modinfo**	None
SuSE	/lib/modules/*version*, /etc/modules.conf	**insmod, kmod, rmmod, depmod, modprobe, lsmod**	None
TurboLinux	/lib/modules/*version* /modules.dep /etc /rc.d/modules, /etc /conf.modules, /etc/rc.modules	**depmod, modinfo, modprobe**	xturbokernelcfg

Table E.2 Boot management in each Linux distribution.

Distribution	Files And Directories	Tools
Caldera	/etc/inittab, /etc/rc.d/, /etc/rc.d/rc#.d, /etc/rc.d/init.d, /etc/sysconfig/, /etc/system.cnf	Lisa, COAS
Debian	/etc/inittab, /etc/rcS.d/, /etc/rc#.d/, /etc/init.d/, /etc/rc.boot/	None
Red Hat	/etc/sysconfig/, /etc/sysconfig /network-scripts/, /etc/rc.d/, /etc/rc#.d/, /etc/rc.d/init.d/	chkconfig, sndconfig, ntsysv
Slackware	/etc/inittab, /etc/rc.d/rc.#/, /etc/inetd.conf, /etc/ttys	None
SuSE	/etc/inittab, /etc/rc.config, /etc/rc.config.d/, /sbin/init.d/rc#.d/, /sbin/init.d/	None
TurboLinux	/etc/inittab, /etc/rc.d/, /etc/rc#.d/, /etc/rc.d/init.d/, /etc/sysconfig/	None

➤ Be able to customize the boot process. Table E.2 outlines the specific files this involves in each distribution, as well as the tools you must use to be able to make the changes outside of a text editor.

➤ Install the distribution. This is where each Linux distribution varies the most. It is also where the general study guidelines apply the most. Become very familiar with installing the distribution in as many ways as possible. If more than one installation program is available, such as with Caldera (LISA and LIZARD), be sure to become familiar with them all. If there are multiple boot disks available, learn which is used in which situation.

➤ Manage packages. Table E.3 lists which distributions use which package-management schemes.

➤ Utilize the distribution's system maintenance tools. Table E.4 lists the tools used in each distribution.

Table E.3 Package management in each Linux distribution.

Distribution	Command Line Tools	GUI Tools
Caldera	rpm, lisa	COAS, kpackage
Debian	dpkg	dselect
Red Hat	rpm	Gnorpm
Slackware	tar	pkgtool
SuSE	rpm	YaST
TurboLinux	rpm, turbopkg	xturbopkg

Table E.4 Administration for each Linux distribution.

Distribution	Command Line Tools	GUI Tools
Caldera	lisa	COAS
Debian	apacheconfig, bindconfig, gpmconfig, pppconfig, sambaconfig, sendmailconfig, smailconfig, update-modules	None
Red Hat	Xconfigurator, XF86Setup	control-panel, linuxconf
Slackware	setup, pkgtool, netconfig, pppsetup	None
SuSE	SaX, SuSEconfig	YaST
TurboLinux	turbodesk, turbopnpcfg, turbosoundcfg	xturbonetcfg, xturbousercfg

➤ Know the location of the system files. Table E.5 lists a good number of these files. Keep in mind that this is not a complete list!

➤ Be able to build a kernel from source under the specific distribution. Notes for each distribution's kernel build process are:

   ➤ **Caldera** Not part of this exam. Caldera provides kernel binaries.

   ➤ **Debian** Utilize the Debian packaged kernel to install a new version, using the depmod, make-kpkg, and update-modules tools.

Table E.5 System file locations.

Distribution	Files
Caldera	/etc/hosts, /etc/resolv.conf, /etc/nsswitch, /etc/system.cnf, /etc/sysconfig, /etc/XF86Config, /etc/passwd, /etc/shadow, /etc/group, /etc/coas, /etc/config.d/shells, /etc/hosts.allow, /etc/hosts.deny, /etc/login.defs, /etc/issue, /etc/issue.net, /ctc/shells, /etc/skel, /etc/skel.d, /etc/crontab.d
Debian	/etc/hosts, /etc/resolv.conf, /etc/nsswitch, /etc/XF86Config, /etc/passwd, /etc/shadow, /etc/group, /etc/hosts.allow, /etc/hosts.deny, /etc/issue, /etc/issue.net, /etc/skel
Red Hat	/etc/hosts, /etc/resolv.conf, /etc/nsswitch, /etc/XF86Config, /etc/passwd, /etc/shadow, /etc/group, /etc/hosts.allow, /etc/hosts.deny, /etc/issue, /etc/issue.net, /etc/skel
Slackware	/etc/hosts, /etc/resolv.conf, /etc/nsswitch, /etc/XF86Config, /etc/passwd, /etc/shadow, /etc/group, /etc/hosts.allow, /etc/hosts.deny, /etc/issue, /etc/issue.net, /etc/skel, /etc/rc.d/inet1, /etc/rc.d/inet2
SuSE	/var/lib/YaST, /etc/rc.config, /sbin/conf.d
TurboLinux	/etc/sysconfig, /etc/resolv.conf, /etc/hosts

Appendix E

➤ **Red Hat** Utilize rpm or gnorpm to install a Red Hat packaged kernel.

➤ **Slackware** Utilize a tarballed source file to build and install the new kernel.

➤ **SuSE** Utilize SuSE provided source in /usr/src/linux to build and install a new kernel.

➤ **TurboLinux** Utilize TurboPkg, XTurboPkg, or rpm to install a packaged version of the kernel.

➤ Manage the default GUI, especially the window manager menus.

GUI MANAGEMENT TOOLS

Although it is important to know how to execute tasks at the command line, a number of distributions also offer GUI (graphical user interface) tools to assist with system administration tasks. For the exams, you are expected to know about three main tools:

➤ Caldera Open Administration System (COAS)

➤ Linuxconf

➤ Yet another Setup Tool (YaST)

This appendix provides an overview of what you can do with the preceding three tools and how to use them. Although, you should keep in mind that nothing beats hands-on experience when it comes to tools, so be sure to explore each tool's interface.

Explanations on how to make decisions and every small feature of all tools are not included in this appendix. You should already know how to accomplish the described tasks at the command line and know how to make the decisions necessary to fill in the information.

COAS

COAS is provided with Caldera OpenLinux. This item is not a specific program, but a suite of management tools. Each tool has a specific function within the general COAS umbrella. To see a list of the tools available in COAS, click the COAS button on the menu bar at the bottom of the screen, or click the K icon on the left to open the main menu and click COAS in the menu. Either way, you get the main COAS menu shown in Figure F.1.

In this appendix, the COAS tools are covered in the order that they are likely to be used, not in the order they appear in the menus.

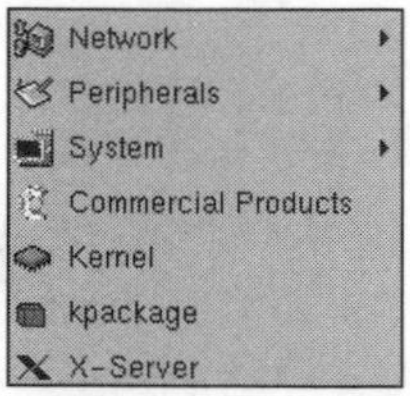

Figure F.1 The COAS main menu.

Configuring Peripherals With COAS

The peripherals that COAS allows you to configure are your mouse and printer. Although the mouse tends to work well enough after most installations, many people dislike working with /etc/printcap and prefer to use tools such as COAS to set up printing. Just keep in mind that you need to know /etc/printcap for the exams—and to fix anything that is accidentally misconfigured by a tool—before you totally rely on GUI tools for getting printers to work.

Setting Up The Mouse

To set up your mouse, perform the following steps:

1. Open the COAS menu.

2. Click Peripherals to open the Peripherals submenu.

3. Click Mouse to open the GPM (General Purpose Mouse) driver via the GPM Mouse Configuration dialog box shown in Figure F.2.

4. If you want to change the model of mouse you are using, click the Model drop-down list box to select a new one.

5. If there is a specific mouse driver you need to use, type its name in the Driver dialog box. Generally speaking, this driver is automatically changed when you choose your mouse type.

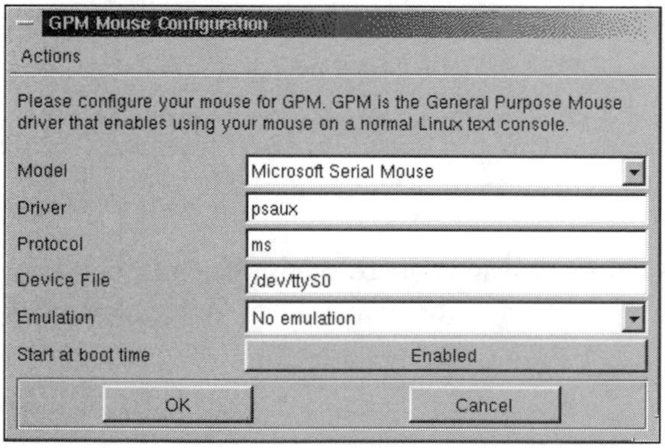

Figure F.2 The COAS GPM Mouse Configuration dialog box.

6. If there is a specific protocol you need to use, type its name in the Protocol dialog box. Once again, this item tends to change automatically to match the mouse type.

7. If you need to change the device driver used by this mouse—for example, because it is in the second serial port (ttyS1) and not the first (ttyS0)—then change the value in the Device File text box.

8. If you are using a two-button mouse but want to emulate a three-button mouse, click the Emulation drop-down list box. Many Linux experts recommend against this option.

9. If you want GPM to start automatically at boot time, click the Start At Boot Time button.

10. Click OK to close the dialog box.

Setting Up A Printer

To configure a printer, perform the following steps:

1. Open the COAS menu.

2. Click Peripherals to open the Peripherals submenu.

3. Click Printer to open the Printer Configuration dialog box.

4. Click Add in the Printer menu to open the Select Printer Model dialog box.

5. Click the printer type you have in the printer listing. The Select Printer Model dialog box closes, and the Printer Name dialog box opens.

6. Assign a name to your printer in the Name text box.

7. Click OK. The Printer Attributes dialog box opens.

8. Choose the paper size and type you intend to use in the Paper Size drop-down list box.

9. Choose the device needed for this printer in the Device drop-down list box. If it is on the first parallel port, then leave it as the default.

10. Change the port communication speed if necessary in the Speed drop-down list box.

11. If you want to do double-sided printing and you have the facilities for it, check the 2 Pages/Sheet checkbox.

12. Click OK to close the dialog box, and click Save to save the changes.

13. Create the printer queue when asked, unless this queue was created before. The print daemon is stopped and restarted, and then the Printer Configuration dialog box reappears.

14. Click OK to close the dialog box.

Appendix F

Configuring Networking With COAS

There is a significant Network submenu in the COAS suite. After all, a good part of system administration is LAN administration. Each of the individual network configuration tools is specialized for a particular task. In the upcoming sections, these tools are covered in the order in which you are most likely to use them.

Setting Up Ethernet Interfaces

To set up one or more Ethernet interfaces, perform the following steps:

1. Open the COAS menu.

2. Click Network to open the Network submenu.

3. Click Ethernet Interfaces to open the Ethernet Interface Configuration dialog box shown in Figure F.3.

4. If you have more than one Ethernet card in the machine, choose the appropriate one in the Network Device drop-down list box.

5. If you intend to set up the machine's networking information via DHCP, choose DHCP in the PNP Configuration drop-down list box.

6. Enter the IP address in the Interface Address text box.

7. Change the Network Mask entry if necessary.

8. Change the Broadcast Address entry to that which is needed by the interface you are configuring.

9. If you want to set a default route for your data to travel, click the Default Route button, then fill in the Default Gateway text box.

10. If you want this interface turned on at boot time, click the Init At Boot Time button.

11. To add a new network device, click the New Device button.

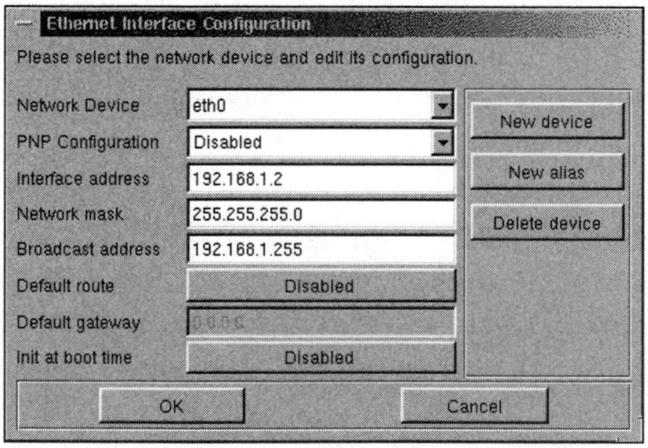

Figure F.3   The COAS Ethernet Interface Configuration dialog box with default values.

12. To add a new network alias, click the New Alias button.

13. To delete an existing network device, click the Delete Device button.

14. Click OK to close the dialog box.

Setting Up Name Resolution

To set up name resolution with COAS, perform the following steps:

1. Open the COAS menu.

2. Click Network to open the Network submenu.

3. Click TCP/IP to open the TCP/IP submenu.

4. Click Resolver to open the Name Resolver Setup dialog box.

5. If you want to change the resolution order from the defaults, click the Information Source button to open the Search Order dialog box. Click the item you want to move, and use the Up or Down button to move it into the appropriate place. When you are finished, click OK.

6. If you want your system to perform a reverse lookup of IP and name information for incoming packets, ensure there is a check in the Try To Prevent Spoofing checkbox.

7. If you have your system watching for spoof attempts and want any suspected spoofing recorded in the system logs, ensure there is a check in the Report Spoof Attempts checkbox.

8. If you want to add to or reorder the list of name servers your system looks to, click the DNS Servers button to open the DNS Name Servers dialog box. Use the Edit menu to add or remove a server, and use the Up and Down buttons to move servers throughout the list. Click OK when you are done.

9. Click OK to close the dialog box.

Setting Up An NIS Client

To set up an NIS client or server with COAS, perform the following steps:

1. Open the COAS menu.

2. Click Network to open the Network submenu.

3. Click TCP/IP to open the TCP/IP submenu.

4. Click NIS to open the NIS Client/Server Setup dialog box.

5. Enter the NIS domain name in the Domain Name text box.

6. If you want to run an NIS client on the machine, click the Start NIS Client On Boot button until it says Enabled.

7. If you want to explicitly set the order in which the machine should use your NIS servers, click the NIS Servers button to open the NIS Servers

dialog box. Click the Edit menu for options to add, change, or remove servers listed. When you are finished altering the order by clicking the Up and Down buttons, click OK.

8. Click OK to close the NIS Client/Server Setup dialog box.

9. Click Save to save your changes. COAS now stops and restarts the NIS daemon.

Setting Up Basic Mail Transfer

To set your machine up for basic mail transfer functionality, perform the following steps:

1. Open the COAS menu.

2. Click Network to open the Network submenu.

3. Click Mail Transfer to open the Mail Transport Configuration dialog box.

4. In the Visible Domain text box, enter the domain information you want to include in outgoing mail. For example, for cherry.fruit.org, you might want all mail to look like it is coming from fruit.org.

5. If the machine is intermittently connected to the Internet or behind a firewall, enter the relay host information in the Mail Relay Host text box. Doing this activates the Transport Method drop-down list box. Select the transport method to use, which is often TCP in such situations. Then, check whether the relay machine is the Internet Hub (the central mail server for the domain that interacts with the Internet) or the Local Hub (the central mail server behind the firewall or among the intermittently connected machines).

6. Click OK to close the dialog box.

Configuring System Information With COAS

One of the largest menus available in COAS is the System menu. This is because COAS, after all, is a tool for system administrators. A variety of items are included in this menu—be sure to take a look at them. The tools are covered in the order you might use them instead of in their menu order.

Setting Your System's Name

To set a machine's name, perform the following steps:

1. Open the COAS menu.

2. Click System to open the System submenu.

3. Click Hostname to open the System Hostname dialog box.

4. Type the fully qualified domain name in the Hostname text box. This means the host name plus the domain name and the extension. For example, blue.colors.org.

5. Click OK. There might be some warnings about changing system settings while in an X session. If so, read the warnings carefully before deciding how to proceed.

Setting System Time

To set your system's clock, perform the following steps:

1. Open the COAS menu.

2. Click System to open the System submenu.

3. Click Time to open the System Time dialog box.

4. If you need to change your system's time, change the values in the Set Current Time text box.

5. If you need to change your system's time zone, click the Your Time Zone button to open the Continent dialog box. Select the continent on which you live and the Continent dialog box closes, then the Country dialog box opens. Select the Country in which you live and the Country dialog box closes. The Region dialog box opens. Scroll to your time zone and choose the appropriate option out of the various geographical regions assigned to it. Click the appropriate option and the Region dialog box closes.

6. Click OK to close the dialog box.

Managing File System Components

To manage which partitions are mounted and unmounted, perform the following steps:

1. Open the COAS menu.

2. Click System to open the System submenu.

3. Click Filesystem to open the File System dialog box shown in Figure F.4.

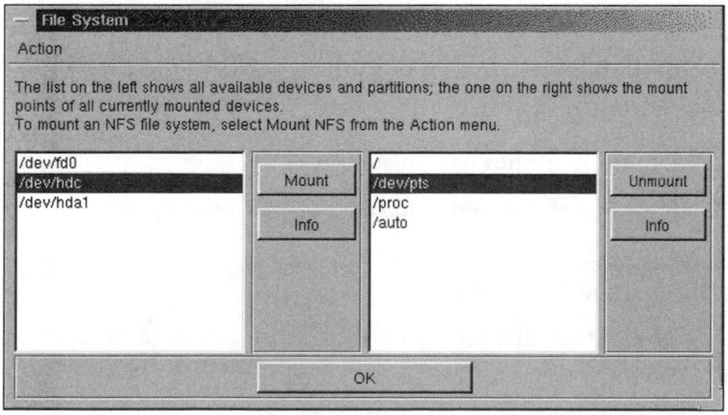

Figure F.4 The COAS File System dialog box.

4. What you do from here depends on whether you want to mount or unmount a device. See the appropriate section for instructions.

5. When finished, click OK to close the dialog box.

Mounting Devices

To mount a device using COAS, perform the following steps:

1. Open the File System dialog box (as described in the preceding section) and select the device you want to mount from the list on the left side of the dialog box.

2. Click the Mount button. The Mount File System dialog box opens.

3. Check to see that the mount point, file system type, and mount options are correct.

4. Click OK to mount the device. The listing is removed from the left column and added to the right.

Unmounting Devices

To unmount a device using COAS, perform the following steps:

1. Open the File System dialog box (as described in the "Managing File System Components" section) and select the device you want to unmount from the list on the right side of the dialog box.

2. Click the Unmount button. The Unmount File System dialog box opens.

3. Read the checkbox options carefully. For example, do not remove anything from /etc/fstab that you always want to have mounted at boot time.

4. Check the appropriate checkboxes.

5. Click OK. The device is removed from the column on the right and added to the column on the left.

Setting Which Daemons Activate At Boot Time

To set which daemons are started at boot time, perform the following steps:

1. Open the COAS menu.

2. Click System to open the System submenu.

3. Click Daemons on the System submenu to open the System Services dialog box.

4. Scroll through the list of services.

5. Uncheck any service that you do not want to start at boot time, and check any that you do.

6. Click OK to close the dialog box.

Managing Users

To work with the accounts on your system, perform the following steps:

1. Open the COAS menu.

2. Click System to open the System submenu.

3. Click Accounts on the System submenu to open the User Accounts dialog box shown in Figure F.5.

There are a number of features in the COAS User Accounts dialog box. What you see by default is a listing of all user accounts. At the top is a set of menus—File, User, Groups, View, and Options. Each of these menus offers its own particular services as described in the following sections. First are the user account options.

Creating User Accounts

The COAS User Accounts tool allows you to create, delete, and modify accounts. To create an account, perform the following steps:

1. Open the COAS User Accounts dialog box (as described in the "Managing Users" section), and click User on the menu bar.

2. Select Create on the User menu to open the Create User Account dialog box.

3. Fill in the account name in the Login Name text box.

4. Click OK. The Edit User dialog box opens as shown in Figure F.6.

5. Type the user's name or alias in the Full Name text box.

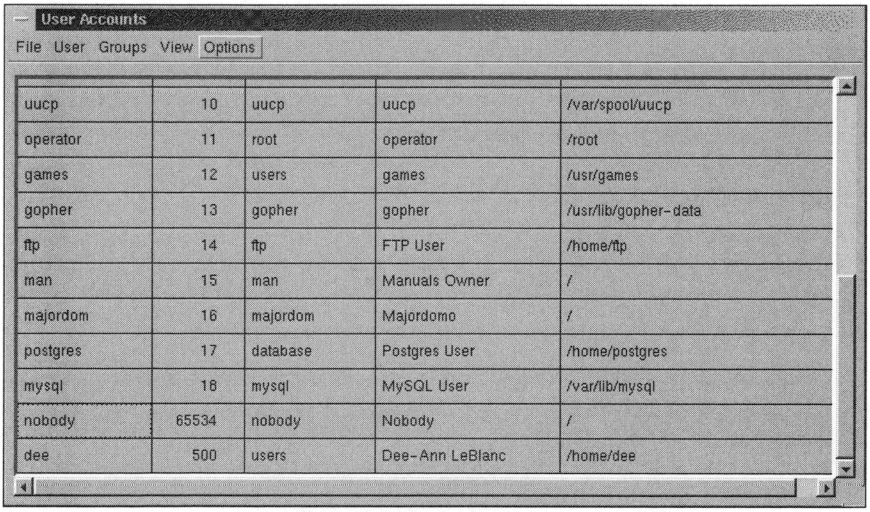

User Accounts				
File User Groups View Options				
uucp	10	uucp	uucp	/var/spool/uucp
operator	11	root	operator	/root
games	12	users	games	/usr/games
gopher	13	gopher	gopher	/usr/lib/gopher-data
ftp	14	ftp	FTP User	/home/ftp
man	15	man	Manuals Owner	/
majordom	16	majordom	Majordomo	/
postgres	17	database	Postgres User	/home/postgres
mysql	18	mysql	MySQL User	/var/lib/mysql
nobody	65534	nobody	Nobody	/
dee	500	users	Dee-Ann LeBlanc	/home/dee

Figure F.5   The COAS User Accounts dialog box.

Appendix F

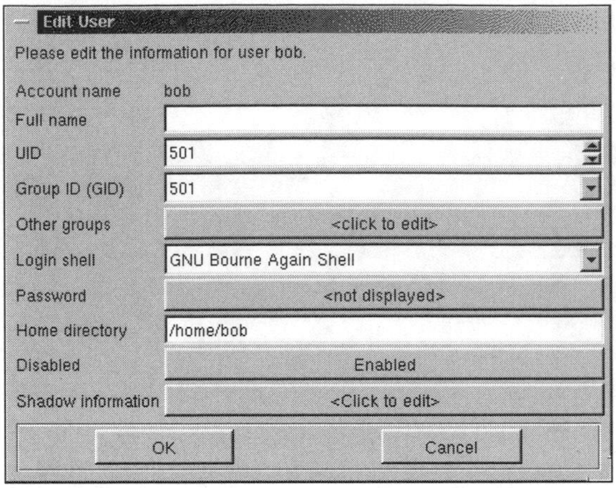

Figure F.6 The COAS Edit User dialog box.

6. If you have specific reason to, change the UID or GID values. Notice that they are identical to one another by default.

7. If you want to add the user to additional groups, click the Other Groups button to open the Groups For User *User* dialog box (*User* will be the name of the user account being edited). Use the left and right facing buttons to add and remove the user from extra groups until you have it set as you want, then click OK to close the dialog box.

8. If you want to change which shell the user's login defaults to, choose a shell from the Login Shell drop-down list box.

9. If you want to change the user's password, click the Password button to open the Change Password dialog box. Enter the password in both text boxes and click OK.

10. If you want to change the home directory that is assigned to the user, do so in the Home Directory text box.

11. If for some reason you want to disable the account now, click the Disabled button to change its reading from Enabled to Disabled.

12. If you want to edit the extra account information stored in /etc/shadow, click the Shadow Information button to open the Password Expiration dialog box. Change the defaults to the new values and click OK.

13. Click OK to close the dialog box. This returns you to the main dialog box.

Editing User Accounts

After you have created an account, you can edit or delete it. Editing is very similar to creating, and, in fact, is identical in process to Steps 5 through 13 in the "Creating User Accounts" section after you perform the following steps:

1. Open the COAS User Accounts dialog box (as described in the "Managing Users" section), and click the account you want to edit.

2. Click User on the menu bar.

3. Select Edit User on the User menu to open the dialog box shown earlier in Figure F.6.

4. Proceed with Steps 5 through 13 in the "Creating User Accounts" section.

Deleting User Accounts

Deleting user accounts is different than editing user accounts. To delete an account, perform the following steps:

1. Open the COAS User Accounts dialog box (as described in the "Managing Users" section), and click the account you want to delete.

2. Click User on the menu bar.

3. Select Delete User on the User menu.

4. Click Yes to delete the user.

5. If you want, click Yes to delete the group.

6. If you want, click Yes to delete the user's home directory.

You can also close the dialog box in the File menu, toggle between seeing all accounts and only accounts that are non-daemon or non-system in the View menu, and set user defaults in the Options menu.

Managing Groups

To manage your groups, perform the following steps:

1. Open the COAS menu.

2. Click System to open the System submenu.

3. Click Accounts on the System submenu to open the User Accounts dialog box shown earlier in Figure F.5.

4. Click the Groups menu to open it.

5. Click Manage Groups under the Groups menu to open the Manage Groups dialog box. What you do from here depends on what you want to do in the Groups menu of this dialog box. See the following sections for instructions.

6. When finished, click OK to close the dialog box.

Creating Groups

To create a group, perform the following steps:

1. Open the Manage Groups dialog box (as described in the "Managing Groups" section), and click the Groups menu to open it.

2. Click Create Group in the Groups menu to open the Create Group dialog box.

3. Enter a name for the group in the Group Name text box. The Create Group dialog box closes and the group name now appears in the group listing.

Deleting Groups

Deleting a group is just as straightforward as creating a group. To delete a group, perform the following steps:

1. Open the Manage Groups dialog box (as described in the "Managing Groups" section), and click the group in the listing that you want to delete.

2. Click the Groups menu to open it.

3. Select Delete Group on the Groups menu to open the Delete Groups dialog box.

4. Click Continue to delete the group. The dialog box closes, and the group is no longer listed.

Renaming Groups

Renaming a group is similar to deleting it. You follow the same process except that you click Rename Group instead of Delete Group, type in a new group name, and click OK before the group's name is moved in the listing.

Clicking on a group in the listing shows you who is in the group in a listing on the right.

Merging Groups

One interesting option that is rarely discussed is merging groups. This idea is useful when you have a number of small project groups, for example, that you want to use to create one larger work group. To merge groups, perform the following steps:

1. Open the Manage Groups dialog box (as described in the "Managing Groups" section), and click one of the groups in the listing that you want to merge. This group should be the one that you want to add the contents of the others to, so you might need to create a new group first.

2. Click the Groups menu.

3. Select Merge Group to open the Merge Group dialog box.

4. Type the name of the group whose users you want to add to the first group in the Group Name text box.

5. Click OK to close the dialog box and complete the merge.

Changing Group Memberships

Finally, if you want to change who belongs to a group, perform the following steps:

1. Open the Manage Groups dialog box (as described in the "Managing Groups" section), and click the group in the listing whose membership you want to alter.

2. Click the Groups menu to open it.

3. Select Group Membership to open the Group Membership dialog box.

4. Use the left and right arrows to move users back and forth until you are satisfied with the group member list.

5. Click OK to close the dialog box.

Getting Information On System Resources

To get information about the resources your system is using, perform the following steps:

1. Open the COAS menu.

2. Click System to open the System submenu.

3. Click Resources in the System submenu to open the System Resource Information dialog box shown in Figure F.7.

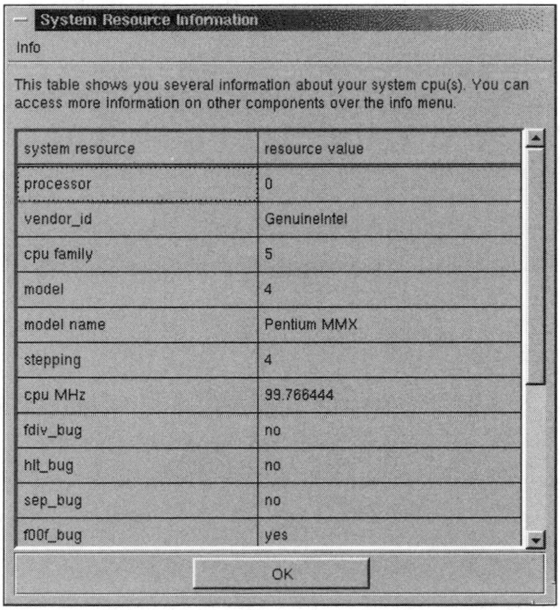

Figure F.7 The COAS System Resource Information dialog box.

4. All of the general resource information is shown in the main dialog box. Clicking the Info menu lists the other segments of resources about which you can get information—Block Devices, Character Devices, Interrupts, System Load Average, Ioports, and DMA.

Managing Kernel Modules

One thing that many people find frustrating is module management. COAS provides a tool to help with this issue. To load and unload kernel modules using COAS, perform the following steps:

1. Open the COAS menu.

2. Click Kernel on the COAS menu to open the Kernel Modules dialog box.

3. The left of the dialog box contains the full list of available modules, whereas the right lists the modules that are actually loaded. Select the item you want to load from the left or unload from the right and then click the Load or Unload button, as appropriate.

4. Carefully read any dialog boxes that open, then close them.

5. When finished, click OK to close the dialog box.

Managing RPMs With kpackage

Although it is simple enough to work with RPMs at the command line, some distributions and GUIs come with components for managing packages graphically. The package included in COAS is kpackage. This is a full-featured tool that takes some of the memorization out of using the RPM commands.

Opening kpackage

To open kpackage, perform the following steps:

1. Open the COAS menu.

2. Click kpackage on the COAS menu to open the kpackage dialog box shown in Figure F.8.

Installing RPMs With kpackage

To install an RPM using kpackage, open the program and then perform the following steps:

1. Select Open on the File menu to open the Select Document To Open dialog box.

2. Click on directory items to navigate to the location of the package. If you want to install an item from the Caldera CD-ROM, navigate to /Packages /RPMS.

3. Click the file you want to install to select it.

4. Click OK. The Install Package dialog box appears.

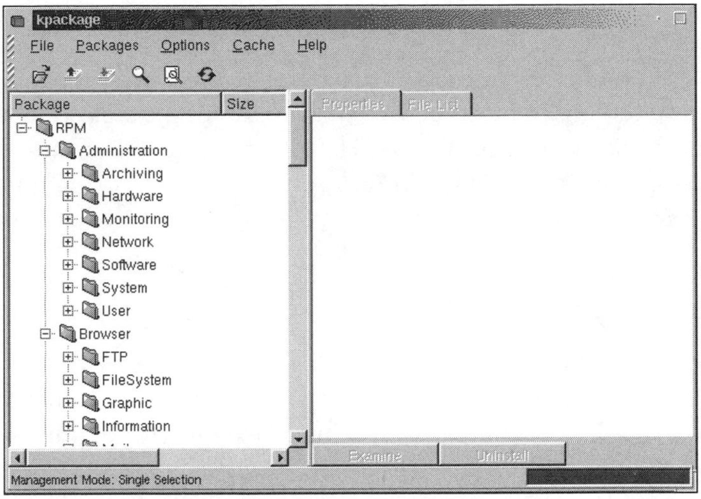

Figure F.8   The COAS kpackage dialog box.

5. Read the contents of the dialog box. Choose and select or deselect the items on the left that make the most sense to you. The available items are: Upgrade, Replace Files, Replace Packages, Check Dependencies, and Test (do not install).

6. Click Install to install the RPM. You are returned to the kpackage dialog box.

Removing RPMs With kpackage

To remove an RPM from the system with kpackage, perform the following steps:

1. Navigate through the package list on the left to find the package you want to remove.

2. Click the package to select it.

3. Click the Uninstall button on the right-hand side to open the Uninstall dialog box.

4. Read the information in the dialog box carefully.

5. In general, it is a good idea to leave the checkboxes as they are. If you have the need to do so, change the checkbox option settings as necessary.

6. Click Uninstall to remove the package.

X-Server

Through COAS, Caldera allows you to run through the X setup routine whenever you need to. This is the same routine that you follow when you install Caldera OpenLinux. To start the X setup routine, open the COAS menu, and click X-Server. Follow the routine all the way through. This is a good way to recover from an X configuration you do not like, without having to fuss with reinstallation or locating the X packages yourself to work with by hand.

Appendix F

LINUXCONF

Linuxconf (see Figure F.9) is a third-party GUI configuration and system administration tool made by Solucorp (**www.solucorp.qc.ca/linuxconf**). This tool is primarily available in Red Hat and derivative distributions. It is well integrated, with data entered in one portion of the tool being properly read into other segments, making your life as system administrators much easier.

How Linuxconf Is Laid Out

Linuxconf is made up of a number of small, integrated functions organized into a menu tree. Part of learning to use this tool involves learning how to navigate through the tree. There are two main branches to the Linuxconf menu tree—Config and Control. This breakdown is fairly intuitive. Basically, all configuration options reside on the Config trunk, whereas all server and service control options reside on Control.

Introduction To The Config Trunk

The Config portion of the tree trunk is broken down into five parts:

➤ Networking

➤ Users Accounts

➤ File Systems

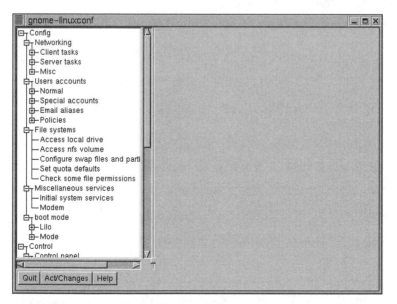

Figure F.9   The Linuxconf main dialog box.

➤ Miscellaneous Services

➤ Boot Mode

Each of these sections is, in turn, even further nested into subcategories. This level is where you encounter actual tools rather than just more branching.

Introduction To The Control Trunk

The Control portion of the tree trunk is broken into five parts as well:

➤ Control Panel

➤ Control Files And Systems

➤ Logs

➤ Date & Time

➤ Features

Parts of the Control trunk are far more shallow than its Config counterpart. Already at this level, you encounter actual tools rather than just menus.

Configuring Client Networking

The first chunk of the Linuxconf Config trunk is Networking. The first chunk of this section is Client Networking, which is where you configure the client aspects of your network services. Each of these items is listed in the order you are likely to use them, so they are covered in that order in the upcoming sections.

Setting Host And Interface Information

To set your host's name and activate network interfaces, perform the following steps:

1. Click Basic Host Information to open the This Host Basic Configuration dialog box.

2. Enter the fully qualified domain name (the host name, domain, and extension) in the This Host Basic Configuration dialog box.

3. Click the Adaptor 1 tab to open the Adaptor 1 dialog box.

4. Be sure that the Enabled button is selected.

5. Click the proper Config mode button—Manual, Dhcp, or Bootp.

6. Enter the fully qualified domain name in the Primary Name + Domain text box.

7. Enter the machine's aliases, IP address, and netmask in the appropriate text boxes.

8. If your Ethernet card is a PCI card, then the Net Device and Kernel Module text boxes are probably already filled out. If not, then fill these in appropriately.

9. If you are having problems with the Ethernet card, consider filling in the I/O Port (opt) and IRQ (opt) text boxes.

10. If you have a second Ethernet card, click the 2 tab to configure it as well. Otherwise, click Accept to close the dialog box.

Configuring Name Service

To configure your name service resolution with Linuxconf, perform the following steps:

1. Click Name Server Specification (DNS) to open the Resolver Configuration dialog box shown in Figure F.10.

2. Ensure that the DNS usage box is selected so that your name server is activated.

3. Enter your domain plus extension in the Default Domain text box. For example, colors.org.

4. Enter the IP address(es) for the nameserver(s) you want to use in the Nameserver 1, 2, and 3 dialog boxes.

5. Click the Accept button to save the changes and close the dialog box.

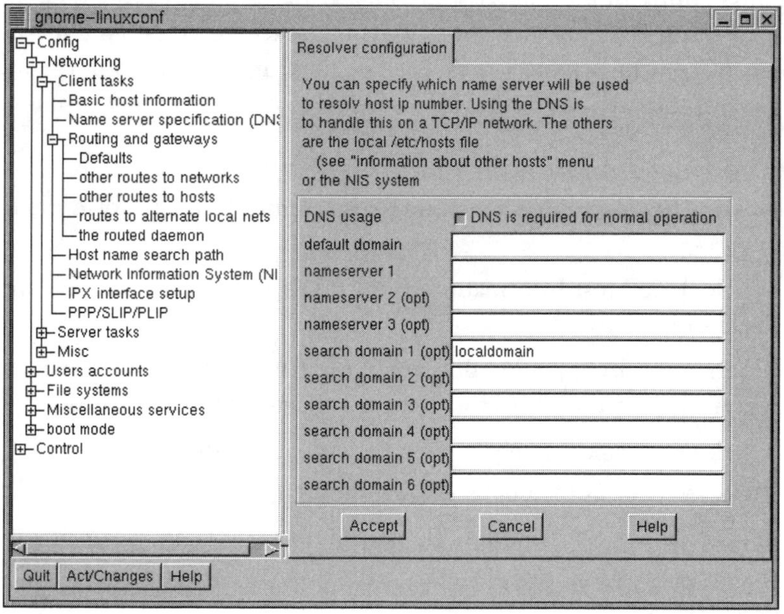

Figure F.10 The Linuxconf Resolver Configuration dialog box.

Configuring Routing In General

Configuring routing in Linuxconf involves a new menu tree. Click the plus next to Routing And Gateways to expand the options. You have the choice of:

➤ Defaults

➤ Other Routes To Networks

➤ Other Routes To Hosts

➤ Routes To Alternate Local Nets

➤ The Routed Daemon

Although you likely need to configure more than one of the preceding options, you probably do not need to configure them all. Give each item some thought to determine whether you need it before you configure it.

Configuring Routing: Defaults

To configure the default routing information, perform the following steps:

1. Click Defaults to open the Defaults dialog box.

2. Enter the default gateway address in the text box. This should be the gateway used to reach the Internet.

3. Select the Enable Routing checkbox if you need the machine to act as a router.

4. Click the Accept button to save the changes and close the dialog box.

Configuring Routing: Routes To Networks

To configure your routing to other networks, such as internal subnets, perform the following steps:

1. Click Other Routes To Networks to open the Route To Other Networks dialog box.

2. Click the Add button to open the Route Specification dialog box, where you set up the new routing scheme.

3. Enter the address for the gateway from the current network to the network you are configuring in the Gateway text box.

4. Enter the network address for the network the gateway passes information to in the Destination text box.

5. If necessary, enter the netmask for the network you are setting routing to talk to in the Netmask text box.

6. Click Accept to save the changes and close the dialog box.

7. Click Quit to close the Route To Other Networks dialog box, or click Add to add another network route.

Appendix F

Configuring Routing: Routes To Hosts

If you want to have hosts that are not on the main LAN considered part of the network, then you need to tell the router how and where to include these machines. To accomplish this task, perform the following steps:

1. Click Other Routes To Hosts to open the Route To Other Hosts dialog box.

2. Click the Add button to open the Route Specification dialog box.

3. Enter the interface to use to talk to the remote host in the Gateway text box.

4. Enter the host's name or IP address in the Destination text box.

5. Click Accept to save the changes and close the dialog box.

6. Click Quit to close the Route To Other Hosts dialog box, or click Add to add another route.

Configuring Routing: Routes To Local Nets

If you have subnets or other networks sharing the same LAN hardware at any point in the configuration, you need to set up routing to local networks. To accomplish this, perform the following steps:

1. Click Routes To Alternate Local Nets to open the Route To Alternate Local Networks dialog box.

2. Click the Add button to open the Route Specification dialog box.

3. Enter the name for the network interface that talks to the other local network in the Interface text box, or select it from the drop-down list box.

4. Enter the other network's network address in the Destination text box.

5. Enter the other network's netmask in the Netmask text box.

6. Click the Accept button to save the changes and close the dialog box.

7. Click Add to create another network definition, or click Quit to close the Route To Alternate Local Networks dialog box.

Configuring Routing: Routed

To configure your actual routing daemon, perform the following steps:

1. Click the routed daemon to open the Routed Daemon Configuration dialog box.

2. If you want your routed daemon to be silent instead of speaking up when requests for a router go out, ensure the Does Not Export Any Routes box is selected.

3. If you want the default route on the machine exported to as the entire network's default route, ensure the Export Your Default Route box is selected.

4. Click Accept to save the changes and close the dialog box.

Configuring The Order In Which Names Are Sought

To configure the order of the files and services your machine looks in to track down host IP addresses, perform the following steps:

1. Click Host Name Search Path to open the Name Service Access dialog box shown in Figure F.11.

2. If you want to allow a machine to have more than one IP address assigned to an interface, or to a range of interfaces, then be sure the Multiple IPs For One Host checkbox is checked.

3. You can only choose one out of the long listing of options. Read each one and understand what you are turning on and off when you choose one.

4. Click Accept to save the changes and close the dialog box.

Setting Up An NIS Client

To configure a machine as an NIS client, perform the following steps:

1. Click Network Information System (NIS) to open the NIS Client Configuration dialog box.

2. Fill in the NIS Domain and Server text boxes.

3. Click Accept to save the changes and close the dialog box.

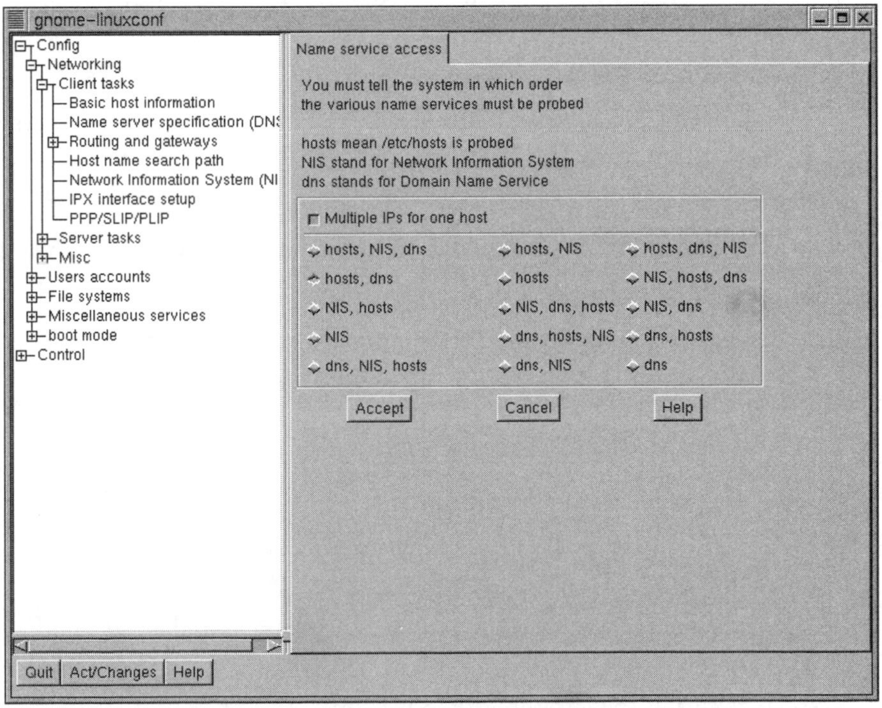

Figure F.11   The Linuxconf Name Service Access dialog box.

Setting Up An IPX Interface

If you need to set up an IPX interface for your network, perform the following steps:

1. Click IPX Interface Setup to open the IPX Interface Configuration dialog box.

2. Fill in the data for each of the three tabs.

3. Click Accept to save the changes and close the dialog box when you are finished.

Configuring A PPP/SLIP/PLIP Connection

If you need to set up your dial-out connection, perform the following steps:

1. Click PPP/SLIP/PLIP to open the PPP/Slip/Plip Configurations dialog box.

2. Click Add to open the Type Of Interface dialog box.

3. Click one of the options—PPP, SLIP, or PLIP.

4. Click Accept to save the changes and open the PPP Interface ppp0 dialog box (this assumes you are setting up a PPP connection, which is the most common today).

5. Fill in the Phone Number, Modem Port, and Login Information text boxes and drop-down list boxes.

6. If you need PAP configuration, ensure the checkbox is selected.

7. Click Customize to save the changes and open the next PPP Interface ppp0 dialog box at the Hardware tab, which is shown in Figure F.12.

8. Set the appropriate hardware information.

9. Click the Communication tab to open the Communication dialog box.

10. Set any necessary connection information.

11. Use the script builder to create your dial-in script. In the Expect text boxes, tell the builder what text to watch for, and, in the Send text box, tell what data to respond with.

12. Click the Networking tab to open the Networking dialog box.

13. Fill in any needed information.

14. If you need to set up PAP authentication, click the PAP tab and fill in the dialog box.

15. Click Accept when finished to save the changes and close all but the original dialog box.

16. Click Quit to close the PPP/Slip/Plip configurations dialog box.

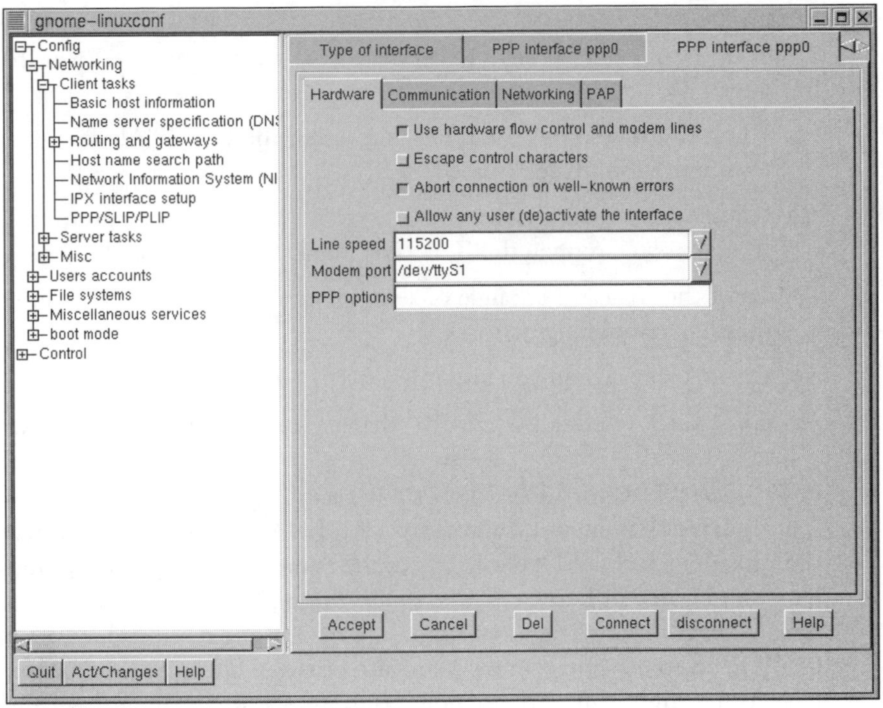

Figure F.12   The Linuxconf PPP Interface ppp0 dialog box, Hardware tab.

Configuring Server Networking

The second chunk of the Linuxconf Config Networking trunk is server networking. This is where you configure the client aspects of your network services. Each of these items is listed in the order you are likely to use them, so they are covered in that order in the upcoming sections.

Exporting NFS Mounts

To set up your machine to export NFS mounts, perform the following steps:

1. Click Exported File Systems (NFS) to open the Exported file systems dialog box.

2. Click the Add button to open the One Exported File System dialog box.

3. Define the file system segment you want to export and its rules.

4. Click Accept when you are finished defining the mount.

5. Click Add to add another file system to export, or click Quit to close the dialog box.

Setting Up IP Aliasing

To set up IP aliasing for any virtual hosts you want to run, perform the following steps:

1. Click IP Aliases For Virtual Hosts to open the Edit IP Aliases Configurations dialog box.

2. Click the network device in the list that you want to assign more than one IP address to, to open the IP Aliases For Device *Name* dialog box.

3. Enter the IP aliases or range of aliases you want to assign to the interface and their corresponding netmask(s).

4. Click Accept when you are finished.

5. Click Quit to close the Edit IP Aliases Configurations dialog box.

Configuring Sendmail In General

Configuring Sendmail in Linuxconf involves a new pair of menu trees. Click the plus next to Mail Delivery System (Sendmail) to expand the options. You have the choice of Basic and Anti-spam filters. Next, you further expand the trees to find that you have a wide range of options to consider. Although you likely need to configure more than one of these filters, you probably do not need to configure all of them. Give each item some thought before you configure it.

Configuring Basic Sendmail: Basic Information

To initially set up your mail server's behavior, perform the following steps:

1. Click Basic Information to get the Basic Sendmail configuration dialog box.

2. Enter your domain name and extension in the Present Your System As text box. For example, colors.org.

3. If the machine is meant to be your primary mail server, check the Accept Email For *Name.ext* box.

4. Enter the IP addresses for the appropriate machines in the Mail Server and Mail Gateway text boxes.

5. If necessary, change the mail gateway protocol.

6. Fill in the Features, Misc, and Aliases tabs appropriately.

7. When finished, click Accept to generate a new Sendmail configuration file. You might receive warning dialog boxes. Read them carefully before closing them.

Configuring Basic Sendmail: Special Routing

If you need to assign special mail routings for certain machines, perform the following steps:

1. Click on Special (Domain) Routing to open the Special Routings dialog box.

2. Click the Add button to open the next Special Routing dialog box.

3. Enter the IP address of the machine that needs special routing in the Destination text box.

4. Enter the IP address of the host that handles the destination machine's mail in the Forward text box.

5. Choose the method by which the mail gets to the destination machine in the Mailer drop-down list box.

6. Click Accept to save the data and close the dialog box.

7. Click Add to add another machine, or click Quit to exit the Special Routings dialog box.

Configuring Basic Sendmail: Redirecting Mail

If you need to redirect mail for specific users, perform the following steps:

1. Click Complex (User) Routing to open the Complex Routings dialog box.

2. Click Add to open the New Complex Route dialog box.

3. Fill in the initial user information in the To text box.

4. Fill in the rerouting information in the remaining text boxes.

5. Click Accept to save the data and close the dialog box.

6. Click Add to add another reroute, or click Quit to exit the Complex Routings dialog box.

Configuring Basic Sendmail: Creating Masquerading Rules

To create a masquerading rule for outgoing mail, perform the following steps:

1. Click Masquerading Rules to open the Masquerading Rules dialog box.

2. Click Add to open the New Masquerading Rule dialog box.

3. Enter the original sender's address in the From text box.

4. Enter the new format for the sender's address in the New From text box.

5. Click Accept to save the data and close the dialog box.

6. Click Add to add another reroute, or click Quit to exit the Masquerading Rules dialog box.

Configuring Basic Sendmail: Creating A Mail To Fax Gateway

To create a mail-to-fax gateway, perform the following steps:

1. Click Mail To Fax Gateway to open the Mail To Fax Gateway Configuration dialog box.

Appendix F

2. Click the Basic Information button to open the next dialog box.

3. Click the Active button to activate the gateway.

4. Enter the command that needs to be run to transmit faxes in the Spool Command text box.

5. Enter the logging file and commands in the appropriate text boxes.

6. Click Accept to return to the main dialog box.

7. Click the Fax Access Rules button to open the Fax Rules dialog box.

8. Click the Add button to open the One Access Rule dialog box.

9. Fill in the appropriate information.

10. Click Accept to return to the Fax Rules dialog box.

11. Click Quit to return to the main dialog box.

12. Click the Fax Users button to open the Fax Users dialog box.

13. Click the Add button to open the Fax Users dialog box.

14. Fill in the appropriate information.

15. Click Accept to return to the Fax Users dialog box.

16. Click Quit to return to the main dialog box.

17. Click the Fax Users button to open the Fax Zones dialog box.

18. Click the Add button to open the One Fax Zone dialog box.

19. Fill in the appropriate information.

20. Click Accept to return to the Fax Zones dialog box.

21. Click Quit to return to the main dialog box.

22. Click the Fax Aliases button to open the Fax Zones dialog box.

23. Click the Add button to open the Fax Alias dialog box.

24. Fill in the appropriate information.

25. Click Accept to return to the Fax Aliases dialog box.

26. Click Quit to return to the main dialog box.

27. Click Quit to close the dialog box.

Configuring Basic Sendmail: Configuring Virtual Email Domains

To set up email service for a virtual domain, perform the following steps:

1. Click Virtual Email Domain to open the Virtual Email Domains dialog box.

2. Click the Add button to open the One Vdomain Definition dialog box.

3. Enter the fully qualified domain name for the virtual domain in the Virtual Domain text box. For example, if you provide email for **www.pretend.org**, then enter the entire address, or you could type "pretend.org."

4. Click the Match Full User Name checkbox to activate the feature.

5. In the Aliases For This Domain text box, enter other domain names that might point to the same users.

6. Click Accept to return to the main dialog box.

7. Click Quit to close the dialog box.

Configuring Basic Sendmail: Managing The Mail Queue

To alter the Sendmail queue, perform the following steps:

1. Click the Mail Queue button to open the Mail Queue dialog box.

2. Click the queue in the list that you want to manage. This opens the One Message Status dialog box.

3. Click Delete to delete the message(s) listed. Otherwise, click Cancel.

4. Click Quit to close the dialog box.

Configuring Basic Sendmail: Creating User Aliases

To create user aliases in Sendmail, perform the following steps:

1. Click User Aliases to open the Edit Global Mail Aliases dialog box.

2. Click an alias to edit it, or click the Add button to create a new one. The One Alias Definition dialog box opens.

3. Name the alias in the Alias Name text box.

4. If you want to pipe all messages to the alias through another program, enter the command to run in the Filter Program text box.

5. If you want the list of people the alias represents to reside in a file, enter the file's path in the List File text box.

6. Below the line, enter the user names one by one that the alias points to. If you need to add more than there are blanks for, click Add.

7. Click Accept to return to the main dialog box.

8. Click Quit to close the dialog box.

Configuring Basic Sendmail: Creating Specific Users On Virtual Domains

If you need to create aliases for user names at any of your virtual domains, perform the following steps:

1. Click Virtual Domain User Aliases to open the Pick The Domain dialog box.

2. Click the domain you want to edit to open the /etc/vmail/aliases.*domain.ext* dialog box.

3. Click Add to open the One Alias Definition dialog box.

4. Follow the instructions in the Configuring Basic Sendmail: Creating User Aliases section.

5. Click Accept to close the dialog box.

6. Click Add to create a new alias, or click Quit to close the dialog box.

7. Click Quit to close the main dialog box.

Configuring Basic Sendmail: Regenerating /etc/sendmail.cf

Whenever you want to regenerate the Sendmail configuration file, click /etc /sendmail.cf. The file is generated automatically.

Configuring Anti-Spam Sendmail: Rejecting Senders

To refuse mail from specific users or domains, perform the following steps:

1. Click Rejected Senders to open the Mail Rejected From dialog box.

2. Click the Add button to open the Rejected Message dialog box.

3. Enter the address you want to reject in the Email Origin text box.

4. Enter the message to be sent back with the rejected mail in the Error Message text box.

5. Click Accept to close the dialog box.

6. Click Add to reject another address, or click Quit to close the dialog box.

Configuring Anti-Spam Sendmail: Setting Who To Relay

To set particular users or addresses as being OK for relaying, perform the following steps:

1. Click Relay For By IP to open the May Relay Mail For dialog box, or click Relay For By Name to open the same dialog box.

2. Click the Add button to open the Allow This Host/Domain To Use Your Server (IP) dialog box, or click the Allow This Host/Domain To Use Your Server dialog box.

3. Enter an IP address for a host or a network address for an entire domain if you chose the By IP option. Otherwise, enter the machine's host name or a domain name.

4. Click Accept to close the dialog box.

5. Click Add to add another definition, or click Quit to close the dialog box.

Configuring Anti-Spam Sendmail: Relay To Hosts

To set up who Sendmail is allowed to relay to, perform the following steps:

1. Click Relay To Hosts to open the May Relay Mail To dialog box.

2. Click the Add button to open the Relay To This Host/Network dialog box.

3. Enter an IP address for a host, a network address for an entire domain, the machine's host name, or a domain name.

4. Click Accept to close the dialog box.

5. Click Add to add another definition, or click Quit to close the dialog box.

Configuring Miscellaneous Networking

The third and final chunk of the Linuxconf Config Networking trunk is miscellaneous networking. This is where you configure aspects of your network services that did not fall under either client or server applications. Each of the miscellaneous networking items is listed in the order you are likely to use them, and so they are covered in that order in the upcoming sections.

Setting Information About Other Hosts

To input information about other machines on or outside of the LAN, perform the following steps:

1. Click Information About Other Hosts to open the /etc/hosts dialog box.

2. Click a host in the list, or click the Add button to open the Host/Network Definition dialog box.

3. Enter the fully qualified domain name in the Primary Name + Domain text box.

4. Enter any aliases you want to assign to that host in the Aliases (Opt) text box.

5. Enter the machine's IP address in the IP Number text box.

6. Click Accept to close the dialog box.

7. Click Add to add another host, or click Quit to close the dialog box.

Setting Information About Other Networks

To input information about your own or outside networks, perform the following steps:

1. Click Information About Other Networks to open the /etc/networks dialog box.

2. Click a network in the list, or click the Add button to open the Host/ Network Definition dialog box.

3. Enter the fully qualified domain name in the Primary Name + Domain text box.

4. Enter any aliases you want to assign to the network in the Aliases (Opt) text box.

5. Enter the network address in the IP Number text box.

6. Click Accept to close the dialog box.

7. Click Add to add another network, or click Quit to close the dialog box.

Appendix F

Setting Up Linuxconf's Network Access

To configure which hosts can be used to access Linuxconf on the machine remotely, perform the following steps:

1. Click Linuxconf Network Access to open the Linuxconf HTML Access Control dialog box shown in Figure F.13.

2. Click the Enable Network Access button to activate the ability to reach Linuxconf remotely if you want to do so. If you activate this capability, be sure to also activate access logging.

3. Enter a network address or host IP address from which Linuxconf can be remotely accessed in the Network Or Host text box.

4. If you want, enter the netmask the network or IP address has to be using in the Netmask text box.

5. Repeat Steps 3 and 4 for the second pair of text boxes if you want.

6. Click Add to access more boxes.

7. Click Accept to save the changes and close the dialog box.

8. Click Quit to close the main dialog box.

Configuring Normal Users Accounts

The second chunk of the Linuxconf Config trunk is Users Accounts. The first chunk of this section is Normal. This is where you configure standard user and

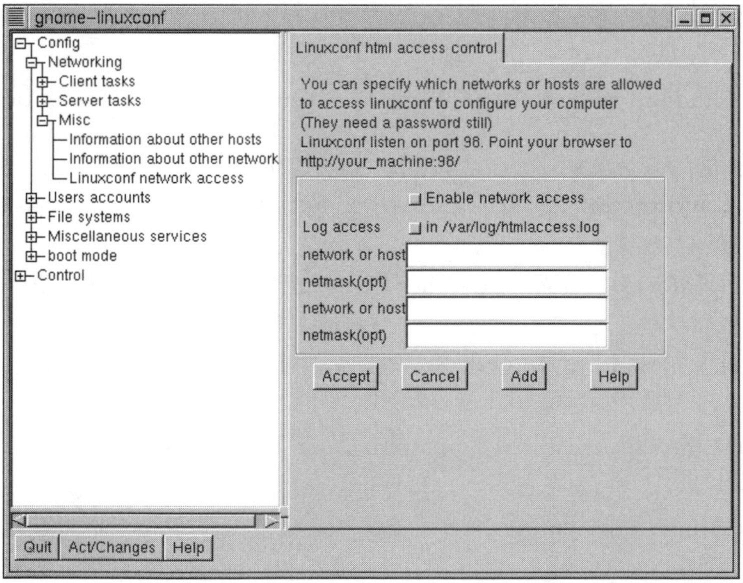

Figure F.13 The Linuxconf HTML Access Control dialog box.

group issues. Each of these items is listed in the order you are likely to use them, so they are covered in order in the following sections.

Configuring User accounts

To set up a user account, perform the following steps:

1. Click User Accounts to open the Users Accounts dialog box shown in Figure F.14.

2. Click an account to edit, or click Add to open the User Account Creation dialog box.

3. Enter the account name in the Login Name text box.

4. Enter the user's name or nickname in the Full Name text box.

5. Enter or choose a primary group in the Group (Opt) text box or drop-down list box.

6. If you want the user to be in more than one group, list the secondary groups in the Supplementary Groups text box.

7. Click the Params tab to access the password parameters.

8. Configure the password parameters if you want to enforce how often a password is changed.

9. Click the Mail Settings tab to access the user's mail options.

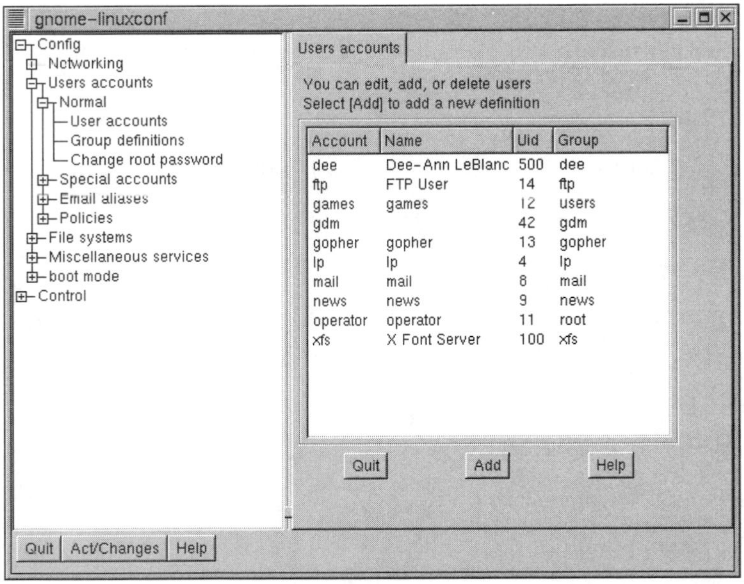

Figure F.14   The Linuxconf Users Accounts dialog box.

10. Forward the mail to another address if necessary, or create mail aliases for the user's account.

11. Click the Privileges tab to access a new set of tabs relating to what the user can and cannot do and access.

12. Configure each tab as necessary.

13. Click Accept to accept the account parameters.

14. Enter the user's initial password and click Accept.

15. Retype the password and click Accept again. You are returned to the main dialog box.

16. Click Quit to close the main dialog box.

Configuring Group definitions

To create a new group, perform the following steps:

1. Click Group Definitions to open the User Groups dialog box.

2. Click a group to edit, or click Add to open the Group Specification dialog box.

3. Fill in the Group Name and GID text boxes.

4. Enter any users you know you want to add to the group into the Alternate Members text box.

5. Click the Directories tab.

6. If you want each group member to have a different main directory, then ensure the appropriate checkbox is selected. Otherwise, enter the path to the group's home directory.

7. Click Accept to return to the main dialog box.

8. Click Quit to close the main dialog box.

Changing The Root Password

To use Linuxconf to change a root's password, perform the following steps:

1. Click Change Root Password to get the New UNIX Password dialog box.

2. Enter the new password in the text box.

3. Click Accept to open the Secondary Password dialog box.

4. Enter the password again.

5. Click Accept to close the dialog box and officially change the password.

Configuring Special Users Accounts

The second chunk of the Users Accounts section is Special Accounts. This is where you configure user accounts that are not straightforward shell logins. Each of the items is listed in the order you are likely to use them, so they are covered in that order in the following sections.

Configuring PPP Or SLIP Dial-In Accounts

To set up a PPP or SLIP dial-in account, perform the following steps:

1. Click PPP Accounts or SLIP Accounts via normal login to open the Users Accounts dialog box shown earlier in Figure F.14, though this item is initially empty of users.

2. Click Add to open the User Account Creation dialog box. Once again, this is the same dialog box you encounter while creating a normal user, except that certain items are already filled in for you to limit the user to a PPP or SLIP account.

3. Follow the instructions in the Configuring User Accounts section to fill in the rest of this dialog box and create the user's password.

4. Click Quit to close the Users Accounts dialog box. The user will not have a shell account to log in to.

Configuring UUCP Or POP Accounts

To set up a UUCP or POP mail account, perform the following steps:

1. Click UUCP Accounts or POP Accounts (Mail Only) to open the Users Accounts dialog box shown earlier in Figure F.14, although this item is initially empty of users.

2. Click Add to open the User Account Creation dialog box. Once again, this is the same dialog box you encounter while creating a normal user, except that certain items are already filled in for you to limit the user to a UUCP or POP account.

3. Follow the instructions in the Configuring User Accounts section to fill in the rest of this dialog box and create the user's password.

4. Click Quit to close the Users Accounts dialog box. The user will not have a shell account to log in to.

Configuring Virtual POP Accounts

To create a POP account for a user at a virtually hosted domain, perform the following steps:

1. Click Virtual POP Accounts (Mail Only) to open the Pick The Domain dialog box.

2. Click the domain you want to create the virtual POP account for. The Users Accounts dialog box shown earlier in Figure F.14 opens, although it is empty.

3. Follow the instructions in the Configuring UUCP Or POP Accounts section.

Appendix F

4. Click Quit to close the Pick The Domain dialog box when you are finished. The user will not have a shell account to log in to.

Configuring Email Aliases

The third chunk of the Users Accounts section is email aliases. This is where you set up mail aliases for various user accounts and virtually hosted accounts. Both of the items in this section are redundant entries that are also used in other sections of Linuxconf. Therefore, pointers are provided.

Setting Up Aliases For User Accounts

To create mail aliases for users, perform the following steps:

1. Click User Aliases to open the Edit Global Mail Aliases dialog box.

2. Follow the instructions in the section Configuring Basic Sendmail: Creating User Aliases section.

Setting Up Aliases For Virtual Domains

To create mail aliases for users on virtual domains, perform the following steps:

1. Click Virtual Domain User Aliases to open the Pick The Domain dialog box.

2. Follow the instructions in the Configuring Basic Sendmail: Creating Specific Users On Virtual Domains section.

Configuring Policies

The fourth and last chunk of the Users Accounts section is Policies. This is where you set various account creation defaults to save yourself time later. Each of these items is listed in the order you are likely to use them, so they are covered in that order in the upcoming sections.

Setting Password And Account Policies

To set default password and account policies, perform the following steps:

1. Click Password & Account Policies to open the Password/Account Setting Policies dialog box shown in Figure F.15.

2. If you want passwords to be longer or shorter than the currently required length, change the value in the Minimum Length text box.

3. If you want to ensure that characters that are not letters of the alphabet are included in the passwords on your system, change the value in the Minimum Amount Of Non Alpha Char text box to declare how many non-letters must be included.

4. The Private Group checkbox refers to Red Hat's policy of creating a private group for each user instead of lumping them all into the users group. If you want to shut this off, uncheck the box.

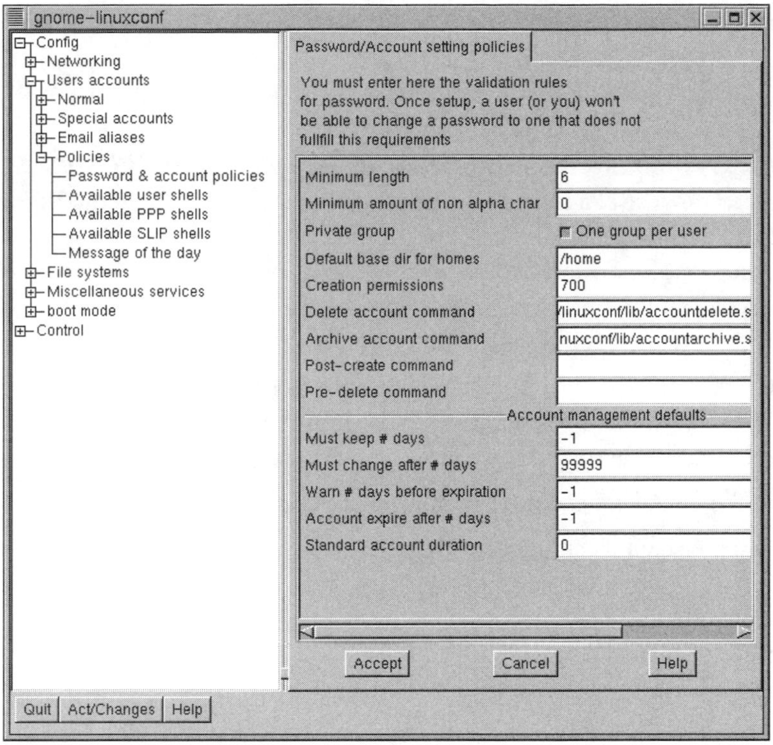

Figure F.15 The Linuxconf Password/Account Setting Policies dialog box.

5. If you want, change the base directory for user home directories or the permissions assigned by default to the home directory.

6. If there are specific commands you want to have run by Linuxconf when you use it to create or remove a user account, enter the commands in the appropriate text boxcs.

7. In the Account Management Defaults section, alter any of the expiry times that you deem necessary.

8. Click Accept when you are finished to close the dialog box.

Listing Which Shells Are Available To Users

To create the master list of the shells you have installed and want to make available during the user creation process, perform the following steps:

1. Click Available User Shells to open the Standard User Shells dialog box.

2. If you want to change which shell is assigned by default, change the listing in the Default Shell text box.

3. If you want any of the shells currently listed to be unavailable to the average user, delete them from the user's text box.

Appendix F

4. If you need more text boxes to list shells, click the Add button to open another text box.

5. Click Accept when you are finished. This closes the dialog box.

Listing Which Shells Are Available To PPP Or SLIP Users

This is somewhat of a trick topic. In general, it is not wise to allow PPP or SLIP users to access a shell. A shell account is intrinsically a security hole, so the fewer shell accounts you offer, the more secure your system. To list which shells—in this case, meaning programs—that should be launched when PPP or SLIP users connect, perform the following steps:

1. Click Available PPP Shells or Available SLIP Shells to open the Available PPP Login Shells or Available SLIP Login Shells dialog box, which are identical aside from their names and the default shells listed.

2. Make any changes to the shell programs listed in the text boxes.

3. Click Accept to close the dialog box.

Setting The MOTD

If you want to set a Message Of The Day (MOTD) for users to see when they log in, perform the following steps:

1. Click Message Of The Day to open the Message Of The Day dialog box.

2. Fill in the text boxes to enter your message. Keep in mind that you are the system administrator. Make your MOTD professional.

3. Click the Accept button to close the dialog box.

Configuring File Systems

The third branch off the Config trunk is File Systems. This is where you set up the various aspects of your file system. Each of these items is listed in the order you are likely to use them, and so they are covered in that order in the following sections.

Manipulating Mount Definitions In /etc/fstab

To use Linuxconf to manage your mount definitions in /etc/fstab, perform the following steps:

1. Click Access Local Drive to open the Local Volume dialog box shown in Figure F.16.

2. Click the line you want to edit, or click the Add button to open the Volume Specification dialog box.

3. Enter the file system location in the Partition text box.

4. Enter the file system type in the Type text box.

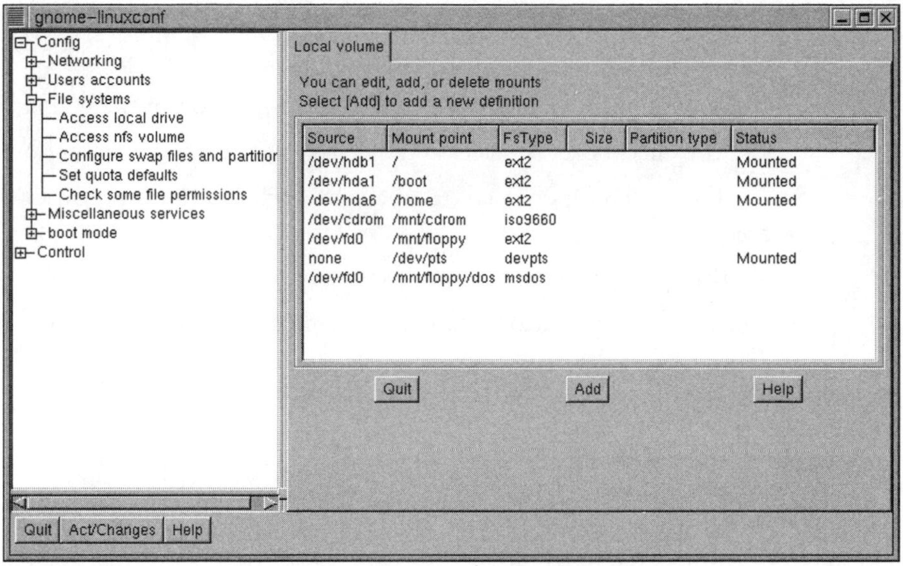

Figure F.16   The Linuxconf Local Volume dialog box.

5. Enter the mount point in the Mount Point text box.

6. Click the Options tab to open the Options portion of the dialog box.

7. Use the checkboxes to select and deselect the various mount options.

8. Set the Dump frequency and Fsck priority as you see fit.

9. Click the DOS Options tab to open the DOS Options portion of the dialog box.

10. In the DOS Options dialog box, set the values that you want assigned to any DOS partition that is mounted onto the file system so it is not left vulnerable and accessible to all.

11. Click the Accept button when you are finished defining the mount.

12. If the mount point does not already exist, Linuxconf offers to create it for you. Click Yes to create the mount point.

13. Click Quit to close the dialog box.

Mounting NFS Partitions

To mount an NFS partition from another Linux box or your own, perform the following steps:

1. Click Access NFS Volume to open the NFS Volume dialog box.

2. Click the definition you want to alter, or click the Add button to open the Volume Specification dialog box.

3. Fill in the server's IP address or domain name plus host in the Server text box.

4. Enter the mount name in the Volume text box.

5. Enter the local mount point in the Mount Point text box.

6. Click the Options tab to go to the Options portion of the dialog box.

7. Use the checkboxes to select and deselect the various general mount options.

8. Click the NFS Options tab to open the NFS Options portion of the dialog box.

9. Set the appropriate NFS mount options using the check and text boxes.

10. Click the Accept button when you are finished defining the mount.

11. If the mount point does not already exist, Linuxconf offers to create it for you. Click Yes to create the mount point.

12. Click Quit to close the dialog box.

Manipulating Swap Files And Partitions

If you want to make changes to your current swap space arrangements, perform the following steps:

1. Click Configure Swap Files And Partitions to open the Swap Space dialog box.

2. Click the item you want to edit, or click the Add button to open the Volume Specification dialog box.

3. Enter the partition's device name (for example, hda1) in the Partition text box.

4. Click the Accept button when you are finished defining the mount.

5. Click Quit to close the dialog box.

Setting Quota Information

If you have a quota-enabled partition, you can manage the quotas by doing the following:

1. Click Set Quota Defaults to open the Default Quota For Users And Groups dialog box shown in Figure F.17.

2. Click the tab corresponding to the partition with the quotas you want to alter or set.

3. Set the User Disk Space Soft Limit, Hard Limit, and Grace Period options.

4. Set the User File Count Soft Limit, Hard Limit, and Grace Period options.

5. Set the Group Disk Space Soft Limit, Hard Limit, and Grace Period options.

6. Set the Group File Count Soft Limit, Hard Limit, and Grace Period options.

7. Click Accept to close the dialog box.

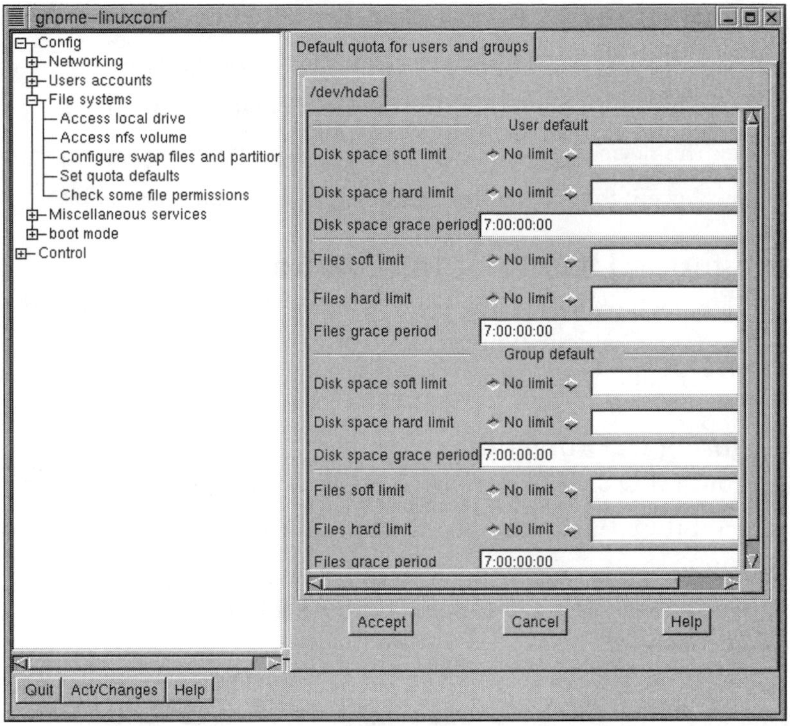

Figure F.17 The Linuxconf Default Quota For Users And Groups dialog box.

Check File Permissions

If you want to have Linuxconf check the permissions set on critical files, then click the Check Some File Permissions option. Linuxconf runs a check on your file system and then displays a dialog box. Typically speaking, the dialog box simply tells you that all is well. Read the response carefully and click OK to close the dialog box.

Configuring Miscellaneous Services

The fourth branch of the Config trunk is Miscellaneous Services. Contained in this section are configuration services that do not fit into any of the other sections.

Changing The Default Runlevel

To change the default runlevel, perform the following steps:

1. Click Initial System Services to open the Init Default Runlevel dialog box.

2. Click the Accept button to close the dialog box.

Setting The Default Modem Port

To set your default modem port, perform the following steps:

1. Click Modem to open the Modem Configurator dialog box.

2. Click the device location that corresponds to your modem.

3. Click Accept to save the information and close the dialog box.

Configuring LILO Boot Information

The fifth branch off the Config trunk is Boot Mode. The first branch of Boot Mode is LILO. Configuration options that control the various functions LILO performs for your system at boot time are contained in the next few sections.

Configuring LILO defaults

To set your LILO defaults, perform the following steps:

1. Click LILO defaults to open the LILO Defaults dialog box shown in Figure F.18.

2. To activate or deactivate LILO, select the LILO Is Used To Boot This System checkbox.

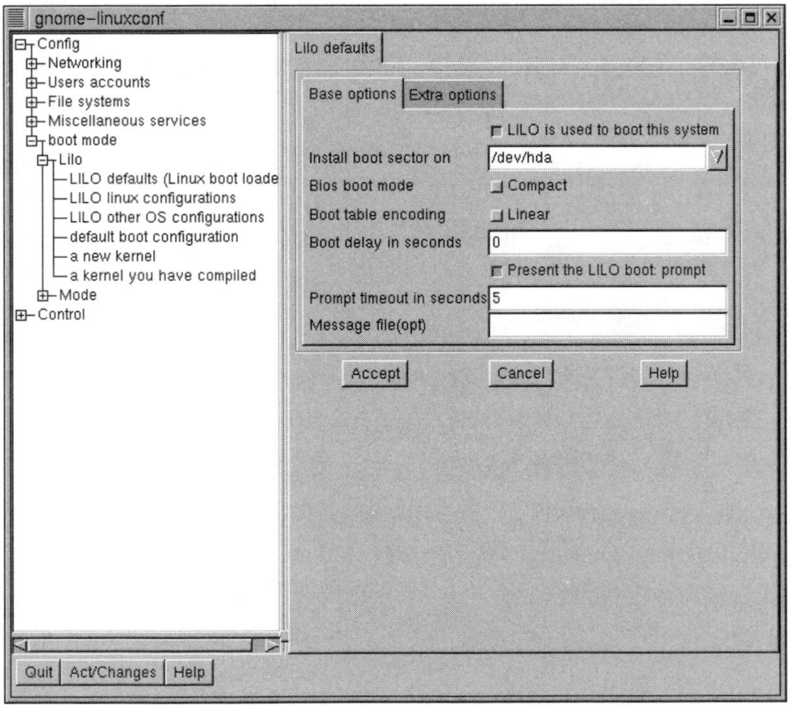

Figure F.18   The Linuxconf LILO Defaults dialog box.

3. Use the Install Boot Sector On drop-down list box to choose where to install LILO.

4. If you need to use the Compact or Linear boot options, activate those checkboxes.

5. If you want LILO to pause and wait before continuing the boot process, enter how long it should wait in the Boot Delay In Seconds text box.

6. To suppress the LILO boot prompt, uncheck the Present The LILO Boot Prompt check box.

7. If you want LILO to print any specific text at boot time, enter the text in the Message File text box.

8. Click the Extra Options tab to open the Extra Options portion of the dialog box.

9. Fill in any boot parameters that you need.

10. Click Accept to activate the changes.

11. You might get a warning dialog box. If so, read it carefully, then click OK.

Adding Linux Boot Options

To add a new Linux boot option to LILO, perform the following steps:

1. Click LILO Linux configurations to open the LILO Linux Configurations dialog box.

2. Click the definition you want to edit, or click Add to open the Linux Boot Configuration dialog box.

3. Enter the new boot label in the Label text box.

4. Enter the path to the kernel image file in the Kernel Image File text box.

5. Enter the root partition for the boot option in the Root Partition text box.

6. Set any other needed parameters.

7. Click Accept to activate the changes.

8. You might get a warning dialog box. If so, read it carefully, then click OK.

Adding Other OS LILO Boot Options

To add a new non–Linux boot option to LILO, perform the following steps:

1. Click LILO Other OS Configurations to open the LILO Other OS Configurations dialog box.

2. Click the entry you want to edit, or click Add to open the Other Operating System Setup dialog box.

3. Enter the label for the new boot option in the Label text box.

Appendix F

4. Enter the partition containing the operating system's boot information in the Partition To Boot text box.

5. Click Accept to activate the changes.

6. You might get a warning dialog box. If so, read it carefully, then click OK.

7. Click Quit to close the dialog box.

Setting The Default LILO Boot Option

To set which OS boots by default, perform the following steps:

1. Click Default Boot Configuration to open the Default Boot Configuration dialog box.

2. Click the boot option in the listing that you want for a default.

3. Click Accept to activate the changes.

4. You might get a warning dialog box. If so, read it carefully, then click OK.

Adding A New Kernel To The Boot Options

To add a new kernel to your LILO boot options, perform the following steps:

1. Click a new kernel to open the Adding A New Kernel To LILO dialog box shown in Figure F.19.

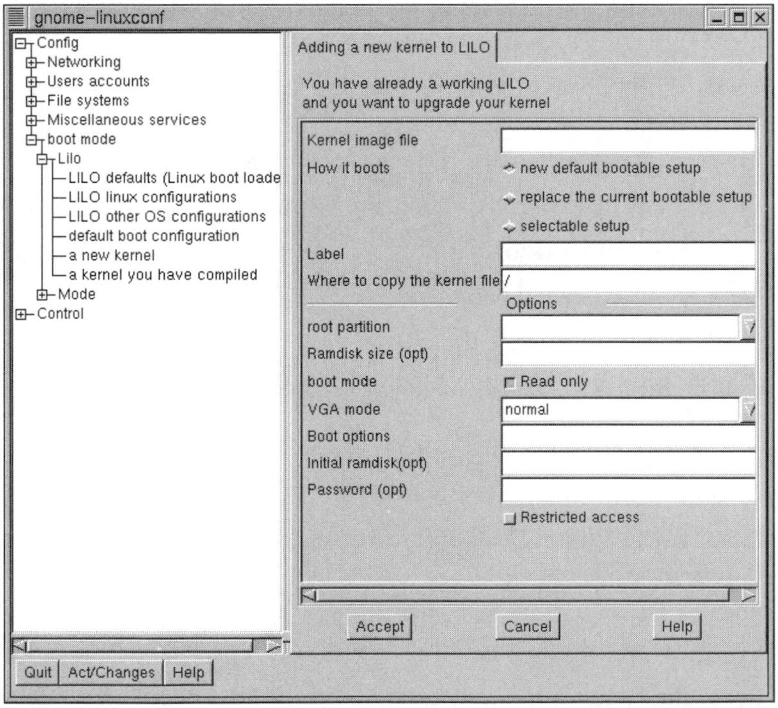

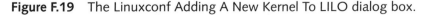

Figure F.19 The Linuxconf Adding A New Kernel To LILO dialog box.

2. Enter the kernel image's path in the Kernel Image File text box.

3. Choose an option among the How It Boots choices.

4. Enter a name for this option under the Label text box.

5. Fill in the special options needed to boot the kernel, if necessary.

6. Click Accept to activate the changes.

7. You might get a warning dialog box. If so, read it carefully, then click OK.

 If you want to add a kernel that you just compiled, use the A Kernel You Have Compiled option instead. It works almost the same as the previous description.

Configuring The Default Boot Mode

The fifth branch off the Config trunk is Boot Mode. The second branch of Boot Mode is Mode. This section only has one option. To set the default boot mode for your system, perform the following steps:

1. Click Default Boot Mode to open the Boot Mode Configuration dialog box.

2. Select or deselect the Boot Time Menu Enabled checkbox.

3. In the Default Operation Mode, check Graphic & Network to boot into the GUI or check Text Mode & Network to boot onto the command line.

4. Set the appropriate delays.

5. Click Accept to activate the changes.

Using The Linuxconf Control Panel

The first chunk of the Linuxconf Control trunk is the Control Panel. This is where you get the system to do things, rather than just set it up. Each of the items is listed in the order you are likely to use them, and so they are covered in that order in the next few sections.

Activating Changes Made In Linuxconf

To activate the changes you made in the Linuxconf tool, perform the following steps:

1. Click Activate Configuration to start the process.

2. You might get some warnings or notices. If so, read each one carefully, and respond accordingly.

3. Finally, you get the Status Of The System dialog box. This is the same dialog box you get if you try to close Linuxconf without activating changes first.

4. Click an option. If you activate the changes, you might get a set of questions explaining what needs to be done, asking if you want to continue the

procedure. Read each question and respond accordingly. After the process is complete, you return to a blank dialog box.

Shutting Down And Rebooting

To use Linuxconf to shut down or reboot your system, perform the following steps:

1. Click Shutdown/Reboot to open the Shutdown Control Panel dialog box.
2. Select either the Reboot or Shutdown & Halt option.
3. Enter a delay if you want the shutdown process to wait before initiating.
4. Enter a message if you want one displayed to the users.
5. Click Accept. The machine immediately begins the process you initiated.

Activating Or Deactivating Services

To activate or deactivate a service, perform the following steps:

1. Click Control Service Activity to open the Service Control dialog box.
2. Click the service you want to alter. A Service *Name* dialog box opens—for example, Service pcmcia.
3. To start the service, click Start.
4. To stop the service, click Stop.
5. If you want, select either the Activate This Service At Startup or Deactivate This Service At Startup checkbox.
6. Click Accept when you are finished manipulating the service.

Mounting And Unmounting: Local File System

To mount or unmount a part of your local file system, perform the following steps:

1. Click Control Configured Local Drives to open the Local Volume dialog box shown in Figure F.20.
2. Click the item you want to mount or unmount. The (Un)Mount File System dialog box opens.
3. Click Yes to mount or unmount, depending on your aim.
4. Click Quit to close the dialog box.

Mounting And Unmounting: NFS File System

To mount or unmount one of your NFS partitions, perform the following steps:

1. Click Control Configured NFS Volume to open the NFS Volume dialog box. This item looks almost identical to Figure F.20.
2. Click the item you want to mount or unmount. The (Un)Mount file system dialog box opens.

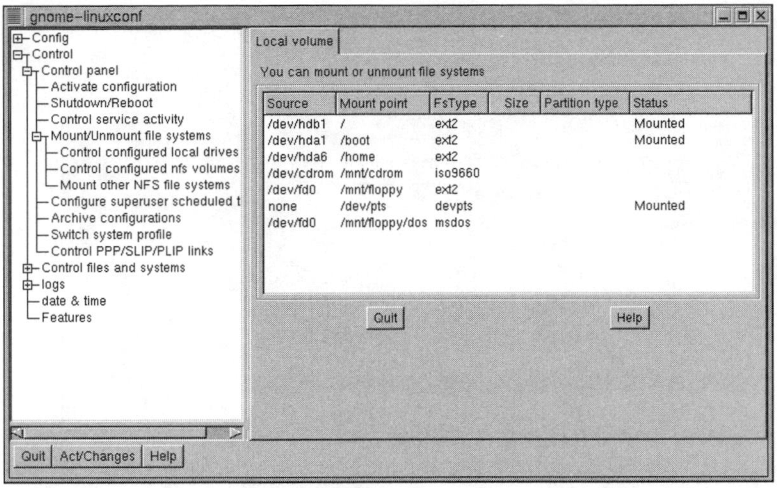

Figure F.20   The Linuxconf Local Volume dialog box.

3. Click Yes to mount or unmount, depending on your aim.

4. Click Quit to close the dialog box.

Mounting And Unmounting: Other NFS Partitions

If you want to mount an NFS partition that you do not already have configured, perform the following steps:

1. Click Mount Other NFS File Systems to open the Mounting Manually dialog box.

2. Enter the NFS server name in the Server text box.

3. Enter the NFS mount name in the Volume text box.

4. Enter the mount point in the Mount Point text box.

5. Click the Accept button. If the mount point does not exist, let Linuxconf create it for you.

Scheduling System Cron Jobs

To schedule a system cron job in Linuxconf, perform the following steps:

1. Click Configure Superuser Scheduled Tasks to open the Schedule Jobs For Account Root dialog box.

2. Click the Add button to create a new job. This action opens the Schedule Job Definition dialog box shown in Figure F.21.

3. Select or deselect the This Entry Is Active button to turn the job on or off.

4. In the Command text box, enter the command that needs to be run when the job activates.

5. Use the various time text boxes to set when the job should activate.

Appendix F

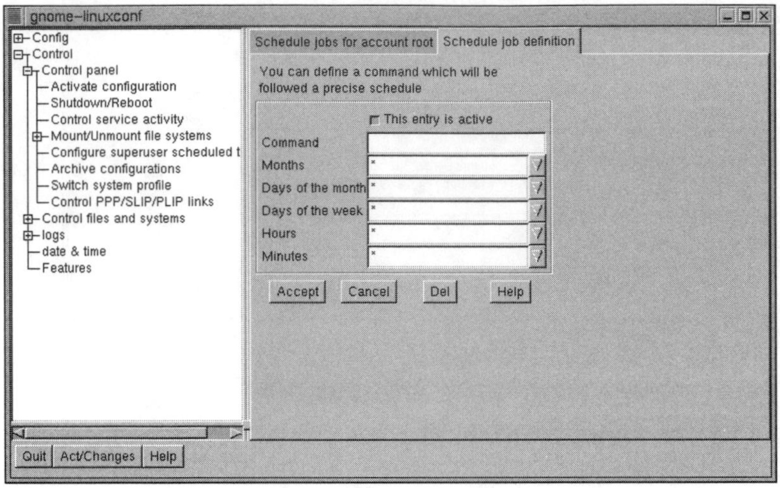

Figure F.21   The Linuxconf Schedule Job Definition dialog box.

6. Click Accept to save the job.

7. Click Quit to close the dialog box.

Archiving Your Configuration

To archive the current settings you have in Linuxconf, click the Archive Configurations option. This action takes care of the archiving automatically.

Switching The System Profile

To change which system profile you are using, perform the following steps:

1. Click Switch System Profile to open the Pick A Version dialog box.

2. There are two basic profiles available by default—Home and Office. The initial one you tend to work within is Home. All the settings you have worked on are saved in the Home profile. If you want, click the right-hand half of the button to change to the Office profile. The dialog box closes automatically, and you switch over to using the Office profile.

3. Now, you can configure the Office profile differently from the Home profile. This is the profile you will boot with until you change the default.

Controlling PPP/SLIP/PLIP Connections

To pull up or bring down a dial-out connection, perform the following steps:

1. Click Control PPP/SLIP/PLIP links to open the PPP/SLIP/PLIP Connection Control dialog box.

2. Click the item in the listing that you want to activate or close. The (De)Activate Link dialog box opens.

3. Click Yes to indicate that you want to (de)activate the link.

Controlling System Files With Linuxconf

The second chunk of the Linuxconf Control trunk is Control Files And Systems. Each of these items is listed in the order you are likely to use them, and so they are covered in that order in the upcoming sections.

Setting Configuration File Locations

Moving your major configuration files is generally not a good idea. Just because Linuxconf knows where a file is located does not mean the programs also know. With this in mind, to specify where your individual configuration files are, perform the following steps:

1. Click Configure All Configuration Files to open the List Of Configuration Files dialog box.

2. Click the file in the listing that you want to move. The Modifying A Config File Path dialog box opens.

3. Change the path to the file in the text box.

 You can revert to the original location by clicking Reset.

4. Click Accept to save the change.

5. Click Quit to close the dialog box.

Setting The Commands Linuxconf Can Control

To set which commands Linuxconf can and cannot control, perform the following steps:

1. Click Configure All Commands And Daemons to open the Netconf Scope dialog box.

2. Click the daemon or program in the list for which you want to modify control issues. The Daemons And Command Config dialog box opens.

3. Check whether Linuxconf is allowed to manipulate the daemon or program.

4. Modify the path to call the command if necessary.

5. Add arguments if necessary.

6. Click Accept to save the changes.

7. Click Quit to close the dialog box.

Modifying Permissions For Linuxconf-Controlled Configuration Files

To change permissions or ownership for any of the configuration files to which Linuxconf has access, perform the following steps:

1. Click Configure File Permissions And Ownership to open the Filter Prefix dialog box.

2. Build your search term if you want to use one, to choose the particular files you want to examine.

3. Type the search term into the Item's Prefix text box, or leave the box blank to see all files.

4. Click the Accept button to open the Permissions Of All Config Files dialog box.

5. Click the config file you want to modify. Changing permissions or owner-ship of such files is not recommended! Be sure you know what you are doing. The One File Permission Setting dialog box opens.

6. Make the permission and ownership changes you want to make.

7. Click Accept to make the changes. This action returns you to the Filter Prefix dialog box.

8. Click Cancel to close the dialog box.

Setting Which Linuxconf Modules Load

To set which modules Linuxconf loads when it starts up, perform the following steps:

1. Click Configure Linuxconf Modules to open the List Of Modules dialog box.

2. Select and deselect modules to load when Linuxconf starts or load when needed.

3. Click the Accept button when you are finished. The dialog box closes.

Setting Up System Profiles

The "Switching The System Profile" section earlier in this appendix describes how to change which profile you are using. Here, you can set up the profiles themselves. To accomplish this, perform the following steps:

1. Click Configure System Profiles to open the Configuration Versioning dialog box.

2. Either click an existing configuration entry (Home or Office), or click Add to open a new Configuration *Name* dialog box.

3. Edit the Title/Comment text box if necessary.

4. Choose a new Default RCS (Revision Control System) archiving family from the drop-down list box if necessary.

5. For each text box corresponding to an item you want archived, provide an archiving family name.

6. Click Accept when you are finished.

7. Click Accept to close the main dialog box.

Adding New Drop-In Add-Ons To Linuxconf

To add new add-ons to Linuxconf, perform the following steps:

1. Click either Override Linuxconf Add-ons or Create Linuxconf Add-ons to open the Dropin Management dialog box.

2. Click the Add button to open the Dropin Configuration dialog box.

3. Fill in the appropriate package information within the dialog box.

4. Click Accept to save the changes.

5. Click Quit to close the dialog box.

Controlling Logs And More

The third chunk of the Linuxconf Control trunk is Logs. After Logs are two items that hang directly off the trunk itself. Each of these items is listed in the order you are likely to use them, and so they are covered in that order in the following sections.

Viewing Boot Messages

To view the last round of boot messages recorded by your machine, click Boot Messages.

Viewing Linuxconf Log Contents

To view the logs generated by Linuxconf as you have used it to manipulate your system, click Linuxconf Logs.

Changing The Date And Time

To manipulate your system's date and/or time, perform the following steps:

1. Click Date & Time to open the Workstation Date & Time dialog box shown in Figure F.22.

2. Change the time zone if you need to by using the Zone drop-down list box.

3. If you want to save the new time setting in GMT to your machine's CMOS, select the appropriate checkbox.

4. Set the Time and Date values accordingly.

5. Click the Accept button to save the changes. The screen might go black for a second.

Setting Linuxconf Features

To set some esoteric Linuxconf features, perform the following steps:

1. Click Features to open the Features dialog box.

2. Choose the Keyboard Map from the drop-down list box.

3. Change the language if you need to by clicking the Language button.

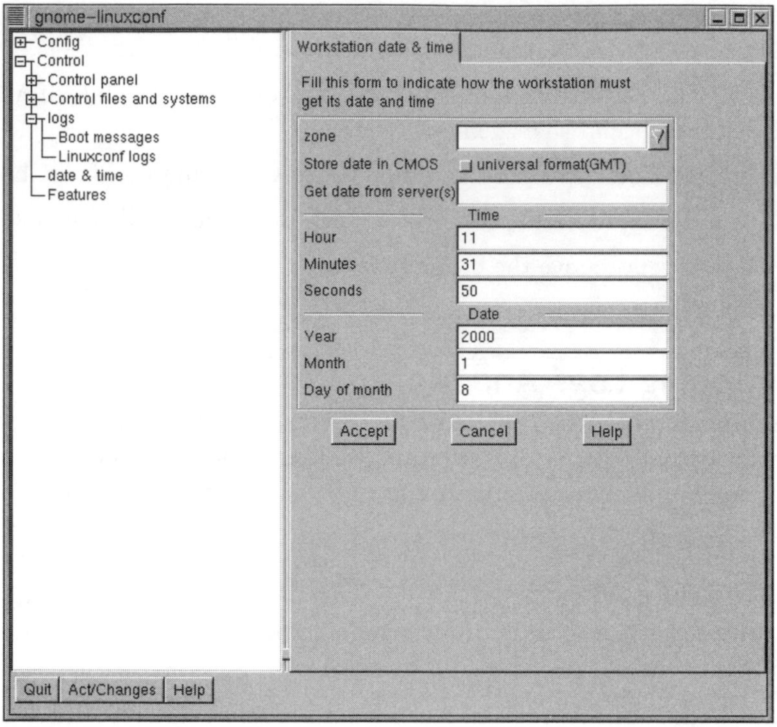

Figure F.22 The Linuxconf Workstation Date & Time dialog box.

4. Change any of the HTML settings if you need to.

5. Click Accept when you are finished.

YaST

YaST is an administration tool provided with the SuSE Linux distribution. It is by far the least graphical of the administration tools, but that does not make it the least functional. This program assists you with managing the installation itself—not a small task because SuSE either comes on six CD-ROMs or a DVD—and system administration through a menu-driven interface as shown in Figure F.23. You can run YaST either from the command line or within the GUI.

Getting Help With The Installation

If you need help with managing the installation, perform the following steps:

1. Select General Help For Installation from the YaST main menu, and press Enter with the option selected to open a help file that discusses installation issues. Although this might seem a bit after the fact, you might have first

```
— w YaST                                                    · □ ×
   ┌─────────────YaST – Yet another Setup Tool───────────┐
   │          YaST Version 1.03 -- (c) 1994-99 SuSE GmbH  │
   │                                                      │
   │  Language:      English                              │
   │  Media:         CD-ROM   /dev/cdrom                  │
   │  Root-Device:   /dev/hda3                            │
   │                                                      │
   │  ┌──────────────────────────────────────────────┐   │
   │  │ General help for installation                │   │
   │  │ Adjustments of installation            ->    │   │
   │  │ Choose/Install packages                      │   │
   │  │ Update system                                │   │
   │  │ System administration                  ->    │   │
   │  │ Show README file for installation media.     │   │
   │  │ Copyright                                    │   │
   │  │ Exit YaST                                    │   │
   │  └──────────────────────────────────────────────┘   │
   │                                                      │
   └──────────────────────────────────────────────────────┘
```

Figure F.23   The YaST main menu.

installed SuSE through the automated GUI interface. Reading this file helps you understand how to do the more controlled installations without pulling hair out in the process.

2. Use the Page Up and Page Down keys to maneuver through the help file.

3. When you are finished reading, press F10 to return to the main menu.

Altering Your Current Installation

Adding new software or removing packages from your SuSE installation can feel daunting because there are so many CD-ROMs involved. Fortunately, YaST provides a tool for managing these changes. You can access this tool by performing the following steps:

1. Select the Adjustments Of Installation menu by using the up and down arrows.

2. Press Enter to open the submenu.

 You can exit the submenu at any time by pressing the Esc key.

Choosing A Language

To select a language in SuSE, perform the following steps:

1. Choose the Select Language menu option if you want to change which language your installation uses. Because SuSE is a German distribution, it has excellent support for those who do not want to work in Linux in English.

2. Use the arrow keys to select the language you want to use, then press Enter.

Choosing A Keymap

If you want to change which keyboard mapping your installation uses, perform the following steps:

1. Choose the Select Keymap menu option. You can quickly navigate this menu if you understand the breakdown of the listings. Each keyboard type is named after the top row of letters and how they are laid out on the left-hand side. A typical American PC keyboard is called qwerty. There is usually no reason to change this setting unless you use something other than a qwerty PC keyboard.

2. To change a keyboard mapping, use the arrow keys to select the keyboard map you want to use, then press Enter.

Choosing The Installation Medium

If you want to add new software and do not plan to do so with the same method you initially installed the system, perform the following steps:

1. Choose the Select Installation Medium menu option. There are a number of options available to you here.

2. Choose one of the following:

   ➤ **CD-ROM** Installs from a local CD-ROM.

   ➤ **NFS** Installs from an NFS mount.

   ➤ **Reachable Directory** Installs from a directory that is part of your SuSE installation.

   ➤ **Partition** Installs from a separate partition that is not part of your SuSE file system.

   ➤ **FTP Site** Installs on the Internet or network installations that do not use NFS.

3. Press Enter. Depending on the option you choose, YaST will ask for more information so it knows exactly how to reach the medium.

Configuring Partitions

To configure partitions in SuSE, perform the following steps:

1. Choose Configure Hard Disk Partitions if you want to manipulate the partitions on any of your system's hard drives.

2. Use the arrow keys to select which drive to alter and then press Enter. This action opens the partition table editor—fdisk with a graphical interface—shown in Figure F.24. A simple function key menu is provided, as shown in Table F.1.

3. Select a function from the options shown in Table F.1.

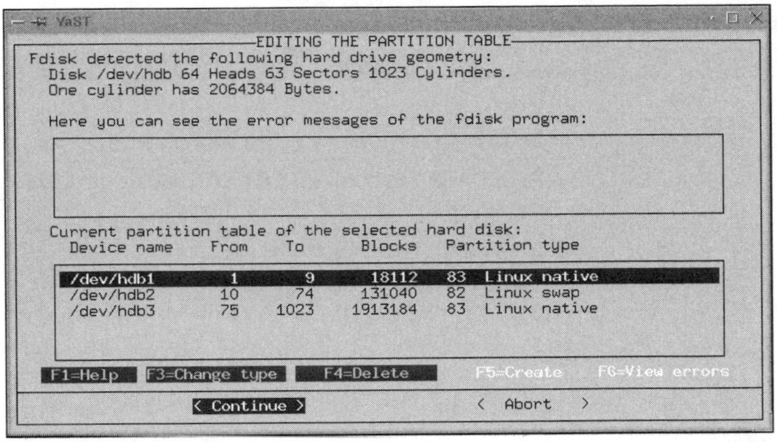

Figure F.24   The YaST partition table editor.

Table F.1   The YaST partition table editor's function key menus.

Key	Menu Option
F1	Help
F3	Change file system type
F4	Delete partition
F5	Add a new partition
F6	View fdisk error messages

4. When you are finished manipulating the contents of the hard drive, use the Tab key to select Continue. You will be asked if you want to write the partition table to disk. After you do or choose not to, you are returned to the Disk Selection menu.

5. Choose Continue to return to the Adjustments Of Installation submenu.

Setting Install Targets

To create a new file system on a partition, perform the following steps:

1. Choose Set Target Partitions/Filesystems. This option opens the File System Creation menu.

2. Use the cursor to select the partition you want to manipulate, and then use the function key menu laid out in Table F.2 to make your changes.

3. After you are ready to put these changes into effect, use the Tab key to select Continue, and press Enter. You will likely receive questions, such as whether you want to do a normal format or a format and check for surface errors.

Table F.2   The YaST file system creation editor's function key menus.

Key	Menu Option
F1	Help
F4	Set the mount point for this partition
F5	Access the Expert menu, which enables you to choose the file system details for the partition
F6	Make a file system on the partition
F7	Reread fstab

4. If you make any changes to /etc/fstab when asked about them, YaST will close, and you will need to reboot your machine to put those changes into effect.

Configuring The Volume Manager

To set up an LVM (Local Volume Manager) installation on the system, choose Configure The Local Volume Manager. For more on LVM and what it can do for you, go to **http://linux.msede.com/lvm/**. Do not choose this option on a whim.

Installing To A Directory

If you want to place your entire Linux installation under a particular directory—there are some reasons for doing this, such as installing to an NFS partition on another machine—perform the following steps:

1. Choose Installation To A Directory.

2. Enter the path for the installation home in the dialog box that opens.

Installing New Packages

After you have manipulated the installation and set up new partitions, set the installation media, and more, you can add packages. To do so, perform the following steps:

1. Select Choose/Install packages on the YaST main menu to open the installation tool.

2. Open Load Configuration and then abort out of the menu. This loads the entire package list that you installed and makes all of the other installer menus accessible.

3. Choose the Change/Create Configuration option to open an alphabetized menu of the available package types.

4. Select one of the items and press Enter to see the list of available packages.

5. When you decide on a package you want to add, select it and press Enter.

6. A dialog box usually opens to inform you of any other packages that need to be installed for the program to function properly. Choose Auto to let YaST automatically mark the dependencies as also needing to be installed.

7. After you are finished marking packages to install, press the F10 key to return to the installation menu. Then, choose Start Installation to install the packages you selected.

8. YaST will ask you to insert the appropriate CD-ROM. After this process is complete, you are returned to the Installation menu.

9. Choose Main Menu to return to the YaST main menu. The SuSEconfig utility launches at this point and makes notes of what you changed in your installation for the next time you launch YaST, as well as alters any configuration files that need to change because of alterations you made in your setup.

Catching Up With The Times

Whenever a new SuSE version comes out, many people like to upgrade their system. However, this is a precarious task if you have to do it by hand. In YaST, choose the Update System main menu option to upgrade. YaST examines your hard drive and makes suggestions about programs that need to be updated, and walks you through the process quite nicely.

Administering Your System

YaST is, among other things, a system administration tool. You get a large submenu of options when you select System Administration on the main menu. These options cover everything from adding new hardware to user and group administration. This is one of the most important sections of YaST for the Sair and LPI exams.

Configuring Your Hardware

To configure hardware, perform the following steps:

1. Select the System Administration main menu option.

2. Select Integrate Hardware Into System.

3. Select one of the following items from the submenu:

➤ **Mouse Configuration** Configures a new mouse or reconfigures the current one.

➤ **Modem Configuration** Sets up the device the modem is attached to.

➤ **CD-ROM Configuration** Reconfigures the CD-ROM.

➤ **Configure Printers** Launches an APSFilter setup script.

➤ **Configure ISDN Hardware** Allows you to fully define the box or card you are using for an ISDN connection.

➤ **Configure Your Scanner** Configures a SCSI scanner (this option will not work with a non–SCSI scanner).

➤ **Configure Your Network Device** Sets all of the necessary options (instead of tracking down the appropriate files to do so).

 Clicking Continue after any of these options launches the SuSEconfig tool.

Configuring Boot Information

To configure boot information, perform the following steps:

1. Choose the Kernel And Bootconfiguration option to open its submenu. This is a slightly misleading label. The only reason the kernel is related to this option is that it is referenced by LILO.

2. Choose the Select Boot Kernel option to open the Kernel Selection menu. This is where you can choose a ready-made kernel that is more optimized for your current system than the default kernel.

3. Choose a kernel and press Enter.

4. YaST installs your choice and offers to test your LILO configuration to ensure that the system will boot properly the next time. Choose Yes for this option.

5. Choose the Create Rescue disk option. This is an important step for good system administration.

6. Place a floppy disk in the drive—the program says it must be formatted, but that is not true—and allow YaST to build the disk you will need if the system will later not boot properly by itself.

7. Label the disk clearly and store it in a safe place, but not one so safe that you will not be able to find it when you need it.

8. Choose LILO Configuration to alter your boot information directly.

Configuring Network Information

Many system administrators appreciate having tools that help them with networking issues. Although these tools do not excuse you—especially for exam purposes—from knowing how to find network information by hand, it is nice to be able to have everything centralized under one interface. To configure network information, perform the following steps:

1. Choose Network configuration to access the networking submenu.

2. Select one of the following options:

➤ **Network Base Configuration** Allows you to manipulate various network devices. You can activate or deactivate interfaces; assign IP, netmask, and gateway information; and, in general, do what you might by hand accomplish with ifconfig.

➤ **Change Host Hame** Sets your machine's name and domain name.

➤ **Configure Network Services** Sets which networking daemons will start at boot time. This includes the superdaemon, the portmapper, and the NFS server. The SuSEconfig script runs after you make the changes, so they are put immediately into effect.

➤ **Configure Nameserver** Sets up nameservice. This option asks you if you want to access a nameserver. If you choose Yes, you are able to enter the IP address for this server and domain information.

➤ **Configure YP client** Configures NIS if you included it among the packages you installed. Otherwise, this menu option is inaccessible.

➤ **Configure Sendmail** Allows you to tell YaST the basic situation the machine runs under, such as whether it is a networked mail client or a standalone machine with no networking. SuSEconfig then changes your sendmail configuration as you exit to reflect the situation.

➤ **Configure ISDN Parameters** Configures an ISDN connection. This option is available only if you have already configured your ISDN device. Although this menu looks accessible to you if you have not configured an ISDN device, you will not be allowed to utilize it unless the device is already set up.

➤ **Configure A PPP Network** Configures a PPP connection. This option opens the WvDial configuration program, which you can use to set up your PPP dial-out connection.

➤ **Administer Remote Printers** Allows you to configure any network printers you need to set up. If you included Samba or Novell support in your installation, then the last two menus for configuring printer support across these items are also available.

Including A Live CD-ROM File System

To include a live CD-ROM file system, perform the following steps:

1. Choose the Configure Live-System menu to open its submenu.

2. Within this submenu, choose Integrate CD Live Filesystem to add a live file system to your SuSE installation, or choose Disconnect CD Live Filesystem to remove it.

Configuring The Login Environment

To change any of the generic login settings, perform the following steps:

1. Choose Login Configuration. This is where you can set whether users log in to command line or GUI mode by default.

2. Choose which display manager to use—SuSE provides XDM or KDM by default.

3. Choose who is allowed to shut down the machine from a range of just root to everyone.

Configuring Susewm

The SuSE Linux distribution comes with its own window manager, susewm, for root. To configure how the window manager behaves, perform the following steps:

1. Choose Configure Susewm.

2. In the resulting menu, choose the default window manager assigned to users.

3. Set up default configuration files for the selected window manager.

4. Choose which window managers and desktop environments you want to have configurations available for users to change to.

Maintaining Your User Base

To create new user accounts and remove existing user accounts perform the following steps:

1. Choose User Administration to open the submenu.

2. Typing the user name and pressing Enter fills in half of the dialog box for you with default values. If you want to accept the defaults, all you need to do from there is fill in the initial password, mark whether this user should have access to the modem if there is one, and enter any description information you want to include.

3. Press F4 to create the user's account.

 If you want to work with an existing account but you do not remember its login name, press F3 to open a list of existing accounts.

Maintaining Groups

The interface for groups is similar to that for users. To add new groups, delete current groups, set a group password, or modify a group's member list, perform the following steps:

1. Choose Group Administration.

2. Press F3 to open a list of existing groups.

3. Press F4 to create a new group when you have the proper information filled in.

4. Press F5 to delete a selected group.

Making System Backups

To create a backup of your system files, perform the following steps:

1. Choose Create Backups. You must choose an installation medium before you choose this option, or you will get error messages.

2. Continue past the messages into the Backup Configuration dialog box.

3. Choose the file system types you want to include in your standard backup scheme, and choose the parts of the file system to add. The list on the right-hand side of the screen tells you what is already included.

4. To add more items, type "+" to be able to enter the path for the directory you want to add to the backup list.

5. To remove an item, select it and type "-". After you finish modifying the list, press F10.

6. The backup utility generates a list of the installed packages. After this task is complete, the program asks if it should search for files that do not belong to installed packages. If you have a tendency to download and install programs from source, answer Yes to this question. If you only tend to install directly from the SuSE CD-ROM or other media, choose No.

7. Next, you are shown a list of configuration files. Choose whether you want each file included in the backup. An X next to an item means it will be included. You can remove an X by pressing the spacebar, and replace it by doing the same. After you are finished choosing which configuration files to include, press F10.

8. Now, you are presented with the actual backup. YaST's automated backup facility uses the **tar** command. Specify a name for the package—including .tar or .tgz—whether to compress the archive, and whether to generate a separate file named by you that contains a list of the archive's contents.

9. To create the backup, press F10.

Configuring Security

There is a certain level of system security that YaST will help you to set up. To access these options, perform the following steps:

1. Choose Security Settings to access the submenu.

2. Choose General Information On System Security. A dialog box opens with a list of security levels you can set for your system.

3. Make your choices, then choose Continue. Wait for SuSEconfig to finish running.

4. Select Configuration Of /etc/login.defs to set up how the login routines behave with respect to failed logins and passwords.

Appendix F

Setting Your Console Font

To select a console font, choose Set The Console Font to test various fonts that can be used at the command line, and choose a font.

Setting Your Time Zone

To configure time zone settings, perform the following steps:

1. Choose Set The Time Zone.

2. Choose your country and time zone region from the submenu, and press Enter.

3. Inform YaST whether your hardware clock is set to local time or GMT.

Configuring X

YaST offers you three options when you choose Configure Xfree86. You can use the SaX (SuSE Advanced XF86-Configurator) utility to set up X, the xf86config text utility, or the XF86Setup graphical but not GUI utility. Choose one of these options, and YaST will launch it for you.

Configuring GPM

If you want to use GPM to allow you to cut and paste at a command-line terminal, then choose the Configure GPM menu option. You are given the option of running GPM at boot time or manually when you need it. Then, you have the chance to test GPM and either keep the current configuration, or change it.

Configuring Environment Variables

SuSE uses a host of environment variables to store its system settings. You can change any of these by choosing Change Configuration Variables. Select the item you want to consider, press F2 to see what the item is set to, then press F3 to change the setting if you want.

Using Final YaST Configuration Options

The last few main menu items for YaST are short and sweet, so they are lumped together in this section. As you can see, YaST is a feature-rich configuration and administration tool even though it is not fully graphical in a GUI sense. The graphics level does not matter, the capabilities do.

Viewing The Install Media README File

If the README file that defines all of the installation media options is installed on your system, you can select Show README File for installation media in order to view it. If the file is not installed, you will receive an error message.

Viewing YaST and SuSE Copyright Information

All information pertaining to both YaST and SuSE's copyrights are available by choosing Copyright on the main menu. Reading this document is especially useful for developers.

Closing YaST

Finally, to close the YaST program, choose Exit YaST. It cleans up its own temporary files and then shuts down the program.

ANSWERS TO REVIEW QUESTIONS

CHAPTER 1 SOLUTIONS

1. **b.** The driver for a device is located in Kernel space. This is because device drivers are a low level activity, which instruct the kernel on how to interact with the device.

2. **b.** A driver is an interpreter between the kernel and the hardware. The kernel itself does not know the commands the hardware accepts without the driver's assistance.

3. **c.** The kernel is the operating system itself. The rest consists of tools that work along with the kernel to make the whole package we tend to refer to as "Linux".

4. **c.** The kernel is responsible for low-level operating system tasks. It works behind the scenes to run the show.

5. **d.** The **kill** command stops a healthy process without any flags.

6. **b.** The **killall** command stops all instances of a command by name.

7. **b.** The **–HUP kill** flag tells a daemon to re-read its configuration file, so is essentially like restarting it.

8. **c.** Generic system calls are held in kernel space, until interpreted by a hardware driver.

9. **d.** Making a kernel module would allow the device driver to be held in memory constantly.

10. **a.** You can add a module that was not provided with the default distribution in /etc/conf.modules.

11. **d.** You can add an append statement to /etc/lilo.conf to pass driver information to the kernel.

12. **a.** User and kernel space are not physically separated from one another. Instead, they are each put into their own "zones" on the hard drive.

13. **d.** The larger your kernel is, the more information the machine has to hold in RAM. The more RAM the kernel takes up, the slower the rest of your machine will perform.

14. **d.** The GNU (GNU's Not Unix) organization has been behind most of the tools currently used with Linux.

15. **d.** Linux can handle multiple users logged in at the same time.

16. **c.** Linux can handle multiple processes running at the same time.

17. **a.** The person who first wrote the Linux kernel was Linus Torvalds.

18. **False.** Device driver lag means that the latest and greatest equipment may not yet be supported under Linux.

19. **a, d.** Free software (or open source software) refers to the philosophy that programming code should be openly available for all to modify, package, and compile to run.

20. **b.** The Free Software Foundation is the financial arm of GNU.

CHAPTER 2 SOLUTIONS

1. **b.** This card will not be supported until someone has had a chance to write a driver for it.

2. **c.** You should have two partitions, one swap and one root, at the very least.

3. **a.** A package manaement tool.

4. **b.** You can always install the updated software from the source code.

5. **d.** You would type

   ```
   ./configure -help
   ```

   to learn how to relay the library's location to the configuration script.

6. **b.** You would type

   ```
   find / -name foo
   ```

   to search for a file named foo.

7. **c.** You would use the **which** command if foo was an executable in your path.

8. **d.** You would type

   ```
   echo LD_LIBRARY_PATH
   ```

   to determine what the invalid path is.

9. **b.** If a program requires libdb version 1.2.17 or higher, libdb.so.1.2.18 is an acceptable file.

10. **a. make** greatly simplifies the compilation process.

11. **c.** The **setserial port 0x03f8 auto_irq uart 16450 skip_test** command would configure a modem with an IO port of 0x03f8, an unknown IRQ, and a 16450 UART that incorrectly reports itself when probed.

12. **b.** Many soundcards claim to be SoundBlaster compatible when they are not.

13. **c.** The BIOS options must be checked and sometimes changed before you install Linux.

14. **a, b, d.** An X server allows the end user to work within a GUI, an NFS client allows them to mount remote network drives, and word processing packages are good for helping them get work done.

15. **a, b, c.** The BIOS may contain SCSI ID, IRQ and port information.

16. **d.** Device port addresses in the BIOS are three digits with an H on the end.

17. **a. fdisk** is available in all Linux distributions for partitioning drives.

18. **d.** You can damage your monitor by setting the video options too high.

19. **b.** You can only get as high a resolution as both devices can handle.

20. **a, b, c.** You would not want to have a GUI on a high traffic Web server, because that would just slow it down. You definitely would not want games played on it, that would be a waste of CPU cycles. Finally, you would not want to be editing HTML documents directly on the server because that would also slow it down and might cause partially edited files to be served to Web surfers.

CHAPTER 3 SOLUTIONS

1. **a, b, c.** Partitions, floppy drives, and Zip drives can all be mounted onto the filesystem either temporarily or more permanently in /etc/fstab.

2. **b.** The **fdisk** command allows you to add, remove, and set partition types.

3. **c.** The **mke2fs** command makes the **ext2** filesystem type on a partition, which is the Linux filesystem type.

4. **a.** The **e2fsck** command checks the filesystem for errors and offers to fix them when found.

5. **c.** The **vfat** filesystem type is for Windows partitions, the second IDE drive on a system is hdb, and the first partition on that hard drive would be hdb1.

6. **a.** To access any files on the mount point /mnt/win, you first must change to the /mnt/win directory, which in this case is akin to being in d:\. Then, to get to the d:\work\faxes directory, you change to /mnt/win/work/faxes.

7. **c.** To remove a partition from the filesystem you use the **umount** command with either the device or the mount point as an argument.

8. **c.** The file /etc/fstab contains information used to mount partitions onto the filesystem at boot time (and data for mounting manually) and the settings to use for those partitions, including whether to use quotas.

9. **a.** To create a quota that a user can exceed for a limited period of time (called the grace period), create a soft quota. On top of this, you can create a hard quota that the user can't go over.

10. **b.** The **repquota** command is a quota report generator.

11. **d.** Remember that an **r** is worth four, a **w** is worth two, and an **x** is worth one. So the permissions **rw-r--r--** amount to (4+2) + (4) + (4), or 644.

12. **b.** A symbolic link's permission set is fully filled out, with an *l* for *link* at the beginning of the listing.

13. **c.** Many daemons are located within /etc and its subdirectories.

14. **a, b, and d.** The **which** command locates programs that exist within the user's PATH statement. The **find** command is the most powerful (and time-consuming) search tool; it searches the live filesystem. The **locate** command looks through a database it refreshes nightly, which consists of the entire filesystem structure as of when the database was last refreshed.

15. **d.** The FSSTND is the Filesystem Standard, which lays out which directories should contain which types of files.

16. **a, b, d.** There is a caveat for b (Partial Filesystem Backup)—the lost permissions must be attached to files included in the partial backup.

17. **c.** rwxr—rw- is rwx r—rw- is 4+2+1 4+0+0 4+2+0, or 746.

18. **d.** An executable bit cannot be set within the umask.

19. **a.** The inverse of rw-r—rw- is —x-wx—x, and the executable bits are not counted for the umask, so it is 020.

20. **a.** A hard link creates another pointer to the same exact inode, so both the original and the link have to be deleted before the file is removed.

CHAPTER 4 SOLUTIONS

1. **b.** The file /etc/fstab is the mount master data file, not an init script.

2. **a.** The command and option **shutdown -r** reboots the system.

3. **d.** The **init** command allows you to set a runlevel of 0 through 6 (except 4, which isn't used).

4. **a.** The **sync** command makes sure to save all buffered information to disk before you unmount the partitions.

5. **c.** The /etc/inittab file contains the default runlevel data.

6. **b.** To enter the full Linux implementation at the command line level, type "init 3".

7. **c.** To enter the full Linux implementation at the GUI level, type "init 5".

8. **c, d.** Either "Linux single" or "Linux 1" will boot you into runlevel 1, which is single user mode. Then, you can change the root password using the "passwd root" command.

9. **b, c.** Sometimes, LILO not booting properly is a fluke and rebooting the machine works. At other times, a number of the symptoms can be caused by pieces of LILO not being placed properly when it was previously installed.

10. **d.** The LILO binary is located at /sbin/lilo.

11. **a.** The delay variable expects its values in tenths of seconds, and so 5000 tenths of seconds is the same as 500 seconds.

12. **d.** Although setting a boot message is a valid /etc/lilo.conf entry, it is not necessary for the Linux OS section to work properly.

13. **b.** The /proc segment of the file system is a virtual segment which is completely held in memory.

14. **d.** The program isapnp helps Linux to automatically configure PNP devices installed in the box.

15. **b.** The /etc/rc.d/rc#.d directories each contain notation for which daemons should run in a particular runlevel, and which should be shut off.

16. **a.** To shut down a machine with a ten-minute wait before it actually begins the shutdown process, type "shutdown -h +10m".

17. **d.** The command to create a custom boot disk is "mkbootdisk".

18. **b.** The root and image items are not used when creating a pointer to a Windows partition. The other and table items are used instead.

19. **c.** The environment variable containing the domain name itself is NISDOMAIN.

20. **d.** To cancel the shutdown command, use **shutdown -c**.

CHAPTER 5 SOLUTIONS

1. **b.** A shell is the login working environment for the Linux or Unix user.

2. **d.** The shells tcsh (enhanced C), bash (Bourne Again), and ksh (Korn) all exist.

3. **b, c, d**. There is no "delete" mode in vi. Deletions are accomplished in command mode, or insert mode.

4. **a, b, c, d.** The c command allows the user to change text, the R command enters overwrite mode, the s command allows text substitution, and the o command opens a new blank line.

5. **d.** A comma (,) is not a metacharacter in vi.

6. **c.** The **PWD** environment variable contains the current directory the user is in.

7. **a.** The master user environment settings file is /etc/profile.

8. **b.** The chsh command lists available shells, and can be used to change a user's default shell.

9. **a, c**. The user is required to make at least one backup floppy when he or she may not need to. And, there is no checking to ensure that the data is the type of data requested, or that anything was entered at all.

10. **b.** Shell scripts are capable of doing anything you can do from the command line.

11. **a, b, d**. The "\<" tells vi to look at the beginning of the word, the period (.) stands for a single unknown character, and the asterisk (*) stands for any number of unknown characters.

12. **d.** A binary program must be compiled; the best process to follow is edit, compile, and then test.

13. **b.** File manipulation requires colon mode, and the **w** colon command saves the file. Colon commands aren't submitted to the editor until the Enter key is pressed.

14. **a.** Environment variables in bash or ksh are typed in all capital letters. You assigned a variable a value by setting the variable equal to the value. When the value is a multiword string, you put it in quotes.

15. **c, d.** The first line in any shell script declares which shell is in use. The shell recognizes this declaration because it starts with #!.

16. **b.** "C" typed in command mode means to change the current line of text.

17. **c.** Typing the forward slash (/) allows you to enter the text or pattern you want to search for.

18. **b.** The **read** command is used to accept data from a user. The script won't take in this data until the Enter key is pressed.

19. **c.** You can't run a shell script by just typing its name unless its permissions are executable.

20. **a.** The Gnu C Compiler (gcc) is the C compiler most commonly used in Linux.

CHAPTER 6 SOLUTIONS

1. **a.** When creating new user accounts, the command is useradd or adduser.

2. **c.** The program used to create new user passwords is passwd.

3. **b.** To see the default user settings you would type "useradd -D" or "adduser -D".

4. **a.** The default user directory setup information is stored in /etc/skel.

5. **d.** The cron daemon oversees automated system tasks.

6. **b, d.** The at program runs a process once at the time specified, and the crontab program allows the user to edit his or her cron configuration file, which stores their repeated process information.

7. **d.** Facilities can be separated by commas, but not priorities.

8. **a.** The cron format is: minutes after the hour, hour in twenty-four hour time, day of the month, month of the year, and day of the week starting with zero on Sunday.

9. **c.** The /usr/sbin/logrotate program does the actual work of cycling the log files.

10. **a, d.** In fact, these items work well in combination. First, use the tar program to store files together in a group with their hierarchy intact, then compress the tar file with gzip.

11. **d.** The userdel command is used to remove users from the system.

12. **d.** There is no /etc/cron.yearly.

13. **b.** The at format allows use of twenty-four hour time and the word tomorrow, and 2 P.M. is 1400 hours.

14. **a.** The find command has an option that allows you to search for files owned by specific users.

15. **c.** Errors in system cron jobs and log rotations are sent by default to root.

16. **b.** Writeable CD-ROMs can only be written-to once, and so are a waste of materials unless used for long-term storage backups.

17. **d**. The shell /bin/false is a keyword meaning that the user has no shell access.

18. **c**. In the month of the year slot the number listed is 15, but there are only 12 months in a year.

19. **c**. The file /etc/passwd contains the user name and shell information for login, though the file /etc/shadow often contains the password itself.

20. **b**. User cron data is stored in /var/spool/cron.

CHAPTER 7 SOLUTIONS

1. **d**. The = character is not a metacharacter used in regular expressions.

2. **a**. Data streams are two directional.

3. **d**. A job creates as many processes as there are individual programs executed by the job.

4. **b**. The **sed** program is best for repeated substitutions in a file.

5. **a**. Grep is a filter—a program that performs a specified operation on a text file.

6. **b**. The command shown is a valid pipe. The sort command redirects error messages to a file, but pipes the output into the grep command. The grep command pipes the output to the **lpr** command.

7. **b**. The **ps** command displays information about processes, obtained from the /proc filesystem. It cannot accept data from stdin.

8. **d**. The regular expression shown will match any lines that have a number anywhere in the line.

9. **d**. The file name is not included in the inode.

10. **c**. The command "renice PID" can be issued by the owner to increase the nice number. Only a privileged account can issue a command to lower the nice number.

11. **d**. The command shown will produce the desired report.

12. **c**. System commands are programs, stored as files in the filesystem.

13. **a**. The man pages provide information on system commands. Help provides information on built-in commands.

14. **b**. The row of special characters would be first.

15. **a**, **b**, **c**, **d**.

16. **a**. The **tr** command can convert special characters.

17. **a, c.** You can see the contents of a .gz text file by typing "gunzip *file*.gz ; cat *file*", or "zcat *file*.gz".

18. **d.** The **wc** command gives counts of lines, words, and characters in a file.

19. **c.** The **killall** command can kill a group of processes running the same command all at once.

20. **d.** There are not enough arguments for the **tr** command.

CHAPTER 8 SOLUTIONS

1. **a.** A Linux program requests a status report via SNMP (Simple Network Management Protocol).

2. **d.** IPX (Internetwork Package Exchange) is a transport protocol used in Novell NetWare.

3. **c.** A TCP connection is a stream based network connection.

4. IP is the network protocol, and TCP is a form of network connection.

5. IP addresses are assigned to a network interface on a specific machine. For example, if you had two different Ethernet cards in a machine, each would get its own IP address.

6. **b.** If a network interface has an IP address of 172.16.0.24 and a netmask of 255.255.0.0, then its broadcast and network addresses are 172.16.255.255 and 172.16.0.0, respectively.

7. No

8. **b.** The IP address described in question 6 is a class B address.

9. **a.** To allow the interface in question six to access the Internet, it would have to go through NAT, or Network Address Translation.

10. **10**

11. 16,777,214. No.

12. **a, d.** The commands used to configure interface eth0 with an IP address of 192.168.0.4 and a netmask of 255.255.255.0 are **ifconfig eth0 192.168.0.4 netmask 255.255.255.0** or **ifconfig eth0 192.168.0.4**

13. **d.** To add an entry in the routing table for an Internet gateway with an IP address of 172.4.25.3, you would use the code:

```
route add default gw 172.4.25.3
```

14. **a, b.** To delete the routing table entry added in the previous question, you would use **route del default** or **route del 0.0.0.0**.

15. **b.** The non-subnetted netmask for a Class B network is **255.255.0.0**.

16. **d.** The PING **−c 6 172.4.0.23** command will send six ping packets to interface 172.4.0.23.

17. **c.** You would use the traceroute command if you suspected packets were being dropped enroute to their destination.

18. **c.** NIS is correct.

19. **d.** whois is correct.

20. **b.** The command ifconfig eth0 netmask 255.255.0.0 would fix the problem in the previous question.

21. **b.** The directory /etc/ppp contains the files associated with pppd.

22. **a**, **b**, and **c.** The ppp login chat script contains the prompts sent by the dialup server, and the answers that should be given to those prompts. The login password is one of those answers..

23. **b**, **c.** You would add the following lines to the /etc/ppp/options file to tell pppd to use serial device ttyS1 with hardware flow control: **/dev/ttyS1** and **crtscts**

24. **a.** A chat script is the major difference between dial-in and dial-out ppp services using pppd.

CHAPTER 9 SOLUTIONS

1. **b.** The superdaemon is inetd, and its configuration file, which defines what processes it controls, is /etc/inetd.conf.

2. **a.** The file /etc/services maps network services to their respective ports.

3. **c.** The daemon commonly used to handle DNS services on network machines is named.

4. **c.** The m4 sendmail configuration process begins with the .mc file, which is in the end converted to a .cf file.

5. **d.** The files /etc/ftpaccess, /etc/ftphosts, and /etc/ftpusers are all valid files used to configure your FTP server.

6. **b.** The files srm.conf, httpd.conf, and access.conf are all valid files used to configure your Apache Web server.

7. **d.** The NFS service allows remote mounting of Linux partitions on Linux machines.

8. **a.** The SMB service allows remote mounting of Linux partitions by machines running other operating systems.

9. **d.** When a networking services daemon has an init script, the cleanest way to close it down so you can restart it is by using the init script's "stop" feature.

10. **c.** The best way to configure inetd to stop managing a service is to comment that service out in /etc/inetd.conf. Commenting it out in /etc/services only removes the port definitions and will cause an error.

11. **b.** The "dnl" string prevents the sendmail.cf file from being needlessly long by removing the blank characters from the end of the text to the end of the line.

12. **a.** The first line in your customized .mc file must be include('../m4/cf.m4') so that the macros are understood when the m4 processor creates the sendmail.cf file.

13. **c.** The m4 processor sends its output to STDOUT so it has to be redirected into the sendmail.cf file.

14. **b.** The end of the file httpd.conf is where you add support for virtual hosting.

15. **d.** The base directory for web files is referred to as the "root" directory for the documents, hence the term DocumentRoot.

16. **a.** The smbclient program lists what shares are available when typed in the form "smbclient –L".

17. **b.** Samba shares are mounted in the format "mount –t smb *device mountpoint*".

18. **c.** The file /etc/exports contains the data for the exported segments of the local file system for NFS.

19. **a.** The file /etc/smb.conf contains the data for the exported segments of the local file system for SMB.

20. **a.** The Samba (SMB) service handles print sharing as well as file sharing.

CHAPTER 10 SOLUTIONS

1. **b.** The print daemon is lpd.

2. **b.** The printer configuration file is /etc/printcap.

3. **d.** The lpc up command enables all printers and print queues, then starts a new lpd. The lpc enable command allows jobs to go to the print queue; and the lpc stop command tells the queue to stop taking new print jobs, and then disables the printer once the queue is empty.

4. **c.** The program used to print a document and add it to the queue is lpr.

5. **c.** The lpq program uses printername, while lpr and lprm use –Pprintername.

6. **b.** The directories and files necessary for printing should be assigned to the daemon group.

7. **c.** A middle line in an /etc/printcap definition just begins with a colon, and ends with a colon and a backslash.

8. **d.** The program used to list the contents of the print queue is lpq.

9. **d.** The if variable defines the input filter, of defines the output filter, and lo defines the log file.

10. **a.** Using the **cat** command in the format cat file > /dev/printerdevice.

11. **c.** The syslog daemon handles lpd's general logging needs.

12. **a.** The program used to manage printers, queues, and jobs is lpc.

13. **b, c.** The printer daemon lpd is not a networking daemon and so is either started by the machine-specific init file /etc/rc.d/rc.local, or as a link in the /etc/rc.d/rc#.d directories.

14. **a, d.** The gs command invokes the Ghostscript program, which handles postscript files directly, and the **lpd** command can handle postscript files when print filters are involved.

15. **c.** The maximum print job size is given in blocks. There are 512 bytes per block.

16. **d.** The sh variable stands for "suppress headers". It is useful for when there are very few users utilizing the printers and so identification pages are not needed for the print jobs.

17. **a, b, and c.** It is a very quick process to see if the printer is turned on, the cables are in place, and if lpd is running. However, debugging an input filter can take some time.

18. **a, b, and d.** An input filter can be a program or a shell script.

19. **b.** The **lpq** command can be used to display the contents of the queue in question, and then the lprm command can be used to delete a particular job in that queue.

20. **d.** Invoking the printer daemon as **lpd –l** looks to /etc/syslog.conf to see how much information to log, and to where.

CHAPTER 11 SOLUTIONS

1. **b.** The Linux operating system itself is the kernel, just as it is with any other operating system.

2. **c, d.** If the second portion of a kernel number is odd, then it is an experimental kernel.

3. **b.** The **insmod** command loads a kernel module.

4. **a.** The **lsmod** command lists all loaded kernel modules and their dependencies.

5. **d.** The **rmmod** command removes a module that is idle, and not required for other loaded modules.

6. **a, d.** If the second portion of a kernel number is even, then it is a production kernel.

7. **a.** The make package is a compilation management program.

8. **c.** The patch program inserts the source code changes necessary to incrementally upgrade the kernel source version (or other source code) to the next level.

9. **b.** The egcs package contains gcc, the GNU C Compiler.

10. **b.** The **make xconfig** command starts the GUI kernel configuration program.

11. **d.** The **make oldconfig** command builds the default configuration file for the kernel.

12. **a.** The **make bzImage** command builds a slightly compressed version of the kernel (compared to **make zImage**).

13. **a, b.** Once the kernel and modules are built, the kernel and its corresponding System.map file have to be copied to the /boot directory for some distributions, and the root directory into others.

14. **c.** Once the kernel is placed in the /boot directory, or even before it is placed there, it must be renamed to "vmlinuz-*version*".

15. **b.** The **make menuconfig** command starts the menu–driven kernel configuration program. This program requires the ncurses packages to run properly.

16. **d.** The **make modules_install** command installs the kernel's modules to where they need to go in the filesystem structure.

17. **a.** The **mkinitrd** command creates the ramdisk necessary to boot the machine, which is then unloaded and replaced by the kernel you just compiled and installed.

18. **a.** The **make config** command starts the long, text questionnaire which walks you through the kernel configuration process.

19. **c.** To show LILO where to find the new kernel and give it a boot menu option, edit the file /etc/lilo.conf.

20. **c.** To have LILO re-set all of its configuration files for the boot loader, run "/sbin/lilo –v".

Chapter 12 Solutions

1. **d.** Groups are managed and created within the /etc/group file.

2. **c.** The tcp_wrappers tool is a method of protecting one particular machine's traffic.

3. **a.** The file used to tell tcp_wrappers where traffic is not allowed to come from is /etc/hosts.deny.

4. **b.** The file used to tell tcp_wrappers where traffic is allowed to come from is /etc/hosts.allow.

5. **d.** All three rules are valid tcp_wrappers statements.

6. **b.** The ssh tool uses encryption to transmit data such as passwords for remote connections.

7. **b and c**, **with one caveat.** The ssh tool may be available through certain distributions that do not come from the US. Since it involves encryption, it falls under legal issues that vary from country to country. The .fi site is the home site for the tool.

8. **b.** The ipchains tool is the IP Filtering firewall discussed in this book.

9. **c.** The SOCKS tool is the Proxying firewall discussed in this book.

10. **c.** The SOCKS wildcard to mean "all" is the dash (-).

11. **b.** The last item stands for what proxy to go to, so it must be a specific machine and also port if non-standard.

12. **a.** The command is **ipchains –L** to list the existing chains.

13. **b.** The ALLOW policy does not exist.

14. **b.** The -p flag specifies the protocol to be used.

15. **c.** The –y flag signals that the TCP packet specifically referred to is the SYN packet, which is used to open a TCP connection.

16. **a.** The -s flag refers to the source address, or where the packet came from.

17. **b.** The -d flag refers to the destination address, or wherever the packet is going.

18. **d.** There is no source (-s) or destination (-d) assigned to the address. The filter needs to know which portion of the header to examine to make its decisions.

19. **c.** The pwconv program converts the machine to using shadow passwords.

20. **b.** The btmp file tracks all failed login attempts.

21. **b.** The **lastb** command displays the end of the /var/log/btmp file.

Chapter 13 Solutions

1. **b.** X11R6 is current.

2. **c.** xdm is not a window manager.

3. **a.** xdm is not a command to start X.

4. **c.** XFree86 is released by the XFree86 Project, not the X consortium.

5. **d.** Configure the mouse first.

6. **b.** The window manager is responsible for moving windows.

7. **d.** wm2 is a window manager.

8. **a.** and **d.** The X server is not responsible for resizing or closing windows.

9. **a.** It is a valid DISPLAY value.

10. **d.** XF86Config is not a utility. It is a configuration file.

11. **d.** The X protocol has nothing to do with bitmaps.

12. **b.** Pixmaps in XMP format are used by window managers.

13. **c.** xhost gives permission for remote X clients to display on the local X server.

14. **b.** startx is a script used to start X.

15. **a.** **xinit** is a command.

16. **c.** You change the runlevel in the inittab configuration file.

GLOSSARY

.

A special character that the shell interprets to mean the current directory.

..

A special character that the shell interprets to mean the parent directory of the current directory.

!!

Command that reenters the last command typed.

/bin

The directory where user commands are stored.

/etc/fstab

The file that contains the filesystem data needed by Linux at boot time.

/sbin

The directory where system administration commands are stored.

/usr/bin

The directory where user commands are stored.

^oldtext^newtext

A command that substitutes new text for old text in the last command entered and reenters the command.

alias

A short name (nickname) for a command. When you type the alias, the command is entered. An alias is useful if you enter the same long command frequently.

ampersand (&)

A metacharacter added to the end of a command that means to send the command into the background.

argument

Information used by a command when executing.

autoprobe

The process of randomly guessing configuration information of a device.

awk

A filter that provides a set of programming functions for non-interactive editing of text files. Awk provides the use of variables, use of arithmetic and string operators, and use of simple programming constructs, such as loops. Awk allows complex reformatting of a structured text file.

background

The commands executing in the background are not connected to the command line. Jobs in the background do not tie up the system, leaving the command line available for other uses. You can run many commands in the background simultaneously.

backslash (\)

A metacharacter used to continue a command from one line to the next line in shell command lines. Also used in regular expressions to escape metacharacters.

bg

A command that sends a stopped job into the background.

binary

A program that is already compiled.

block device

A data storage media that saves data in chunks called "blocks", which have addresses described by cylinders and sectors.

broadcast address
Generic address used to access all nodes on a network simultaneously.

built-in commands
Subroutines in the shell program itself that are run when the correct command syntax is entered at the command line.

cable lock
A piece of security equipment used to secure computers to tables or within the room so they cannot "walk away".

caching nameserver
A nameserver that caches keeps a record of the names it has resolved through DNS into IP addresses and, the next time it goes to resolve those names, gets the information from the cache instead.

cat
A program that reads files and sends them to STDOUT. This program is often used in conjunction with redirections and pipes.

child process
A new process created in the current, exist-ing process. The new process is the child; the process in which it was created is the parent.

chmod
The command used to change the permis-sions on a file.

chown
The command used to change the owner-ship of a file.

client/server computing
A model of computing in which the client software requests a service (processing or data) from the server software and the server software responds to the request with the appropriate service. The client and server software can be located on the same computer or on different computers.

command
Instructions typed at the command line. Commands consist of the name of the com-mand, followed by options and arguments.

Commands instruct the computer to per-form a task.

command line
The interface provided by the shell for entering commands. The shell displays a prompt to signal that it is ready to receive a command.

commercial
Software that the admin or user must pur-chase before using. Sometimes a trial version is available for free.

compile
The act of turning source code into actual executable programs.

compiler
A program that turns code written in a programming language such as C into an executable file called a binary, which is in machine language.

console
A physical machine with keyboard and monitor.

cracker
Someone who specializes in breaking into user accounts by guessing or otherwise gaining passwords.

cron job
An item added to the system cron files or the user crontab, which is then run by the cron daemon at the specified time and date.

Ctrl+C
A command that halts a job. The job is ended and the command must be reentered.

Ctrl+Z
A command that suspends a job. The stopped job can be resumed at the point where it stopped with either the **bg** or the **fg** command.

daemons
Programs that run in the background, listen-ing for activity on specific input ports, then responding to that activity as designed.

debugging
The process of finding and eliminating the errors in a script or program.

default route
Where packets go if no specific route exists for their destination address.

dependency
Something required to make a program compile or run.

desktop environment
A suite of applications that provide an integrated GUI environment on the user's screen. A desktop includes, in addition to a window manager, a file manager, a panel control center, and many other components.

device
Hardware item used to input or output information from a Linux system.

dgram
Short for "datagram", which is the type of data packet sent by the UDP networking protocol.

diff
A command that compares two files and outputs each line that is different.

directory
A special file that contains a listing of the files in the directory. The entry for each file contains the name of the file and a pointer to information about the file.

DISPLAY
Environment variable that designates the display where the X client output will be painted.

display management
Actions performed by X server software, including opening a window and painting the display requested by the X client.

distribution
A Linux package that normally includes GNU tools and other software.

dotted quad
Common term used to describe an IP address which consists of 4 bytes separated by dots.

downstream
The direction of a data stream that is toward the device.

driver
The piece of software that interprets generic system calls into hardware language.

echo
Command that displays one line of text.

edquota
The command that enables a system administrator to edit quotas.

environment variables
Variables whose values remain the same and accessible throughout the shell, regardless of session or sub-shells.

escape
The process of telling a shell or program command that what normally would be a special character (metacharacter) is instead meant to be taken at face value.

export
The process of taking the value of the variable out of the sub-shell or process and making it available to all portions of the shell as an environment variable.

facility
The type of program or daemon generating a log message, as used in /etc/syslog.conf.

fdisk
A command-line program used to create, remove, and manage drive partitions.

fg
A command that brings a job into the foreground.

file
A command that displays the type of a file.

filesystem
The entirety of the devices that a Linux system and its files span.

filter
A command that operates on a text stream. A filter is designed to perform specified, distinct operations on text as it passes through the filter.

find
The command used to search the live file-system for where something exists within it.

firewalls
A physical unit or piece of software that regulates the traffic going through it to the protected network or machine behind it, and perhaps the traffic going out as well.

firmware
A piece of software contained inside a hardware device.

foreground
The command executing at the command line, with which the user can interact, is said to be in the foreground. Only one job can be in the foreground at a time.

format
Prepare a partition to house files for a particular type of operating system, such as Linux.

freeware
Software that is often copyrighted by the author, but freely available to the public to use without cost.

function
A subroutine within a program or shell that returns a value.

gawk
GNU version of awk.

GID (group identification) number
The number used by the Linux system to track which groups users belong to.

GNU (Gnu Isn't Unix)
Part of the FSF (Free Software Foundation). The GNU organization collectively writes programs and documentation which are available for free. For more information, go to **www.gnu.org**. The GNU project is where most Linux software comes from.

GNU Network Object Model Environment (GNOME)
A desktop environment built entirely of free, open-source software. It includes a panel (for starting applications and displaying status), a desktop (where data and applications can be placed), and a set of standard desktop tools and applications, such as a calendar and an address book.

grace period
The amount of time a user with a soft limit has before his or her account is disabled.

graphical user interface (GUI)
The display on a high-resolution bitmap display screen that provides a graphical interface by which users access computer resources.

grep
A filter that searches through one or more files to find specified text strings and outputs information resulting from the search.

grpquota
Command used to assign quotas to groups.

hacker
Originally a person who "hacked" with code, meaning a programmer. Today, used generically to mean people who break into systems.

hard limit
The maximum amount of disk space available to someone with a quota.

hard link
A link between files where the two files share the same inode.

head
A command that displays first few lines of a file. Displays 10 lines by default.

head of a stream
The application end of a data stream.

help
A command that provides information about built-in shell commands.

host
A computer on the network, it is identified by a hostname, not an IP address.

How-To
The form that the general Linux documentation comes in.

info
A command that provides a hyperlinked information system containing information on various topics.

inode
A data structure that contains information about the file and pointers to the physical location of the data in the file. There is one inode for each file in the filesystem.

interface
What connects the host to a network, an interface is usually a network card, but not always. The interface is known by the IP address.

IP chain
A grouping of TCP/IP packet types used within an IP filtering firewall.

job number
A number that is assigned and displayed when a command is sent to the background. The first job sent to the background is 1, the next is 2, etc. The job number is used to monitor the status of the background command.

jobs
A command that displays information about background jobs.

K Desktop Environment (KDE)
A complete, integrated desktop environment that is both free and open source and runs on most flavors of UNIX. It includes a file manager, a help system, a configuration system, a terminal emulator, tools and utilities, and an ever increasing number of applications, including mail and news clients, drawing programs, a PostScript and a DVI viewer, etc.

kernel space
Virtual "zone" in Linux where low-level processes are contained.

key
The item used in encryption situations to prove that the user is indeed who he or she claims to be.

keymap
The file which contains the layout of what characters correspond to which keyboard keys.

kill
A command that deletes processes and jobs.

killall
A command that deletes several processes at once.

less
A command that displays a file to screen one page at a time. Has more options than the **more** command.

libraries
A collection of functions and subroutines used by programs. Linked into code at compile time, adding the code to the executable.

library
A collection of commonly used functions.

LILO (Linux Loader)
The default program that manages booting a machine with Linux—and other operating systems if included.

line printer
A particular model of printer built for fast, high-volume output.

link
A method of allowing a file to appear to exist in two places at once.

literal character
A normal character, with no special meaning. An a is an a with no meaning other than one of 26 letters in the alphabet.

ln
The command used to create a link.

local printer
A printer connected to the specific machine in question.

locate
The command used to search the locate database to find where something lies within the filesystem structure.

log
A file containing a history of the behind-the-scenes goings on with the process it tracks.

loopback device
Virtual interface to allow a computer to address itself without having any other network settings.

ls
A command that lists the files in a directory.

mail forwarder
A sendmail session that does not process mail except to pass it to the server, which then packages it to go to the Internet or LAN.

make
A command that simplifies the compilation process by acting on a set of rules specified by the programmer in the form of a makefile.

make targets
An argument used to tell the make package which section of the makefile to execute.

man
Command that provides information about system commands.

mask
A file or directory's permissions.

metacharacter
A special character that is recognized by a program or operating system to have a special meaning when used in an instruction or command.

mkdir
A command that creates a new directory.

mke2fs
Program used to format a partition to hold Linux files.

module
A driver that can be dynamically loaded and unloaded from the kernel.

module
A piece of the kernel that represents one particular piece of functionality, such as a hardware device driver.

more
A command that displays a file to screen one page at a time.

motif
GUI standard developed as an alternative to OPEN LOOK. It is now provided on almost all standard distributions of UNIX.

mount
Add a device to part of the filesystem.

mount point
The location in the filesystem where a device is added during the mount process.

mv
A command that moves a file or a directory.

nameservice
The resolution of Internet name addresses into their IP addresses.

NAT (Network Address Translation)
A process typically used to allow computers on a LAN using reserved address to be addressed on the internet.

netmask
The mask that is applied to an interface's IP address to determine what network it is on.

network address
Defines the subset of addresses that can exist on a network.

newsgroup
Discussion forums on the Internet often used for problem solving, information dissemination, or general chat.

nice
A command used to regulate how much CPU time a process uses.

nice number
A number that represents the priority of the process relative to other processes. The nice number (being nice to allow other processes to use the system) is set by the user or the system administrator.

noclobber
A system variable that determines whether existing files will be overwritten when new files are created by redirection. When noclobber is on, an error message is returned saying the file already exists and the command will stop executing. Noclobber is off by default in the bash shell.

octal
A numerical system that has the digits 0 - 7, so is base 8.

OPEN LOOK
A GUI standard that was developed by Sun to provide a unified look and feel for different workstations.

open source
A guideline some software is released under that says the source code must be provided

along with the executables, so that people can modify it or send in improvements if they want.

option
A command-line instruction that changes the way a command executes. Most options consist of a minus sign (-), followed by a keyword, consisting of one or more characters.

owner
The person who has full rights to the access and use of a file.

package management
A way to simplify the installation and upgrades of software.

packet
One chunk of data to be sent over a network.

parent process
The process that was running and in which a new process was created. The new process is the child; the process in which it was created is the parent.

partition
A portion of a hard drive, or an entire hard drive, that is blocked off into a separate entity.

patch
A small file generated with the **diff** program which contains the differences between the original source and the new version of the source. Then, this file can be applied against the same original source elsewhere to update it to the new version.

pattern
A collection of characters used to build a search term, incorporating wildcards to fill in unknown segments.

permission
A quality of an item in the filesystem that sets who is allowed to read, write, or execute it.

PID (process ID) number
The unique number assigned to a process when it is created.

pipes
A construct of UNIX that allows you to connect the stdout of one command directly to the stdin of another command. The metacharacter, |, is used to connect two programs.

plug and play
A method for (sometimes) auto-configuring a device properly.

POP (Post Office Protocol)
A method of collecting and storing email until the user uses an email client to collect it.

port
A virtual access point on a computer that is essentially an internal address through which a machine can connect to the outside LAN and/or Internet.

PPP (Point-to-Point Protocol)
The preferred dial-in protocol used by ISPs because of its flexibility, including the fact that it recognizes more than the Internet's TCP/IP protocol.

print job
A document, picture, or other such data waiting to be printed.

print spool
The directory containing all of the jobs waiting to go to a specific printer.

priority
The level of logging that should be used by the program or daemon defined in /etc/syslog.conf.

priority number
A number that represents the absolute priority of the process. The priority number is computed dynamically by the scheduler, based on the nice number, the process status, recent resource use of the process, other

available processes, and other factors. This number cannot be changed by the user or the system administrator.

process
A set of sequentially executed software instructions, usually taking the form of a program; although, a program may have more than one process for operations that can be performed in parallel.

profile
A file containing login configuration information.

protocol
A set of rules to guide communication of a network.

ps
A command that displays information about processes.

pstree
A command that displays all the processes in a tree structure, showing the parent/child relationships.

queue
A numbered list of the print jobs waiting to go to a specific printer, numbered according to the order they arrived.

quota
An amount of space that a user or group can be limited to using within a partition.

ramdisk
A "virtual disk," or piece of code held in memory as a kind of boot disk to assist in the boot process.

redirection
The process of using metacharacters to change the input and output streams for a program.

regular expressions
Patterns of literal characters and metacharacters that enable you to selectively process text. Regular expressions are used by many Unix commands and utilities.

Regular expressions allow quite complicated text processing via pattern matching.

renice
A command that changes the nice number of a running process.

repquota
A command that generates reports on quota use.

rmdir
A command that deletes an empty directory.

rotate
Close the current log file, rename it, and immediately create a new log file in its place to continue capturing data.

runlevel
A parameter that is set in the inittab file and determines the system state while running. You set the runlevel to start xdm at boot time. Different runlevels have different meanings for different distributions of Linux. Runlevel 5 starts with xdm for Red Hat and Caldera.

scheduler
The part of the kernel responsible for timesharing decisions. The scheduler swaps processes in and out of memory for execution, maximizing CPU usage and ensuring that all processes get some time, no matter how low their priority.

sed
A filter that provides non-interactive editing of text files. sed offers the same basic editing commands that are available for interactive editing, e.g., inserting text, deleting text, substituting text. You can create a set of editing instructions and apply them to the entire file in one step. The set of instructions is saved in a script that can be used to edit any number of files.

shadow
A method of password storage that protects the passwords themselves behind a root-only accessible file, instead of leaving them in the globally accessible /etc/passwd.

shared libraries
A collection of functions and subroutines used by programs. Referenced by code, not compiled into the executable itself. Must be installed for program to run.

shareware
Software freely available for download from the Internet that people are expected to pay for if they like. Often "crippled" in some way so that some features are not available without paying, or it will only function for a specific amount of time unless payment is made and a key code is obtained.

shell
The working environment during a login session.

SLIP (Serial Line Internet Protocol)
The less used dial-in protocol by ISPs because of lack of flexibility.

soft limit
The amount of space available to someone with a quota before they get a warning and an allotted amount of time to trim back down if they exceed it.

sort
A filter that sorts the lines of text in a file.

spam
Uninvited barrage of email or newsgroup postings most often containing advertising material.

standard error (stderr)
A data stream for displaying error messages that is connected to every process when it is created. By default, stderr is connected to the video display, but it can be redirected to another file. It is assigned file descriptor 2.

standard input (stdin)
An input data stream that is connected to every process when it is created. By default, stdin is connected to the keyboard, but it can be redirected to another file. It is assigned file descriptor 0.

standard output (stdout)
An output data stream that is connected to every process when it is created. By default, stdout is connected to the video display, but it can be redirected to another file. It is assigned file descriptor 1.

startx
A script file that starts the X Window System. It executes the **xinit** command.

stream
A single-byte connection between an application and a device that is used to transfer data for all I/O operations.

subnet
A subsection of a network.

superdaemon
The inetd daemon that manages any other networking daemons the administrator configures it to watch.

symlink
A link between files that have different inodes, and yet all refer to the same original.

system commands
Programs, stored as files in the filesystem, that are run by typing the command name.

tail
A command that displays last few lines of a file. Displays 10 lines by default.

telnet
Program used to remotely log in to external machines, either on the same LAN or outside. No dial-in capability; the machine must already be connected to a network or the Internet.

text stream
A stream of single characters, including the character that marks the end of the line. The stream flows into the processing program and out, displaying on the screen.

theme
A well-developed combination of settings that define a specific look and combination of functions.

thread
See *process*.

timesharing
A method of sharing the CPU time among all the active processes, based on a priority number. A program is moved into memory and begins executing. If no waiting time is encountered, the program executes for its designated time slice, a fraction of a second, and is swapped out. Another program is swapped into memory and begins executing. The swapping continues for one process after another.

top
A command that displays information about the processes that are using most of the CPU time.

touch
A command that updates the last access and last modified dates of a file.

UID (user identification) number
A number used by the system to keep track of the users themselves.

umask
The permission bits that are explicitly not set upon file creation.

unmount
A command that removes a device from the filesystem.

UPS (uninterruptible power supply)
A device used to prevent computers from immediately crashing during power outages or brown-outs.

upstream
The direction of a data stream that is toward the application.

user space
Virtual "zone" in Linux where user programs are contained.

usrquota
Command used to assign quotas to users.

vi
A small text editor.

which
The command used to search the PATH environment variable for the program in question.

wildcards
Metacharacters used to signal unknowns in search patterns.

window
An area of the screen allocated to a given application program.

window manager
X client software that is responsible for managing windows under the X Window System. It controls the appearance of windows and provides the means by which you interact with them. The window manager is responsible for positioning a new window, providing window titles and borders, moving the location of an existing window, changing window size, iconifying windows, switching the focus from one window to another, and removing a window.

X client
Any application that requires the use of display graphics. When the client requires a graphics display, it sends a request to the X server, which paints the requested display.

X consortium
A worldwide consortium, called X.Org, that is empowered with the stewardship and collaborative development of the X Window System technology and standards. Official releases of X are provided through X.Org.

X protocol
A language used for communication between an X server and an X client. It specifies the format and meaning of the data transmissions exchanged by the client/server software. The X protocol is freely available so that computer vendors can implement their own X server and/or clients. As long as the software understands the X protocol, the programs will work with any other X servers or clients.

X server
Software that drives the graphics and input hardware. The server, located on your Linux system, is windowing software that can organize the physical display area into subareas known as windows and can control and manage many activities simultaneously. The server monitors input and renders drawings on the display. The server is hardware-dependent and knows how to communicate with your video card, keyboard, and pointing device.

X Window System
A hardware-independent, distributed windowing system that provides a GUI to make computer use easier and more intuitive for users. It is portable, network-transparent, and runs on almost all types of computers.

X11
The widely released eleventh version of the X Window System. It initiated popular acceptance of X and its continuing position as the dominant standard for UNIX systems. Successive releases of X11 have added extra functionality while attempting to remain largely backwards-compatible. The current release is Release 6 (X11R6.4).

xdm
The display manager that is used to start X at boot time. X starts when the system is booted and users log in through an X login screen, a useful setup for multi-user machines.

XF86Setup
A utility used to configure the hardware for XFree86.

XFree86
The version of the X Window System designed, implemented, and distributed by the Xfree86 Project. It is free software The Xfree86 Project, a member of the X Consortium that ports the X Window system to many Intel-based Unix and Unix-like operating systems. It is provided with all Linux distributions. It is free software—designed, implemented, and distributed by The XFree86 Project, Inc., a not-for-profit corporation, initiated in 1992 by four developers who were unhappy with the existing support for Intel-based Unix platforms and funded by contributions. The Xfree86 Project is a member of the X consortium and provides enhancements to the X Window System software, with ports to many Intel-based Unix and Unix-like operating systems. Xfree86 includes all of the required binaries, support files, libraries, and tools.

xinit
A command that starts the X Window System, starting the X server and one client program.

xman
A utility for viewing man pages in a GUI.

INDEX

Index

Index

Index

Index

Index

Z